Gustav Kawerau, Wilhelm Moeller

History of the Christian church

Gustav Kawerau, Wilhelm Moeller

History of the Christian church

ISBN/EAN: 9783337263331

Printed in Europe, USA, Canada, Australia, Japan

Cover: Foto ©Lupo / pixelio.de

More available books at **www.hansebooks.com**

HISTORY
OF THE
CHRISTIAN CHURCH

UNIFORM WITH THIS VOLUME.

(1.) HISTORY OF THE CHRISTIAN CHURCH.
A.D.—1—600.

BY THE LATE DR. WILLIAM MOELLER.

TRANSLATED BY ANDREW RUTHERFURD, B.D.

"Characterised by all the thoroughness that marks most of the productions of German scholars. A distinct advance on Kurtz."—*Review of the Churches.*

"To say the least, entitled to rank with the very best works of the kind."—*Bookman.*

"The orderly, consecutive, readily apprehensible statement. . We have no hesitation in saying that the book is a great improvement on the manual of Kurtz, the work with which it most invites comparison . . . . Thorough knowledge, clear method, lucid statement, a power of seizing and distinctly exhibiting the main points in a period of movement—these are the qualities which are likely to put it in the front rank among our text books of Church History."—*Critical Review.*

"This work furnishes a much-needed desideratum to students of early Church History."—*Religious Review of Reviews.*

"The book is a text or hand-book, and the best of its kind we are acquainted with."—*Modern Church.*

"The place which Dr. Moeller's History was sent to fill was unfilled till it came. It is a student's volume, the kind of book which a student delights in, loves to handle, loves to conquer and know."—*Expository Times.*

"To the teacher who wants references, to the priest or minister who wants to keep up his theological library, to the public librarian who wants to be able to send his inquirers to a practical and scientific authority, and to be himself directed to the choice of the best books on the subject, as well as to the student, this book may be heartily recommended."—*Manchester Guardian.*

(2.) HISTORY OF THE CHRISTIAN CHURCH.
THE MIDDLE AGES.

"Has deservedly taken a first place among works of its kind. The present volume is one of great interest, covering as it does the whole march of events ecclesiastical, from Gregory the Great to the Renaissance. It has all the qualities which made the former volume so suitable as a text-book—clear and concise statement, a sufficient reference to authorities, a careful and unprejudiced estimate of men and movements."—*Critical Review.*

"There is an unbroken testimony to its industry and scholarship. It will be a well-thumbed and well-loved book by the sincere student, and that is the only reward the distinguished author would have cared for. It will henceforth be referred to by English writers as the standard of authority."—*Expository Times.*

"A book of extraordinary comprehensiveness, the amount of information compressed into it is marvellous, and, where so much is attempted, it is extraordinary that so much should be done so well. It is a work of immense industry and of remarkable power, both of analysis and synthesis. There can be no question of its value as a book of reference."—*Guardian.*

"All the substantial excellences of Dr. Möller's work continue to be found in it, his profound learning and his calmly judicial temper being conspicuous among them. The book is primarily a book of reference. It does not pretend to give vivid and detailed descriptions, but it supplies the student with the means of making himself master of the subject. It is scarcely too much to say that from this point of view it is indispensable."—*Spectator.*

"Will be welcomed by every teacher and preacher who wishes to keep abreast of modern theological research, and by all students of Church History, who desire to have at hand a thoroughly reliable scientific authority on the subject. It combines perspicuity with thoroughness, and method with style."—*Dundee Advertiser.*

HISTORY

OF THE

CHRISTIAN CHURCH

A.D.—1517-1648.

THIRD VOLUME

REFORMATION AND COUNTER-REFORMATION

BY

THE LATE DR. WILHELM MOELLER
Professor of Church History in the University of Kiel

EDITED BY

DR. G. KAWERAU
Professor of Theology in the University of Kiel

TRANSLATED FROM THE GERMAN BY

J. H. FREESE, M.A.
Late Fellow of St. John's College, Cambridge

LONDON
SWAN SONNENSCHEIN & CO., LIM.
NEW YORK: THE MACMILLAN COMPANY

1900

Printed by
H. S. NICHOLS, LTD.,
3 SOHO SQUARE, LONDON, W.

PRELIMINARY NOTE.

AFTER the death of Dr. W. Möller, the publisher entrusted the completion of the unfinished work to the author's colleague, Dr. G. Kawerau.

Owing to the fact that the greater part of Dr. Möller's work, as he left it, treated of subjects that would naturally have been included in a later volume (the Greco-Russian Church, English Methodism), Dr. Kawerau may be regarded as being mainly responsible for the present instalment. Divisions I. and VII. were written by him independently, as well as several chapters in other divisions.

The references to books bearing upon the subject (which could have been greatly increased) have been purposely limited.

The present Volume carries the history only down to the year 1648, as being the *terminus* recommended by the course of German Ecclesiastical History.

The Editor's standpoint is thus described in his own words: "A History of the Reformation is essentially influenced by its author's position. I gladly acknowledge myself a disciple of Luther. But for that very reason I have always kept before my eyes his exhortation to every historian, "intrepidly to write *what is true*," and I have endeavoured not to forget this duty. The cause of truth can be served only if we keep inviolate the *prima lex historiae, ne quid falsi dicere audeat, deinde* **ne quid veri non audeat,** *ne qua suspicio gratiae sit in scribendo, ne qua simultatis* (CICERO, De Oratore, II., 15)."

ABBREVIATIONS.

ABA	= Abhandlungen der bairischen Akad. d. Wissenschaften, histor. Classe.	PpStA	= Publikationen aus den preuss. Staatsarchiven.
ADB	= Allgem. deutsche Biographie.	PrJb	= Preussische Jahrbücher.
AG	= Archiv für Geschichte.	RE	= Real-Encyclopädie von Herzog, Plitt u. Hauck. 2. Aufl.
ALG	= Archiv für Lit.-Gesch.	RQ	= Römisch. Quartalschrift.
AÖG	= Archiv für österr. Gesch.	SBBA	= Sitzungsberichte der bairischen Akademie.
ASB	= Acta Sanctorum Bollandi.	SBWA	= Sitzungsberichte der Wiener Akademie.
BA	= Braunschweiger Lutherausgabe 1889 ff.	Schaff	= Bibliotheca Symbolica, ed. Schaff. New York 1877.
BM	= Bullarium magnum, Turiner Ausgabe.		
CA	= Confessio Augustana.	StBlV or StlV	= Stuttgarter Bibliothek des liter. Vereins.
CR	= Corpus Reformatorum.		
Denzinger	= Enchiridion Symbolorum ed. Denzinger. 6 Wirceb. 1888.	StKr	= Theologische Studien und Kritiken.
DevBl	= Deutsch-evang. Blätter.	ThLB	= Theolog. Liter.-Blatt.
DLZ	= Deutsche Literatur-Zeitung.	ThLZ	= Theolog. Lit.-Zeitung.
DZGW	= ZGW.	ThQ	= Theolog. Quartalschrift (Tübinger).
EA	= Erlanger Luther-Ausgabe.	UN	= Unschuldige Nachrichten.
Enders	= Luthers Briefwechsel, herausg. von Enders.	Vg	= Vulgata.
		VRG	= Verein f. Reform.-Gesch.
FC	= Formula Concordiae.	WA	= Weimarer Luther-Ausg.
FdG	= Forschungen zur deutschen Geschichte.	Walch	= Walch'sche Luther-Ausgabe.
FRA	= Fontes rerum Austriacarum.	ZdA	= Zeitschrift für deutsches Alterthum.
GGA	= Göttinger gelehrte Anzeigen.	ZdCG	= Zeitschrift für deutsche Culturgeschichte.
GGN	= Göttinger gelehrte Nachrichten.	ZfTh	= Zeitschrift für Theologie (Tübinger).
GV	= Geschichtsverein.	ZG	= Zeitschrift f. Geschichte.
HJb	= Historisches Jahrbuch (Münchener).	ZGW	= Deutsche Zeitschrift für Geschichtswissenschaft.
HpBl	= Historisch-politische Blätter.	ZhTh	= Zeitschrift f. historische Theologie.
HpZ	= Historisch-politische Zeitschrift (L. Ranke).	ZhV	= Zeitschrift des historischen Vereins.
HTb	= Historisches Taschenbuch.	ZKG	= Zeitschrift für Kirchengeschichte.
HZ	= Historische Zeitschrift.	ZkTh	= Zeitschrift f. katholische Theologie.
JdTh	= Jahrbücher für deutsche Theologie. (NJdTh = Neue Jahrbücher).	ZkW	= Zeitschrift für kirchliche Wissenschaft u. k. Leben
JGG	= Jahrbuch der Görres-Gesellschaft.	ZlTh	= Zeitschrift f. lutherische Theologie (Rudelbach-Guerike).
JprTh	= Jahrbücher für protest. Theologie.	ZPGLK	= Zeitschrift f. preuss. Geschichte u. Landeskunde.
KL	= Kirchenlexikon, kath. 2. Aufl.	ZprTh	= Zeitschrift f. praktische Theologie.
KO, KOO	= Kirchenordnung, Kirchenordnungen.	ZSKG	= Zeitschrift für sächsische Kirchengeschichte.
KZ	= Kirchenzeitung.	ZThK	= Zeitschrift für Theologie und Kirche.
MIÖG	= Mittheilungen des Instit. f. österr. Geschichte.	ZwTh	= Zeitschrift für wissenschaftliche Theologie.
NA	= Neues Archiv.		
Niemeyer	= Collectio confessionum in eccl. reformatis publicatarum. Leipz. 1840.		

CONTENTS.

PRELIMINARY NOTE	v
LIST OF ABBREVIATIONS	vi
ERRATA	xii

CHURCH HISTORY OF MODERN TIMES.

FIRST PERIOD—REFORMATION AND COUNTER-REFORMATION (1517-1648).

INTRODUCTORY SURVEY	1—4
FIRST DIVISION. THE REFORMATION IN GERMANY UP TO THE YEAR 1555	5—162
CHAPTER FIRST. LUTHER'S RUPTURE WITH ROME	5—40
1. The Course of Luther's Development, up to the commencement of the Struggle	7—10
2. The Dispute about Indulgences	11—15
3. The Negotiations with Cajetan and Miltitz	15—17
4. The Leipzig Disputation	17—20
5. Melanchthon	20—21
6. The Humanistic Allies and the New Emperor	21—24
7. The Great Reformation Treatises of the Year 1520	24—26
8. The Papal Ban	26—29
9. The Diet of Worms	29—33
10. The Sojourn at the Wartburg, and the Return to Wittenberg	33—38
11. The Formulating of reformatory Ideas in Melanchthon's Loci Communes	38—40
CHAPTER SECOND. THE MOVEMENT IN THE NATION	41—57
1. The Political Situation	41—45
2. The Spread of the Reformation in Germany	45—46
3. The beginnings of the Institution of Evangelical Communities	46—49
4. U. Zwingli and German Switzerland	49—57
CHAPTER THIRD. THE YEARS OF CLEARING UP AND SEPARATION	58—69
1. Erasmus and Luther	58—61
2. The Severance of the Reformation from the Mystico-Revolutionary Circles	61—63
3. The Severance of the Reformation from the fanatic Anabaptist Circles	63—66
4. Separation of the Reformation from the Revolution of the Peasants' War	66—69

CONTENTS

	PAGE
CHAPTER FOURTH. DEVELOPMENT OF THE REFORMATION: ECCLESIASTICAL TERRITORIES AND CONFESSIONS OF FAITH	70—114
1. Emperor and Pope	70—71
2. The Gotha-Torgau League	71—73
3. The Diet of Spires, 1526	73—74
4. The Beginnings of the Established Churchship	74—81
5. The Consolidation of the Reformation in German Switzerland	81—82
6. The Eucharistic Controversy	83—87
7. The Endangering of the Reformation by Anabaptist Propaganda in Germany	88—96
8. The Protestation of Spires and the Marburg Colloquy	96—102
9. The Diet of Augsburg	102—114
CHAPTER FIFTH. THE SCHMALKALDIC LEAGUE IN ITS PRIME	115—138
1. Zwingli's Death and the Nuremberg Truce	115—119
2. The Growth and Development of German Protestantism	119—124
3. The Concord of Wittenberg	124—125
4. The Catastrophe in Baptism	125—130
5. The Schmalkaldic Articles and the Truce of Frankfort	131—135
6. Fresh Victories of the Reformation	135—138
CHAPTER SIXTH. THE WEAKENING OF THE LEAGUE AND THE IMPERIAL POLICY OF REUNION	139—148
1. The Religious Discussions of Worms and Ratisbon	139—143
2. Weakening of the Schmalkaldic League by Philip's Bigamy	144—146
3. The Respite before the Catastrophe	146—148
CHAPTER SEVENTH. THE OVERTHROW OF THE SCHMALKALDIC LEAGUE	149—153
1. The Approach of the Catastrophe and Luther's Death	149—152
2. The Schmalkaldic War	152—153
CHAPTER EIGHTH. THE INTERIM AND THE RELIGIOUS PEACE	154—162
1. The Interim	154—159
2. The Treaty of Passau and the Religious Peace of Augsburg	159—162
SECOND DIVISION. THE REFORMATION OUTSIDE GERMANY. CALVINISM	163—217
CHAPTER FIRST. THE FOUNDATION OF LUTHERAN ESTABLISHED CHURCHES IN THE SCANDINAVIAN NORTH	163—170
1. Denmark	163—167
2. Sweden	168—170
CHAPTER SECOND. (FRENCH) SWITZERLAND AND CALVIN	171—189
1. German and French Switzerland after the death of Zwingli	171—173
2. Calvin until the time of his arrival at Geneva	174—177
3. Calvin's early activity in Geneva, his Expulsion and Recall	178—181
4. Geneva and Switzerland under the influence of the Spirit of Calvin	181—187
5. The Reformation in the Grisons	187—189
CHAPTER THIRD. THE REFORMATION MOVEMENTS IN FRANCE	189—195
1. The Beginnings of Lutheranism under Francis I.	190—192
2. The Propaganda of Calvinism	192—195

CONTENTS

	PAGE
CHAPTER FOURTH. THE REFORMATION MOVEMENTS IN THE NETHERLANDS	195—198
CHAPTER FIFTH. THE ECCLESIASTICAL REVOLUTION IN ENGLAND	199—211
1. Henry's Breach with Rome	199—204
2. Henry's Established Church Government	204—207
3. Evangelical Reforms under Edward VI.	207—211
CHAPTER SIXTH. THE REFORMATION IN POLAND, HUNGARY, TRANSYLVANIA, AND AMONGST THE SOUTH SLAVS	212—217
1. In Poland	212—214
2. In Hungary and Transylvania	214—217
3. The Gospel amongst the South Slavs	217
THIRD DIVISION. THE RESTORATION OF CATHOLICISM	218—275
Preliminary Remarks	218
CHAPTER FIRST. THE CATHOLIC REACTION AND THE EXTINCTION OF THE REFORMATION IN ITALY	219—227
1. Evangelical Movements and Catholic Reforms	219—223
2. The Annihilation of the Italian Reformation Circles	223—227
CHAPTER SECOND. THE ORDER OF THE JESUITS	228—236
1. St. Ignatius	228—232
2. The Society of Jesus	232—236
CHAPTER THIRD. THE COUNCIL OF TRENT	237—248
1. Its External Course	237—243
2. The Theological and Ecclesiastical Results of the Council	243—248
CHAPTER FOURTH. THE POPES OF THE RESTORED CATHOLICISM	249—254
CHAPTER FIFTH. THE INTELLECTUAL CURRENTS AND FORCES IN POST-TRIDENTINE CATHOLICISM	255—272
1. Catholic Learning in the Service of the Counter-Reformation	255—258
2. The Decline of Augustinianism	258—260
3. Gallicanism and its Opponents. The Jesuit Doctrine of the State	260—265
4. The Corruption of Moral Teaching by the Jesuits	265—268
5. The Cultivation of Mysticism	268—270
6. Orders and Congregations at the Service of the Counter-Reformation	270—272
CHAPTER SIXTH. THE MISSIONARY CONQUESTS OF CATHOLICISM	273—275
FOURTH DIVISION. THE DISRUPTION AND CONFESSIONAL SEPARATION OF GERMAN PROTESTANTISM	276—314
CHAPTER FIRST. DOGMATIC CONTROVERSIES IN LUTHERANISM	276—282
1. The Points of Difference between Melanchthon and Luther	277—279
2. The Controversies after Luther's Death	280—282
CHAPTER SECOND. PHILIPPISTS AND GNESIO-LUTHERANS	283—288
CHAPTER THIRD. THE WORK OF CONCORD	289—298
1. The First Attempt and the Overthrow of the Philippists in Saxony	289—291
2. The Concord	291—296
3. The Downfall of Crypto-Calvinism in Saxony	296—298

CONTENTS

	PAGE
CHAPTER FOURTH. THE ADVANCE OF CALVINISM IN GERMANY	299—314
1. The Electoral Palatinate	300—303
2. Nassau	304—305
3. Bremen	305—306
4. Anhalt	306—307
5. Baden	307
6. Hesse and Lippe	307—309
7. Electoral Brandenburg	309—311
8. The Lower-Rhenish Church	311—314
FIFTH DIVISION. THE STRUGGLE BETWEEN REFORMATION AND COUNTER-REFORMATION	315—381
CHAPTER FIRST. THE COUNTER-REFORMATION IN SPAIN AND THE NETHERLANDS	315—322
1. The Extinction of Evangelical Movements in Spain	315—318
2. The Religious Struggles in the Netherlands	318—322
CHAPTER SECOND. THE RELIGIOUS STRUGGLES IN FRANCE	323—329
1. The Massacre of St. Bartholomew	323—326
2. The Edict of Nantes	326—329
CHAPTER THIRD. THE STRUGGLES IN ENGLAND AND SCOTLAND	330—357
1. Bloody Mary	330—331
2. Elizabeth	331—336
3. Ireland	336
4. Scotland	337—345
5. England and Scotland under James I.	345—348
6. The Struggle of Catholicising Episcopalianism with Puritanism	348—354
7. Independency	354—357
CHAPTER FOURTH. THE STRUGGLE WITH THE COUNTER-REFORMATION IN SWEDEN, POLAND, AND HUNGARIAN TRANSYLVANIA	358—363
1. Sweden	358—359
2. Poland	359—362
3. Hungary and Transylvania	362—363
CHAPTER FIFTH. THE CONDITION OF GERMANY AFTER THE RELIGIOUS PEACE OF AUGSBURG	364—374
1. The Period of Suspense	365—369
2. The Counter-Reformations	370—372
3. The Presages of the War of Religion	372—374
CHAPTER SIXTH. THE THIRTY YEARS' WAR AND THE PEACE OF WESTPHALIA	375—381
SIXTH DIVISION. THE INTERNAL CONDITION OF THE EVANGELICAL CHURCHES	382—427
CHAPTER FIRST. THE CONSTITUTION	382—390
CHAPTER SECOND. THE DEVOTIONAL LIFE	391—400
CHAPTER THIRD. THE DEVELOPMENT OF THE THEOLOGICAL SPIRIT FROM THE TIME OF THE CONFESSIONAL SETTLEMENT	401—420

CONTENTS

1. Lutheran Scholastic Theology	401—404
2. The mystical and practically-religious Current	404—407
3. Fresh Controversies	407—409
4. The Reformed Theology	409—410
5. Arminianism and the Synod of Dort	410—415
6. The Peacemakers and G. Calixtus	416—420
CHAPTER FOURTH. THE INFLUENCE OF THE REFORMATION UPON MORALITY AND EDUCATION	421—427
SEVENTH DIVISION. THE SMALLER NON-CATHOLIC GROUPS	428—465
CHAPTER FIRST. THE WALDENSIANS	428—430
CHAPTER SECOND. UTRAQUISTS AND BOHEMIAN BRETHREN	431—436
CHAPTER THIRD. THE ANABAPTISTS	437—443
1. The Baptist Congregations after 1535	437—442
2. New Prophets	442—443
CHAPTER FOURTH. ANTI-TRINITARIANS AND SOCINIANS	444—457
1. The first anti-Trinitarians	444—446
2. Michael Servetus	446—451
3. The Italo-Polish anti-Trinitarians	451—453
4. Socinianism	453—457
CHAPTER FIFTH. MYSTIC SPIRITUALISM	457—465
1. Sebastian Franck	457—462
2. Caspar Schwenkfeld	462—465
GENERAL INDEX.	

ERRATA.

Page 72 line 17 *for* "case" *read* "cause."
,, 102 ,, 34 *for* "day" *read* "diet."
,, 185 ,, 32 *delete* "the" *before* "Martyr."
,, 197 ,, 9 *for* "Propst" *read* "Probst."
,, 263 ,, 45 *for* "Sextus" *read* "Sixtus."
,, 301 ,, 25 *for* "Schnepp" *read* "Schnepf."
,, 307 ,, 19 *for* "church beadles" *read* "ministers and schoolmasters."
,, 363 ,, 18 *for* "Nikolsburg" *read* "Nicolsburg."
,, 399 ,, 31 *for* "*canonical*" *read* "*canonicae*."
,, 403 ,, 34 *for* "Tarnor" *read* "Tarnov."
,, 407 ,, 23 *for* "Tarnor" *read* "Tarnov."
,, 429 ,, 1 *for* "Waldesians" *read* "Waldensians."
,, 422 ,, 27 *for* "Leonhard" *read* "Hutter."
,, 424 ,, 1 *for* "Patrick Hamilton" *read* "Church History."
,, 425 ,, 10 *for* "Raticius" *read* "Ratichius."

CHURCH HISTORY OF MODERN TIMES.

Literature: E. L. TH. HENKE, *Neuere Kirchengeschichte*, 3 vols., Halle, 1874-1880. *Nachgelassene Vorlesungen* (edited by W. Gess and A. Vial). J. J. HERZOG, *Abriss der gesammten Kirchengeschichte*, 2nd edition by G. Koffmane. Vol. ii. Leipzig, 1892. K. VON HASE, *Kirchengeschichte auf der Grundlage akadem. Vorlesungen.* Parts iii. and iv. Leipzig, 1891-1893. G. J. PLANCK, *Geschichte der Entstehung, der Veränderungen und der Bildung unseres protestantischen Lehrbegriffs.* 6 vols. Leipzig, 1781-1800; continued in *Geschichte der protestantischen Theologie von der Konkordien-formel bis in die Mitte des 18 Jahrhunderts.* Göttingen, 1831; the writings of WERNER, FRANK, DORNER (see vol. i., p. 24).

FIRST PERIOD.

Reformation and Counter-reformation (1517-1648).

Introductory Survey.

NOTWITHSTANDING the assertion of more recent Romish Church historians to the contrary, the modern period of Church History commences with Martin Luther. In the first place, the result of his appearance upon the scene was a split in Western Christendom, so considerable and far-reaching, that all the schisms which the Middle Ages witnessed appear by comparison insignificant, more or less local severances, and from that time forth the name "Catholic" Church is claimed for the party that resisted the Reformation; in the second place, the process of construction, which the Christian Church underwent in the system of Catholicism, is negatived on principle in all crucial points, and replaced by a new edifice founded upon a new understanding of the Gospel. In spite of numerous points of contact in detail, Luther's Reformation by no means stands on the same footing as the formation of various sects in the Middle Ages,—still less is it the continuation of the internal ecclesiastical reforms of the 15th century, but indicates a new phase in the development of Christianity. Wiclif and the so-called pre-reformers, on the one hand, may have, to a great extent, prepared the way in individual details, in religious knowledge and criticism of what was already existent, as, in like manner, on the other hand, the opponents of Curialism (Marsilius and others), and lastly also, Humanism may have done in its criticism of Christianity and

Scholasticism, and by reason of its application *ad fontes*,—to the Scriptures and the Fathers of the Church: yet Luther is not historically to be considered the man who collected, renovated, and carried out their ideas. He was not guided to the mission of his life by these men's school, but on an entirely different path: in the case of theology, he was led from nominalistic Scholasticism to Augustine (partly also to German mysticism) and by way of Augustine to Paul and the Scriptures generally; in the case of religion, from the search after the most manifold guarantees of happiness beyond the grave to the discovery and knowledge of happiness as the certainty of forgiveness of sins founded on belief in the divine purpose of grace made manifest in Christ. His knowledge of salvation, guided and confirmed by the Scriptures, shatters, as far as he is concerned, the Catholic idea of Belief, Grace and the Church, and, at the same time, the Catholic ideal of piety. He lays a new foundation on the crucial points, in a renewal of the religious ideas of Paul and in the understanding of the essential nature of the Gospel. The development of the ecclesiastical struggle of necessity forces him out of the papal Church, and drives him to a new edifice, in the first instance, **evangelical communities:** then the Princes (and magistrates) interfere and organise established churches. The religious becomes the national question, and soon, that of the interests of the different States. The division of Germany into Catholic and Evangelical States (the religious peace of Augsburg) and also the division into Lutheran and reformed denominational churches, is decided by protracted struggles, processes of purification, and schisms (Anabaptism, Mysticism, Antitrinitarianism). However, the new foundation was largely built upon with material that had been handed over, the Evangelical notion of belief combines anew with the Catholic, the work of Theology, amidst the struggles raging on the right and on the left, drifts rapidly into a new Scholasticism. The Churches, which are the product of the struggle, are, on the Lutheran side, schools of pure doctrine and educational establishments for a people as yet under age, rather than priestly communities of the faithful. The struggle with Rome drives men to set up the authority of the infallible word of Scripture in opposition to that of the Church, tradition, and the Pope, but at the same time to make the symbols, or, in other words, a rapidly confirmed tradition of pure doctrine, the canon of interpretation of the Scriptures. Particularism of the most varied kind paralyses the German Protestants' capacity for action, weakens them in the face of Rome's methodical advance, and causes them to lose again much of what they possessed: finally, they are only enabled to hold their ground, by means of assistance obtained outside Germany, during the terrors of the Thirty Years' War. **Calvinism** enters into the development of events as an independent factor in ecclesiastical history: a descendant of Lutheranism, but of an independent stamp. Distinguished from Lutheranism, not so much by searching theological differences as by its **theocratic** character, it appears by the side of the former (which, politically self-sufficient, is busied solely with the purity of the Gospel and of doctrine developed in continually increasing detail and with the consolation of the conscience of the individual) as a politically **aggressive** power, waging the wars of the Lord and everywhere encroaching, with full consciousness of its aim, upon the domain of public life. Its history accordingly becomes a history of war, and a martyrology without parallel. In Germany, certainly, where it continues its victorious march almost entirely on already Lutheran soil as a "purifying" of Lutheranism from papistical leaven, and conquers all the territories which were driven by the continuous development of Lutheranism to the theology of the Formula of Concord, its theocratic character becomes less pronounced, but in the struggle with its deadly enemy, the idolatrous Papal Church, in the West of Europe, it acquires a pure characteristic stamp.

The end of the Thirty Years' War, the middle of the 17th century, is the close of the Reformation period. But at the end of the latter, in Germany, the prophet of further developments of Protestantism appears in Germany in the person of Calixtus with his wide historically well-posted view and his eminently conciliatory disposition, while in England, where a properly national Reformation now for the first time commences, the ideas of complete separation of Church and State, of the exchange of the established and national Church for the free association of the faithful, the principle of toleration and the like, prepare the way for further ecclesiastical development. In the meantime, the Roman Church has recovered from the shock which the Reformation dealt it, found its leaders in the struggle in the Order of the Jesuits, and rejected the Reformation at Trent, and at the same time established itself so extensively, that it is in a position to commence the work of reconquest (Counter-reformation) with success. But its great victories, frequently made too easy for it by the weakness, discord, and short-sighted policy of its opponents, frequently gained by secular weapons, injure its internal development: the saviour of Catholicism, the Society of Jesus, proves fatal to it: the reduction of religious life to something purely mechanical, like the struggle for power, introduces with itself a new secularisation. The Eastern Church, almost entirely unaffected by the course of events in the West, disappears for awhile from our consideration, not to become the subject of our narrative until the conclusion.

FIRST DIVISION.

The Reformation in Germany up to the year 1555.

Sources for the history of the Reformation in Germany: LUTHER'S WORKS, Wittenberg, 12 German (1539-1559), 7 Latin folios (1545-1558): more correctly, Jena: 8 German, 4 Latin folios, 1555-1558: Eislebener Suppl. (J. Aurifaber) 2 folios, 1564-1565: Altenberg, 1661-1664, 10 folios (only the German); Leipzig, 1729-1740, 22 folios (German): Halle (G. Walch) 24 vols. 4°, 1740-1753, the Latin in a German translation, with the addition of documents and treatises by opponents; Erlangen—Frankfurt—Calw. (Irmischer, Schmidt, Enders), 67 vols. German, 1826-1857, a part of the same (1-20, 24-26) in a second, essentially improved edition, 1862-1885: 28 vols. *opp. exeg. lat.* 3 vols. *Comm. in ep. ad Gal.*, 7 vols., *opp. var. argumenti; Briefwechsel* (Enders) up to the present, 5 vols., 8°; WEIMAR (KNAAKE and others) from 1883 in 4°, up to the present i-vi., viii., xii-xiv. *Briefe*, besides those in DE WETTE, 6 vols. (the 6th by K. SEIDEMANN), Berlin, 1825-1856; *Luthers Briefwechsel* by BURKHARDT, Leipzig, 1866; KOLDE, *Analecta Lutherana*, Gotha, 1883. *Tischreden*: FÖRSTEMANN-BINDSEIL, 4 vols., Berlin, 1844-1848. BINDSEIL, *Colloquia*, 3 vols., Lemgo, 1863-1866, WRAMPELMEYER, *Tagebuch des C. Cordatus*, Halle, 1885. SEIDEMANN, *Lauterbachs Tagebuch.* Dresd. 1872. PREGER, *Tischreden.* Leipzig, 1888. LÖSCHE, *Analecta Luth. et Mel.* Gotha, 1892.—Best (annotated) popular edition (Selections): Braunschweig, 8 vols. 1889-1892.

MELANCHTHON'S WORKS. Basil. 1541, 5 fol.; Viteb. 1562. 4 fol. *Corpus Reformatorum* ed. BRETSCHNEIDER and BINDSEIL, 28 vols. 4°. Hal. and Brunsv. 1834 to 1860 (vol. i-x. *The Letters*). Completion of the *Letters* in BINDSEIL, *Ph. Mel. Epistolae.* Hal. 1874; C. KRAUSE, *Melanthoniana*. Zerbst, 1885; HARTFELDER, *Anal. Melanth. paedag.* Leipzig, 1892. On ZWINGLI see later. *Briefwechsel d. J. Brenz* ed. PRESSEL, Tüb. 1868; *d. J. Jonas*, ed. KAWERAU. 2 vols., Halle. 1884-1885; *des* BUGENHAGEN ed. VOGT: Stettin. 1888.

Other publications dealing with the *Sources*: LÖSCHER, *Vollst. Ref.-Acta* (1517-1519), 3 vols. Leipzig, 1720 ff. TENTZEL-CYPRIAN, *Hist. Bericht vom Anfang und Fortg. d. Ref.* 2 vols., Leipzig, 1717, 1718, containing, in addition to many useful documents, SPALATINI *Annales* (up to 1543), F. MYCONII, *hist. reform.* KAPP, *Kl. Nachlese nützl. Urkunden.* 4 parts, Leipzig, 1727 ff. RIEDERER, *Nachrichten zur K., Gelehrten-u. Büchergesch*, 4 vols., Altdorf, 1764-1768: STROBEL, *Miscellaneen, Beiträge u. Neue Beiträge.* Nürnb. 1778 ff.; 1784 ff.; 1790 ff. FÖRSTEMANN, *Archiv f. d. G. d. R.* Halle, 1831; the same, *N. Urkundenbuch*, Hamb, 1842. M. LENZ, *Briefw. Landgr. Philipps mit Bucer*, 3 vols., Leipz. 1880-1891 (Pp St A. 5. 28. 47). NEUDECKER, *Urkunden aus der Ref.-Zeit.*, Kassel, 1836. the same, *Merkw. Aktenstücke*, Nürnb, 1838. the same, *N. Beiträge*, Leipz., 1841, 2 vols. J. C. SEIDEMANN, *Erläuterungen zur Ref.-Gesch.* Dresd., 1844. *Beiträge zur Ref.-Gesch.*, 2 parts, Dresd., 1845-1848. K. LANZ, *Corr. des Kaisers Karl V.*, 3 vols.

Leipz., 1844-1846. G. HEINE. *Briefe an Karl V.* (1530-1532), Berlin, 1848. *Polit. Corr. der Stadt Strassb.*, edited by VIRCK and WINCKELMANN. 2 vols., Strassb., 1882-1887, *Nuntiaturberichte aus Deutschl.*, edited by W. FRIEDENSBURG. First Division, 2 vols., 1533-1538, Gotha, 1892. HORTLEDER, *Von den Ursachen des teutschen Kriegs*, 2 vols., Frankf., 1617-1618, (1522-:558). A. VON DRUFFEL, *Briefe und Akten zur Gesch. des 16 Jhs mit bes. Rücksicht auf Baierns Fürstenhaus.* 3 vols., München, 1873-1880.

Literature: JOH. SLEIDANUS, *De statu religionis et reip. Carolo V. Caesare commentarii:* Argent. 1555; edited at the end of vol. 3, Francf. 1785. A. SCULTETUS, *Annalium evangelii saec. 16 per Europ. renovati decades I. et II.*, (1516 to 1536) in VON DER HARDT, *Hist. litteraria ref.*, Frcf. 1717. V. L. VON SECKENDORF, *Comment. historicus et apolog. de Lutheranismo*, 1517-1546,[2] Lips., 1692. SALIG, *Vollst. Hist. d. CA.* (1517-1562), 3 parts. Halle, 1730-1745. GERDESIUS, *Introductio in Hist. Evglii sec. 16 passim per Europam renovati*, 4 vols. Groning, 1744. MARHEINEKE, *Gesch. der teutschen Ref.*, 4 parts, Berlin, 1831 to 1834. L. RANKE, *Deutsche Gesch. im ZA d. Ref.*, Berl., 1839, 6 vols., *Works*, Vols. i.-vi. K. HAGEN, *Deutschlands lit. u. rel. Verhältnisse im Ref.-ZA.* 3 vols., Erl. 1841-1844. J. DÖLLINGER, *Die Ref., ihre innere Entwicklung und ihre Wirkungen*, 3 vols.,[2] Regensb., 1848. K. F. A. KAHNIS, *D. d. Ref. I.*, Leipz., 1872. J. JANSSEN, *Deutsche Gesch. seit dem Ausg. d. MA.*, vols. ii. and iii., Freib., 1879-1881. F. v. BEZOLD, *Gesch. d. deutschen Ref.*, Berlin, 1866 ff. G. EGELHAAF, *Deutsche Gesch. im 16 Jh bis zum Augsb. Rel.-Frieden.*, 2 vols., Stuttg., 1889-1892. F. B. v. BUCHOLTZ, *Gesch. d. Regierung Ferdin. I.* 8 vols., and volume of documents. Wien, 1831-1838. VON ROMMEL, *Philipp d. Grossm.*, 2 vols., and volume of documents. Giessen, 1830 ff. H. BAUMGARTEN, *Gesch. Karls V.*; up to the present 3 vols., Stuttg., 1885-1892. (HEFELE) *Conciliengesch.* Vol. 9, by HERGENRÖTHER (1517-1536). Freib., 1890.

Biography of Luther: MELANCHTHONS *kurzer Abriss von* 1546, in CR VI., 155 ff. (originally the Preface to Vol. II. of the Wittenb. edition of Luther's Works); JOH. COCHLEUS *Commentaria de actis et scriptis Lutheri.* Mogunt., 1549, (well informed, but hostile and self-complacent). M. RATZEBERGER, *Handschriftl. Gesch. über Luther und seine Zeit*, edited by NEUDECKER. Jena, 1850 (written from the party standpoint of the anti-philippistic Lutheran). J. MATHESIUS, *Historien von des ehrwürd. D.M. Lutheri Anfang, Lere, Leben und Sterben.* Nürnberg, 1566, and since that time, in numberless edns. (Sermons of the loyal and pious pupil) J. KÖSTLIN, *M. Luther*, 2 vols.[2] Elberf. 1883. TH. KOLDE, *M.L.*, 2 vols., Gotha, 1884-1893. (These two scientifically independent works render the mass of older literature out of date). Add to these G. PLITT *Einleitung in die Augustana.* Vol. I. *Gesch. der evg. K. bis zum Augsb. Reichstag.* Erl. 1867. (*The Biography of Luther* in 6 volumes by the convert G. EVERS, Mainz, 1883-1891, is spiteful, a work written with a purpose only to be considered as a pamphlet. Against this, as against the abundant ultramontane Luther-literature of recent years, its misunderstandings and misrepresentations, cp. W. WALTHER, *Luther im jüngsten röm. Gericht.*, 4 parts, Halle, 1886-1892; LUTHEROPHILUS, *das 6 Gebot und Luthers Leben.*, Halle, 1893.

CHAPTER FIRST.

Luther's Rupture with Rome.

1. The course of Luther's development up to the commencement of the Struggle.

Sources: WA I., III., IV.; Enders I.
Literature: K. JÜRGENS, *Luther von seiner Geburt bis zum Ablasstr.*, 3 vols., Leipz., 1846-1847. J. KÖSTLIN in St Kr 1871, 7 ff. TH. KOLDE, *Die deutsche Augustinercongreg. und Joh. v. Staupitz*. Gotha, 1879. H. HERING, *die Mystik Luthers*, Leipz., 1879. F. W. KAMPSCHULTE, *die Univ. Erfurt*, 2 vols., Trier 1858-1860. OERGEL, *Beitr. z. Gesch. des Erf. Humanismus, in Mitth. d. Ver. f. d. Gesch. u. Alterthumskunde von Erf.* XV. O. SCHMIDT, *Luthers Bekanntsch. mit den Klassikern*, Leipz., 1883. For STAUPITZ: his *Opera*, ed. KNAAKE I. Potsdam, 1867; add RITSCHL in JdTh. 1869, 555 ff. GRIMM in ZhTh 7, 2, 58 ff.; N. PAULUS in JGG XII 309 ff., 773 ff.; the same in JGG XII. 68 ff. on the Journey to Rome. DIECKHOFF, *Luthers Lehre in ihrer ersten Gestalt*, Rostock, 1887. LOOFS, DG³ 1893, pp. 344 ff. F. NITZSCH, *L. u. Arist.*, Kiel, 1883. F. BAHLOW, *L.s Stellung z. Philos.*, Berl., 1891.

The German Reformation commences with the course of the inner development of a personality, which in itself fully tested the religious and ecclesiastical training for Catholic piety, but, in striving after the assurance of salvation on the path of religious knowledge, attained to a new understanding of the Gospel, the practical consequences of which were bound to bring the true son of the Church irresistibly into conflict with the organs of the Catholic Church. Up to the year 1521, the history of the Reformation is consequently almost identical with the history of Martin Luther's development, searchings, and struggles.

Luther sprang from a German peasant family, which had settled at Möhra in Thuringia. His father, Hans Luther, had removed from there to Eisleben, to look for work in the mines: here his son Martin by his wife Margaret (maiden name Ziegler, StKr 1881, 684 ff.) was born on the 10th of November, 1483.[1] After a few months, the family went on to Mansfeld, where it gradually worked its way up from its original state of poverty to a financially improved and respected position. Both the parents were pious Catholics, although the father certainly had little liking for monks and clergy (cp. EA 44, 235). Rendered shy by the harshness of his bringing up, the boy made but slow progress in the

---

[1] There is no doubt that Luther was born in this year, not in 1484, although in later years, he himself varied in his statements.

schools at Mansfeld and Magdeburg; it was at Eisenach, where he was for a time admitted into the highly respected family of one Cotta, a merchant,[1] and became acquainted with a more refined mode of life, that he first attained a freer development and commenced to display his abundant talents. In 1501, he entered the University of Erfurt,[2] to study law in accordance with his father's wish. This institution was still completely dominated by the medieval spirit and system of instruction, although a minority of Humanists still existed by the side of the representatives of Scholasticism. Although he attended a course of lectures on the humanities (on Reuchlin's Sergius) and by private study made himself familiar with the writers of antiquity (especially Virgil, Cicero, and Terence), and further, contracted personal friendship with individual younger Humanists, he remained far removed from the humanistic turn of mind. He never belonged to the league, which here gathered round CONRAD MUTIANUS,[3] Canon of Gotha. Its members regarded him as "the Philosopher," but at the same time, as a "lively, genial comrade," and "a musician." However, it was no linguistic or æsthetic interest that attracted him to the classical authors, but his liking for their practical worldly wisdom. Having taken his Mastership in Arts in 1505, he was about to commence the special study of the law, when he suddenly (July 17th) disappeared in the Augustinian Convent. The question "How can I find a merciful God?" had laid hold upon him: the sudden death of a friend, and the terrors of a thunderstorm had deeply shocked him, and impelled him to utter the vow: "Help, dear St. Anna, I will become a monk." His intention was, by "becoming pious and giving satisfaction," to procure for himself a merciful God: in this, the "complete sacrifice" of his life in monastic self-sacrifice was to assist him. He chose a convent of the order of Augustinian Hermits of the Observance.[4] The convent of Erfurt belonged to the "German Congregation," regulated by PROLES, and now under the Vicarship of JOH. VON STAUPITZ. In the convents, which had come under the guidance of these men zealous for monastic holiness, there existed in many cases a seriousness combined with monastic ideals; and, side by side with these, scientific strivings, fervour in preaching and the care of souls, and careful superintendence of the brotherhoods that had become popular in the second half of the 15th century. No trace is to be found in the Order of a freer, evangelically disposed Theology, such as has frequently been supposed. The theologians of the Order defended papal absolution, were zealous promoters of the worship of Mary, vigorous advocates of the system of indulgences, and the like.[5] Luther took his monasticism very seriously—his father became angry. After his novitiate, a period of continued self-denial for the youthful Master of Arts, he entered a monastery and then

---

[1] The "juvenile" Frau Ursula Cotta has been transformed, in the light of more recent investigation, into a matron who was probably at the time already advanced in years; cp. SCHNEIDEWIND, *Das Lutherhaus in Eisenach*, 1883.

[2] Cp. NIC. PAULUS, *Barth. Usingen*, Freib. 1893.

[3] Cp. KRAUSE, *Briefwechsel des Mutianus Rufus*, Kassel, 1885. GILLERT, *Briefwechsel des Conr. M.*, Halle, 1890.

[4] *De observantia*: see Vol. ii. of this work, pp. 460, 539.

[5] Staupitz was not the first to introduce diligent reading of the Holy Scriptures: it had already been prescribed in earlier constitutions. Cp. N. PAULUS, *Joh. Hoffmeister*, Freib. 1891, p. 7.

commenced the study of scholastic theology, in which he showed a preference for the later school-men, Occam, d'Ailly, Gerson, and Biel, whose shrewdness attracted him. But, with all his progress in his studies, he never forgets the question of justification and salvation. "If ever a monk reached Heaven by monkish life, I also resolved I would reach it." He cannot do enough in the matter of asceticism: but the more earnestly he struggles with his sins, the more he discovers in himself anger, envy, and pride. The object of admiration in the convent owing to the strictness of his life, he is tormented by the feeling of being abandoned by God. Staupitz,[1] whose attention was directed to him on one of his visitations, took upon himself the care of Luther's soul. Certainly he did not understand the depth of the needs of Luther's soul, but he referred him from subtle speculations concerning predestination to the fact of expiation, to the shepherd Jesus, who allows no one to be torn from his arms. He taught him that penitence does not commence with fear of the God of punishment, but with love of the God, who will justify sinners. On his advice, Luther commences the study of the Scriptures, together with Augustine and Bernard. This private study leads him further. In 1507, he was ordained priest and held his first mass. The year after, in accordance with a resolution of the Order, his convent sends him off to that of Wittenberg, to finish his theological studies at the new University (founded 1502), and commence his academic activity. There he became *baccalareus* and *sententiarius* in 1509, and then Erfurt suddenly recalled him. Disputes between Staupitz and a number of the convents placed under his control, amongst which was that of Erfurt (not that of Wittenberg), excited the German Congregation: and Luther, who was treated with great confidence by Staupitz and enjoyed a high reputation amongst the brethren, was well fitted to act as negotiator and advocate. This dispute also occasioned his being sent (in 1511) to the Pope as the deputy of the seven convents concerned in it. This journey to Rome, on which occasion he successfully represented the standpoint of the convents at the Curia, subsequently proved extremely instructive to him from the gloomy insight which it afforded him into foreign, Romish piety, but at the time in no way shook his devotion to the Papacy and the Church. Returning again to Wittenberg, he finished his graduation in Theology, and became a Doctor in that faculty in the autumn of 1512. Contrary to the usual custom, he now delivered exclusively exegetical lectures,—on the Psalms, and the Epistles to the Romans and Galatians. In 1515, he was appointed district-vicar of eleven convents in Saxony and Thuringia, and devoted himself with pastoral earnestness to the guidance of the brethren entrusted to his care. At the same time, at the urgent request of Staupitz, he also began to turn his attention to preaching, in which his practically popular method soon broke through the scholastic forms of preaching. The writings of the later German Mystics (TAULER [Vol. II. p. 469]) and "German Theology" have a powerful attraction for him, without specifically mystic speculations having gained a hold upon him.

During this period of study and the commencement of teaching, the foundation of Luther's "New Theology" is completed in a number of religious fundamental ideas, which for the most part

---

[1] Staupitz also first underwent a continuous development under the influence of Luther's development. At that time he was simply the practically experienced Christian, who—without any definite system—was Luther's adviser.

flashed upon his mind as a new understanding of individual passages of Scripture: that, e.g., in *Romans* I. 17, God's justice does not denote that *qua deus iustus est et peccatores iniustosque punit*, but that *qua nos deus misericors justificat per fidem*: that *Genesis*, iv. 5, means, that the person must be just, before works well-pleasing to God can be performed by him, but that the person does not become just by works: in like manner, according to *Isaiah*, xxviii. 21 (Vulg.) the difference between God's *opus alienum* (wrath against and crushing of the sinner) and *opus suum* (showing mercy and forgiveness). In his view, *Justificatio* is identified, with ever increasing definiteness, with the idea of forgiveness of sins, but at the same time also is on principle regarded as *Sanctificatio*, as the awakening of a new life; *Gratia* again (according to biblical usage), according to him, is used to indicate God's feeling towards us = *Misericordia*; *Fides* still more decidedly = confidence in God's promise and the work of Christ. These simple fundamental views of religion, due to the influence of Augustine, are combined with the conviction of the absolute incapacity of the natural man for good, and its predestinarian conclusions. At the same time, he takes up an attitude of ever keener opposition to the **piety** of his time (not to the doctrine and constitution of the Church), the superficial, formal, and self-righteous nature of which he attacked both in the lecture-room and in the pulpit; at the same time, the forms of devotion exhibited in the worship of the Saints, pilgrimages and the like, which were cultivated with especial fervour at the end of the Middle Ages, are criticised by him with ever increasing keenness and recognised as caricatures of genuine religious feeling.

On the other hand, he is left almost unaffected by the quarrels between the Humanists and Dominicans (Vol. ii., p. 533); certainly, in REUCHLIN's dispute with the monks of Cologne, he declares against the latter, but only because there were things more necessary to be done in the Church of the Lord than to burn Jewish books, and the famous pamphlet of the younger contentious Humanist, the *Epistolae virorum obscurorum*, offends him by its tone; " *votum probo, opus non probo* " (ENDERS, I. 62). Neither has he any enthusiasm for the Erasmus-cult of these days; however valuable the Greek New Testament (1516) and the *Adnotationes* upon it are to him, to whatever extent he recognises Erasmus's erudition, he clearly detects traces of the difference of mind; as Erasmus feels drawn towards Jerome, so does Luther towards Augustine. But he certainly commences, of his own accord, a struggle against the domineering position of Aristotle in the sphere of Theology; it is in his Ethics that he sees the scientific source of the Pelagian character of scholastic theology; " back from Aristotle to Paul and Augustine " becomes the watchword of a new " Wittenberg " Theology, for which Luther more and more inspired his colleagues (Carlstadt, Armsdorf, and others) with enthusiasm.

2. The Dispute about Indulgences.

Literature: KAPP, *Schauplatz des Tetzel'schen Ablass-Krams.*[2] Leipz. 1720; the same, *Sammlung einiger zum . . . Ablass . . . gehörigen Schrifften*, Leipz. 1731. GRÖNE, *Tetzel und Luther*, Soest., 1853; the same, *Der Ablass.* Regensb. 1863. KÖRNER, *Tetzel*, Frankenberg, 1880. BRATKE, *Luthers 95 Thesen*, Göttingen, 1884. DIECKHOFF, *Der Ablassstreit*, Gotha, 1886. GRUBE in lit. *Rundschau für das kath. Deutschl.*, 1889. No. 6. J. MAY, *Card. Albrecht II. von Mainz u. Magdeb.*, 2 vols., München, 1865-1875. G. KAWERAU, *Sobald das Geld im Kasten klingt*, Barmen, 1889. DIETTERLE, *die franciscan. Summae Confessorum und ihre Bestimmungen über den Ablass*, Döbeln, 1893 (Progr.).

In 1513, the warlike Julius II. was succeeded by the Medicean Leo X. (Vol. II., p. 530), the man of refined enjoyment of life, the sympathiser with the culture of the Renaissance,[1] and the clever financial politician. The general tithe imposed upon Christendom for the purpose of carrying on war against the Turks, for which the fifth Lateran Council of 1517 had given permission, and financial operations such as the appointment of numerous Cardinals, the creation of new offices, posts of honour, an order of Knights and the like, were not sufficient to fill the treasuries; he also had recourse to the favourite method of granting indulgences.

Julian II. had already issued (in 1506) an indulgence for the new building of St. Peter's Church (in place of the Basilica of ancient fame) and caused it to be promulgated by Franciscans in Italy and the Slavonic countries (BM V 481 f.). After this, in 1514, the same indulgence had been offered for sale by Arcimboldi in North Germany and in the Scandinavian North, and by Franciscans in Switzerland. In 1513 and 1514, the Archbishoprics of Magdeburg and Mainz had fallen to the Margrave ALBERT, the youthful brother (born 1490) of Joachim I., Elector of Brandenburg, in addition to the administration of the bishopric of Halberstadt. He had promised his Mainz electors that he would pay the heavy expenses of the papal *pallium* himself, the Fuggers having advanced him the money for the purpose. At his earnest entreaty and for a cash payment of 10,000 ducats, Leo, on April 15th, 1515, made over to him the right of promulgating this indulgence for eight years in his ecclesiastical parishes and in the Brandenburg countries; half of the money that was got in, after deducting expenses, was to be paid into the Papal exchequer. But, as the claim of the Archbishop to the second half of the moneys was not explicitly mentioned in Rome, he waited, after opening up the transaction, until this matter was settled. It was not until 1517 that the affair began to progress. The Dominican JOH. TETZEL[2] of Leipzig, who had already in many ways shown

---

[1] Hence the German Humanists at first received him with loud applause; so, even as late as 1518, PETR. MOSELLANUS, *de variarum linguarum cognitione*, Ausg. Jenae, 1634, p. 9 f.

[2] As yet we possess no account of his life, which satisfies all requirements; SCHIRREN's animadversions in *Arch. f. d. Gesch. Livlands* VIII., p. 198, f. still hold good; at present, the best account is KÖRNER's.

his activity as an agent for indulgences since the year 1502, entered Albert's service and, in the summer, travelled through the districts of Magdeburg and Brandenburg. It was an indulgence *in forma Jubilaei*, whereby, by way of a fiction, Rome with its places of mercy, which people formerly sought out as pilgrims, was conveniently brought before their door; *perpendat populus, quod hic est Roma*.[1] The kind of grace it offered was announced in the *Instructio summaria pro subcommissariis*[2] issued by Albert on the lines of earlier examples, and the method of puffing up these acts of grace may be learnt from Tetzel's sermons composed for his assistants.[3] There were four different graces to be obtained: 1. On the supposition of previous confession, a *plenaria remissio omnium peccatorum*, i.e., recovery of the *gratia Dei* and complete cancelling of every *poenae in purgatorio luendae*, in return for certain devotional exercises and a *contributio in cistam* taxed according to the amount of a man's property; 2. By the purchase of a "confessionale" was obtained the *facultas eligendi confessorem idoneum*, who, amongst other things, even in cases reserved for the apostolic chair, would be able to give absolution *semel in vita et in mortis articulo*, to grant exemption from vows, and once in life and then in peril of death to bestow plenary indulgence (as in 1); 3. By paying indulgence-money, a man could obtain for himself and his parents, provided they *in charitate decesserunt*, the *participatio omnium bonorum ecclesiae universalis;* lastly 4. Also in return for a contribution according to a fixed rate, the *plenaria omnium peccatorum remissio* for particular souls in purgatory; this remission of sins was administered to these souls by the Pope in proportion to the *charitas in qua defunctus decessit* and the *contributio viventis*.—Consequently, the theory of indulgences, which had already long ago obtained a certain ecclesiastical sanction not by resolution of a Council, but by the authority of theologians of repute and the practice of the Church, was here correctly represented. The indulgence does not refer to the **guilt** of sin, but to the remission of censures decreed by the church, and not only to that, but also to **punishments** of sin meted out by the justice of God to the sinner, in this case, that is to say, in purgatory. The doctrine of indulgences forms a complement of the doctrine of the Sacrament of repentance. But, while the later school-men pretty generally declared the *attritio*, the imperfect penitence ("gallows'-repentance"), which had its origin in fear of punishment, to be sufficient in order to obtain the sacramental forgiveness of sins, while the indulgence conveniently put aside punishments themselves here and in purgatory, **guarantees of happiness and exemption from punishment,** which ruined the religiousness of the people, were procured **without real conversion.**

It was, in addition, notorious that the Curia, like the prelates, managed these concessions of indulgence purely as financial speculations, and it is obvious that, in the sale of these spiritual wares, the loudest "crier" was the most welcome to those who undertook the financial operation; lastly, it was no secret that the indulgence-money was afterwards frequently devoted unblushingly to purposes quite different from the pretended spiritual ones.[4]

[1] KAPP, *Schauplatz*. p. 44.
[2] KAPP, *Sammlung* p. 117 ff.
[3] V.D. HARDT, *Hist. litter. ref.* iv. 14. ff. KAPP, *Schauplatz.*, p. 43 ff.
[4] Cp. on this point BOMHOVERS, *Schone historie* (about 1508) in the *Archiv für die Geschichte von Liv-, Est- und Curland,* VIII. (1861) p. 170 ff, 191 f.

Tetzel, who was no worse than others of his profession, was a preacher who knew how to lay on the colours most effectually without exactly distorting the traditional doctrine of indulgences, a man of by no means irreproachable morals, who had already been involved in frequent quarrels in consequence of his pretentious bearing. In the autumn of 1517, while plying his trade, he had reached Juterbogk and Zerbst in the neighbourhood of Wittenberg —he had been forbidden to carry on business in the Electorate of Saxony—where damaging stories were told of the methods by which he puffed up the indulgence.[1]

Luther, in his intercourse with members of the community, who had hastened thither to buy *confessionalia*, witnessed its evil effects: he saw the doctrine of the penitence of the Christian reduced to utter confusion. He accordingly resolved, after he had on several occasions preached upon the indulgence to the community, to clear up, to his own satisfaction and that of others, the real nature of the indulgence, which the Church approved of and which nevertheless brought in its train consequences so injurious to the religiousness of the people. This he endeavoured to do by means of 95 disputation theses[2] or propositions which, in accordance with academic usage, he affixed to the door of the castle church on the 31st of October, as the vigil of All Saints' Day, the dedicatory festival of the church, which was endowed with an indulgence. He sent his theses to his superiors, the Archbishop Albert and the Bishop of Brandenburg Hieronymus Scultetus, and drew their attention to the doubtful proceedings that went on.

The theses are nothing but a programme of Reformation. In them, he does away with the dangerous identification of penitence with penitential sacrament; the **whole** life of believers is to be a change of mind, a conversion. He seeks to limit the competency of papal indulgences to the remission of canonical ecclesiastical punishments and, consequently, to the living; on the one hand, he develops evangelical ideas, the consequence of which is the negation of an ecclesiastical mediatorship in reference to the forgiveness of sin and punishment; on the other, his endeavour is to understand absolution, like indulgence,

---

[1] There can be no doubt of the genuineness of the saying attributed to Tetzel, "As soon as the money chinks in the box, the soul leaps forth from Purgatory." Silvester di Prierio declared it to be a *mera et catholica veritas* (EA *opp. v. a.* I. 357). Subsequently, Tetzel, in his theses (EA *opp. v. a.* I. 300 cp. WIMPINA, ANACEPHALAEOSIS 1528, 44 b.) did not **dispute** the statement, but rather **went further**: "The soul is released from Purgatory more rapidly than the indulgence-money can reach the bottom of the box."

[2] Facsimile reprint, Berlin, 1892; WA I 229 ff., in a new German version BA I 99 ff.

as a *declaratio remissionis divinae*. He consoles himself with the idea, that the practices of the preachers of indulgences were unknown to the Pope, and consequently regards it as a duty enjoined upon him by the Church, to tell the people that he (the Pope) desires their prayers rather than their money. The effort to make the way of salvation clear for the sinner is as pronounced as the endeavour to elicit a tolerable interpretation for the ecclesiastical arrangement of indulgences. Even good Catholic circles rejoiced at this protest against the traffic in indulgences.[1]

No one presented himself for the discussion challenged by Luther; there was no reply from Albert. Nevertheless, the affair closely concerned the latter, as the proceeds of the sale of indulgences were bound to suffer from such a protest, especially as a reprimand had just been sent from Rome, to the effect that the commissaries were injuring "the holy business" by excessive expenditure. In consequence of the unseemly behaviour of his people, Tetzel received a reprimand, but, for the rest, the trade was to be continued. Luther's bishop, on the other hand, in an answer couched in friendly terms, warned him to keep silence and not to interfere with the authority of the Church. Tetzel himself, however, replied in some theses composed for him (by CONR. WIMPINA)[2] and posted up in Frankfort on the Oder. These theses correctly develop the medieval doctrine of indulgences—indulgence extends to **all** punishments of sins, even to souls in purgatory; those who are *attriti* and *per confessionem contriti* have already obtained forgiveness, **minima** *contritio sufficit ad peccatorum remissionem*—; Luther answered, in 1518, with his *Sermon von Ablass und Gnade*.[3] Tetzel replied in his *Vorlegung wyder einen vormessen Sermon*,[4] and subsequently, in a second series of theses (May, 1518); whereupon Luther, by his *Freiheit eines Sermons päpstl. Ablass belangend*, put an end to this dispute in June.

In the meanwhile, he completed a detailed elucidation of his 95 theses (**Resolutiones**) which, while waiting for the verdict of the Church, he dedicated to the Pope,[5] and sent to his bishop with an accompanying letter couched in humble terms. Significantly enough, although still uncertainly and inconsistently, recourse is had from the Pope, as a human being liable to error, to the verdict of a Council, but not unconditionally, and the papal authority over the Church is only recognised according to *Romans* xiii., 2; a new idea of the Church makes itself noticeable in contrast with the prevailing one.

---

[1] GESS in ZKG ix. 590.
[2] WIMPINA, *Anaceph*. I. Bl. 39 indicates himself (*nos*) as their author.
[3] Cp., against WA I 239, KOLDE in GGA 1884, p. 986 f.
[4] In KAPP, *Sammlung*, p. 317 ff.
[5] In regard to a still more humbly worded outline of this letter cp. ThLB 1892, 360.

Joh. Eck of Ingolstadt, who had previously approached Luther in a friendly spirit, was the first who mixed himself up in the quarrel between Luther and Tetzel. In March, his essay *Obelisci*, circulated only in MS. form, came into Luther's hands; it consisted of carping remarks upon the theses, in the course of which Luther was attacked as a "Bohemian" and as the *novus Propheta, qui egreditur terminos, quos constituerunt patres nostri*. Luther issued a rejoinder in his *Asterisci*, also in MS.[1]

3. The Negotiations with Cajetan and Miltitz.

Literature: JÄGER in ZhTh 28, 431 ff. SEIDEMANN, *Miltitz*. Dresd. 1844.

The Pope had at first regarded the dispute about indulgences as a monkish quarrel; he then commissioned the general of the Augustinians "to pacify the man." However, before he had taken any steps, the Dominican SILVESTER Mazzolini PRIERIAS, master of the palace and papal censor of books, bestirred himself, and within three days, wrote a counter-treatise (June, 1518), which unreservedly espoused the cause of Tetzel, even in the matter of "the money in the box"; it was of even still greater importance that he placed at the head of it a number of rigorously curialistic propositions[2] relating to the Church, which is virtually included in the infallible Pope; any one who dissents from the doctrine of Rome and the Pope is a heretic, consequently, everyone who asserts *ecclesiam Romanam non posse facere id quod de facto facit*. Luther confronted this opponent with the infallibility of the Holy Scriptures. But Rome was already preparing to bring a charge of heresy against him. Roman judges (amongst them Prierias) were appointed, and on the 7th of August, the summons to Rome reached Wittenberg. Immediately afterwards, the Saxon Provincial of the Augustinians was directed by the General of the Order to have Luther imprisoned.[3] The latter begged FREDERICK the Wise to intercede for him at Rome, with a view to his being examined on German territory. Frederick, who at the time was in Augsburg at Maximilian's last imperial diet, by negotiation with the papal legate, Cardinal CAJETAN (vol. ii. p. 530), succeeded in obtaining permission for Luther to be examined by the legate on German soil, at Augsburg, at the end of the diet. On the 7th of October, Luther presented himself at Augsburg, where, at the

---

[1] The two Essays were first printed in 1545.
[2] EA opp. v. a. I. 346 f.
[3] ZKG II. 476. KOLDE, *Augustinercongr.* p. 411 f.

request of the electoral councillors, he at first waited for the imperial letter of safe conduct.

On the 12th of October he entered the presence of the learned Dominican, who received him in a fatherly manner, but, at the same time, curtly demanded the recantation of his errors, his promise not to be guilty of them again, and a vow that he would abstain from everything calculated to produce confusion in the church. During the conversation that ensued about the errors of Luther alluded to by the Cardinal, the curialism of the latter came into unyielding collision with Luther's assertion, that papal decretals had frequently perverted the Scriptures. The next day, Luther read a "protestation," in which he submitted his previous writings to the judgment of the Church and *omnibus melius sentientibus*, and declared his readiness to accept the judgment of the Universities of Bâle, Freiburg, Louvain, or Paris. The Cardinal, on the other hand, curtly demanded recantation, but finally allowed him to present a written defence. When Luther handed this in on the 14th, Cajetan for the third time demanded recantation, refused to allow Luther to speak, and dismissed him ungraciously with a threat of excommunication. At this critical moment, Staupitz prudently released Luther from the vow of obedience to the order and left the city himself, to avoid being obliged to take any proceedings against his friend. The latter now appealed (Oct. 16) in due form *a papa non bene informato ad melius informandum*, notified the same to the Cardinal, and, as the latter persistently maintained a suspicious silence, secretly took flight from the city, not without reason, for, on the 23rd of August, the papal order had already been issued, to arrest Martin "the heretic" and convey him to Rome.[1]

On his return home, Luther published the *Acta Augustana Minutes of the Augsburg Conference*].[2] Meanwhile, Cajetan had demanded from Frederick Luther's extradition to Rome or, at least, that he should be expelled from Saxony; the Elector immediately showed his letter to Luther, whereupon the latter begged him not to give him up, at the same time expressing his willingness to leave the country. But as he even declared himself ready to allow himself to be confuted, the Elector was not yet willing to let the ornament of his University go. In the meantime (Nov. 25), Luther solemnly appealed from the Pope to the Council. But at Rome, people were hesitating about the ban and bringing pressure to bear upon Frederick, since, owing to political reasons (Election of Emperor) they desired to keep him well disposed towards them. The papal chamberlain, KARL VON

---

[1] Concerning the genuineness of the papal brief, which Luther was at first disinclined to believe, cp. KOLDE, *Luthers Stellung zu Concil und Kirche*. Gütersloh, 1876, p. 115 f.; WA II. 22; *Conc. Gesch.* IX 69; EVERS, II. 102, 547; H. ULMANN, DZGW, X 1 ff.

[2] WA II. 1 ff., and StKr 1888, p. 166 ff.

MILTITZ, a Saxon nobleman, was commissioned, when conveying the "golden rose" intended for the Elector, to press for the extradition of Luther to Rome at the same time. But, on his arrival on German soil, he learned with astonishment what keen interest was already being extensively taken in Luther's case by all the nation, and he accordingly resolved to leave the "golden rose" in keeping somewhere for awhile, and, on his own responsibility, before presenting it, to enter upon the path of amicable intervention.

Tetzel had to be sacrificed for this purpose. Miltitz summoned him to Altenburg, but he declared that he could not travel in safety, considering the excited state of the people. Accordingly, Miltitz visited him in the Dominican convent at Leipzig, searchingly investigated the manner in which he had carried out his office and his manner of life; the result was unfavourable, and Tetzel was treated very ungraciously; a few months later, he died, utterly broken down by this unexpected disgrace. Luther, on the other hand, obeyed the summons to Altenburg. As Miltitz was unsuccessful in his demand for recantation, he condescended to negotiations lasting several days, the result of which was as follows: both parties were henceforth to remain silent, and Luther's case was to be submitted to the judgment of an intelligent German bishop, who should indicate the points in which Luther had gone too far. He was further to write an essay, to prevent his earlier writings being misunderstood, and to confess to the Pope that he had been too hasty.

The affair seemed happily settled by prudent diplomacy. Luther wrote the letter desired and the pacifying essay *(Unterricht auf etliche Artikel, die ihm von seinen Abgönnern aufgelegt und zugemessen werden)*,[1] half submitting and vigorously rejecting the conclusions of his premises, but still it was only "an episode, which could not arrest his development." And could the Curia approve of this patching-up of fundamental differences?

4. The Leipzig Disputation.

Sources: WA II. Enders II. Add Luther's correspondence with Eck, recently discovered, in Enders V.

Literature: SEIDEMANN, *die L. Disp.* Dresden, 1843. ALBERT in ZhTh 43, 382 ff. SEIFERT, *die Reform. in Leipzig.* Leipz. 1883. WIEDEMANN, *J. Eck.* Regensb., 1865. HpBl 108, 241 ff.

ECK deserves the credit of having put an end to this cessation of hostilities which could not possibly last. This learned authority on Scholasticism and famous disputant, after his *Obelisci* (see p. 15) became known, was challenged by CARLSTADT, who as dean of the theological faculty, thought himself obliged to champion

---

[1] [Information on certain articles, laid to his charge and attributed to him by his enemies].

its honour, in some theses (May 9th, 1518), upon sin, grace, and free will, which were more closely worked out at Wittenberg in several disputations. Eck first declined the challenge, then answered with counter-theses, and demanded a disputation at Rome, Paris, or Cologne. Carlstadt answered and conditionally agreed to the proposal of a disputation. In the personal negotiations that took place between Luther (representing Carlstadt) and Eck at Augsburg, Leipzig or Erfurt was agreed upon. Eck decided in favour of Leipzig, where he applied for leave to hold the debate. At the same time, he published (at the end of December) twelve theses, in which, as Luther observed with indignation, he himself, rather than Carlstadt, was attacked. Hereby Luther considered himself released from the promise he had given to Miltitz—certainly Eck knew nothing of this agreement—and, breaking through the bonds of that arrangement without any qualms of conscience, he replied, at the beginning of February, 1519, with twelve counter-theses. Eck now inserted in his theses, by way of supplement, a proposition directed against Carlstadt. Luther accordingly subjoined a new counter-thesis: Carlstadt also now published his defence.

The most important thing in Eck's challenge was the fact that he again insisted upon the teaching of the **Church**; Luther had observed in his *Resolutiones* that, even in the time of Gregory I., Rome possessed no primacy over the whole Church, at least, not in the East (WA I 571); Eck now affirmed that this precedence was already in existence in the times before Pope Silvester (314-335), since the Pope was the successor of Peter and general Vicegerent of Christ. Luther now rejoined, that the supremacy of the Roman Church was only founded on the *frigidissima decreta* (only 400 years old) of the Popes, whereas the history of the first eleven centuries, the Scriptures, and the Council of Nicaea bore witness to the contrary. Again, just before the disputation, he issued a special essay against this thesis of Eck (WA II. 183 ff.) In this, serious questions connected with the history of the Church were concerned. He denies the *ius divinum* of the papal primacy, bases its authority only upon *Romans*, xiii, and declares that *Matthew*, xvi, does not refer to Peter alone, but to him as the *commune organum omnium Apostolorum*. The keys belong *ecclesiae, communitati*; the priest who exercises office *non suo iure, sed ministerio ecclesiae clavibus utitur* (II. 189-191).

The University of Leipzig, pressed by Duke GEORGE, had only consented against its will to the disputation between Eck and Carlstadt; George also had scruples, when Luther was drawn into it. Negotiations were protracted. Miltitz now summoned Luther to appear before the Archbishop of Treves in conformity with the agreement; but, under the altered conditions, Luther refused (May

17th). The disputation began without permission having arrived for Luther to take part in it: he could only set out upon the journey as Carlstadt's companion. After the settlement of tedious negotiations about the conditions of the disputation, on the 27th of June, Eck and Carlstadt opened the debate (on Free Will) in the presence of a large concourse of hearers, some of whom had hurried up from a distance; on the 4th of July, Luther was able to take part and the discussion was now directed to the question of the papacy.

Here Eck succeeded in exposing Luther as a **heretic.** In Constance, the view that subordination to the Pope was not necessary to salvation, had already been condemned as a heresy of Huss. Thereupon Luther replied: *certum est, inter articulos J. Hus vel Bohemorum multos esse plane Christianissimos et evangelicos, quos non possit universalis ecclesia damnare* (WA II. 279). Terrified at the conclusions, which Eck at once drew from this, Luther endeavoured to move back a step, and suggested that perhaps those Articles were only foisted in the acts of the Council; but that certainly only the word of God, not a council, was infallible; and then, in order partly to withdraw this proposition from Eck's attack and to make a concession, that resolutions of the Council were certainly binding in matters of belief (WA II. 303). The disputation then turned upon purgatory and indulgence; on the 14th of July, Carlstadt again took part in it. In the end, it was agreed to lay the proceedings of the disputation before the Universities of Erfurt and Paris. Both parties claimed the victory; however, Luther himself looked back with uneasiness upon a struggle, in which cleverness, not truth had gained the day. On his return home, he wrote an explanatory essay upon his disputation theses; he recognises the Pope, but rejects his *ius divinum* as a *novum dogma ;* the whole constitution of the Church is an ecclesiastical, not a divine arrangement (WA II. 432 ff); some Erfurt friends brought the proceedings of the disputation before the public.[1]

The proceedings at Leipzig, as may easily be understood, attracted the attention of the Bohemians to Luther; Utraquists entered into correspondence with him, and Huss's treatise *de ecclesia* was sent him. On the other hand, a new Catholic opponent, HIERONYMUS (Jerome) EMSER of Dresden, seized upon the opportunity of drawing Luther out, by undertaking, in an apparently friendly manner, to defend him against the suspicion of being an ally of the Bohemians. This gave rise to a quarrel, which, during the years immediately following, caused both parties frequently to take up the pen.[2] Although the disputation made Duke George Luther's decided enemy, on the other hand, from the time of his conflict with Eck, the increasing sympathy of the humanistic circles (*e.g.*, in

---

[1] Cp. HEUMANN, *Documenta litter,* p. 248.
[2] ENDERS, *Luther und Emser,* 2 vols., Halle, 1889-91.

Erfurt), which soon grew to a positive offer of a stormy alliance, inclined in his favour.

Eck, in the proud consciousness of victory, at once applied to the Elector Frederick, demanding that he should now have Luther's books burnt, and then repaired to South Germany and on to Rome, in order to press for Luther's condemnation. The biting satire *Eccius dedolatus* [the planed Eck (corner or angle)], of which the humanist W. Pirkheimer was indicated as the author[1] pursued him from Nuremberg. MILTITZ now really wanted to present the golden rose to the Elector, but only succeeded in seeing the Councillors; his part was played out. Luther, however, gladly returned from the controversial questions of the day to the cardinal question of the way of salvation in his **Commentary upon the Epistle to the Galatians** (WA II. 436 ff.).

5. Melanchthon.

Literature: HEYD, *Mel. und Tübingen.* Tübg. 1839. C. SCHMIDT, *Ph. M.* Elberf. 1861. K. HARTFELDER, *Mel. als Praeceptor Germaniae.* Berlin, 1889. PLITT-KOLDE, *die loci comm. Ph. Mels.*[2] Erlangen, 1890.

Meanwhile, a colleague was introduced to Luther, with whom his life and work were henceforth to be indissolubly connected in mutual giving and receiving, influencing and being influenced. PHIL. MELANCHTHON (Schwarzert, who writes his name "Melanthon" after 1531), the son of an armourer and great nephew of Reuchlin, born (1497) in Bretten, where (and in Pforzheim) he received his early education, had already studied at the University of Heidelberg when twelve years old, and afterwards migrated (1512) to Tübingen, where he found capable humanistic teachers; after taking his Master of Arts in 1514, he worked as a teacher of the Classical languages, a philologer in the best sense of the world, interesting himself not only in the grammar (he wrote a *Griechische Grammatik*, 1518), but also in the spirit and views of life of the ancients. Reuchlin's quarrel had made him a decided humanistic enemy of the Schoolmen, "the Sophists"; on the other hand, Luther's appearance on the scene left him as yet unaffected[2]—as the task of his life, he conceived the plan of editing the **genuine** Aristotle (CR I. 26). In the summer of 1518, on Reuchlin's recommendation, he went as teacher of Greek to Wittenberg, where "the puny little creature" speedily captured all men's hearts, aroused a general enthusiasm for the study of Greek (Luther also took lessons with him), and also, being of an impressionable turn of mind, in the atmosphere of Wittenburg acquired an interest in the religious question aroused by Luther's vigorous

---

[1] Reprinted by SZAMATOLSKI (Berlin, 1891), who, without sufficient reason, calls Pirkheimer's authorship into question (cp. ThLZ, 1891, Sp. 380 ff.)

[2] He has been described, against the facts of history, as having "placed his universal knowledge at the service of theology while still at Tübingen" (von Bezold p. 280.)

nature. Luther's cause became his, the interest in Aristotle waned, the humanist became the theologian. And Luther himself urged his friend to take up theology. On September 9th, 1519, he became bachelor of theology; the propositions, which he defended on this occasion, breathe Luther's spirit,—even in part go beyond him.[1] The accession of this humanist to the cause of the Reformation was of eventful importance for the latter. Not only did Melanchthon exert himself to put Luther into correspondence with the leaders Reuchlin and Erasmus (Enders I. 320 ff. and 488 ff.), not only did numerous younger humanists, following his example, complete the accession to Luther, (and thus the results of humanism subsequently proved especially beneficial to Protestanism in matters of education), but it became the task of his universal learning and formally trained gifts to transform Luther's ideal world into clearly intelligible, acceptable doctrine. "Luther's ideas have only been historically realised in the form, which Melanchthon gave them. On the other hand, Melanchthon's statements cannot be understood without the chief motives and catchwords given by Luther."[2] While Melanchthon placed all his knowledge at the service of theology, he not only brought humanism into relation with the Church, but it thus also became possible for the Protestant University system to follow the analogy of the medieval *studium generale*: the entire *orbis litterarum* became an organic whole, of propaedeutic and subsidiary value for the *princeps omnium artium, Theologia*.[3]

6. The Humanistic Allies and the new Emperor.

Sources: HUTTENI *opp.* ed. Böcking.

Literature: KAMPSCHULTE, *de Croto Rubiano*, Bonnæ, 1862. EINERT, *Joh. Jäger*, Jena, 1883. STRAUSS, *U. v. Hutten*, 3 parts, Leipz. 1858-1860. SZAMATOLSKI, *Huttens deutsche Schriften*, Strassburg, 1891. WERCKSHAGEN, *Luther und Hutten*, Wittenb. 1888. REINDELL, *Luther, Crotus und Hutten*, Marb. 1890. H. BAUMGARTEN, *Gesch. Karls V.* (see above p. 6); the same, *Karl V. und die deutsche Reform*. Halle, 1889; the same, in FdG 1883, 521 ff.

After the Leipzig disputation, the humanistic circles began to take an interest in Luther. CROTUS RUBIANUS (Joh. Jäger), one of the authors of the Letters of Obscure men (*Epistolae obscurorum virorum*) on the plea of old acquaintance, in October, 1519, endeavoured to get into communication with Luther from Italy.[4]

---

[1] See PLITT-KOLDE p. 260 ff. The ostensibly "meaningless" *sine cicotibus* in Thesis 13 is the Greek ἄνευ εἰκότων cp. CR XIII. 617 f.

[2] TRÖLTSCH, *Vernunft und Offenbarung bei J. Gerhard und Mel.* Göttingen, 1891 p. 139.

[3] Cp. HARTFELDER p. 160 ff. Tröltsch, p. 68.

[4] The frequently alleged correspondence between Crotus and Luther in the autumn of 1518, only rests upon a misunderstanding of the passages in the letters (ENDERS I. 227 and 303). We only know of one letter from Crotus to Luther at Augsburg, but this did not reach him (ENDERS II. 208).

In stormy language, he invited him as *pater patriae*, upon whom the eyes of all would be turned, to take part in the struggle against the *fraus Romana*, declaring that the people must be stirred up by *publice clamare*. Somewhat later, he was also approached by ULRICH V. HUTTEN, whose edition of Laurentius Valla's treatise upon the so-called *Donation of Constantine* had just reached Luther's hands, and confirmed him in the apprehension, which had already occupied his attention ever since the Augsburg negotiations had left their impression upon his mind, that the **Antichrist** had arisen in the Papacy. Hutten, "a wandering poet with the pretensions of a cavalier," had worked his way up through the struggles and trials of an adventurous life, in numerous literary quarrels, to the position of mouthpiece of the national enthusiasm for the liberation of Germany from Roman tyranny, a protest glowing with anger against the practices of the degenerate Church of the World, and fostered, in widely extended circles, hatred of the Romanists. This deadly enmity was "of purely worldly, half humanistic, half national origin and does not exhibit a single trace of any religious interest whatever."[1] Consequently, the positive aims of his efforts always remained obscure. If he had at first criticised Luther's behaviour as due to a monkish quarrel, he now sought a reconciliation. He offered Luther Sickingen's protection at this critical moment, and proposed fresh assaults upon Rome. Further, recognising that the struggle against Rome would in this case be carried on from **religious** motives, he now exerted himself to the utmost to strike this note in his conduct of the dispute. Thus, in the spring of 1520, his dialogues *Vadiscus sive Trias Romana* (directed against the corruption of Rome and its exploitation of Germany) and *Inspicientes* (attacking the papal legate Cajetan) were published and added fuel to the flame.

For Luther, however, this alliance was neither personally a matter of indifference nor, in reality, without influence. Certainly, the **German** was not now for the first time awakened in him, and the idea that he borrowed the materials for his accusations against Rome from Hutten, is shown on closer examination, to be unsupported[2]; it is doubtful whether he was acquainted with the *Vadiscus* at all, when he wrote his Essay to the Christian nobility. Far stronger than such direct influences or borrowings, which certain persons

---

[1] v. BEZOLD, p. 286.
[2] Compare against KAMPSCHULTE, MAURENBRECHER and WERCKSHAGEN, especially WA VI. 381 ff. and REINDELL (also GGA 1890, 484 ff. ZdA 1891, 220 ff.

thought they had discovered, was **the indirect influence of the contemporary parallel intellectual movement.** He also began to regard his cause as the cause of the nation; he had an inkling of a rising of the German people against oppression that had already been patiently endured too long; it roused him to believe that, in case of eventualities, he might rely upon human protection in the struggle. While inwardly renouncing the Roman Church which he had so long loyally reverenced, his mission now rises before him—not to suffer alone as a martyr to his cause, but **to lead his people to the fight for freedom.** Accordingly, the tone of his writings changes; theological discussion makes way for **the appeal to his people.** He believes in a reorganisation of things, which will be carried out, but not without noise and tumult: his intention certainly is, to carry out this *bellum domini* only with his own weapon, the word of God, but at the same time he hopes that all appeals amongst the people will also co-operate. Luther would have broken with Rome even without that national movement; but its development may well have hastened the rupture. Although Luther has adopted much from its *gravamina* in his programme, yet everything has been driven into the light of the religious question. Thus, for a short time, the religious and the humanistic-national movements meet; **both combined** stir the German nation in these spring days of the Reformation to its very depths. In numerous pamphlets, for the most part anonymous, the soul of the people declares its assent.[1] In sight of most people both movements blend into one—the peculiar characteristics of both reasserted themselves soon enough.

At this time, when the German people was in the highest state of excitement, Luther was expecting the overthrow of the Papacy. For him, also, the question had now grown beyond the purely religious aspect: all in the nation, who desired help and a reorganisation of things, looked to him, filled with expectation. He expected an explosion, but not in the form of a tumult, but as the exercise of a right of necessity in opposition to the authorities of the Curia. He even—and many with him—hoped for the goodwill of the youthful Emperor Charles. His Essay to the Christian nobility was dedicated to this " gentle blood," and a special section devoted to the independence of his imperial dignity as far as Rome was concerned. But even here Luther mistook the actual condition of things.

On the 12th of January, 1519, Maximilian died, after he had received the promise of the Electors, while still in Augsburg, that they would elect his grandson Charles (born at Ghent in 1500) King of Rome. But now, in addition, Francis I. of France appeared as a candidate for the throne; both courted the votes of the Electors. All, with the exception of Frederick the Wise, showed themselves open to bribery. Francis paid ready money and had the Pope on his side, his power seemed in the highest degree dangerous to the independence

---

[1] SCHADE, *Satiren und Pasquille.* ² Hannover. 3 vols. A. BAUR, *Deutschl. in den Jahren* 1517-1525. Ulm 1872.

of the Electors; nevertheless, he finally lost the favourable chance, as the dislike of the German people to the Frenchman was mightily stirred on the Rhine at a decisive moment. The Pope attempted, even at the last hour, to guide the choice of the Electors to Joachim I. or Frederick the Wise, and the latter had a chance of being elected. but he did not consider his dynastic power strong enough for this position. Thus, at last, on the 28th of June, 1519, the votes were united in favour of Charles. The agitation of the Pope for the election of the Frenchman as Emperor had been the first of those serious tactical errors, whereby the Popes of the Reformation period injured their cause. But it was a mistake for people to expect far and wide a national anti-Romish policy from the young Emperor who was distasteful to the Pope.

Charles regarded his new office as bestowed upon him by God for the purpose of acting against Turks and heretics. From religious conviction—for he was a faithful son of the Roman Church—he looked upon himself as protector of the Church. But his political interest also pointed in the direction of the same task. For, in the enormous kingdoms in three quarters of the globe, over which he had to rule, the unity of the Roman Church was the indispensable support of his authority. Hence, political instinct had always made him anxious for the friendship of the Pope, however disloyal and untrustworthy this friend might prove towards him. He tore up the confidential letter which Luther addressed to him.

7. The Great Reformation Treatises of the Year 1520.

Literature: LEMME, *die drei grossen Reformationsschriften Ls.*[2] Gotha. 1884.

Luther's **Sermon Von den guten Werken**[1] had grown into a book, in which he joyously gives expression to his new understanding of the Gospel; the central meaning of belief, which is a firm trust in God's mercy and moves men's hearts to keep God's commandments with joy in free love, limited by each man's professional duties. Never had the *Summa* of the Gospel been preached so clearly and with such telling effect to the German people. The incredibly foolish defence of the *ius divinum* of the Holy See which was undertaken by the Franciscan Augustin **Alveld** of Leipzig, gave Luther the opportunity of an immediate and sharp rejoinder in his *Vom Papstthum zu Rom*,[2] and of propounding the religious idea of the Church to the laity,—the community of the believers in Christ, the existence of which is recognised by its signs, the Gospel and the Sacraments. But even here the tone, which characterises the succeeding essay to the nobility, makes itself visible: the national idea breaks forth, the hope of measures of emancipation carried out by the secular orders: his language becomes more aggressive. These ideas find expression unreservedly in the Essay (which appeared in the middle of August) addressed **"an den christlichen**

---

[1] [Discourse on Good Works].

[2] [Concerning the Papacy at Rome].

Adel deutscher Nation von des christlichen Standes Besserung."
[To the Christian nobles of the German nation: concerning the reformation of the Christian Estate.] [1]

He overthrows the three walls [2] of the Romanists, first, the elevation of the "ecclesiastical" order above the "secular" by the proclamation of the royal priesthood of the faithful: Christendom only recognises differences of service and function, not a priestly order set over the laity: the "clergy" are the mandatories of the community of believers. With this, consequently, the two other walls,—that they alone claim the right of interpreting the Scriptures, and that the Pope alone should have the power of summoning a Council—fall to the ground of themselves. A free Council is needed, as a subject for the debates of which he proposes the injury done to the Church, so far as it is caused by Roman ecclesiastical government: hence this bill of indictment is concerned chiefly with the actual administration of the Church, scarcely at all with the injuries inflicted in the matter of doctrine. Here Luther becomes the spokesman of the manifold *gravamina* of the German nation. But not only does he complain, he also formulates demands: decentralisation, the establishment of a German Church under the Primate of Germany, so that there may be left to the Pope something of the importance of a representative of the unity of the nationally organised ecclesiastical bodies; pilgrimages are to be forbidden, the celibacy of the priests abolished, the number of festivals reduced, the Universities reformed, all usurious trafficking forbidden, trading-companies limited, brothels done away with, the poor to be systematically cared for and the nuisance of beggars minimised, and the like,—in short, an abundant programme of ecclesiastical and social reorganisation.

The theological tract **De captivitate babylonica Ecclesiae praeludium** (A prelude concerning the Babylonish captivity of the Church) followed in October.[3] This endeavours to shatter the ecclesiastical methods of power, whereby it forces the life of the Christian into dependence upon the priestly church,—its seven Sacraments.

Of these, only Baptism and the Lord's supper, and, in a certain sense, the penitential Sacrament are allowed to stand; their common strength is the word of promise, which contains forgiveness of sins and requires belief. He criticises the withholding of the cup from the laity, and transubstantiation, for which (with Ailly and Occam) he would prefer to substitute a *con*substantiation without change of the elements, but, above all, the conversion of the Lord's supper into an act of sacrifice. He shows how Baptism excludes self invented works and vows, and how all the Christian's penitence is only a return to baptism; he

---

[1] WA VI. 381 ff. Of the special editions that by BENRATH holds a distinguished place, VRG Part 4. Halle, 1884.

[2] Cp. VIRGIL. *Aen.* VI. 549 (Tartarus): triplici circumdata muro.

[3] In 1519, Melanchthon already speaks of the 400 years "Babylonish Captivity" of the Church, CR I. 71. See Luther's Essay, translated into German with notes, in BA II. p. 375 ff.

criticises the practice of confession, the *character indelebilis* of the priesthood, the tyranny of the marriage legislation, and so forth. Here, certainly, the foundations of Roman Christianity were shaken. For Christianity in the Catholic acceptation stands and falls with the mediating grace of the Church and the piety that is to be founded upon a man's own performance of religious exercises. Nevertheless, Luther was convinced that he was no "heretic," since indeed he only represented the cause of "evangelical truth against the superstitious opinions of human tradition" (Enders I. 469).

But, at the same time that he had poured out the vials of his wrath upon Rome, Luther showed wonderful internal composure in his thoughtful Essay **Von der Freiheit eines Christenmenschen** (concerning the freedom of a Christian) (in both Latin and German).[1]

Here he teaches the grandeur of belief, which makes the Christian a free master in all things, since, in believing, he has Christ; but, at the same time, in his external life, he remains engaged in battle with sin, and, in affection, bound to serve his neighbour. Luther at the same time made use of the Latin edition of this Essay as a letter, which the indefatigable Miltitz had suggested to him he should send to the Pope, to show that he had never desired to attack him personally. But, during the negotiations on this matter, the papal bull threatening excommunication had already become known. Miltitz and the electoral court accordingly induced Luther to antedate his treatise the 6th of September. It is not easy to understand, how anyone could expect any good results from a letter, which, notwithstanding its courteous tone, contained so much that was offensive to the Pope.

8. The papal ban.

Literature: v. DRUFFEL in ABA 1880, I 5, 571 ff. HEFELE, *Conc.-G.* IX. 129 ff.

In January, 1520, Eck had taken a journey to Rome, where he succeeded in securing Luther's condemnation. Frederick the Wise, pointing to the excitement of the German people, vainly endeavoured to persuade Rome to consent to a refutation of Luther by the testimony of the Scriptures.[2] After lengthy deliberations in the papal consistory, the bull *Exsurge Domine* was issued under date June 15th.[3]

"Foxes will lay waste thy vineyard, a wild boar out of the forest seeks to destroy it, etc." (*Pslams*, 74, 22. 80, 14). Forty-one propositions from Luther's writings are censured (amongst them that *Haereticos comburi est contra voluntatem*

---

[1] Reprinted by KNAAKE, Halle, 1879.
[2] EA opp. v.a. V. 7 ff.
[3] BM V. 748 ff. A letter of Hoogstraten to Leo. X. was made use of in drawing it up, WA II. 384.

spiritus), particularly propositions dealing with the Church and its plenary power, and only indirectly propositions referring to his doctrine of belief and justification. It is already proof of his heresy, that he has appealed to a Council. His heretical books are to be destroyed, and he is to be deprived of his professorship and authority to preach; the faithful are to avoid intercourse with him and his followers; every place which receives him is to be placed under interdict. He is granted sixty days for recantation.

Leo forwarded the bull to Frederick the Wise with a letter of advice, dated July 8th, and called upon him to withdraw his protection from the now convicted heretic.[1] At the same time, Eck appeared in Germany, to make the bull public everywhere, but met with little encouragement from the bishops in face of the excited disposition of the people. Authority was granted him to include in the bull, at his discretion, the names of some of Luther's followers: in addition to Carlstadt and Feldkirchen of Wittenberg he selected his personal enemies, above all Pirkheimer (see p. 20) and Laz. Spengler, the town-clerk of Nuremburg, who, in 1519, had earnestly and manfully taken Luther's part in a "Vindication" written in German: in addition, Adelmann, Canon of Augsburg, whom he hated as joint author of Oecolampadius's satire *Canonicorum indoctorum responsio* (1520); lastly, Joh. Silvius Egranus the preacher of Zwickau was included in the threat of excommunication in consequence of a theological quarrel, which he had had with a Leipzig theologian. First, Adelmann, then Pirkheimer and Spengler humbled themselves before Eck and obtained absolution from the ban.[2] Luther acted differently. The University of Wittenberg, acting in concert with the Elector's councillors, delayed the publication of the bull: Luther himself was at first inclined to look upon it as a forgery of Eck. On the 17th of November, he repeated the appeal to the Council, demanded the Emperor and Princes, as representatives of the Christian Community, to espouse his cause, and, in his essay *Adversus execrabilem Antichristi bullam*, opposed the papal excommunication with his sentence of excommunication against the Antichrist in Rome: *Christus index viderit, utra excommunicatio apud eum valeat* (EA *opp. v.a.* V. 153).

Meanwhile, the Emperor Charles had made his appearance in

---

[1] BALAN, *Monum. ref.* p. 1 ff.
[2] DREWS, Pirkheimer. Leipz. 1887, p. 59 ff. ROTH, *Augsburgs Reformationsgeschichte.* München 1881, p. 65 ff.; the same, *Einführung der Ref. in Nürnb.* Würzburg, 1885, p. 71 ff.; the same, PIRKHEIMER, Halle 1887, p. 39 ff. BUCHWALD on *Silvius Egranus* in ZSKG IV. 163 ff. For *Adelmann* see ZhV Schwaben VII. 85 ff.

Germany, had been solemnly crowned at Aix-la-Chapelle on the 23rd of October, and with full conviction had taken an oath to maintain the Catholic belief as handed down to him, and to be submissive to the Pope and the Romish Church. The papal nuncios, Caraccioli and Aleander, had previously, in Flanders, handed him the bull against Luther, and had also obtained his promise that he would at any rate order Luther's writings to be burnt in the Netherlands and Burgundy. (In regard to the ban of the empire, they had been put off until the coronation should have taken place.) Aleander,[1] who was specifically commissioned for the proceedings against Luther, at once began at Louvain with an "act of faith," with which he expected to create a great impression upon the laity. On the 10th of December, Luther replied by burning the papal decretal and the bull of excommunication. "Since thou hast afflicted the Holy One of the Lord (*Mark,* I. 24) so may eternal fire consume thee!" The attitude of **Frederick** the Wise was now bound to be of decisive importance. In Cologne, on the 4th of November, the nuncios had handed him the bull together with the Pope's letter, and demanded the execution of the bull and Luther's extradition to Rome. Frederick wanted to think the matter over. **Erasmus,** who was in Cologne at the time, being questioned by him, advised him to demand that the matter should be investigated and settled by a court of arbitration of men who were beyond suspicion and capable of judging (EA *opp. v. a.* V 241 f).[2]

Thereupon Frederick replied to the nuncios, that Luther should be examined under safe conduct, before learned judges who were beyond suspicion: and then, if his writings were convicted of heresy, he would prove himself an obedient son of the Church.

With this commences the diplomatic game, which Frederick continued to play to the end of his life with wonderful cleverness, against Rome and then also against the Empire: to every demand to take steps against Luther he immediately raises an objection: to every complaint against Luther's or his own

---

[1] BALAN, *Monumenta reformationis Luth.* Regensb. 1884. BRIEGER, *Al. u. L.* Gotha, 1884. KALKOFF, *Die Depeschen des Nuntius Al.* Halle, 1886.

[2] On this occasion, he gave utterance to the sarcastic expression: *Lutherus peccavit in duobus, nempe quod tetigit coronam Pontificis et ventres monachorum.* Shortly before, at a council which has erroneously made its way into Zwingli's works (*Opp. lat.* I p. 1 ff.), he had given similar advice in the matter of a court of arbitration, but had at the same time admitted that **Luther had undoubtedly deviated from the truth** (cp. Geiger in ALG V. 554 ff). Side by side with this, the same man, when it suited him, could declare that he had never read Luther's writings.

attitude, he has a rejoinder: and he knows how to hold in suspense his actual partisanship of Luther and therewith his conflict with the ecclesiastical as well as with the imperial power. Hence it remains uncertain, whether, how far. and since when, he heartily made Luther's cause his own. Originally loyal and devoted, in a medieval spirit, to the Church and its guarantees of salvation. he **at first** endeavoured to protect, in the person of Luther, the famous Professor of his University: then Luther's piety. as exhibited in his practically edifying writings (e.g. the consolatory letter *Tessaradecas consolatoria* (1519) addressed to himself) won him over, the religious movement in his country affected him, and the role of mediator cleverly played by his court chaplain and private secretary, G. SPALATIN, had its share in preventing him from abandoning Luther even in most critical situations: finally, this game of hide and seek against Curia and Empire was entirely congenial to the skilled diplomatist[1].

9. The Diet of Worms.

Sources: FÖRSTEMANN, N. Urkundenbuch p. 1. ff. Aleander's dispatches in Balan, Brieger, Kalkoff (see above, p. 28). EA *pp. v. a.* VI. 1 ff. Account by SPALATIN, *Annales,* p. 38; by Peutinger in KOLDE, *Anal.* 28: by Spengler in M. MAYER, *Spengleriana* p. 13 ff.

Literature: BRIEGER in *Marburger Festschrift zur Lutherfeier,* 1883. KOLDE, *Luther und der Reichstag zu Worms.* Halle, 1883. SOLDAN, *Der Reichstag zu Worms.*[2] Worms, 1883. ELTER, *Luther und der Wormser Reichstag.* Bonn, 1886. BURCKHARDT, *Luthers Wormser Rede* in Spalatins Wiedergabe in St Kr 1894. p. 151 ff.

After his coronation, the Emperor proceeded to Worms, where he awaited the assembling of the States, whom he summoned thither on the 1st of November to the diet. The question, whether Luther would now be condemned unheard, as the Curia demanded, or whether he would be summoned before the imperial diet, was variously answered, according to the information that came in as to the Pope's position in relation to Charles and King Francis: first, it was said, he was to be summoned, and then only, if he were willing to recant; then (December 29th) that he was to be condemned unheard by imperial mandate. The arrival of the States and the respect that was necessarily paid to them again rendered Luther's prospects more favourable. Meanwhile, on the 3rd of January, 1521, **Leo** solemnly published the ban *Decet Romanum Pontificem*[2], and called out the secular sword against the heretic.

---

[1] Cp. KOLDE, *Friedr. d. W.* Erl. 1881; KÖSTLIN in StKr 1882, 700; the same, *Friedr. d. W. u. die Schlosskirche zu Wittbg.* Wittbg. 1892 (also StKr 1893, 603 ff.). That Frederick, as late as 1522, caused relics to be bought up, perhaps was a part of the role, in which he wanted to protect Luther.

[2] BM V 761 ff.

On the 13th of February, Aleander appeared before the imperial diet and, in a long speech,[1] described Luther as a man who was politically dangerous, in whose case the Pope had now exhausted his leniency: he added that they should not allow themselves to be blinded by his show of piety, but, without further ado, should comply with the sentence of the Church, and not venture, as laymen, to claim to be judges in this matter. The Emperor also was ready to act in this manner, but the States, who were acquainted with public feeling, and who also had their *gravamina* against the Curia, wished notwithstanding to examine him: perhaps, said they, he recanted his "unchristian" propositions and only upheld his criticism of abuses. A committee of the States accordingly recommended that he should be summoned, and the Emperor, who really wanted to bring a number of demands before the States, and perhaps also was really again beginning to entertain suspicions of the papal policy,[2] gave in on the first point. Accordingly, the summons was drawn up (March 6th, but not sent until the 15th): it commenced in a most respectful manner, "Honourable, dear, beloved, etc." In the meantime, on the 10th, Charles signed a mandate, according to which all Luther's writings were to be delivered up to the authorities. It was made public on the 26th, when Luther was already on his journey, during which the approval of the nation showed itself to him in many places. When he heard of the mandate on his way, he was taken aback, but still continued his journey, and refused to allow himself to be dissuaded from finishing it, either by the efforts of the Emperor's confessor Glapio, who wanted to make him turn aside and go to Sickingen at his castle at Ebernburg, or by a warning from Spalatin, who feared the worst for him at Worms. To Aleander's amazement, he entered Worms on the 16th of April, eagerly welcomed by crowds of people. At noon on the 17th, he stood in the presence of Emperor and Empire.

The Official[3] of Treves, Joh. v. Eck, instructed by Aleander, laid Luther's books before him, and asked him whether he were willing to recant. Luther answered in a low voice ("as if he were frightened and terrified"), that he asked for time for reflection. This *début* was generally disappointing: "in any case,

---

[1] FÖRSTEMANN, *N. Urkundenbuch.* p. 30 ff. Add Aleander's despatches of February 14th.

[2] Cp. on this point BRIEGER, p. 3 ff. BAUMGARTEN, *Karl V.*, I 441. ULMANN in Fd G XI 638 ff.

[3] [The Catholic representative of the Bishop in secular matters].

he has lost much of his earlier reputation," triumphantly exclaimed Aleander: the great crisis had been too much for him, and the peasant's son had been confounded amidst this brilliant company.[1] On the following day, Eck addressed him ungraciously in the presence of the assembly of the States with respect to his request for time for reflection; but Luther this time gave a final answer "in a bold and fearless voice." He distinguished three classes of his writings: the devotional, which even his enemies appreciated: the polemical treatises against the Pope and Papists, which he said he could not possibly recant: lastly, his controversial writings against private individuals—in these he admitted that he might have been too violent, but even these he could not materially recant. He could only recant if he were confuted by the writings of the prophets and evangelists. A promise had previously been given to Aleander that no one should argue with Luther: accordingly, it was impossible to agree to his request. Eck then declared to him that his erroneous doctrines had long since been refuted by the Church as errors of Wiclif and Huss: would he not at least be willing to recant what had been already been condemned at Constance? Luther rejoined, that he could believe neither Pope nor Councils alone, that he required written testimony or clear arguments. On being questioned, he again affirmed his conviction, that even the Council of Constance had been at variance with the Scriptures in many points. This led to an excited argument between Luther and Eck, but the Emperor rose angrily and cut short further dispute. Amidst the general confusion which this produced, Luther was heard to exclaim: "I cannot do otherwise! here I stand, God help me! Amen."[2]

Frederick the Wise was satisfied with Luther's first appearance. But what next? On the following morning, Charles, in an autograph message,[3] unreservedly declared himself a "Catholic" Emperor, and that as such, although he would certainly give the monk safe-conduct, in other respects he would proceed against him as against a declared heretic. Not so the States, some of which were personally favourably disposed to Luther, while others were subject to the pressure of public opinion, which now vented itself in anonymous, threatening placards. They accordingly endeavoured to bring the influence of clever mediators to bear upon Luther.

The Elector of Treves conducted these negotiations, the Chancellor of Baden, Dr. Vehus,[4] was spokesman. Although extensive concessions were made, it was at least desired to extort from him compliance with the demand of the Council, but he persisted in declaring that the Word of God was the only court he recognised. JOH. COCHLAEUS,[5] who had been brought up as a human-

---

[1] Cp. WALTHER, *Ls Beruf.* Halle, 1890, p. 139 ff.

[2] These words have produced an extensive controversial literature, for which see KÖSTLIN, II² 800 (453); add v. GRUNER in FdG 1886, 141 ff. v. DOMMER, *die Lutherdrucke auf d. Hamb. Stadtbibl.* Leipz. 1888, p. 113 ff.

[3] BAUMGARTEN I 456 ff.

[4] SEIDEMANN in Zh Th 21, 80 ff.

[5] GESS, *Joh. Cochl.* Oppeln 1886. KOLDE in *Kirchengesch. Studien.* Leipz. 1888, 197, ff. (on the other side, DITTRICH in JGG X 110 ff.)

ist, had previously been well-disposed to the Reformation; but, alarmed by Luther's *Babylonish Captivity* and, in short, converted by his connection with the Court of Mainz into an opponent of Luther, even he now pressed upon him and challenged him to a discussion, in return for which he was to give up all claim to safe conduct: a proposal, to which Luther was ready to assent, but it was rendered void by the Elector's Councillors.[1] Luther laid open his heart to the Archbishop of Treves in the form of a confession; Aleander eagerly desired to hear what this confession was, and asked the Archbishop (but in vain) to break the secret of the confessional. But the negotiations themselves remained altogether fruitless: Luther could neither submit unconditionally to the verdict of a council, which it was desired to induce him to do, nor did the offer from the Archbishop of a benefice as the reward of submission, make any impression upon him. Thus this attempt on the part of the States had to be abandoned.

Against the advice of his Councillors, Charles gave the heretic safe-conduct and allowed him three weeks more for the return journey: he only forbade him to preach on the way. By command of the Emperor he left the city on the 26th of April. Aleander now urged that he should be proclaimed an outlaw and drew up the draft of the ban himself, but was unable to induce the Emperor to issue the edict in his own name without the States. Charles preferred to settle all the other affairs of the diet, before he proceeded with this affair, which was not to the liking of many. It was not until the 25th of May, when Frederick and the Count Palatine had already departed—and even then not at an official assembly of the States, but when the Princes happened by chance to be with him—that he surprised them by having the edict read to them (not laid before them for decision). The Elector Joachim thereupon, without authorisation, declared his assent: no one ventured to gainsay him. Thus it seemed as if Emperor and States were in this case unanimous! Under date (wrongly) of the 8th of May,[2] the **Edict of Worms** was promulgated in the different countries: it declared Luther an outlaw in the harshest terms and demanded that he should be delivered over to the Emperor. His followers were to be apprehended, their property confiscated, his own and his followers' writings burnt, the censorship of his books to be exercised by the spiritual authorities.

Under normal conditions, Luther would now have been lost, and the Reformation crushed. But, in the German Empire of that time, imperial laws were only valid so far as the interest of the individual States permitted, while,

---

[1] ZhTh 21, 91 ff. GESS, p. 13 ff. JANSSEN II 166 ff. WEDEWER, *Dietenberger*. Freiburg 1888, p. 51 f. *Briefwechsel des Jonas* II 346. Enders III 174 ff.

[2] As to the question whether this proceeding is to be regarded as a deceitful ante-dating, cp. TESDORPF and BRIEGER in ZKG IX 129 ff. 132 ff.

in regard to the latter, **popular opinion**, which impetuously espoused the cause of Luther,[1] played a part which was by no means to be underrated. Matters would certainly have been different, if Charles had now remained in Germany and had been able to apply his will and authority to carrying out the edict: but, on the 22nd of May, the French Ambassador in Worms resigned his office, the Frenchman's war of revenge for his defeat in the imperial election was directly impending, and Charles's years-long struggles for the defence of his vast possessions, which for a long time withdrew him from Germany and German affairs, commenced. This was destined to save Luther and the Reformation.

10. The Sojourn at the Wartburg and the Return to Wittenberg.
Sources: WA VIII. Enders III.
Literature: M. LENZ in the *Marb. Festschrift zum Lutherfest.* 1883.—C. F. JÄGER, *Andr. Bodenstein v. Carlstadt.* Stuttgart, 1856.

As early as the 28th of April, Luther had written to Wittenberg from Frankfort: "I am going to hide myself, I do not yet know where. We must keep silent and suffer for awhile."[2] The day before his departure from Worms, the electoral councillors disclosed to him the plan, in accordance with which the prudent and cautious Frederick wanted to get him out of the way for a time,[3] so that it remained officially unknown, where he was really staying. The Elector so arranged it, that he did not even know himself, in which of his castles Luther was, and hence could affirm his ignorance. Indeed, the secret was so loyally kept and the plan so successfully carried out, that both friend and foe were at first misled and e.g. Cochlaeus, even after Luther's death, was unable to ascertain, where his "Patmos" had really been.[4]

Luther, while visiting his relatives in Thuringia, was to all appearance violently attacked with hostile intent near Altenstein, and carried off to the Wartburg. Aleander at once rightly conjectured that Frederick the Wise had a hand in the game, although the latter in all respects kept up the part of one who knew nothing with considerable skill.[5] The people's attention was occupied by the most varied conjectures and apprehensions regarding Luther's fate. A. Dürer lamented, in touching language, the lot of him who had been carried off, perhaps murdered by his enemies, and called upon Erasmus now to take the command in the struggle as protector of the truth.[6]

---

[1] Cp. the pamphlets, *M. Luthers Passion, Neukarsthans, Kuntz und Fritz* and others, in A. BAUR, p. 97-157; v. BEZOLD, p. 351 ff.

[2] De Wette I 588.

[3] It was, however, with quite a different idea that Charles V. recommended Frederick at Worms *ut fratrem Martinum in aliqua arce detineat* (BALAN, p. 94): accordingly we must not, with EGELHAAF I 350, speak of a certain consideration for the Emperor's wishes.

[4] Cp. MYCONIUS, Hist. Ref. p. 42. G. KAWERAU, *Agricola*, p. 42.

[5] Cp. KALKOFF, p. 192 ff.

[6] ZUCKER, *Dürers Stellung zur Reformation.* Erlangen, 1886, p. 14 ff. For the widely circulated view, that the cause of Erasmus and Luther was one and the same, cp. the passages in HARTFELDER HTb 1892, 123 f.—For Dürer's religious position see also DANKO in ThQ 70, 244 ff. Dürer's lament for Luther's disappearance is also discussed by K. LANGEN and F. FUHSE, *Dürer's schriftlicher Nachlass.* Halle, 1893, p. 161 ff. For his religious position, see the same, p. 66 ff. 380, and elsewhere.

Luther found rest at the Wartburg after the storm, in the character of *Junker Georg* (Squire George). It was no doubt at the same time a severe trial of patience for the soldier ready for battle. The unusual mode of life brought on bodily ailments, and his keeping himself hidden seemed to him a desertion of his colours. The restriction placed upon his reading drove him to intense study of the Bible, and he soon proved his existence to the world by weighty writings. JAC. LATOMUS, the Louvain theologian, by a polemical treatise called forth from him the *Rationis Latomianae Confutatio*, an exhaustive exposition of his doctrine of sin and justification by faith. Then followed *Von der Beichte, ob die der Papst Macht habe, zu gebieten*, a loud protest against the tyranny of the Romish practice of confession, a keen criticism of the untenable proof of the same adduced from Scripture, but also the eulogy of an evangelical order of confession and excommunication. Through all this time he also worked at his *Kirchenpostille* (Book of Homilies)[1], which the Elector had previously urged him to write. In December, he commenced the **Translation of the New Testament** from the Greek (First Edition, September, 1522).

The Old Testament followed in single parts in the following years: the first complete and at the same time revised edition, of the Bible appeared in 1534, after a second thorough revision, the edition of 1541; the editions of 1543 and 1545 were also revised and improved. For Luther's independence of the medieval German Bible (Vol. II. p. 543) see WALTHER, *L.s Bibelübersetzung kein Plagiat*, Erl. 1891, although this work was not unknown to him, at any rate in later years, as BILTZ has shown, *Beiträge über deutsche Sprache und Literatur*. Berl. 1891, p. 125 ff.

His Catholic contemporaries already took delight in accusing him of having deliberately **falsified** the Bible in his translation (*e.g.*, by interpolating "alone" in *Romans*, 3, 28 and elsewhere), and, since **Döllinger**, Ref. III., 131 ff. has attempted to establish the charge afresh, it is confidently repeated by many. He himself had already (1530) answered it with a clear conscience and carefully considered sarcasm, EA 65, 104 ff., in a circular letter, in which he treats of the task of the "interpreter" as a pioneer and in advance of his contemporaries. For a justification of Luther in detail compare WALTHER, *Luthers Glaubensgewissheit*, Halle, 1892, p. 61 ff., 91 ff. For Luther's "fine and almost unerring linguistic feeling," cp. P. PIETSCH, *L. und die hochdeutsche Schriftsprache*, Bresl. 1883, and KEYSSNER, *die drei Psalterbearbeitungen Luthers*, Meiningen, 1890. Owing to the publication of H. Emser's New Testament 1527, and Joh. Dietenberger's Bible, 1534, both of whom made Luther's work the foundation of their own, his Bible obtained a wide circulation even amongst the Catholics;

---

[1] It appeared piecemeal, the Advent sermons in 1521 before the departure for Worms; then, in 1522 and 1525, the winter homilies; lastly, 1527-1528, the summer half and the festival sermons. (These homilies were Sermons on the Gospels and Epistles for the Church year).

for Luther's work now compelled his opponents to meet the popular demand for German Bibles. Emser certainly, in his concluding remarks, **warned** the laity against the Bible; "let every layman concern himself about a godly life more than about the Scriptures, which are commended to the learned alone." Zürich provided itself with a German Bible partly its own, Luther's work being taken as the foundation of the New Testament and the historical books of the Old, while a special version of the Prophets and Apocrypha was attempted by Leo Jud (Judah Leo); the Bible, thus put together, then underwent severe revisions (Breitinger, 1629) and touching up (from 1661: cp. J. J. Mezger, *Gesch. der deutschen Bibelübersetz. in der schweiz. ref. Kirche*, Basel, 1876; add ThLZ 1877, no. 9; ZKG III., 558 f.) An important work, which deserves notice by the side of Luther's, was the translation of the Prophets by the Anabaptists L. Hetzer and J. Denck, Worms, 1527.

Luther was driven to other deeply trenchant works by the reports as to the development of ecclesiastical affairs in Wittenberg during his absence. The University, in spite of the edict of Worms, was now more flourishing than ever: Joh. Bugenhagen (Pomeranus) of Treptow on the Rega and Just. Jonas of Erfurt had entered with Carlstadt, Amsdorf, and Melanchthon. Carlstadt, to gratify his ambition, now strove to obtain the leadership,—a doubtful prospect, considering the unsteadiness of his development and the crudeness of his ideas.

People were pressing on to practical reforms: individual clergy married; their bishops took steps against them, a literary defence of their action followed. Carlstadt now drew the further conclusion, that monks and nuns also could leave the convent and marry. Luther was taken aback when he heard of this; was there, then, no difference between the celibacy that was **forced upon** the priests by ecclesiastical law and the virginity (of those belonging to an order) which depended upon a **free** vow? Carlstadt further asserted, that marriage was enjoined upon the priests, not only permitted, by the Scriptures; that the breaking of the vow by monks and nuns was certainly a sin, but not so great as that of living an unchaste life. At the same time, he began the struggle against the adoration of images and the worship of the Saints, and on behalf of the granting of the cup to the laity. The question of monastic vows was especially serious; Carlstadt's argument was evidently untenable, and also Melanchthon endeavoured (but in vain) to find a more tenable position. Then Luther intervened with his Essay *de votis monasticis*, in which he examined the motive with which vows were taken. In most cases it was the sinful motive of obtaining special holiness, justification by one's own act. Monastic life is to so small an extent a higher grade of morality, that it much rather signifies selfish neglect of the duties of love of one's neighbour. Vows taken in this sense must be done away with. But certainly the freedom of the Gospel can also exist with subordination to a definite rule of life.

Even before this Essay appeared, steps had already been taken in Wittenberg, actually to abolish monastic life. In November, thirteen monks left the Augustinian convent, some of them becoming mechanics and citizens. Shortly before, the Augustinian

Gabriel Zwilling had denounced daily mass without a communicating congregation; the Augustinians discontinued the daily reading of the mass: Luther supported them in this with his Essay *Vom Missbrauch der Messe* (also in Latin: *de abroganda missa privata*). When Archbishop Albert now ventured upon the attempt to reopen the traffic in indulgences in his Cathedral at Halle with an exhibition of relics, Luther, by a letter from his Patmos, in which he threatened him with an angry essay, so alarmed the frivolous prelate, that he humbled himself before him. A secret visit to his friends at Wittenberg (in December) was the occasion of his writing his " exhortation to all Christians, to keep themselves from disturbance and sedition." He told them that his Gospel did not teach disturbance, that the authorities, not the *Lord Omnes*, should be left to deal with the removal of abuses: that it was a matter of being indulgent to the weak and showing themselves " Lutherans " by something better than railing at the Pope and reckless use of the freedom of the Gospel.

Meanwhile, the Reformation went on in Wittenberg: Carlstadt (at Christmas) celebrated the holy communion without confession, without sacrifice, in both kinds, without priestly vestments: it was considered a new evangelical law, to take the host itself into the hand (Take, eat) and to pass the wine round in an ordinary drinking-cup. At Epiphany 1522, an Augustinian chapter, under the Grand Vicar Wenzel Link[1], was held, which portended the breaking up of the "German Congregation." For everyone has the right to secede; begging and votive masses are abolished, those who remain behind in the convent are regarded as a free association, the members of which, according to their several capacities, can preach the Gospel or support themselves by some handicraft. The side-altars and images of the Saints in the convent church were forcibly removed under Zwilling's direction. Carlstadt now also commenced social reforms: he established a "common chest" for the church and the poor, and for lending money.[2] In addition, some "prophets" from Zwickau had immigrated here on the 27th of December 1521. At Zwickau, **Thomas Münzer** (amongst others) had preached, a man in whom medieval mysticism and apocalypticism were combined with passionate zeal against the existing ecclesiasticism. Further, unmistakably **Taboritic** influences from the neighbouring Bohemia produced their effect amongst the cloth-makers of the city. Thus, an enthusiastically socialistic spirit of reformation grew up here in conventicle circles. The punishment of priests and godless persons is close at hand; God's spirit works in revelations and visions, not through the letter of the Scriptures, not through an ecclesiastical office; infant baptism is also reprobated. When Münzer was obliged to withdraw from Zwickau, some of

---

[1] W. REINDELL, W. Linck, I. Marb. 1892.

[2] RICHTER, *Ev. Kirchenordnungen des 16. Jahrhunderts*, Weimar, 1846, II. 484 f.

these prophets determined to try whether restless Wittenberg might be soil better suited to their seed, amongst them the cloth-maker **Nic. Storch** and the former student **Marcus Thomä Stübner.** Melanchthon was confounded and perplexed in face of the new spirit; in particular, he could not agree with their polemic against infant baptism. In his need he turned to Luther, who advised him to ask the enthusiasts for their call to their prophetic mission, and to test them in their spiritual knowledge,[1] but to use no violence against them. He firmly supported infant baptism, and he was certain that the intercessory prayer of the god-parents awoke actual belief in children under age. The mysticism of the enthusiasts met with a sympathetic reception from Carlstadt. He began to fraternise with this awakened laity and, for example, to despise academical degrees, since God manifested himself to those under age. Schools and a learned education were now regarded as a hindrance to salvation. The schoolmaster at Wittenberg implored the parents to remove their children from the school for conscience sake. The school was broken up; the students also left the University in large numbers, preferring to learn a trade. The Elector could not avoid making the anxious complaint, "They act so strangely and in so many different ways at Wittenberg, that the result is, that so many sects are formed, that each and every one is mistaken and no one knows which is which." (Enders III., 295). He was undecided and helpless in face of the confused state of affairs.

At the end of February, Luther informed him: " I myself, God willing, will be there at once. Your Highness need not be concerned about me."[2] The Elector certainly recognised that only Luther could stem the tide of confusion, and consequently in his heart himself desired Luther's return. But respect for the Council of Regency at Nuremberg, where his jealous neighbour, Duke **George**, had a seat, and caused all his actions to be suspiciously watched, so that his ambassador, Hans v. d. Planitz, had the hard task of continually proving his master's loyalty, forbade him to express this wish; only when Luther returned **against** his command and **acknowledged to him**, that he came against his orders, was help afforded him. He accordingly drew up an intricate list of instructions (Enders III., 292 ff.), which formally prohibited Luther from returning. The latter clearly understood what was meant, and assisted in the time of need, but also drew up for the cautious diplomatist so vigorous a letter, containing a most contemptuous protest of belief against the protection of princes, that Frederick was obliged to ask him in all haste for a revised letter, softened down and rendered more serviceable for his purposes. At last, after the letter had been re-written for the third time, it expressed Frederick's views (De Wette II., 137 ff., 141 ff., 146 ff.), and in this form Planitz was obliged to go round and lay it before the Council of Regency.

On the 6th of March, Luther was again in Wittenberg[3]: on the next Sunday he occupied his pulpit and made himself completely master of the situation by preaching for eight days. As the three

---

[1] Cp. GOTTSCHICK in ZThK I. 155 ff.

[2] DE WETTE, II., 137.

[3] For his meeting with some Swiss students on his journey, see J. KESSLER, *Sabbata*, ed. Götzinger. St. Gallen, 1866, I. 145 ff.

chief articles of Christianity[1] he preached to them confession of sin, acknowledgment of God's grace in Christ, and love towards one's neighbour. To the latter also belongs tolerance for the weak. Hence he blames the excessive haste of their reforms, their adherence to externals. They are on the point of making freedom a new law. His success was obvious: Carlstadt sulked in silence, Zwilling became thoughtful, Melanchthon again reserved. The "Prophets" first attempted to convert Luther in private conversation, but as he steadily opposed the Scriptures to their revelations, they left the city in anger. The Council honoured the outlaw with presents. He had, in fact, saved the progress of the Reformation from precipitancy and the spirit of fanaticism. He then continued the work of restraining and regulating, which had been commenced at Wittenberg, in those places which had been most deeply stirred,—in Zwickau and Erfurt.

And it was well that the Reformation again came into his firm hand: for, shortly afterwards, the projects of that Knighthood, actuated by humanistic and reformatory ideas, which was represented in its literary aspect by **Hutten** and in its material by **Sickingen**,[2] miserably collapsed. The latter was quite in earnest in his belief, but still more in regard to a violent change of the political situation. In the summer of 1522, he attacked the Elector of Treves, partly pretending to be acting on the Emperor's orders, in order to punish the Elector for his partisanship of the Frenchman at the imperial election, partly as if he desired to obtain the electoral dignity for himself—in reality, a fierce interested struggle of the Knight of the Empire against the power of the princes under the colour of the "Gospel." But he succumbed, and, on the 7th of May, 1523, lost his last stronghold, that of Landstuhl, and his life at the same time. In August, 1523, Hutten, a fugitive after the unsuccessful result of this insurrection, sickly and poverty-stricken, also died, on the island of Ufnau in the lake of Zürich. In Sickingen's downfall Luther, deeply affected, saw the judgment of God: Hutten had already completely disappeared from his range of vision.

11. The Formulating of reformatory Ideas in Melanchthon's Loci Communes.

Sources: CR XXI. PLITT-KOLDE, *Separat-Ausgabe*.[2] Erlang. 1890 (add KNAAKE in StKr, 1891, 301 ff). Also worthy of special notice are: the *Declamatiuncula D. in Pauli doctrinam* (1520) in PLITT-KOLDE p. 262 ff. and CR XX. 703 ff. (1522).

---

[1] Unfortunately, these most effective sermons of Luther are only preserved in scanty marginal notes, and in a double recension, in the Augsburg imprint of 1523 (= EA 28, 252 ff.) and in the Eisleben supplementary volume of 1564, (= EA 28, 203 ff.), the latter perhaps only a more copious revision of the former.

[2] ULMANN, *Fr. v. Sickingen*. Leipz. 1872: THIKÖTTER in DevBl. 1888, 77 ff.

Luther's main ideas, as they had been developed by the first years of the Reformation, found classical expression in Melanchthon's *Loci communes*[1] *rerum theologicarum seu hypotyposes theologicae*, December, 1521. The whole of the evangelical understanding of salvation and ideal of life is here set forth eloquently and with the directness of fresh impulses, the first text-book of "our theology." We can here survey the hitherto existing theological result of the new movement. All the other authorities have collapsed in the presence of the Holy Scriptures: in these it is Paul who, before all others, has been the guide to the understanding of Christ and salvation: *nullius literis propius cognosci posse Christum atque adeo salutis nostrae summam quam Paulinis* (Pl.-K. 264).[2] With this is connected the clear knowledge of having derived from Paul a theology, which had been lost to the Church soon after its beginnings, in consequence of the irruption of Greek philosophy: *nostram theologiam videntur adiuvare* **nulli neotericorum neque veterum** *scriptorum praeter Augustinum et pauculos Graecos. Origenes nimium philosophatur* (CR XX. 704). *Statim post ecclesiae auspicia per Platonicam philosophiam Christiana doctrina labefactata est* (XXI. 86). But the peculiar thing about the new understanding of salvation is, that its interest is only directed towards those articles, *qui* **nostra** *maxime referunt* (anthropology and soteriology), *peccatum, lex, gratia : tribus his summa iustificationis nostrae comprehenditur :* the others (*e.g.*, the one *de Deo uno trino, Verbi incarnatione*) *magis curiosas quam utiles disputationes continent* (xxi. 49). *Mysteria divinitatis rectius adoraverimus quam vestigaverimus* (xxi. 84). Further, the sharp distinction between *historica cognitio* and *fiducia in promissionem divinam*. No *historica cognitio de Christo* (*quod est deus et homo*, etc.) justifies; in itself it stands on the same footing as any other profane *cognitio historica : non fides, sed opinio est :* the *fides Evangelii* first begins with the fact that *Christus* **pro me** *datus sit,* **mea** *deleat peccata, vivificet* **me**; it is *fiducia misericordiae* (xx. 706, xxi. 161, 163). It is a **pernicious** use of language for us, in spite of this, to call that *historica cognitio* "faith" (xx. 708), as we usually do. *Hoc est Christum cognoscere, beneficia eius cognoscere, non . . . . eius naturas, modos incarnationis contueri* (xxi. 85). It is the business of the divine law, to point out our sins and to make criminal, *legis opus occidere et damnare;* the Gospel, on the other hand, is a promise of mercy, revealed in the person and work of Christ; that we are able to believe, is the result of the Gospel, the object of belief is the promise. *Sola fides iustificat. Quia illa fides nos Christo incorporat et inserit, ideo iustificamur, i.e., ideo nos vult reputare pro iustis* (xx. 706). Where this belief exists, *spiritus dei occupat corda :* hence, good works necessarily follow belief, but they *fiunt in carne adhuc impura*, and are hence still *immunda* even in those who are justified. *Coepta enim iustificatio est, non consummata*. Hence, even these works lack the credit of *meritum :* it is only to belief that they owe it that they are no longer regarded as sins: at every step of the Christian life *fidei* (= *misericordiae dei*) *iustificatio tribuitur* (xxi. 178). The Christian must be **certain** of this divine grace; this certainty is the characteristic of the Christian (186, 187). *Quatenus credimus, liberi sumus, quatenus diffidimus, sub lege sumus*. But Christian freedom does not mean, failure to carry out the law, but *sponte ab animo velle ac cupere quod lex poscit* (xxi. 197, 196). The pernicious distinction between generally valid

---

[1] For this expression cp. PLITT-KOLDE 33 ff. TRÖLTSCH, p. 59 ff.

[2] *Christum nostris temporibus ex unius Pauli literis cognoscere datum est* (p. 268). *Aliquamdiu prope ignoratus nunc reflorescit* (Paulus) (p. 277).

praecepta and *consilia evangelica* left to the Christian's discretion is done away with (124). The Sacraments, only two of which—Baptism and the Lord's Supper—are established by Christ, are *signa, testimonia divinae voluntatis erga nos*: they do not justify us, salvation is not necessarily bound up with them, but only with belief; they are, however, *pignora misericordiae*, a means of strengthening belief, to assist our weakness (209, 210). It is in keeping with the Pauline-Augustinian origin of this theology and the contrast in which it stands to the scholastic doctrine of *liberum arbitrium* and *meritum*, that it is drawn up in a **sharply predestinarian** spirit, even to a decided affirmative reply to the question, *utrum deus mala faciat* (87 f. xx. 705). Luther called these Loci an *invictum libellum, non solum immortalitate, sed canone quoque ecclesiastico dignum*.[1] The later editions and revisions of the Loci (especially those of 1535 and 1543) are the instructive documents of the further development, but also of the alteration, of that first understanding of the Gospel by (Luther and) Melanchthon.

---

[1] *Opp. v. a.* vii., 117.

CHAPTER SECOND.

The Movement in the Nation.

1. The Political Situation.

Literature: C. v. HÖFLER, *Papst Adrian VI.* Wien, 1880. NIPPOLD in HTb, 1875. O. R. REDLICH, *der Reichstag von Nürnberg,* 1522-1523. Leipz. 1887. ST. EHSES, *die Politik des Papstes Clemens VII.* in JGG VI. 557 ff. VII. 553 ff. *Notizenblatt des Arch. für Kunde österr. GQuellen.* 1852, 97 ff. A. RICHTER, *der Reichstag zu Nürnberg,* 1524. Leipz. 1888. EGELHAAF, I. 493 ff. H. BAUMGARTEN, *Differenzen zwischen Karl V. und Ferdinand,* 1524. DZ f. GWiss, II. 1. ff. E. BRASSE, *G. d. Speierer Nat.-Concils,* 1524. Halle 1890. J. WEIZSÄCKER in HZ 64, 199 ff. W. FRIEDENSBURG, *der Regensb. Convent in Hist. Aufs.,* dem Andenken an G. Waitz gewidmet. Hann. 1886, p. 502 ff. F. P. DATTERER, *Matth. Lang.* Freising, 1890, p. 37 ff.

After the Emperor had left Germany, the **Council of Regency** (at Nuremberg) under the presidency of **Ferdinand,** the Emperor's brother, as lieutenant of the Empire, took over the conduct of affairs. At first, chiefly at the instigation of Duke George of Saxony, it adopted an attitude hostile to the Reformation, and demanded the execution of the mandate of Worms, but did not meet with success even in Nuremberg itself, partly since perpetual want of money paralysed its efficiency. Thus also, the intervention against Frederick the Wise was not carried out, and Luther's successful action against the radical elements in Wittenberg **brought about a change of opinion in his favour.** Force, if it had been now employed against him, would have infallibly again let radicalism loose. In addition, the members of the government who had Catholic leanings also had many causes of complaint against Rome. Luther and the Reformation were thus, as a matter of fact, allowed a free hand. The brief **Diet of Nuremberg** (March, 1522), being only concerned with the question of assistance against the Turks, did not even mention his case. In the autumn of 1522, another diet assembled at Nuremberg, personally presided over by Ferdinand, at which the new Pope was represented by his nuncio Chieregati.

On the 1st of December, 1521, Leo X. had suddenly died. The self-seeking and worldly-minded conclave elected, to the general astonishment, a pious, scholastically educated Netherlander of strictly Catholic views, **Adrian VI.**, Cardinal of Tortosa. Of humble origin, he had gradually worked his way up in his ecclesiastical career, had been Charles's tutor, and for a considerable time his representative (**gobernador**) in Spain. His scholastic training rose in revolt against Luther's heresies: but, on the other hand, he had a lively sense of the fact that there were violent abuses in the Church to be contended against. By honourably removing these, he hoped to regain the goodwill of the Germans. He owed his election not to any pious zeal of the Cardinals for the welfare of the Church, but only to their mutual rivalry. His honourable efforts met with the strongest opposition in the circles of the Curia: the Italians grumbled at the barbarian, who could not even speak their language: the contrast between his austerity and parsimony and the dazzling magnificence, the love of art and luxury of the Medicean was too great. His efforts in the direction of reform led to characteristic negotiations, which showed the helplessness of goodwill in the bonds of system and conflicting interests. He also soon quarrelled with the Emperor Charles, since he did not afford him support against France, but demanded the reconciliation of the contending princes and speedy mobilisation against the Turk.

At Nuremberg, like Ferdinand, he demanded the execution of the Edict of Worms, but at the same time he desired to counter-balance defection from the Church by its reformation. Accordingly, his nuncio was obliged to make **a confession of the sins** of the Curia before the diet to the following effect. The great falling away was a punishment for sins, especially those of the prelates. The corruption had proceeded from the head to the limbs, from the Pope to the prelates. They had all sinned. But the Pope was ready to begin with the reformation of the Curia, *unde forte omne hoc malum processit*. Certainly, time was necessary to bring about this improvement: but in any case proceedings must be taken against the sects. In his judgment of Luther there was no difference between him and his predecessor. The States refused to carry out the Edict of Worms as being impossible, since it would mean civil war. They demanded that a Council should be summoned on German soil within the space of a year: till then the pure Gospel should be preached "according to the true Christian sense." (A more rigorous definition of this ambiguous formula in the Catholic sense was not carried through). Censorship regulations were to check the spread of writings calculated to occasion disorder. The resolutions were a fresh **adjournment** of a decisive opinion. Luther rejoiced at resolutions more favourable to his cause and made use of them for a public complaint against the States, who "perverted the meaning of the mandate" (WA XII. 48 ff.). As early as the 14th of

September, however, Adrian succumbed to the heavy burden of fruitless labour. Meanwhile, the internal affairs of Spain and the war with France claimed all the Emperor's attention.

The new diet, which was summoned for Martinmas, 1523, at Nuremberg, could not be opened until January, 1524. The new Pope, **Clement VII.**, Leo's cousin, Cardinal Julius di Medici, who had now at last obtained the object of his desires, was personally a man of blameless life and character, but a thorough Italian, without religious sympathies, but inclined to political intrigues, hitherto an enemy of France, and hence apparently made to be Charles's ally. He sent Cardinal Campeggi[1] as his Ambassador to Nuremberg, with instructions to demand the suppression of the heretics. The Emperor also issued an emphatic warning that the Edict of Worms was to be carried out. The majority in the diet, which was still entirely inclined to Catholicism—Frederick the Wise had left the diet before Campeggi's arrival—also recognised the edict a second time, but only declared its willingness to carry it out "as far as possible." The cities on the other hand declared that the disturbance that was to be feared rendered its execution impossible: other individual States supported them in this. Then the demand for a "common free universal council" in the German nation was repeated: but its summoning was certainly not to be thought of for a moment, as long as the Emperor and France were at war. Accordingly, the more general demand, especially urged by Bavaria, followed: to summon a "**common assembly of the German nation**" (National Council), in the autumn, at Spires, with a view to the provisional settlement of the ecclesiastical question. Consequently, there was a fresh adjournment of a decision. In addition, the electorate of Saxony and others protested against the resolution. But the chief achievement of the diet was the abolition (carried through by the princes) of the Council of Regency at Nuremberg which was too powerful for them, and the resolution passed for a central authority to be newly constituted at Esslingen. The Pope and the Emperor received the resolution of the diet in regard to the ecclesiastical question very angrily: the latter forbade the national assembly that had been planned, at which hopes had already been

---

[1] For the proposals which were submitted to him by the Franciscan A. Bomhauer for the effectual putting down of the Lutheran heresy, see JGG X. 810 ff.

entertained that Luther would appear before the German nation,[1] but against which Campeggi warned him as a dangerous opportunity for a *schisma aeternum :* Ferdinand also was terrified at this project, considering that there the princes would be able to bring about the election of a Roman King. The Emperor again demanded the carrying out of the Edict of Worms. Luther, in an essay blazing with wrath, printed the latter by the side of the fresh Nuremberg resolution as " two imperial orders that were incompatible and contradictory" (EA 24^2, 220 ff.). Enraged at the internal contradictions in the latter, he overlooked in his wrath how favourable to his cause on the whole this last resolution had turned out. The States were again indignant at the annulling of their resolution. Evidently, in view of the opposition of the Emperor (who was far from the Empire and at the time powerless) to the resolution of the States, the imperial organisation was in danger of being broken up. It was no wonder that fresh forces now took the lead in the Empire; the **territorial** powers were obliged to proceed independently, and the States were obliged to seek protection and furtherance of their interests on the path of **coalition**. The Catholic party made the first start in this direction; Ferdinand, on the advice of Campeggi,[2] in order to be able to meet the day of Spires with a firm front, at the end of June 1524, united the Dukes of Bavaria and the majority of the South German bishops at **Ratisbon** in a solid **league** against the heretics. The prohibition of Luther's writings and of studying at the University of Wittenberg, as well as certain reforms extorted from Campeggi,—such as a diminution of the number of holidays, the lightening of the ecclesiastical imposts—belonged to the programme of the league, in which for the first time the modern anti-reformatory Catholicism became an organised reality. Ferdinand himself took the lead mercilessly in the persecution of the heretics in Austria and in Breisgau. Pope and Emperor rejoiced at this convention,[3] without

---

[1] THOMAS, *Mar. Sanuti Diarium* p. 46 : *a Spira dove vegnirà Martin Lutherio in persona.* The *Wittenberger Nachricht* of April 8th, 1524, certainly refers to this: *Lutherum aiunt petiturum Wormaciam absque omni fide publica et praeter voluntatem ducis Saxonici etc.* HARTFELDER, *Melanchthoniana paedag.* p. 133.

[2] He had already, on April 25th, 1524, recommended to the Bishop of Strasburg a *mutuus consensus foedusque principum ad pellendos haereticos.*

[3] Cp. Charles's letter to Ferdinand dated the 31st of October, 1524, in DATTERER, p. lx.

considering **that it was just in this that German unity was shattered.** Only the Protestant Upper German States at first followed the Catholic model; they combined for preaching the simple Gospel and for purposes of mutual assistance, in case the attempt should be made to force the Edict of Worms upon them.

2. The Spread of the Reformation in Germany.

Literature: For C. Güttel see Biography by G. KAWERAU. Halle 1882; Link see above p. 36; Stiefel: G. KAWERAU in RE XIV. 702 ff.; Propst: JANSSEN. ²Amsterd. 1866; H. Zütphen: IKEN. Halle 1886; Brismann: Zh Th 20, 502 ff.; Myconius: LOMMATZSCH. Annab. 1825 and MEURER in *Altväter der luth. K.* IV.; Eberlin: B. RIGGENBACH. Tübing. 1874, and M. RADLKOFER. Nördl. 1887; Kettenbach: B. RIGGENBACH in RE VII. 648 ff; Lambert: J. W. BAUM. Strassb. 1840, and HASSENCAMP in *Väter der ref. K. IX.* Elberf. 1860; Bucer: J. W. BAUM, *Capito und Bucer* in *Väter der ref. Kirche III.;* Blarer: KEIM. Stuttg. 1860. Oecolampadius, see below; Rhegius: UHLHORN. Elberf. 1861; Spengler: HAUSSDORF. Nürnb. 1741; H. Sachs: W. KAWERAU. Halle 1889. For pamphlets, see SCHADE and BAUR p. 23 above; further, J. VOIGT in HTb 9, 321 ff. Strassburg: A. BAUM, *Magistrat u. Ref. in Strassb.* Strassb. 1887. Ulm: TH. KEIM, *Ref. d. Reichsst.* Ulm. 1851. Augsburg: FR. ROTH. München, 1881. Nürnberg: MÖLLER, *A. Osiander.* Elberf. 1870; FR. ROTH. Würzb. 1885. Schwäbisch-Hall: HARTMANN and JÄGER, *Joh. Brenz,* 2 vols. Hamburg, 1840-1842. Magdeburg. FR. HÜLSSE. Magdeb. 1883. Ostfriesland: CORNELIUS, *der Antheil Ostfrieslands an der Ref.* 1852; FRERICHS, *Blicke in die Ref.-G. Ostfrieslands.* Emden, 1883. For the Dutch martyrs cp. WA XII. 73 ff. For the beginnings of the Reformation in the Baltic provinces. XII. 143 ff. Prussia: TSCHACKERT, *Urkundenbuch zur Ref.-G. Preussens.* 3 vols. Leipz. 1890; the same, *P. Speratus.* Halle, 1891.

Under these circumstances the Reformation was able to spread and strengthen itself. In nearly every part of Germany voices were raised in favour of Luther's belief. At first in his own order: amongst many, Joh. Lang in Erfurt, C. Güttel in Eisleben, Wenz. Link in Altenburg, M. Stiefel in Esslingen, Jak. Probst and Henry of Zütphen in the Netherlands. They were supported by a large number of Franciscans, Brismann in Cottbus, then in Königsberg, Fr. Myconius in Gotha; in South Germany, the popular preachers and pamphleteers Eberlin of Günzburg and Henry of Kettenbach; Lambert of Avignon, who fled from France to Luther. Add to these, the Dominican Bucer in Strasburg, the Benedictine Ambros. Blarer in Constance, Joh. Oecolampadius on the Ebernburg and then in Bâle, the Carmelite Urb. Rhegius in Augsburg and others. The voices of the laity joined with those of the theologians; the town-clerk Laz. Spengler, the master-singer[1] and shoemaker Hans Sachs in Nuremberg (Wittenberg. Nachtigal. 1523), the nobleman Hartmuth of Cronberg, and Argula of Grumbach. Pamphlets in large numbers, the sermons of wandering preachers

---

[1] [The "master-singers" were a corporation of German poets from the 14th to the 17th century].

and "escaped" monks, the inspired activity of Luther's numerous personal disciples, and also the propagandist zeal of wandering artisans spread the news of the new preaching of faith over the whole land, often in purely evangelical enthusiasm, often also more in the desire of throwing off the yoke of manifold statutes, in noisy abuse of the old Church and its adherents and boasting of a mistaken freedom. In the cities, especially the **free imperial cities,** numerous centres of the evangelical movement were formed: **Strasburg** (Matthias Zell already since 1578, followed by Bucer, Capito, Hedio), **Ulm** (Eberlin, Kettenbach, Diepold, Conr. Sam), **Augsburg** (Oecolampadius, then Urb. Rhegius) **Nuremberg** (Andr. Osiander), **Schwabisch-Hall** (Joh. Brenz.), Nördlingen, Reutlingen, Constance: Frankfort on the Main: Erfurt, Goslar, Magdeburg (Nic. Amsdorf) and elsewhere.

The waves of the Reformation may be traced advancing from the Netherlands, where the Augustinians Henry Voes and John of Essen (Esch) were burnt on July 1st, 1523, the first martyrs of the Reformation, as far as Livonia (Andr. Knöpken) and from East-Friesland, Holstein (Henry of Zütphen, killed at Heide, December 10th, 1524) and Pomerania as far as Austria and Hungary. Besides Frederick the Wise, who, officially neutral, as a matter of fact everywhere promoted the appointment of evangelical communities in his lands and his brother **John,** who openly came forward as Luther's adherent,—**George** of Brandenburg (of Frankish lineage, at the same time Duke of Jägerndorf), the grand-master **Albert** of Prussia, who visited Luther at Wittenberg in 1523, asked for some clergymen (Paul Speratus and Brismann) from him, and whom Luther, by his essay *An die Herren Deutsch Ordens* [1] (WA XII. 228 ff.) assisted to prepare the way for the conversion of the land of the Order into a secular duchy, Henry and Albert Dukes of Mecklenburg, and Count Albert of Mansfeld especially, amongst others, devoted their sympathy and showed more or less open solicitude for the cause of the Reformation. It was a matter of the highest significance, that the young Landgrave **Philip** of Hesse, in spite of the obstacles raised by his father-in-law, Duke George of Saxony, in the spring of 1524 decidedly espoused the cause of the Reformation (cp. SEIDEMANN, in ZhTh 19, 175 ff.). The great hopes, which Luther, in 1523, placed in an evangelical movement of the Utraquists of Bohemia, soon showed themselves to be vain (WA XII 160 ff.); even the negotiations, which he had carried on with the Bohemian "Brethren" since 1522, making advances in a spirit of joyous expectation, had at first only resulted in an aggravation of the differences that existed between the two parties.

3. The beginnings of the institution of evangelical communities.

Sources: WA XII.; EA 22, 140 ff. (BA VII. 109 ff.); RICHTER, Ev. KOO I. (W. LÖHE) *Samml. liturg. Materialien III.* Nördl. 1842, (here p. 37 ff. the alleged regulations for divine service by Bugenhagen, 1524, p. 42 ff. A. Döber's *Nürnb. Gottesdienstordnung* 1524, p. 51 ff. *Strassb. Ordnung d. Messe);* TH. KOLDE, *Die älteste Nürnb. Liturgie* in St Kr 1883, 602 ff.; Mittheil. aus dem Antiq. v. S. Calvary I. 57 ff.; (*Strassb. Messordn. von* 1524); another in RÖHRICH, *Mitth. aus d. Gesch. d. evg. K. des Elsasses*, I. 191 ff.
Literature: EHRLE, *die Armenordnungen von Nürnberg und Ypern* in JGG IX 450 ff.; B. RIGGENBACH, *das Armenwesen der Ref.* Basel 1883; TH. BRIEGER, *die angebl. Marb. KO.* Gotha 1881. (For the literature of church hymns, etc., see below in division vi., chapter 2).

---

[1] *i.e.,* to the Order of Teutonic Knights.

In German countries it was already possible to speak, not only of adherents of Luther, but even of evangelical **communities** with a new order of divine service, a recognised clerical office, and a municipal constitution: but they were still isolated communities, without regular union, without hierarchical organisation, in reality emancipated from episcopal jurisdiction, but also without any definite settlement of their relation to the sovereign government, or to the communal arrangements—a period of transition, during which the existing legal arrangements were broken through in numberless cases in the name of "divine" right, and a new ecclesiastical right was now for the first time to be created.

In his treatise *Von Ordnung Gottesdiensts in der Gemeinde* (1523) Luther indicated the general main outlines of ritual, laying stress upon preaching the word as the chief thing, and in his *Formula missae et communionis* (1523) described, for others to imitate freely, the conservative Wittenberg practice which had hitherto been observed with careful regard for custom. In his *Taufbüchlein*[1] (1523) he commenced to turn the service into German, while, for the sake of the pupils, he was desirous of still leaving a place for the Latin language in choral singing and parts of the liturgy. By numerous modifications and gradations, divine service in the evangelical communities was altered to an evangelical "Mass," simplified and purified from the idea of sacrifice: the celebration of the Lord's Supper by as many members of the community as possible was to form the regular culminating point of the Sunday service, and the communion was to be celebrated even at week-day services, if there were communicants present. The *communio sub utraque*, which was at first still treated by Luther as optional, speedily drove out the Romish withdrawal of the cup. The low masses of the priests without a congregation to participate in them were abandoned, and with them died the significance of the side altars and the numerous attendants on the priests of the Church. Hereby, as well as in consequence of the cessation of the established masses, especially those for the soul, the finances of the Church were in need of a new adjustment. Luther's struggle against mendicancy and his demand for regular relief of the poor required the establishment of municipal relief-funds. The now generally created regulations of a "common chest" served to solve this task—the arrangements of the chest in the little town of Leisnig were published by Luther himself (1523) as a model for other towns. The need of evangelical preachers for the communities sought satisfaction in asserting the right of the Christian community to appoint and remove from office: Luther himself proclaimed it in 1523, in his treatises *Dass eine christliche Versammlung Recht und Macht habe, Lehrer zu berufen* and *De instituendis ministris*, and thereby succeeded in bringing it about that, frequently in defiance of existing rights of patronage, the communities provided themselves with evangelical "priests" and "preachers" (deacons). In such proceedings of the community, the organisation of the civil communities served as the form in which the ecclesiastical proceeded in its acts and resolutions; thus, the "right of the community" could easily and without contradiction pass into a patronage of the council. In 1524, Luther commenced with the publication of some German hymns; in the same year the first hymn-books (the *Wittenberger*

---

[1] Little book of Baptism,

Achtliederbuch, the Erfurt *Enchiridion*, and John Walther's *Gesangbüchlein*) appeared. These hymns soon proved a most effectual means of furthering the Reformation. At first, ordination was not substituted for the Romish consecration of priests; the mandate of the community was regarded as a sufficient legitimation for office. Confirmation and supreme unction were likewise suppressed, without anything being substituted for them. Compulsory confession was done away with, at first without any definite fresh regulation being made; but on Maundy Thursday, 1523, Luther announced one,—a notification to communion with an examination of the communicants, in order to check the religious ignorance of the multitude and prevent communicating without due consideration. Private confession entered into combination with this *exploratio* as a means of training and instruction for the simple. But matters did not stop at the mere initiative of the community in reference to the spread of the Reformation. However strongly Luther accentuated the separation of spiritual and temporal power, however firmly he adhered to the principle: *nemo ad pietatem et fidem cogi potest nec debet*, and hence interposed in cases in which preachers desired to drive the people to violent reforms (de W. II 438), yet the other was connected with it: *scelera tamen publica tollenda sunt* (Enders IV 54), and from this point of view he endeavoured—at first in vain—to induce the Elector to do away with Catholic forms of worship (*e.g.* in the Castle Church of Wittenberg). Thus, as early as 1522, he advised the Count of Schwarzburg to "take away their benefices" from those monks, who would not preach the Gospel, "and to fill them by pious learned men" (de W. II 258).

It was in the free imperial cities in particular that reorganisation was carried out unceasingly after the example of Wittenberg. The people were urgent, zealous preachers took the lead in reforming, the Council was in the habit of tacking about for a short time, but afterwards took the same road, sometimes on its own initiative, sometimes rather under pressure. Different German translations and evangelical revisions of the mass appeared in print, all of which, however, adhered more or less closely to tradition. In Strasburg, *e.g.* on February 16th, 1524, the Lord's Supper was for the first time celebrated *sub utraque*, then divine service and the baptismal service were conducted in German; the municipal authorities at first took no notice, but soon took the work of reform in hand themselves, did away with images and relics, and began to abolish established masses. Almost at the same time (Passion week, 1524) innovations in public worship were introduced at Nuremberg, thanks to the courageous example of the Augustinian prior Volprecht; the provosts of both parish-churches combined, and Osiander prepared a German baptismal service. The Bishop of Bamberg attempted to proceed against the provosts and the prior with threats of deprivation of office and excommunication; but the Council ignored these ecclesiastical censures and thereby practically wrested the city from episcopal jurisdiction. It was the same in other places. It is obvious that secular reasons, in the imperial cities, co-operated, which made liberation from episcopal rights of jurisdiction appear desirable; the efforts of the larger communities (that had grown strong in self-government) in the direction of independence contributed valuable assistance. Already, even now, by the side of the conservative method of Luther's reforms, a more radical method in the treatment of ecclesiastical tradition unmistakably showed itself here and there. In Strasburg, not only did the people resort to violent measures against the images, to noisy interruptions of Catholic services, but also to more radical ideas of feast days, and the substitution of tables for altars; a leaning to far simpler forms of worship manifested itself prominently: *quid enim commune Christianis cum papistis?*[1] The model of the Church of Wittenberg was imitated in that of Zürich.

4. U. Zwingli and German Switzerland.

Sources: Opera: Zürich, 1545, 4 vols.; ed. Schuler and Schulthess., 8 vols., Zürich, 1828-1842. *Oecol. et Zwinglii epist.* libri IV., Basil, 1536. HERMINJARD, *Corresp. des Réformateurs* I. and II., Genève, 1866 f. *Briefw. d. Beat. Rhenanus*, by HORAWITZ and HARTFELDER, Leipz., 1886. H. BULLINGER, *Ref. gesch. (1519-1532)*, edited by HOTTINGER and VÖGELI, 3 vols., Frauenf., 1838 to 1840. J. J. SIMLER, *Samml. alter und neuer Urk.*, 2 vols., Zürich, 1757 to 1763. *Eidgenöss. Abschiede*, Vol. IV. Ia and Ib (1521-1532), revised by STRICKLER. Brugg and Zürich, 1873 and 1876. J. STRICKLER, *Actensamml. zur schw. Ref. gesch.*, 1521-1532, 5 vols., Zürich, 1878-1884. E. EGLI, *Actensamml. zur G. d. Züricher Ref.*, 1519-1533, Zürich, 1879; *Archiv f. d. schw. Ref. gesch.*, edited by the Swiss Piusverein, 3 vols., Soloth., 1868-1876. TSCHUDI's *Chronik der Ref. jahre, 1521-1533*, edited by STRICKLER, Bern 1889.

Literature: For Zwingli's biography: O. MYCONIUS, *de vita et obitu Zw.*, 1536. R. CHRISTOFFEL, Elberf., 1857. J. C. MORIKOFER, 2 vols., Leipz., 1867-1869. R. STÄHELIN, Halle, 1883. PH. SCHAFF, *Hist. of Chr. Church, VII.*, New York, 1892. M. USTERI, *Initia Zwinglii* in StKr, 1885. 607 ff.; for his theology, see E. ZELLER, Tübing. 1853; CH. SIGWART, Stuttg. and Hamb., 1855, but especially A. BAUR, 2 vols., Halle, 1885-1889. A. BAUR, *die erste Züricher Disputation*, Halle, 1883. Bern: VAL. ANSHELM, *Berner Chronik*, edition by STIERLIN and WYSS, 2 vols., Bern, 1884-1886. M. V. STÜRLER, *Urkunden der Berner K. Ref.*, 2 vols., 1855-1877. M. KIRCHHOFER, *B. Haller*, Zürich, 1828. C. PESTALOZZI, *B. H.*, Elberf., 1861. For N. MANUEL: GRÜNEISEN, Stuttg., 1837. BÄCHTHOLD, Frauenf., 1878. Basel: *Basler Chroniken*, edited by W. VISCHER, Leipz., 1872. K. R. HAGENBACH, *Kirchl.*

---

[1] KAPP, *Kleine Nachlese* II 650.

Denkwürdigkeiten z. Gesch. Basels seit d. Ref., Basel, 1827. W. VISCHER, *Actenstücke z. Gesch. d. Ref. in Basel* in *Basler Beiträge*, 1854. J. J. HERZOG, *das Leben Oecolampadius*, 2 vols., Basel, 1843. HAGENBACH, *Oecolamp. u. O. Myconius*, Elberf., 1859. St. Gallen: JOH. KESSLER, *Sabbata. Chronik der Jahre 1523-1539*, edited by E. Götzinger. St. Gallen *(Mitth. zur vaterl. Gesch. V—X)*. St. Gallen, 1866, 1868, 2 vols.

Meanwhile, under **Zwingli's** leadership, an evangelical movement, parallel to the Wittenberg Reformation, had taken place in German Switzerland, which, although not so independent of Luther as its promoters affirmed,[1] nevertheless had a different origin: besides, in accordance with the character of the people and the political conditions of the confederacy, it pursued other paths of reform, and hence, notwithstanding all points of relationship, the longer it continued, the more its peculiar nature and independence asserted themselves.[2] Its advent at first promoted the victorious spread of reformatory ideas: on the other hand, it weakened the resistance to Rome by the quarrels which soon broke out between the two reformation circles, while the efforts of the theologians as well as of the youthful communities were demanded by the dogmatic declarations in respect to the questions of doctrine that were in dispute between them. This struggle itself, then, in many ways checked the consistent, quiet development of reformatory principles

Ulrich (Huldreich) **Zwingli**[3] was born January 1st, 1484, at Wildhaus, in Toggenburg. Like Luther, he was descended from the peasant order, but grew up under far easier and more favourable conditions of life. Early destined by his father for a learned profession, he passed his school (in Bâle and Berne) like his student days (in Vienna and Bâle) free from material want and also undisturbed by severe internal struggles. At an early date he was trained by humanist teachers (such as Celtes in Vienna) to take delight in ancient writers and to dislike Scholasticism—" a full and complete humanist, who fills up his intervals of rest with cheerful enjoyment of life, in particular

---

[1] As to the dependence of the evangelical movements in Switzerland in general upon Luther's work, cp. R. STÄHELIN in ZKG III., 558.

[2] " Not springing from the depths of an anguish-stricken heart, but uplifting itself on the foundation of a humanistically perfected understanding, the anti-Catholic piety of the Swiss strengthened its base in the granite pillar of the idea of the absolute God, whose majesty, alone worthy of adoration and alone ordaining, stands elevated above every creature. If the German reformation sees, in Catholicism, mankind cheated of its salvation, the Swiss sees in it the Godhead cheated of its honour."—G. FRANK, *Gesch. d. prot. Th.*, I., 41 f.

[3] In the Bâle matriculation list, May 1st, 1502: Udalricus Zwyngling de Liechtensteig.

seasoned with music."[1]   He took his Master of Arts in 1506 at Bâle, and, soon afterwards, being appointed pastor of Glarus, he introduced a humanistic enlightenment into his ecclesiastical office through the instrumentality of his teacher, Thomas Wyttenbach of Bâle, and still more through the study of the writings of Erasmus. This enlightenment at first did not conflict with the obedience to the Pope, which he rendered both as pastor and politician; he certainly vigorously opposed his countrymen entering upon service in France, but on the other hand upheld service under the Pope as the duty of a Christian, accompanied as chaplain, on at least two occasions, the troops of Glarus to Italy on a campaign in defence of the Pope, and enjoyed a papal pension until the year 1520. In consequence of the hostility of the French party he was obliged to leave Glarus. At the end of his stay in that place (which lasted till 1516), his interest in theology, under the influence of Erasmus, perceptibly increased, yet even now, from a moral point of view, he remained under the spell of the lax views of the humanist circles. He began to study seriously the fathers and the New Testament. But even during the time of his pastorate at Einsiedeln, a famous resort of pilgrims (1516-1518), his standpoint was no higher than that of a reformer as Erasmus understood it. After the latter had settled in Bâle (1516) for a considerable time, a circle of admirers (Glareanus, Beatus Rhenanus, Conrad Pellicanus, Oswald Myconius, Joachim Vadianus, and others) gathered round him, with whom Zwingli also entered into correspondence. His letters were dominated by the taste for declamation and literary sympathies of these circles,—also by delight in the struggle of humanistic illumination against the obscurantists. As a preacher, he soon acquired a reputation: he combated the moral diseases of popular life in the spirit of a lively national feeling. But, even at Einsiedeln, his insight into the abuses of the Catholic Church increased; he recognised with increasing clearness the sharp contradiction between the prevailing ecclesiastical system and the Bible: he was a free-thinking, enlightened Catholic, who fell back upon a simpler, biblical method of instruction, but did not yet manifest his call to be a reformer. As late as September, 1518, the papal legate Pucci appointed him papal chaplain. Even the appearance of **Bernard Samson,** the trader in indulgences, in Switzerland (in the winter of 1518[9]), although it certainly aroused his disapproval, did not drive him to any decisive action. The ecclesiastical huckster met with almost general opposition in Switzerland. The assembly of the States at Zürich vigorously resisted the imposition, and the Pope, who did not wish to fall out with the Confederates, considerately left it to them to decide whether Samson should be granted or refused permission to carry on his traffic,—even his commissioner for Switzerland unceremoniously abandoned him. The politic bishop of Constance, Hugo von Landenberg, apart from this, was not favourably disposed towards this papal indulgence, as it was an unpleasant rival to the episcopal indulgence; he accordingly approved of the opposition of Zwingli and others to it. On the first day of the year 1519, having been called upon by the chapter of the canons to offer effective resistance to the French party, he entered upon his office as *Leut*-priest (*i.e.*, a priest who held a regular pastorate, who preached, and undertook the cure of souls) at the great cathedral of **Zürich.** Here he commenced with a series of sermons upon the biblical books, which were highly approved by

---

[1] A. BAUR, I, p. 18.

the congregation. His pastoral activity during the plague epidemic in the summer of 1519 confirmed his reputation: having been brought to the brink of the grave himself by sickness, he devoted more serious attention to his religious life.[1] Under the influence of Luther's writings, he now began to investigate the Pauline Gospel teaching more thoroughly. His continued patriotic opposition to the system of pensions and foreign service, and also to the luxury that crept in in their train, and, in addition, his contestation of the divine right to demand ecclesiastical tithes excited opposition both amongst the clergy and also amongst those who were humanistically inclined and politically influential. A mandate of the Council (1520), which in this case by its orders interfered in a remarkable manner in ecclesiastical matters, commanded that the Gospels and Epistles should be preached in accordance with the Spirit of God and the Holy Scriptures, and that nothing should be said about any adventitious innovations and dogmas,—obviously a hint for Zwingli to confine himself to what was purely religious. In Switzerland, a combination of Zwingli's activity with the cause of Luther (whose works were much pirated and read) had already been begun: he was already reckoned as the foremost amongst Luther's adherents in that country. Nevertheless, he always vigorously denied that he had been influenced by Luther. "Before any man in our land knew anything of Luther's name, I had already begun to preach the Gospel of Christ in the year 1516" (I 253). This was undoubtedly in part self-deception: he even asserts that he scarcely knew anything of Luther's writings, whereas it can be proved against him, with how large a portion of them he was really acquainted before 1522, so that his reformatory ideas **in the matter of religion** were at least strongly influenced by Luther.[2] And yet his assertion, that he was no pupil of Luther, is subjectively correct, since he gradually advanced, without a break with the past, from Erasmus to Luther, and even then his Christianity, like his theology, preserved the traces of having originated from another source. The Pope and his representatives in Switzerland, at first, however, treated Zwingli quite differently from Luther. While the papal legate, at the assembly of the States at Baden (1520), demanded that Luther's writings should be burnt, he endeavoured, by entreaty, cajoleries or menaces, to keep Zwingli from proceeding further. Yet it was greatly to the interest of the Pope to keep on his side the zealous opponent of the temptations held out by France to Switzerland. But Zwingli renounced the papal pension in 1520, and received for it a small prebendary's benefice at the cathedral: he was, however, unable to prevent Zürich from again affording military assistance to the Pope on the ground of a previous agreement.

His reformatory labours proper began in the spring of 1522. Several citizens (amongst them Zwingli), who had violated the ordinances in regard to fasting, appealed to their evangelical conviction, fostered by Zwingli, that it was only a matter of human ordinances. The Council, on the advice of the chapter and the clergy, ordered (March 19th, 1522) that no one should eat meat on fast days without sufficient reasons, and the Bishop of Constance

---

[1] Cp. his poems on the plague. Works II 369 ff.
[2] Usteri in StKr 1886. 142 ff.

despatched a commission to uphold the ecclesiastical ordinance. Then, on April 12th, 1522, Zwingli wrote *Von erkiesen und fryheit der spysen*[1] (I, 1 ff.). Attempts were immediately made to silence him. The Bishops of Constance and Lausanne bestirred themselves, the Curia demanded that his chapter should take proceedings against him, the assembly of the States at Lucerne forbade all preaching that tended to produce error in belief. But Zwingli would not allow himself to be intimidated.

In July, together with some friends who held similar views (amongst them Leo Jud [Judä]), he wrote a *Supplicatio* (in Latin to the Bishop of Constance, III, 17 ff., in German to the same effect, I, 30 ff.), petitioning for the free preaching of the Gospel, for permission for the priests to marry, or at least that their marriage should be tolerated.[2] This was followed by his *Archeteles* (III, 26 ff.), a moderate but yet decisively offensive and defensive treatise, in which he opposes the Scriptures as the normative authority to the ecclesiastical principle of authority. The struggle of parties now became inflamed, calumnies were heaped upon him, and his life was threatened by the one side, while tumultuous impetuosity was shown on the part of several of his adherents. The Council of Zürich itself could no longer keep out of the movement. "After the most careful consideration of a difficult matter" it resolved to arrange a public disputation,[3] at which discussion should be carried on "with the aid of truly divine writings and in the German language." While the **Council** reserved for itself the decision "in accordance with truly divine writings" in this disputation which was appointed for January 29th, 1523, to which all the clergy in its jurisdiction were invited, he confidently took the work of religious reform in hand. Evidently, the leading personalities in the Council had already made up their minds beforehand: the disputation would only solemnly authenticate the actual revolution of public opinion at a large assembly (RE 15, 596). Rome, which was still in debt to Zürich for arrears of pay, had hitherto still endeavoured to hold the latter to the old political connection. The new Pope, Adrian VI., not only wrote

---

[1] [Of choice and free use of meats].

[2] At that time Zwingli had already secretly married Anna Reinhard, widow of Johann Meyer, of Knonau; the marriage was not publicly blessed until 1524.

[3] A. BAUR, I, 174 ff.

to Zürich, at the same time loudly extolling the services rendered by the city to the papal chair, but, at the beginning of 1523, sent his legate Ennius thither with fresh commissions, wrote to Zwingli's friend Franz Zingg of Einsiedeln to win the former over to the cause of Rome by his assistance, and even sent (January 23rd, 1523) a flattering letter to his "beloved son" Zwingli in recognition of his distinguished services, offering him special favours, if he would show himself compliant.[1] When this letter arrived, the decisive step had already been taken.

Zwingli had drawn up for the disputation sixty-seven "Conclusions" (I 153 ff.), "the model of a Christian confession of belief."[2] The Gospel carries its authority in itself, and needs no previous confirmation by the Church. The sum of it is the revelation of the will of God, redemption and reconciliation to God through Christ, who is therefore for us the only way to eternal happiness. No other teaching is to be compared to that of the Gospel or to be looked upon with greater respect. The Church is the community of the Saints, the body of Christ, the members of which are only attached to their head and his word. The salvation and condemnation of mankind depend only upon belief or unbelief in regard to the Gospel. Christ is the only high priest. The result of these fundamental principles is the rejection and criticism of the Romish papal, priestly, and sacramental church. The authority of the Pope conflicts with that of Christ, the mass with His sacrifice, the intercession of the Saints with His mediation. Further, justification by works, prohibition in the matter of food, feast-days, pilgrimages, monastic orders, prohibition of marriage, usages of worship are subjected to religious criticism. The ban is assigned to the individual community as a reaction against public offences in their midst. All magisterial authority is disputed with the Church: **all functions connected with the government of the Church are, on the other hand, adjudged to the Christian authorities,** so far as they do not order what is against God. If any authority acts thus, it has forfeited its office and may be "deposed by the will of God."

The confederate States invited to the disputation, even the friendly-disposed Bâle, officially declined, with the exception of Schaffhausen. Only a few friends of Zwingli attended in a private capacity, Vadian from St. Gall, Sebastian Meyer from Berne, and others; but the Bishop of Constance sent a deputation, the spokesman of which was his general-vicar **Joh. Faber** (Fabri). The latter endeavoured to avoid the disputation (I 105 ff.) as much as possible, but was finally drawn into it by Zwingli,[3] when he attempted to screen himself under the authority of the Church

---

[1] Works VIII 266, 300. BULLINGER I 82, 84.

[2] Cp. RITSCHL, *Rechtfertigung.*,[2] I, 168. NIEMEYER, *Coll. Conf.*, 3 ff. SCHAFF, *Bibl. symb.*, I, 363 ff.; III, 197 ff.

[3] For the importance of this moment of the disputation, cp. NIPPOLD in HAGENBACH, *KGesch.*, [5]III, 697 ff.

and the fathers, and only exceptionally soared to a feeble proof drawn from the Scriptures. At noon the resolution of the Council (I 143) was announced to the great assembly: Zwingli was to continue, as hitherto, to preach the Gospel and the genuine divine Scripture in accordance with the spirit of God and to the best of his ability, until he should be better informed. All the preachers in the country were also to preach nothing but what they could uphold by the authority of the Scriptures, but were at the same time to refrain from all accusations of heresy and from abuse. This decided the victory of the Reformation in Switzerland. Faber subsequently attempted (but in vain) to conceal his defeat by his literary efforts. Zwingli, with heart uplifted with joy, now produced his *Auslegung und Begründung der Schlussreden* (I. 169 ff.), a treatise of fundamental importance for the religious side of the Swiss Reformation.

Practical reforms followed in rapid succession. The Council permitted withdrawal from the monasteries, several priests took the step of marrying: Leo Jud, who had been Zwingli's colleague in office at Zürich since the beginning of the year, translated the baptismal service into German: the chapter of the great Cathedral was reformed, its revenues partly allotted to educational purposes. In the autumn, the impatience of the populace pressed on to violent reforms: images, ever-burning lamps, and crucifixes were destroyed by men who had been stirred to iconoclasm by a pamphlet written by the restless and hot-headed **Ludw. Hetzer** in Wädenschwyl. Zwingli disapproved of such action as being an excess, certainly not as an act of sacrilege. The Council interposed with a punishment of imprisonment, but, in the face of the great sensation which these events excited in Switzerland, thought it desirable to settle the matter at a second disputation "concerning the mass and images." This took place on October 26th-28th (I, 459). No competent opponent presented himself; every speech that was not supported by Scriptural proofs was cut short. Zwingli and Leo Jud represented the radical standpoint in the attack upon images, the pious Commander [of the Knights of St. John], Conrad Schmid of Küssnacht, spoke fervently in favour of sparing the weak, but the spirit of fanaticism was already excited in Conrad Grebel, for whom the work of reform could not be pushed on rapidly enough, and, in Simon Stumpf, the enthusiastic prophetic spirit, the subjectivism of which refuses to submit to any authority. Zwingli's and Leo Jud's propositions, that God forbade images, that the mass was no sacrifice and had hitherto been celebrated with many abuses, obtained recognition: but at the same time, in view of the sudden appearance of an extravagantly radical party, the Council determined to proceed cautiously and tenderly, and to take further reforms in hand only in combination with previous **instruction**. With this object, Zwingli, under the authority of the Council, wrote the *Kurze christliche Einleitung* (I, 541 ff.), which was followed by the order of the Council, that images were no longer to be carried round in processions, and that the mass should be freely administered: a definitive arrangement was to come into force at Whitsuntide (1524).

Zwingli's *Einleitung* was sent to the bishops and the confederate cantons. Subsequently, on January 24th, 1524, at Lucerne, the twelve cantons decided upon the unconditional maintenance of the old Church and sent a solemn embassy to Zürich, to formulate complaints and issue a warning. But Zürich replied on March 21st, 1524: that it intended to support the confederate alliance loyally, but at the same time not to deviate from what God's word and the salvation of souls required. Meanwhile, the reforms in public worship advanced (organ-playing also was done away with). After Zürich had made certain of the assent of its country-parishes, the abolition of monasteries, the limitation of the number of festivals, the establishment of civil and ecclesiastical regulations in regard to the poor, of a school and theological seminary out of church property, the change of the mass into a simple communion-service (Easter, 1525), the substitution for the altar of a table covered with a white cloth with wooden plates and goblets for unleavened bread and wine, the abolition of all singing (even singing by the congregation being discouraged), emancipation from the liturgical model of the Romish mass,—all these reforms were introduced. The rupture with the Catholic constitution of the Church followed. The civil authorities (the Council of the Two Hundred) took over the government of the Church "as a Christian authority and instead of their common church" and appointed a "court of discipline" and a "marriage court" for marriage affairs and moral discipline, consisting of four members of the Council and two pastors, to which the *Stillstände* (presbyteries) in the parishes corresponded as a local board of control. Thus the Reformation attained to a clerical organisation more rapidly in Switzerland than in Saxony.[1]

But already Zürich no longer stood alone. In **Appenzell** (Ausserroden) evangelical preaching obtained a free course by a resolution of the general assembly in 1524: in the imperial city of **Mühlhausen** (united with Bâle) allegiance to the Bishop of Bâle was renounced in the same year. In **Berne** the Swabian Berthold Haller and Sebastian Meyer had already, several years before, by outspoken preaching, and the painter **Nicolas Manuel**, by his satirical poems, stirred up a movement amongst the population; still, the Council did its utmost to maintain an ambiguous position midway between the two parties, while it combated certain abuses, drove Sebastian Meyer, as well as his

---

[1] This organisation was completed by the foundation of the **Synod**, composed of all the pastors, municipal deputies and government representatives (*assessores publici*).

opponent, a Dominican, from the city, but allowed Haller to do as he pleased. In **Biel,** Zwingli's former teacher, Thomas Wyttenbach, courageously espoused the cause of the Reformation, was deprived of his office for getting married in 1524, but in the next year the community secured free preaching of the Gospel. In **Bâle, Wolfgang Fabricius Capito** had, up to 1520, devoted himself to the study of the Bible in an Erasmian spirit and criticised outspokenly the abuses of the Church: then, Caspar Hedio and the Franciscan Conrad Pellicanus had fostered the first humanistic enthusiasm for Luther. But, in 1522, **Joh. Oecolampadius** (Hussgen, Hausschein, born 1482 at Weinsberg), who had already shown literary activity in 1521 as an adherent of Luther, arrived there. By his preaching and his activity as Reader in the Scriptures at the University, he soon obtained a reputation amongst the citizens: the bishop in vain forbade attendance at his lectures. Two disputations in December, 1524 (the one by Stör, a priest, against celibacy, the other by Wilhelm Farel, who had fled from France) encouraged the evangelical party. In February, 1525, the Council appointed Oecolampadius minister of St. Martin, and allowed him to take in hand alterations in conformity with the Word of God. Nevertheless, the complete victory of the Reformation here was still in abeyance. Oecolampadius was already connected with Zwingli by an intimate friendship. Schaffhausen also had found in Sebastian Hofmeister (Wagner), St. Gall in the humanist Vadian and in the pupil of the Wittenbergers, the learned saddler Joh. Kessler, active promoters of the knowledge of the Scriptures. On the other hand, Lucerne and the original cantons firmly closed their gates against the evangelical movement. Hence the victory of the Reformation was in sight only for a part of Switzerland: but already, together with the Old Church opposition, another dangerous enemy showed itself, the fanatically Anabaptist propaganda. The attempt of statesmen of Catholic views in the interior of Switzerland (the assembly at Lucerne, January, 1525), to avert the danger of civil war by means of a system of state church reforms (without and against the Pope) did not lead to an agreement.[1]

---

[1] OECHSLI, *das eidgenöss. Glaubensconcordat von* 1525 *in J. f. schw. Gesch.*, XIV 263 ff.: the same, in *Anz. f. schw. G.*, XXI, l 18 ff.

CHAPTER THIRD.

The Years of Clearing Up and Separation—1524, 1525.

1. Erasmus and Luther (Separation of the humanist and evangelical parties).

Literature: For Emser, P. MOSER, Halle, 1890; Murner, WALDAU, Nürnb., 1775; STROBEL, Strassb., 1827; RÖHRICH in ZhTh 18, 587; W. KAWERAU, 2 parts, Halle, 1890, 1891; O. WINCKELMANN in ZG d. Oberrheins. 1891, 49 ff.; Faber, A. HORAWITZ, Wien, 1884; Dietenberger, H. WEDEWER, Freib. 1888 (add WALTHER in HZ 63, 311 ff., KOLDE in GGA, 1889, 27 ff.); Schatzger: A. v. DRUFFEL in SBBA, 1890, II 3. For Erasmus, *Opp.* ed. Lugd. Bat. 1703 ff., Tom. III and X; CHLEBUS in ZhTh 15, 2, 1 ff.; G. PLITT in ZThK, 1866, 479 ff.; R. STÄHELIN, *Er.' Stellung z. Ref.* Basel, 1873; HARTFELDER in HTb 6. F. XI 148 f.; F. O. STICHART, *Er. v. R.*, Leipz., 1870.

A whole host of literary adversaries of Luther had entered the field: in addition to Eck, Emser, Cochleus and the satirist Th. Murner, the general-vicar Joh. Faber, the Dominican Joh. Dietenberger, the minorite Schatzger and others, supported by foreign theologians (Clichtoveus, John Fisher and others). Luther, who at the commencement had always been ready with an answer, after his return from the Wartburg as a rule left the task of defence to his younger friends and pupils. It was only exceptionally that he himself took up the challenge: thus, in 1522, when Henry VIII. of England defended the seven sacraments against him, in return for which he obtained from the Pope the title of *Defensor fidei* and received a guarantee of an indulgence for every reader of his book,[1] he wrote the recklessly insulting Essay *contra Henricum Regem Angliae* (EA *opp. v. a.* VI 385 ff.) and, in 1523, curtly repulsed all Cochleus's repeated efforts to enter into a quarrel with him (VII 46 ff.). But hitherto the man, who had long since been exhorted on the Catholic side to come forward against Luther, namely, **Erasmus,** had remained silent. The Popes, the Emperor, King Henry, his English friends and others had hitherto vainly waited for his word of command in the struggle, although it had been represented to him that he was the only man who was Luther's literary equal or superior. But Erasmus, however conscious he was of being at heart different from Luther, and however important he considered it to keep the cause of *belles lettres* separate from the dangerous tendencies of the

---

[1] Cp. LÄMMER, *Anal. Rom.*, p. 148. WILKINS, *Conc. Britann.* III 693 ff., 695 ff., 702. BRIDGET in *Dublin Review*, 1885, 243 ff.

reformatory movement, had hitherto only made his dissent known by occasional sallies in letters and essays. Luther's Reformation had brought him into an uncomfortable position midway between two parties: on both sides he aroused expectations,—but also distrust. His original assent to Luther's criticism of the state of affairs in the Church was soon transformed by the "tumultuous" course of procedure into a nervous apprehension *ne res exiret in tumultum* (III 639); to this was added a feeling of anxiety lest the reformatory movement should drive humanist sympathies, which had hitherto dominated the noblest of the nation, into the background, and at the same time weaken his own dominant position (*ubicunque regnat Lutheranismus, ibi literarum est interitus!* III 1139); but soon he felt what was heterogeneous in Luther's religious position. It was just the crucial religious statements of Luther (*omnia opera sanctorum esse peccata; liberum arbitrium esse nomen inane; sola fide iustificari* [Zwinglii *opp.* VII 308]) that were *aenigmata absurda* to his moralism. In 1521, in consequence of the hostile attitude of the monastic party, he had retired from Louvain to Bâle. But, at the end of 1522, he had renounced his old friendship for Hutten, who had fled thither, and was in consequence publicly accused by the latter in his *Expostulatio* of falling away from the Gospel and of weakness of character, whereupon he found himself compelled to describe his intermediate position in his *Spongia*: he declared that both sides were united in all the main points, and that only exaggerations on both sides prevented an understanding. He thought he would be able, by the aid of moderation and dispassionate negotiations carried on by the learned, to calm the excitement of the time. Vigorous attacks from the Lutheran camp (O. Brunsfels and Er. Alberus) followed. At the beginning of 1524, he asked Pope Clement's pardon for the audacious tone of his earlier writings, and informed him of an essay written against Luther; the Pope rewarded him in hard cash and ordered the monastic opponents of Erasmus to keep silence.

In April, Luther again attempted, in a letter to Erasmus (de Wette II 499, Enders IV 319), to prevent the feud which he had long expected from breaking out between them: but the arrogant manner, in which Luther—with a true estimate of facts—endeavoured on this occasion to assign to him, as feeble and aged, the part of a spectator in the battle of belief, deeply wounded Erasmus. Greatly irritated, he replied in a letter (Enders IV 335): in the autumn appeared his *de libero arbitrio* διατριβή.[1] In this he could pick a quarrel with Luther, without being obliged to withdraw his earlier criticism of ecclesiastical abuses: in this the point was set forth in which the humanistic culture felt itself, as far as religion was concerned, separated from Luther and was the representative of Catholicism: and at the same time the point at which Luther's ideas, in the form in which they had been brought forward, afforded a convenient object of attack.

---

[1] *Opp.* IX 1215 ff., in German in WALCH XVIII, Sp. 1962 ff.

In 1520 Luther had written: *Liberum arbitrium est figmentum in rebus seu titulus sine re, quia nulli est in manu sua quippiam cogitare mali aut boni, sed omnia (ut Viglephi articulus Constantiae damnatus recte docet) de necessitate absoluta eveniunt* (EA opp. v. a. V 230). He employed all his efforts, not only to show these propositions absurd—which was easy enough—but also to keep the right mean between Manichaeism and Pelagianism, and to examine carefully the share that grace and free will respectively have in the salvation of mankind. Thereby results a Synergism,[1] which allows the beginning and end to grace, the intermediate step to free will. "The best of all his writings, but an entirely worldly one and most deeply irreligious."[2]

Luther's answer was put off owing to the intervention of the Peasants' War, his marriage, and the change of government in Saxony. It was not until the end of 1525 that it appeared: *De servo arbitrio* (EA opp. v. a. VII 113 ff.), with a German version by Jonas, who had formerly been an enthusiastic admirer of Erasmus, entitled "*Dass der freie Wille nichts sei*" (Walch XVIII 2049 ff.). In calm, polished language he demonstrates how he is concerned in the assertion of a "servile will": that what medieval theology had always treated as **the act of man**, which God only more or less supports by acts of grace and methods of salvation, namely, belief, is much more **the experience of an act of God** in the case of sinful man. This practically religious, inviolable kernel of his ideas,—his experience of belief, he endeavours to justify dialectically, as if it were not a religious experience, but a dogma of philosophical metaphysics, and thus irrevocably rushes into a deterministic, supralapsarian[3] doctrine of predestination, the practical conclusions of which he then again seeks to evade by a distinction of the *Deus absconditus* and the *Deus revelatus*, the revealed will of God for the salvation of all and the concealed, which disposes of the salvation or condemnation of the individual.

Luther, as late as 1537, expressly acknowledged this essay of his before others (de W. V 70)—a stumbling-block for his descendants, which it was endeavoured to explain away by violent exegetical devices (cp. Walch XVIII Introd. p. 140 ff.). Erasmus's essay had made no special impression on Melanchthon, who at first had been delighted that Luther should find in him (Erasmus) a cautious adversary (CR I 674); nevertheless, since 1527

---

[1] [In the Lutheran church, a Synergist was one who held that divine grace required a corresponding action of the human will to make it effectual].

[2] HARNACK, DG III 714.

[3] [The supralapsarian Calvinists held that the fall of Adam was part of the original plan of God, as also His decree of election as regards the eternal salvation of some and the eternal reprobation of others].

(Commentary on the *Epistle to the Colossians*), he had abandoned the paths of deterministic predestinarianism and henceforth sought ethical means of intercession for the efficacy of divine grace.

Erasmus, now freed from the suspicion of being a secret Lutheran (although to the end of his life zealous Catholics annoyed him by saying *Erasmus est pater Lutheri, Erasmus posuit ova, Lutherus exclusit pullos*[1]), replied with irritation in his *Hyperaspistes* (X 1249 ff.). **From this time forth, those who shared his views withdrew from the Reformation together with him, the chief of the humanists,** although individuals knew how to assert other special reasons for doing so: the jurist Zasius alleged Luther's abuse of the papacy, Pirkheimer his special Nuremburg relations, Crotus the absence of good fruits. In reality, the obstacle in the case of all was Luther's doctrine of grace. Even Mutianus, now advancing in years, joyfully welcomed Erasmus's vote in favour of free will.[2]

2. The Severance of the Reformation from the mystico-revolutionary Circles.

Literature: M. GÖBEL, *A. B. v. Carlstadt* in StKr 1841-1843; JÄGER (see above, p. 33); SEIDEMANN, *Th. Münzer*, Dresd. and Leipz., 1842; O. MERX, *Th. M. u. H. Pfeiffer*, I, Gött., 1889. For J. Strauss, see G. L. SCHMIDT, J. Menius, Gotha, 1867, I 105 ff.; BOSSERT in RE XIV 781 ff.

Luther's return from the Wartburg had at first paralysed **Carlstadt's** activity. But secretly he was arming for a fresh struggle with Luther.[3] A protest against academical degrees and fraternisation with the peasants as "Neighbour Andrew" was combined with mystic writing, which raised up the spirit against the letter and treated the forms of ecclesiastical life with contempt. In the autumn of 1523, he got himself chosen pastor by the congregation of Orlamünde, the pastorate of which was incorporated with the archdeaconry of the Wittenberg collegiate church which was held by him. Here he soon began a crusade against images and introduced reforms in church-worship: he deduced from the Old Testament the right of bigamy and the identification of Sabbath and Sunday. Recalled by the University of Wittenberg to his post, although he resigned his ministry, he still remained

---

[1] R. STÄHELIN, *Briefe aus der Ref. zeit*, Basel, 1887, p. 24.

[2] GILLERT, *Briefw. des Mutianus*, II p. 300.

[3] Cp. Melanchthon's description CR II 31.

as a "citizen" in the community that was blindly devoted to him. Meanwhile, **Thomas Münzer**, after all sorts of wanderings, had settled at Allstedt in Thuringia as minister, where he established a German form of worship, decked out with mystical whimsicalities, and began to collect a "community of saints" here and there in "leagues," in which communistic were already combined with mystical ideas, and the prospect was opened out of the speedy judgment of the "godless," the princes and lords first and foremost, which the good are called upon to execute. At Easter, 1524, he commenced deeds of violence by storming and plundering a neighbouring pilgrims' chapel. The Elector Frederick hesitated about taking proceedings against the dangerous fanatic. In the summer of 1524, Luther, in his *Brief an die Fürsten von Sachsen vom aufrührischen Geist* [letter to the Princes of Saxony concerning the spirit of disturbance] (de Wette II 358 ff.),[1] recommended that the teaching of the fanatics should be tolerated ("let the spirits dash against one another"), but that, as soon as they interfered with the fist, the disturbance should be opposed by punitive measures. Being summoned to Weimar for examination, Münzer, without waiting for the verdict, secretly left Allstedt and repaired to the neighbouring imperial city of Mühlhausen. Carlstadt, in spite of Münzer's cajolery, had resisted the appeal to force. But now he opened the campaign against Luther in the matter of his doctrine of the Eucharist, which appeared to him equivalent to the Romish; he required "heavenly" instead of "sacramental" ideas, and interpreted the τοῦτο (not οὗτος) of the sacramental words ("this is my body") to mean that Jesus simply referred to his own *body*, but expressed no opinion as to the *bread*. A meeting between Luther and Carlstadt at the Black Bear at Jena led to no result; an attempt to bring about a discussion with his excited adherents at Orlamünde was equally unsuccessful; amidst the execrations of the mob Luther was obliged to retire without having effected anything. The Elector still thought of clearing up the situation by a public discussion, to which, in addition to Luther and Melanchthon, Carlstadt, the preacher Jacob Strauss of Eisenach, the fabricator of plans of social reforms, and even Münzer, should also be summoned: but, on Luther's opposition, the idea was abandoned and Carlstadt, with two of his adherents, was banished from the country.

---

[1] For the date cp. de W. VI 580.

Carlstadt turned towards South Germany, where together with his Eucharistic doctrine he at the same time spread dislike of Luther personally. His appearance made a special impression in Strasburg, so that Luther in his *Brief an die Christen zu Strassburg* (de W. II 574 ff., Enders V 83 f.) attempted to resist the "fanatical spirit." There, however, the controversy was regarded as a simple contest of words. He then rose up with the full weight of his eloquence against the immoderate attacks, which had in the meantime been made in Carlstadt's writings, in his Essay *Wider die himmlischen Propheten von den Bildern und Sacrament* [Against the heavenly Prophets concerning the Images and the Sacrament] (EA 29, 134 ff.), in which his Eucharistic doctrine attained full development (see below). Carlstadt's contrite endeavour to become reconciled to Luther was hindered by the refusal of the Elector to grant him safe-conduct. Nor would any such understanding have been able to delay the outbreak of the dispute about the Eucharist.

Münzer had found in Mühlhausen a soil already explored by the Cistercian Henry Pfeiffer. The Council still exerted itself against the new preacher of disturbance and drove him out. He wandered through South Germany as far as Switzerland, had his incendiary essay *Wider das geistlose, sanftlebende Fleisch in Wittenberg* [1] [Against the godless, easy-living flesh at Wittenberg] printed at Nuremberg on the way and entered into relations with the Zürich Anabaptists: but he soon appears again with Pfeiffer in Mühlhausen, attacks the authorities and nobility, commences an assault upon the monasteries, overthrows the Council; peasants and townspeople league together: the war of extermination against the "godless" under the leadership of the new prophet was ready to break out. Before the princes had agreed upon counter-measures, the storm burst.

3. The Severance of the Reformation from the fanatic Anabaptist Circles.

Literature: HEBERLE in JdTh 1858, 225 ff. CORNELIUS, *Gesch. des Münsterischen Aufruhrs, II.*, Leipz., 1860, p. 15 ff. EGLI, *die Züricher Wiedertäufer der Ref. zeit*, Zürich, 1878; the same, *die St. Galler Täufer*, Zürich, 1887. STRASSER in *Berner Beiträge*, edited by NIPPOLD, 1884, p. 166 ff. BURRAGE, *History of the Anabaptism in Switzerland*, Philad., 1882. NITZSCHE, *Gesch. der Wiedert. in der Schweiz*, Einsiedeln, 1885. LOSERTH, *die Stadt Waldshut u. die vorder-österr. Regierung, 1523-1526*, in *A. f. öst. G.* 77, 1 ff.

At the same time, in Switzerland, those who considered that Zwingli's reforms proceeded too slowly and whose ecclesiastical ideal only found satisfaction in the conventicle, had in like manner

---

[1] Reprinted by L. Enders, Halle, 1893 (Niemeyer's reprints No. 118. p. 17 ff.).

separated from him. As early as the second conference at Zürich (see p. 55) spirits of the kind had come forward. Socialistic tendencies also showed themselves in Simon Stumpf, and in others, such as Conrad Grebel, a youthful humanist who had suddenly awakened from a dissolute life, and Felix Manz, the desire for a **visible representation of the community of the Saints.** As Zwingli combated their endeavours as a "rebellion," they from that time regarded him as the enemy of Christianity. Münzer's writings against Luther here found a ready hearing, and his assistance, as well as that of his partisan Balthasar Hübmör (Hubmaier) of Waldshut, was in request.

In 1523, the latter, after having already delivered reformatory sermons at Ratisbon, had in a short time won over the town of Waldshut on the frontier of Switzerland to the new doctrine as understood by Zwingli. The anterior-Austrian government, like the Bishop of Constance, had in vain endeavoured to call him to account or to procure his dismissal. It was only when preparations were made for proceedings against the town, whose defection and accession to the confederates were feared, that Hubmaier withdrew, in the summer of 1524, to Schaffhausen, but to the joy of the citizens returned soon afterwards, after volunteers from Zürich had marched into the town to defend the word of God. But, in the meantime, Hubmaier had entered into personal relations with Th. Münzer, abandoned Zwingli and joined the Zürich *Stürmer und Dränger*.[1] Anabaptism was begun, although "weak" parents were still not forbidden to have their children baptised. He thereby brought dissension into his congregation and deprived it of the sympathies of evangelical Switzerland. (After the end of the Peasants' War the town, which in vain invoked the protection of Switzerland, was handed over to the Austrian government, Hubmaier just managing to save himself by flight: Joh. Faber again triumphantly restored the Catholic service.)

The conventicles of the fanatical society, which in its radical Bible Christianity recklessly sacrificed its connection with the history of the Church, and felt elevated in the consciousness of having no other than true Christians as fellow-members, were recruited from the artisan classes. In these circles **the rejection of infant baptism**—"the greatest cruelty of the devil and of the Romish Pope"—was uplifted as the standard: by **Ana**baptism, as the independent act of the individual, who desired to live as a citizen of the Kingdom of God, a man severed the bond with the rest of Christendom and separated from it to join a new,

---

[1] *Literally*, "Stormers and Stressers," but it is impossible to give an adequate equivalent.

enthusiastic community.¹ Neither Zwingli's private negotiations with the leaders, nor two public discussions (January 17th and March 20th, 1525), appointed by the Council of Zürich, were able to arrest the baptist movement, which, *e.g.*, in St. Gall, was joined by the people in large numbers, after the baptism of the monk Blaurock[2] by Grebel had given the signal. In spite of extravagant manifestations of the most whimsical kind, this movement notwithstanding maintained a **peaceful** character, in pronounced contrast with Münzer's warlike aspirations.[3]

It was here that **the Baptist community** received its first characteristic, full development: in the return to the regulations of the Apostolic Church, in the assertion that Christians ought not to hold any magistracy nor wear a sword; in the rejection of the paid office of preacher; in the opinion that the taking of interest and tithes was sinful: in the demand that "all things should be common and heaped up together." In the question of the Eucharist, they followed Carlstadt. In addition, there were special rules in regard to clothes (coats of coarse cloth, wide grey hats) and a vagabond horror of the forms of social life—"monks without cowls."

The Council of Zürich endeavoured to protect infant baptism with threats of punishment, while Zwingli, in his Essay *Vom Tauf, vom Wiedertauf und vom Kindertauf* [On Baptism, Anabaptism, and Infant Baptism] defended it as a sign of allegiance and not to be withheld from children as members of the people of God, after the analogy of circumcision; in a second Essay *Vom Predigtamt* he combats the proceedings of the Separatists, which threatened to destroy the church, refusing them divine legitimation for their separation.[4] But it required increasingly severe mandates of the authorities to suppress the strong, popular movement in favour of the proscribed unlicensed sect. The rigorism of the authorities,

---

[1] As a matter of course the name **Ana**baptists was always rejected: it was asserted that there were no Anabaptists, since the *first* baptism was nothing. EGELHAAF, II, 32.

[2] For BLAUROCK, see FRITZ JECKLIN in the 21st *Jahresber. der histor. antiq. Gesellsch. von Graubünden*, 1891, p. 1 ff.

[3] Cp. Grebel's Letter to Münzer, September 5th, 1524: Man sol das Evangelium und sine annemer nit schirmen mit dem schwert oder sy sich selbsz ... rechte gleubige Christen sind Schaf mitten unter den wölfen, etc. [Men should not defend the Gospel and those who accept it, or themselves with the sword: the real faithful Christians are as sheep in the midst of wolves.] In CORNELIUS, *Gesch. des Münsterischen Aufruhrs*, II 244.

[4] For a third Essay, his *Elenchus*, cp. Baur in ZKG X 330 ff. USTERI in ZKG XI 161 ff.

which has made the history even of the peacefully disposed portion of the baptist communities a history of suffering without parallel, is partly to be explained by the coincidence of the first appearance of the Baptists with the revolutionary convulsions in the German peasantry and the many points of contact between the two movements which in themselves were **entirely distinct.**

4. Separation of the Reformation from the Revolution of the Peasants' War.

Literature: W. VOGT, *Vorgeschichte des Bauernkrieges*, Halle, 1887; the same, *die bairische Politik im Bauernkriege*, Nördl., 1883; the same, *die Bodenseebauern*, Augsb., 1892. For the supposed "Bauernparlament" see v. KLUCKHOHN in GGN, 1893, 276 ff. For the twelve articles see DOBEL, *Memmingen in Ref. zeitalter*, I² 69 ff. STERN, *über die 12 Artikel*, Leipz., 1868; the same, FdG XII 475 ff. BAUMANN, *die oberschwäb. Bauern und die 12 Art.*, Kempten, 1871; BOSSERT in *Bl. württ. KG*, II 73 ff; VOGT in ZkW, 1885, 413; RADLKOFER in ZhV f. Schwaben XVI 1 ff.; HÖHLBAUM in FdG XVII 345 ff. EGELHAAF, I 569 ff. FALCKENHEINER, *Philipp d. Grossm. im Bauernkriege*, Marb., 1887. SEIDEMANN, *das Ende des Bauernkr. in Thür.* in N. Mitth. aus d. Gebiet hist. antiq. Forsch. XIV 392 ff.

Disturbances amongst the peasants had already commenced, decades before the Reformation, in which the religious question of the latter originally had no share at all. The condition and treatment of the peasants living in serfdom just in the territories of the Church are in great measure responsible for them. After the culture of the towns had rapidly advanced, the peasantry began their war of emancipation, not entirely because the burden of their condition was unendurable, but because they objected to be looked down upon from a legal standpoint as compared with others. Special grounds of complaint acted as inflammatory material: first, devastating campaigns, then, the reception of the Roman law, which bestowed upon their masters fresh legal claims to territory, the change of hereditary into revocable fief, the limitation of right of settlement, the unlimited exercise by the masters of the right of hunting: to these were added apocalyptic voices, astrological announcements, the impression which the Hussite victories had made upon the ordinary man, and the biblical catch-words, which had penetrated the masses: then, especially in the small-citizen circles, writings like the *Reformatio Sigismundi* of 1438 with its religiously democratic programme of reform, full of promises and supposed to have been devised by that Emperor himself, and its doctrine of "divine justice," *i.e.*, the treatment of the Bible as the authority also for civil and social justice. The end of the 15th and the beginning of the 16th century had already witnessed numerous explosions amongst the peasants and in the townships, but all of strictly limited area. Luther's demands for reform, further intensified by the inflammatory preaching of a number of preachers and by fugitive literature, had naturally afforded fresh nourishment to this frame of mind: the discontented peasantry appropriated them as fresh *gravamina*, and the regularly planned establishment of an "evangelical community" now combined with the social revolution. The abolition of the Nuremberg Council of Regency finally aggravated the pessimistic feeling. Certainly, the isolated risings of the year 1524 had for the most part nothing to do with the "Gospel": at Waldshut (August, 1524) the agrarian and the religious movements went hand in hand; in the succeeding winter, the blending of the social revolution with certain catchwords and demands of the Reformation was more definitely completed. The fact that a large number of country parsons and priests who said matins joined the peasants is to be explained by their own oppressed condition and their peasant origin. On the 24th of February, 1525, the peasants of Allgäu (in Upper Swabia) constituted themselves "a Christian union" and proclaimed the holy Gospel as their fundamental law, but at the same time, manifesting peaceful intentions, they turned to the Archduke Ferdinand, as the representative of the Emperor, with the demand for social assistance. When then the different South German bands of peasants combined, the evangelical tendencies were at first checked in March, but immediately afterwards gained the upper hand in the acceptance of the **Twelve Articles of the entire peasantry,**[1] the author of which was the furrier Sebastian Lotzer, who was assisted by the Memmingen preacher Christopher Schappeler. These articles put in front of an agrarian, economic programme the demands, that the congregations should be allowed to exercise the right of choosing and dismissing their ministers (see above, p. 47), since they are in need of "pure" preaching of the Gospel, and that the tithe, which they further are willing to give, should be appropriated by the congregation itself to the support of the parson, the maintenance of the poor and as a reserve fund for the needs of the country. Also, the succeeding socio-economical demands of their programme at the same time appeared with a religious colouring, as founded on the Bible. But it is a programme of reform, not of revolution; reconciliation, not a civil war is desired. **The evangelical Spirit, which penetrated the movement, had a moderating effect.** But the Swabian league, encouraged by the defeat of France before Pavia (February 24th) and by the failure of Ulrich of Wurtemberg's campaign to recover his country, rejected all the demands of the peasants. Then the radical elements broke out amongst the peasantry, deeds of violence began on the 26th of March: but the defeats of Leipheim (April 4th) and Wurzach (April 14th) and the treachery of the commander of the Lake of Constance peasants before Weingarten on April 17th sealed their fate. The peasants on the Neckar and in Franconia fought with better success; but even in these cases the defeat at Böblingen (May 12th) bade the movement halt. On April 26th, Pfeiffer broke out from Mühlhausen: within a few days the whole of Thuringia was in revolt. Frederick the Wise, seriously ill and at the point of death, refused to believe in the seriousness of the danger. Luther, on his way to Eisleben, came across the Twelve Articles, and, while still travelling, wrote (April 19th) his *Ermahnung zum Frieden auf die 12 Artikel der Bauernschaft in Schwaben* [Exhortation to Peace] (EA 24² 269 ff.), without knowing that his advice was too late. He reminded the Princes of their offences and begged them to deal kindly with the peasants: he approved of the 1st Article: as for the others, he did not materially interfere with them,

---

[1] The foundation of these are the ten Articles of the Memmingen peasantry; DOBEL, *Memmingen im Reformationszeitalter* I² 69 ff.; the Twelve Articles are printed in STROBEL, Beitr. II 1 ff., in Low German FdG 1877, 343.

but only on principle set forth the moral duties of the authorities towards their subjects.[1] But he pointed out to the peasants that they forfeited all claim to take the lead in a Christian cause, the moment they proceeded to violence. At the risk of his life he attempted—but without success—to oppose personally the peasants in the Hartz Mountains and in Thuringia. Meanwhile, Frederick the Wise died on the 5th of May, seeing with resignation God's judgment of the Princes in the revolt of the peasants. In this critical situation, Luther with all his might opposed the revolt, in the interests of the Gospel. Satan desires to spoil his sowing, by making his Gospel the license for the revolution. He accordingly writes the rude and violent essay *Wider die mörderischen und räuberischen Rotten der Bauern* (EA 24^2 300 ff.).[2] He calls upon the authorities to discharge the duties of their office; he asks them to acknowledge that they have deserved this storm, but at the same time once again to offer to do justice to the peasants, and, if this is of no avail, to grasp the sword immediately; and then again, to show mercy to the large numbers amongst the prisoners who had been misled. He recognised, sooner than many others, that energetic management of authority in times of sedition is the right kind of compassion to be shown towards a country. On the 15th of May, the decisive blow was struck at the battle of Frankenhausen, by the combined forces of Philip of Hesse, the Elector John, Duke George, and the Counts of Central Germany. Münzer was taken prisoner and executed in camp. The more recklessly the Princes took vengeance upon the peasants, the heavier became the weight of odium, which Luther had to bear. He had lost his popularity amongst the peasants, the Romanists despised him as a man who could not be depended upon,[3] and even his friends were partly taken aback: was he not to blame for this bloody reaction?[4] He justified himself with a good conscience in a circular letter (EA 24^2 309 ff.). Never before had Luther been so isolated, and yet he had remained true to his profession.

The defeat of the peasants was the hour of the birth of the Catholic reaction: people now thought they had tested the fruits of the Reformation and now desired likewise to tear up the

---

[1] Cp. on the other hand Melanchthon, who, in CR XVI 441 has curtly denoted this essay as *impius ac seditiosus libellus:* cp. further XX 641 ff.

[2] [Against the murderous and plundering gangs of the peasants.] He wrote this at the time when he did not as yet know who would gain the victory (cp. EA 242, 307). Certainly, in the writings of ultramontane pragmatists, from COCHLEUS and FABER to HERGENRÖTHER (*Conc. Gesch. IX 434*), we find such statements as the following: "No sooner had the news of the first defeat of the peasants echoed through the land, than Luther etc.;" *quos ubi vidit superari, affligi, confici, hortatus est nobilitatem, ut etc* (FICKER, die Konfutation, Leipz., 1891, p. 185).

[3] Cp., e.g., FABER in FICKER, *die Konfutation*, Leipz., 1891, p. 184 f.

[4] Cp. Poliander's defence of Luther in TSCHACKERT, *Urkundenbuch* II 131 ff. The Austrian government showed itself especially cruel: the more beneficent was the effect produced by the mildness of Strasburg: cp. FdG 1883, 284 f.

"root" of the revolution,—the Reformation.¹ The clear brightness of Luther's name grew dimmer in the lower circles of the people—the spread of baptist principles in succeeding years proves this. He also, since that time, bore a grudge against the Lord *Omnes*, and lost his joyful reliance upon the national movement. Henceforth, in his eyes the essential task of the Church was, the education of the uncultivated and stiff-necked ordinary man. The spring days of the Reformation were over.

Cochleus, with odious meddlesomeness, had connected Luther's **marriage** with the defeat of the peasants: the whole of Germany lamented that he celebrated a joyous wedding!² A connection actually existed, in so far as the need of the time had awakened in him the idea of an approaching death and hence, the desire ("to spite the devil before I die") to set the seal of his own example (de W. III 13) upon his written testimony in favour of the marriage of the priests, "even should it be no more than a 'Joseph's' marriage" (de W. II 678). On the 13th of June, he quickly made up his mind and concluded a marriage with Catherine von Bora, a nun who had fled from the convent at Nimptschen: compassion for the woman who had been abandoned by a wealthy suitor had rapidly changed to affection. A fortnight later the marriage was publicly solemnised. Melanchthon, who had not been taken into confidence owing to his timidity, was beside himself at what Luther had done: the full tenor of his malicious letter, more characteristic of him than of Luther, has only recently become known.³ Erasmus took occasion to circulate false and odious tittle-tattle about this marriage. It forms no special turning-point in Luther's **public** activity: it is frequently forgotten, that he was already at that time in his forty-second year.

---

¹ For Duke George (and equally for the Pope) the victory of Frankenhausen was simply a *sigk widder die Lutterischen* "a victory over the Lutherans" (ZhTh 1847, 644). Cp. FRIEDENSBURG, *Zur Vorgesch. des Gotha-Torgauischen Bündnisses*, Marburg, 1884, p. 6 ff. J. Brenz had already successfully defended the Reformation against such accusations: see JÄGER and HARTMANN, *J. Brenz* I 70 ff. Cp. also Philip's declaration to Duke George in v. ROMMEL, *Philipp d. Gr.* II 85: that there had been less disturbance where people followed the Gospel, than where they persecuted it.

² *Comment.* 1549, p. 117 f.

³ W. MEYER in SBBA of November 4th, 1876. DE LAGARDE, *Mittheilungen* IV 416 ff.

CHAPTER FOURTH.

Development of the Reformation: ecclesiastical territories and Confessions of faith.

1. Emperor and Pope.

Literature: W. HELLWIG, *die politischen Beziehungen Clemens' VII. zu Karl V* im *J. 1526,* Leipz., 1889. GRETHEN, *die politischen Beziehungen Clemens' VII. zu Karl V. 1523-1527,* Hannover, 1887. M. BROSCH, *Gesch. des Kirchenstaates.* Gotha, 1880, I 106 f. GREGOROVIUS, *Geschichte der Stadt Rom. VIII.*

At the beginning of the year 1525, the Emperor's position had unexpectedly become most brilliant. The great victory before Pavia had almost annihilated the French army, Francis I. was his prisoner. Charles now resolved to leave Spain as soon as possible for Italy for his coronation and then to proceed to Germany to exterminate the "sect." He also regarded the Peasants' War simply as a Lutheran movement: a fresh reason for annihilating Lutheranism. Protestantism had to thank **the Pope,** that it did not now feel the Emperor's strong arm immediately. Certainly Clement VII., after the victory (terrible for him) of the imperial arms at Pavia, was driven to an alliance with Charles: but, at the same time, he began to conspire against the latter in France, England and Italy, attempted to entice Charles's general, Pescara, to treason, persuaded Francis to break the oath he had taken at the Peace of Madrid (Jan. 14th, 1526), and gave him absolution—in short, instead of supporting the Emperor in the struggle against the Reformation, he forced upon him a struggle against himself. On the 22nd of May, Clement, Francis, Milan, Venice and Florence, under the protection of Henry VIII., combined in the "Holy League" at Cognac, avowedly for the purpose of bringing about a lasting peace amongst the Christian princes, in reality to crush the Emperor. A correspondence followed between Pope and Emperor, in which the former (June 23rd, *Non opus esse credimus*[1]) charged the Emperor's policy with ambition and trampling upon the papal rights, while the latter (September 17th) brought forward crushing material for accusation in reference to the faithlessness of the Pope, and, lastly, appealed to a general council[2] against the Pope, who from a shepherd had become an invader (*non pastor sed invasor*). In November, the Emperor despatched his troops against the Pope: recruiting for this purpose had also taken place in Germany, and Lutheran mercenaries hurried up right willingly,

---

[1] In BALAN, Mon. saec. XVI. I. 364 ff.

[2] The Emperor himself repeatedly published his accusation in 1527. The author of the comprehensive document was probably the imperial secretary, Alfonso de Valdés. Cp. also LANZ, Corresp. Karls V. I 219 ff.

eager to advance against Rome. On the 6th of May, Spaniards, Italians, and Germans stormed the walls of Rome, and a fearful avenging judgment broke over the city:[1] the undisciplined host kept the Pope prisoner until November. The idea was now mooted in the Emperor's Council to deprive the Pope of secular authority altogether, or to remove the papal chair from Rome, and to bring him entirely under the imperial control: but the Emperor refused to listen to these suggestions. He certainly allowed the Essay by Alfonso de Valdés (Dialogo) to issue from his chancery, which excuses the Emperor before Christendom for the plundering of Rome, but, at the same time, demonstrates God's judgment upon the rottenness of the Curia, the greedy profanation of the Holy One, the corruption in the high spiritual association. But further: Christ's teaching is here contrasted with that of Rome. If the Pope will recognise his errors, and heal the wounds of the Church, then the terrible fate, which has befallen Rome, will turn out a blessing. The first work with reformatory tendencies was thus written in the Spanish language to defend the Emperor against the Pope![2] It was not until June, 1529, that peace was concluded between Emperor and Pope—thanks to the political errors of the Papacy, a valuable respite was afforded the German Reformation, which enabled it to take firmer root.

2. The Gotha-Torgau League.

Literature: SEIDEMANN in ZhTh 1847, 638 ff., 656 ff. FRIEDENSBURG, *Zur Vorgeschichte des Gotha-Torgauischen Bündnisses*, Marb., 1884. STOY, *Erste Bündnissbestrebungen evg. Stände*, Jena, 1888.

The overthrow of the peasants had encouraged the Catholic princes to energetic proceedings against Lutheranism. In South Germany, in the districts of the members of the Ratisbon league (p. 44), the triumph over the peasants became at once a bloody persecution of the evangelicals, especially of the "preachers." In many of the towns also the re-establishment of order was combined with that of the old Church. A similar result was to be expected in the North. Duke George,—after he had already, in camp before Mühlhausen, urged a league of the princes for the future prevention of disturbances amongst the peasants,—invited the Electors Joachim of Brandenburg and Albert of Mainz, as

---

[1] Cardinal Cajetan judged that the *iustissimum Dei iudicium* so ordered it in this case. GREGOROVIUS, VIII 568. Cp. Kilian Leib, *Annales* in DÖLLINGER, *Beitr.* II 506 ff. For the "Sacco di Roma" cp. C. RAVIOLI in *Archivio della societa di Roma di storia patria* VI (1883) 303 ff.; a hitherto unpublished bull of Clement VII., threatening with the punishments of the Church the oppressors of that Church in *Archivio storico Italiano* IV I ff. Further the letters JGG XII 751 ff.

[2] *Reformistas antiguos espanoles* IV 325 ff. WILKENS, *Gesch. des span. Protestantismus*. Gütersloh, 1888, p. 31 ff.

well as the Dukes Eric and Henry of Brunswick, to Dessau on the 19th of July, 1525, where it was agreed to "extirpate the root of this disturbance, the damned Lutheran sect."[1]

It was hoped, in view of the Peasants' War, that the Elector John and Philip of Hesse also would be converted from Lutheranism: they were accordingly invited to enter into the league. Both princes refused the demand in a united declaration (September 15th) and conditionally avowed their adhesion to the "Lutheran action in so far as it agreed with the Holy Gospel and the Word of God," declaring that it was impossible for them to help root out the latter.[2] Thereby they saved North Germany from a decided Catholic reaction. As a diet had been convened at Augsburg for Martinmas in the current year, at which the Catholic party again intended to demand the execution of the Edict of Worms, Saxony and Hesse, at Philip's instigation, at first entered into an agreement on the 8th of November, at the Castle of Friedewald, in the case of the Gospel "to stand together as one man," but to reject the Edict of Worms as "quite unendurable." The diet was so poorly attended that it was deferred till the next year at Spires. Meanwhile, the cathedral chapter of Mainz assembled the suffragan chapter, and decided to send a petition to the Emperor with the object of violently exterminating Lutheranism[3]: with the same object, the Dessau confederates sent Henry of Brunswick with a memorial to Spain.[4] This rendered further understanding and agreement between the Evangelicals necessary. Certainly, princes and cities were not yet able to become united, but, on the 27th of February, 1526, Hesse and Saxony entered into a close brotherhood (the so-called Torgau league) at **Gotha,** and, on the 12th of June, the Dukes Ernest and Francis of Brunswick-Lüneburg, Philip of Brunswick-Grubenhagen, Henry of Mecklenburg, Prince Wolfgang of Anhalt, Count Albert of Mansfeld and the city of Magdeburg entered into the alliance at the latter place. Albert of Prussia, who, on the 10th of April, 1525, had handed over the land belonging to the Order to Sigismund King of Poland at Cracow as liege-lord and had got it back as a secular dukedom in fee, soon followed

---

[1] FRIEDENSBURG, p. 113. Consequently it was not a question of only a harmless defensive league.

[2] FRIEDENSBURG, p. 114 ff.

[3] A sharp rejoinder by Luther (EA 65, 22 ff.) was suppressed by the Elector John.

[4] SCHMIDT, G. der Deutschen XI 279 ff.

suit at the Königsberg agreement (September 26th).[1] In Poland, an heretical but dependent Prussia was preferred to a Catholic but independent one. In like manner, the Evangelicals sought union with Frederick I. of Denmark and Gustavus Vasa. Thus, on both sides, measures for "defence" were organised.

3. The Diet of Spires, 1526.

Literature: FRIEDENSBURG, *der Reichstag zu Speier,* 1526, Berl., 1887. NEY, *d. Reichst. z. Sp.*, Hamb., 1889; the same, in ZKG VIII 300 ff., IX 137 ff., 593 ff.

In the meantime, **the diet at Spires** had been opened (June 25th). The Catholic States were still decidedly in the majority, but were not agreed as to the extent to which the Edict of Worms admitted of being carried out: in addition, they now heard of the great coalition of the powers against Charles (p. 70), and consequently felt that his active interference in the affairs of Germany could no longer be counted upon. The Emperor's proposals demanded the prohibition of all innovations until the next Council, the punishment of the refractory, and the ultimate carrying out of the Edict. Secret additional instructions were couched in still stronger language. But now the cities (Nuremberg, Strasburg and Ulm) boldly took the lead in acknowledging that the Edict of Worms was simply impracticable. In consequence of the impression produced by this declaration, the idea of only provisional stipulations, favourable to reform, to remain in force until the next Council, began to be entertained: on the other hand, Frederic now brought forward his stringent additional instructions. In the excitement which was thereby aroused in the diet, recourse was finally had in the existing embarrassment, to the formula that every State "should so behave, rule, and believe, as it should hope and trust to answer before God, the imperial majesty, and the Empire." The **Evangelical** States were only able to accept this formula,—in which the original "before God **first of all** and **afterwards** before the imperial majesty" had been struck out, and thus responsibility to God and Emperor had been placed on the same footing,—since at the same time it was decided to send a message to the Emperor, to enlighten him as to the real state of affairs and the necessity of bringing about a peaceful reconciliation between the two parties in the

---

[1] TSCHACKERT, *Urkundenbuch* II 275.

Empire by means of a general or national Council and to beg him to come to Germany.

The resolution passed at Spires was subsequently denoted as the legalisation of the territorial treatment of the religious question, and people discovered in it the sanctioning of national churchdom. This was certainly not its original purport: it was at first only the repeated adjournment of the imperial decision.[1] But, owing to the fact that the embassy, thwarted by the Catholics, remained in abeyance, that political conditions rendered the general council impossible, that Charles would not listen to the idea of a national council, and refused even to go to Germany, the provisional resolution obtained a much more far-reaching importance: **the condition of affairs itself created a free path for the evangelical States** to arrange ecclesiastical affairs in their districts in whatever manner seemed suitable to them. And they rapidly accustomed themselves to interpret the resolution of the diet as the license for this procedure on their part.[2] The Emperor was certainly engrossed by public affairs: but Ferdinand, who, notwithstanding all his hatred of the Reformation, as Archduke of Austria had hitherto only possessed trifling authority, was now diverted from the persecution of the Evangelicals by great increase of power. After King Louis of Hungary and Bohemia, in the summer of 1526, had fallen at Mohacs against the Turks, his brother-in-law, Ferdinand, was crowned King of Bohemia in February 1527, and in November also King of Hungary. But just for that reason the Turk was henceforth his chief adversary. Against him Ferdinand needed the assistance of the Empire, also for this purpose the votes of the Evangelicals. Thus political reasons from this time forward drove him to adopt a completely different attitude towards the Reformation, even to endure the heretics in his own country. The territorial enlargement of the evangelical communities to established churches was hence able to proceed.

4. The Beginnings of the Established Churchship.

Literature: L. RICHTER, *Gesch. d. evgl. KVerfassung.* Leipz. 1851. H. FRANTZ, *die evg. KVerf. in den deutschen Städten des 16 Jhs.* Halle 1876. O. MEJER, *zum KRecht des 16 Jhs.* Hann. 1891. LORENZ, *L.s Einfluss auf die Entwicklung des evg. KRegiments.* Gumb. 1891. TH. BRIEGER, *die kirchl. Gewalt der Obrigkeit nach der Anschauung Luthers* in ZThK II 513 ff. C. A. H. BURKHARDT, *Gesch. der sächs. Kirchen-und Schulvisitat.* (1524-1545.) Leipz. 1879. Hessen: *Lamberti paradoxa* in v. D. HARDT, *Hist. lit. ref.* V 98 ff.; his *Ep. ad Colonienses* in UN 1740, 30 ff. CREDNER, *Philipps hess. KRef.-Ordn.* Giessen 1852. BAUM, *Lamb. v. Avignon.* Strassb. 1840. A. RITSCHL in ZKG II 49 ff. MEJER in RE VI 268.

The **reigning princes** and city authorities now came forward as administrators and organisers. This was no unheard-of inno-

---

[1] Cp. BRIEGER DLZ 1891, 16.

[2] Thus, on the 20th of October, 1526, the Synod of Homburg: "according to the resolution of Spires they might make ecclesiastical regulations *de quibus parati sumus Deo et Caesari reddere rationem.*" RICHTER KOO I 56. Responsibility to the Emperor, *i.e.*, to his Edicts, was transformed into readiness to endeavour to justify their conduct to him from God's word.

vation. If it did not correspond to the curialistic theory, it was in harmony with the actual course of the development of the relation of State and Church in the 15th century. In like manner the aspiring city constitution, like the princely "liberty," had, in fact, ignored the "independence" of the Church and claimed and exercised a number of rights, of which that theory knew nothing. Yet the Church itself, during the 15th century attempts at reform, *e.g.*, the reforms in the monasteries, had called in the aid of the State and granted it rights in numerous ecclesiastical matters.

Even before the Reformation, the authorities had come to regard themselves as responsible only to God, and that also in regard to the condition of the Church. In order to uphold peace and public order, they employed their police, and did their duty unhesitatingly even in face of the Church. The regulations for the country in the 15th century already bore unmistakably the character of regulations for the Church. The penetration of the Roman law promoted the theoretical justification of these views of the executive: and, while the Popes continually made use of the ruling princes against the bishops and had thus broken through the constitution of the Church, that sweeping right of reform had been granted to the princes, the conclusions of which were now drawn, and the reformers themselves appealed to this right.

Some amongst them might directly deduce from the combination of membership of the Christian community and possession of secular power the duty incumbent upon the holders of such authority to arrange everything for the benefit of their subjects, "which Christ, in a Christian assembly, had ordered them to do";[1] others might deduce from the fact that the episcopal jurisdiction had in reality ceased, and that no other man—not even the chiefs of the reformers—had received the call from God to hold a vacant episcopal office, only a right of **necessity** *i.e.* a **charitable** duty of the authorities under prevailing circumstances, to fill the gap to the best advantage of the Christian communities:[2] in practice it amounted to the same thing.

For Luther, state and church theoretically fall completely asunder: the former has control over the person and property of man, in the latter, God governs souls by his word. Nevertheless, he is not untrue to himself, in driving his Elector on to the path of the regulation of ecclesiastical affairs by the sovereign. For the authorities are appointed for the purpose of maintaining peace, consequently of preventing confusion, factions, and discord in the Church: they have to punish blasphemy, consequently blasphemous forms of worship and doctrine: they have to protect the property of the Church, and prevent its being wasted: they are under the obligation of carefully providing for the religious education of the young. But, to these duties of the authorities

---

[1] See e.g. Joh. Brenz, RICHTER KOO I 40.
[2] So Luther: de Wette II 493.

qua authorities are to be added those which arise from the fact that the bearer of authority is at the same time himself **a member of the Church**. As such, the Prince, at a time when the Christian communities are distressed, exercises his duty as a Christian in causing them to be visited and so assisting them by his position. The only condition attached is that the possessor of authority should himself submit to the word of God. Luther completely gave up the idea of coming to an understanding with the bishops in regard to the new constitution of the Church: in regard to these he could only give the advice (in 1526). "that they should consent to their order being changed to a secular one, and that certain properties should be taken in fief from the Empire and bestowed upon those who were found worthy of it" (EA 26², 8).

Since, further, it was an established principle of the reformers, that "only one kind of preaching should be allowed in one place" (de W. III. 89),[1] civil and ecclesiastical communities could be identified and the former made the executive organ of the ecclesiastical administration.

The church of the youthful duchy of **Prussia** was reorganised most rapidly and under most favourable circumstances. Bishop George von **Polentz**[2] of Samland had joyfully supported the cause of the Reformation: on the 30th of May, 1525, he placed his secular authority entirely in the hands of his ruler,[3] but reserved to himself the episcopal right of visitation and ordination, as well as the supervision of the clergy. Erhard von Queiss, who had been selected, but not confirmed by the Pope as Bishop of Pomesania, followed his example in 1527, after having in like manner made a declaration to his clergy in 1525: there were still to be bishops, but such as " preach and teach, and interpret God's word in its purity and **govern** the Church."[4] When he died in 1529, he was succeeded by Speratus, but not, as Queiss had wished, by the election of the clergy, but by decree of his ruler. For in this case also Albert regarded himself as the proper bishop (by necessity) of the land (*coacti sumus alienum officium, hoc est, episcopale, in nos sumere*)[5], and the two established bishops as persons entrusted by him with the *cura divinorum*.[6] By a ducal mandate of the 6th of July, 1525, evangelical preaching was decreed for the whole land, and a proposition of the duke was agreed to by the diet, whereby the right of nomination, the limitation of parishes, the endowment of pastorates, the church finances and the like were reorganised, while an episcopal "ecclesiastical order" was announced for the "ceremonies."[7] The latter followed later, in 1526.

It is worth noticing that, in these regulations, the community is allowed to co-operate in the choice of ministers and in exclusion from the Communion: the latter right, however, was not practically exercised. A **visitation** of the

---

[1] Bucer reckons the idea of tolerating religious points of view of different kinds within the limits of the same country as one of the "errors of the Baptists," ZhTh 1860, 7.—Cp. also EA 39, 252.

[2] TSCHACKERT in *Kirchengesch. Studien*. Leipz. 1888: add DITTRICH in JGG X 112 ff.

[3] TSCHACKERT, *Urkundenb*. II. 120.

[4] TSCHACKERT, *Urkundenb*. II. 101.

[5] RICHTER, *Gesch. d. KVerf.* p. 36.

[6] TSCHACKERT, I 168. "Not a separation of Church and State, but only a division of the duties of the government."

[7] TSCHACKERT, I. 127 ff.

parsonages by secular commissioners of the duke and theologians immediately followed (1526, continued in 1528). Finally, in 1530, synods of the clergy were summoned, before which a first confession of doctrine was laid: but, instead of the latter, the Augsburg Confession was almost immediately introduced in the land.[1]

In **Saxony,** Frederick the Wise, during his lifetime, had kept up the appearance of abstaining from public participation in the reorganisation of the Church. His brother John[2] acted differently: even before he came to power, he had much more openly taken up a definite attitude towards the Reformation, but was for a time so caught by the ideas of **James Strauss** of Eisenach—who wanted to re-establish the Law of Moses as the norm in the evangelical community—that his son, **John Frederick,** becoming uneasy, entreated Luther, in 1524, to visit Thuringia and examine the preachers in reference to fanaticism and to dismiss those who were worthless "with the assistance of the authorities" (Enders IV 356 f.). But Luther refused, while Strauss, commissioned by the Prince, actually officiated as inspector, in January, 1525, in the neighbourhood of Eisenach, accompanied by a lawyer. Meanwhile, in the autumn of 1524, the preacher, N. Hausmann, of Zwickau, had applied to the Elector, on pretence that the position of the Church in the country required regulation by the authorities. His idea was, that a synod should be summoned *pro unitate ceremoniarum statuenda*: but Luther decidedly rejected this proposal, in order to leave the independence of the communities unimpaired (de Wette II 563, VI 54). In a memorial to Duke John, Hausmann subsequently (in May, 1525) developed the following plan:[3] as the proper bishops do not trouble themselves about the abuses of the Church, the ruler must interpose as the **supreme protector**: he should take heart and, making allowance for necessity, above all arrange **visitations.** The precedent of King Jehoshaphat (Chron. II. 17, 6 ff.) serves as a biblical authorisation, and the procedure of the Margrave Casimir of Anspach (Richter, KOO I 50) shows that other princes have already entered upon similar paths. In order to provide evangelical clergy for the whole country, the introduction of the right of the communities to elect is requisite.[4] He also harks back to his scheme of summoning synods. At the same time, Spalatin, just before Frederic's death, had endeavoured to induce him to issue a "Reformation decree."[5] Soon Luther himself also called upon the new ruler to do away with the existing Catholic clergy, and to employ the revenues of the Church to the benefit of the preachers of the Gospel (de Wette III 15). The confusion, which the Peasants' War had caused, and the spoliation of church property by the nobility under the cloak of the Gospel had convinced him that the regulation of the affairs of the Church must now be carried out with a strong hand. On the 1st of October, 1525, Spalatin informed the

---

[1] TSCHACKERT, I 165 ff.

[2] J. BECKER, *Kurfürst Johann und seine Beziehungen zu Luther*, I, Leipz., 1890.

[3] ZhTh 22, 365 ff.

[4] The Lutheran Reformation did not follow up this idea further. Bugenhagen (1526) in his Essay *Von dem christlichen Glauben* (VOGT, Bugenhagen p. 249) has expressed its position in regard to the question of the right of election of ministers "In this point we should be content with **the usual right**.... What does it matter by whom it is established?"

[5] KOLDE, *Friedrich der Weise*, p. 68.

Elector of Luther's present readiness to lend a helping hand to such procedure on the part of the authorities,[1] and, on the 31st of the same month, in a highly characteristic cry of distress, he himself appealed to the Emperor, as a matter of conscience and as being the man who "is required and demanded by us and by necessity itself as also assuredly by God," (de Wette III. 39) to remedy with vigour the confusion existing in the Church. John followed the cry although he prudently rejected all possible claims upon the state-chest (Burkhardt, Briefwechsel, p. 92). The financial support of the ministries he declared to be the duty of the parishioners. Luther now made positive proposals (de Wette III. 51 f.): that the land should be divided into four or five visitation-districts; that the revenues of the livings should be regulated by secular visitors; that old or inefficient ministers, provided only they were not hostile to the Gospel, should be treated with forbearance, with the aid of the homily, from which they could read. Accordingly, in January, 1526, the **visitation** of the country commenced, at first by way of experiment in individual districts. In connection with this arrangement and the institution of a national church, Luther's *Deutsche Messe* (German mass)[2] appeared in January, 1526,—the important advance in the direction of a German language for purposes of worship and further emancipation from the Romish mass, certainly also the evidence of the **lowering of his community ideals.** For the service of God now serves "for the most part the simple and the young people." By the side of this, he develops the plan of the separation of a closer sacramental community, uniting in works of love and moral restraint, for the realisation of which, however, the time does not appear to be as yet ripe.[3] In the summer of 1527, Melanchthon, in view of the visitations that were now to be generally undertaken, drew up some shorter instructions in Latin for the purpose of testing the teaching and doctrine of the clergy: *articuli de quibus egerunt per visitatores* (CR 26, 7 ff.),—an attempt to equip the Church for effective, religiously moral education of the people, and at the same time a reaction against the manner in which many evangelical preachers misused the preaching of grace, the preaching of penitence (to be based upon the law) being put before the preaching of faith as indispensable: *intelligi quid sit fides non potest nisi praedicata poenitentia: praedicatio legis ad poenitentiam provocat.* This emphasis laid upon the law called forth the first conflict amongst Luther's companions: **Joh. Agricola** (at that time head-master of the school and preacher at Eisleben) exercised his censorship at the electoral Court upon the new method of instruction as in the case of Luther, and raised the complaint that Melanchthon "was again creeping backwards." However, Luther still endeavoured to soothe his friend and materially supported Melanchthon, who as a matter of fact in this case had followed Luther's footsteps,[4] so that, after some hesitation at Court, it became possible for the longer essay in German, *Unterricht der Visitatoren* [Instructions to

---

[1] Kolde, p, 70 f.

[2] EA 22, 226 ff. BA 7, 161 ff.

[3] As early as 1523 WA XII 485 and again in 1527 (de Wette III 167). He even had in his mind the idea of gathering the "real" Christians together at special preaching services in the convent church, and of having sermons delivered to the rest by the chaplain in the parish church: cp. Kolde in ZKG XIII 552 ff.

[4] Cp. *e.g.* EA 27, 180, 194, 270 f., 42, 112.

Visitors] to follow.¹ This was certainly not, as Luther's preface sets forth, "a strict injunction that we should not raise fresh papal decretals, but a history and, in addition, an evidence and a confession of our faith." but it is intended that the secular authorities by virtue of this norm, should see to it that "discord, faction and disturbance do not arise amongst the subjects." The "Instruction" arranges the teaching in reference to the controversial questions of the day, settles the form of divine worship, appoints **Superattendents**,² whose duty it is to exercise supervision over the teaching, administration and manner of life of the ministers; to make reports at Court in certain contingencies through official personages: to interrogate and examine ministers to be newly appointed before their investiture with the office in question: it is also their duty to settle the **normal plan of instruction** for the Latin schools of the country. A catechism, which Melanchthon had already begun to print, was not completed, in consideration of the conflict with Agricola.³ Yet something of the kind was obviously an urgent necessity, in order to create a fixed tradition of instruction and to regulate as a uniform whole both material and form for the now prescribed catechismal sermon as well as for instruction in church, at school, and at home. Luther himself put his hand to the work and, in 1529, brought out in rapid succession, first, the "**large**," then the "**small Catechism**,"⁴—the former, which had its origin in his own sermons on the main points,⁵ as a specimen for catechismal sermons, the latter for the exercise of young men and servants, a remedy for the alarming religious ignorance of the people. A marriage manual as well as a revision of the baptismal manual of 1523 (see p. 47) completed the liturgical apparatus of the established Church.

Hesse seemed desirous of striking out a strongly divergent path of ecclesiastical organisation. Landgrave Philip convoked a synod at Homberg for October, 1526, to which he summoned, in addition to the clergy, deputies from the nobility and towns. At this meeting, the eccentric **Francis Lambert** of Avignon, who had been summoned by him from Strasburg, defended a number of reformatory theses (*Paradoxa*), on the basis of which the Synod instituted a commission, in which he played the part of leader. This commission handed

---

¹ It is characteristic, that Melanchthon himself hoped that this essay of his would meet with the approval of Erasmus, and that John Faber, on the basis of the same, made the attempt to invite him to return to the Catholic camp with an offer of a favourable provision being found for him, CR I 947, 998. Even the later edition of 1538 was regarded by the papal nuncio as *retrattatione de molte case male*. FRIEDENSBURG, *Nuntiaturberichte* II 288.

² The name was the familiar translation of Episcopus, especially in the form *Superintendens*. Cp. Jerome. ep. 85, *ad Evagr*: Augustine *de civitate dei* 19, 19: on *Psalm* 116; Rab. Maur. *de cler. inst.* 1, 5: Gabr. Biel in IV *Sent. dist.* 24, 9, 1; EA 24,² 219; CR II 283.

³ The Zwickau library contains the only copy of the uncompleted impression.

⁴ On the 16th of May, copies of the small catechism were ready for distribution; on the 26th, it was adopted for use in the monastery of Nimptschen: by the middle of June, the third edition had already been printed. Cp. AGd Buchh. XVI 91; GROSSMANN, *die Visit.-Acten d. Diöc. Grimma*. I. Leipz., 1873, p. 78.

⁵ Recently discovered by G. BUCHWALD.

the Landgrave the outline of a constitution,[1] which presents the peculiarity that its purport is to complete the separation of the *congregatio fidelium* from the mass of the parishioners and make it the foundation of the constitution. The names of all who are willing to submit to the regulations of the community, are entered in a list, and henceforth form the community of the Lord's Supper, bear the name of brethren, and are subject to the discipline of the community. In connection with divine service, they meet to discuss communal affairs, and are the administrators of ecclesiastical government in the local community. They appoint and dismiss the minister, and exercise the right of excommunication. On the deputation of the minister and a delegate from the community, they constitute the **Synod,** which meets every year and performs the functions of ecclesiastical government as a higher court. It nominates three standing visitors of the communities, and also a synodal committee, which carries on the government during the intervals. All this is the only order of things that is in conformity to the Scriptures. That Luther's ideas, as expressed in the "German Mass" (see p. 78), exercised an influence upon this scheme, is evident: on the other hand, the influence of Waldensian or Franciscan institutions, asserted by more recent authorities, is uncertain. The only concession made to the principle of sovereignty was, that the Prince, the Counts and the Knights should have a right of voting in the Synod, without this right being expressly connected with their belonging to the community of the faithful: further, the government of the Church was provisionally handed over to the Landgrave for a year, and the new order of things was not to enter into force until this period had elapsed. But Luther, before whom Philip laid the scheme, warned him against introducing it, declaring that it was too much innovation at once, that the arrangement was premature. Above all, there was still a lack of the clergy to take it in hand. Experience would show that many alterations must be made, that much must be reserved entirely for the authorities (de Wette, VI. 80 f.). Here also, therefore, instead of Lambert's plans being followed, the mode of procedure in Electoral Saxony was adhered to. The only permanent result of his activity in Hesse was the foundation of the University of **Marburg** (1527), the first founded by Protestantism, which was due to his instigation. But Archbishop Albert of Mainz, by an agreement, dated the 11th of June, 1528, formally handed over to the Elector and the Landgrave the ecclesiastical jurisdiction in their lands, until the time of a free Christian council.[2] **Joh. Bugenhagen** created the model for numerous churches in North Germany in the Brunswick Church ordinances of 1528. In this case the affairs of the Church form part of the **city** administration: the Council and the community appoint a superattendent, especially charged with the supervision of instruction in the case of church and school servants: the management of the "cash box" is entrusted to "cash box keepers" chosen by the Council and representatives of the community. "Deacons," summoned from the community, whose qualifications are established in accordance with *Timothy* I, 3, are appointed to look after the poor. Bugenhagen's numerous church ordinances (Hamburg, 1529, Lübeck, 1531, and later) exercised a most important influence upon the conservative character of the worship and customs of the church in the Lutheranism of North Germany, in the ecclesiastical year, mass-vestments, the maintenance of certain Latin parts of the liturgy, private

---

[1] Richter, KOO I 56 ff.
[2] Rommel, *Philipp d. Grossmüthige.* Giessen., 1830, I 156; II 116 f.

confession, and, further, in the value attached to frequent catechismal preaching. **Joh. Brenz** in the church ordinances of Schwäbisch-Hall (1526) proposed a committee of the elders of the community to be appointed by the Council, which should administer ecclesiastical discipline together with the minister.

In Strasburg, the Reformation gained a decisive victory in 1529: in Hamburg, thanks to the cooperation of Bugenhagen, in 1528: in Brunswick-Lüneburg it dated from 1527.

5. The Consolidation of the Reformation in German Switzerland.

Literature: Continuation of p. 49: TRECHSEL in RE II 313 ff. WIEDEMANN, Eck. p. 206 ff. HERGENRÖTHER, *Conc.-Gesch.* IX 659 ff. H. ESCHER, *die Glaubensparteien in der Eidgenossenschaft und ihre Beziehungen zum Ausland 1527 bis 1531.* Frauenfeld, 1882. ROHRER, *das christliche Burgrecht.* Luz., 1876. Archiv f. d. G. der Republik Graubünden II 286 ff. E. BLÖSCH, *eine neue Quelle zur Gesch. der Berner Disp.* in Theol. Z. aus der Schweiz. 1891, p. 157 ff.

After the Peasants' War, the Catholic reaction had in like manner made itself felt in **Switzerland**. Eck had there repeatedly offered his services for a victorious disputation with the leaders of the Reformation who had hitherto always been successful in their efforts in that direction. The Catholic party now accordingly urged such a debate. As Zwingli and Eck could not agree upon the conditions, the former kept away from the religious colloquy— to the detriment of his reputation (II, 2, 393 ff.). In May, 1526, the new disputation took place in **Baden** (Aargau) in the presence of the four bishops and a distinguished assembly. Only Oecolampadius held his ground against Eck, Faber and Th. Murner (at that time in Lucerne); the Catholic party was already sure of its victory in advance. Eck's theses were the foundation of the proceedings. Eighty-two of those present gave the victory to Eck, only ten to Oecolampadius: it was a great momentary success for the Catholic party,[1] a shock (although it certainly soon passed away) to the position, which the Evangelicals had up to the present obtained.

A resolution of the diet threatened Luther and his associates with the great ban; common measures were to be henceforth taken for the suppresion of the innovation. Zürich was required with threats to reduce Zwingli to silence. But it was just the certainty of victory that paved the way for a repulse. It was not only that

---

[1] Cp. however, in regard to the favourable impression produced by the disputation in Strasburg, KOLDE, Anal. 83.

Zwingli lifted up his head in a courageous counter-declaration (I. 2, 506): in Berne and Bâle also opinion veered round in favour of the Reformation: the five forest cantons, feeling their isolation, sought to enter the confederation with Freiburg and Valais. The grand council of Berne now ordered a fresh disputation, for which Francis Kolb and Bercht. Haller drew up the theses.[1] It commenced on the 6th of January, 1528, attended by numerous deputies from Switzerland and South Germany (Bucer, Capito, A. Blaurer and others). A great success was gained: not only did Berne completely throw in its lot with the Zwinglian Reformation, but Bâle, St. Gall, and Schaffhausen followed its example; in other districts (Graubünden,[2] Glarus, Solothurn) the evangelical party grew: the movement was now also introduced into French Switzerland by Farel. At the same time this disputation indicated the victory of the Zwinglian doctrine of the Eucharist over the Lutheran in Switzerland and the friendly communities of South Germany.[3] Both parties now hastened to strengthen their position also politically. On the Catholic side, a league was formed with Austria (February 18th, 1529): Zürich, on the other hand, hastened to conclude a "Christian league"[4] with the evangelical cantons of Switzerland, which at the same time sought assistance in the Empire (Strasburg). Thus the confederacy was divided owing to the dissension caused by the religious question. The burning of the minister Kaiser of Zürich at Schwyz in 1529 had given the signal for war: the armies already stood face to face at Kappel, but this time—against Zwingli's wish—a reconciliation was effected between the hostile parties and a public peace brought about (June 25th, 1529). The five Catholic cantons were obliged to abandon their league with Austria: yet it was in that country that the Catholic cause possessed its strongest bulwarks.

---

[1] Printed in NIEMEYER 14 f. HENKE I 188. SCHAFF., *Bibl. symb.* I. 365 f. III. 208 ff.

[2] The disputation of Ilanz, 1526, followed by a law, in accordance with which each of the parties was allowed free movement in the three confederacies and persecution of the others forbidden.

[3] This caused great ill-humour at Wittenberg (de Wette III 290).

[4] Or, "to enter into Christian *burgher-rights*" *(Burgrecht)*.

6. The Eucharistic Controversy.

Literature: HOSPINIANUS, *Hist. Sacramentaria* II. Tig. 1598. V. E. LÖSCHER, *Hist. motuum zw. Luther u. Ref.* Frkf. 1723. A. W. DIECKHOFF, *die evgl. Abendmahlslehre im Reformationszeitalter.* I. Gött, 1884. J. KÖSTLIN, *L.s Theologie.*[2] II. Stuttg. 1883. TH. HARNACK, *L.s Theologie,* 2 parts, Erlg. 1862 and 1886. A. BAUR, *Zw.s Theologie.* Vol. II Die DGG by THOMASIUS-SEEBERG Vol. II. and LOOFS,[3] p. 391 ff.

In 1519, Luther had at first taught (EA 27, 38) that the Eucharist was to be regarded as a promise of God offered under visible signs to be adopted in faith: and then, from the sacramental words of Christ, developed the idea of a testament, the purport of which is forgiveness of sins. This promise of Christ is on the one hand sealed for us by his death, on the other hand our weak sensual nature **needs,** in addition to the word of promise, "a powerful, most precious seal and sign," the Sacrament, an external and yet in purport and meaning a spiritual thing, which, however, can effect nothing without belief in the promise (27, 147 f. 151, 164). Further, following Peter d'Ailly, he had criticised (see p. 25) the dogma of transubstantiation as a contradictory attempt of Scholasticism to make the mystery intelligible, and having been attacked by Henry VIII. on the point, had rejected this dogma as *impium et blasphemum* (opp. v. a. VI. 428). The expression "This bread is Christ's body," he wishes to be judged like "This Man Jesus is God," as a judgment formed, not by any philosophy, but by faith (WA VI. 511). The Dutch advocate **Cornelis Henricxs Hoen** of the Hague had directed a letter to Luther, probably in the summer of 1522[1]), in which, referring to several passages of Scripture, he explains the *est* of the sacramental words as equivalent to *significat: hoc quod trado vobis, significat corpus meum, quod do vobis dando istud: diiudicemus ergo inter panem ore susceptum et Christum quem fide accipimus.*[2] (Enders III. 422 ft). Luther sent back the letter, and also combated the interpretation here put forward, in his essay (1523) on the adoration of the Sacrament (EA 28, 393). The bearer of the letter, the principal of the house of brethren at Utrecht, **Hinne Rode,** went on with it to Switzerland. Oecolampadius, upon whom he called in January, 1523,[3] at first reserved his opinion, but the letter made an impression upon Zwingli. This was the impulse that gave his doctrine of the Eucharist its definitive form. He had already selected *John,* VI., as the starting point for this doctrine: from this time forth he regarded the purely symbolic interpretation as the only possible one—the expression "the flesh profiteth nothing" appears to him the clear canon of interpretation for the obscure sacramental words. In the letter to M. Alberus dated November 16th, 1524,[1] and then in the *Commentarius de vera et falsa religione* (III. 589 ff., 239 ff.) he put forward his doctrine: in the Sacrament we think of the death and

---

[1] For the date cp. ENDERS III. 424, LOOFS[3] 387: on the other side L. SCHULZE in RE 18, 235 f.

[2] [This which I hand to you signifies my body, which I give unto you, by giving it (*i.e.* the bread): let us therefore distinguish between the bread taken in the mouth and Christ, whom we receive by faith.]

[3] Cp. PLITT I. 469.

[4] KEIM in JdTh 1854, 556.

shedding of the blood of Christ: by taking part in the Lord's Supper, we prove ourselves members of Christ and bind ourselves to a Christian life: *est = significat:* the cup is a symbol of the Testament of Christ. He rejected Carlstadt's interpretation of the sacramental words that had become known in the meantime as an exegetical perversity. In 1524, Rode also looked up the inhabitants of Strasburg and won Bucer over to the new doctrine of the Eucharist.[1] The **literary struggle** was opened by Urban Rhegius, in the autumn of 1524, with a polemic against Carlstadt:[2] then followed Luther's writings (mentioned above on p. 62) in like manner directed against Carlstadt. Here Luther had already been obliged to defend himself against the argument that Christ could not come down from Heaven into the Sacrament, with the counter-declaration, that he does not ascend and descend in the Sacrament, but is present in all places and fills all (Ephesians, I, 23), and yet we are not bidden to enquire how it happens that the bread becomes the body of Christ (EA 29, 288 ff.). Accordingly, Zwingli[3] also now took up this argument against Luther: that Christ's body sits on the right hand of God, which he will not leave until his coming again. Nevertheless, Luther himself did not yet directly enter the lists against Zwingli: but **Bugenhagen** published a circular letter to John Hess in Breslau *Wider den neuen Irrthum,* in which he somewhat hastily and briefly snubbed Zwingli, who answered (October 23rd, 1525) with a keen and detailed rejoinder (III 604 ff.)[4] Meanwhile, Oecolampadius had taken Zwingli's side in his Essay *de genuina verborum Domini expositione,* and had thereby at the same time transferred the controversy to the examination of the patristic evidence. Oecolampadius explained *corpus* in the sacramental words figuratively as *figura corporis.* He dedicated his learned and acute essay to the preachers of Swabia. Fourteen of these, who agreed with Luther on the question of the Eucharist, met, on October 21st, 1525, at the house of **Brenz** in Hall, and drew up an answer (*Syngramma Suevicum,* translated into German by Agricola, 1526, Walch 20, 667 ff.),[5] in which they insist upon the sacramental words, utilise the three different interpretations of these words by Carlstadt, Zwingli and Oecolampadius as evidence against them, and set against the symbolical interpretation as alone in conformity with the Scriptures the other view,—that Christ's word of promise included the true body and the true blood for the believer. They see, in the mutilation of Christ's words practised by the others, the cunning of the devil, who in appearance undoes God's effective acts,—the symptom of a false principle, which lifts up intelligence against the word of God.[6] A deputation of the inhabitants of Strasburg, sent to Luther (October, 1525), with the object of settling the dispute, failed completely. On the other hand, Pirkheimer attacked Oecolampadius in three polemical Essays, renouncing his old friendship, and, after beginning with a defence of Luther's point of view,

---

[1] BAUM, *Bucer und Capito,* 1860, p. 304.

[2] UHLHORN, *U. Rhegius,* 1861, p. 89. JdTh 1860, 3 ff.

[3] In 1525, he published, in addition to the *Commentarius* and Hone's *Letter to Luther,* his *Subsidium* or *coronis de eucharistia* (III 326 ff.), besides *the Letter to Edlibach,* published by O. FR. FRITSCHE in ZhTh 13, 3, 123 ff.

[4] VOGT, Bugenhagen, p. 77 f.

[5] STROBEL, *Miscellaneen* III 155 ff.

[6] HARTMANN and JÄGER, *Joh. Brenz,* 1840, I 135 ff.

drew still closer to the Catholic doctrine.¹ The learned **John Fisher**, Bishop of Rochester (Roffensis), took part in the controversy and endeavoured to adduce traditional evidence for the *Semper, ubique et ab omnibus* of the Catholic dogma (*De veritate corporis et sanguinis Christi in eucharistia*, Coloniae, 1527). **Bucer** also became involved in the dispute, in consequence of his venturing, in his translation of Luther's homilies and Bugenhagen's Commentary on the Psalms, to traduce Zwingli's Eucharistic doctrine, against which both raised a vigorous protest.² But elsewhere also Luther took a personal part in the struggle, at first in July, 1526,³ in his Preface to the German edition of the *Syngramma Suevicum* (EA 65, 180 ff.); the *Sermon vom Sacrament* (EA 29, 328 ff.) composed of three sermons, that appeared at Michaelmas, had been published without his co-operation: "Christ is also everywhere present by virtue of his humanity . . . . he is about us and in us, in all places . . . . our words cannot draw him hither, but are given us as an assurance that we know how we can certainly find him" (337). Zwingli answered him in the *Amica exegesis* (April 1st, 1527; III 459 ff.). But, in the meantime, Luther's polemical essay *Dass diese Worte, das ist mein Leib, noch feststehen* (EA 30, 19 ff.) was completed (April, 1527). Zwingli replied *Dass diese Worte . . . ewiglich den alten einigen Sinn haben werden* (II, 2, 16 ff.),⁴ and Luther issued a rejoinder (March, 1528) in the (large) *Bekenntniss vom Abendmahl* (EA 30, 151 ff.); Zwingli and Oecolampadius in August (II, 2, 94 ff.). Luther had previously declined to listen to the idea how "Christ was brought into the Sacrament" and had made it a reproach against Scholasticism that, by means of speculations and distinctions, it endeavoured to render comprehensible the judgment of faith, that Christ is here present, and now he himself puts his hand upon the armoury of the "Sophists" (EA 30, 207).⁵ He combats the objection of the *absurditas* of the presence of the body and blood of Christ asserted by him by a doctrine of omnipresence, the Christological distinctions of which subsequently passed over through the Formula of Concord from the *communicatio idiomatum* into the didactic creed of the Lutheran churches. Christ's body has a share in the properties of the Deity. Locally, certainly, he is only in **one** place, but repletively in **all places**, and definitively **where he pleases** (*Multivolipraesentia*). But this omnipresence is only comprehensible for us, in cases in which he desires to be present for us by special promise—on such an occasion, in fact, as the Eucharist. If the presence of the body of Christ is thus founded upon the *communicatio idiomatum* and the special will of Christ, it exists not only for belief, but unconditionally, so that **even the unbelievers** enjoy Christ's body (29, 246. 30, 180. 355 f., 31, 381 f.). He meets the objection that in this case a **superfluous** miracle is maintained (since, even according to Luther, the Sacrament offers nothing which is not existent for the believer even without it) by reference to the **individual appro-**

---

¹ Drews, *Pirkheimer*, p. 89 ff.
² See Luther's letter in de Wette III, 201, September 13th, 1526 (not 1527).
³ Cp. ZKG XI 474.
⁴ Here Zwingli's republican pride shows itself against the Elector of Saxony in the remark that glass windows were "transparent," but not princes (cp. Strobel, *N. Beiträge*, V 386 f.); an expression which Luther could not have forgotten. *Tischreden* (Först.-Binds.) II 416.
⁵ *Revocavit nos Lutherus ad Scotica et Thomistica*, writes Zwingli, August 30th, 1528.

priation of the forgiveness of sins offered generally in the preaching of the Gospel. If he herewith remains essentially in the sphere of ideas, which from the commencement had fixed his Eucharistic doctrine from a religious point of view, yet the spirit of controversy drives him at the same time to take up again the old Catholic view of the Eucharist as φάρμακον ἀθανασίας; he speaks of a life-distributing effect of the same upon the **body** of the Christian, "that he may live for ever and rise again at the day of judgment" (30, 135 and often), without, however, allowing a determining influence to this reflection.[1] Zwingli now again confronts the *communicatio idiomatum* with a doctrine of ἀλλοίωσις, according to which all the passages of Scripture, which Luther brought forward in defence of the former doctrine, are interpreted as figures of speech: the tendency is towards the separation of the two natures in Christ. The different attitude assumed by the two leaders in the controversy in regard to the question whether *John* vi deals with the Eucharist, is characteristic: it is still more significant, that Luther, in spite of the starting point which he adopts in the case of the sacramental words, as a matter of fact abandons this attitude, and refers the body, of which Christ speaks, to the glorified resurrection-body.—The split was complete, the Romanists rejoiced: many communities were excited and divided on the question of the Eucharist.

At the same time, behind the theological discussion, which on the one hand, led back into the abandoned paths of Scholasticism, and, on the other, demonstrated the influence of Erasmian enlightenment,[2] stood more deeply-seated religious differences, for the arrangement of which on matters of principle the Eucharistic question afforded **an opportunity.** Luther's religious need found in the Sacrament **the act of God** in regard to man that sealed the consolation of the forgiveness of sins in divine condescension in a manner that appealed to the senses, the means of grace, which the individual needs to strengthen his belief, so that, according to him, in view of the communion with God the importance of the Sacrament as a communion of the community almost disappeared: Zwingli never felt this religious need of Luther, and hence was able to convert the Sacrament into an act of confession or duty performed by the faithful in the presence of the community. But what inevitably rendered the controversy more acute and made the breach irremediable, was that Zwingli never understood Luther's position **from a religious point of view,** in regard to the Sacrament, but only looked upon it as a folly that was contrary to common

---

[1] We should notice the correction, which Luther himself, in the large Catechism, makes in reference to the assertion of a *medicine for the body*: "When the soul has recovered, the body also is helped" (EA 21, 152).

[2] Cp. on this point PLITT I 468. Melanchthon writes CR IV 970: *Cinglius mihi confessus est, se ex **Erasmi** scriptis primum hausisse opinionem suam de coena Domini.*

sense: further, Zwingli, whom Luther did not know, set his face against the latter, as an ally of Carlstadt, whom he had seen through as a fanatical enthusiast: and lastly, Zwingli's rationalistic cavilling at the Scriptures,[1] in connection with the simultaneous fanatical depreciation of the external word, was regarded by him as a symptom of a serious, far-reaching revolt of the intelligence against the Scriptures. Thus in Luther's eyes, Zwingli was entirely in a line with the "fanatics," while Luther's doctrine of the Eucharist still seemed to Zwingli only a tinge of the Catholic doctrine. Thus, although the Eucharistic controversy divided the evangelical ranks into two camps and thereby weakened their capacity for action, **yet at the same time it saved the Lutherans from giving their adherence to Zwingli's lofty political plans.**

But the most serious result was, that the Eucharistic controversy obscured the evangelical idea of faith. Henceforth, Luther speaks of "points" of Christian belief, and makes the membership of the Christian church dependent upon the acceptance of the same in a definite theological coinage: as the result of this view, he declared all his life long that Zwingli was a non-Christian, whose "errors" were accounted to him as a "sin."[2] The latter in his turn, regards Luther and his followers as hardened heretics: *stultitia Fabrum superat, impuritate Eccium, audacia Cocleum!*[3] [He surpasses Faber in folly, Eck in impurity, and Cochleus in audacity!] A great portion of the Swabian communities (Constance, Lindau, Ulm and others) approved of Zwingli's views, but, in nearly all, a Zwinglian party henceforth arose by the side of the Lutheran: Zwinglianism advanced victoriously from Bâle down the Rhine by way of Strasburg as far as the Netherlands: it even made its way successfully, as early as 1526, into East Friesland, where it was proclaimed by Rode himself. The split in the matter of the Eucharist had thus also become a fact on the soil of Germany.

---

[1] Cp. Melanchthon's complaint CR I 694: *hoc dogma arridet* **sensui communi.**

[2] Cp. EA 32, 399 f. Loofs[2] 365 ff.

[3] R. Stähelin, *Briefe aus der Reformationszeit.* Basel 1887, p. 21; cp. also Zwingli's works. III. 21.

7. The Endangering of the Reformation by Anabaptist Propaganda in Germany.

Sources: Jos. v. BECK, *die Geschichtsbücher der Wiedertaüfer in Oesterr.-Ung.* Wien 1883. (Fontes rer. Austr. II, XLIII).
Literature: ERBKAM, *Gesch. der prot. Sekten im Zeitalter der Reformation.* 1848. CORNELIUS, *Gesch. des Münst. Aufruhrs.* 2 vols., 1855, 1860. L. KELLER, *Gesch. d. Wiedert.* 1880. RITSCHL, *Gesch. des Pietismus.* I. Bonn. 1880. UHLHORN in RE I. 361 ff. For HUBMAIER see UN 1746; SCHELLHORN in *Acta hist. eccl.* Ulm 1738, I 100 ff.; CORNELIUS II., 281 ff.; SCHREIBER in *Tagebuch für Geschichte und Alterthümer in Süddeutschland.* 1839-1840. CUNITZ in RE VI. 344 ff. LOSERTH, B. Hubm. und die Anfänge der Wiedert. in Mähren. Brünn 1893. JOH. DENK: HEBERLE in StKr 1851 and 1855; KELLER, *ein Apostel der Wiedert.* Leipz. 1882. GERBERT, *Gesch. d. Strassb. Sektenbewegung.* Strassb. 1889, p. 25 ff.; L. SCHWABE in ZKG XII. 452 ff. (against the latter KELLER in *Monatsh. d. Comen. Gesellsch.* I. 225); KOLDE in *Kirchengesch. Studien.* Leipz. 1888, p. 228 ff. HETZER (Hätzer): KEIM in JdTh 1856, RE V 527, VII 630. HUTT: ROTH, *Augsb. Ref.-Gesch.* 199 ff. HOFMANN; KROHN, *Gesch. d. Wiedert.* Leipz. 1758. LEENDERTZ and ZUR LINDEN, *M. Hofm.* Haarlem 1883 and 1885. For the whole subject, see also KESSLER, *Sabbata* (page 46), I. 258 ff. II. 120 ff.

After the end of the Peasants' war and the violent suppression of the Baptists in Switzerland the propaganda of Baptism advancing by way of Waldshut and Constance, in an incredibly short time overspread the whole of Germany. Strasburg, **Augsburg**, and Nuremberg became the chief meeting-places. The leaders, partly yielding to persecution, and partly imitating the example of the Apostles, travelled through the countries of Germany, gathering together conventicle-communities of "brethren:" the wandering artisans, from whom their ranks were specially recruited, became in like manner wandering apostles of the doctrines of the Baptists. In a short time the traces of the new, completely unknown formation of communities became perceptible not only in Central Germany (*e.g.* Hesse and Thuringia, where Münzer's adherents were won over to baptism),[1] but also in countries where Slav languages were spoken. In **Nicolsburg** in Moravia, Herr Lienhard von Lichtenstein had, since 1525, afforded the brethren domicile and protection, and also underwent baptism at their hands. In consequence of additions from Austria, South Germany and Switzerland a solid community was formed, which increased in numbers to 15,000 souls. In the Catholic districts the Lutheran propaganda gradually disappeared in the face of the baptist; in

---

[1] *e.g.* Melchior Rink, cp. HOCHHUTH in RE XII. 799 ff.

the evangelical, the Reformation suddenly found itself **seriously threatened** in its occupation, especially amongst the lower classes.

Many things co-operated to promote this rapid spread of Baptist doctrines: the popular style of the apostles of Baptism, the courage that defied death, which they exhibited amidst all persecutions, the biblical radicalism, which, boldly overleaping the historical development of the Church, started directly from the Apostolic period, and seemed to restore the latter to its primitive form; the world-shunning piety of its professors,[1] which held itself aloof externally from the children of "the world" and the Babylon of the church of "the world," austere, but in most cases indisputable, in glaring contradiction with the often undoubtedly worldly behaviour even of the evangelical clergy and their communities: the stress laid upon the imitation of Christ in good works and the self-sacrificing brotherly love in the Baptist communities, in contrast to the reliance upon a belief, which only too frequently was wanting in the fruit of the works; the fanatically apocalyptic, millenarian character, which produced the hope of speedy revelations of God, the gathering together and separation of the Communion of Saints visibly represented,—all these things exercised a wonderful effect upon the people. A number of highly gifted and inspired leaders put themselves at the head of the movement: and, the more the ruling powers endeavoured to crush it by brutal persecution, the more deeply the soul of the people was roused by it. But, under the continuous pressure of persecution, the Baptists did not succeed in attaining a uniform stamp in their views of belief or a uniform organisation. Hence, they were not a spiritual power, everywhere homogeneous, whose ranks presented a firm front. It afforded all possible individual opinions, whether of a mystic or rationalistic kind, the opportunity of germinating, for which the whole body, cannot as yet be held responsible. By the side of peaceful, quiet and harmless conventicle-Christians, dreamers and agitators of a most dangerous kind were concealed in their midst: by the side of biblical Christians, the inspired, who received revelations directly from the Spirit, by the side of strict ascetics, the proclaimers and practisers of an evil libertinism.

Already however, out of the muddy ferment was formed **the solid core of the movement,** which alone was able to weather the times of storm and stress: Swiss and Swabian Baptists, on the 24th of February, 1527, at Schlatten,[2] agreed upon seven articles, the result of which is a clear ideal of a community: 1. Rejection of infant baptism: baptism presupposes penitence, belief, spiritual life and personal desire; 2. Amongst the brethren the ban is enforced in the degrees of admonition prescribed in Matt. xviii; 3. In the breaking of bread in memory of the death of Christ the union of the brethren in the body of Christ, which takes place by baptism, is represented; 4. The brethren sever themselves from all abominations, above all from the worship of the papists as

---

[1] Cp. Capito's testimony in ZhTh 1860, 40.
[2] At the foot of the Randen.

well as from that of the anti-papists (the Reformation churches), both of which are "bondage of the flesh"; 5. The community chooses for itself pastors for purposes of instruction and admonition, for pronouncing the ban and superintending the breaking of bread; 6. The use of the sword is a divine ordinance, which is necessary for the world; but the "perfection of Christ" knows only the ban, not the sword: Christians do not draw the sword, do not sit in judgment, and consequently do not accept any office of authority; 7. Disciples of Christ abstain from the oath in every form.[1] For the rest, the Apostolicum or Apostles' Creed was regarded by these circles as the simple foundation of the confession which connects them with the Church of the Apostles.

What was the origin of this violent movement? It must be observed that these baptist circles themselves[2] sought their home in **Switzerland**, extolled the year 1525, as the time of the rising of the "true morning star," and Grebel, Manz, Blaurock and Hubmaier as the founders of the "separation from the world." Luther and Zwingli certainly possessed the merit in their eyes of having attacked, as it were with thunderbolts, the malice and trickery of the Romish church of the World: but they had substituted nothing better for it, but immediately attached themselves to the secular power and authorities, and hence only brought up a shameless people to the service of sin. They regarded themselves as most nearly related to the Bohemian brethren or Waldensians, who at least have preserved "some small appearance of truth." But, even as compared with these, they are sensible of a new, complete separation.[3] In spite of this independence, which they attributed to themselves, the task is imposed upon the historian, of enquiring for the connecting links in the case of this phenomenon.

The Baptists have often been called the most consistent and the most genuine sons of the Reformation, or it has been thought that they have been excellently characterised by the name of the "Ultras" of the Reformation: but this view is supported only by the very extraneous circumstance, that many of their members had previously been adherents of Zwingli or Luther, and that the Swiss Reformation prepared the way for their doctrine of the Eucharist and their biblical radicalism. Even the attempt of Cornelius to explain their rise as the effect of the Bible in the hand of the ordinary man, is only sufficient to account for certain formalities and singular eccentricities. To judge from their collective view of the world, measured by their motives and aims, they belong, not to the Reformation, but to **medieval** Christianity, a continuation of the opposition (which grew up in the second half of the Middle Ages on Catholic soil) to the secularised church. A. Ritschl deserves the credit of having

---

[1] BECK, p. 41-44.

[2] Such at the present day is the historiography of the Mennonites, cp. A. BRONS, *Ursprung, Entwicklung, und Schicksale der Mennoniten.*[2] Norden 1891, p. 13 ff. CHR. SEPP, *Kerkhist. Studiën* (Leiden 1885, p. 3 ff.) discusses the nature and origin of Anabaptism very cautiously.

[3] BECK p. 11, 13, 15 ff.

paved the way for this opinion of the movement.¹ **Different** currents of the religious and social life of the 18th century here work continuously: Mysticism, Asceticism, and Apocalypticism, and, by the side of these, the Waldensian and Wicliffian ideas which were finally gathered together in Taboritism. They belong to the Catholic stage of Christianity by virtue of their treatment of the Gospel as the new law, which is normatively to settle the ecclesiastical and the civil community; and, in like manner, by virtue of their world-renouncing and world-denying system of Ethics, their leaning to asceticism, their esteem for contemplation and ectasy, their opposition to Luther's doctrine of justification, which they meet with the theory that God's merciful feelings must be won by the individual. In all this, they betray their origin in the ideas of the Middle Ages. On the other hand, the complete banishment of the sacramental and priestly Church from their ideas separates them from ecclesiastical Catholicism. The authority of the Bible, in other words, of the natural law is opposed to the authority of the Church, a new order of prophets to the clergy. Their judgment of civil and state regulations as the consequence of the Fall is a heritage from the Middle Ages, their ideal of perfection by means of the separation of conventicles of the holy is a retroflection of monastic ideals. The Reformation's only part in them is, that the strong religious excitement, which it aroused in the German people, also revivified these religious ideas which had their origin in the 15th century; and the importance attached to the Bible was at least greatly enhanced by the influence of the Reformation. The large number of those who hailed in Luther only the reformer of Christian life and of civil society were soon undeceived, and either returned to Catholicism or sought the realisation of their hopes in baptism. That the latter proceeded **directly** from the circle of the Franciscan *tertiarii* (Ritschl) is an hypothesis,² for which no sufficient proof can be adduced, although, without doubt, these influences may have exercised a subsequent effect, especially amongst the artisan circles: the movement also is thereby too one-sidedly imputed to a single branch of medieval reaction against the church of the world. That Waldensianism, that is to say, Hussitism **also** had a share in it, is not to be doubted: certainly L. Keller has hitherto defended this proposition with great learning, but with such over-hasty combinations, that he has introduced more confusion than certain knowledge.³ Unquestionably, many partly very dissimilar medieval remnants of sects meet together in the Baptist movement, and unite to bring about the by no means uniform mixture of Anabaptism.⁴ Yet, even amongst the educated amongst its adherents, the influence of the writings of Erasmus should be taken into consideration. In regard to this, there is great need of investigation by fresh enquiry into authorities.

Amongst the prominent leaders we may mention: **Balt. Hubmaier,** formerly Eck's pupil and *protégé*, professor at Ingolstadt, minister of the Cathedral of Ratisbon, where he became involved in a violent conflict with the Jewish

---

[1] Luther already calls them *fratres Papistarum. Caudis enim sunt coniunctae istae vulpes, sed capitibus diversae.* EA Comm. in Gal. I. 8.
[2] Against it cp. ThLZ 1883, 369 (KOLDE) and SEPP, as above, p. 9.
[3] Cp. HZ 55, 477 ff. GGA 1886, 353 ff.
[4] *Nulla est veterum haeresium, quae non videatur his auctoribus repullulare* (Melanchthon, CR I 955).

community[1] which trusted in Austrian protection, and subsequently, having been seized by revolutionary ideas, minister at Waldshut in 1522: now influenced for a time by Zwingli and then by Münzer, at Easter 1525, he was re-baptised (see above p. 65), and gave his literary support to Anabaptism against Zwingli. In Zürich, whither he had fled for refuge, a recantation was extorted from him after he had been imprisoned, but this recantation proved so unsatisfactory, that he was sentenced as a punishment to severer imprisonment (the rack was applied!)[2] Having been released at Easter, 1526, he proceeded by way of Augsburg to Nicolsburg, where he carried on an effective propaganda and, in numerous writings, vigorously combated infant baptism, and also described the baptismal and communion service of the brethren. Having been imprisoned by King Ferdinand, he steadfastly suffered death at the stake at Vienna in 1528: in spite of his many changes of mind, a moderate and sincere apostle of Baptism. Of greater intellectual importance was **Joh. Denk,** an able humanist, whom Oecolampadius had recommended, in the autumn of 1523, to Pirkheimer as principal of the school of St. Sebaldus at Nuremberg: it was here that his antagonism to the Reformation doctrine of justification developed in connection with a mystic rationalism: he worked zealously and quietly to spread his doctrines, until Osiander's observation denounced him to the Council and he was banished from the city (January 21st, 1525). He now commenced a wandering life (St. Gall, Augsburg, Strasburg, Bergzabern, Worms—then, again, Switzerland and South Germany), everywhere agitating with great effect, until persecution drove him on. Worn out and finally unable to comprehend the doctrines of the Baptists he succumbed (1527) to the plague at Bâle. His doctrines of the inner light, to which the Scriptures are subordinate ("God works without any means") and of which Christ only enters into consideration as a pattern (Jesus "the man, in whom love was shown in the highest degree"), of the capacity of the enlightened man to fulfil the law without sin, of the conversion of the devil and of the apocatastasis are evidences of his fondness for speculations and give his activity a peculiar significance. Friend and foe saw in him one of the most important leaders of the movement. He co-operated with **L. Hetzer** in a translation of the Prophets into German. The latter, as chaplain at Wädenschwyl, near Zürich, had drifted towards iconoclasm; driven from Zürich in 1525, he removed to Augsburg, where he agitated against infant baptism and in favour of Carlstadt's doctrine of the Eucharist, but was again expelled in the same year as a seditious person. Apparently repentant, he returned to Zwingli, whose confidence he once more regained, but soon lost by his own fault. Having been subsequently banished and giving offence at Bâle by his looseness of morals, he proceeded to Strasburg, where, renouncing his Anabaptism, he was welcomed by Capito. Here he united with Denk, to whose superior intellect he adapted himself, and at the same time, going beyond his ideas, proceeded to contempt of the external word, to rejection of the merit and the godhead of the "brother" Christ. They carried on a combined agitation in the Palatinate, where they gained over the evangelical preacher

---

[1] Cp. V. TRAIN, *Gesch. der Juden in Regensburg.* ZhTh 7, 3, 129 ff.; the same, in ZhTh 14, 2, 81 ff.

[2] Cp. Zwingli's account in R. STÄHELIN, *Briefe aus der Reformationszeit.* Basel 1887, p. 20.

Jakob Kautz, but by their provoking demeanour, not only brought about their own expulsion, but also a Catholic reaction against the evangelical preaching. After much wandering about, Hetzer prepared for himself an inglorious death at Constance, where he was executed (1529) as an adulterer.[1]

The influences of Denk and Münzer cross each other in **Hans Hutt**, a restless book-seller and book-binder of Franconia. He adopted from Münzer the idea that God puts the sword into the hands of His holy ones to execute judgment upon the godless: a victorious campaign of plunder against the Turk will take place, then the believers will gather up the gleaning.[2] With mighty eloquence, in the style of the language of the Old Testament, he fascinates and fanaticises the multitude: he strikes by preference and with most effect the note of apocalypticism. The communistic and apocalyptic propositions of the so-called Nicolsburg articles have their origin in him—if he is not even the author of all of them.[3]

Having been imprisoned at Augsburg in 1527, he endeavoured to secure an opportunity of escape by setting fire to the prison, but was nearly suffocated in the smoke, and died a few days after: the burning of the author of "seditious and heretical articles" was completed in his dead body. Lastly, amongst these characteristic types of Baptism we may mention **Melchior Hofmann**, a furrier from Schwäbisch-Hall. It was not until late that he formally gave his adherence to the Baptists, and then made this community take up a fateful attitude. His principle is the subjectivity of the lay preachership that comes into conflict with every ecclesiastical regulation, in combination with the megalomania of the inspired. He commenced his lay preaching in Livonia in 1523, at first as a tumultuous, unrestrained follower of Luther, who as late as 1525 recognises him as one of his disciples. But his arbitrary subjectivity soon gave such offence amongst the evangelicals, that he left Livonia and proceeded to Sweden as preacher to the German community. Gustavus Vasa expelled him as a visionary. He turned towards Holstein, where King Frederick granted him license to preach throughout the country. As he propagated Luther's Eucharistic doctrine (with special modification) he was in this case also banished, after the religious conference held at Flensburg (under the presidency of Bugenhagen) in 1529.[4] He then proceeded by way of East Friesland and turned up in Strasburg; here he was at first hailed with joy as the champion and martyr of the Swiss Eucharistic doctrine, but here also people were frightened by the visionary prophet, who contrasted his "office of clearness" with the "literal office" of the preachers. Here he soon completed his adherence to the Anabaptist community. He now turned back to East Friesland (1530), where he founded the Emden Baptist community and planted the germs of the subsequent Anabaptist Kingdom of Münster, which pulled down his spiritual ideas into the flesh. For his followers saw in him

---

[1] It is idle for A. BRONS, p. 414, to refer the unfavourable aspect of Hetzer's life entirely to calumny. Cp. on the other side, Th. Blaurer's account in KESSLER, Sabbata II 190 ff.

[2] In **Denk's** *Vom Gesetz Gottes* we read: "He (the believer) may not resist a judge, if he judges rightly. He himself may not judge or promise further than it is of service to the Kingdom of Heaven."

[3] Cp. CORNELIUS II 279 ff.

[4] HOFMANN's *Dialogus* of the Flensburg disputation is reprinted in STROBEL, *Beitr. zu Lit.* II 501 ff.

the prophet, who should arise before the great day of the Lord and establish the Gospel throughout the world. A prophetic voice announces to him that he would first be imprisoned six months in Strasburg, and then be liberated and convert the whole earth. Accordingly, being again driven out, he proceeds by way of the Netherlands to Strasburg, cheerfully allows himself to be imprisoned and waits for the fulfilment of the prophecy. This city is for him the spiritual Jerusalem, from which 144,000 apostolic messengers are to set out with all speed into the world, and offer it alliance and Anabaptism. At the same time the judgment of wrath will visit those who have hitherto persecuted the brethren. But the liberation from prison did not come to pass, none of the dates given by the prophet proved true. Under the influence of Schwenkfeld Hofmann now also developed the principle that harked back to Docetism: that the *Logos* did not assume our nature (the accursed flesh of Adam), did not even derive its human nature from the Virgin Mary, but itself became the bodily Word (flesh). The people of Strasburg spared his life, convinced that "his errors were not due to wilfulness" (Leendertz, p. 362). In 1543, he died in prison at Strasburg: in the meantime his adherents had long since selected another city as Jerusalem and endeavoured to establish the kingdom.

Everywhere throughout the Empire measures were taken against the Baptists.[1] At Zurich, in 1527, Felix Manz was drowned by order of the Council and other Baptists were removed in a similar manner: Strasburg, in 1527, protected itself by expelling them. By the existing law Anabaptism was a capital crime: in accordance with this, an imperial mandate of the 4th of January, 1528, decreed the punishment of death against the Baptists. An edict of the Swabian diet (Feb. 16th, 1528) treated the Baptists (and Zwinglians) as beyond the pale of the law: divisions of cavalry scoured the country and executed judgment on the guilty and suspected, without sentence having been judicially pronounced. The Catholic authorities in Wurtemberg, the Palatinate, Austria, and Bavaria behaved with especial cruelty: "he who recants shall be beheaded, he who does not recant shall be burnt" (Duke William of Bavaria).[2] Thousands were the victims of this Baptist persecution,[3] amongst them also many evangelicals (Leonh. Käser). A fresh imperial mandate (April 23rd, 1529), ordered the pardon of those who repented, but the death-penalty for the teachers and backsliders or the refractory amongst those who were baptised. The evangelical authorities were visibly embarrassed. Should false doctrine be visited with secular punishment? Did this come

---

[1] Cp. KELLER, *die Reformation* p. 443 ff.

[2] JÖRG, *Deutschland in der Revolutionsperiode* p. 715. Cp. also the opinion of the Catholic theologian Dungersheim EA 26², 328.

[3] A list of the brethren of 1531 already reckons more than 400 executions, BECK, p. 310 ff.

within the jurisdiction of the authorities? Must not the erroneous doctrines of the papists also be punished? Luther (and similarly Brenz) advised that punishment should only be inflicted, "in cases where offenders refused to acknowledge and obey the secular authorities" (de Wette II. 622), and, for the rest, demanded "that every man should be allowed to hold what belief he pleased. It is not just and it causes me real sorrow, that such miserable people should be so pitifully murdered, burnt, and cruelly put to death," (EA 26² 283; de Wette III. 347). Melanchthon on the other hand, undertook to demonstrate, from divine and secular law, the duty of the authorities to proceed against the false doctrine of the former as against blasphemy (CR II. 18; III. 197 ff.); he taught, besides, that every man who held Baptist views, even if he were personally most peaceably inclined, should be regarded as a political criminal owing to his theoretical refusal to recognise the State. In principle, Osiander considered it justifiable, at least to put their teachers to death; in practice, however, he dissuaded it. Thus then the behaviour of the evangelical States was very different: in many places, an attempt was made to manage with milder punishments, expulsion, imprisonment, and the like; yet much Baptist blood was shed, *e.g.*, in Augsburg. The Elector of Saxony was in favour of severity, Philip of Hesse for gentler measures.[1] Nuremberg hesitated longer, but finally decided for expulsion. The Catholic practice of suppression of books now also found ready imitators amongst the evangelical party. "The arm of the civil authority was frequently invoked too soon, and still more frequently the assistance only too readily offered by it was gladly accepted, and thus rights, which it did not possess, were conceded to it in a matter that concerned the Church."[2] This worldly cleverness in dealing with the Baptists was subsequently destined to exact a bitter revenge from the evangelical national churches. On the other hand, the manner in which the German Reformation had up to the present developed into an ecclesiastical organisation, under the protection and care of the authorities, which promoted the education of the people, caused its inability to carry out in the abstract the principle of personal freedom of belief; a free church organisation, resting simply upon free, individual

---

[1] Cp. SCHMIDT, *J. Menius*, I 176 ff. ARNOLD, *Kirchen- u. Ketzer-Hist.* Frankf. 1700, II. 274 f. HOCHHUTH in ZhTh 28, 538 ff.

[2] PLITT, I 416.

association could not come into being.[1] These violent measures proved successful in stemming the Baptist movement and driving it into concealment; but, in spite of all the blood that was shed, it was not really destroyed.

8. The Protestation of Spires and the Marburg Colloquy.

Sources and Literature: WALCH XVI. 315 ff. *Politische Correspondenz der Stadt Strassburg.* I. Strassb. 1882. J. J. MÜLLER, *Hist. v. d. evg. Stände Protestation.* Jena 1705. JUNG, *Gesch. des Reichstags zu Speier.* Strassb. 1830. NEY, *Gesch. des R. zu Sp.* Hamb. 1880. For the extensive literature of the Marburg Conference, see KÖSTLIN II² 645, KOLDE II 589: add EA 36, 320 ff.; REDLICH in Chr. W. 1891, No. 6 ff., BAUMGARTEN, *Karl V.* III. 11 ff. For the Schwabach Articles, see ENGELHARDT in ZhTh 1865, 532 ff. PLITT I 513 f. KÖSTLIN II² 651. For the Pack affair, see SCHOMBURGK in HTb 1882, 175 ff. EHSES, Freib. 1881; the same, *Landgraf Philipp und O. v. Pack.* Freib. 1886; H. SCHWARZ, Leipz. 1884; M. LENZ in ThLZ 1883, 345; NIEMÖLLER in HpBl 104, 1 ff. LENZ in ZKG III.

While the Emperor still held aloof from German affairs, and the combination of the States in offensive and defensive leagues called forth suspicion and anxiety,[2] a downright forgery was able to take in Germany, in the year 1528, immediately before the outbreak of the religious war. OTTO VON PACK, one of Duke George's prominent officials, who had frequently been engaged in political missions, a man whose affairs were in disorder and who possessed the natural talents that go to make a fashionable swindler, had informed Landgrave Philip, at the end of 1527, of the existence of a Catholic offensive league against the Protestants secretly concluded at Breslau in May. Philip demanded the production of the original document: in February, 1528, Pack handed him a pretended copy, which spoke of a great Catholic coalition, which had for its object an attack upon Electoral Saxony, Hesse, and Madgeburg, for the purpose of deposing the evangelical Princes and carrying out sentence upon Luther. Philip hastened to anticipate the attack of his opponents by a counter-federation on the evangelical side and rapid preparations, at the same time threatening the frontiers of the bishops on the Main. Like the Elector, Luther, and Melanchthon, he was convinced of the genuineness of the "Breslau league": only Luther successfully warned his Elector against an **offensive** war, but approved of preparations, in case self-defence should become necessary. When Philip made the document public in order to justify his warlike attitude, the forgery was discovered. Yet Pack for some time lied so cleverly on both sides in order to get out of it, that at any rate the suspicion that the league might have a real existence continued to be

---

[1] The struggles of the 17th century in England, the result of which was the free churches of the Dissenters, show what had to be carried out before a free course could be cleared for such formations.

[2] It was probably at this time that Luther's *Ein feste Burg ist unser Gott* was written. It is certain that it was printed in 1529, probably in the spring of 1528. Cp. KNAAKE in ZkW 1881, p. 39 ff.

entertained for some time by Philip (and on the other hand by Luther). The danger of war that threatened rapidly passed over, but the evangelical cause was appreciably damaged, not only by the uncritical credulity which had made people allow themselves to be deceived by Pack, but from the fact that the Catholic States had now been threatened by the evangelical with armed force. This again led Luther personally into a stubborn and unrestrained paper-war with Duke George, occasioned by one of Luther's private letters having fallen into his hands.[1] For the first time the Landgrave had shown himself a politician, who had no scruple, in the interests of his religious position, about entering into relations with France and making use of Ferdinand's adversary, the Hungarian John Zapólya. He had also entertained the banished Duke Ulrich of Wurtemberg and secured his return to his Duchy.

The political situation now assumed a more peaceful appearance in the summer and autumn of 1528: the conclusion of peace between the Emperor and Pope was discussed, and this was bound to make its influence felt at once in dealing with the religious split. Accordingly, the Emperor ordered Ferdinand to convoke another diet at Spires for 1529, with the object of first rendering imperial aid against the Turkish danger, and then of again taking up the ecclesiastical question.

The Pack affair had roused the Catholic States from their indolence and Ferdinand, by his zeal, succeeded in gathering round him a compact Catholic party at the diet. Since the termination of the Peasants' War, they no longer feared popular opinion, and the most zealous anti-Lutheran theologians were on the spot and added fuel to the flame. But the imperial proposition so far took the state of affairs into consideration, that it no longer, as hitherto, directly demanded the **complete** execution of the Edict of Worms, but was willing, until the Council met, for which the Pope was now prepared, to be content with punishing severely the **further spread** of the Reformation. It declared the Spires Recess[2] of 1526—which had been hitherto egregiously misunderstood—to be annulled. The majority essentially agreed, at first limited the execution of the Edict of Worms to Catholic districts and, in regard to evangelical territories, desired that no further innovation should be taken in hand, but that the Romish form of worship should here also remain unmolested: further, that all the sects hostile to the Sacrament of the Eucharist (the Zwinglians) should be rooted out, and that no clerical order should be deprived of its authorities, property, and profits. The jurisdiction of the bishops was thereby again

---

[1] De Wette, III 340, 397; EA 31, 1 ff.
[2] [Decree of an Imperial Diet].

secretly set up, and a one-sided legality claimed for the Catholic form of worship, without any equivalent being allowed for the Evangelicals on the part of the Catholic States. The evangelical States in vain laid stress upon this inequality: but as they were powerless against the majority and yet could not bring themselves to submit, they raised **a protest** on the 19th of April, appealing to the Spires "recess" of 1526, which would render the new resolutions "of no effect and not binding." Amongst the princes only John, Philip, George of Brandenburg, Ernest of Lüneburg and Wolfgang of Anhalt gave support to it: but the fourteen Upper German cities,—Strasburg, Nuremberg, Ulm, Constance, Lindau, Memmingen, Kempten, Nördlingen, Heilbronn, Reutlingen, Isny, St. Gall, Weissenburg and Windsheim gave in their adherence. Next day the Princes handed over their protest further elaborated.[1] The immediate result was a secret defensive league, which was concluded on the 22nd of April between Electoral Saxony, Hesse, and the cities of Strasburg, Nuremberg, and Ulm.

On the same day, Philip wrote to Zwingli, asking him to assist in the promotion of a religious discussion between the representatives of the two evangelical parties who were divided upon the question of the Eucharist. The more sharply the Catholic policy now accentuated this internal evangelical dissension, and endeavoured to separate the Zwinglians also politically from the Lutheran States, the more urgently did it appear to the far-seeing politician to be required by duty, that this division should be healed, and Duke Ulrich of Wurtemberg, who had been gained over by Oecolampadius had not in vain inspired Philip with enthusiasm for the idea of an agreement between the disputants.

Melanchthon, who was present at Spires, showed himself ready to accede to the plans of the Landgrave: as early as the 8th of April, he wrote to Oecolampadius (CR I 1050), *satius esset, hac de re aliquot bonos viros in colloquium una venire* [it would be better that several good men should enter into a conference concerning this matter], while at the same time he placed himself on Luther's side in the struggle. On the other hand, the plan met with difficulties

---

[1] They laid their protest in a special deputation before the Emperor, who at first kept them waiting a long time for an answer, and then, when the Turkish danger was averted, decisively rejected it, and when the deputies on the other hand appealed to a free Christian Council, even threatened them with imprisonment.

at Wittenberg from Luther and the Elector who was advised by him, and even Melanchthon's assent yielded to anxious reserve. At the diet held at Rotach (June) the dislike of the Elector to enter into any connection with the "Sacramentarians" made itself manifest: it thus appeared as if the result would be separate combinations of the States which favoured Luther and Zwingli respectively. If, in the case of Luther, it was simply his strong courage of belief, which caused political leagues and human aid to appear to him unnecessary, and he was able to imagine a union always only on the basis of complete agreement, Melanchthon felt with ever-increasing clearness that fraternisation with Zwingli meant renunciation of the Catholic Church, to which it was still intended to adhere on the Lutheran side as the authorised party, and of the holy Roman Empire.[1] But Electoral Saxony was far more inclined to come to an understanding with Ferdinand than with the Swiss. At last (June 22nd) the importunity of the Landgrave gained the day, but all felt certain that they were going to engage in a work which would be without result. The Landgrave, who had hitherto carefully concealed from the Lutherans his plan of inviting not only Oecolampadius, but Zwingli as well, fixed the discussion for Michaelmas Day at Marburg. Melanchthon armed himself for the struggle by a collection of *Sententiae veterum aliquot scriptorum de coena domini* (CR XXIII, 727 ff.).[2] Besides Luther and Melanchthon, there appeared on the Lutheran side Jonas, Cruciger, Myconius, Menius, and (later) Osiander, Brenz, Steph. Agricola (Augsburg); on the other side, Zwingli and Oecolampadius, Bucer, Hedio, Jak. Sturm, head of the civil corporation of Strasburg, and others.

In order to avoid more violent conflicts, Luther and Oecolampadius, Melanchthon and Zwingli were at first confronted by the Landgrave at a private discussion on the 1st of October; this first meeting on the Eucharistic question led to no result, but at least prejudices and misunderstandings on the part of the Wittenbergers in regard to other points disappeared. The Strasburg jurist Nic. Gerbel had already, in 1527, denounced the Zwinglians to Luther as persons who boldly penetrated the *secretissima Trinitatis arcana, nescio quid de*

---

[1] *Universae ecclesiae ac toti imperio minatur horribilem mutationem (ista controversia).* CR XXIII. 749. *Cingliani . . . . seditiosissima consilia ineunt opprimendi Imperatoris.* II 104. An obvious invention of a later period is Melanchthon's pretended letter from Marburg to his brother, in HARTFELDER, *Melanchthoniana Paedagogica.* Leipz., 1892, p. 37.

[2] Perhaps printed in July, 1529, as Chr. W. 1891, 126 affirms. In any case it was already written at that time. BINDSEIL, *Mel. Epp.* 39 ff.

personis excogitaturi.[1] This insinuation had made an impression: Luther had accordingly solemnly protected his Essay against Zwingli in 1528 with a confession of the trinitarian creed (EA 30, 363, cp. 30, 19). Suspicion had continued to rest specially upon the Strasburg theologians (CR I 1099, certainly on account of their relations to Hetzer, see page 92). Further, amongst other things, Zwingli's doctrine of original sin (*morbus non peccatum*, Opp. III. 629) had given well-grounded offence and caused Luther to characterise him as a "new Pelagian" (EA 30, 365). Melanchthon was now able to announce success with satisfaction: "they have received instruction from us, and have given way in all these points" (CR I 1099), *i.e.*, misunderstandings were removed, and partly Zwingli adapted himself as far as possible to their form of language. The public discussion on the following day, at which Luther disputed alone against the two Swiss, was devoted essentially to the Eucharistic dissension: Luther again laid stress upon the cogent force of the sacramental words, meeting with God's omnipotence, all objections to the possibility of their literal interpretation as they upon did *John* vi. and the mathematical impossibility that a body can be in more than one place.[2] Zwingli offered brotherly union in loving words: but as no one gave way from his position, Luther lacked the indispensable foundation for such mutual understanding. The debate was continued without result on the 3rd of October, and finally broken off, both sides begging that the bitter speeches which had been uttered might be forgiven. The theologians of Strasburg still endeavoured to obtain Luther's assent to their method of teaching on the most diverse points: but Luther cautiously and mistrustfully refused it: he declared that his mind and theirs were not in harmony: did they teach in their native place in the same manner as Bucer now discoursed?[3] The next day passed in individual interviews, from which the Strasburgers took away the impression, that their really irreconcilable opponent was Melanchthon, and were imbued with the apprehension that any connection with the Swiss would completely destroy any chance of coming to an understanding with the Emperor and Ferdinand. But, in spite of Zwingli's acknowledgment that there were no people on earth with whom he would rather be in harmony than the Wittenbergers, Luther stuck to his opinion: "You have a different spirit from ours."

However, the Landgrave and the Swiss, with a view of establishing the important consensus between them, succeeded in inducing Luther to draw up a confession in 15 articles (**The Marburg Articles**). In 14 articles complete agreement was declared—the Swiss conformed to Luther's terminology, although certainly, if left to themselves, they would have adopted a different wording in several matters (original sin, baptism, private confession); in the 15th, they declared their agreement in reference to the communion in both kinds and the rejection of the mass as a

---

[1] KOLDE, Anal. 87.
[2] It is this that Melanchthon calls the *geometria*, the *geometricae speculationes* of the Zwinglians. CR I 1049, XXIII. 752.
[3] Jonas found in Bucer a *calliditas vulpina, perverse imitata prudentiam et acumen*, CR I 1097.

sacrifice, and agreed in the formula that the Eucharist was "a sacrament of the true body and blood of Christ," that "the **spiritual** manducation is especially necessary to every Christian," also that "the use of the Sacrament, like the Word, was ordered by God, in order to move weak consciences to belief by the Holy Spirit." But there remained a disagreement in regard to the question, "whether the true body and blood of Christ was **bodily** in the bread and wine:" "however, one party should exhibit Christian love towards the other, so far as each man's conscience would allow it." Both parties signed their names to two copies.[1] In addition, they promised to give up violently attacking each other in writing. An outbreak of "English sweat" in the city rendered an adjournment necessary.

Luther, however, had acquired the belief in a reconciliation as a result of the personal meeting. His opinion was on the whole friendly, he only saw a *dissensus* still existing *de peccato originis* and in regard to the bodily presence of Christ. Nevertheless, "the position of the matter is a hopeful one. I do not say that there exists a **brotherly** unity, but a kindly, friendly agreement,"[2] yet he hoped that the prayer of Christians would also render it "brotherly." (EA 36, 321 f.). In Zwingli's repeated entreaties for recognition as a brother he saw the admission that he really felt himself overcome and only declined to submit completely out of regard for his party: this was a grievous error, for Zwingli had rather left Marburg in the proud consciousness of having gained a manifest victory over Luther's "shamelessness and conceit." In fact, he had completely gained over the Landgrave there, although the latter did not yet publish the fact abroad. And he had gained him over to admission into his "burgher rights" (page 82). But Philip's plan of a strong, politico-religious league of all the Evangelicals was frustrated: its realisation would have made the Landgrave and Zwingli the leaders of a Protestantism that would have been henceforth political, and would have involved results that would have been incalculable, but momentous for the Empire as well as for the Reformation.[3]

On return from Marburg, the Wittenbergers were summoned by the Elector to Schleiz,[4] where he intended to meet the Landgrave George of Anspach. For them, Luther drew up a confession of faith, which the Elector desired to make the foundation of the political combination of the evangelically-minded

---

[1] Cp. KÖSTLIN II.² 646, CR 26, 113 ff. ["According to Osiander, three copies were signed at Marburg: two have been recovered and published by HEPPE and USTERI from the archives at Cassel and Zürich." SCHAFF, *Chr. Ch.* x. 647].

[2] In 1533, Luther defines the love which they here promised each other as the love, "which keeps peace even with enemies and prays for them." EA 31, 267.

[3] Cp. M. LENZ, *Zw. und Landgr. Philipp* in ZKG III.

[4] According to KOLDE II 590, however, neither the Elector nor Luther actually entered Schleiz.

States. This was the origin of the so-called **Schwabach Articles** (CR XXVI, 138 ff., EA 24^2 334 ff.).

Thrown off in haste, they are a revision of the Marburg articles, but consciously couched in severer terms, especially against Zwinglianism. For the Elector was determined only to enter politically into connection with the Upper German States, "if they were of a proper Christian belief" with the rest, "and also, now and henceforth, held the same Baptism and Sacrament." Consequently, the Articles, as Luther subsequently rightly insisted, were not drawn up "for the sake of the Papists" (EA 24^2 337), but as a line of demarcation against Zwinglianism. Hence they sharply accentuate the christological assertions (Art. 2 and 3), the doctrine of original sin (Art. 4, "not only a simple weakness or infirmity"), of baptism (Art. 9) and especially of the Eucharist (Art. 10), while the presence of the body and blood of Christ is brought prominently forward, as against "the opposite party," and in Art. 8 stress is laid upon the fact that God "offers and gives faith and his spirit by the Sacraments." At the same time, also, the antithesis of the Papacy is further worked out. The Church (so Luther here declares in Art. 12) "is nothing else but the believers in Christ, who keep, believe and teach the above-mentioned articles and doctrines." (EA 24^2 343).[1] At this point, consequently, "the community of Saints" begins to change into the Lutheran denominational Church, which is rejected by Zwingli and his followers as non-Christian.

The practical result of these articles was, that Strasburg and Ulm refused to accept them at the **Schwabach** convention (October 16th). The same thing took place on the 29th of November at the **Schmalkald** convention. **The league with the Upper Germans had become impossible.** The Lutheran alliance in South Germany remained limited to **Nuremberg**, Ulm entered the burgher rights of Zürich. The single connecting link was formed by the person of the Landgrave, who kept up his intercourse with Zwingli. But the latter hoped, by gaining over Hesse, finally to isolate Wittenberg politically, and in this manner to be able to render it obedient to his plans. Such were the antecedents of the day of Augsburg.

9. The Diet of Augsburg, 1530.

Older collections of *Authorities* by CHYTRAEUS. Rostock, 1576; COELESTINUS. Frankf. a. d. Oder, 1597; WALCH XVI 542 ff.; J. J. MÜLLER (see above p. 96); E. S. CYPRIAN. Gotha, 1730; G. G. WEBER. Frankf., 1783; FÖRSTEMANN, *Archiv. f. d. Gesch. d. kirchl. Ref.* Halle 1831; the same, *Urkundenbuch zur Gesch. des Reichst. zu Augsburg.* 2 vols., 1833-1835;

---

[1] Cp. on this, EA 31, 250 (1533). where Luther assigns a central position to "the word of grace and forgiveness of sins as the **chief article**, which has been the source of **all** our doctrine."

CR II and XXVI; de Wette IV; Kilian Leib, *Annales* in Döllinger, *Beiträge* II 538 ff. Lämmer, in ZhTh 28, 142 ff. J. Ficker, *Die Confutation.* Gotha, Leipz., 1891; Strobel, *Beitr. z. Lit.* I 413 ff.; Rotermund, *Geschichte des Glaubensbekenntnisses.* Hann., 1829; Plitt (see above p. 6); Zöckler, *Die CA.* Frankf., 1870. Schaff, *Bibl. symb.* I 225 ff. Schirrmacher, *Briefe und Acten.* Gotha, 1876. Pastor, *Die kirchlichen Reunionsbestrebungen.* Freib., 1879, pp. 17-70. For Melanchthon at Augsburg, see Spieker in ZhTh 15, 1, 98. Virck in ZKG IX. Brieger, *Beiträge zur Gesch. d. A.R.* in ZKG XII 123 ff.

On the 29th of June, 1529, peace had been happily concluded between the Emperor and the Pope at Barcelona,—"indissoluble peace, friendship, and alliance"; the Emperor was to proceed immediately to Italy, render obedience to the Pope, and receive the crown from his hands; he and his brother bound themselves to check, by every means, the pestilential malady of the new opinions, and eventually to punish, to the utmost of their power, the insult offered to Christ. On the other hand, not a word was said about the Council.[1] The treaty of Cambray (August 5th) also brought about a reconciliation between the Emperor and France. Charles now appeared able to devote himself unreservedly to German affairs and to carry out his plans against the heretics. On the 12th of August he landed at Genoa, acceded to the wishes of the Pope, and on the 22nd and 24th of December, 1529, for the last time in German history, the double coronation-ceremony, which represented Pope and Emperor in peaceful union as the two lights of the world, took place at Bologna. Not one of the German electors had been invited to the Emperor's coronation. Subsequently, on the 21st of January, 1530, the summons[2] to the diet of Augsburg was issued from Bologna.

Its peaceful tone was surprising: the diet was to discuss the settlement of the differences that had arisen in the holy faith, and in such a manner that "every man's judgment, view, and opinion, should be listened to in love and kindness, in order to compare and bring them to a united Christian truth, and to dispose of everything that had not been rightly explained on both sides." Consequently, the Emperor was desirous of **negotiating** with the Protestants and of listening to them, and did not desire to subject them dictatorially to the Edict of Worms. Nevertheless, Charles had not such strong confidence in his own power, the peace with France and the friendly feelings of the Pope, that he would not have preferred the method of negotiations, to which his appearance in person lent due weight, to the way of reckless violence. He was confident of reaching his aim in this manner more surely and

---

[1] *Conc.-Gesch.* IX 561 f. Baumgarten, *Karl V.* II 692 ff.
[2] Förstemann, *Urkundenb.* I 2 ff.

rapidly. Even the Pope agreed that an attempt should **first** be made by the "*via dulcis*":[1] other counsellors who pressed for bloodshed and violence (EA 25², 16 f.) were not listened to at the time.

On the 15th of June, the Emperor rode into Augsburg surrounded by imperial pomp, after he had already sent on a prohibition against evangelical preaching during the diet. The Corpus Christi procession of the following day gave the evangelical princes the opportunity of at once definitely disclosing their position in the matter of conscience: in the matter of preaching they yielded to the imperial desire, in accordance with which from that time only preachers appointed by himself might preach. The diet was opened on the 20th of June. It was proposed that the Turkish question should be first discussed and then the question of belief, the States giving him their written opinion in both Latin and German; but the evangelicals succeeded in securing precedence for the question of belief. On the 24th of June they had their "complaints and opinion in regard to belief" ready, and asked for permission to read them aloud. The Emperor decided to yield to their importunity and to fix the following day for the reading, which accordingly took place on the 25th of June, in the chapel of the bishop's palace: Beier, Chancellor of Saxony, read loudly and distinctly the German copy of the Confession, in accordance with the desire of the Elector, that the German, not the Latin, copy must be read on German soil. Both copies were afterwards handed to the Emperor.

This document had been drawn up before the departure for the diet. As early as the 14th of March, the Elector had summoned Luther, Jonas, Bugenhagen and Melanchthon to Torgau; he declared that it would be necessary, before the diet commenced, to come to a decision upon all points, in regard to which there existed disagreement in matters of belief and ecclesiastical usages, as to whether and how far they might form the subject of compromise and negotiation between the contending parties. Chancellor Brück had made the practical proposal, that the opinion of the evangelicals "should be regularly collected together in writing, together with well-grounded justification of the same from Holy Scripture, since it was hardly likely that the preachers, but only the princes and councillors would be allowed to speak" (CR II 25 ff.). The common efforts of the theologians in that direction may be seen in CR 26, 171-182,[2] a collective opinion, drawn up as an apologia against the reproach, that it was unfairly said of the Elector that "he did away with

---

[1] BAUMGARTEN III 24
[2] Cp. especially ENGELHARDT in ZhTh 1865, 550 ff. and BRIEGER in *Kirchengesch. Studien.* Leipz., 1888.

all service of God and set up a godless, dissolute life and disobedience." Against this it is set forth in ten articles, that he rather established, in all seriousness, a right and true service of God, and also what induced him to drop certain abuses. The second part of the CA is modelled upon these **Torgau Articles** (CR II 47). The theologians, who had been summoned by a second note from the Elector (March 21st, CR II 33), repaired with these to Torgau. In addition to the order of visitation (see above p. 78), they took with them the Marburg and Schwabach Articles. Luther, Melanchthon and Jonas accompanied the Elector on his journey, being joined on the way by Spalatin, Joh. Agricola, and Casp. Aquila. At Coburg, it was decided that Luther could not be taken further, since not only was Augsburg closed to the outlaw, but Nuremberg also, out of respect for the Emperor, refused him safe-conduct.[1] During a stay of several days at Coburg, Melanchthon had already commenced the composition of the "Saxon counsel," which he himself designated as an *Apologia*, for it was at first intended as a justification of the deviations, which the ecclesiastical system of the evangelicals exhibited in contrast to Catholic tradition and practice. But, in the further course of the work, Melanchthon was obliged to recast it in two directions: he was obliged to abbreviate, *neque enim vacat Caesari audire prolixas disputationes* (CR II 45), and he was obliged to change the *Apologia* into the *Confessio*, in order to parry an attack made by Eck upon the Evangelicals, which he had put into the Emperor's hands on the 14th of March. In 404 propositions, in which Luther, Zwingli, and the Anabaptists were wilfully confused, he had denounced Luther to the Emperor as the man to whom the Church owed the "Iconoclasts, Sacramentarians," yea, even "*Anabaptistas, novos Epicureos, qui animam mortalem assererent . . . . novos item Cerinthianos, qui Christum deum negarent.*"[2] Now, the Emperor's standpoint was, that, amidst the manifold reports as to what was really the doctrine of the Evangelicals, he wanted above all to assure himself whether the doctrine of these people was in harmony with the "Twelve Articles of the Christian Faith" or not. Only in the first case did he consider an attempt at agreement or reunion possible.[3] Thus it was clearly necessary to touch upon *omnes fere articulos fidei* in the *Apologia*, as a *remedium* against Eck's insinuations (CR II 45). The Marburg and Schwabach Articles served as models in this case. On the 11th of May the draft of the CA was presented to Luther: he gave his assent with the characteristic remark: "for I cannot tread so softly and gently" (de Wette IV 17). But, from this time forth, Melanchthon altered and revised his work unceasingly (the German text more than the Latin), and, the longer he worked, the more anxiously he strove to soften all acerbities against Rome (CR II 57, 60, 140)—and, the more he softened, the more he found that he had still written far too severely: "*satis est meo iudicio vehemens* (CR II 142); he would gladly have toned it down still more, but the evangelical theologians who were gathered together with him at Augsburg put their veto upon it (CR II 140). Chancellor Brück, who was familiar with the curialistic style, wrote the introduction and conclusion: Jonas prepared the Latin translation from these materials. It was not until shortly before its presentation, that the other Evangelical States, which had in part

---

[1] BURCKHARDT in ZkW X 97 f. KOLDE in *Kirchengesch. Studien.*, p. 251 ff.
[2] WIEDEMANN, *Eck*, p. 580 ff. PLITT I 526 ff. CR II 45. DE WETTE IV, 27.
[3] G. KAWERAU, *Agricola*, p. 100. MAURENBRECHER, *Kath. Reformation* I 209.

already prepared confessions of their own, made the "Saxon counsel" their collective confession. But it was of special importance that the Landgrave Philip, although undoubtedly under the influence of the Zwinglian doctrine of the Eucharist, and in spite of his earnest efforts to restore the "brotherhood" between the contending evangelical camps, was sufficiently politic not to isolate himself from Saxony.[1] Thus, in addition to the Elector John, the Confession was also signed by the Margrave **George** of Anspach, Duke **Ernest** of Brunswick-Lüneburg, the Landgrave **Philip**, Prince **Wolfgang** of Anhalt [the Latin copy also by the Electoral Prince **John Frederick** and Duke **Francis** of Brunswick-Lüneberg][2] and the cities of Nuremberg and Reutlingen. During the session of the Diet, Weissenburg (in Franconia), Heilbronn, Kempten and Windsheim followed their example. The Latin original (Melanchthon's rough copy) made its way into the imperial archives at Brussels: King Philip II. demanded (in 1569) that it should be sent thence to Spain, that "so damnable a work might be for ever destroyed."[3] The German version was sent to the archives of Mainz, whence (in 1546) it was taken to the Council of Trent. Since then it has disappeared, although Mainz for a long time duped the Protestants by the pretence of possessing it, and thereby sadly confused the textual history of the CA.

Melanchthon himself had almost frustrated the presentation of the CA: for, since the arrival of the Emperor, he had, with incredibly blind confidence, sought to come to an agreement with the imperial party. He had declared to Alf. Valdés, the imperial secretary, that reunion was possible, provided only the cup, the marriage of priests and the abolition of the *missa privata* were agreed to, and the settlement of other disputed points was left to the Council (CR II 122 f. Lämmer, *Monum. Vatic.* 43 f.). The Emperor and the legate Compeggi were ready to agree, only the abolition of the private mass was rejected by the latter. Melanchthon received a commission, and was ready to formulate these conditions of arrangement in writing: but Nuremberg and the Princes insisted upon the presentation of their Confession.[4]

The CA claims to be estimated historically as a proof that the protesting States, in spite of their innovations, belonged to the

---

[1] His opinion must not be judged according to KOLDE, *Anal.*, p. 125 (*non sentit cum Zwinglio*): LAMBERT's testimony in FUESLIN, *Epist. Ref. Cent.* I 71 and his own statements (CR II 97, 100), are much more important. He relies upon the agreement laid down in the 15th Marburg article on the doctrine of the Eucharist (see above p. 101): this agreement is so close that it renders brotherhood and mutual tolerance possible. But, in the controversial question, Zwingli teaches him "in accordance with faith and the Scriptures," while Luther's doctrine "cannot be made certain from the plain text, without a gloss." He signed the CA, but at the same time declared *sibi de sacramento a nostris non satisfieri* (CR II 155).

[2] Cp. KÖLLNER, *Symbolik* I 201 ff.—EA 48, 128. ZKG XI 216.

[3] DÖLLINGER, *Beiträge zur polit., kirchl. u. Culturgesch.* I 648. KÖLLNER, I 312.

[4] VIRCK in ZKG IX 92 f.

Catholic Church.[1] They meet their opponents as a party struggling for its right of existence on the territory of this Church, anxious to show their agreement with the recognised articles of faith of the Church (*nos nihil docere contra ullum fidei articulum*, de Wette II 190), to defend their special form of doctrine not only by the Scripture but also by the testimony of recognised Catholic authorities, and to prove that all their innovations were the abolition of abuses that had crept in, and, consequently, that there is nothing in their doctrine *quod discrepet a Scripturis* **vel ab ecclesia catholica vel ab ecclesia romana**, *quatenus ex scriptoribus nota est* . . . **Tota** *dissensio est de* **paucis** *quibusdam abusibus* (CR XXVI, 290).[2] They distinguish as sharply as possible their position from that of the Zwinglians and Anabaptists: they accommodate their doctrine of the Eucharist as closely as possible to that of the Catholics, without expressing dissent in the matter of transubstantiation. The papacy is not even mentioned, "for certain reasons." Conformably to this, their articles of doctrine are set forth in accordance with the scheme of Catholic dogmatics; important elements of the Lutheran gospel (*e.g.*, the priesthood of the faithful) are not mentioned. Nevertheless, Melanchthon succeeded in giving classical expression to the reformation doctrine of salvation and in bringing out its importance with telling effect in crucial points (especially in Article 20), and, in fact, in spite of his harking back to ecclesiastical authorities, the normative authority of the Scriptures turns the scale. **Formally**, the preface of these articles as a whole offers material for negotiations for an **arrangement** together with the offer of sacrificing *quae* **utrinque** *in scripturis secus tractata aut intellecta sunt*, but, of course, **materially**, from the certainty that, if it came to such negotiations, the rights of their position would be clearly revealed. Luther on the one hand always joyfully recognised the CA (de Wette IV 71, 82 and often); on the other hand, he blamed Melanchthon's optimistic judgment of their

---

[1] The Evangelicals, in 1546, still advocated this view: *nostri* . . . *affirmant* . . . . *confessionis Augustanae doctrinam* . . . . *esse consensum catholicae Ecclesiae Dei*: hence they protest against the reproach *quod ab Ecclesia defecerint.* CR VI 35. At Wittenberg also ordination testimonials were drawn up, in which the *doctrina catholicae ecclesiae Christi* was acknowledged: *e.g.*, de Wette, V 78.

[2] Such was the wording of the document as handed to the Emperor, which was subsequently toned down by Melanchthon in the 2nd edition of the *editio princeps*.

opponents (de Wette IV 68) and his intentional silence (*dissimulatio*) upon important points in the contrary propositions (*de purgatorio, de sanctorum cultu* [he also considers Article 21 too feeble] and *maxime de Antichristo Papa*, de Wette IV 110).[1] But the attempt to discover in the CA a specifically Melanchthonian method of teaching, deviating from Luther's, was distinctly perverse: Melanchthon himself subsequently made the striking remark that "he had been drawn to the Confession as a poor pupil" (of Luther) (CR XXII 46).[2]

[The CA became henceforth at first the **federal charter** of the Schmalkaldic League; but very soon found employment as the **rule of instruction** for the Lutheran national churches, for instance, in 1530, in the Duchy of Prussia (Tschackert I 172); the Saxon Articles of Visitation of 1533 ordered that the CA and Apologia must be provided in all parishes (Richter, KOO I. 228): a vow of adherence to the CA was introduced at Wittenberg in the same year as necessary for theological degrees (CR XII. 6 ff): the same obligation for pastors in the matter of teaching was insisted upon in the Pomeranian liturgy (Richter I. 248)—since that time the treatment of the CA as a symbol become more and more general. The diet of Schmalkalden in 1534 required of all members of the league who were to be newly admitted, "that they would cause instruction to be given and sermons to be preached in conformity with the word of God and the pure doctrine of our confession, and should and would firmly abide by this (Strassb. *Pol. Corresp*. II. 322).[3]]

As the efforts of the Landgrave to obtain for the Upper German cities a union with the Lutherans failed, and the request of the Strasburgers to be allowed to sign the CA without Article 10, was refused by the Princes (CR II 155), the Strasburg deputies caused

---

[1] Cp. also de Wette, IV 52: **Plus satis** *cessum est in ista Apologia*." Luther's own "Augsburg Confession" is before us in his severely worded pamphlet "Vermahnung an die Geistlichen, versammelt auf dem Reichstag zu Augsburg" [An exhortation to the clergy assembled at the diet of Augsburg] (EA 24² 356 ff.): he declares that not he, but the opposite party, is responsible for all the harm suffered by Germany during the last ten years. He accordingly delivers a singularly sharp penitential sermon to the Romanists: "We and you know, that you live without God's word, but we possess God's word." At the beginning of June the pamphlet was published: the Emperor prohibited its being sold at Augsburg.

[2] His later complaint is valueless: *Lutherus ipse non voluit scribere talem aliquam confessionem, cujus tamen erat scribere*, and, therefore, he himself was obliged to (Sachs. *K.-u. Schulbl*.) The letter to his brother, in which he exclaims, "other theologians wanted to write the book and would to God they had been allowed to!" is foisted in. HARTFELDER, *Melanchthoniana paed*. p. 38.

[3] Cp. K. MÜLLER in Pr Jb LXIII 124 ff. STROBEL, *Beitr. zur Lit*. II. 192 ff.

a confession of the four cities Strasburg, Constance, Memmingen and Lindau (Tetrapolitana)[1] to be drawn up by Bucer and Capito. The Emperor decidedly refused to have it read aloud to him, but it was presented to him on the 11th of July. Ulm completely isolated itself and refused to join the four cities.[2] More violent in its attack upon Romish doctrine and practice (violent also in its attack upon the use of images), more decided in the importance it attached to the authority of the Scriptures, but also broader than the CA, it endeavours, in the eighteenth article (on the Eucharist), to bring forward a middle theory, expressed in extremely Lutheran language, which shares Zwingli's protest against the *manducatio oralis*, but at the same time asserts something more than a commemoration meal. (They consistently evaded the question subsequently put to them by the Emperor, whether they were Zwinglians or Lutherans, by referring to the confession handed in by them). Zwingli, however, forwarded to the Emperor at Augsburg a confession dated July 3rd (*Fidei ratio ad Carolum Imperatorem:* Opp. IV. I. ff., Niemeyer 16 ff., Schaff, Bibl. symb. I. 366 ff.)

The reading of the CA had certainly made a favourable impression upon individual Catholic princes: but when the Emperor asked the Council of the Catholic States what he should do, they recommended him (June 26th) to have the document tested, or in other words, confuted by a body of intelligent and learned men, but at the same time to endeavour to find a means of reforming abuses. The papal legate Campeggi also zealously brought his influence to bear upon Charles: he declared that much of the real doctrine of the Protestants was concealed in the CA, that other parts of it, so far as they were good, were adopted from the Catholic doctrine, and, so far as they were false, could be shown to be a *réchauffé* of heresies long since condemned. . He declared that a confutation of the contents ought to be composed and then read before the diet as the final decision of the question of belief.[3] The Emperor thereupon commissioned the legate to undertake the task of seeing to the written confutation of the CA, but was at the same time unwilling to lose sight of the removal of abuses.

---

[1] NIEMEYER, *Collectio confessionum* 740 ff. SALIG I 387 ff. SCHELHORN, *Amoenitates litt.* VI. (1727) p. 305 ff.

[2] Cp. ZhTh 19, 445 ff.

[3] LANZ in StBlV XI 45 ff.

Campeggi called together about twenty Catholic theologians to draw up the Confutation, amongst them Eck, Faber and Cochleus, the most hostile opponents of the Reformation.

In the meantime Melanchthon at once sought reunion with the Romish party. He not only again entered into connection with the imperial Court as soon as possible, but, on the 6th of July, he took the unwarrantable step of writing a letter to Campeggi, which, together with the grossest flatteries, contained the declaration: "*Dogma nullum habemus diversum ab ecclesia Romana. Parati sumus obedire ecclesiae Romanae, modo illa pro sua clementia, qua semper erga omnes gentes usa est,* **pauca quaedam** *vel dissimulet vel relaxet, quae iam mutare ne quidem si velimus queamus.*" They would certainly be slandered by the ill-disposed, but "*Romani pontificis auctoritatem et universam politiam ecclesiasticam reverenter colimus . . . . Nullam ob rem aliam plus odii sustinemus in Germania, quam quia ecclesiae* **Romanae** (!) *dogmata summa constantia defendimus . . . levis quaedam dissimilitudo rituum est, quae videtur obsistere concordiae*" (CR II 170). He now reduces his demands to the cup for the laity and permission for priests to marry: as for the mass, the learned would certainly be able to come to an agreement. In return he volunteers *obedientiam reddere et iurisdictionem Episcopis* (173). The legate delayed with his answer: he hoped *cunctando* to gain over the Protestants at a smaller sacrifice. Fortunately, in the meantime, Melanchthon's too ready attitude of concession had become suspicious to his associates: they informed Luther of his timidity and disposition to yield, who thereupon endeavoured to combat his blind confidence (de Wette IV 68).

On the 9th of July, the insidious question was put to the evangelical States, whether they had any other disputed articles besides those put forward in the CA: they gave an evasive answer (CR II 181 ff.). The Catholic theologians had now on their side finished their confutation (*Catholica et quasi extemporalis responsio*). Eck was chiefly responsible for it; Faber and others had contributed additions. It is a voluminous, violently-worded indictment, dominated by the idea that the CA persistently concealed and kept silence upon the real teaching of the Evangelicals and its pernicious results.[1] It was handed (in German and Latin) to the Emperor on the 12th of July. But the Emperor, who was anxious to bring the Protestants again into submission to the Church by the mildest possible measures, and at the same time to meet the wishes of the friends of reform on the Catholic side, could do nothing at all with it. He (and also the Catholic States) insisted upon a thorough revision. Accordingly, the confutation was again taken in hand; an indictment by theologians was converted into a reply by the Emperor to the CA, shorter and couched in milder and

---

[1] It was printed for the first time in Ficker 1 ff.

more dignified language (CR XXVII. 81 ff.). In it the Emperor speaks as the patron of the Church and advocate of the Catholic faith. By dint of continuous alterations and improvements, in which Campeggi's severity was finally obliged to yield to the milder attitude of the imperial policy, the confutation finally received the form in which, on the 3rd of August, it was read before the States of the Empire by the imperial secretary Alexander Schweiss; even then it was in many points a decidedly weak defence of Romish ecclesiastical policy and rather an accusation than a confutation of opponents. The Emperor declared that the Protestants were hereby confuted. They were now required to return to their obedience to the Church, otherwise he would treat them as "the Patron and as the Protector" of the Catholic Church. They asked for a copy of the confutation: as their request was only granted on condition that they would neither reply to it nor make it public (ZKG XII. 158), they abandoned it, but at the same time firmly rejected the imperial demand. The more severely they were threatened, the more steadfastly the evangelical parties held up their heads. The Landgrave of Hesse suddenly left the diet on the 6th of August (probably because he had heard that Zürich had accepted its Hessian burgher rights), after having declared that he would rather lose his life, than consent to give up the Confession: the Elector John was equally firm in face of the alternative, "to deny God or the world" (ZKG IX. 103 f.).

Only Melanchthon again deluded himself with a *spes transactionis* (CR II. 261). By the end of July[1] he had again offered his conditions to Campeggi, in which he confined himself to the demand for the cup and the marriage of priests, expressed the hope of a peaceful agreement in regard to the mass, and, for the rest, abandoned the Reformation as *temerarii motus* (CR II. 246 ff). This attitude of Melanchthon, in such sharp contrast with the loyal adherence of the Princes to the Confession, only made Campeggi more confident that it would be possible to obtain all from Melanchthon: however, on this occasion he caused an ample reward to be offered him for further good services (LÄMMER, Mon. Vatic. 53)!

The Emperor, however, hesitated at this moment about employing the violent measures that had been threatened against the refractory princes: the Council, which he had again exhorted the Pope to summon, and the convocation of which would have been of the greatest moment for the Reformation at this stage, was dreaded more than anything else and hindered by Clement: it

---

[1] For the date cp. ZKG IX. 300.

accordingly seemed best to take advantage of Melanchthon's yielding disposition, and to enter upon the path of **negotiations.**

A committee of seven persons on each side commenced to hold amicable meetings on the question of religion. Eck and Melanchthon were the chief spokesmen. An actual understanding was arrived at in regard to the different articles of the CA (1, 3, 7, 9-11, 13, 16-19): the **sola** *fide* was, at least formally, allowed to drop. On the Catholic side, the administration of the cup to the laity was allowed for Protestant districts,—provided it should be ratified by the Pope until the matter was decided by the Council—and on condition that the Protestants should teach the legality also of the *communio sub una:* the sacrifice of the mass was reduced to "a memorial sacrifice, in memory of the death of Christ" (*sacrificium repraesentativum*): they were willing to tolerate the married priests of the evangelical party ("in order to spare the misguided women"), but refused to allow further marriages to be concluded: the confiscated properties of the monasteries were at once to revert under ecclesiastical control. The evangelical members of the committee certainly did not agree to these proposals for self-annihilation, but their counter proposals (FÖRSTEMANN, *Urk.-buch*, II 256 ff.) also offered most far-reaching concessions. While negotiations were going on, Luther's opinion was appealed to, and his replies of the 26th of August (de Wette IV 140 ff.; VI 118 ff., and EA 65, 46 ff.) turned the scale, "as a freeing from evil enchantment." The demands of their Catholic opponents were refused: the Elector John requested leave of absence from the Emperor.

Once more, the work of reunion originated from the imperial Court in the form of peace negotiations, in which the earlier conditions of agreement substantially reappeared. We again have a readiness on the part of Melanchthon to make concessions, accompanied, however, by increasing indignation of the Protestants against him; and now, in the case of the latter, a complete change took place: the more obstinately they resisted the Romish allurements and threats, the more—to Melanchthon's surprise—**a mutual understanding with the Upper Germans** resulted. **Bucer** had managed things so cleverly, that the four cities had not confessed themselves Zwinglians, but had in all essentials declared their doctrine of the Eucharist to be the consensus arrived at at Marburg: after that, undeterred by manifestations of unfriendliness, he had indefatigably sought an agreement with the Wittenbergers at Augsburg: finally, he visited Luther himself on the 25th of September at Coburg, and succeeded in drawing from him the opinion that he regarded an agreement with the Strasburgers on the sacramental question as henceforth possible (de Wette IV 191).[1]

---

[1] Cp. Bucer's account in *Epp. Schwebelii*, p. 148 ff.

Although Article 10 of the CA is undoubtedly a protest against Zwingli, and from this point of view lays stress upon agreement with the Catholic Church, yet the judgment of the Upper Germans in regard to the same was strikingly friendly: they found it "quite modest in tone" and expressed the opinion that, if it had been brought forward at the negotiations of 1529 instead of the 10th Schwabach article, "we should never have separated from each other."[1] The Emperor, also induced by the Turkish danger and lack of warlike preparations to defer yet again the decision by force,[2] finally proposed a "recess" of the diet, since all negotiations led to no result. This decree declared the CA confuted, but allowed the Protestants till the 15th of April of the following year to make up their minds to accept the articles in regard to which no agreement had as yet been come to: during that time he would consider what it would then be his duty to do. But also, during that time, they were strictly forbidden to introduce further ecclesiastical innovations. Lastly, they were to make common cause with the Emperor and the Catholic States against the Anabaptists and "those who do not keep the holy reverend Sacrament." The Supreme Court of Judicature would take proceedings against any violation of this "recess." The evangelical States replied with the protest, that their Confession was not confuted, that the Emperor might accept only Melanchthon's **Apologia** (the first draft, drawn up from notes taken during the reading of the Confutation, CR XXVII 247 ff., 275-378),—but he refused. In their final consultation (held on the 23rd September) they even summoned up courage to refuse to join in the proceedings against the Zwinglians, "since it was still to be hoped that they might yet agree herein with a common Christian Church." They demanded a copy of the recess and time (until the 15th of April) to think over whether they could accept it or not. On the same day the Elector John left the diet. The course of affairs at this very menacing diet, in spite of the friendship of Pope and Emperor, and in spite of Melanchthon's "timidity" (*Blödigkeit*)[3] had

---

[1] DOBEL, Memmingen IV 32.

[2] See the description of the political situation in WINCKELMANN, *der Schmalk. Bund*, Strassb., 1892, p. 3 ff.

[3] During the years immediately following the diet of Augsburg, the efforts of the Romish party were exerted to persuade Melanchthon to return to the Catholic Church. Cp. for 1531-1532 LÄMMER, *Monum. Vatic.* p. 85, 97, 103, 128; for 1553, *Nuntiaturberichte*, I 140 and HARTFELDER, *Melanchthoniana paedag.* p. 202; for 1539, LÄMMER, p. 230.

had been a success for the Reformation: decision by the sword was again put off. "If it has not turned out for Pope and Emperor as they expected at Augsburg, it shall not so turn out for them in the future": with this result Luther was able to console himself (de Wette IV 203). Certainly, on the 25th of October, the violent confutation of the Tetrapolitana drawn up by Faber, Eck and Cochleus was read to the four cities, which they then in like manner met by an Apologia: but **Strasburg**, at the Schmalkald Convent (December 22-30, 1530) had already given its assent to the CA, so that the accession of the Lutheran States to the league was thereby introduced.

On his return home, Melanchthon worked up his apologia to an exhaustive defence of the CA: it appeared in April 1531, the Latin text prepared by Melanchthon himself, a German version by Jonas:[1] Melanchthon's **private** answer to the theologians, who had prepared the confutation (CR 27, 420 f.), but in the central details so masterly a work that, especially as it was printed together with the CA, it very soon acquired importance as a charter of the Confederation (at the Schweinfurt agreement, 1532) and then, also as a symbol of doctrine.

---

[1] Dobel IV 18 ff.; in Latin in Müller, *Formula confutationis*, Lips. 1808, p. 191-224.

CHAPTER FIFTH.

The Schmalkaldic League in its prime.

1. Zwingli's Death and the Nuremberg Truce.

Sources: Strassburgs politische Correspondenz II. 1887.
Literature: LENZ in ZKG III. O. WINCKELMANN, *der Schmalkald. Bund und der Nürnberger Rel.-Friede.* Strassb. 1892. NOACK in *Fd Gesch.* 1882; the same, *Prog. d. Realsch. zu Crefeld.* 1886. BAUMGARTEN III. 38 ff. ESCHER, *die Glaubensparteien in der Eidgenossenschaft.* Frauenfeld, 1882. FICKER in ZKG XII. 613 ff. LÜTHI, *die berner. Politik in den Kappelerkriegen.* Bern 1878. EGLI, *die Schlacht von Kappel.* 1873.

On the 19th of November, the Emperor had published the "Recess" of the diet, in which the summoning of a council was declared to be imperatively necessary. Not only was the decision, which the approaching 15th of April was to bring, menacing for the Evangelical party, but also the intention to take proceedings against them by the imperial court of judicature (strengthened as it was by Catholic councillors) for their confiscation of ecclesiastical properties: in addition to this, Charles's desire to procure the election of his brother Ferdinand as King of Rome, in order to secure the succession in the Empire for his house, and to have him as his standing representative in Germany, had to be taken into account. The votes of the remaining Electors were soon (November 13th) won over with gold: but it was difficult to gain that of the Saxon. The rest of the Electors opposed the idea of excluding him from the election as a heretic, for which purpose the Pope was ready to supply a bull. Accordingly, on the 29th of December, the Emperor summoned him to Cologne for the election. **This decided him to come to an understanding at Schmalkalden with the Oberland cities.** Not only did **Strasburg** (Bucer and Jakob Sturm), with its politically freer view, and its tendency to unite **all** the evangelicals, thereby acquire authoritative influence, but an important change was now being accomplished in the views of the Elector John as well as of the Wittenberg theologians in regard to the imperial power and the right of self-defence (EA 25², 12; 113 ff.).[1] Protestantism there-

---

[1] Cp. WINCKELMANN p. 36 ff. KOLDE, *M. Luther* II. 377 ff.

by became a political party in the Empire. (Only George of Brandenburg and the City of Nuremberg did not follow this course, and hence became isolated. On the 25th of December, the evangelical princes assembled at Schmalkalden protested against Frederick's election, and the plan of a league was drawn up. John did not appear at Cologne at person, and on the 5th of January, (Saxony protesting against the validity of the whole proceeding) Ferdinand was elected King. The Emperor was also asked by the Schmalkaldeners to suspend the proceedings of the Court of Judicature against the Protestants in matters of belief.[1] On the 27th of February, at a second meeting, the league for the defence of the Gospel was formally concluded.[2] In addition to Saxony and Hesse, the members of the league were Brunswick-Lüneberg and Brunswick-Grubenhagen, Prince Wolfgang of Anhalt, the two Counts of Mansfeld, the cities of Strasburg, Ulm, Constance, Reutlingen, Memmingen, Lindau, Biberach, Isny, Lübeck,[3] Magdeburg, and Bremen. It was a league for purposes of common defence against anyone who should attempt to drive them or their subjects violently from the word of God: it was to last for six years at first, and new members were to be admitted with the knowledge and consent of all. The Emperor's hopes of the disunion between Lutherans and Zwinglians were thereby destroyed: Upper and Lower Germany held together. The resolution to hold an evangelical general synod to arrange a common ritual was dropped, since the outbreak of differences was feared. As the effect of the league on the one hand was, that the appointed limit of the 15th of April passed without any momentous consequences for the evangelicals, it on the other hand paralysed Zwingli's political plans. The Upper Germans, under Bucer's guidance, in order to find support in the Empire, had also drawn near as far as possible to Luther. In this Zwingli was unable to follow them: Zürich and Berne even rejected the Tetrapolitana: the efforts of Strasburg and the Landgrave to bring about their adhesion were now rebuffed by Switzerland, and the Landgrave's desire to enter into an alliance with Switzerland in preference to Saxony was checked by Jakob Sturm's thoughtfulness. Thus Zwingli lost the

---

[1] The Emperor returned an evasive answer.

[2] The charter of the league is given in the *Politische Correspondenz* of the city of Strasburg.

[3] The mention of this city was premature, but on the 3rd of May it formally declared its adherence.

importance which he had obtained for a great part of Germany. This was the more significant as, under the influence of Strasburg, "Bucerism" had now gained the victory in Ulm, Augsburg, Biberach and Esslingen. But Zürich rose up so defiantly against the five Catholic cantons that it brought war within measurable distance: in addition to this, Zwingli drew up a plan involving so complete a political change of the confederacy that even the confederate towns raised objections. Even in Zürich a strong opposition grew up against the theological politician. The latter, on the 26th of June, 1531, alarmed his fellow-citizens by demanding his discharge and thereby once more regained his authoritative position for a short space of time. The blockade of supplies, which Zürich and Berne had proclaimed over the five cantons,—a half-measure which Zwingli had in vain opposed,—was answered unexpectedly, on the 9th of October, by the latter by a declaration of war. On the 11th, Zürich suffered a decisive defeat at Cappel: Zwingli, who had been ordered by the Council to accompany the troops as chaplain, was wounded and then struck down. His corpse was quartered and afterwards burned by the executioner.[1] Oecolampadius also, deeply affected by Zwingli's death, succumbed to illness at Bâle on the 24th of November. Zürich and Berne were obliged to abandon their league at the **Peace of Cappel** and to allow the Catholic faith scope in their district. Zwingli's "Burgrecht"[2] was annulled, the progress of the Reformation was checked, all the aggressive plans of Zürich for the transformation of Switzerland came to nothing. The Protestantism that endeavoured to carry out vast political designs was now carried to the grave with Zwingli.

In individual districts a violent rehabilitation of the Catholic Church took place: in any case the religious split in Switzerland was irrevocably decided. The counter-reformation soon began its work. Zürich itself suffered least, as it found an excellent substitute in **Bullinger.**

The Catholic world rejoiced. Ferdinand and the papal legate importuned Charles to crush the German heretics also: but he prudently hesitated, feeling doubtful about France and not even certain that he would meet with general assistance amongst the

---

[1] Luther could only regard his opponent's death, as also the Peace of Cappel, from the point of view of a divine judgment: cp. de Wette IV. 322 f., 332 and elsewhere. On Oct. 24th, Zürich was again defeated.

[2] [See p. 82. Schaff translates the word by "Co-burghery."]

Catholic princes of Germany. But the Peace of Cappel finally settled the disputed question of the admission or rejection of the Swiss: they had no longer to be reckoned with, and the Upper Germans had now still more reason to combine staunchly with the Lutherans. At the same time, the princes thereby gained preponderance over the cities. Germany remained the country of the Lutheran Reformation, but still with a manifest distinction between a North German and a South West German type.

Thus the organisation of the league proceeded in a highly satisfactory manner. On the 19th of December the Elector and Landgrave were elected chiefs of the league at Frankfort: Goslar and Eimbeck were fresh recruits. At Schweinfurt (April 1532) the organisation was completed. The Upper Germans recognised the CA and Apology by the side of their own special confession, in return for which they were spared the express rejection of the "Zwinglian".[1] "It would be contrary to brotherly love," so Strasburg declared, "to pledge ourselves to show no favour to anyone who acknowledges the common Christ with us, even though he should not be at one with us in regard to some article, more in the letter than in the spirit."[2] The Schmalkaldic League received peculiar support from the old hostility of Bavaria to the Habsburgs. On the 24th of October, 1531, the Dukes of Bavaria entered into a formal league at Saalfeld with the evangelical princes of the league against Ferdinand. Anti-imperial alliances were also entered into with France, England, Zápolya, King of Hungary, Denmark and Duke Charles of Gueldres partly through the Landgrave and partly through Bavaria.

It was a melancholy necessity for the Reformation, that it needed foreign alliances against the Emperor, whose power rested upon vast kingdoms outside Germany, and particularly, that the hostility between the Emperor and France necessarily formed an important factor in all political calculations. Certainly the Schmalkaldic League as such never sought alliance with France: it was its individual members that did so. Thus the Reformation, which commenced as a mighty national development, as it went on, at first actually proved a serious **weakening of the nation,** since it had not been able to take hold upon the **entire** nation, and had the might of the Emperor against it. It strengthened particularism and made Germany's fortunes dependent upon foreign countries. In this particularism, to which it was driven by force of circumstances, it suffered harm itself, inasmuch as, split up into numerous established churches, **it was obliged to seek its unity in the sphere of rigid formularies of doctrine.** Thus, the longer Protestantism lasted, the more it pressed forward in the direction of dogmatism. Cp. **Baumgarten,** *Karl V. und die deutsche Reformation*, p. 65 f.

The invasion of Hungary by the Turks rendered it an imperative duty for the Emperor to come to an understanding with the Protestants somehow or other. Very humiliating offers of peace, which Ferdinand made up his mind to offer, were rejected by the Sultan. Charles accordingly began to

---

[1] Strasburg's *politische Correspondenz*. II 107 ff.
[2] Ib., p. 112.

negotiate with the Schmalkaldeners, first at Schweinfurt and then at Nuremberg. Even the Pope now advised an attempt to come to terms, in order to be able to resist the Turks. He even laid the CA before some Romish theologians for examination, who expressed themselves in favour of the possibility of an understanding on matters of dogma. The Evangelicals demanded the inclusion, not only of the present, but of all future subscribers to their Confession in this peace and the abandonment of the persecution of their fellow-believers in the Catholic provinces. (Luther himself considered these demands far too high-pitched: the opposite party, he declared, would never accept the former, for then "without a doubt all their people would soon be overturned").[1] They further demanded the dropping of all suits that were hanging over them in the Court of Judicature and the summoning of a Council, at which alone a decision should be come to in accordance with God's word.

They were finally obliged to be content with a **truce,** which assured their religious position until the time of the Council which would be convened by the Pope. The dropping of the religious suits was certainly promised them, but only at a secret by-agreement, which was not communicated to the Catholic States, and in such a manner that they were obliged to move for it in each individual case; and even then it was only to hold good in the case of the actual associates of the league. This "truce,"[2] ratified at Nuremberg on the 23rd July, was not adopted into the Recess by the diet that was sitting at Ratisbon at the same time,[3] but was made public by an especial imperial mandate on the 3rd of August. If not much was gained by it, yet the Emperor had been driven a little from the attitude he had hitherto held towards the evangelicals: he had proclaimed the principle of toleration. But, in the autumn of 1532, Charles returned from Ratisbon and Vienna by way of Italy[4] to Spain, and it was only after a lapse of nine years that he was again able to turn his whole attention to German affairs.

2. The Growth and Development of German Protestantism.

Literature: HEPPE, *Gesch. d. ev. K. v. Cleve-Mark.* Iserl. 1867. WOLTERS, *Conr. von Heresbach.* Elberf. 1867. L. KELLER in HTb 1882, 123 ff. WOLTERS, *Ref.-Gesch. d. Stadt Wesel.* 1868. J. GECK, *die deutsche KReform. mit bes. Berücksichtigung Soests.* Soest, 1874. HEYD, *Ulrich, Herz. z. Württ.* 3 vols. Tüb. 1841-1844. KUGLER, *Christoph, Herz. z. Württ.* I. Stuttg. 1868. VON STÄLIN, *Württ. Gesch.* IV. Stuttg. 1873. HARTMANN, *E. Schnepff.*

---

[1] DE WETTE, IV 369.
[2] Walch XVI 2210 ff.: Strassb. polit. Corr. II 168 ff.
[3] J. FICKER in ZKG XII 583 ff.
[4] See the agreement entered into between Pope and Emperor at Bologna (February 24th, 1533) printed in RQ V 301 ff.

Tüb. 1870. WILLE, *Phil. v. Hessen und die Restit. Ulrichs.* Tüb. 1882; the same, in *Z. f. Gesch. d. Oberrh.* 37, 263 ff. E. SCHNEIDER, *Württ. Ref.-Gesch.* Stuttg. 1887. ROTHENHAÜSLER, *der Untergang der kath. Rel. in Altwürtt.* Stuttg. 1887. *Württ. KGesch.* Calw. 1892. WILLE in ZKG VII 50 ff. WINCKELMANN in ZKG XI 211 ff. VON STETTEN, *Gesch. der Reichsst. Augsb.* 1743 I; ZAPF, *Chr. v. Stadion.* Zürich 1799, p. 81 ff. *Werke des Fürsten Georg von Anhalt.* Wittb. 1561; BECKMANN, *Hist. des Fürstenthums Anhalt* 1710. VI; O. SCHMIDT, *N. Hausmann.* Leipz. 1860; STIER in Mitt. d. Ver. f. Anh. Gesch. IV 1 ff.; KRAUSE, *Melanthoniana.* Zerbst 1885. VON MEDEM, *Gesch. der Einführung der evg. Lehre in Pommern.* Greifsw. 1837. HERING, *Bugenhagen.* Halle 1888, p. 97 ff.; the same in StKr 1889, 793 ff. BAHRDT, *Gesch. d. Ref. d. Stadt Hannover,* 1891. *Die Pommersche KO von* 1535, edited by M. WEHRMANN. Stettin 1893.

The conclusion of the religious peace at Nuremberg had made it possible for a successful resistance to be offered to the invasion of the Turk. The Emperor also pressed the Pope hard in the matter of the desired Council. The Pope secretly disclosed his opinion of this Council to Ferdinand, to whom he represented that anything of the kind would infallibly bring about a fresh separation: for either it would proclaim the superiority of the Pope to the Council and then a split would at once arise: or it would declare the supremacy of the Pope, and then the Protestants would say that it had not been left free to act and would in like manner bring about a split.[1] Finally, a course of procedure was agreed to, which, with apparently good intentions, was bound, in fact, to make the Council unacceptable to the Protestants. Inviolable submission to its decisions was required of them; in addition to this, the summoning of the Council was made dependent upon the assent of France and England, which it was known beforehand would refuse it. In June, 1533, the papal nuncio Rangoni actually presented himself to the Elector John Frederick, who had succeeded his father (who had died on the 16th of August, 1532) in the government of Saxony, and, as was to be anticipated, was put off by him until a joint answer should be received from the Schmalkaldener confederates, from whom he got a decided refusal on the 30th of June.[2] The question of the Council was difficult for the Protestants: they could not at the outset reject this means of coming to terms, they had desired it often enough: but they could not submit to every judgment of a majority of the Council, and hence were bound to propose such conditions in regard to it, to which again no Pope could assent. The cause of the Reformation had, in fact, long outgrown submission to a Council. Only in places where the Erasmian ideas of a cautious ecclesiastical reform prevailed would a Council have been of any service at that time. As a matter of fact, Erasmian ideas of reform asserted themselves in a larger German territory, in the powerful Duchy of Jülich-Cleve, which, apart from that, had been rendered very independent ecclesiastically by earlier papal favour. The autocratic John III., the friend and patron of the Humanists—his son's education was entrusted to Conrad of Heresbach—owing to the influence of the latter, as early as 1525 had decreed, without taking episcopal advice, an "order or reformation" in church matters, after he had

---

[1] BUCHHOLTZ, IV 288.
[2] WALCH XVI 2268 ff., 2281 ff.—For the opinions of Luther and Melanchthon see de Wette IV 454 ff., CR II 655 f, also Strassb. Polit. Corr. II 150 ff.

just before very prudently warned his country against Luther's teaching in an edict.[1] Here preaching of the word of God was called for "without any disturbance, scandal or self-interest": masses for the soul and payment of money for spiritual ministrations abolished: the elevation of the spiritual order taken into consideration. The order afforded many a handle for the increasing evangelical frame of mind, without, however, being able to satisfy the latter. In 1532, a new ritual, which had been eagerly awaited, appeared,[2] but which suffered still more from incompleteness and indefiniteness, and revealed the incapacity of the Erasmians for understanding the religious question and for a productive renovation of the affairs of the Church. Even the "Declaration" of the 8th of April, 1533,[3] which was more evangelically coloured in some points, and the visitation that was held on the basis of the same were not able to keep the parties together as was desired: each party put its own interpretation upon it, and, especially in Wesel, Soest (de Wette IV 364, 376) and other towns the evangelical movement proceeded vigorously under its flag. But at the same time the incompleteness of the reforms promoted sectarian growths. But, impressed by the catastrophe at Münster, the Duke soon lost the desire for further steps.

Although the Emperor, in accordance with the Nuremberg truce, had charged his Fiscal (Attorney-General) at the imperial court of judicature to stop proceedings against the evangelicals, this official was able to render the Emperor's concession ineffectual by not ranking *causae possessoriae* and actions for restitution amongst "matters that concerned belief": accordingly, in January, 1534, the Schmalkaldic League raised a "recusation," and rejected the majority of the members of the Court as too "mistrustful and partisan" for processes in matters of religion.[4] But the restoration of **Ulrich** of Wurtemberg to his dominions was far more effectual than this protest.

The Swabian league, by which the powerful duke had been driven out in 1519, had handed over the country on the 6th of February, 1520, to Charles V. as Archduke of Austria; in 1522, Ferdinand had been appointed vice-regent and the country had been allotted to him as his inheritance at a secret treaty of partition. Ulrich's attempts (1524 and 1525) to regain possession of his country had failed: he had been for some years the guest of the Landgrave. As the Hispano-Austrian government had made itself hated in the country, the sympathies of the population were strongly aroused in favour of the old lord of the land, since in his misfortune he had turned evangelical, and had introduced the principles of the Reformation in the county of Mömpelgard.

---

[1] He had illegally allowed his subjects, Adolph Clarenbach and Peter Fleisteden, to be imprisoned for a year and a half at Cologne without interfering: on the 29th of September, 1529, they were executed as Gospel martyrs.
[2] Richter, KOO I 160 ff.
[3] Richter I 212 ff.
[4] Strassb. Pol. Corr. II 205.

His son Christopher, who had been seized by the Habsburgs, had escaped from his "guardians" in 1532, and asserted his own and his father's claims. With the assistance of money from France, the Landgrave Philip (in spite of the opposition of Luther, who tried to dissuade him from thus taking the offensive, **Seckend.** III 74) in a brief campaign defeated and routed the Austrians at Lauffen: after which, at the **peace concluded at Kaaden** (Cadan, in the northwest of Bohemia) on the 29th of June, 1534, he compelled Ferdinand to acknowledge Duke Ulrich's claim to the government of Wurtemberg, although, to Ulrich's disappointment, only as a rerefief of Austria, with, however, a seat and vote in the diet. He further extorted the promise, which was certainly not carried out in real earnest, that all processes against the evangelicals in the imperial court of judicature should be suspended: on the other hand, the members of the league of Schmalkald from that time dropped their opposition to Frederick's election. But the articles of peace also allowed Ulrich the right of carrying out a future ecclesiastical reformation in the country; only the lords and sovereign bishops settled there, who had royal prerogatives of their own, were assured their Catholic belief. It was due to John Frederick that this stipulation found acceptance. The Sacramentarians, however, were to be excluded.

Thus Wurtemberg was rendered accessible to the Reformation it had so long desired. Ulrich appointed two men of a different turn of mind to assist him; in the upper country (south of Stuttgart) **Ambrose Blaurer** of Constance, who held the same views as Bucer, who had recommended him to the Duke; in the lower country, the zealous Lutheran **Erhard Schnepf** of Marburg. The meeting of the two tendencies of the Reformation which were laboriously combined in the league caused difficulties;[1] Blaurer and Schnepf, however, agreed upon a formula of the Sacrament (the Concord of Wurtemberg), " that the body and blood of Christ is present and is administered veritably, that is substantially and essentially, but not quantitatively, qualitatively, or locally." The disputed question of the partaking of it by the unworthy was left open. The reforms in the Church service bore the impress of Strasburg rather than Wittenberg. The Duke himself supported neither the CA nor the Tetrapolitana. These proceedings, which, however, did not exclude misunderstandings, again brought an understanding between Wittenberg and the Oberlanders in the matter of questions of doctrine within measurable distance.

The influence of **John Brenz**, that had for a long time been put to the test in Schwäbisch-Hall, was secured by Ulrich for two years, to set ecclesiastical affairs in order in his country (Ritual, Order of Visitation, Catechism, University reform; cp. **Richter**, KOO I 265 ff.; **Pressel**, *Anecdota Brentiana*, Tübingen,

---

[1] Cp. Strassb. Pol. Corr. II 219 ff.

1868, p. 156 ff.). The efforts of the Landgrave were successful in securing the work of the Reformation against agitations from the opposite side (especially Bavaria), in getting Ulrich to join the Schmalkaldic League (1536), finally, in reconciling him to his son Christopher, who was still a Catholic, and converting the latter to the evangelical faith. Thus the evangelical character of the country was assured. The Swabian league was dissolved: in its place, Bavaria, in 1536, brought about a Catholic alliance at Donauwörth with the Emperor and Ferdinand, the Counts of the Palatinate, Otto Henry and Philip, and the bishoprics of Salzburg, Augsburg, Eichstedt and Bamberg. The imperial cities significantly held aloof from this new league: in them the Reformation rather made fresh progress. **Augsburg**, where the contending parties had hitherto opposed each other, now resolved, without heeding the bishop or the influential house of the Fuggers, to allow no papal preaching and no celebration of mass, except in the churches that belonged directly to the bishop (1535); this powerful city also subsequently joined the Schmalkaldic League.[1] **Frankfort-on-the-Main** acted in the same manner.

But in the North also important victories of the Reformation were to be recorded. **Anhalt**-Köthen, under the pious prince Wolfgang, had already declared its adherence to the CA: in 1532 the three brothers of the **Dessau** line followed suit: under the leadership of Prince **George**, the provost of Magdeburg Cathedral, they summoned Nicolas Hausmann as minister, and, in spite of the counter-efforts of Duke George and Cochleus, entered into increasingly friendly relations with the Wittenberg reformers. In 1534, the whole country had become Lutheran; the princes joined the Schmalkaldic League. In **Pomerania** also, after a period of violent party spirit, after the death of the Catholic-minded Duke George, the Reformation was introduced by Duke Barnim (who had studied at Wittenberg) and George's son Philip. The diet of Treptow on the Rega (December, 1534), to which they had invited their countryman John Bugenhagen, decided that the Gospel should be preached throughout the land, all popish practices and ceremonies contrary to divine law abolished, and the service arranged in accordance with the ritual drawn up by Bugenhagen (**Richter**, KOO I 248 ff.), who himself conducted the first visitation. In **Hanover**, also, the Reformation gained a decisive victory in 1534 amidst violent constitutional struggles: **Urbanus Rhegius**, by literary and personal intervention, assisted in the ecclesiastical reorganisation: the new ritual appeared in 1536 (**Richter**, I 273 ff.). In 1536, Hanover joined the League together with **Hamburg**.[2] The happy conclusion of the Concord of Wittenberg above all served to strengthen the league **internally**.

---

[1] Strassb. Pol. Corr. II 357.

[2] Strassb. pol. Corr. II 342. The idea spread by **Ranke** (IV 55) that John Frederick, in the summer of 1535, induced Ferdinand to extend the Peace of Nuremberg to new members of the league, is erroneous. Cp. Strassb. pol. Corr. II 316, 320 f. ZKG XI 230 ff.

3. The Concord of Wittenberg.

Sources and *Literature*: KOLDE in RE XVII 222 ff.; the same, *Anal. Luth.* 200 f., 214 ff. WINCKELMANN in Strassb. pol. Corr. 675 ff.; STROBEL, *Beitr. zur Lit.* I. 247 ff.

In July 1533, Bucer had already proposed to the Landgrave another conference, "more thorough and leisurely than that at Marburg." Since 1531, Melanchthon had been perplexed about Luther's doctrine of the Eucharist; he now inclined towards the Strasburgers and eagerly desired an understanding. On the invitation of the Landgrave, Bucer and Melanchthon first met at Cassel (Christmas, 1534), where the former gave explanations, which satisfied even Luther. A number of Lutheran theologians (Brenz, Osiander, Rhegius), with whom Melanchthon negotiated further, also showed themselves inclined for reconciliation: only Amsdorf raised difficulties. Bucer now canvassed the South, also Switzerland, and, after overcoming much opposition, advanced matters so far that it was agreed that the peace assembly should be held at Eisenach on the fourth Sunday after Easter, 1536. Representatives attended from Strasburg (Capito and Bucer), Augsburg (W. Musculus), Memmingen, Ulm, Esslingen, Reutlingen, Frankfort, and Constance. But they learned, on reaching Eisenach, that Luther had been detained on his journey by illness. Thereupon, they repaired to Wittenberg, accompanied by the Lutherans, Menius (Eisenach) and Myconius (Gotha). After negotiations that lasted several days (CR III 75 ff.) it was agreed: *cum pane et vino vere et substantialiter adesse, exhiberi et sumi corpus Christi et sanguinem: sacramentali unione panem esse corpus Christi, h.e. porrecto pane simul esse et vere exhiberi corpus Christi.* And this sacramental gift is as independent of the *dignitas ministri* as of that of the *sumens: porrigi corpus et sanguinem Christi etiam indignis et indignos sumere, ubi servantur verba et institutio Christi, sed tales sumere ad iudicium.* At the same time, those who appeared declared their assent to the CA and the Apology. Consequently, a **thoroughly Lutheran** formula had gained the victory in this case, only without accentuating certain points that were keenly disputed (there was no doctrine of ubiquity; Bucer distinguished between *infideles* or *impii* and *indigni;* in the case of the former he denied, and only in the case of the latter admitted the partaking of the Sacrament).

The Oberlanders, who had herewith completed their adhesion to Luther, also united with him on the question of infant baptism and the value of private confession. But Bucer was now desirous of extending the Concord to the Swiss, and finally presented their First Confessio Helvetica,[1] which had been settled in January at Bâle, but hitherto kept secret: it was not a Zwinglian Confession, but one that met Lutheranism in a conciliatory spirit. It declared that Christ really offered his body and blood at the Lord's Supper: certainly, there existed neither *naturalis unio* nor *localis inclusio* nor *carnalis praesentia*, but, by virtue of its institution, the bread and wine are *symbola, quibus ab ipso domino per ecclesiae ministerium vera corporis et sanguinis communicatio exhibetur*, certainly not to feed the belly, but *in aeternae vitae alimoniam*. Luther expressed himself fairly well-disposed towards this Confession. In November, consultations actually took place at Bâle about the Concord: but here the "substantial" presence, which Bucer had admitted, was rejected. Courteously conducted negotiations were carried on subsequently from time to time (cp. Hospinianus Hist. Sacr. II 150b; de Wette V 83 ff.); but the Swiss never really accepted the Concord. Only the acrimony of political controversy was moderated for several years. On the other hand, the Upper Germans also were drawn, from a religious point of view, into the community of Lutheranism, but in such a manner, that there was still left them a peculiar acceptation of their own of the Eucharistic doctrine. When hostilities broke out afresh, the conflict with the Swiss was certainly bound to be all the keener, as now the strong moderate party between the opposite camps could no longer assert itself.

4. The Catastrophe in Baptism.

In reference to the *Sources* cp. **Cornelius**, *De fontibus, quibus in hist. seditionis Monasteriensis*, etc. Monast. 1850; the same, *Geschichtsquellen des Bisthums Münster*. Vol. II. Münster, 1853. Hase, *Das Reich der Wiedertäufer*. Leipz. 1860, p. 150 ff.
Literature (Jochmus, 1825. Hast, 1836. Fässer, 1852): Cornelius, *Gesch. des Münst. Aufruhrs*. 2 vols. Leipz., 1855, 1860. Hase, *l.c.*; L. Keller.

---

[1] Niemeyer I 338 ff., III 211 ff. This had been preceded by the "Confession of Bâle" (Hagenbach, *Krit. Gesch. der I. Basler Conf.*, Basel, 1827), drawn up under the influence of Oswald Myconius, Oecolampadius's successor. This also was an attempt to go beyond Zwingli's ideas (*confitemur, Christum in sua S. Coena omnibus vere credentibus praesentem esse*). **Niemeyer**, p. 78 ff. **Schaff** I 385 ff.

Gesch. der Wiedertäufer und ihres Reiches. Münster, 1880; the same in HZ 47, 429 ff. H. KAMPSCHULTE, *Gesch. der Einführung d. Prot. in Westfalen.* Paderborn, 1806. STEITZ, *Abhandlungen zu Frankfurts Ref.-Gesch.* Frankf., 1872, p. 150 ff. BOUTERWEK in Ztsch. d. Berg. Gesch.-Ver. I 280 ff. For the Battenburgers: NIPPOLD in ZhTh, 1863, 96 ff.; KELLER in Westd. Z. f. Gesch. u. Kunst, 1882, 455 ff.; SCHAUENBURG, *die Täuferbewegung in der Grafsch. Oldenb.* 1888. D. JORIS: ARNOLD, *K. u. K. Hist.* Frankf., 1700, II 283 ff. (important as containing certain authorities); MOSHEIM, *Anderw. Vers. einer Ketzergesch.* Helmst., 1748, II; NIPPOLD in ZhTh 1863, 1864 and 1868; CRAMER in Kerkhist. Archief. XVI and XVII; RIGGENBACH in RE VII 93. V. D. LINDE, *D. Joris. Bibliographie.* Gravenhage, 1867. M. SIMONS: Werke. Amst., 1581. A. M. CRAMER, *MS.* Amst. 1837. DE HOOP-SCHEFFER in RE IX 560 ff. NIPPOLD in ZhTh 1863, 141 ff. CHR. SEPP, *Uit het predikantenleven van vroegere tijden.* Leiden, 1890. WULLENWEVER: BARTHOLD in HTb VI 1 ff.: WAITZ, *Lübeck unter J.W.* 3 vols. Berl., 1853, 1856. KELLER, *Gesch. d. Wiedert*, 186 ff. ZKG XII 566 ff.

Since the beginning of the decade, the Westphalian cities also had brought about the triumph of Lutheranism, although as a rule not without communal conflicts in co-operation with a democratic current; this was the case *e.g.* in Minden (1529), Herford (1530),[1] Lippstadt, Lemgo, Bielefeld. In a greater or less degree the Gospel had at the same time been obliged to serve political aims. The corporations were victorious over the patricians; but the small artisans and workmen soon followed suit and demanded a purely democratic constitution. But these were the classes of society amongst which the doctrines of the Baptists had chiefly gained admission. Thus, the Lutheran was followed by a Baptist movement. Melchior Hofmann (see p. 93) had left behind him numerous "Melchiorite" adherents in East Friesland. Their community spread rapidly from Friesland over Holland;[2] prophetic utterances on the one hand, and bloody persecution on the other gave the sect the fervent zeal of a socio-revolutionary fanaticism. In the autumn of 1533, the baker of Haarlem, Jan Mathys (John Matthias), appeared in Amsterdam, announced himself as the second witness foretold by Hofmann, the prophet Enoch, and speedily obtained the undisputed leadership. He sent out "Apostles" two and two, who in a short time overspread the Netherlands with a network of Anabaptist communities. This spirit was especially observable in **Münster**. In this episcopal city, the preaching of Lutheranism by the chaplain **Bernt Rothmann** (Bernard Rottman) had (since 1531) met with great approval amongst the burghers. The democracy of the guilds protected him against the bishop as well as against the Council and the aristocratic patrician families. Driven out at first, he had during his flight been affected by Zwinglianism at Strasburg: hence, after his return to the city, the Reformation assumed a decidedly Zwinglian complexion in the matter of worship. The community, contrary to the wishes of the Council, appointed him minister of St. Lambert's Church; all the churches were occupied in rapid succession by the evangelical party.

---

[1] HÖLSCHER, *Ref.-Gesch. der Stadt Herford.* Gütersloh, 1888.

[2] FRERICHS (*Blicke in die Ref.-Gesch. Ostfrieslands.* Emden, 1883, p. 26) has endeavoured to dispute altogether Hofmann's influence upon the West-Friesian and Dutch Anabaptists; but the connecting link is found in the person of Tripmaker.

At this period, Luther and Melanchthon again issued fruitless warnings against the encroachments of Zwinglianism (de Wette IV 424 ff. ZKG VIII 293. CR II 619 ff.). On Christmas Day, 1532, the burghers surprised and captured the cathedral chapter of Telgte and compelled the newly-elected bishop, Francis of Waldeck, to come to an agreement (February 14th, 1533), whereby all the parish churches were to be given up to the evangelicals, only the cathedral being left to the bishop and chapter. But, in the summer of 1532, the immigration of a mystico-revolutionary unlicensed company of preachers from the little Jülich town of Wassenberg had begun; and these people drew Rothmann more and more into their practices. The Landgrave Philip, by sending two Hessian preachers, in vain endeavoured to clear up the position and bring about a consolidation of the dispassionate evangelically-minded party; the radical party continually gained strength from the accession of Netherland fanatics.

On the 4th of January, 1534, two apostles of Jan Mathys appeared, and rebaptised Rothmann and many others. After a few days, two fresh emissaries followed, one of whom was **Jan Beuckelssen** (John Bockhold), of Leyden, the youthfully beautiful and eloquent tailor; shortly afterwards, the prophet Mathys himself appeared. The gospel of endurance and martyrdom, which Melchior Hofmann joyfully fulfilled in the prison of Strasburg, now changed into the message, to take up arms for the restoration of the new Jerusalem; it was reported in the Netherlands that God had rejected Strasburg by reason of its unbelief and chosen Münster as the new Jerusalem. Rothmann himself came forward as the publicist of the new kingdom: in October, 1534, his book appeared, entitled *Restitution rechter und gesunder christlicher Lebre* [The restoration of correct and sound Christian doctrine] (reprinted, Halle, 1888), in which he defended polygamy as a fulfilling of the divine command "Be fruitful," according to which "men more richly blessed by God" needed several wives. In December, this was followed by *Van der wrake* [concerning Revenge], in which he successfully spread the new preaching of disturbance[1]; this again by the Essay (February, 1535), *Von Verborgenheit der Schrift des Reiches Christi und von dem Tage des Herrn* [Of the secret mystery of the writings of the Kingdom of Christ and of the day of the Lord] (reprinted, Gotha, 1857). In the meantime, events had followed one another in rapid succession. The Münster cloth-maker, **Bernd** (Berendt) **Knipperdolling** joined the Prophets; by a bold *coup de main*, the constitution of the city was overthrown, Knipperdolling raised to the rank of first

---

[1] Zeitschrift d. Berg. Gesch.-Ver. I. p. 345 ff. KELLER, p. 151 f.; see further, SEPP, *Geschiedk. Nasporingen* I 91 ff., 115 ff.

burgomaster, and a community of goods proclaimed. The well-to-do abandoned the city, and Bishop Francis laid siege to it. The siege worked up fanaticism to theocratic frenzy. Mathys fell heroically and John of Leyden took his place as a "King" instead of a prophet, on the authority of certain predictions: twelve elders supported him, Knipperdolling became the viceroy and executioner of the theocratic despot. Certainly, community of wives was not proclaimed, but as no woman was to remain without a husband, a compulsorily-established polygamy was established. Two violent assaults by the episcopal army were successfully repulsed by the Baptists. The bishop (in addition to the support he received from Catholic neighbours, Cologne and Jülich-Cleve) was finally obliged to accept the aid of auxiliary troops from Hesse. Movements amongst the Netherland Baptists to relieve Münster were put down with much bloodshed.[1] And when, in October, 1534, the Baptists sent out twenty-eight Apostles, to proclaim the new King of Zion to the world, they met with a pitiable end. The fanatical Baptists braved the terrors of hunger in the beleaguered city, and John of Leyden put down with an iron hand all murmuring against his rule. It was not until the 24th of June, 1535, that the city fell into the hands of the besiegers through treachery. Rothmann fell in the engagement, the King and others fell victims to the cruel vengeance of the conquerors. The city lost its independence: enthusiastic Anabaptism (and certainly, at the same time also the cause of the Reformation) was annihilated in Münster. Catholic worship was restored in all the Churches, in spite of the counter-efforts of Hesse and the imperial cities. Although, therefore, the Reformation in this case also locally sustained a perceptible loss, yet the defeat of Anabaptism was an important event **for the consolidation of Lutheran ecclesiasticism in North Germany.**

For, all along the line of Baptist propaganda in the North, the catastrophe of Münster exercised a most momentous effect. Revolutionary Baptism sank, in the "Battenburg faction," to ordinary brigandage, upon which the rejection of infant baptism was only able to confer with great difficulty the faint light of a religious principle. Battenburg, for some time burgomaster of Steenwyk, organised the rising of "the little man" with the watchword "Extermination of the godless," but, in 1537, he was imprisoned and executed in the county of Artois. **John David Joris**, a glass-painter of Delft (born at Bruges or Ghent), who, since 1536, had for a considerable time taken upon himself the part of leader in wide Baptist circles,—a man who all his life was unable to master the difference

---

[1] Cornelius in ABA XI 51 ff.

between highly unnatural, ecstatico-mystical piety and the mazes of unbridled sensuality,—sent his adherents (even his own mother) to the heroic death of martyrs: he himself, with long-headed adroitness, preferred to disappear at the right moment, and withdrew to Bâle, where (from 1544), under the name of John of Bruges, he played the ecclesiastically blameless Zwinglian for a year, but at the same time, with the aid of numerous devotional tracts,[1] kept his "Jorists" or "Davidians" to the belief in his Messiahship and the opening up of an antinomistically sensual Kingdom of God. Corresponding to the three ages of the world—during the second of which Christ Jesus rules (whose kingdom is destroyed by the King of Babylon, the Pope), while Christ David (Joris) builds the eternal house in the third and last,—there are three purifications and a triple birth. In the Kingdom of Christ David the old laws of marriage are abolished, the perfect are no longer bound by these restrictions, and need only practise prudence and moderation, in order to avoid offence to the weak and their own danger.[2] Certainly Joris persistently disowned (in Arnold II 290 ff.) all that was charged against him in his doctrine, but the counter-proof, which Ubbo Emmius has produced from his letters and writings, cannot be confuted.[3] It was not until some time after his death (1556) that Bâle recognised that it had so long had the arch-heretic in its midst, and then inflicted the punishment of a heretic upon his corpse.

After the catastrophe at Münster, when Low German, Dutch, and English Baptism broke up into parties of the most different kind (the Münsterites and Battenburgers, who favoured violent and revolutionary measures, the Melchiorites and Ubbonites, named after Ubbo Philips, who were opposed to violence as well as the establishment of polygamy), it had been Joris who, at the meeting at Bocholt (August, 1536), had brought about a kind of agreement between the parties, without, however, overcoming all opposition: the points of difference had been declared unessential in comparison with the doctrines they held in common.[4] But, in the meantime, a reorganiser had arisen for the Baptists in the person of **Menno Simonis,** who knew how to unite the community of the Saints in a simply practical Christianity, eliminated the fanatical, revolutionary and antinomistic elements, and thereby assured the continued existence of the community. Born at Witmarsum in Friesland in 1492, holding the office of a Catholic priest, incited by the martyrdom of an Anabaptist to serious study of the Scriptures, he had been (since 1532) introduced to the circle of the Melchiorites, but continued to hold his priestly office.[5] It was not until January 12th, 1536, that he resigned it; after this, he was chosen elder by the most moderate and cautious party, the Ubbonites: in this capacity, by his

---

[1] See a list of them in NIPPOLD ZhTh 1863, 163 ff.; 1864, 557 ff.; 1868, 475 ff.

[2] For the Adamitic practices of his adherents cp. the Confessions of 1538 in ZhTh 1863, p. 91 ff.

[3] *Grondelike onderrichtinge van de leere ende den geest des Hoofketters D. Joris.* Middelburgh, 1599. Cp. ZhTh 1864, 649 ff.; 1868, 580 ff.

[4] ZhTh 1863, 52 ff.

[5] The polemic against John of Leyden, frequently attributed to him and alleged to have been composed by him in 1535, while he still held his Catholic office, but of which we know of no impression previous to 1627, is rightly disavowed on his behalf by Sepp.

personality, his visitations, and popular tracts, he soon obtained a decisive influence,[1] and especially endeavoured also to convince the authorities, that his communities had nothing in common with those of Münster. In 1542, having been banished from West Friesland by an imperial proclamation, he found room for his organising activity in East Friesland (Emden), then in the district ot Cologne, the Baltic provinces (Wismar), and lastly in Holstein (Wüstenfeld by Oldesloe). He successfully protected his communities from the invasion of anti-Trinitarianism. At his death in 1559, he left behind him an organised community of quiet, industrious people, averse to all idea of disturbance, although certainly, in its attitude towards the Reformation, it was characteristically separated from it in its efforts to pick out a community of saints by the exercise of excommunication, in its avoidance of the world as shown in dress and manner of life, in its judgment of the state *régime* as something belonging to the world (hence, the members of the community were not allowed to serve in war, to hold positions of authority, nor to take the oath), as well as in the thoroughly medieval stamp of its doctrine of salvation.

The bold schemes of **Jürgen Wullenwever** of Lübeck have recently been brought into closer connection with the course of events in Münster. Here also the victory of the Reformation was followed by victories of the democratic party over the aristocratic constitution and the rise of the triumvirate composed of Wullenwever, John Oldendorp and Mark Meyer, when foolhardy plans were formed of contesting, on behalf of Lübeck, the right of conferring the crown of Denmark and Sweden, and of restoring the power of the Hanseatic Union throughout Scandinavia. It has been affirmed that only Wullenwever's fall (1535, he died 1537) frustrated the victory of Baptism throughout the entire North. But the evidence in favour of any direct part played by Baptism in that episode in the history of Lübeck is decidedly weak: partly "confessions" subsequently extorted by the rack, partly the fact that Wullenwever sought **political** connection with the democracy of Münster. Herman Bonnus, the excellent Lutheran superintendent of the city, removed from office by Wullenwever, only fell a victim to his adherence to the old aristocratic constitution of the Council, and, in his bold address "to the irregular council," only referred the people of Lübeck to Münster, in order to remind them of the misfortunes that the overthrow of the constitution brings upon a city.[2] Certainly a victory of democratic principles in the North would have been indirectly a decided advancement of the cause of the Baptists; but it cannot be proved that a change "according to the views of the Anabaptists" had been planned in Lübeck.[3] Democratic agitations were for a long time buried in Wullenwever's grave; and, in like manner, the type for the development of the Lutheran churches in the North was for a long time fixed.

---

[1] Cp. Micronius's complaint about the *magna vis librorum Mennonis*, CR 45, 68.

[2] In SPIEGEL, *H. Bonnus*, ed. 2, Götting. 1892, p. 154.

[3] JANSSEN, III 312.

5. The Schmalkaldic Articles and the Truce of Frankfort.

Sources: Nuntiaturberichte, Vols. I and II. Gotha, 1892. Strassb. pol. Corr. II. HTb X 465 ff.
Literature: KOLDE in RE XIII, 591 ff. BAUMGARTEN III 287 ff.; the same, in ZGW VI 281 ff. ZÖPFFEL in RE XII 321 ff. VIRCK in ZKG XIII 487 ff.

In the meanwhile, Clement VII had died (in 1534); his successor, Alexander Farnese (born 1468), elevated by a combination of the Italian and French parties to the Holy See, after previous vain attempts, under the title of **Paul III,** had already declared in conclave that the summoning of a Council was necessary, and expressed his conviction that it would only be possible to put down heresy by a salutary reformation of the Church. The Emperor's power had been considerably enhanced by his personally conducted and victorious campaign against the ruler of Algiers and Tunis, Khaireddin Barbarossa (1535); his return through Italy was a triumphal procession, and, conscious of his power, he now energetically demanded the Council. The Pope had already sent his nuncio, Peter Paul Vergerio, to Germany, to announce to the German States his decision to summon a Council, but in an **Italian** city (Mantua). Paul knew, however, that the Germans would never accept such a Council, especially as he demanded, as a preliminary condition, the submission in advance of the Protestants to his authority and the renunciation of their doctrines. This embassy met with a very different reception in the Catholic States: the nuncio, on his journey, had a conference with Luther and Bugenhagen at Wittenberg (November 1535), at which Luther adopted a tone of defiant assurance, while at the same time he declared his readiness to appear at a Council.[1] The Elector of Saxony refused to give the nuncio a definite answer. But the Emperor's position soon changed for the worse owing to a fresh outbreak of hostilities with France about the Duchy of Milan: and, when Paul III., on June 4th, 1536, actually convoked the Council for the 23rd of May, 1537, at Mantua, the possibility of this resolution being carried out was removed to the distant future by the general political situation. Nevertheless, Emperor and Pope sent their ambassadors to Germany, to induce the Protestants also to send representatives to the Council. Consequently, the Evangelicals were confronted by the question what attitude they should adopt.

---

[1] Nuntiaturberichte I 540 ff. KÖSTLIN II² 378 ff.

While the Elector of Saxony wished from the outset to decline taking part in it (CR III 99 ff.), the theologians and jurists advised him not to refuse point-blank, but to wait and see whether they would be summoned as heretics or invited like the other States (CR III 119 ff.) John Frederick's adventurous scheme of getting Luther "and his auxiliary bishops and ecclesiastics" to convoke "a common, free Christian Council" as a counter-council (CR III 141), was dropped on the protest of the theologians (III 127); in return, the latter strengthened the Elector's conscience in the matter of the resistance that would be more or less necessary, in case the papal Council should attempt to proceed against the Evangelicals with unjust demands. Further, at the bidding of the Elector, Luther had to draw up certain articles, which were first laid before a meeting of Saxon theologians to sign and subsequently taken to Schmalkalden to the meeting of the league (the so-called **Schmalkaldic Articles**)[1] in view of their being presented to the Council.

The result of the Elector's commission was to make it a matter for reflection "on what articles and points it might be possible to yield or give way for the sake of peace and harmony or not." (Burkhardt, *Luther's Briefwechsel*, p. 271.) Luther, accordingly, gives prominence in the first part to the "high articles of the divine Majesty," which would be acknowledged without dispute by both parties: he then introduces the articles, which, according to him, are the *ceterum censeo* of Protestantism in contrast to Rome: the articles, which would cause a difference of opinion at the Council, as the Pope and his followers would condemn them and would not give way in the least in regard to them: (1) Christ alone is the Redeemer and *sola fide*: "it is impossible to give up this article or make concessions, should Heaven and earth fall, on this article depends all that is opposed to the Pope, the devil, and the world in our life and doctrine; (2) the rejection of the "dragon-tail" of the mass with its "filth," purgatory, pilgrimages, brotherhoods, relics, indulgences, invocation of saints; (3) the abolition of convents and monasteries, or their conversion into schools; (4) the rejection of the *ius divinum* of the Papacy. A third part treats of points or articles, which "we desire to discuss with learned and sensible men or amongst ourselves," consequently, points of doctrine, in regard to which the hope is firmly entertained that at least the sensible men of the Romish party will listen to reason; sin, law, confession, sacraments, marriage of priests, and the like. It was not that Luther was ready to admit his doctrine to be open to dispute in these points, but he thought that concessions in regard to them might possibly be obtained from the opposite party. However, nothing would have been gained by such concessions, as Rome would never have given way in regard to the Articles

[1] EA 25² 163 ff. Facsimile of the autograph copy, published by ZANGEMEISTER, Heidelberg, 1883; edition by MARHEINECKE, Berlin, 1817. BERTRAM-RIEDERER, *Gesch. des symbolischen Anhangs der schmalkald. Art.* Altdorf, 1770. KÖLLNER, *Symbolik*, 1 439 ff. PLITT, *de auctoritate artic. Smal. symbolica*, 1862.

of Part II. At the beginning of 1537, the theologians subscribed these articles at Wittenberg. Melanchthon gave utterance to the optimistic remark that, if the Pope were willing to allow free course to the Gospel, his superiority to the Bishops *iure humano* might well be admitted for the sake of peace. Luther had originally wished to word the article dealing with the Eucharist (EA 25^2, 197) according to the text of the Wittenberg Concord (see p. 124), but, persuaded by Bugenhagen, formulated it more sharply in conformity to his turn of doctrine. Melanchthon, who had raised no objection to this article at Wittenberg, then had recourse to the Landgrave at Schmalkalden and advised him to reject Luther's articles and to appeal to the fact that the CA and the Wittenberg Concord had been accepted.[1]

On the 9th of February, 1537, the Convention met at Schmalkalden. On the 15th, the imperial vice-chancellor Held[2] addressed the members of the league and demanded, in his master's name, that they should attend the Council, for which they had always clamoured, in considerable numbers, declaring that no State, which had accepted the "recess" of the Augsburg diet, would now be justified in leaving the Catholic Church. After a few days the Protestants replied: that a council was not to be thought of in the present political situation; that they felt bound to reject the idea of a council that was to be summoned in an Italian city, above all a council, at which the impenitent papacy, which still persisted in its abominations, was to be judge; that they were obliged to maintain the Peace of Nuremburg extended to all the States, which had since then joined them. The papal nuncio, Van der Vorst (Vorstius), who had in the meantime appeared at Schmalkalden, was treated by John Frederick with affected disregard.[3] In regard to the articles drawn up by Luther, Melanchthon's secret advice had been successful; they were not officially discussed at all; instead, those concerned testified their agreement to the CA and the Apology, but, while Luther was dangerously ill, Melanchthon

---

[1] Strassb. pol. Corresp. II 430. Cp. CR III 292, 370 ff. KOLDE in StKr, 1894, p. 157 ff.

[2] The Emperor had given him two sets of instructions to suit the condition of affairs: in the most extreme case, it was left to his discretion, in accordance with his secret instructions, to offer the Protestants an agreement with the Emperor and a German national assembly [Assemblée nationale] (LANZ II 268 f.); his official instructions in regard to the Protestants were, however, quite different. Cp. BAUMGARTEN III 284 f. G. HEIDE in HpBl 102, 713 ff. Nuntiaturberichte II 29 ff.

[3] Strassb. pol. Corr. II 424. Nuntiaturberichte II 128. BAUMGARTEN III 298. Cp. Melanchthon's brief but sharp criticism: that the two ambassadors were treated *sane* φορτικῶς. CR. III 297.

composed the *Tractatus de potestate et primatu Papae* (and *de potestate et iurisdictione Episcoporum*), under the influence of the bluntly anti-papal frame of mind of the States, in a much more incisive style than usual. The States accepted **this tractate** and had it subscribed by the theologians present, together with the CA and Apology (CR III 286 f.).

Luther's articles were then submitted to the theologians by Bugenhagen, but, as Bucer and his friends declined to subscribe (CR III 371), were not officially accepted: the greater part of them only subscribed in their private capacity. All the theologians gave their assent to the CA and the Wittenberg Concord. Luther, who subsequently (in 1538) published his articles as "articles which would have been delivered to the Council at Mantua," does not seem to have ever rightly understood how it had fared with his work during his illness: he says (EA 25² 169) that they were "accepted, unanimously acknowledged and decided upon by our party." This (erroneous) assertion has essentially contributed to the fact that his articles have been reckoned (since 1544)[1] amongst the symbols of the Lutheran Church as "Schmalkaldic." (The official Latin text of the Book of Concord, a version which frequently destroys the spirit of the original, is by **Selnecker**, 1579.)

After the refusal of the imperial requests by the Protestants at Schmalkalden, Held did his utmost to unite the Catholic princes of Germany in a **league** against the Schmalkaldic. After numerous partly vain attempts he succeeded in getting a plan of alliance for this "defensive league" drawn up at Spires in March, 1538, which was subscribed at Nuremberg in the following June. Besides the Emperor and Ferdinand, only Bavaria, George of Saxony, the Dukes Eric and Henry of Brunswick, Albert of Mainz (but only for Madgeburg and Halberstadt) and the Archbishop of Salzburg took part in it—a considerable number of the Catholic princes, especially those on the Rhine, would have nothing to do with the league, which consequently could only combine to act on the "defensive," and could not, on its part, think of taking the offensive. The position of the Schmalkaldeners was certainly not improved by the cessation of hostilities between the Emperor and France, which was brought about by the mediation of the Pope at Nice on the 17th of July, and the subsequent meeting of the two princes at Aigues-mortes,—the prospects of their being able to fall back on France thereby disappeared. But Charles knew best, how little reliance could be placed on the new reconciliation and what damage his political power had suffered in consequence of the last war with

---

[1] NEUDECKER, *Urkunden*, p. 689.

France; in addition, all his strength had to be called out against the Turks. He accordingly resolved to enter upon the path of **friendly negotiations** with the Protestants, in order at least to calm people's minds in Germany and to secure a free hand for the struggle against the Turks. The Elector, **Joachim II.** of Brandenburg, who still hesitated between Catholicism and Evangelicalism, and **Louis,** Count of the Palatinate, undertook the part of mediators; the Archbishop of Lund received extensive powers to pave the way for negotiations with the Schmalkaldeners. The result was that, on the 19th of April, 1539, a fresh "**truce**"[1] was agreed to at **Frankfort,** by which the Protestants obtained, not indeed a distinct peace and recognition, but a truce for fifteen months,—subsequently reduced, with the consent of both parties, to six—the suspension of all processes pending in the Court of Judicature and the agreement that representatives of both parties should assemble for a religious discussion on behalf of a "laudable Christian union." Charles, however, never ratified this truce: he regarded it only as a means to gain time.

In the meantime, under pressure from the Emperor, the Council was actually convoked at **Vicenza** for the 1st of May, 1538, in order once again to be postponed indefinitely by pointing to the opposition of the Protestants and the quarrel between the Emperor and France. It was not until the meeting at Lucca (1541) that Charles succeeded in getting the Council convoked at **Trent** for the 22nd of May, 1542; it was actually opened, but, in view of the war between Charles and Francis I., so poorly attended, that Paul again adjourned it (to the 6th of July, 1543).

6. Fresh Victories of the Reformation.

Literature : K. W. HERING, *Gesch. der im Markgrafenthum Meissen .... erfolgten Reformation.* Grossenhain, 1839. HOFMANN, *Ref. Hist. der Stadt Leipzig,* 1739. GRETSCHEL, *Kirchl. Zustände Leipzigs,* 1839. SEIFERT, *Ref. in Leipzig,* 1883; the same, *Joh. Pfeffinger,* Leipz. 1888. DIBELIUS, *Einf. der Ref. in Dresden,* 1889. MÜLLER, *Gesch. d. Ref. in d. M. Brandenburg.* Berlin, 1839. HEIDEMANN, *die Ref. in d. M. Brandenburg.* Berlin, 1889. UHLHORN, *A. Corvinus.* Halle, 1892. O. MEJER, *Zum Kirchenrecht des Ref.-Jhs.* Hann. 1891. SCHRÖDER, *Ev. Mecklenburg.* I. Rost, 1788.

At this period the evangelical party obtained considerable accessions, in the shape of fresh territories. In Albertine Saxony, the old, high-minded Duke **George,** who, although by no means insensible of the abuses of the Church, had

---

[1] HORTLEDER (see p. 6), I 126 ff. Strassb. pol. Corr. II 546 ff.

once and for all declared himself emphatically against the Reformation of Luther, the refractory monk, was fated to witness the unexpected death of the heir to the throne, the good Catholic **John**, in 1537, and the public declaration by his widow Elizabeth, the Landgrave's sister, of her adherence to the principles of the Reformation. There now only remained to him his weak-minded son Frederick, whom he provided with a wife (1539) in the hope of his having children, but he suddenly died four weeks afterwards. The Reformation was now only waiting for his own death, in order to invade his country. His brother **Henry** had already opened his little territory (including the town of Freiberg) to the new doctrines and had joined the Schmalkaldic league. George now vainly endeavoured to exclude him from the government or, at any rate, to make him abandon the league by the offer of all kinds of conditions and to bind him firmly to the Catholic cause: he even had the idea of handing over his country by will to the Habsburg Ferdinand. The idea of conciliatory ecclesiastical reforms was also mooted, for which the Erasmian, **George Witzel**, who had returned from the evangelical ministry to the Catholic Church, was to plead, and by which evangelically disposed minds were to be appeased.[1] George died on the 17th of April, 1539; his brother hastened to take possession of the country and, supported by John Frederick and his theologians, rapidly spread the Reformation throughout the land by means of a visitation of the Churches, without paying any heed to the half-hearted reforms now offered by the Bishop of Meissen (Misnia).

Immediately afterwards, the revolution was also carried out in the March of **Brandenburg**. **Joachim I.**, one of the most influential and important princes of the empire, had strenuously opposed the Reformation until his death in 1535. However, he had not been able to suppress completely the numerous evangelical movements in his country: one of his three established bishops, Matthias von Jagow, of Brandenburg (since 1526), not only discontinued the persecution of the Lutherans, but inclined more and more to reformatory views. But his wife Elizabeth,[2] sister of Christian II. of Denmark, had been early won over to Luther's doctrines through the influence of her relatives. and secretly had the Sacrament administered to her at Easter, 1527, by a Lutheran minister: this inflamed the wrath of her husband, who gave her a certain time to reflect, at the expiration of which she was to be imprisoned in one of his castles. On the 24th of March, 1528, she fled from Berlin to Electoral Saxony, where she was able to live in the castle of Lichtenberg unmolested in her belief and in constant intercourse with Luther. From that time Joachim regarded Luther as the destroyer of his conjugal happiness: and when the latter interfered with his relation to a lawful wife, who had been turned from her husband by him with warnings of conscience, he was still more annoyed.[3] After having loyally supported the policy of the Habsburgs and also (at Halle, 1533) concluded an alliance (with George of Saxony, Albert of Mainz, and the Dukes Eric and Henry of Brunswick, for the purpose of upholding the old doctrine), into which his sons were obliged to enter, he further bound them by his will, " at all times to continue steadfast and unchanged in the old Christian faith, religion,

---

[1] Leipziger Religionsgespräch, January 2nd, 1539; *Literature* in RE XVIII 247. CR IV 623 ff. LENZ, *Briefw. Landg. Philipps mit Butzer*, I 63 ff.
[2] RIEDEL in ZPGLK II. 90 ff.
[3] ZIMMERMANN in ZPGLK XX 310 ff. KOLDE, *Anal. Luth.* 106 ff.

ceremonies, and obedience to the Christian Church"; at the same time, contrary to the family-statute, he bestowed the New-March upon the younger, John, in order to bind him in this manner to the Catholic faith and the alliance of Halle. Nevertheless, after his father's death (June 11th, 1535), he broke from the alliance, allowed perfect freedom to evangelical preaching, and in 1537 became a member of the Schmalkaldic league. **Joachim II.**, on the other hand, had been hesitating for four years before he came to a decision. The Landgrave Philip at once endeavoured to acquire an influence over him and advised him to allow reformatory preaching to make its own way by observing neutrality towards it. Joachim drew up for himself, in accordance with his personal inclinations, his own programme of reformation: a mean between Wittenberg and Rome, a combination of evangelical doctrine with an episcopal constitution and full Catholic ceremonial presented itself to him under an alluring aspect, in which partly political considerations and partly his fondness for show and elegance exercised their influence. In the meantime, he behaved as a Catholic prince, who only showed much indulgence to the *de facto* irruption of Lutheran preaching. However, in the spring of 1538, Melanchthon was summoned to Berlin, to give his opinion upon a plan of reformation which had been handed to the princes; this scheme was again abandoned for a time, as Joachim offered his services as agent for the Emperor's negotiations for reunion which were now commencing. After his return from Frankfort (p. 135) he found that the Lutheran movement had grown mightily in the country; the death of his father-in-law, Duke George, relieved him of burdensome obligations; accordingly, in the summer of 1539, he summoned a commission of theologians to draw up an ecclesiastical ordinance; George Witzel (p. 136) sat by the side of the Lutherans Stratner and Buchholzer: Melanchthon was summoned for the second time, and assisted in the discussion of the ordinance and the further steps to be taken. On the 1st of November, Joachim—without his wife, who remained a Catholic[1]—received the communion *sub utraque* from the hand of the Bishop of Brandenburg at Spandau: this was the signal for the public conversion of the whole country: the city of Berlin followed suit on the 2nd.[2] The ordinance was now again laid before the Wittenberg theologians for examination. Luther was ready to put up with much in the matter of ceremonial, if only the article of justification were secured; in March, 1540, the diet accepted the ritual, which occupies a position of its own amongst the Lutheran rituals with its preservation of the established bishops and its worship inclining to Catholicism. Joachim succeeded in inducing the Emperor to recognise his ordinance, on condition that he would submit to any future resolutions of diet or council. But, in this case also, experience soon showed that episcopal hierarchy was not compatible with the idea of a national church of the Lutheran profession. Not only did the Bishops of Havelberg and Lebus simply reject the ordinance and thereby compel the Elector to look for another ecclesiastical administration, but conflicts still continued between the Lutheran Bishop of Brandenburg and his clergy, in the course of which the latter appealed from the "tyranny" of the bishop to the Elector. Thus, here also (1543) a consistorial hierarchy was established: superintendents-general appointed by the princes took over the functions

---

[1] She was the daughter of Sigismund, King of Poland, and his second wife
[2] The statements of FREGE in ZhTh 7. 4. 149 are erroneous.

properly reserved for the bishops, as the Elector had already (1540 appointed Stratner his superintendent-general for the visitation of the country and originally had not even provided an episcopal commissioner. Thus, the bishops were practically pushed aside. On the death of the Bishop of Brandenburg (1545), the post was again filled, but only as a sinecure; at Havelberg, the Elector filled the episcopal see with a prince of the house (1548) and thereby introduced Protestantism, although a Catholic party still maintained itself in the cathedral-chapter until 1561; at Lebus he was obliged to allow the election of a Catholic bishop again for political reasons, but when the see fell vacant for the second time in 1554, in this case also he secured the election of a prince; the chapter then gradually died out.

In the Archbishopric of Magdeburg and the bishopric of Halberstadt, again, Archbishop **Albert** was unable in the long run to check the progress of the Reformation. Always in need of money, he was obliged to depend upon the goodwill of the States of the country and found himself obliged to make one concession after another. Thus, for instance, it became possible for Justus Jonas to introduce the Reformation at Halle (1541). Joachim's sister **Elizabeth**, on the advice of Antony Corvinus, while acting as regent during the minority of her son, Eric the younger, made use of the opportunity to provide the district of Calenberg and Göttingen with an excellent church ordinance (**Richter** I 362 ff.) and to carry out the Reformation (at least externally) by means of visitations.

In **Mecklenburg**, also, Luther's doctrines made visible progress. Its rulers were the brothers, the evangelical Duke Henry and the Catholic Duke Albert; the bishopric of Schwerin had fallen to Magnus, the son of the former, while he was still under age (1516), and he had entered upon its "administration" in 1532. With 1539 commences the calling of evangelically disposed clergy into the country and the *de facto* organisation of the church in accordance with the Lutheran model, although it was the death of Albert (1547) that first formally threw the country open to Lutheranism.

The Reformation, just about this time, also made considerable progress in the most advanced outpost of the empire—in **Livonia**. Here, the States with their German population, in spite of the opposition of the Master of the Order, Walter of Plettenberg (died 1535) and the prelates (the Archbishop of Riga and the Bishops of Dorpat and Oesel), had shown themselves at an early date favourably disposed to the Reformation; Riga in particular, in consequence of the summoning of **John Brismann** (1527) had attained to a settled establishment of an evangelical church system, and, as early as 1535, had sought to join the Schmalkaldic League. But now, Duke Albert of Prussia had succeeded (in 1529) in promoting his brother William to be coadjutor of the Archbishop of Riga; and thus (in 1539) the Roman Catholic metropolis of the East came into evangelical hands. Albert wanted to obtain for his brother the papal ratification in due form; he consulted Luther on the matter, but he energetically warned him against "worshipping the devil at Rome," "come what might" (de Wette V 308). Notwithstanding, Albert made an attempt to get his brother to accept the "mummery," but without success at Rome. But anyhow, under the new Archbishop, the Reformation was now able to spread, unhindered and victorious.

CHAPTER SIXTH.

The weakening of the League and the imperial policy of Reunion.

1. The religious discussions of Worms and Ratisbon.

Sources and *Literature:* WALCH, XVII 389 ff.; CR IV; ROEDER, *de Colloquio Wormatiensi.* Nürnb., 1744. BRETSCHNEIDER in ZhTh 2, 283 ff. MOSES, *die Religionsverhandlungen zu Hagenau und Worms.* Jena, 1889. VETTER, *die Religionsverhandlungen auf dem Reichstage zu Regensburg.* Jena, 1889. PASTOR, *die kirchlichen Reunionsbestrebungen.* Freib. i. Br., 1879. BRIEGER, Art. *Gropper* in Ersch und Gruber. HERGANG, *das Religionsgespräch zu Regensburg.* Cassel, 1858. DITTRICH, *Miscellanea Ratisbon. 1541.* Braunsb., 1892. BRIEGER, *Contarini und das Regensb. Conc.-Werk.* Gotha, 1870. L. PASTOR, *die Corresp. d. Card. Contarini, 1541,* in JGG I 321 ff., 473 ff. DITTRICH, *die Nuntiaturber. Morones, 1541,* in JGG IV 395 ff., 618 ff.; the same, in *Quellen und Forschungen aus dem Gebiet d. Gesch.,* I 1. Paderb., 1892 (add Friedensburg in GGA, 1892, No. 24. H. Baumgarten in DLZ, 1892, No. 49); the same, *Regesten und Briefe des Card. G. Contarini.* Braunsb., 1881 f. SPIEGEL in ZhTh 42, 36 ff.

Impressed by the greatly increased power of the Protestants, Charles attempted to come to an agreement with them by the path of **religious discussion**.[1] The meeting, which was at first convoked at Spires (HORTLEDER I 157), assembled in June, 1540, at **Hagenau**, under the presidency of Ferdinand. Melanchthon was obliged to be absent, since he was taken very ill on his journey at Weimar, having been greatly upset by the bigamy of the Landgrave Philip (see below); Cruciger was obliged to take his place. But, almost at the outset, the meeting was so hopelessly at variance as to the manner in which the negotiations should be carried on, that the majority of the Protestant theologians left before the end of the day: it was seen to be necessary to break off the unsatisfactory negotiations and to defer them till an assembly at **Worms** in the autumn. Eleven deputies attended

---

[1] He thereby fell back upon a proposal that had already been made (1538) by the Elector Joachim II. to Ferdinand. Cp. Nuntiaturberichte II 294 f. The Wittenberg theologians, in February, 1540, had formulated their position, as a matter of principle, in regard to all such negotiations: see de Wette V 260 ff.

from each party, amongst them Melanchthon, Bucer and Calvin on the one side, and on the other Eck, Cochleus and Gropper.[1] The president of the meeting was Granvella, the imperial councillor. In spite of the great courtesy with which the latter treated the Protestants—even going so far as to behave with striking impoliteness towards Campeggi, the papal legate (CR III 1125)—here also the discussion was uselessly protracted by petty disputes in regard to formalities, since, considering the uncertainty of some Catholic votes, it was necessary to prevent any decision by voting. At last, on the 14th of January, 1541, Eck and Melanchthon commenced the disputation on the basis of the CA, during which the former at once pointed out the deviations of the edition of 1540 from the *editio princeps* (CR IV 33 ff.); after the question of original sin had been debated for four days, and a form of compromise devised, an imperial decree broke off the negotiations and ordered their resumption at the diet at **Ratisbon**, which was opened in the presence of the Emperor on the 5th of April, 1541. The collocutors nominated were Julius von Pflug, Gropper, Eck, Melanchthon, Bucer, and Pistorius of Hesse; Frederick the count-palatine and Granvella undertook the presidency. The noble Cardinal **Gasparo** (Caspar) **Contarini** appeared at the diet as papal legate—a man who was regarded in Italy as the representative of reformed ecclesiastical ideas. Of the Catholic collocutors Gropper and Pflug were also the most moderate representatives of Catholic principles that could have been found. The CA was not to be again made the basis of discussion on this occasion, but a secretly prepared scheme of agreement (*liber Ratisbonensis*).[2] This document was the result of secret discussions,[3] for which Granvella and the Landgrave Philip had made arrangements while still at Worms, where Bucer and Capito had repeatedly conferred with Gropper and Granvella's secretary Gerard Veltwyck from December 15th, 1540, and had discussed certain articles of compromise prepared by Gropper. These were then sent by the agency of the Landgrave to Joachim II., that he might confidentially submit the anonymous articles to Luther's consideration. The latter had replied, that certainly the authors' intention was good, but "the proposals were impossible," such as the Curia could not accept, and which also

---

[1] W. Schwarz in JGG 7, 392 ff., 594 ff.
[2] For the original draft see Lenz III 31 ff. CR IV 190 ff.
[3] CR IV 578 ff. Lenz I 271 ff.

would fail to satisfy the evangelical party in many points (de Wette VI 281 f.). Without attempting to amend the articles, he had again presented them to the Elector. In spite of this rejection, an attempt was now made with this book, to Eck's indignation: the negotiations began on the 27th of April.

The Catholic collocutors, before the negotiations commenced, visited Contarini every day to consult with him. After the first four articles (*de conditione hominis, de libero arbitrio, de causa peccati* and *de originali peccato*) had been lightly passed over, a serious dispute began about the fifth article *de iustificatione*. Eck, and also Melanchthon, decidedly rejected the diffuse and ambiguous document. The fresh formularies attempted by Eck and Contarini, as well as Melanchthon, were also rejected; finally, on the 2nd of May, a draft drawn up on the Catholic side was so greatly altered by Melanchthon that the evangelical party also was able to assent to it,—a draft of which certainly Gropper was the author, but in which the superiority of justification by faith and the exclusion of *meritum* was asserted. A distinction was made between *iustitia imputata* and *iustitia inhaerens;* we obtain the former by faith, which is understood not only as belief in all divine doctrines, but also, evangelically, as *fiducia propter promissionem Dei;* and this justification by faith is at the same time the commencement of *iustitia inhaerens*, as the faith that justifies is at the same time *fides efficax per charitatem*. The Christian is consequently *iustus* in a two-fold sense: *iustus reputatus* by faith and grace, and actually just for his just works. But, as the latter justice is always imperfect, the Christian's certainty of salvation always rests only on the former, on the *iustitia Christi nobis donata*. But, at the same time, the divine reward of the *iustitia inhaerens* of those who advance in good is assured, both in this life and in the next. In conclusion, the doctrine *sola fide iustificamur* is approved, on the supposition that the doctrine of penitence and good works always remains closely connected with it. Granvella, highly pleased, himself committed to paper the article thus happily agreed upon: only Eck gave an unwilling assent.

Contarini, well satisfied, sent the article to Rome, with the assurance that it could be interpreted in good Catholic fashion, but, on the 27th of May, it was rejected in the consistory: the omission of the idea of *meritum* had given special offence. On the other hand, John Frederick at once demanded Luther's opinion of it. The latter characterised the formula as a "patched up thing," which he could only accept, if the opposite party admitted that their teaching had hitherto been at variance with what was here intended, and would also, in the following articles, draw the right practical conclusions from the doctrine of justification by faith (de Wette V 353 f.). Thereupon, the Elector instructed Melanchthon that this article should only be considered as accepted on condition

---

[1] Cp. DITTRICH in JGG XIII 196.

of an agreement in regard to those that followed, and warned him against further concessions.

Thus Rome and Wittenberg had decided against the laborious work of arrangement. Yet it indicates an important moment for the inner development of Catholicism: for it proves the existence of a Catholic under-current, which was able at least to approximate to the idea of faith and the certainty of salvation, and it was of momentous importance that this tendency was at once rejected from Rome. But Contarini's share in it and the credit due to him have been overrated. For neither was he the father of that formula of agreement, nor did he correctly reproduce it. His famous tractate *De iustificatione* (1541) certainly takes the twofold justification into account, but teaches that *iustificatio nihil aliud est quam iustum fieri* **ac propterea** *etiam haberi iustum*, consequently harking back in the main to the doctrine of St. Thomas: according to him the actual justification precedes the declaration that a person is just in the forgiveness of sins.[1]

Articles 6-8 (*de ecclesia, de nota verbi, de poenitentia*) were subsequently accepted with slight alterations, the discussion of Article 9 (*de auctoritate ecclesiae*) suspended for a time owing to serious differences: but in regard to 10-13 (the Sacraments, ordination, baptism, confirmation) some sort of an agreement was arrived at. Article 14, however (on the Eucharist) led to a violent controversy, in which the Catholic party under Contarini's influence—Eck had fallen ill—fought for the direct attestation of transubstantiation with its practical consequences, while, on the other hand, Melanchthon, who was greatly troubled by Bucer's unlimited concessions, boldly held out against all allurements and intimidation: on this the laborious work of reconciliation was shattered. The conflict raged again round Article 15 (Absolution), 19 (*de hierarchico ordine*), 20 (Mass), 21 (the marriage of priests). On the 22nd of May, the discussion of the book was over, but the schemes of reunion were also wrecked.

The Emperor now thought of proclaiming at least the articles as to which an agreement had been come to as a common doctrine for the Empire, and of demanding, in regard to the rest, mutual forbearance until the meeting of the Council (Scheme of Toleration). Contarini, however, made a decided protest, fearing that Catholicism in Germany would be thereby greatly imperilled. Then the Emperor made the desperate attempt, **to win Luther himself over to his scheme.** Apparently in the name of the Elector of Brandenburg and the Margrave George, but in reality by order

---

[1] Against BRIEGER and WEIZSÄCKER (RE 3, 350) cp. SEEBERG in ZkW X 657 ff.

of the Emperor, princes John and George of Anhalt, accompanied
by a councillor and the theologian Alesius, journeyed to Wittenberg and transmitted their proposal. Luther replied (Burkhardt,
385; de Wette V 366) that he regarded the imperial attempt at
an arrangement as entirely impracticable; the agreement in regard
to the first articles could not be seriously meant, otherwise
there would also have been unanimity as to its logical
results and practical ecclesiastical questions. However, if only
the Emperor would provide for preachers who should preach the
articles agreed upon in Catholic countries, then further agreement would follow of itself. Thus the scheme of toleration also
fell through: in addition to this, the tension of parties at Worms
itself had continually grown more acute. After protracted negotiations, the Emperor and the States agreed upon a "recess," which
the Protestants accepted on the basis of an imperial declaration
that was granted them: the results of the colloquy were to be laid
before a universal or national council that was to be summoned,
and eventually the Emperor would convoke a new diet within
eighteen months: until then the Protestants were to abide by the
articles agreed upon, while the Catholic prelates were to press on
the reform of their clergy. The peace of Nuremberg was renewed,
and also the Augsburg "recess" (CR IV 612 ff.). But the declaration also guaranteed the Protestants that their ecclesiastical
possessions should be protected, that Protestant assessors should
be admitted at the Court of Judicature, and that the "recess" of
Augsburg should not be applied to religious matters: the Christian
reformation of monasteries and the maintenance of churches and
schools from church properties was granted them (CR IV 623 ff.).
But, however favourable this result was, and however well-disposed
the Emperor had shown himself, he had notwithstanding prepared
a severe blow for the cause of the Protestants: not only had he
drawn the Elector Joachim from the common cause and secured
his services in the interest of his policy, but he had also separated
the Landgrave Philip (and his son-in-law, Duke Maurice) from his
allies and bound him to himself by a pact. This had only been
rendered possible by Philip's melancholy matrimonial affair.

2. Weakening of the Schmalkaldic League by Philip's Bigamy.

Literature: HEPPE in ZhTh 22, 263 ff. STROBEL, *Beiträge zur Lit. des 16 Jhs.* II 395 ff. VON ROMMEL, *Gesch. von Hessen* IV 230 ff. HASSENKAMP, *KG Hessens* I. M. LENZ, *Briefwechsel Landgr. Philipps mit Bucer* I and II. StKr 1891, p. 564 ff. KOLDEWEY in StKr 1884, 553 ff. *Argumenta Buceri pro et contra:* edited by L(öwenstein). Kassel 1878.

The Landgrave Philip, who had married the daughter of Duke George, by whom he had seven children and for whom he had little affection, was frequently overcome by his sensual nature; but the religious influences to which he was subjected continually caused him qualms of conscience. For fifteen years this inward compulsion had kept him away from the Communion; he earnestly sought after a tolerable means of escape. In addition, he had long since formed the idea that bigamy was permitted by God. In the Old Testament, openly permitted to the patriarchs, nowhere forbidden in the New —indeed, presumably left open to all other Christians by passages like *Timothy* I. iii. 2, which indeed only prohibited two wives in the case of the clergy—bigamy appeared to him a perfectly lawful resource in his present position. He had observed carefully that Luther in his *Babylonish Captivity* (1520) had declared bigamy to be more tolerable than divorce (*Opp. v. a.* V 100)[1]; again, in 1524, Luther had expressed the opinion that he did not know how to prevent bigamy *nec repugnat sacris literis* (although the practice should be resisted, Enders IV 283); similarly, in the sermons on Genesis delivered at the same time, but not printed until 1527: "I could not prevent it at the present day, but I would not advise it" (EA 33, 324). Certainly, when Philip, in 1526, had put the question directly to him, he had answered with a decided refusal, since there was no positive divine command in such a case: "it is not enough for a Christian to consider the acts of the patriarchs, he must also have the divine word on his side" (de Wette, VI 79; cp. also III 139 f.).[2] Now, in 1539, Philip had made the acquaintance of Margaret von der Sala, a maid of honour at the court of his sister, the Duchess Elizabeth von Rochlitz, and had obtained her mother's assent to a left-handed marriage, in case it should be publicly defended by him or at least concluded before princely witnesses, that is to say, their deputies. Philip, who had become acquainted with the declarations of the Reformers favourable to bigamy in the case of the matrimonial affairs of Henry VIII (1531), subsequently took Bucer into his confidence, whose conscientious scruples were entirely outweighed by the apprehension that otherwise Philip might be alienated from the evangelical cause.

Philip personally felt so certain about the matter that, when the storm broke out, he was able to strengthen his conscience with the maxim that "all God's causes shall suffer persecution" (Lenz I 365). But, in the face of publicity, he sought protection against attack from behind[3] at first among the Reformers. They assented and expressed themselves ready to take upon themselves his public justification: then he had a mind to defy the Emperor and public law; otherwise, he thought of eventually gaining his end by obtaining a dispensation from the Pope, by negotiating with the Emperor.

---

[1] Luther further defended this position, de Wette, IV 296.

[2] For a treatise in defence of bigamy, which was said to have appeared in 1527, cp. AG deutsche Buchh. XVI 67.

[3] [*Rückendeckung:* a military term, Fr. and Eng "parados."]

Even in the latter case, he certainly meant to remain true to his belief, but saw himself confronted by the necessity of politically "attaching himself more closely to the Emperor than was advantageous to this (Schmalkaldic) league" (Lenz I 354). On the 10th of December, 1539, Luther and Melanchthon gave their opinion (de Wette VI 238 ff.), which was to the following effect. There was not and ought not to be any law in Christendom that allowed bigamy; for monogamy alone was confirmed by the order of creation and by Christ, and polygamy was an "importation contrary to the first rule." However, they recognised cases of conscience in which a person might, "not indeed to bring in a law but to consult his own need," choose a left-handed marriage as the lesser of two evils, as "a dispensation in accordance with divine permission." Hence, if necessity urged him to take such a step, absolute secrecy in the eyes of the world was an indispensable condition. They accordingly advised, in the first place, that the Landgrave should earnestly endeavour to purify his immodest life; but if that were impossible, they would have him "be in a better state in the sight of God and live with a good conscience" by contracting a left-handed marriage. The perversity of this advice is obvious, the moment we consider the part they thereby required the "left-handed wife" to play, who, according to the opinion expressed by them, was bound to be degraded to the position of a concubine in the eyes of the world: the theory of the "lesser evil" had been elsewhere rightly limited by Luther to *res corporales*, but, on the contrary, excluded in matters affecting morality. The fact that, when the bigamous marriage became known, Luther could only advise "a good downright lie" (Lenz I 373) as a help in need, proved how inadmissible this "confessional advice was."[1] Further (in addition to CR III 863, 1079), Luther's statement (in Lauterbach's *Tagebuch*, p. 197), that they would have given their vote, "in order to anticipate" the Landgrave's decision to apply to the Emperor and the Pope, shows more than anything else that the reformers' advice was not without a political tinge. Philip also obtained his wife's assent to the step; on the 4th of March, 1540, his court-chaplain, Dionysius Melander, performed the momentous ceremony at Rothenburg, in the presence of Melanchthon, Bucer and an envoy from the Elector of Saxony (for the nuptial address see ZhTh 22, 272 ff.). By this act of marriage the Landgrave had gone further than Luther had advised, who had only had a private marriage in mind. The secret was speedily revealed by the Landgrave's sister at the Court of Dresden, and soon became public property. The ranks of the Protestants were divided; while the majority saw in what had happened a stigma upon the evangelical cause (cp. instar omnium, Anecd. Brentiana 210, 212), Melanchthon had the courage to defend the act of bigamy in his writings and sermons; but the Wittenberg theologians now advised that the world should be deceived by falsehood, and were obliged to hear from the Landgrave the following words: "I will not lie, for lying sounds bad; no Apostle ever taught it to any Christian—nay, more, Christ most strictly forbade it."[2] (Lenz I 383.)

---

[1] KOLDE II 488 rightly brings into prominence the after effect of the medieval depreciation of the wife, and the misunderstanding of the meaning of the public written law.

[2] Certainly, however, the Landgrave himself had repeatedly deceived his own sister by untruths in the course of the matter (LENZ I 332).

Momentous political results soon showed themselves: John Frederick refused to make this matter a concern of the Schmalkaldic League. The Landgrave, who was thereby left to face the Empire alone, subsequently concluded a separate pact with the Emperor at Ratisbon on the 13th of June, 1541 (LENZ III 91 ff.); he bound himself, not to conclude or allow any alliance for himself or on the part of the Schmalkaldeners with France or other foreign princes, not even to admit the evangelical Duke William of Cleve to the league, in other words, to sacrifice this neighbour of the Dutch possessions of the Emperor. Thus, the alliance with King Francis, which had been most zealously fostered, and to which Electoral Saxony also showed itself inclined,[1] had to be broken off; Denmark and Sweden were obliged to be rejected. The politician of the Schmalkaldic League was himself obliged to paralyse the league politically. "The dreaded champion of the Gospel had become an instrument of the imperial policy."

3. The Respite before the Catastrophe.

Literature: Pfalz-Neuburg: BROCK, Nördl., 1848; Naumburg: Mitt. d. thür.-sächs. Ver., 1835, 1863 and 1864. Meissen: O. RICHTER, *Ueber die Verdienste des sächs. Fürstenhauses um die Aufhebung des Bist. Meissen.* Döbeln, 1874. Braunschweig: KOLDEWEY, *Heinz. v. Wolfenb.* Halle, 1884; the same, in Zh Ver. Niedersachs., 1869, 243 ff. F. BRUNS, *Vertreibung Herz. Heinrichs von Br.*, I. Marb., 1889. Köln: STROBEL, Neue Beitr. V 273 ff.; VARRENTRAPP, *Hermann v. Wied.* Leipz., 1878. CHR. MEYER, *Stadt und Stift Köln im ZA d. Ref.*, Hamb., 1892. C. KRAFFT in Arb. d. rhein.-westf. Pred.-Vereins., 1891, 152 ff. Merseburg: A. FRAUSTADT, *Einf. d. Ref. im Hochst. Merseb.* Leipz., 1843.

Still, however, important political affairs gave the Protestants a fresh respite. Ferdinand was hard pressed by the Turks and the Emperor, in order to divert the Turk from his Austrian hereditary dominions, undertook an unsuccessful campaign against Algiers (October and November 1541): there was a prospect of another war with France. At the diet of Spires in 1542 the Protestant States agreed to give aid against the Turks in return for the promise of a prolongation of the state of peace for five years. Thus, at first, Protestantism was again enabled to make fresh acquisitions.

At **Ratisbon** the evangelical feeling of the population now asserted itself victoriously (**Nicolas Gallus**). The **lower Austrian** constitutional estates applied to Ferdinand, the **Bavarian** to their dukes, for leave to preach the Gospel. In

---

[1] P. VETTER in NA für sächs. G. XIV 21 ff.

Palatine Neuberg, under **Otto Henry**, a brother-in-law of the Dukes of Bavaria, who in addition solicited the co-operation of a theologian from Nuremberg (Andrew Osiander), the result was a real, though carefully restricted Reformation. Here the conservative Brandenberg ritual, which the Emperor had allowed the Elector Joachim to use, was taken as the model. In the see of **Naumburg-Zeitz**, which was under the protectorate of Electoral Saxony, John Frederick successfully endeavoured to extend his right of reform to a bishopric and to exercise "annexion" under title of the Gospel. The cathedral chapter, after the death of the bishop (January 6th, 1541) had at once elected the Erasmian **Julius von Pflug**. But the Elector set aside the election, claiming a formal right of assent. In spite of the warnings of his chancellor and also of Luther, in spite of the dissuasion of the Emperor, he took upon himself the secular control of the see, and appointed it a **bishop** in the person of **Nicolas Amsdorf**. (Prince George of Anhalt, who had been proposed to him by Luther, in case he persisted in following this risky course, was rejected by him on various pretexts). Luther agreed to ordain this evangelical "bishop." A wealthy parish-priest became a poor bishop, who had to appear with episcopal dignity without corresponding means, while the secular government of the see was administered by an electoral "vidame."[1] A similar attempt of the Elector to extend his rights in the bishopric of **Meissen**, in which both Saxon lines exercised a protectorate in common, and to introduce evangelicalism by force, nearly led to a conflict with **Maurice** of Saxony, which the Landgrave Philip succeeded in averting. The disputants divided the protectorate of the see. But Maurice now opportunely secured for himself the disposal of the bishopric of Merseburg. Then the Schmalkaldeners turned against the Catholic Duke **Henry** (Heinz) of Brunswick. The free imperial city of **Goslar** had pulled down a few neighbouring monasteries, to deprive the Brunswicker of positions of attack; the supreme court of judicature had laid it under an interdict, but the diet of Ratisbon settled the matter, and declared the sentence void. Nevertheless, Henry endeavoured to get it carried out upon the hated city. His scandalous private life, frequent acts of incendiarism, which were said to have been instigated by him, in addition to acts of violence against the city of Brunswick had created excessive bitterness against him in evangelical circles.[2] In July, 1542, Saxony and Hesse jointly occupied his dominions, declared that they would only restore them to his sons, and introduced the Reformation by force. In the episcopal city of **Hildesheim** also evangelical principles were victorious.

At the same time an extremely favourable prospect presented itself to Protestantism in the West. Not only did the Reformation make gratifying progress in Metz (de Wette V 508): a German archbishop, an ecclesiastical Elector, **Hermann**, Count of Wied, Archbishop of Cologne, declared his adherence to the principles of the Reformation. Since the Münster riots had been put down, he had felt the need of ecclesiastical reforms: and, in combination

---

[1] [The deputy of a bishop in temporal affairs].
[2] It was against him that Luther wrote his treatise *Wider Hans Worst.*, 1541.

with Duke **John of Cleve**, whose country belonged to his diocese, and who was under the influence of the Erasmian Conrad of Heresbach (p. 120), he had introduced negotiations for reform. Gropper and Heresbach had held a consultation at Neuss at the end of 1535; a provincial council in 1536 had subsequently adopted the *summaria capita* of the former, and, included in them, a reformation of various abuses, which however did not satisfy the Archbishop's intentions. At the religious discussions of Worms and Ratisbon he had had personal intercourse with Bucer. Relying upon the Ratisbon "recess," in accordance with which the prelates also were to take in hand "a Christian order and reformation," and strengthened by the entreaties of the States of his country (Bonn, March 11th, 1542), he summoned Bucer at the end of 1542 and also Melanchthon in the summer of 1543. A ritual, essentially Bucer's work, was arranged, which, although it excited the indignation of Luther and Amsdorf by its indecisively Lutheran Eucharistic doctrine, nevertheless showed an evangelical tendency throughout. When laid before the diet it met with much sympathy, but, at the same time, violent opposition on the part of the cathedral chapter and the clergy of Cologne; Gropper himself was the soul of the opposition, and the cathedral chapter invoked the assistance of the Emperor. But also Duke William of Cleve (since 1539) had shown himself well disposed to the new doctrine and the Bishop of Münster, Minden and Osnabrück, **Francis of Waldeck**, a very unspiritual lord, now desired to join the Reformation. "We are daily becoming fewer," was the lament of Cochleus in those days. In 1544, the bishopric of Merseburg also became vacant; Maurice handed over to his brother Augustus the secular, and to Prince George of Anhalt the spiritual administration of the see.

CHAPTER SEVENTH.

The Overthrow of the Schmalkaldic League.

Literature: VON DRUFFEL, *Karl V. und die röm. Kurie 1544-1546* in ABA 1881, 1883 and 1887. A. DE BOOR, *Beiträge zur Gesch. des Speierer Reichst. 1544.* Strassburg, 1878. MAURENBRECHER in HTb 6. F. V 147 ff. J. SPRINGER, *Beitr. zur Gesch. des Wormser Reichstags.* Leipz., 1883. MAURENBRECHER, *Karl V. und die deutschen Protest., 1545-1555.* Düsseld., 1865. VON DRUFFEL in SBBA 1888, II 2, 279 ff. ISSLEIB in NA für sächsische Gesch. N.F. II. P. KANNENGIESSER, *der Reichst. zu Worms, 1545.* Strassb., 1891. N. PAULUS, *Joh. Hoffmeister.* Freib., 1891. TH. KOLDE, *Luthers Selbstmord.* Erlg., 1890 (written against P. MAJUNKE's libel, *Luthers Lebensende.* Mainz., 1890). M. LUTHERS *letzte Streitschrift*, edited by G. Buchwald. Leipz., 1893.

1. The Approach of the Catastrophe and Luther's Death.

All this, to some extent doubtful, extension of power was unable to check the momentous counteraction. In the summer of 1543, the Emperor made his appearance in the Empire, prepared for war. Philip's pact with him (p. 146) now bore bitter fruits. The duchy of Guelders, with the assent of the States, had been sold by the childless and heavily involved Duke Charles of Egmont to Duke William of Cleve; the Emperor, on the other hand, claimed the dukedom as an imperial fee which had reverted to himself. William, who since 1539 had united Guelders and Cleve and was inclined to the principles of the Reformation (he introduced them at Wesel), might have been able to bring considerable reinforcements to the Schmalkaldic League in league with Cologne, but Philip was obliged to refuse his admission into it, and the Schmalkaldeners were obliged to leave him without support, as the Emperor now threw himself upon him, humbled him at the treaty of Venlo (September 6th, 1543), took Guelders from him, and compelled him to put an end to his ecclesiastical innovations and to support the imperial interests. They were obliged to submit to the Reformation being now abolished by force by the Emperor at Metz. This at the same time sealed the fate of the Reformation at Cologne. Hermann was accused by his opponents in the chapter before Pope and Emperor, and the Schmalkaldic League left him in the lurch.

Yet, at the time, the Emperor still had need of the Protestants. At the **Diet of Spires** (1544) he succeeded in securing considerable help from the States both for Ferdinand against the Turk and for himself against the ally of the Turk—the French—in return for which the Protestants obtained the confirmation of the promises made at Ratisbon, and the prospect of further amicable attempts at a settlement, so that they again regarded the situation with blind confidence,[1] while the Pope entered an angry protest (August 24th) against the resolutions of Spires. Disillusion speedily followed. Charles, allied with England, victoriously made his way into France, and compelled Francis I. to make peace at Créspy (September 14th, 1544); he sought reconciliation with France, in order to deprive the Protestants of this reserve, and France bound herself never to assist them again. The Elector-Palatine Frederick II. also commenced the work of reform in 1545, and even the successor of Cardinal Albert of Mainz, Sebastian von Heusenstamm, showed an inclination to follow the example of Cologne. But the Schmalkaldic League was seriously weakened internally; there was no lack of friction between the members of the league. The diplomatic Duke Maurice had already left it (1542) and had drawn nearer to the Emperor (cp. p. 143). Joachim II. persistently held aloof from the league; the Electoral-Palatinate refused to be gained over to it. The constitution of the league was unwieldly, and lacked vigorous and uniform leadership. In addition, just at this time Luther's suspicion of Bucer and his followers was again increased, and he uttered his protest against the Swiss, who had been annoyed by his publicly expressed opinions of Zwingli and their doctrine of the Eucharist. He harshly renounced the Swiss and their " scandalous " doctrine (de Wette, V 587; cp. Lenz, Briefwechsel II 222, 241 f.): in Sept. 1544, his *Kurz Bekenntnis vom heiligen Sakrament*[2] (EA 32, 396 ff.) appeared, a definitive, abrupt renunciation of the connection. And, just at this time, Paul III. again convoked for the 15th of March, 1545 (in the bull *Lactare Hierusalem* of the 19th of November, 1544) the council which had already been appointed for 1542 at **Trent**, but had not commenced proceedings in consequence of warlike alarms (see p. 135), in order, on his side, to hinder the independent arrangement of religious controversies **by a German assembly,** and also invited the European rulers to take part in the council.

---

[1] At Strasburg alone certain persons showed clearer political judgment.
[2] [Brief Confession or Creed of the Holy Sacrament.]

However, in conformity with the "recess" of the diet of Spires, different plans of reform were drawn up as the basis of an agreement, by Bucer in several treatises (BAUM, p. 604 ff.), by Hesse (NEUDECKER *Urkunden*, 681), and especially from Wittenberg by Melanchthon *(Reformatio Witeberg.)*, January, 1545.

Under the erroneous opinion, that the Emperor was serious about a peaceful arrangement, far-reaching concessions were made in the last-named treatise: the episcopal constitution and the secular position of the prelates was to be recognised in return for full liberty of evangelical preaching. But when the diet was opened at Worms in March 1545, the Saxon ambassador hung back. The impending council filled the Protestants with grievous apprehensions: they were entirely without guarantees of impartial procedure: they accordingly refused to recognise it at Worms or to take any part in it. At the desire of the Elector, Luther had written his tractate *Wider das Papstthum zu Rom vom Teufel gestiftet*[1] (March, 1545), a reply to the arrogant brief addressed by the Pope to the Emperor (August 24th, 1544). This tractate, which was written in a very coarse style, although objectively its contents was of great intrinsic value, excited great anger at the diet.[2]

In the autumn of 1545, Henry of Brunswick, supported by French money and also by German prelates, invaded his dominions, of which he had been deprived, and at once everywhere abolished evangelical ecclesiastical institutions: but on the 11th of October, he was defeated by the Landgrave and taken prisoner, together with his eldest son. At the desire of his reigning prince, who wanted to exert definite influence upon Philip, Luther now took part in politics and recommended that the prisoner should not for the present be released. On this occasion, also, the special policy pursued by Maurice as imperial middleman was distinctly prominent and the sequestration caused differences amongst the allied princes.

But still the Emperor held back, proposed fresh negotiations and declared that he had no idea of employing force in matters of religion; but at the same time he revealed to the Pope, who had sent his grandson Farnese to him as legate, that he contemplated entering upon the path of force, but was obliged to hold back until a suitable time: he declared that all negotiations were only intended to amuse the Protestants. The Pope hastened to offer

---

[1] [Against the Papacy founded by the devil at Rome.]

[2] "A production written in anger, which contains more thorough discussion of the true and false idea of 'church,' than even many evangelicals imagine." (Niedner.)

him (June 17th) troops and money[1] for the war against the heretics and was greatly disappointed, when the Emperor even now still hesitated, convened another meeting for religious discussion (at Ratisbon), and put forward the demand for the council to take in hand decretals of reform before decretals of doctrine. The Emperor sought to put pressure upon the Pope and the Protestants at the same time. In December, 1545, the former actually caused the Council to be opened and, without delay, contrary to the Emperor's wishes, Protestantism was excluded by important doctrinal statements: immediately afterwards, and quite independently, **the religious conference** desired by the Emperor took place at Ratisbon, under the presidency of the Bishop of Eichstädt: on the Catholic side were the Spaniard Malvenda, Cochleus, John Hoffmeister, an Augustinian monk of Colmar, and Billik, a Carmelite: on the Protestant, G. Major, Schnepf and Brenz: Malvenda and Bucer were especially prominent. The Catholic collocutors found themselves bound by respect for the Council: there was no hope of an understanding, as they refused to recognise the points agreed upon in 1541 (see p. 142) as a basis for discussion. In March, 1546, the Protestant States recalled their collocutors to spare them further useless trouble. At the diet of Ratisbon, which was sitting at the same time, the Catholic States now assigned the religious question to the Council, while the Protestant sought to protect themselves by the resolutions of Spires. In these anxious times, Luther was called away (on the 18th of February) at Eisleben by a peaceful death, rejoicing in the faith: the peaceful work of reconciling the Counts of Mansfeld who were disputing about certain privileges had called the invalid thither at an inclement season. During his last years, bodily suffering, excess of work, struggles without and calamities in his own circle had exhausted his vital powers, and frequently made him bitter, irritable and pessimistic. He was mercifully spared from witnessing the outbreak of the unhappy war and the disorders that arose amongst his adherents.

2. The Schmalkaldic War.

Shortly afterwards a young Spaniard of evangelical views, named **John Diaz**,[2] was treacherously murdered at the instigation of his own brother at Neuburg: both the perpetrator and the instigator of the deed remained unpunished. It was the presage of the war of

---

[1] 500 horse, 12,000 foot and 300,000 ducats.
[2] VEESENMEYER in ZhTh 7, 3, 156 ff. CR XX 515 ff.

religion, for the Emperor now showed his intentions without any attempt at concealment. He soon came to an understanding with Ferdinand: on the 26th of June, Paul III signed the deed of alliance, whereby he furnished the Emperor with troops and a sum of ready money, and also gave him permission to dispose of the ecclesiastical revenues in Spain for purposes of war; the Pope also summoned the Catholic powers (German and those outside Germany) to a holy war and prescribed prayers for the faithful to use for the victory of the Catholic arms. Certainly, the Emperor even now sought to keep up the appearance of desiring only to punish the political refractoriness of the princes of the Schmalkaldic League: it was only by disavowing the character of the war as a religious one that he gained over Maurice of Saxony, to whom he promised the electorate of Saxony, and secured the services of the evangelical Hans von Küstrin as colonel of cavalry. Also Eric of Brunswick and the Margrave Albert of Brandenburg entered his service. Hence, it was very awkward for him that papal indiscretion lifted the veil prematurely.[1] But this very thing drove the Schmalkaldeners to arm hastily, so that they might be able to march against the Emperor, before his foreign troops were brought up. After an initial success gained by the Schmalkaldic princes, which however was not energetically followed up and was checked by the skilfulness of the Emperor, Maurice and Ferdinand brought about the crisis of the war by invading Saxony. The South German cities were abandoned to the Emperor and were obliged to decide upon a separate agreement with uncertain promises as to their religious position. Archbishop Hermann of Cologne was deprived of his office: the battle on the heath of Lochau (Mühlberg, April 24th, 1547) decided the fate of Saxony. At the capitulation of Wittenberg the Electorate, in addition to half the country, was surrendered to Maurice, and John Frederick became the Emperor's prisoner. Julius von Pflug had previously been re-instated as bishop of Naumburg. In spite of the victory of the Low German troops over the imperial at Drackenburg (May 23rd), the Landgrave Philip gave up all for lost, and, in misplaced hopes of the Emperor's mercy, surrendered at Halle on the 19th of June, where Alba, by command of the Emperor, took him prisoner.[2] (A regular breach of promise on the Emperor's part in this matter cannot be proved.) North Germany also submitted to the imperial conqueror; Magdeburg alone set him at defiance and was outlawed.

Von Druffel in ABA XX 294.

[2] For Philip's imprisonment, cp. Issleib in NA für sächs. Gesch. XI 177 ff.

CHAPTER EIGHTH.

The Interim and the Religious Peace.

1. The Interim.

Literature: J. E. BIECK, *das dreifache Interim.* Leipz., 1721. PASTOR, *Reunionsbestrebungen.* Freib., 1879. G. KAWERAU, *J. Agricola.* Berlin, 1881; the same, in ZPGLK XVII 398 ff. VON DRUFFEL, *Briefe und Akten*, Vols. I. and III. BEUTEL, *über den Ursprung des Augsb. Interim.* Dresden, 1888. VON DRUFFEL, *die Sendung des Card. Sfondrato an den Hof Karls V., 1547 bis 1548* in ABA XX, II, 293 ff. SPIEKER, *Beiträge zur Gesch. d. Augsb. Int.* in ZhTh 21, 345 ff. ISSLEIB in NA für sächs. Gesch. XIII 207 ff. WITTER, *Beziehungen und Verkehr des Kurfürsten Moritz mit Ferdinand.* Neustadt a.d. H. 1886. W. KAWERAU in Magd. GBlätter, 1893; Alberus in Magd.

The attitude **of the Pope** in regard to the Emperor was again destined to prevent the Catholic cause from reaping the full fruits of victory. The Pope had already greatly annoyed Charles by having ordered doctrinal decretals to be at once drawn up at the Council, so that the Emperor, in May, 1546, had entered a formal protest against its conduct; again, when the war went in favour of the imperial arms, the Pope, feeling some anxiety as to the Emperor's influence upon the Council, had transferred it to Bologna, for he did not, like Charles, desire to make entrance to it possible for the Protestants. In January, during the course of the campaign, he had recalled his auxiliary troops and thereby greatly irritated the Emperor; and, *vice versâ*, he had not hesitated to charge the Emperor with the murder of his son Pierluigi (September).[1] Charles, however, caused a protest against the sins of the Curia to be read at Bologna (January 18th, 1548), which reminds us of the period of his violent conflict with Clement VII (p. 70). Thus the Emperor, at the "armed"[2] Diet of Augsburg (since September 1st, 1547) set to work to settle the affairs of Germany **by himself without the assistance of the Pope.** Here the Emperor also compelled the Protestant princes to submit to the Council, holding out the

---

[1] Cp. Spicilegio Vaticano I 1. Roma, 1890.
[2] [So called because his troops were stationed in the neighbourhood.]

promise of safe-conduct and its retransference to Trent. But, as he himself was afraid that the Pope might delay its meeting for years, he now earnestly set to work to "settle" ecclesiastical affairs in Germany provisionally *(interim)*.

He had already (in January, 1547) entered into negotiations with Ferdinand in regard to this:[1] **Pflug** was commissioned to draw up a scheme *(Formula sacrorum emendandorum*, ed. Chr. G. Müller, Leipzig, 1803). After a religious committee, chosen from both Catholic and Protestant States, had sat without result, an imperial commission that had long since been secretly formed, consisting of Pflug, Michael Helding, and (as Protestant member) John Agricola, Joachim's vain court-preacher, set to work. All their efforts to obtain the co-operation of Bucer were fruitless; but the Spaniards Malvenda and Soto joined it. Owing to the differences that arose between Agricola and the Spaniards, Pflug's copy was abridged and revised. Thus a work was completed, the doctrines of which were in the main points Catholic. (Justification = making just: distinction between the works commanded by God and the *consilia evangelica:* the Church, under control of the bishops, legitimised by apostolic succession, equipped with power to interpret the Scriptures and propagate binding traditions, laying down the law at councils, placed under the successors of Peter for the sake of the necessary unity: however, every bishop in his diocese, by virtue of divine right, is a true bishop [a rejection of the curialistic theory]; the seven sacraments: the sacrifice of the mass as an imputation and commemoration of the merit of the sacrifice of Christ upon the cross: intercession and merits of the Saints: intercession for the dead at the sacrifice of the mass, as we do not know whether they are already sufficiently "purified"; daily masses in the towns, at which participation by communicants would certainly be "useful": arrangement of fasts: Corpus Christi day: allowance of the marriage of priests and the toleration of communion in both kinds until the final decision of the Council). It was cleverly so arranged, that two Protestant princes (of Brandenburg and the Palatinate) delivered the work to the Emperor when completed, and it thereby came before the States as if it corresponded to the wishes of the Protestants. The evangelical States were led to the mistaken idea, that the Interim was to be valid **also for the Catholic States of the Empire**,—at least, this seems the only possible explanation of Agricola's infatuation, and exhaustive negotiations were carried on with the Elector Maurice on this basis. Nevertheless, the latter insisted on making his acceptance dependent upon the advice of his learned men and the assent of his Estates. He showed the Interim to his theologians without delay and asked their opinion. In April, 1548, Melanchthon, Major, Cruciger and Pfeffinger held a consultation at Altzella. The doctrines of justification, the saints, masses for the dead and private masses were decisively rejected. In regard to the doctrine of the Church and the sacraments they were ready to make concessions. At this critical period, when Melanchthon was alarmed by the report of the Emperor's wrath against him as well as by the general condition of affairs, he wrote the melancholy letter to Christopher von Carlowitz (CR VI 879 ff.), in which he threw the responsibility for the

---

[1] BUCHHOLTZ, *Gesch. Ferdinands* V 553 ff.

reformation of the Church upon Luther and lamented the servitude which he had so long been obliged to endure at Luther's side. Meanwhile, the Catholic States at Augsburg declared to the Emperor, that the Interim could naturally have no application to them. Thus, on the 15th of May, the Interim (*liber Augustanus*, the Augsburg book) was officially laid before the States as binding upon the Protestants: a consultation followed, at which Maurice expressed his reservation and indignation at the restriction of the Interim to the Protestant States; lastly, the Archbishop of Mainz proclaimed the obedience of the Empire. On the 18th Maurice handed his protest to the Emperor.

On the 30th of June the Interim, by virtue of the "recess" of the diet, became **a law of the Empire**, together with a *Formula reformationis* (originally Part III. of Pflug's draft)[1] for the Catholic States, dealing with the removal of certain abuses. The bishops made this Formula of Reformation known at numerous diocesan synods during this and the following year, but no important improvements were arrived at.

The majority of the Protestant States at heart opposed the Interim that had been forced upon them, recognising that it meant the death of Protestantism; but only a few (as Hans of Küstrin and the Count Palatine Wolfgang of Zweibrücken) ventured to protest openly.[2]

In South Germany, the Emperor, by his superior power, was able to compel the free imperial cities, and also Wurtemburg, formally to accept the Interim. His threat, "You shall still learn Spanish," was terribly fulfilled in the case of the cities. Constance lost its freedom, became Austrian and was forced to return to Catholicism.[3] Spanish soldiers obtained votes by force; numerous evangelical ministers wandered about the country as *exsules Christi*, others, like those of Ulm (Frecht), were imprisoned by the Emperor; only a few of the leading personalities submitted. The evangelical population for the most part offered a passive resistance to the hated Interim-service, for which in many cases there was a complete lack of clergy. Where it was possible, recourse was had to formal submission without consequent performance (*e.g.* in Nuremberg, Brandenburg-Anspach, Strasburg).

The situation was more favourable in North Germany. The Elector Maurice desired on the one hand to satisfy the Emperor, and on the other to respect the feelings of his country. He accordingly caused discussions to be held at numerous diets and conventions of theologians throughout the year (at Meissen, Pegau,

---

[1] In GOLDAST, *Constitutt. imper.* II 325 ff.

[2] For what follows cp. especially VON DRUFFEL, *Briefe und Akten* III 109 ff.; HIRSCH, *Geschichte des Interim in Nürnberg*. Leipz., 1750; *Württ. KG.* Calw., 1893, p. 367 ff.; Frecht's *Briefe aus der Gefangenschaft* in Württ. Vierteljahrshefte IV and V.

[3] HpBl 67, 659 ff.

Torgau, Zelle; at the Jüterbogk convention an understanding was arrived at with Brandenburg); and finally, on the 24th of December, the so-called **Leipzig Interim** was decided upon by the States at Leipzig. On this occasion Melanchthon succeeded in restoring the evangelical doctrine of justification, although without any keen opposition, and in persuading the Bishops of Meissen and Naumburg to approve this pretended transcription of the section in question of the Augsburg Interim. Subordination to episcopal jurisdiction and much Catholic ceremonial was retained, but accompanied by (dogmatically) less offensive arguments (fasting on Friday was to be observed as a regulation of the secular authorities: mass was only to be celebrated when a sufficient number of persons was present): the canon of the mass was done away with, other objectionable practices (*e.g.*, Corpus Christi procession, and the offertory) were nominally retained, but in the *Agenda*[1] drawn up in 1549 practically rendered harmless. Melanchthon saw in this Interim an act of "compulsion"; but he regarded even this as more tolerable than the complete abandonment and subversion of the communities. In other places (East Friesland) only a modified Interim was introduced. At Brandenburg the Elector behaved like the serf who says Yes and then does not carry out his master's bidding: he soon allowed himself to be persuaded by his theologians to deceive the Emperor with the mere appearance of an introduction of the Interim. Nor could anything serious be done in Hesse, although the imprisoned Landgrave tried to persuade his sons. But the North German **cities** resisted bluntly.[2] Hamburg, Lübeck, Bremen, Lüneburg, Brunswick, Hanover, Hildesheim, Göttingen, and Eimbeck, after common consultation, rejected it: the princes of Anhalt did the same: others desired to abide by it "as far as possible." The imprisoned John Frederick could not be induced to accept it, either by threats or harsh treatment: his sons at Weimar rejected it, by agreement with their theologians. But **Magdeburg** ("the chancery of our Lord God") became the meeting-place of the fugitive opponents of the Interim, and, under the leadership of Amsdorf, Matthias Flacius (Flacich) of Illyria, Erasmus Alberus,

---

[1] On the Interim-ritual see FRIEDBERG in ZhTh 41, 36 ff.; the same *Agenda, wie es in des Kurf. zu Sachsen Landen gehalten wird*. Halle, 1869.

[2] Aepinus of Hamburg drew up the exhaustive vote of the Hanse towns against the Interim; for the hesitation of the Pomeranian theologians, see ZhTh 13, 4, 36 ff.

Nicolas Gallus, and others, the starting-point of a fresh, uncompromising polemic against the Interim and its authors (especially Agricola), and even still more against Melanchthon and others who, like him, were ready to make concessions (Major, Eber, Cruciger, Bugenhagen).[1] The evangelicals listened with joy to the voice of these unyielding opponents: numerous pamphlets and satirical poems kept Luther's spirit alive amongst the people during these critical times: the "Interimists" and "Adiaphorists" had a difficult task to defend their undecided attitude in face of this **popular** Lutheranism. For the first time, the gnesio-Lutheran party separated distinctly from the Philippist: in the person of Flacius, a pupil of Melanchthon suddenly grew up a weighty, but also irreverent opponent, who now rendered never to be forgotten services to evangelical Germany.

The progress of the introduction of the Interim was impeded by the fact that the Pope,[2] and with him the strictly Catholic party, contested not only the trifling imperial concessions to the Protestants in the Interim, but the interference generally of the secular authority in the ecclesiastical question. It was only after lengthy negotiations that Paul III. found himself prepared to send legates to reincorporate with the Church the Protestants who submitted, and to promise very carefully restricted dispensations in the matter of the marriage of priests, the administering of the cup to the laity, fasts and feast days. Charles indignantly declared that no one had done more than the Pope to prevent the perfect remedying of evils in Germany: he threatened him with an appeal to the Council, and, eventually, with a schism: but Paul did not hesitate to advise Henry II. of France to unite with the German Protestants in an attack upon the Emperor.[3] It was not until shortly before his death that he yielded to the imperial will and broke up the Council at Bologna, which, supported by France, he had desired to transfer to Rome itself (Sept. 1549.) His successor, **Julius III.** (John Maria Giocci), although elevated to the pontificate by the party of the Farnese to alarm the imperialists, immediately took up a different position and declared his readiness to acquiesce in the imperial intentions. Thus, in spite of the counter-efforts of France, **the Council of Trent** was able to be reopened again in May, 1551. The Emperor expressly required the Protestants to send representatives. Joachim II., who desired the episcopal sees of Madgeburg and Halberstadt for his son Frederick, declared his willingness to send representatives. Other evangelical States were obliged to prepare to do so whether they liked it or not. Melanchthon drew up as the basis of negotiations for Saxony the carefully-written *Confessio Saxonica* (*Repetitio Confessionis Augustanae*, CR XXVIII 339 ff.),[4] and Brenz for Wurtemberg the *Con-*

---

[1] GÖTZE, *die Magd.Presse zur Zeit der Reichsacht* in Magd. Blätter f. Handel. etc., 1876, no. 21; further, Magd. GBlätter VI 61 ff.; XV 29 ff.; XVII.

[2] G. DE LEVA in Rivista stor. ital. V 251 ff. VI 40 ff.

[3] VON DRUFFEL, Briefe und Akten I 211.

[4] SCHAFF., *Bibl. Symb.* I 340 ff. HEPPE, *Bekenntnissschriften der altprotestantischen Kirche.* Kassel, 1885, p. 407 ff.

fessio Virtembergensis.[1] The secular delegates of Wurtemberg and Strasburg, and also of Saxony actually appeared at Trent, and obtained a hearing, but not at a solemn sitting, but at a congregation (January 24th, 1552) at which the Wurtembergers handed over their confession, and together with the Saxon delegates formulated their demands: that the arrival of their theologians who were on the way ought to be awaited: that the previous resolutions of the Council should be taken up again and the bishops released from the oath administered to them by the Pope as long as the negotiations lasted. This proceeding made an impression on part of the assembly: but in this manner only inadequate results could have been obtained. Then the position of affairs was on a sudden totally altered by Maurice of Saxony.

2. The Treaty of Passau and the Religious Peace of Augsburg.

Sources: LEHMANN, *de pace religionis acta publica.* Francf., 1707. LANZ *Corresp. Karls V.*, Vol. III.

Literature: J. VOIGT, *der Fürstenbund gegen Karl V.* in HTb 3, F. 8, 3 ff. MAURENBRECHER, *Studien und Skizzen.* Leipz., 1884. VON LANGENN, *Moritz von S.;* 2 vols. 1841. CORNELIUS in ABA 3, Cl. X.; the same, in München. HJb, 1866. WENCK in FdGesch. XII. SCHÖNHERR, *der Einfall des Kurf. v. S. in Tirol.* 1868. J. TREFFTZ, *Kursachs. und Frankr., 1522-1557.* Leipz., 1891. G. FISCHER, *die pers. Stellung und politische Lage K. Ferdinands, 1552.* Königsb., 1891. ISSLEIB in NA f. sächs. Gesch. VI 210; VII 1; VIII 41. M. RITTER, *der Augsb. Rel.-Friede* in HTb 6, F. 1. L. SCHWABE, *Kursachsen und d. Augsb. Rel.-Friede* in NA f. sächs. G. X. G. WOLFF, *Der Augsb. Rel.-Friede.* Stuttg., 1890. K. KÖHLER, *der Augsb. Rel.-Friede* in JdTh 23, 376 ff. J. GRIESDORF, *der Zug Karls V. gegen Metz, 1552.* Halle, 1891. HEPPE, *der Convent der evg. Reichsstände zu Naumburg.* Marburg, 1877. VOIGT, *Albrecht Alcibiades;* 2 vols. Berlin, 1852.

Maurice felt that he had been deceived by the Emperor in regard to his father-in-law Philip of Hesse, whose release became the more a point of honour with him, the more disgracefully Philip was ill-treated in prison. The indignation of evangelical Germany weighed heavily upon him, as it deservedly held him responsible for the unfortunate issue of the Schmalkaldic War. In March, 1551, Charles had induced his brother Ferdinand to agree that, after the death of the latter, he should be succeeded also in Germany by his (Charles's) son **Philip**, not by Ferdinand's son Maximilian, who had shown a leaning towards evangelicalism. Thus Charles thought he had secured his life work, the recovery of the Protestants for the Catholic church. But his autocratic behaviour in the height of his power displeased even Catholic princes and made them by no means disinclined to join a coalition against him. Henry II. of

---

[1] SCHAFF. I 343 ff. HEPPE, p. 491 ff.

France, although he had far stronger Catholic sympathies than Francis I. had had, was jealous of Charles's growing power, and was ready to enter into a league against him, although now, in face of the politically humiliated Germans, only at the price of the Lothringian bishoprics of Metz, Tull and Verdun. Maurice employed the time, during which he was carrying out the sentence of outlawry upon defiant Magdeburg by command of the Emperor, in getting up a coalition against him. After the capitulation of the city (November 4th, 1551) he suddenly came forward with the most serious accusations against the Emperor, marched against him while he lingered in a state of unpreparedness at Innsbruck with a rapidly increasing army, while France at the same time attacked the Netherlands. The imperial power was broken at a single blow; neither Ferdinand, who had become estranged from his brother in consequence of his plans of succession, nor the Catholic States helped him; indeed, the former left the passes of the Tyrol open to the enemy. On the basis of negotiations that took place between Maurice and Ferdinand at Linz, at which the Emperor showed himself very tenacious on the religious question, the victors now obtained, at the diet at **Passau**, in which Charles took no part in person, and lastly, in the camp before Frankfort, the so-called **Treaty of Passau** (August 2nd, 1552). True to his convictions and his Catholic conscience, Charles attempted to keep back negotiations and to cling tenaciously to the leading idea of his church policy, the ecclesiastical unity of the Empire. Hence, a **definitive** recognition of equality of privileges and mutual toleration on the part of both religious parties was not yet attained, but, in the first instance, only an **amnesty** and **truce** until the next diet, which was to decide in what way (whether by council, a resolution of the Empire, or a colloquy) the difference should be removed. A supplementary treaty (not signed by the Emperor) settled that, even if no agreement should be come to, the state of peace should notwithstanding continue. The captive princes were to be released. But the definitive settlement which was held out was long in coming.

Warlike troubles intervened, in which religious interests were on all sides ousted by political and the parties were completely upset (the Emperor's campaign against France and the futile siege of Metz; the wild Margrave Albert of Brandenburg, who at first continued the war on his own responsibility, ravaging Nuremberg, Bamberg and Würzburg, then fighting on the Rhine in the interests of France, then suddenly turning round and taking service with the Emperor, and finally (July 9th, 1553) defeated at Sievershausen by Maurice who however paid for the victory with his life : subsequently, the efforts of the Ernestines to recover electoral dignity and electoral dominions; it was not until a year later that Albert, the wild disturber of peace, was driven to France).

The more urgent the desire of a peaceful arrangement on all sides throughout the Empire, the more Charles abandoned German affairs. In the summer of 1554, he empowered Ferdinand to bring matters to an end **on his own responsibility.** He himself refused to have anything to do with this conclusion of peace, which went against his conscience.[1]

In February, 1555, **the diet of Augsburg** assembled under Ferdinand's presidency. At a by-assembly at Naumburg sixteen evangelical princes had agreed at all events to abide firmly by the CA : the offer of another religious discussion, as well as the idea of having recourse to the Interim, was thereby set aside: firmly combined, they now obtained a " permanent, abiding, and unconditional " **peace**, recognition of their rights of possession, suspension of episcopal jurisdiction over their territories, security in regard to their confiscation of ecclesiastical property, so far as " immediates "[2] had not by law the right of control over it. But now they also demanded an assured legal foundation for the further progress of the Reformation : to this the Catholic party would not and could not agree. Negotiations nearly came to a standstill on this point; but finally, Ferdinand induced the Protestants to allow him to insert in the " recess " the *reservatum ecclesiasticum* (*i.e.*, the proviso whereby prelates who joined the evangelical church were to renounce their secular authority)[3] and to leave the settlement of it to his own conscientiousness, but their counter-demand—free practice of religion for evangelical subjects under spiritual authorities—did not find a place in the " recess," but was only guaranteed them by a royal **declaration**, which was not presented to the Imperial Chamber. The right for the moment of holding both faiths was assured to the free imperial cities in the interest of the Catholic minorities. Thus **the religious peace** was made public on the 25th of September, 1555. It essentially surrendered the future of the church to the **territorial** power (*cuius regio, eius religio*) ;[4] heterodox subjects obtained the right of emi-

---

[1] LANZ III, 622 ff.
[2] [Persons subject only to the imperial government.]
[3] On this point, cp. Melanchthon's hesitation, CR VIII 477 ff.
[4] "Nam ubi unus Dominus, ibi sit una religio."   LEHMANN p. 49 ff.

grating without loss of honour or property—a considerable mitigation of the medieval proceedings against heretics; it assured to the Catholic Church the continued existence of **the ecclesiastical States**: it created **ambiguities,** which contained the germ of fresh struggles; but it sealed the **disruption** of Germany in matters of belief and gave the "adherents of the Augsburg Confession,"[1] subject to certain limitations, a recognition in the Empire on a footing of equality.[2] Continued disputes, which however seldom led to open war, as to the interpretation of the conditions of peace were the unavoidable result. Paul IV., passionately excited at the concessions, which the heretics had obtained, exclaimed: " Had Ferdinand been already Emperor, he must have been deposed." The Romish ecclesiastical historian **Raynaldus** declares that, by this peace **Satanas** *Germaniae imperium ex aequo cum* **Christo divisit.**[3] "This recess is **somewhat milder** than the recesses of former diets since 1521" was the cautious verdict of Wittenberg upon the achievement of the Religious Peace (CR VIII 652). No party was contented.

---

[1] No declaration was made as to which recension of the CA was intended, although an attempt had been made on the Catholic side to get the CA of 1530 expressly mentioned.

[2] Extension of religious freedom to the "subjects" was also discussed, especially owing to the efforts of the States, but decidedly rejected by Ferdinand. MAURENBRECHER, *Karl V und die Protest.* p. 171 f.

[3] In BARONII *Annales* XXI 133. Raynaldus's words are to be found in the edition of Mansi, Vol. XXXIII, 570.

SECOND DIVISION.

The Reformation outside Germany.

Calvinism.

CHAPTER FIRST

The Foundation of Lutheran established Churches in the Scandinavian North.

The conquests which Lutheranism made in the North were intimately connected with the efforts of the royal authority to break the too powerful influence of the bishops: the Reformation served to strengthen the royal power and hence, from the outset, bore a conservative character in regard to the State Church, was a reform from above, without a deeper stirring up of the soul of the people. But still, Lutheranism proved itself a power, which here gradually took firm root and penetrated deeply into the life of the people.

1. Denmark.

Sources: A. SCHUMACHER, *Gel. Männer Briefe an die Könige in Dänemark* (1522-1663). 3 vols. Kopenh. u. Leipz., 1758, 1759. *Dänische Bibliothek*, Kopenh. u. Leipz., 1738-1743. *Aarsberetninger fra det kongelige Geheime-archiv*. 1852 ff. I 215 ff.

Literature: E. PONTOPPIDAN, *Kurzgefasste Ref.-Hist. der dän. Kirche*. Lübeck, 1734; the same, *Annales ecclesiae Danicae*. Vols. II. and III. Kopenh., 1744 and 1747. F. MÜNTER, *KGesch. von Dänem. u. Norw. III*. Leipz., 1833. CH. TH. ENGELSTOFT, *Reformantes et Catholici in Dania concertantes*. Hauniae, 1836. F. C. DAHLMANN, *Gesch. von. Dän. III*. Hamb., 1843. Considerable information may also be found in *Kirkehistoriske Samlinger*. Kjöbenh. 1849 ff. For H. TAUSEN see Biography by P. Rön. Hafn., 1757. J. S. B. SUHR, Ribe, 1836. RÖRDAM in Kirkehist. Saml. V and VI. For Bugenhagen in Denmark see B. MÜNTER, *Symbolae ad illustr. Bugenhagii in Dania commorationem*. Hauniae. 1836. HERING, *Bugenh.*, Halle, 1888. C. H. CLAUSS, *Christian III*. Dessau, 1859. For the Reformation in ICELAND, see L. CHR. MÜLLER in ZhTh 20, 384 ff. (SCHLESWIG-HOLSTEIN: G. J. TH. LAU, *Gesch. der Einführung u. Verbr. der Ref. in Schlesw.-Holst*. Hamb. 1867. JENSEN-MICHELSEN, *Schl.-H. KGesch. III*. Kiel, 1877. L. SCHMITT, *der Carmeliter Paulus Heliae*. Freib., 1893.

Queen Margaret's Union of Calmar (1397), in accordance with which the three northern kingdoms were to have only **one** king, had not, however, been able to bring about lasting tranquillity. In 1448 it was broken up, Sweden separated under Karl Knudson, without accepting as king Count Christian of Oldenburg, who had been chosen by the Danes and, after some hesitation, recognised by the Norwegians. However, **Christian I.** (1448-1481) after defeating the rival king (1457), succeeded in reuniting the kingdoms; in 1460 Schleswig-Holstein also fell to his share (after 1490, divided between his sons Hans (John) [Segeburg] and Frederick [Gottorp]. But **John,** as ruler of the northern kingdoms, did not succeed in holding his ground in Sweden against the two powerful Swedish vice-regents the Sten Stures. But as the Archbishop Gustavus Trolle actively supported the interests of Denmark, John's energetic, brutal and bloodthirsty son **Christian II.,**[1] relying on his party, ventured to reclaim the Swedish crown: repulsed in 1518, he again landed in 1520, being now further assisted by the papal sentence of excommunication pronounced against those who proved refractory. Sten Sture the younger fell in battle, Trolle was reinstated in his office, from which he had been ousted and had fled to Denmark, and Christian was crowned at Stockholm: but the fearful **massacre,** by which he now thought to establish the union permanently, became the prelude to the revolt of Sweden under Gustavus Vasa.

Immediately after his victory, Christian wrote to his uncle Frederick the Wise and asked him to send a theologian of the school of Luther and Carlstadt to Copenhagen. The Reformation was intended to aid him in weakening the power of the bishops and securing by force the possession of their landed property for the State. Martin Reinhard (Rhynhart) arrived at the end of the year 1520 and preached, his sermons being interpreted by the Carmelite prior, Paul Eliä, who soon, however, turned against the foreigner; the King sent Reinhard back, in order, if possible, to get Luther himself for Copenhagen. The latter did not come, but Carlstadt did,[2] although he in like manner returned after a brief stay.

In the meanwhile, Christian was occupied with the scheme of reforming his people by legislative measures. All appeals to Rome were to cease, the clergy were to be allowed to marry, the secular power of the bishops, who were to be kept to the religious administration of their office, was to be curtailed, and the monasteries reformed. He certainly abandoned this bold scheme as impracticable; but, by an order which had in view the amelioration of the state of affairs in the city (1522), he introduced many reforms in ecclesiastical matters. But the Jutes, dissatisfied with his rule, rose against him and, in 1523, offered the throne to his uncle **Frederick** von Gottorp from Denmark; Christian, at variance with himself, deserted his cause, in order to seek help from his

---

[1] [1513-1523].

[2] H. GRAM in *Kiöbenh. Seldkabs Skrifter,* 1747. III 1 ff. D. SCHÄFER in ZKG XIII 311 ff. (against VIII 283 ff.).

father-in-law, Charles V., and his German relatives. His code was burnt, and Frederick recognised as King by Denmark and Norway. At heart attached to the Reformation, he nevertheless swore that he would resist Luther's heretical pupils and punish them in person and property; in reality, he rendered no assistance to the Reformation, but neither did he violently check it in its irresistible progress from the duchies to the North. At the diet of Odensee (1527), he succeeded in carrying a law of toleration, which allowed free scope to the preaching of the new doctrines by the side of the old until a general council had given its decision; he declared that he had only sworn to protect the Catholic church, not its errors. The nobility saw in the abolition of the excessive power of the bishops a strengthening of their own position, and accordingly supported Frederick. The clergy were allowed to marry, and the bishops, instead of fetching the *pallium* from Rome, had to get it from the King. Protected by this law, the Reformation made rapid progress.

Hans Tausen (Tausanus, the "Danish Luther") occupied a prominent position as its spiritual promoter. The son of a peasant of Fühnen (born 1494), a monk of the Order of St. John at Antvorskov, he studied from 1516 at Rostock, where he gave philosophical lectures; he afterwards became (in 1523) a pupil of the German reformers at Wittenberg (Alb. acad. Viteb., p. 118); imprisoned in his native country as a Lutheran and subsequently released, he repaired to Wiborg in Jutland, which he made the starting-point of the evangelical movement, until he was again imprisoned. The King now took him under his protection and appointed him his chaplain, which enabled him to carry on his work unhindered. Numerous writings, amongst them two translations of the New Testament into Danish (by Michelsen, 1524, and a better one by Petersen, 1529), Tausen's version of the baptismal service, hymns original and translated from the German—all these carried the movement into wider circles; on the other side, Paul Eliä came more prominently into notice as the literary defender of the old order of things. Evangelical communities were formed, which in a few instances succeeded in gaining possession of certain churches with the co-operation of the magistrates. At the diet of 1530, held at Copenhagen, the King requested the bishops and prelates on the one side, and the Lutheran preachers, Tausen and his followers on the other, to present their confession and to discuss the question how **one** Christian religion might be established in the kingdom. Tausen handed in a confession consisting of forty-three articles;[1] the bishops opposed to it a confutation in the form of a bill of indictment; the preachers replied with an Apologia.[2] The intended disputation did not take place, since it was found impossible to come to an agreement as to

---

[1] In MÜNTER III 308 ff.

[2] *Apologia Concionatorum Evangelicorum* . . . . edita cum ipsa accusatione a M. WÖLDIKE. Hafniae 1739 ff. ENGELSTOFT, *de confutatione latina, quae apologiae Evangelicorum* . . . . *1530 opposita est.* Havniae, 1847.

the language in which matters should be discussed or the choice of judges whose decision would be accepted. The King thereupon decided that the Protestants should be allowed to remain unmolested until the meeting of the Council. In 1531, there was an outburst of iconoclasm, at Copenhagen, which however Tausen decidedly opposed.

In 1533 Frederick died, after Christian II., relying upon the discontent of the prelates and the Catholic party and having made his peace with the Pope, had in vain attempted to reconquer the kingdoms, and was subsequently rendered harmless by being kept in strict confinement. The States, at the new election, now hesitated between Frederick's son, **Christian III.,** who had made Luther's acquaintance as a youth at the diet of Worms, and as vice-regent of the duchies[1] had already accepted Luther's doctrines, and the youthful John, who was decidedly favoured by the bishops; the claims of other German princes were also considered. The ambitious and far-reaching schemes of Wullenwever and Mark Meyer for the extension of the Hanseatic League, a democratic constitution and the introduction of the Reformation at the same time (p. 130) had a disturbing influence upon affairs; but it was just the revolutionary character of this movement that caused the conservative elements of the population to look to Christian III. for support. The Knights of Jutland and the islands did homage to him, he conquered Fühnen, and afterwards proceeded to besiege Copenhagen. Wullenwever's influence collapsed in Lübeck itself: the peace, which Christian concluded with Lübeck in February, 1536, was followed by the submission of Malmös, and (in July) by that of Copenhagen.

Hereby the kingdom and also the victory of a conservative Reformation, regulated from high quarters, was made safe. All the Danish bishops were imprisoned, their chapter-properties confiscated, and subsequently, at a council of the kingdom, in which nobles, burgesses, and peasants were represented, the reorganisation of the Church in the State was decided upon. The power of the bishops was broken, their properties became crown-lands, a third of the tithes was appropriated to the advancement of learning and

---

[1] HERMANN TAST had worked since 1522 at Husum in the spirit of Luther: the prelates, in 1526, had further attempted to check the progress of the movement by large supplies of money, but in the same year the Reformation already proved victorious in the majority of the towns. In the north of Schleswig its victory was decided in the year 1528. The Flensburg disputation between Tast (and others) and Melchior Hofmann (under the presidency of Bugenhagen) about the Eucharist and Baptism (1529, see p. 93) decided the rejection of the Zwinglian doctrine of the Eucharist and of mystic enthusiasm. During the reign of Christian III. Bugenhagen (in 1541) introduced the first Lutheran "bishop" in Schleswig, and in 1542 the modified Danish ritual also came into force in the duchies. The bishopric of Schleswig, after the precedent of affairs in Germany, till 1624 further served as a maintenance for the princes of the house. The monasteries were allowed to die out and their estates assigned to the crown, the four nunneries of St. John, Schleswig, Preetz, Jtzehoe and Uetersen were handed over to the Knights as aristocratic ladies' seminaries.

science. **Bugenhagen**, who had been summoned to Copenhagen in 1537, crowned the King, consecrated seven superintendents,[1] who still, however, retained the **title** of bishop, and assisted in completing a very conservative ecclesiastical order which had been drawn up by certain Danish theologians.[2] The monasteries were secularised, the owners of property received important rights of patronage. Attention was paid to the improvement of the university and educational affairs. Christian entered into relations with the leaders of the Schmalkaldic league, but then drew back again.

In **Norway**, the independence of which was to be abolished, Christian III. was only recognised in its southern part in 1536; in the North, opposition threatened in favour of the imprisoned Christian II. under the leadership of the Archbishop of Drontheim, Oluf Engelbrechtson. But, on the King's approach, the latter fled with his treasures to the Netherlands. Thus, here also, the old Church fell, the church-property was confiscated by the crown, the archiepiscopal office done away with and the church reorganised on the Danish model: nevertheless, the disinclination of the population to submit caused difficulties for a considerable time. It was found even more difficult to make **Iceland** bow to the will of the King. Certainly Luther's New Testament had been secretly circulated in an Icelandic translation,[3] and Bishop Gisser Einarsen of Skalholt, who had been educated in Germany, had begun (in 1539) to reform the Church after the Danish model. But, in 1548, a violent Catholic reaction followed under Bishop Aresen, who refused obedience to Copenhagen. He was executed as a traitor in 1550; however, his adherents rose in revolt and were not put down till 1554. The Lutheran ecclesiastical order was now introduced, in many instances by force.

But danger still threatened the Lutheran Danish royal throne from the German Empire, the Habsburgs supporting the claims of Christian II. until the peace of Spires (1544) brought about an amicable understanding, after which the prisoner was allowed greater liberty.

The Lutheran Church in Denmark and Norway now essentially developed itself in the forms and tendencies of German Lutheranism. After the fall of the bishops, the great superiority of the nobles, whereby the servitude of the peasants was now for the first time introduced, was dangerous to church matters. This authority exerted itself ecclesiastically in the case of rights of patrons. However, Christian was obliged to establish a law in 1551, that the children of ministers should not be treated as serfs of their patrons. The CA was also accepted as the basis of confession for Denmark and Norway; Tausen's confession of 1530, on the other hand, was ousted. The Formula of Concord, on the other hand, was rejected (see below).

---

[1] The Danish Church boasts of an uninterrupted episcopal succession. Peter Palladius, a disciple of the Wittenbergers, became bishop of Roeskilde, Tausen received an appointment at the newly-organised university.

[2] In this the prohibition of any formula of administering the Sacrament is peculiar.

[3] Printed in 1540, cp. Dän. Bibl., 8 Stück, p. 20 ff.

2. Sweden.

Sources and *Literature :* Skrifter och Handlingar, til Uplysning i Swenska Kyrko och Reformations Historien; 5 parts. Ups. 1790, 1791. JOH. BAAZIUS, *Inventarium Eccles. Sveogothorum.* Lincopiae, 1642. THYSELIUS, *Handlingar till Sverges Reformations och Kyrkohistoria undar Konung Gustaf I.* Stockh., 1841-1845. For more important information, see also ZhTh 17, 183 ff.; the same, in ZhTh 16, 238 ff. J. WEIDLING, *Schwed. Gesch. im ZA der Ref.* Gotha, 1882. E. G. GEIJER, *Gesch. Schwedens II.* Hamb., 1834. A. FRYXELL, *Leben Gustavs I. Wasa.* Neustadt a.d.O. 1831. AUG. THEINER, *Schweden und seine Stellung zum hl. Stuhle;* 2 parts. Augsburg, 1838 (as far as the text is concerned one of the worst productions of Ultramontane history-making, but it contains valuable additions from the archives).

In consequence of the massacre of Stockholm (p. 164), **Gustavus Vasa**, a young connection of the family of the Stures, was elected regent in 1521; and, when Christian II. retired from Denmark, whither he was followed by Frederick I., who now claimed recognition in Sweden on the basis of the Union of Calmar, the diet of Strengness elected Gustavus King (1523). The overthrow of the too wealthy and powerful bishops was here also of vital importance to the new monarchy which, being without means, had to rely upon the support of the people.

At the diet of Strengness, an eloquent and undaunted adherent of Luther had already arisen in the person of **Olaus Petri** (Olaf, or Olave Peterson). In 1516 he had gone to study at Leipzig, but had soon migrated to Wittenberg to hear Luther; in 1519 he returned home and, as deacon of Strengness, had found an intelligent superior in Archdeacon Laurence Andreä (Anderson), so that the cathedral pulpit as well as the cathedral school was opened to the new doctrines. But, just at this moment, the legate of Adrian VI., John Magni, appeared at the diet, and demanded the suppression of the Lutheran heresy; he even for the moment obtained a promise from the cathedral chapter, that it would abstain from the new doctrines. At the moment, the King's chief anxiety was to prevent the Pope again forcing upon him Archbishop Trolle, who had Danish leanings, and to get him to approve his expulsion; he was clever enough to interest the legate on his behalf, and caused him to be elected Trolle's successor himself. A papal brief arrived, demanding the re-acceptance of the latter. Then Gustavus (certainly influenced by the course of events in Germany, *e.g.,* the Diet of Nuremberg) presented a kind of ultimatum to the Curia; that if he should be opposed there, *nos per liberam et regiam nostram auctoritatem ita de ecclesiis et Christiana religione in terris nostris disponemus, secundum quod Deo et omnibus Christianis principibus placere credamus;*[1] if patience and friendliness should prove of no avail, *ad iustitiae rigorem procedemus, non sinentes populum nostrum sub alienorum intolerabili iugo servire.* Shortly after this, Adrian died, and Clement VII. at first conceded that Magni should act as archbishop until Trolle's affair should be decided. In the meantime,

---

[1] THEINER II *Urkunden,* p. 13.

Gustavus had afforded effective support to the evangelicals; he summoned Laurence Anderson to Court as his chancellor and took care that Olave Peterson should be appointed not only a preacher at **Stockholm** itself, but at the same time town-clerk. Evangelical preaching now resounded unchecked through the capital. Luther's writings were allowed to be publicly offered for sale; and when the leader of the old church party, Bishop Brask of Linköping, endeavoured to obtain the prohibition of these writings, the King replied that hitherto these writings had not been condemned by unbiassed persons, but only by opponents. Thus protected, Olave Peterson in 1525 was able to marry; the King himself caused the Bible to be translated into Swedish, and cleverly paralysed any counter-action on the part of the episcopate by inviting the vain Magni to render a service to Sweden by undertaking the work. While this work of Magni's was in preparation, a translation of the New Testament prepared by the evangelicals (Laurence Anderson and others) appeared in 1526,[1] and became an important factor in the spread of Lutheranism. Melchior Hofmann, who was now also stirring up men's minds in Stockholm, was driven out of the country (p. 93). Gustavus continued his ecclesiastical policy with heavy taxation of the large property of the church, and, while preparing the decisive blow, got John Magni out of the way by sending him as ambassador to Russia and Poland.[2] Charles's struggle with Clement (p. 70), and the scandalous union of the latter with the Turk created for him the favourable moment to strike the first blow.

He planned a disputation at a church synod of the kingdom, for which twelve articles were drawn up, which were discussed by Peter Galle on the Romish, and by Olave Peterson on the evangelical side.[3] He then summoned (at Whitsuntide, 1527) a diet at Westerås, and laid certain proposals before it, which were at first indignantly rejected by the bishops and nobles: Gustavus then suddenly declared his intention of solemnly laying down his authority, whereupon, in the greatest confusion and thoroughly disheartened, they begged him to resume his authority, and humbly conceded all his demands: the surrender of the episcopal castles and strongholds to the King, the latter to have free liberty of disposal of their revenues: the right of the nobles to withdraw their donations which had been given to the Church since 1454: free preaching of the "pure word of God and the Gospel." The episcopal power was broken by the King's well-directed policy; Bishop Brask, the leader of those who held by the old doctrines, resigned his office and secretly left the country. Gustavus summoned a number of new bishops, having divided the large dioceses

---

[1] Reprinted by Acksel Andersson. Upsala, 1893.

[2] On his journey, Magni importuned the Pope to confirm his appointment as archbishop and to furnish him with the fullest powers; he would then, he said, oppose the apostasy of Sweden, but without the archiepiscopal *pallium* he would not venture to return there. THEINER II., *Urkunden*, p. 21 ff.

[3] Skrifter och Handlingar I., 1 ff. BAAZIUS, p. 165 ff.

and thus increased their number, who were consecrated by the old bishop, Peter Magni of Westeräs, as the only holder of the Catholic episcopal consecration, although he earnestly resisted. Surrounded by these new bishops, Gustavus caused himself to be crowned in 1528, and Olave Peterson preached the sermon at the ceremony.

Peterson worked indefatigably, by means of pamphlets and tractates written in Swedish,[1] to spread the ideas of the German reformation; he was a disciple of Luther, who, in the matter of the Eucharist, steadfastly adhered to Luther's older, dogmatically undeveloped method of teaching. By translations and poetry of his own, he also began to furnish the Swedes with an evangelical hymnology (the first hymn-book was published in 1530), and in 1529 composed the first liturgy in the Swedish language[2] on Lutheran lines; in 1531 followed the " Swedish mass "[3] quite after the model of the conservative Lutheran services. Numerous young men repaired to Wittenberg for purposes of study. Under the presidency of Laurence Anderson (now archdeacon of Upsala) a synod was held at Oerebro in 1528, which allowed evangelical preaching, but at the same time instituted only very sparingly reforms in ecclesiastical practices, and showed itself especially conservative in the matter of ritual. Although the episcopal title was retained, the control of ecclesiastical matters was still in the hands of the ruling prince, to whom the control of the Church was made over. The twelve bishops (of whom the Bishop of Upsala bore the title of Archbishop) formed no union: the Archbishop was only *primus inter pares*, upon whom devolved the coronation of the Kings, the *actus ministeriales* in the royal house and the office of spokesman of the ecclesiastical order at the diet, but he possessed no jurisdiction over his colleagues. Olave Peterson's younger brother, Laurence, was the first Archbishop of Upsala (1531).[4] As the majority of the old clergy remained in office, while the younger were eager for innovations and reforms, disputes were unavoidable. At first no violent changes were made, even the monasteries being allowed to continue; further steps were only taken gradually as the result of several synods. The " Gustavus" Bible, prepared by the brothers Peterson, did not appear till 1541. In the succeeding year, discontent with the alterations forced upon the Church led to a revolt.

In supporting Gustavus, the people had at first only intended to aid the victory of the national monarchy, not that of the new doctrines. In the end, his inconsiderate interference with church property and church government was bound to evoke opposition and resistance in the country even on the part of the Protestants. At the time Sweden was but little affected by the spirit of the Reformation and only in limited circles.

---

[1] See specimens in Skrifter och Handl. I—V.

[2] Een Handbock pää Swensko. Skrifter III 41 ff.

[3] Skrifter III 147 ff. (Formula of administration: May the body [blood] of our Lord Jesus Christ preserve thy soul to everlasting life).

[4] Clement now first appointed in opposition John Magni Archbishop and Primate of Sweden. Dantzig became the meeting place of the northern Catholic fugitives.

CHAPTER SECOND.

(French) Switzerland and Calvin.

1. German and French Switzerland after the death of Zwingli.

Literature: BULLINGER: *Biography* by PESTALOZZI. Elberf., 1858. MÖRIKOFER in ADB 3, 513 ff. J. HEER in RE II 779 ff. K. KRAFFT, *Aufzeichnungen des schweiz. Ref. H. B.* Elberf., 1870. USTERI, *Vertiefung der Zwingli' schen Sakramentslehre bei Bull.* in StKr 1883, 730 ff. O. MYCONIUS: *Biography* by KIRCHHOFER. Zürich, 1813. HAGENBACH. Elberf., 1859. B. RIGGENBACH in RE X 403 ff. FAREL: *Biography* by KIRCHHOFER; 2 vols. Zürich, 1831 (the same, in StKr 1831, 282 ff.). FAREL and VIRET: C. SCHMIDT. Elberf., 1860. P. GODET, *Viret.* Lausanne, 1892. In addition: F. W. KAMPSCHULTE, *J. Calvin, seine Kirche und sein Staat.* I. Leipz., 1869. ROGET, *Hist. du peuple de Genève;* 7 vols. Genf., 1870 to 1883. K. PIETSCHKER, *die luth. Reform. in Genf.* Cöthen, 1875. CALLET, *Ph. Berthelier, fondateur de la républ. de Gen.* Paris, 1892. RUCHAT, *Hist. de la réf. de la Suisse.* Gen., 1728. FLEURY, *Hist. de l'égl. de Gen.;* 2 vols. Gen., 1880. M. PHILIPPSON, *Westeuropa im ZA Philipps II.* Berlin, 1882. HUNDESHAGEN, *die Conflicte . . . . in der Berner Landeskirche.* Bern, 1842.

After the unhappy issue of the War of Cappel, the excellent **Henry Bullinger** had taken Zwingli's place. He was the son of a minister and dean of the chapter of Bremgarten, born in 1504 as the result of a marriage which was tolerated by the Church, although it was not legitimate, and for which his father subsequently received the blessing of the Church (in 1529). Educated at Emmerich, at the school of the "Brethren of the Common Life," he commenced the study of theology at Cologne, where, by a steady process of development, he first turned from Scholasticism to the older fathers of the church, and then, by secret perusal of the writings of Luther and Melanchthon, to the study of the Scriptures. When the youthful *magister* returned to his native place (1522) and obtained a post at the Cistercian school at Cappel, he independently and decidedly took his stand on the side of the Reformation. He took an active part in the establishment of the principles of the Reformation in the city and monastery of Cappel, and accompanied Zwingli to the disputation at Berne. In 1529, he married a former nun, succeeded his father at Bremgarten, but, after the unlucky war of 1531, was obliged to leave his native place and repair to Zürich, where he was appointed preacher at the great cathedral. Here, where under pressure of events those who showed decidedly evangelical tendencies were driven back and the secret or political friends of the old state of things made more and more headway, in spite of a resolution of the Council whereby preachers were forbidden to say a word about political matters, he succeeded in preserving for them the right of free speech, and at the same time, by careful reserve, brought about better relations between the clergy and the authorities. During the tension that existed between the orthodox and reformed cantons in consequence of the counter-reformatory current, his declaration at Zürich to abide "stoutly and steadfastly" by the Gospel, since it contained some cutting remarks against the Romish mass, was interpreted as a breach of the peace; too weak to defend himself, he was again obliged to acquiesce in a humiliating agreement (Einsiedeln, 1533). But the prosperous development of the reformed church at Zürich quietly proceeded, and Bullinger above all worked indefatigably as a fascinating popular preacher and as a spiritual guide, in his solicitude for higher and lower school education, by founding and carrying on the arrangements for preachers and synods, and in his devoted care for banished co-religionists. At the same time, he exerted himself to continue to teach Zwingli's Eucharistic doctrines by bringing into prominence the mystery of the divine effect of grace upon believers in the direction in which an agreement with Calvin's interpretation subsequently became possible. (For the First Confession of Bâle and the Helvetic Confession, see above, p. 125.)

In 1534, the maintenance of the Reformation was confirmed by oath at **Berne** by the whole district. At **Bâle**, the place of Oecolampadius was taken by **Oswald Myconius**, the friend of Zwingli, but less abrupt and more temperate, who had previously held a post as schoolmaster at Zürich.

Now, however, French Switzerland came equally into prominence with German Switzerland. In the French-speaking districts of the modern cantons of Berne and Biel, the fiery, turbulent Frenchman, **William Farel**, had been preaching since 1526 (for his disputation at Bâle, see p. 57). Born in Dauphiné, a pupil of Faber Stapulensis, he had at first lived with Bishop Briçonnet, of Meaux, and then, when the latter was no longer able to protect him, had sought refuge at Bâle, which he was obliged to leave after the disputation. After a short stay at Strasburg, where he became intimate with Bucer and Capito, he commenced his stirring campaign in the French districts of Switzerland. After breaking the images at the hospital chapel, he gained Neuchâtel over to the Reformation. In the course of his wandering life as a preacher he reached **Geneva** in 1532.

This city, which originally fell to the German Empire together with New Burgundy, had lost many liberties and rights to the bishop, who relied upon the support of the Dukes of Savoy; the dukes, as lord-protectors, occupied the castle. Since the beginning of the 14th century, Geneva had been regarded as a city of Savoy, and still more so in the 15th, since the bishops had been for the most part princes of Savoy. At the beginning of the 16th century, luxury and immorality had become very prevalent at the episcopal court and also amongst the clergy. In 1526, the political situation was altered; an attempt of the duke and his episcopal relative to annihilate the republican order of things and simply to incorporate Geneva with the duchy, was repulsed with the aid of Berne and Freiburg; the ducal troops were driven out, and a decidedly republican constitution introduced; the bishop was limited to his ecclesiastical rights. Philip Berthelier had been the leader of the "Confederates." Years of stormy movements and struggles with Savoy followed: but at the same time also the new religious ideas, exercising their effect from Berne, began to make themselves plainly heard.

While matters were in this state of ferment, Farel made his appearance in 1532, with a defiant demeanour; he was soon obliged to withdraw, but sent the young **Antony Froment** to Geneva in his place. At the end of 1533, he returned to Geneva under the protection of Berne, accompanied by **Peter Viret**. A religious discussion, held in January, 1534, in the presence of delegates from the town council of Berne, which was followed by a second, assisted progress; the populace was carried away by Farel's stirring words; in several of the city churches the service of the mass was forcibly abolished by him. The majority of the Great Council took his side and, after the autumn of 1535, Geneva became an evangelical city: by a resolution of the assembly of the citizens (May 21st, 1536) the papal religion was abolished and the new church elevated to the dignity of the state church: the reformed ideas had won the victory. Charles of Savoy still attempted to take measures against the rebellious city, but Berne liberated Geneva and conquered Vaud for itself. The bishop transferred his see to Annecy. A resolution of the Council established a simple service, daily early sermons in place of the mass, celebration of the Eucharist with ordinary bread, and introduced strict moral discipline. The way was entered upon, which would inevitably lead to a state church police as in the evangelical cantons of German Switzerland. On Farel alone fell nearly all the work of the re-organisation of the church—Viret was now working in Lausanne—and that amongst a deeply roused population, intoxicated by its young political and ecclesiastical freedom, only slightly penetrated by deeper evangelical conviction, and still less inclined to strict moral discipline. Then the man appeared in Geneva, whom Farel immediately endeavoured to secure for the accomplishment of the great task: **John Calvin.**

2. Calvin until the time of his arrival at Geneva.

Sources: Opera Calvini in CR (edited by BAUM, CUNITZ, REUSS and others) Vols. 29-73 (1-45). Braunschweig. 1863-1892 (containing in 38b—49[=10b —21] the highly important *Thesaurus Epistolarum*, consisting of 4,271 letters; Calvin's Biography by BEZA 1564 and *Annales Calviniani;* Indices in 50 [22]; from 51 [23] onwards the *opera exegetica* and *homiletica*). HERMINJARD, *Corresp. des réformateurs dans les pays de langue française.* VIII vols. Gen. and Paris 1866-1893.

Literature: See above p. 171; add Biographies by H. HENRY. 3 vols. Hamb. 1835; HERZOG, Basel 1843; E. STÄHELIN, 2 vols. Elberf. 1861. LEFRANC, *la jeunesse de C.* Paris 1888; M'CRIE. *The early years of John Calvin*, Edin. 1880; A. LANG, *die ältest. theol. Arbeiten C.'s*, in NJdTh II 273 ff. BERTHAULT, *Mat. Cordier.* Paris 1876. PIERSON, *Studien over J. Kalvijn.* Aust. 1881. USTERI, *Calvins Sakr. u. Tauflehre* in StKr 1884, 417 ff. On the *Institutio*, see J. KÖSTLIN in StKr 1868, 7 ff., 410 ff. On his stay at Ferrara: SCHELCHER in ZkW 1885, 498 ff.: SANDONNINI in Rivista storia Italiana 1887, 531 ff. and *Ancora del soggiorno di C. a F.* Modena 1889; FONTANA in Arch. della soc. Rom. di storia patria, 8, 101 ff. F. KATTENBUSCH; J. C. in JdTh 23, 353 ff. E. MARCKS, *Coligny:* I. I. Stuttgart, 1892, p. 281 ff. For CALVIN's *Theology* see LOOFS ³426 ff. I regret that the valuable Essays of H. LECOULTRE (in the Revue de Théologie et de Philosophie) on Calvin did not come into my hands until it was too late for me to make use of them in the text.' On Calvin's conversion (XXIII 1 ff.), he says that it was *ni une conversion de l'intelligence, ni une conversion du sentiment, mais une conversion de la volonté* (p. 28); for the Commentary on Seneca, see XXIV. 51 ff.; for Ferrara, XIX 168 ff. and XXIV 225 ff.; for Calvin's banishment from Geneva, XIX 522 ff. My doubts of the Calvinistic authorship of the speech of Cop (see page 175) are founded, apart from considerations of style and material, upon the striking phenomenon that the French edition of Beza's *Vita Calvini* (Geneva, 1663, p. 16) **omits** the statement of the Latin *suggessit eam Calvinus* and makes the latter withdraw from Paris only in consequence of his *familiarité* with Cop (Copus). But the expression "probably spurious" is somewhat too strong. DALTON, *Calvin's Bekehrung* in Dev Bl 1893, 529 ff.

John Calvin (Jean Cauvin or Caulvin) was born on the 10th of July, 1509, at Noyon in Picardy. His father was procurator-fiscal and the bishop's secretary; he was not a wealthy man, but favoured by position and connections. The son, from early youth, exhibited not only zeal in all ecclesiastical exercises, but also seriousness and strictness in his views of morality; it is said of him who lost his mother early, that he never played as a boy; the weaker sides of sentimentality remained unfostered. Destined from an early age to an ecclesiastical career, he was brought up and educated in the house of a noble patron, to whom he was indebted for the aristocratic traits in his character, and from whom when only twelve years old he received a prebend. At the age of fourteen, he repaired to Paris, where Maturin Cordier became his tutor; at eighteen, he intended to begin his theological studies at the Sorbonne and had already received the tonsure as usufructuary of a prebend that had been procured for him, when the ambitious desires of his father led him to the study of law, to which he applied himself with energy and success at Orleans and Bourges. In addition, he had already been fascinated by the study of the Bible, with a translation of which his kinsman Robert Olivetanus was occupied. At Bourges he also received instruction in Greek from the German Melch. Wolmar of Rottweil, a man who had been seized by the Lutheran movement, and in whose house he first came into contact with Theodore de Beze (Beza). His studies, which had become more and more humanistic since the death of his father (1531), who had died under the ban in strife with the clergy, led him back again to Paris; his first attempt at authorship was a Commentary on Seneca's treatise *de Clementia* (1532). Even at that early date, when a band of persons interested in the study of the Bible gathered round Faber Stapulensis, and the Court, especially under the influence of Margaret, sister of Francis I., had not shown itself inaccessible to the evangelical trend of ideas, Paris had already witnessed severe persecution of the " Lutherans " and the martyrdom of many a heretic. But just at the time of Calvin's presence, remarkable fluctuations took place. Under the protection of Margaret, several pulpits were thrown open to different professors of the new doctrines, in spite of the determined opposition of the old orthodox party. To this stay at Paris (interrupted by a second course of study at Orleans)[1] belongs the sudden conversion of Calvin: *Deus animum meum subita conversione ad docilitatem egit* (CR 59, 21).[2] The hand stretched out by a burning heart became his symbol. Convinced that salvation depended alone upon God's mercy in Christ, he felt equally convinced of his own election;[3] on the other hand, he was henceforth dominated by the fundamental idea that he was the absolute property of God and at his disposal alone. By inclination a man of learning, he now thought to serve the Reformation as an author. At first, restless years of wandering followed. When King Francis, on his return from his meeting with Pope Clement at Marseilles, was on the point of taking decided steps against the heretics, on All Saints' Day, 1533 (according to the old statement of Calvin's biographers), the rector of the University and student of medicine, Nicolas Cop, delivered a speech which Calvin is said to have assisted him to compose, and which, with slight concealment, set forth the principles of the Reformation as the task of the century (CR 38, 2, 30 ff.). It is said that Cop and Calvin had to flee from the wrath of the monks. However, in regard to this incident all is uncertain; the traditional report is probably spurious; neither Calvin's share in it nor his flight occasioned by it can be clearly proved. Under the name of Charles d'Espeville he stayed with the Canon Du Tillet at Angoulême, where he diligently applied himself to his studies. On the occasion of a visit to his native town, on the 4th of May, 1534, he formally laid down his ecclesiastical dignity and was imprisoned as a heretic; he then repaired to the residence of Margaret of Navarre, the refuge of the evangelicals, Nerac in Béarn, where Faber (Le Fèvre), Roussel and others were staying at the time; in the autumn of 1534 he returned to Paris once more, just at the time when the embittered evangelicals, during the night of the 13th-14th of October, posted up violent placards attacking the mass and the like[4] on the

---

[1] Bulletin littér. et historique 1877, p. 177. CR 49, 191.

[2] This event, however, cannot have taken place as early as 1532 (as is usually assumed), but not until the spring of 1534.

[3] " He is a stranger alike to Luther's exultation and his inward struggles." KATTENBUSCH.

[4] Printed in CRESPIN, *Hist. des martyrs* 1619, 111a.

church doors and walls, even on the door of the royal bedchamber, and thereby afforded opportunity for fresh persecution. A friend of Calvin, Stephen de la Forge, was at that time burnt with others on the Place de Grève. Calvin left Paris, and, not without trouble and adventures, reached Metz, accompanied by Du Tillet: he then proceeded by way of Strasburg, where he made Bucer's acquaintance, to Bâle, where he was friendly received by Simon Grynaeus.

The persecution of the "Lutherans" in France, which Francis I. represented to the German princes as being merely directed against political agitators, violators of the Sacrament and Anabaptists, caused Calvin[1] to come forward with his *Institutio religionis christianae* (Institutes of the Christian Religion) as a testimony of the belief of the evangelicals, to which he prefixed a letter to the King (August 1st, 1535), of which he says (CR 59, 23): *Silentium meum non posse a perfidia excusari censui, nisi me pro virili opponerem*. In addition to its primary apologetic purpose, the Institutio is at the same time intended to satisfy the need of a concise representation of evangelical doctrine—which, in the first edition, it was. It first appeared in Latin (March, 1536);[2] in a number of the later editions it increased in bulk, but contained no important alteration in its dogmatic views; for it was the work of a man, whose views were fixed.[3]

While Calvin, in this work, from a theological point of view appears mainly as a pupil of the Lutheran Reformation, in regard to the **doctrine of the Eucharist** in particular, certain modifications of his own were introduced. He is at one with Zwingli in the symbolic interpretation of the words *hoc est*, in the rejection of the ubiquity of the glorified body of Christ, and in laying stress upon the celebration of the Holy Communion as a *communio* for mutual love; but he goes far beyond Zwingli in the attempt to maintain a "real" communication of the body of Christ as the *cibus vitae nostrae spiritualis*, not indeed a communication of the substance of the body of Christ, but of all the **beneficia,** *quae in suo corpore nobis Christus praestitit*, the effect of which is the certainty of eternal life and hope of resurrection; in this the bread and wine do not act as a material vehicle, but as signs whereby belief is elevated to that which they signify.

---

[1] Similarly, Zwingli, shortly before his death, had composed a vindication of the Reformation, addressed to Francis I.; *Christianae fidei expositio* (NIEMEYER, p. 36 ff. SCHAFF I 368 f.).

[2] Not, as originally assumed, in French: cp. Prolegomena in CR 29, XXIII ff. For the *editio princeps* see CR 29, 1-248.

[3] For the editions of 1539-1554 see CR 29, 253 ff.; that of 1559, in CR 30; the French edition of 1560 in CR 31 and 32. On the Institutio compare, besides KÖSTLIN, GASS, *Gesch. der prot. Dogm.* I 100 ff. KAMPSCHULTE I 251 ff. Separate edition of the Institutio (1559) by THOLUCK. Berl., 1834, 1835. German translation of the edition of 1536 by B. SPIESS. Wiesb., 1887.

At the same time Calvin was now collaborating in a **French** translation of the Bible. After Faber's earlier attempt, Calvin's uncle, Robert Olivetanus had undertaken an improved version. The **Waldenses** of the mountain valleys of Piedmont gave the first impulse towards defraying the cost of printing. They had already entered into relations with Zwingli, Bucer and Oecolampadius; on the 12th of September, 1532, they had already, at a meeting at Angrogne, declared their adhesion to the churches of the Reformation, discussed the subject of the publication of the French Bible, and in spite of their poverty had sent five hundred gold thalers for this purpose to Neuchâtel. Olivetanus's first edition of the New Testament appeared in 1534. Calvin had already rendered assistance, though not of an important nature, in the work; he rendered far greater service in the complete edition (Old and New Testament) of 1535, for which he wrote the introduction "to all Emperors, Kings, Princes, and peoples, who live under Christ's government" (CR 37, 787 ff.).[1]

We strongly hold, with Kampschulte, that, in the spring of 1536, Calvin, accompanied by Du Tillet, left Bâle and repaired to Italy to the court of the Duchess Renée of Ferrara (daughter of Louis XII. and wife of the Duke of Ferrara of the house of Este), a princess, who had already been connected in France with the Faberian circle and was under the influence of Margaret. At Ferrara, a large number of highly educated persons of evangelical leanings had assembled, amongst them some who had been obliged to leave France for the sake of their religious convictions. Soon, however, Calvin was again obliged to retire before the inquisition, however without any disturbance of his relations with Renée, with whom he kept up a continuous correspondence.[2] He returned once again to France to settle his family affairs, converted two of his brothers and sisters to his own religious views and, accompanied by them, left his native country. "If truth does not deserve to dwell in France, neither may I dwell there; I will submit to *her* lot." The war between Charles and Francis blocked the way through Lorraine, so he proposed to travel by way of Geneva to Bâle, but was detained at the former place by Farel (July, 1536). He endeavoured to excuse himself on the plea that he needed quiet to pursue his studies, and that he knew that his natural shyness made him useless for such work, and so forth. But Farel declared to him in the name of God that, if he refused his help, when the Church was in such sore need, God would curse his studies and his rest. Calvin accordingly remained, at first as a teacher of theology.

---

[1] In the edition of 1540 (Lyons) Calvin's name alone appeared; a later edition was revised by Calvin, assisted by Beza and others (Geneva, 1551, **Robert Stephanus**); a translation, which, together with the "Institution chrétienne" attained great importance for the development of French prose.

[2] More recent enquiries have tended to make even the meagre fragments of this Italian journey, which KAMPSCHULTE considered the historical germ of all kinds of fabulous travelling adventures, uncertain. Opinions are especially at variance in regard to the date of the journey: SANDONNINI transfers it to the autumn of 1535, makes the Institutio appear anonymously in August, 1535, and Calvin withdraw to Italy, in order to conceal his authorship; PHILIPPSON places the journey at the end of 1535; FONTANA fixes the stay at Ferrara between March 23rd and April 14th, 1536. Special notice is also due to Rilliet's treatise which for the first time unmasks the legend: *Lettre à M. Merle d'Aubigné.* Genève, 1864. Add C. A. CORNELIUS in DZGW IX 203 ff.

3. Calvin's early activity in Geneva, his Expulsion and Recall.

Literature: Continued from p. 174. RILLIET and DUFOUR, *le Catech. français de C. en 1537 réimprimé.* Gen. 1878. C. A. CORNELIUS, *die Verbannung C. s aus Genf* in ABA XVII; the same, *Die Rückkehr C. s nach Genf. I,* in ABA XVIII; VIGUIÉ, *C. à Strasbourg.* Paris, 1880; STRECKER, *J. C. als erster Pfarrh. d. ref. Gem. in Str.* Strassb., 1890. HUNDESHAGEN, · *Conflicte,* etc., p. 109 ff.

The citizens soon appointed Calvin preacher. In October, 1536, he accompanied Farel to the weighty religious disputation at Lausanne, where, together with Viret, they championed evangelical principles. The activity of his preaching soon became noticeable; above all, his work was directed towards ecclesiastical legislation, in view of realising the ecclesiastical ideal set forth by him in the Institutio. The establishment of an organised supervision of all the members of the Church conducted by the elders of the laity, with excommunication as the last ecclesiastical corrective, preceded, however, by the constituting of the community by means of a confession of faith to be rendered by each individual, is the object for which he strives. The Council accepted his proposal in January, 1537. He composed a "Catechism," not only intended for the instruction of youth, but also as an epitome of the doctrine that demanded acceptance at Geneva, which accordingly was also communicated abroad as an authentic expression of the same: *Instruction et confession de foy dont on use en l'église de Genève,* 1537.[1] He demanded and obtained from the Council the binding of the whole body of the citizens by oath to **a confession of faith,** which is an abstract of the Catechism, composed by Calvin or Farel.[2] The Council had to tender the **oath** of belief first, then the citizens by tens: future recalcitrants were liable to punishments, both civil and ecclesiastical; those who refused to take this oath were to lose their rights as citizens, a measure which could not, however, be

---

[1] In this treatise, the doctrine of predestination is expressed more definitely than in the Institutio: the seed of the word of God only takes root and bears fruit in those who are predestined for God's children by eternal election. "A tous les autres qui par mesme conseil de Dieu devant la constitution du monde sont réprouvéz, la . . . prédication . . . ne peult estre aultre chose sinon odeur de mort en mort." This doctrine has set its stamp on Calvinism,—the courage bold in death, the invincible tenacity of its professors, but also the abrupt contrast and harshness to the crowds of the " rejected." Calvin's *Catechismus Genevensis,* not composed till 1545, is different from this. NIEMEYER, p. 123 ff.
[2] RILLIET ET DUFOUR, p. 101 ff.

completely carried out and met with increasing opposition. Calvin and Farel further demanded the introduction of an ordinance,[1] which handed over the maintenance of strict ecclesiastical discipline to certain pious men to be chosen from the body of the citizens, who were to keep watch over morals, to offer admonition in common with the clergy, and to threaten the refractory before the assembled congregation with eventual exclusion from the Communion. Further, a fitting order of divine service (inclusive of congregational singing), precepts for the instruction of youth and matrimonial statutes were provided. But the Council only partly agreed to these measures, and refused to permit the monthly Communion Service and the naming of the excluded in the presence of the congregation: it recognised in the proposals accepted in January a limitation of its magisterial rights: it made the proposal in regard to ecclesiastical discipline rather a **State** ecclesiastical police regulation.

It prescribed the observance of the Sabbath, forbade games and ribald songs, and took measures against parents who did not send their children to school. The strict execution of the moral regulations appeared to have good results. But a reaction soon set in, which had its origin in the elements that were unfavourable to such rigorism, and opposed the rule of the clergy. As early as September, 1537, it was seen that no small portion of the citizens had refused to take the oath, while others went back from their word. The inhabitants of an entire street declared that they would neither leave the city nor acquiesce in the new moral constraint: they had bought their freedom dearly enough. The preachers now demanded the right of excluding from communion, together with naming of the offender, which was not allowed them for fear of disturbance. In February, 1538, the people elected the most pronounced enemies of the preachers to the city offices and as its representatives; the moral regulations which were again promulgated were derided: disorder and immorality increased. In addition, difficulties originated from **Berne**. There a more **Lutheranising** tendency (represented by Kunz) had obtained the superiority over the Zwinglian (Megander) and now claimed the adherence of the Genevese in ecclesiastical observances (the keeping of certain feasts besides Sundays, the baptismal font, and the holy wafers). The Council of Geneva took advantage of this against the preachers, but here also met

---

[1] GABEREL, *Histoire de l'église de Genève I*, pièce justific. 102.

with resistance, as they first sought a synodal agreement—for which in fact the basis was found almost entirely at the meeting at Lausanne (which was dependent upon Berne) between Calvin and Farel and the Bernese. But Calvin desired that ecclesiastical matters should be left not to magisterial but to ecclesiastical decision and hence demanded an adjournment of the innovations, until a synod should have decided. The old blind preacher Couraud was forbidden by the Council to enter the pulpit, owing to his invectives against the authorities, and, when he refused to obey the order, was imprisoned. At the Easter festival, the Council wanted to force Calvin and Farel to celebrate the Communion according to the Bernese ritual: on their refusal to do so, another preacher was substituted for them. Then they continued to preach in spite of the prohibition of the authorities, but at the same time declared to the whole congregation that it was unworthy to receive the Communion. The day after, they were **deposed** from office by the Council for contempt of the authorities. The general body of citizens, as a final court, increased the severity of this resolution: they were commanded to leave the precincts of Geneva within seventy-two hours. Eagerness to see the Church independent of the State, and also the lack of moderation and consideration exhibited by the twenty-nine year old Calvin had conjured up the conflict.

Calvin and Farel proceeded respectively to Berne and Zürich: attempts at mediation set on foot by these places proved useless; Geneva declined to resume them. Calvin went on to Grynaeus at Bâle, whence Bucer summoned him to **Strasburg,** while Farel found a post at Neuchâtel. It was of far-reaching importance to Calvin that he now came more closely into contact with the German reformers and that Strasburg's wide political horizon extended his own view. Here he received a commission from the authorities to collect and manage the congregation of French refugees, in whose case he attempted to realise his ideals of Church discipline. At the same time, he delivered lectures at the Academy, and also, in the name of the Church of Strasburg, took part in the German religious negotiations (the Frankfort Convent, the religious discussions at Hagenau, Worms and Ratisbon), feeling himself at one with the position of the Strasburgers and drawing near to Melanchthon, as he accepted the CA in the sense of its author. Here, in 1539, he thoroughly recast his Institutio, being decided by a mechanical idea of the revealed nature of the Bible, and in particular he carried out to a much greater extent the doctrine of predestination and his theocratic ecclesiastical constitution.

But, in Geneva, the continued and increasing party-struggles soon rendered a firm hand necessary again. The members of the congregation who were ecclesiastically most zealous regarded as intruders the successors in office of those who had been banished;

the fact that Calvin himself exhorted them to recognise the latter, after a sort of reconciliation had been brought about by the mediation of Berne, created a good impression in Geneva. Calvin's previous opponents partly agreed to a compromise: the sensible elements shrank from the consequences of undisciplined liberty; his energetic reply[1] to the humanistically superficial letter of Cardinal James Sadolet, Bishop of Carpentras, to the Genevese, in which he exhorted them to seek salvation in a return to Catholicism,[2] successfully assisted in changing men's minds. On the 20th of October, 1540, he was recalled by a resolution of the Council: in September, 1541, he actually returned.

4. Geneva and Switzerland under the Influence of the Spirit of Calvin.

Literature: (continued). CORNELIUS, *die Gründung d. Calv. K Verfassung* in ABA XX 251 ff. ELSTER, *C. als Staatsmann, Gesetzgeber und Nationalökonom* in Jb. f. Nationalökon. 1878, p. 163 ff.; G. GALLI, *die luth. u. calvin. Kirchenstrafen im Ref.-ZA*. Bresl. 1878, 149 ff. J. HEITZ, *C.s kirchenrechtl. Ziele*. I. ThZ aus d. Schweiz 1893, p. 10 ff.; CASTELLIO, *Biogr.* by J. MÄHLY. Basel 1862; F. BUISSON. 2 vols. Paris 1892. BOLSEC's libellous work *De la vie, moeurs, actes, doctrine, constance et mort de J. C.*, printed amongst others in *Archives curieuses de l'histoire de France*, V. Paris 1835 p. 301 ff.; add *La France prot.* [3]II 745 ff. and *die Controverse zwischen* GALIFFE *und* BORDIER 1880-1881; GALIFFE, *Quelques pages d'histoire exacte*. Genf and Basel 1868 (written in a party spirit against Calvin). BEZA: Biography by SCHLOSSER. Heidelb. 1809; BAUM, 2 vols. Leipzig 1843. 1851 (not completed); HEPPE. Elberf. 1861, also RE II 356 ff.; VIGUIÉ in Lichtenberger's Encyclopædia II 255 ff.; literature dealing with the WALDENSES in Division 7, 1; with SERVETUS, Division 7, 4. A. HOLLÄNDER in HZ 69, 385 ff.

With the *Ordonnances ecclésiastiques* 1541[3] (drawn up by Calvin, altered by the Council and accepted by the community on the 20th of November 1541), the radical transformation of Geneva from **theocratic points of view began.**

Certainly, Calvin theoretically desires the complete separation of Church and State as two different spheres. For Church administration he teaches the **divine institution** of four *ordres d'office*, the pastors (for worship and the care of souls), the doctors (for searching and interpreting the Scriptures), the elders (for moral discipline), and the deacons (for the tending of the poor). But, above all, together with pure doctrine and the administration of the Sacrament, he demands, to ensure the stability of the Church, strict **ecclesiastical discipline,**

---

[1] *Responsio ad Sadoleti epistolam*, CR 33, 385 ff.

[2] Sadoleti epistola ad senatum populumque Genevensem. Lugd., 1539. CR 33, 368 ff.

[3] RICHTER, KOO I 342 ff. CR 38a. 15 ff.

which he regarded as the sinew and substance of the Church. To carry this out, is the task of the "Consistory" or "Court of the Elders," in which clergy together with lay-elders exercised their moral and corrective office, which is to be extended rigorously to the entire civil and family life, and which has control over the primitive measures of censure, reprimand, church penance, a humble apology on one's knees before the community and excommunication. But, at the same time, this presbyterian constitution was not thoroughly developed in Geneva, where the church was not divided into communities and hence there were no communal presbyteries. The "Consistory," composed of the six city clergy and the twelve lay deputies of the Council, appeared to secure the preponderance of the latter. The choice of pastors was vested in the clergy, but the Council had the right of confirming the appointment. In this, the influence, which the state churchship of German Switzerland exercised upon Geneva became evident. But, as a matter of fact, the influence of the pastors was dominant in Geneva. "The ecclesiastical moral discipline, which elsewhere continued, in the main, theory, might be put into practice at Geneva, but theory had never gone so far elsewhere as practice at Geneva." But further, Calvin demanded from the State not only express recognition of the Church and its order of discipline, but the citizen community, at the demand of the consistory, is also to follow up the censure of the Church with further civil punishment inflicted by its instruments. Also, for the State God's word is to be the highest authority and is to carry out its requirements (which are partly drawn up under the influence of Old Testament points of view). As now the holders of the spiritual office are the summoned *ministri verbi divini*, it follows that their voice must be heard and respected by the State: as in fact Calvin himself demanded the most deep-searching influence on civil and state life and also knew how to maintain it—although certainly with severe struggles. Only **the one true faith** is to be tolerated in Geneva; suspected and convicted heretics are to be punished and coerced by the authorities; falling away from the true faith is a crime against the state. Not only did the libels of the "libertine" **Jacques Gruët** upon the clergy and his insults against the person and history of Jesus bring about his execution in 1547; but also **Michael Servetus's** (Servede) distinctly theological, although fierce attack upon the church doctrine of the Trinity fell under the point of view of the crime of blasphemy, and Calvin considered it entirely in order that he ended his life at the stake in 1553. (See more in detail in Division 7, chapter 4.) Elsewhere, also, the state authority placed itself at the service of the demands of the Consistory: for instance, when it deprived of office the excellent humanist **Sebastian Castellio**, rector of the School of Geneva, who fell out with the dogmatically abrupt and legal spirit of Geneva; in 1544, further measures taken against him obliged him to flee to Bâle: again, in punishing the physician **Jerome Bolsec** for his opposition to the strict doctrine of predestination with imprisonment and subsequently (only against Calvin's will) with banishment. Calvin in the main pressed for the severest penal laws possible and the merciless execution of the same: pious authorities must be strict. In fact, he obtained a purely Draconic justice. Within five years, 58 death sentences and 76 banishments were carried out amongst the inhabitants of Geneva, who numbered about 20,000. The old Geneva, not only the so-called "libertines," who elevated licentiousness to a principle by an appeal to the old liberties, but **the party of the old community in general,** which desired to maintain the sovereignty of the Council, kicked against this theocratic severity.

From 1546 to 1555 Calvin, supported by numerous evangelical refugees from France, was obliged to contend, in many instances with terrible harshness, against the attempts to shake off the iron yoke of his discipline. In the year 1555 the "revolt" of the city commandant (captain-general of the republic), Ami Perrin, which was exaggerated into a long prepared revolt and, at Calvin's desire, punished with cruel severity, marks Calvin's final victory. From that time resistance is broken, Calvin is master of Church and State; the latter accustoms itself to ask his opinion even in most trifling questions; and Calvin asserts his influence unbendingly, harshly, and not without imperiousness. The enemy of all recreation and amusement, he abolished popular festivals, theatres, card-playing and dancing, caused strict supervision to be kept over the few houses of entertainment which were still tolerated, and regulated private life by rules for food and clothing. The Consistory performed the functions of a keen police board of morals, exercising a strict watch and acting on Calvin's principle that it is better that many innocent persons should be punished, than that **one** guilty person should remain unpunished. During those struggles a new race, brought up by Calvin, had grown up, in which the immigrant French exercised an authoritative influence. The strict moral commands changed into morality: Geneva became the model of a well-ordered, honourable and pious community, in which prosperity flourished without luxury and crime was unknown.

But Calvin's universal genius extended beyond his local task. He keenly felt the need of first bringing into living connection the different reformed districts of Switzerland. In his struggles (*e.g.*, with Bolsec and Servetus) intercourse with the neighbouring communities had served him more than once as a point of support: but the decisiveness with which he asserted his standpoint in opposition to the Zwinglian conception, and his intellectual superiority again aroused the opposition of the various locally conditioned Swiss churches. In contrast to Zwinglianism, dogmatically independent and capable of better appreciating Luther's spirit and the advantages of Lutheran views, he recognised the need of going beyond the specifically Zwinglian institutions. He thereby created mistrust, especially as he had declared his unconditional adherence at Strasburg to the church of that place, and had subscribed to the CA (variata) at Worms (in 1540).

Zealous Zwinglians, *e.g.* in Zürich, where people had been full of mistrust since the Concord negotiations, regarded Calvin as a Lutheran. In Bâle, offence was taken at the moral and doctrinal rigorism of the Genevese; in Berne, political reasons also worked in the direction of an attitude of rejection; for the pieces of French Vaud and Savoy that had fallen to the share of Berne gravitated, after the fashion of the Romance nations and under the influence of Farel and Viret, rather in the direction of Geneva than Berne, and resisted the State churchship of Berne that opposed the theocracy of Geneva, so that jealousy of the peculiar development of Geneva was excited in Berne, especially as people saw in Calvin the origin of the diminution of their own influence upon Geneva. Certainly, the Lutheranising Bernese party had drawn nearer and nearer to Calvin, but it was driven back in 1548 by the Zwinglian: the Vaud clergy who adhered to Calvin were obliged to submit to inconsiderate treatment from Berne.

In spite of these hindrances, Calvin, in company with Farel, first succeeded (in 1549) in coming to an agreement with Zürich (Bullinger) in regard to the doctrine of the Eucharist (**Consensus Tigurinus**).[1] This consensus certainly accentuated the divergence from Luther,[2] and brought into prominence the points of contact with Zwingli,[3] but in reality did not assert Zwingli's view, but represented a compromise between Bullinger and Calvin; the latter renounced the full development of his ideas of the effect of the flesh of Christ upon believers brought about by the mediation of the Holy Spirit, while Bullinger vigorously expressed with Calvin the stress laid upon a real effect of grace in the Eucharist, which had always been opposed by him (*Christum spiritualiter cum spiritualibus eius donis recipere; Christus nos in coena facit sui participes*). Although Berne did not accept the Consensus, to which several Swiss churches soon gave their adherence, it was, notwithstanding, hailed extensively, inside and outside Switzerland (by Bucer, Lasco and others) as a joyful event.

Calvin was less successful in another point. Jerome Bolsec had, as already mentioned, publicly declared (in 1551) against his strict doctrine of predestination, which possessed fundamental importance for him, first at Geneva, then at Vevey, then, goaded on by the "libertines," at a so-called congregation, a devotional gathering, at which everyone present might make some remarks. He was at once overwhelmingly refuted by Calvin, and almost immediately imprisoned by one of the authorities. This gave occasion to the symbolic establishment of this doctrine in the **Consensus pastorum Genevensis ecclesiae, 1552** (CR 36, 249 ff. NIEMEYER, p. 218 ff.).[4] But the German cantons (Zürich,

---

[1] In NIEMEYER, p. 191 ff.; CR 35, 689 ff. SCHAFF., *Bibl. symb.* 1 471 ff.

[2] *Tollenda est quaelibet localis praesentiae imaginatio . . . perversa et impia superstitio est ipsum (Christum quatenus homo est) sub elementis huius mundi includere.*

[3] *Per metonymiam ad signum transfertur rei figuratae nomen.*

[4] SCHAFF, *Bibl. Symb.* I 474 ff. This confession contains only one detailed tract: *de aeterna Dei praedestinatione et de providentia.*

Berne, Bâle) recommended reserve in regard to this divine secret, and in Geneva itself there was no lack of opposition. Bolsec, banished from Geneva, directed abuse from the Bernese Vaud country against Calvin;[1] in Berne also he was violently attacked. The Bernese Council prohibited all useless disputations, also in regard to predestination, and forbade the Vaud clergy, who took offence at the lack of ecclesiastical discipline in the Bernese church, to communicate in Geneva (1555). A Genevese deputation, conducted by Calvin, vainly endeavoured to obtain satisfaction for the accusations and behaviour of the Vaud church. (From 1549, Viret had had the assistance of the highly educated, humanistically trained **Theodore Beza,** teacher of Greek at the school of Lausanne. He was French, like Calvin, and had advanced from humanism to evangelical views; he had already entered into personal relations with Calvin.)

French Switzerland took a lively interest in the fortunes of the Evangelicals throughout France, especially in the suffering of the **Waldenses,**[2] who were seized and driven on by the reformation movement. As the French Government, after 1556, threatened the Piedmontese Waldenses with violent measures, a resolution was come to at Geneva (in 1557) to beg the prominent Swiss cantons and evangelical princes in Germany to intercede for them with the French crown. Beza and Farel were entrusted with the commission who, after having pressed on the matter in Berne, Bâle, Zürich and Schaffhausen, repaired to Strasburg to Otto Henry of the Palatinate and Duke Christopher of Wurtemberg. Here it was a matter of overcoming **the mistrust** shown by the Lutherans (Marbach at Strasburg, Tilemann Hesshusen at Heidelberg, Duke Christopher) towards the Swiss doctrine.

In Germany men's minds had begun to be again stirred up by the opposition between the Gnesio-lutherans and Philippists in the matter of the doctrine of the Eucharist. In 1552, Joachim Westphal at Hamburg had attacked the Consensus Tigurinus, Calvin and Peter Martyr, certainly with the intention of reaching the German Philippists. The Calvinistically inclined **John a Lasco,** driven by bloody Mary from London (1553) with his Franco-Belgian reformed community, had been unable to find a welcome either in Denmark or North Germany. Calvin and Bullinger had come forward in defence of their confession thus attacked; a lively and embittered war of the pen went on. Calvin avowed his adherence to the CA, as it had been laid down at Worms (see above, p. 240), and laid stress upon his agreement with Melanchthon. The zealots all the more regarded the Philippists as Crypto-Calvinists, especially as Melanchthon was silent.[3] In addition, the embittered dispute had broken out

---

[1] His libellous tractate *De la vie, moeurs, actes, doctrine, constance et mort de J. Calvin* (see p. 181) appeared in 1577.

[2] See Division VII, chap. I.

[3] Nihil me peius habet, quam quod ille (Calvinus) audeat scribere, Philippum secum consentire et **quod Philippus publice se non purget,** writes HENRY SIIIER 1558 (in HUMMEL, *Epistolarum Semicenturia,* p. 50).

in Bremen between Timann and Hardenberg in consequence of the reformatory tendencies of the latter.

Beza now put forward a declaration[1] in regard to the doctrine of the Eucharist, which he represented as the doctrine of the Swiss and Waldenses; in this, so far as this is possible from Calvin's standpoint, the doctrine was approximated to the Lutheran conception, the points of difference were concealed, and an essential advance was made upon the Consensus Tigurinus. While people in Germany were inclined to regard this as a conversion of the Swiss, Beza's conduct, being regarded as unauthorised, aroused great discontent in German Switzerland in Bullinger, Martyr, and Haller, which Calvin could only allay with difficulty. The deputation of the Swiss and German princes on behalf of the Waldenses which was successfully carried through would have had no result, had not the complications in the interior of France drawn people's thoughts away from the poor dalesmen. They kept quiet for a time.

Calvin and his party soon afterwards displayed the same sympathy for the sorely persecuted evangelicals in Paris. Intercession with Henry II. was again desired. Beza again went as ambassador to Germany to the theologians who had assembled at Worms for a religious discussion with the Catholics. But Melanchthon and his friends found themselves compelled by the mistrust of the party of Flacius to act with the greatest caution in regard to Beza and the French Protestants. They demanded an explanation of their doctrine, in order to be able to show the princes, that they were not being employed on behalf of sectarians, but of co-religionists. Beza and Farel accordingly drew up a "Confession of the French Church," as they did not venture to propose again the disavowed "declaration." In this, they declared their adherence to the CA of 1530 with the exception of Art. 10, in regard to which there were doubts, but an understanding seemed possible. They declared that the Communion was not only a sign to them, but that Christ is present, who makes us his members through faith.[2] The Germans found this explanation "somewhat obscurely set forth," but subsequently declared that they could recommend the French Protestants to their princes as Christian brethren. Beza returned home with hopes of reconciliation, but the sensitiveness of the inhabitants of Zürich and all the non-Calvinistic (=French) Swiss broke out afresh, especially in Berne. After Beza had visited Frankfort for the third time (1558) in the interest of the Huguenots, he was summoned by Calvin from the discomfort caused him by the condition of the Bernese state-church and the conflicts that grew out of it to the newly-founded **Academy of Geneva.** Soon afterwards, Berne expelled the majority of the Vaudois clergy who resisted the Council. These internal strained relations between the representatives of the two tendencies of thought in the Swiss Reformation continued, but were unable to check the mental superiority and universal importance of Calvinistic **Geneva.**

---

[1] In BAUM, *Th. Beza*, I 405.
[2] CR IX 332. BAUM I 409.

The Academy of Geneva, under the direction of Calvin and Beza, became the seminary of a higher, especially theological education, to which foreigners crowded; Calvin's mind here obtained power over them. He set his impress upon the whole of **West European** Protestantism. In the struggle for existence, under the counter-pressure of hostile executive authorities, the latter needed the strict organisation and harsh discipline, which Calvin taught, in order that, under all pressure and entirely self-governing, it might be able to keep itself pure and remain capable of resistance. Geneva became the refuge of those who were persecuted for belief's sake, first the French, soon also the Italians, Dutch, English and Scotch, and therewith the model of the Christian community of far-reaching influence. Calvin, harsh in his ecclesiastical discipline, blunt in his teaching, nevertheless developed a great, truly oecumenical capacity, in that he on all sides maintained and promoted, by his correspondence, advice and intervention, the great interests of European Protestantism, so far as the latter did not shut the door against him. After Calvin's death (May 27th, 1564), **Beza**, who shared his opinion, continued his life's work.

But even now the strained relations were happily adjusted, which had existed between the two branches of the Swiss Reformation since the badly-received negotiations of Farel and Beza with the German Protestants in German Switzerland. When the reformed Elector Frederick III. who sided with the Reformation was in danger of being excluded from the religious peace at the Diet of Augsburg (1566), Bullinger came to his assistance with a Confession at first drawn up by him in 1564 as his private testimony. The approval which this document met with from Frederick, encouraged the people of Zürich to propose it to all the Swiss churches as a common Confession; Geneva and Berne assented at once; the others (and, last of all Bâle) gave in their adherence. The Scotch, Hungarians, French and Poles soon also joined, so that in this **second Helvetic Confession,**[1] the reformed churches found a strong bond of union.

It teaches the doctrine of predestination to eternal happiness, but with avoidance of all practically dangerous consequences, without scientific solution of the problems, in biblically edifying detail. The Lord's Supper is a recollection of Christ's Redeemer's-death with effects mighty for salvation but at the same time a renewing of the latter, a spiritual reception (through the mediation of belief) of the body and bood of Christ.

---

[1] NIEMEYER, p. 462 ff. SCHAFF. I 390 ff.; III 233 ff. ed. FRITZSCHE, Turici, 1839; E. BÖHL, Vindob., 1866.

5. The Reformation in the Grisons.

Literature: ULRICH CAMPELLI, *Hist. Raetica* (bis 1582) ed. Plattner. 2 vols. Bâle, 1877, 1890. An abstract in German in the Archiv f. G. d. Rep. Graubünden. Vol. II., Chur 1853. DE PORTA, *Hist. ref. eccl. Rhaeticarum.* 3 vols. Chur, 1771 to 1786. CHR. J. KIND, *Die Ref. in den Bist. Chur und Como.* Chur, 1858. M. VALAER, *Joh. v. Planta.* Zürich, 1888. Archiv f. Gesch. d. Rep. Graub. Part 25-27. Chur, 1857. F. MEYER, *die evg. Gem. von Locarno.* 2 vols. Zürich, 1836. PH. SCHAFF, *History of the Christian Church*, VII 130 ff.

The Reformation had also penetrated into **the Grisons** allied to Switzerland, with its three languages and three republican leagues, the league of the house of God (since 1396, in the neighbourhood of Coire), the grey league (since 1424, Disentis) and the league of the ten jurisdictions (1436, Davos). Zwingli, and later Bullinger, had devoted themselves to the old Rhaetian land, and had prepared for them messengers of faith.

The Reformation first stirred itself in the German district (see p. 82). Since 1524 **Comander** (d. 1557) had preached evangelical doctrines in Coire: the disputation at Ilanz (January, 1526), which the diet had arranged on the ground of a complaint of the Cathedral chapter about the innovator and in which Sebastian Hofmeister of Schaffhausen took part, proved a victory for the Reformation,[1] so that now the diet proclaimed **religious freedom** also for the adherents of the new doctrines, on the other hand excluded the Anabaptists and generally prohibited persecution of any kind for the sake of religion (Archiv. II 309 f.); in 1526, the right was bestowed upon the congregations of appointing and dismissing their own ministers, and the episcopal jurisdiction was thereby paralysed. After the disputations at Süs (1537 and 1538)[2] the evangelical doctrine was extended by **Philip Gallicius** through the valleys of the Engadine; he also looked after the first evangelical literature in the Rhaetio-romance language. **Ulrich Campell**, the meritorious historian (d. 1582), further continued this work. A resolution of the majority in the individual communities decided the character of their confession of faith, and two-thirds of them were soon allotted to the Reformation. Here, on the soil of political freedom and self-government, both churches found a peaceful existence side by side. Since 1537, the evangelical

---

[1] COMANDER's *Disputationsthesen* im Archiv. f. Graub. II., 290 f. HEROLD in ThZ aus der Schweiz, 1891; p. 129 ff.

[2] Archiv. II 342 ff.

churchship was managed by a synod that sat daily, at which the clergy came together with representatives of the government: a special theological educational establishment at Coire looked after the preliminary education of the clergy. The acceptance of the *Confessio Helvetica posterior* testified its spiritual adhesion to the Swiss Churches. From the Engadine the Reformation also advanced into the Italian portions of the Grisons and into the districts won from Milan at the commencement of the sixteenth century on the South side of the Alps (Veltlin,[1] Bormio, Chiavenna). Refugees from Northern Italy found protection here, but at the same time brought antitrinitarian and anabaptist leanings with them. Vergerio (see below) worked here from 1549-1553.

But here also the fanaticism that was awakened in the counter-reformation and fostered by Carlo Borromeo in Milanese territory threateningly asserted itself. The Catholic family of Planta entered into rivalry with the evangelical family of Salis. In 1570, a papal bull empowered John of Planta to retake from the evangelicals all the ecclesiastical benefices, which had been seized by them from the Catholic church. But when he endeavoured to carry out this bull, the evangelical preachers called upon the people, and Planta was executed in 1572 as a traitor to his country. But, as early as 1583, the Catholic party planned the entire annihilation of their evangelical fellow-citizens. The Protestant "Strafgericht"[2] at Thusis (1618), to which some Catholic clergy fell victims for conspiracy with Spain, was followed in July, 1620, by the **Veltlin Massacre,** in which political discontent at the strict rule of the Grisons was combined with religious fanaticism. After the Protestants were slaughtered, Veltlin declared its independence; Austrians and Spaniards occupied the little country, but France did not permit the Habsburgers to enjoy their booty; the Duc de Rohan drove them out and conquered the district in 1635, whereupon the Grisons regained their possession, but under condition that they only allowed the Catholic faith to be taught.

We must also mention the community of **Locarno** on Lago Maggiore. In this city, which at that time belonged to the Swiss Confederation, an evangelical community began to flourish; a disputation, which its leaders carried on in 1549 with the Romish party, was however decided against them by the president. Thus they were faced by the alternative of emigration or submission; in 1556, they chose the former: part of them chose the Grisons, part **Zürich** as their new home. This Italian community in Zürich then became the rendezvous for numbers of their fellow-countrymen, who had been driven from their native land by the Inquisition.

---

[1] Valtellina.
[2] A sort of tribunal of inquisition.

CHAPTER THIRD.

The Reformation Movements in France.

Literature: General. *Hist. des églises réf. de France.* Genf, 1580 (ed. BAUM and CUNITZ), Paris, 1883-1889; Bulletin de la Soc. de l'hist. du Protest. fr. Paris, 1853-1865; Bullet. hist. et littér. 1866 ff.; EUG. and EM. HAAG, *la France prot.* Paris, 1846-1859. 10 vols. F. PUAUX, *Hist. de la réf. franç.* Paris, 1859-1863. 7 vols. DE FELICE, *Hist. des Protest. de Fr.* ⁴Paris, 1861; in German, Leipzig, 1855; the same, *Histoire des synodes nationaux.* Paris, 1864. A. CROTTET, *Petite chronique protest. de France. XVIe siècle.* Paris. 1846. E. ARNAUD, *Hist. des Protestants du Dauphiné.* Paris, 1875-1876. 3 vols; the same, *Hist. des Prot. de Provence.* Paris, 1884. 2 vols. SOLDAN, *Gesch. d. Protestantismus in Frankreich bis Karl IX.* Leipz., 1855. L. V. RANKE, *Franz. Gesch. im 16 und 17 Jh.* 6 vols. (Works VIII-XIII); G. VON POLENZ, *Gesch. d. franz. Calvinism.* 5 vols. Gotha, 1857-1869. (Vol. I. up to 1560). C. SCHMIDT, *Beitr. z. Gesch. d. Ref. in Fr.* in ZhTh 20, 3 ff. Faber Stapulensis: Biography by GRAF, Strassb. 1842 (ZhTh 1852); Roussel: Biography by C. Schmidt. Strassb., 1845. E. MARCKS, *Coligny* I, 1, p. 256 ff.

1. The Beginnings of Lutheranism under Francis I.

In France also, movements in the direction of a purer biblical Christianity started from humanistic studies, and at the same time from mysticism. The humanist Le Fèvre d'Étaple (**Faber Stapulensis** see Vol. II. p. 536) proceeded from the study of the Bible to the composition of biblical commentaries (after 1512), and collected a number of pupils round him, amongst them Farel and Gérard Roussel. Himself a mystic, who edited a work by Ruysbroek, the pseudo-Dionysius and Richard of St. Victor which was regarded by him as genuine and considered one of the purest sources of the Christian religion, he never separated from the old church, but could only lament the split that was beginning; but some of his pupils, going beyond their teacher, decidedly gave in their adherence to the Reformation. The preaching of the Bible found a protector in his pupil and patron, Bishop Briçonnet of Meaux; but the latter, more deeply involved than Faber in a mysticism which was in conformity with ecclesiastical tradition, was only able, in face of the commencing struggle, to retire into the tranquil sphere of mystic contemplation. This mystic quietism, during the times of persecution that followed, offered itself to many (especially among persons of distinction, *e.g.*, at the Court of Navarre) as a welcome rest. People were content with internal piety and quietly performed mass, etc.; these forms indeed possessed no importance. Hence, further developments brought about the hatred of the decided Protestants against these who were neither one thing nor the other, "Nicodemites." Faber at first enjoyed the favour and protection of King Francis and his sister Margaret. The news of Luther's appearance on the scene had the effect of a "trumpet-blast." Many circumstances appeared favourable to the reformatory movement. At the royal court free humanistic culture prevailed, Francis himself was looked upon as its patron; in this direction he was strengthened by his highly intelligent sister (who had been since 1525 the wife of Henry II. of Navarre). The French Church had at all times been the centre of opposition to papal pretensions, the promoter of reforming tendencies and episcopalism; even at the beginning of the century, the French crown, during the political struggles in Italy, had declared itself on the side of the national church and episcopalian tendencies (Vol. II. p. 528). French royalty, already far advanced in the concentration of the monarchical authority, had shown itself capable of connecting the national church closely with the latter. Francis I. (1515-1547) had concluded his peace with Leo X. (The Concordat, see Vol. II. p. 530), whereby the latter theoretically gained the victory, while the actual advantage rested with the King, since he was to enjoy a considerable portion of the ecclesiastical revenues and a practically unlimited right of nominating the prelates. The hierarchical organism was *de facto* placed in his hands, strengthened his power and served him as a support. Hence it was his interest to maintain it intact : a French, and at the same time a royal church, the higher clergy of which were deeply involved in the worldly life of the Court. The Pope's privileges met with only lukewarm support; but people were far more enthusiastic for the rights and power of the existing church, against all inconvenient reforms, and hence also, for the ecclesiastical doctrine and against all religious innovation. The Sorbonne, the representative of French theology, which had somewhat deteriorated but lived upon hereditary fame, had already (1521) declared itself against Luther (WA VIII p. 258 ff.). The personally free-thinking attitude of the King and the influence of his sister, who sought to interest him on behalf of the New Testament, was the less able to resist his politico-ecclesiastical interests as he lacked all deeper religious and moral earnestness, being " a man of pleasure of true Gallic fickleness and iron constitution." Faber, having been condemned by the Paris theologians on the occasion of an exegetical dispute (1521) concerning the number of the Marys in the New Testament, withdrew to Meaux, whither he was followed by his friends and pupils and an evangelical movement began. But Briçonnet strictly forbade them to preach or read Lutheran writings. Nevertheless, the pamphlets of the German Reformation carried on an effective propaganda. Farel worked here and there; some repaired to Germany, to make the personal acquaintance of the chiefs of the Reformation, a small band of fugitives collected in Bâle, whence they worked upon their native land by means of pamphlets and translations. Soon (1525), Lutherans were persecuted and put to death in France. The disaster of Pavia was attributed to the indulgence which had been shown to the Lutherans,[1] and a commission to deal with the heretics was immediately appointed by the Parliament. From that time the blood of heretics was shed in abundance. But the movement grew, especially amongst the nobility and educated citizens,—in the South more than in the North. Timid friends were struck dumb and retired. Yet this unfavourable attitude towards the Reformation in his own land did not prevent Francis from seeking political connections with the German Protestants, who opposed the Emperor Charles; in connection therewith, in the middle of the thirties, remarkable negotiations were carried on with the

---

[1] BALAN, *Monum. saec. XVI.* p. 344.

German princes, in which Francis represented his persecution of the French Protestants as a legitimate campaign against fanatical and sectarian revolutionists,[1] but at the same time declared his readiness to agree to a compromise on the religious question, to a purification of the doctrines taught without a violent subversion of the ordinances of the Church.[2]

In 1533, he caused negotiations to be begun with Bucer at Strasburg by his councillor Guillaume du Bellay, and, in 1534, had a judgment (*consilium*) laid before him by Melanchthon (CR II 741 ff.)[3]; in 1535 he even invited the latter and Bucer to further conversations and negotiations with the theologians of the Sorbonne. Melanchthon was inclined to go, in the hope that the French crown might be won for the cause of carefully considered ecclesiastical reforms without any break with Rome being necessary. However, in spite of Luther's intercession, John Frederick refused his permission (chiefly owing to political reasons), and so Bucer also stayed away. Just about this time embittered persecutions again took place in France (see above, p. 176), and again in 1545 the Waldenses were cruelly persecuted. Hitherto, French Protestantism had mainly borne the character of the **German** Reformation, without politically aggressive tendencies.

2. The Propaganda of Calvinism.

When **Henry II.** (1547-1559) ascended the throne, the number of the Evangelicals in France was notwithstanding considerable and continually increasing, against whom persecution was soon directed with increased severity. The evangelical movement now naturally received its stamp more and more strongly from **Geneva** (Farel and Calvin). Calvin's envoys and letters were continually arriving in France, hosts of exiles took refuge at Geneva, and large numbers of preachers again set out for France in contempt of death.

<small>Henry had married a niece of Clement VII., Catherine de' Medici: although she subsequently played a most important *rôle*, her influence now and again gave way before that of the notorious Diana of Poitiers, Duchess of Valentinois, whose influence was supreme at Court. Just like her, the Constable de Montmorency, Henry's all-powerful minister and chief general, was a fanatical</small>

---

[1] Cp. his letter of Feb. 1st, 1535, in FREHERUS *Script. rer. Germ.* ed. Struve III 354.

[2] C. SCHMIDT, *die Unionsversuche Franz' I.* in ZhTh 20, 25 ff.

[3] Cp. STROBEL, *Von Mel.s Ruf nach Frankreich.* Nürnb. 1794. DANZ in ZhTh 11, 2, 80 ff. C. SCHMIDT, *Melanchthon*, p. 268 ff. BUCERS Gutachten in der Centuria epp. ad Schwebelium, p. 258 ff. For the reply of the Sorbonne see STROBEL, p. 178 ff.

opponent of the Protestants. His side was now taken by **the Guises**, *i.e.*, the sons of the wealthy large land-owner, Duke Claude of Guise, especially Charles, Archbishop of Rheims, the "Cardinal of Lorraine," and Francis, Count of Aumale. Their sister Mary, the wife of King James V. of Scotland, was the mother of the unfortunate Mary Stuart, who was at the time being brought up at the frivolous French Court as the intended wife of the Dauphin Francis II. On the other hand, Margaret of Navarre and Béarn (died 1549), in correspondence with Calvin and Beza, favoured and protected the Protestant movement in her district. Her daughter, the highly gifted heiress Jeanne d'Albret, decidedly pronounced herself in favour of the Reformation; Prince Antony of Bourbon (to whom she had been married since 1548), together with his brother Duke Louis of Condé, took the same side. Consequently, it was in Navarre (*i.e.*, the part of the kingdom of Navarre that still remained on the northern slope of the Pyrenees), in Béarn (the possession of the house of Albret), and in the different Bourbon possessions, which were now incorporated with it, that the Reformation had its point of support. Amongst the most prominent representatives of Protestant convictions was **Gaspard de Coligny**, who belonged to the oldest nobility of France, elevated to the rank of Admiral of France in 1552, the purest representative of the Huguenot[1] piety, so full of character, and of its strictness of morals in the midst of a frivolous, dissipated, distinguished Court society, a nephew of Montmorency through his mother and an intimate friend of youth of Francis of Guise. (He had previously declared himself opposed to the oppression of the Protestants, and with full personal conviction he became a Huguenot, after 1556 in exile). In 1549, numerous executions of Protestants again took place; the King was present in person as a spectator during a burning at the stake. Certainly, his alliance with German Protestant princes (Maurice) against Charles V., which unfortunately cost the Empire Metz, Toul and Verdun, appeared to be favourable to the French Protestants,—in the French army a large number of nobles who had embraced the Reformation fought under the leadership of Francis de Coligny, the Seigneur d'Andelot, the admiral's brother. But, after the Passau Treaty, Henry again approached Pope Paul IV. (Treaty of December 16th, 1555).

Nevertheless, it was just now that the first organisation of the numerous Protestants into congregations, the transition from private family-devotion to regular services with administration of the Sacrament and a presbyterial communal constitution, first began in Paris itself (1555); other places soon followed the example. But a stringent royal edict of 1557 ordered the secular courts to pass sentence of death whenever any religion but the Catholic was practised either privately or publicly.

---

[1] The name, started by their opponents, first appears in 1560. It has been proposed to derive it from Hugo Capet, that is to say from a gate named after him at Tours, from a hobgoblin at Tours *roi Huguet* (from their nightly gatherings). But the most probable derivation still seems to be from "Eidgenossen": *Eignots* had been, since 1518, the name of a party in Geneva, where it was already mutilated into *Huguenots*. Cp. SOLDAN I 608 ff. MARCKS I, 1 p. 371.

The blood of martyrs now flowed in streams; but the "Lutheriens," as they were still called, so increased in numbers, that in 1558 they were estimated at 400,000—some years later 2,150 congregations were counted. In fanatically-excited Paris (May, 1559) the preachers of numerous reformed communities of the country (*spreto certae necis metu*) assembled at the suburb of St. Germain at a **first national or general Synod,** under the presidency of the preacher Francis de Morel. They agreed upon a confession of faith (*Confessio Gallica* in Niemeyer 311 ff.) and an **ecclesiastical ordinance** (*discipline ecclésiastique*) both composed entirely under the spirit and influence of Calvin, probably by the Parisian preacher Antoine de Chandieu.

The constitution[1] is erected upon a democratic foundation; every congregation creates for itself, by direct choice on the part of the "people" acting on the advice of the preachers, a *consistoire*, composed of lay and clerical elders (for preaching and strict moral discipline);[2] there were also deacons (to attend to the sick and poor). But, though the congregation is thus constituted at first, the *consistoire* supplies its lay fellow-members further by co-optation (only a veto remaining to the congregation), the preachers are nominated by the provincial synod (consequently, a transition to oligarchy). The political situation naturally of itself brought it about that this self-governing church remained completely independent of the State authority and had no positive relation to the State. The further organisation of the congregations into a church takes place through the steps of *consistoire, colloque, synode provinciale, synode nationale*. Moral strictness and sharp, even harsh rejection of everything papistical became the principles of French Calvinism: they are "ceux de la religion" in contrast to the worldly, secular nature and the combination of the ecclesiastical with the monarchical court interest of the opposite side. The peculiar situation of things soon drove these Calvinists into the position of an opposition that was also **political,** as on the other side, royal absolutism identified itself with ecclesiastical interests.

Henry, who had proposed to Philip II. a campaign for the destruction of Geneva, died in the year of the first French national synod. The Guises at first gained possession of power under the rule of **Francis II.** still a minor, (—1560), the husband of Mary Stuart. Frequent burning of heretics at the stake betokened the spirit of the governing powers. In the **Conspiracy of Amboise** (February, 1560) malcontents from Catholic and Evangelical ranks united to overthrow the power of the Guises under the secret leadership of the Prince de Condé, to whom the reformed clung as their patron, who considered that the leadership of a prince of the blood legitimised armed resistance to the "tyrannis" of two foreigners.[3] The Guises, to whom the plot was betrayed,

---

[1] Ebrard in ZhTh 19, 280 ff.

[2] This was exercised without respect of person; even men like the Prince de Condé, Henry of Navarre, and Du Plessis-Mornay were obliged to bow to it on occasion.

[3] Cp. on the other hand Calvin's more cautious judgment CR 46, 38; further 46, 21. 70. 425 ff. Henry, Calvin III, Beil. 14, p. 153 ff.

were victorious. In view of the threatening situation, the upright and tolerant L'Hospital was appointed Chancellor, who in the Edict of Romorantin endeavoured to secure some protection for the Protestants, and an assembly of notables resolved (March 31st, 1560) to hold a **national Council** of the Gallican church with a view of reforms, but the Pope at once raised an objection to it. Immediately afterwards, fresh measures of punishment were taken against the heretics. It was thought that the execution of the ringleaders would deal Protestantism its death-blow. Antoine of Navarre and his brother Louis of Condé were imprisoned: the latter was only saved by the sudden decease of Francis II. from the death which was already hanging over him, and the Huguenots from destruction.[1]

---

[1] BEZA to BULLINGER, Jan. 22nd, 1561: quum nullum iam humanum auxilium superesset et infiniti omnium aetatum et ordinum mortales gladium iam haberent intra iugulum, ecce Dominus Deus noster evigilavit et miserabilem illum puerum [Francis II.] non minus foedo quam inexspectato mortis genere sustulit. (In BAUM, Beza II, App. p. 18.) "The King is dead: this tells us to live." COLIGNY (in Marcks I 1, 422).

CHAPTER FOURTH.

The Reformation Movements in the Netherlands.

Literature: G. BRANDT, *Hist. d. Reformatie.* Amst. 1671 ff. 4 vols. H. L. BENTHEM, *Holl. Kirch-und Schulen-Staat.* Frankf. 1698. D. GERDESIUS, *Origines eccl. in Belgio reformatarum.* Gron. 1749; G. DE HOOP-SCHEFFER, *G. d. Ref. in den Niederl.* (bis 1531), 1870 (in Dutch): in German by Gerlach, Leipz. 1886; K. TH. WENZELBURGER, *G. d. Niederlande.* 2 vols. Gotha. 1879. 1886. J. REITSMA, 100 *Jaren uit d. Gesch. d. Hervorming in Friesl.* Leeuwarden, 1876; the same, *Gesch. van de Hervorm. en de Hervormde Kerk d. Nederlanden.* Gron. 1893; HOFSTEDE DE GROOT, 100 *Jaren uit d. G. d. Hervorm. in de Nederl.* (1518-1619). Leiden 1884, in German by Greven, Gütersloh, 1893; C. HILLE RIS LAMBERS, *De Kerkhervorming op de Veluwe.* Barneveld 1890. J. REITSMA, *Gesch. van de Hervorming I.* Gron. 1892. CHR. SEPP, *Bibliogr. Mededeelingen.* Leiden 1883; the same, *Bibl. van Nederl. Kerkgeschiedschryvers.* Leiden 1886. Monumenta ref. Belg. I. Leiden 1882 (Reprint of the "Summa der göttlichen Schrift" by TOORENENBERGEN); BENRATH, *Die Summa d. hl. Schr.* Leipz. 1880; the same, in JprTh 1882, 681 ff.; the same, in ThJahresbericht VI 196; J. FREDERICHS, *De Secte der Loisten.* Gent 1891: C. A. CORNELIUS, *Die niederl. Wiedertäufer während der Belagerung Münsters* in ABA XI. Prohibited Books: REUSCH, Index I. 98 ff.

In the wealthy, flourishing Burgundian heritage of Charles V.,—the Netherands (the union of which was greatly desired by him, although their connection with the German empire might thereby be loosened or broken) Luther's ideas found approval and circulation in the towns with their developed spirit of independence and attitude of mind (fostered by the activity of Erasmus) already to a considerable extent anticlerical, and in the already awakened desire for the Scriptures in the language of the country. Certainly, the University of Louvain was a tenacious representative of the old school, and, in February, 1520, had already published its *doctrinalis condemnatio* of the teaching of Luther and Professor Jacobus Latomus (see p. 34) had continued the dispute, in order to attack in Luther the hated opponent of Scholasticism and spokesman of a new education, Erasmus (WA VI 170 ff. VIII 36 ff.). But, in the flourishing towns of Flanders and Brabant, as well as in the northern Low-German, Dutch communities, Luther's writings in the original (soon also in numerous Dutch translations)[1] found active circulation: the Augustinian monasteries were the natural starting-point for an evangelical movement. In addition, in 1523 the *Summa der godliker Scrifturen*, the author of which was certainly the Utrecht priest **Henry Bomelius**, opened the list of native testimony on behalf of the Gospel, with especial stress upon its ethical side. But Charles here also sought to carry out what had met with so much opposition in Germany: he caused the Edict of Worms to be promulgated without delay, which was followed by a second

---

[1] Cp. DE HOOP-SCHEFFER, p. 112 ff. 361 ff.

(April 29th, 1522) for the "complete extirpation of the heresy": his councillor, Francis van der Hulst, was appointed heretical inquisitor. Here (in 1523) the first stakes for Lutherans were set up; on the 1st of July, 1523, Henry Voes and John von Essen (Esch), both of Antwerp, were the first victims of the Inquisition at Brussels (see p. 46), whereupon Luther, in a circular letter "to the Christians in the Netherlands," and in his hymn, "Ein neues Lied wir heben an," praised God, who through the blood of martyrs gave testimony of the genuineness of the Gospel preached by him (WA XII 73 ff.). Other Augustinians, as James Propst, Melchior Myritsch, and Henry of Zütphen had already been previously exposed to this danger: Propst had recanted Luther's doctrines in prison, then regained courage to testify anew, but escaped a martyr's death by flight; Myritsch had saved himself by ambiguous declarations; a rising of the people had freed Zütphen from prison and assisted him to flee. The Emperor issued one edict after another, against the printing and circulation of heretical books as well as against the heretics themselves. In like manner, in Guelders, Charles of Egmont persecuted reformatory agitations with fierce hatred. In 1524, the Pope established a clerical inquisitional council for the Netherlands, on which great powers were conferred; but the execution of the measures still depended upon the good will of the provincial and city officials, who often were little inclined to support this foreign jurisdiction, watched jealously over their privileges, frequently applied the edicts as leniently as possible, and even to a certain extent actually favoured reform. Thus, in spite of the Emperor's zeal, the Protestant movement was able to spread in many places, although it could only carry on its work in secret. In addition, the Stadtholderess Margaret of Savoy, Charles's aunt, was moderately inclined; after her death (1530) she was succeeded by Charles's sister, Maria, the widowed queen of Hungary, who was not altogether ill disposed towards the Reformation. While ecclesiastical reform made way amongst the people, the nobles (who were for the most part worldly minded) showed themselves indifferent. Luther's influence here soon partially ceased, since Hoen and Rode had come to an agreement with Zwingli on the question of the Eucharist (see p. 83); from these "Sacramentarians" the movement soon proceeded further to the Anabaptists, especially in the lower ranks of the people, here pressing on to martyrdom and for a time threatening the order of society. In 1525, Luther had warned the Christians of Antwerp in a "circular letter" (EA 53, 341 ff.) against the fanatical bluster[1] of the slater Eloy Pruystinck, who had visited him at Wittenberg, and afterwards called into being a sect in Antwerp (the Loists), according to whose doctrine all men, according to the flesh, revert to the judgment of God, but also, according to the spirit, eternal happiness is prepared for all; this produced libertinist practical consequences (cp. also JprTh 1877, 286 f.). It was just here that the fanatical baptist efforts found a soil already prepared. Melchior Hofmann (see p. 93) had reached Emden, and, having been expelled from thence, remained some time in the Netherlands, like others who had been driven away from Germany. Tripmaker collected a community in Amsterdam; his execution (1531) only brought accessions to it. It was from here that the Münster Anabaptist Kingdom was principally reinforced. Friesland fell to the share of Anabaptism; the number of adherents increased with the number of martyrs. David Joris (see p. 128) also found adherents here. A violent outburst of the new social ideas was not lacking; thus we read of an attempt to seize Amsterdam, and elsewhere at least of attacks on

---

[1] [*Rumpelgeist:* lit. a noisy hobgoblin.]

monasteries. Other manifestations, partly fanatical, partly foolishly extravagant, partly libertinist, followed. It was only the fall of Münster that cooled the glowing heat. Thus it came about that the adherents of the Reformation were thrown together with fanatical anarchists and anabaptist fanatics—the latter had been rendered sober and disciplined since 1536 by Menno Simonis' salutary organisation (see p. 129). Judgments against heretics continued to be enforced: thousands fell victims to them, chiefly the aggressive Anabaptists. However, the mass of the people were not yet attacked by the movement. The situation was growing worse, when Philip II. received the Netherlands from his father and took up his residence there himself (1555-1559).

But, in spite of all persecution (assisted by informers), the number of the Protestants increased, amongst whom the Lutheran influence now completely gave way before that of French Calvinism. The latter first found the way to the heart of the people; it at first gained a firm footing in the South Walloon provinces, and from there gained an ever-increasing hold upon the German North through the agency of theologians and statesmen. During the rule of Mary Tudor (1553-1558) English refugees also strengthened this tendency. By it the people were rendered capable of the resolute death-defying struggle for freedom of belief against "idolatry." In 1559 (the year of the *Confessio Gallica*, p. 194) a Walloon minister, **Guido de Bres**, drew up a scheme of confession of faith in French, which was communicated to several other persons, including foreign theologians, for examination, revised in 1561 according to the judgment of the Genevese, and in 1562 sent to Philip II. for authorisation.[1] The apologetic preface gives the number of the Netherland co-religionists as 100,000. In its doctrine of the Lord's Supper and predestination the Confession follows Calvin. The co-religionists had already met at synods; the Antwerpers solemnly accepted the Confession as the **Confessio Belgica** (abridged). But, in the case of Philip, no impression could be looked for. In 1559 he had left the Netherlands never to return. Here the struggle for life and death was now to begin.

---

[1] BENTHEM, p. 146 ff. NIEMEYER, p. 360 ff. SCHAFF I 502 ff.; III 383 ff. Cp. SEPP, *Geschiedkundige Nasporingen* III 191 f., according to whom there had already been an imprint of 1561.

CHAPTER FIFTH.

The Ecclesiastical Revolution in England.

Sources : Calendar of State Papers, Lond. (Papers of the reign of Henry VIII. [—1538], of the reign of Edw. VI.), WILKINS, *Concilia Britanniae* vols. III and IV. London 1737.
Literature : G. BURNET, *The history of the Reformation.* 3 vols. Lond. 1679. 1681. 1715. J. LINGARD, *A history of England.* Vol. VI. ⁴Paris 1826; FROUDE, *History of England from the Fall of Wolsey.* I. Lond. 1856 (according to the national legend); J. R. GREEN, *History of the English People.* II. Lond. 1890. J. J. BLUNT, *Sketch of the Reformation in England* (German translation by H. FICK. Frankf. 1863; L. v. RANKE, *Englische Geschichte,* I and II. Berlin 1859; WEBER, *Gesch. d. akath. Kirchen und Secten in Grossbrit.* 2 vols. Leipz. 1845; W. MAURENBRECHER, *England im Ref.ZA.* Düsseld. 1866; M. BROSCH, *Gesch. v. Engl.* VI. Gotha 1890.

1. Henry's Breach with Rome.

Literature: E. NÖLDECHEN, *Lutherthum und Lutheraner unter Heinrich VIII.* Magdbg. 1870; W. BORÉE, *Heinrich VIII. und die Curie,* 1528-29. Gött. 1885; HERGENRÖTHER, *Conc.-G. IX.* SEEBOHM, *The Oxford Reformers, J. Colet, Erasmus, and Thomas More.*² Lond. 1869; R. PAULI in *Aufs. zur engl.* G. Leipz. 1869, p. 98 ff. On the divorce: POCOCK, *Records of the Reformation. The Divorce* 1527-1533. Oxf. 1870; P. FRIEDMANN, *A. Boleyn.* Lond. 1884; J. A. FROUDE, *The Divorce of Catharine of Aragon.* Lond. 1891 (an apology for Henry); BENDER in ZkTh VII 401 ff.; EHSES in JGG XII 24 ff. 209 ff. 607 ff. XIII 470 ff.; the same, in RQ VII 180 ff.; the same, *Röm. Dokum. z. G. d. Ehescheid. Heinr. VIII.* Paderb. 1893. W. BUSCH in HTb 6. F. 8, 273 ff., 9, 39 ff. For Cranmer: STRYPE, *Memorials of Archbishop Cranmer,* London, 1693; H. J. TODD, *The Life of Archbishop Cranmer,* London, 1831; J. GAIRDNER in Dictionary of National Biography XIII 19 ff. For More: Biography by RUDHART, Nürnb. 1829; by BRIDGETT, Lond. 1891. For Fisher: Life in Annal. Bollandiana X 121 ff.; Biography by M. KERKER, Tübing. 1860; by BRIDGETT, Lond. 1888; cp. also BELLESHEIM in Kath. 1890, 2, 71 ff.

Wiclif's ideas had maintained themselves in the conventicles of the Lollards up to the time of the Reformation, where the Bible circulated in copies and many had also committed it to memory to a considerable extent. At the beginning of the 16th century measures of persecution became more frequent against them. To this was added a deep-seated political and social discontent with the powerful and independent clergy, whose ignorance, immorality, greed and ambition gave offence here, as elsewhere. Discontent was equally directed towards the coarseness of the monks. Here also a humanistic culture spread (William Grocyn, John Colet and others), which fostered the study of Greek, the worship of Erasmus[1] and a desire for religious reform, which certainly need not have led to a breach with the Church. But now Luther's appearance on the scene also exercised its effect across the Channel. The old Wicliffian current of thought (that preponderated in the lower strata of society) flowed side by side with the now more powerful Lutheran stream (helped on its course by the educated). The despotic Henry VIII. of the house of Tudor, who was certainly unusually well educated in the circle of the humanists (Colet, Thomas More), a devoted admirer of Erasmus, but also familiar with Scholasticism, since as a second son he had originally been destined for an ecclesiastical career, sharply opposed the religious innovations (see p. 58). The younger generation at Oxford and Cambridge devoted itself energetically to reformatory ideas. Luther's writings were prohibited in 1521;[2] the celibacy of the priests was enforced anew. John Frith and William Tyndale, driven from Oxford, worked from outside by circulating evangelical writings,[3] Tyndale also by his translation of the Bible (New Testament, first published at Antwerp, 1526, followed by the Pentateuch; completed by Coverdale (1535) who made special use of the Zürich Bible).

Entirely different reasons brought Henry, *defensor fidei*, into a conflict with the Pope, which ended in a breach. The immediate cause was the matter of his divorce. By a dispensation from Julius II., he had married Catharine of Aragon, the widow of his brother Arthur (who died in 1502) and the Emperor's aunt. She was older than Henry, but bore him five children, of which only one daughter Mary (born 1516) grew up. Catharine fostered her husband's leaning towards Charles V., and hence exercised a political influence, although quietly and unobtrusively. But, in 1525, England's policy wavered between a Spanish and French alliance. The desire for a male heir to the throne and his passion for Anne Boleyn (which showed itself in 1526), whose sister was already one of

---

[1] He stayed in Oxford from 1498 to 1500, and received from Colet the impulse to lead theological study back to the Scriptures; he also revisited that city (1509-1514), when at the height of his fame and influence, where he wrote the satirical *Encomion Morias*, or " Praise of Folly."

[2] WILKINS III 689.

[3] For a list of the evangelical literature that made its way to England see WILKINS III 707, 719 ff., 739. Cp. also REUSCH, Index I 87 ff. Dictionary of National Biography, XX 277 f.; XII 363 ff.

his mistresses, suddenly caused him to feel scruples of conscience[1] as to the legality of his marriage (Leviticus, XVIII, 16. XX, 21; but also Deuteronomy, XXV, 5) and the validity of the papal dispensation;[2] these were fostered by his ambitious minister Cardinal **Wolsey** for political reasons (in order to bring about a political alliance with France in opposition to Charles V.) and also from a desire to secure his own position. Clement VII. was at the same time (in 1527) to empower Wolsey to pronounce judgment upon the existing marriage and to grant Henry a dispensation from any objection to marriage with a sister-in-law, in order that he might be able to marry Anne, the sister of his concubine. Clement at once (Dec. 17th, Wilkins III 707) bestowed the latter dispensation, but in regard to the former he only bestowed insufficient powers, so that Wolsey could not by virtue of it dissolve the marriage.[3] In 1528, Henry asked for a decretal bull, which should declare the dispensation granted by Julius II. to be invalid. The politic Pope thereupon empowered Wolsey and Archbishop Warham to examine the case of the marriage and eventually to pronounce in favour of divorce, while at the same time he reserved the right of ratifying their judgment. But, as Wolsey recognised that even this bull would be no security against the Queen's appealing to Rome, he asked the Pope for a decretal bull, which was to be kept strictly secret, and requested that Campeggi might be sent to investigate the divorce process with him. Clement yielded, **drew up the bull**,[4] and sent Campeggi—one of the bright lights of his quarrel with Charles V. But, as his hopes, which were at this moment placed in the French, were not fufilled (owing to the disaster to the French arms before Naples), he could not venture to fall out with the Emperor, who at once protested against the papal decision in the case of Henry; he accordingly sent orders to Campeggi, to keep back the matter, until he should have received fresh powers. Campeggi appeared in England in October, 1528, but delayed instituting the process: Wolsey could not make a beginning alone, and was accordingly suspected by Henry of not looking after his interests sufficiently. An attempt on the part of Campeggi to induce Catharine to agree to a divorce and take the veil was

---

[1] But "what he wanted was not the salving of his conscience, but a divorce," as BUSCH (HTb 6, F. 8, 285) justly observes in opposition to English attempts at palliation.

[2] The Anglicans even now are of opinion that the King's marriage was illegal from the outset. Archbishop Parker established it as a law of the Church in the reign of Elizabeth, that no one might marry his brother's widow.

[3] The advice, which Clement gave the English ambassador Casale was peculiar: that Henry might speedily enter into the second marriage, as it would be easier for him to confirm the complete marriage subsequently. (Ehses would understand this only of the legitimation of children who might be born of the marriage concluded in *bona fide*, but which remained invalid.) But Wolsey took care not to relieve the Pope of the responsibility for the divorce.

[4] Its purport remained unknown, as, although it was read to Henry and Wolsey, it was immediately burnt by Campeggi. It is dated April 13th, 1528, was not despatched till the 8th of June, now published by Gairdner in the English historical Review, 1890, July, 544 ff. from the rough draught at Rome. It gives as a reason: The prohibition of marriage in the first degree of affinity is an element of divine law and therefore indispensable.

unsuccessful;[1] she produced the copy of a brief of Julius II. preserved by Charles, which formerly declared unmistakably the legitimacy of her marriage with Henry (in spite of the consummation of the first marriage, which she, however, solemnly contested). Wolsey in vain endeavoured to prove this brief a forgery: but Charles would only show the original in Rome itself, whither Henry did not wish his case to be transferred. Clement, who had entered into an alliance with the Emperor, at the treaty of Barcelona (June 29th, 1529), caused a resolution to be carried in the Consistory, that the marriage-controversy should be transferred to Rome: he now considered himself strong enough to face Henry's anger. Thus, the process which was now at last instituted by Campeggi, but spun out, was broken off without being settled and transferred to Rome. The failure of Wolsey's scheme of divorce, and Henry's hankering after the property of the Church, that was now beginning to show itself, led to the fall of Wolsey, who had ascended to a giddy height and already coveted the papal tiara: he died as a prisoner while being conveyed to London. The noble Thomas More took his place as Chancellor; but in the matter of the divorce the King, acting on the advice of **Thomas Cranmer** (at that time professor at Oxford) consulted the universities of Christendom, but their opinions were only partly such as Henry desired. The attempt to dissuade Charles V. from defending his aunt's marriage by the offer of a large sum of money was unsuccessful. The Parliament now (July, 1530) applied to the Pope with a threatening remonstrance: **therewith began the struggle of England against Rome,**—a policy which attacked Rome and hence introduced an ecclesiastical reformation, in which the King might venture to look with confidence for the support of the pliable Parliament. He raked up against the clergy (as he had already done against Wolsey) the old **Statute of Praemunire** of the year 1353 (see Vol. II. p. 490) which forbade the recognition of a foreign jurisdiction and all appeal to the same, the penalty for transgressing which was confiscation of property. The clergy were said to have violated it by recognising Wolsey as papal legate, while Henry himself had notwithstanding recognised him as such. The Convocation[2] of the clergy of York and Canterbury was obliged to confess itself guilty, to purchase pardon by a large sum of money and at the same time to acknowledge the King as "protector and lord and (*quantum per legem Christi licet*)[3] sole supreme head of the Church and clergy," and, consequently, to transfer to him the papal prerogatives (February, 1531). Catharine was banished from the Court. Clement again issued a warning in a brief, which was sent to England by the agency of the Emperor. The Parliament thereupon resolved to discontinue the payment of the annates to the Pope. Thomas More, as a pious Catholic, now resigned his office. All power of independent action in the matter of ecclesiastical legislation was subsequently withdrawn from Convocation, and it was made dependent upon the royal pleasure. Meanwhile, Luther and Melanchthon also were applied to for their advice in the matter of divorce. Luther had decisively

---

[1] The legate hence complained of the "obstinatione" of the Queen, who refused to follow this "sano consiglio," to help Rome and England out of all embarrassment. LÄMMER, Monum. Vaticana, p. 28.

[2] Cp. SCHOELL, *Die Convocation der englischen Kirche* in ZhTh 23, 85 ff.

[3] This clause was inserted to calm people's minds. See the Acts in Wilkins III 742 ff.

rejected the proposed divorce, and eventually expressed his preference for bigamy (de Wette, IV 294 ff.), after Melanchthon had recommended the latter proposal as *tutissimum propter magnam utilitatem regni* (CR II 520 ff. Cp. ZKG XIII 576). At the end of January, 1533, Henry was secretly married to Anne Boleyn:[1] it was not until afterwards that a decree of the Parliament forbade cases connected with marriage being transferred to Rome; Cranmer, who had been elevated to the Archbishopric of Canterbury and Primacy of all England, now pronounced sentence of divorce,[2] and the Parliament added the resolution, that Mary, as being the fruit of a marriage that was null and void, was illegitimate and forfeited all right of succession to the throne. The Pope answered (July 4th, 1533) with a declaration that the new marriage was null and void, demanded the dismissal of Anne Boleyn, and threatened Henry with the ban.[3]

There now followed a succession of measures on the part of the King and the Parliament, whereby the English church was to be definitively torn away from the Romish primacy. The "Bishop of Rome" was denied all jurisdiction in England, and was declared to possess no more authority than any other foreign bishop.[4] All the ecclesiastical ordinances, which did not run counter to the rights of the crown, were to remain valid for a time; an appeal from the archbishop to the King was to take the place of the appeal to Rome; the annates were to fall to the King, Peter's pence was to be abolished. The King is to settle the bishops to be elected by the chapters, and they are to take the oath to him alone.[5] Any attack upon these enactments, the divorce or the royal supremacy, is to be regarded as high treason. Finally, it was decided by the **Act of Supremacy** (November 3rd, 1534) that the bishops should renounce the Pope, forswear all recognition of his authority, and take the oath of supremacy to the King unconditionally. But, notwithstanding this abrupt breach with the Romish system, at the same time, by the King's wish, the scholastic orthodoxy was firmly adhered to, on both sides with tyrannical persecution of every deviation as high treason, with due legal formalities, but with despotic pressure. Hence victims fell on both sides. After

---

[1] For this date cp. BROSCH VI 253 f. Elizabeth was born on the 7th of September, 1533; hence the subsequent eagerness to antedate the day of the marriage.

[2] WILKINS III 759. Three years later, the same Cranmer declared, also at Henry's request, that his marriage with Anne was invalid. III 803 f.

[3] On the 23rd of March, 1534, the Pope again threatened the employment of all ecclesiastical legal remedies.

[4] WILKINS III 772 ff.

[5] See the forms of oath in WILKINS III 780 ff.

John Frith, amongst the reformers, had been burnt in London in 1533, on the papal side, Thomas More, an honourable character, formerly so dear to Henry, fell a victim—the Reformation appeared to him over-hastiness on the part of the youthful generation. In April, 1534, he was imprisoned because he refused to recognise the King as head of the Church; in the summer of 1535, he was "granted the favour" of having his head cut off. For refusing to take the oath of supremacy, Bishop Fisher of Rochester lost his head shortly before; he had formerly assisted Henry in his literary feud with Luther, but had now asked the Emperor to take armed measures against the King. The Pope had injudiciously promoted him to be Cardinal when a prisoner. The Pope now (August 30th, 1535) in vain fulminated all the dire results of excommunication, interdict and release of Henry's subjects from their obedience to him, and called upon Christendom to rise against him.[1]

2. Henry's Established Church Government.

Literature (continued): GASQUETT, *Henry VIII. and the English monasteries;* 2 vols. Lond., 1888, 1889 (in German, Mainz, 1890, 1891). For Cromwell: A. PAULI, *Aufs. zur engl. Gesch.* N. F. Leipzig, 1883, 293 ff. CH. HARDWICK, *A history of the Articles of Religion* (1536-1615)[2]. Cambridge, 1859.

The King, who up to 1540 had left his absolutist church government in the hands of the violent and irreligious Thomas Cromwell[2] (formerly Wolsey's secretary), met with only slight opposition amongst the clergy, but considerably more amongst the monks (mendicant friars and Carthusians), where it amounted to fanaticism. In 1534, measures began to be taken against the monasteries; in 1536, a visitation of the same took place, in consequence of which more than 300 monasteries were confiscated by the Crown, on the convenient pretext that they had been found greatly neglected,[3] a measure which has certainly proved very beneficial to the welfare of England. The natural consequence of the confusion which these revolutionary measures brought about was that part of the nation broke through Henry's ambiguous and untenable position between the two parties and, by shaking off the authority of Rome, was driven into Pro-

---

[1] Cp. FRIEDENSBURG, Nuntiaturberichte I 463, 466 f. However, at the desire of France, the Pope suspended this ban and did not issue it until 1538. WILKINS III 792 ff.; 840 f.

[2] Cromwell was "the instrument which made the Church of England so securely a part of the State, that it could not not release itself from its embrace." For his appointment as *Vicarius generalis in ecclesiasticis* see WILKINS III 784 f.

[3] Wolsey had been beforehand in this, acting on the basis of a papal bull (1524-1529) in the interest of the endowing of colleges. WILKINS III 704 ff., 715 ff.

testantism. The one party (Cranmer, Cromwell, Latimer, Fox and others)[1] consciously carried on not only a royal, but also a **Protestant** opposition to the papacy: the other desired to hold fast by Catholicism (but without the Pope) together with the King. The resistance of the papal party, which found its support chiefly in the North (York) and the monasteries, and proceeded to serious disturbances (at first in Lincolnshire), was the cause of measures of increased severity being taken, and of the suppression of all the monasteries (1539). The Articles of Reformation, drawn up by the King in 1536 and accepted by Convocation (Wilkins III 817 ff.) certainly exhibit as yet only a feeble approximation to an evangelical reformation of doctrine and worship. They uphold transubstantiation, auricular confession, intercession and mass for the dead, but declare the Scriptures to be the foundation of faith together with the old symbols, reduce the number of the Sacraments to three, and speak in very modified language of images and saints. Of greater importance was the issue, at Cranmer's instigation, and by royal permission, of an English bible (Matthews' [really Rogers'], a new edition of the Tyndale-Coverdale version, with prefaces and notes), followed in 1539 by Coverdale's own revised translation without notes (the edition of 1540 contained a preface by Cranmer, and is therefore commonly known as "Cranmer's," or "The Great Bible"). To this period also belong various **attempts at an approach** to German Protestantism. In 1535 Henry proposed an alliance and union of doctrine and invited Melanchthon to England,[2] an invitation which he no more accepted than a similar one to France. In 1538, the Saxon councillors Burkhard and Boyneburg, together with the theologian F. Myconius, negotiated without success in England.[3] At this time the **downright anti-evangelical** party opposed these tendencies. The Articles of Reformation of 1536 were further enlarged in 1537, and worked up into "*The godly and pious institution of a Christian Man*" drawn up at Lambeth (cp. Wilkins III 830 ff.). It was written in essentially the same spirit, but it was not sufficient for the King's increasing need of defending the Catholic orthodoxy against the successes of the reformatory party. Under the pressure of his personal authority and his "superior argumentation and theological learning" the Act of Parliament "for the suppression of diversity of opinion in certain articles of religion" was passed in 1539, the "bloody statute" (Wilkins III 845 f.), which proclaimed (1) Transubstantiation; (2) The non-necessity of Communion in both kinds; (3) The prohibition of the marriage of priests;[4] (4) The obligation of vows of chastity; (5) The retention of private masses; (6) The expediency and necessity of auricular confession. Contravention of these articles was in most cases punished by death and confiscation of property. This harsh procedure was due to the fact that the Catholic (secretly papal) party (the Duke of Norfolk and Gardiner Bishop of Winchester) obtained increased influence over Henry by cleverly taking advantage of the circum-

---

[1] Queen Anne, who favoured this party, had been obliged (1536) to make room for the King's new flame, Jane Seymour. Melanchthon rightly observes (CR III 89) that Anne was *magis accusata quam convicta adulterii*.

[2] Henry's letter of invitation, CR II 947 f.

[3] Letters and papers XIII 480 ff. TODD I 241 ff. HARDWICK, *History of the Articles*. Appendix II. p. 261 ff.

[4] Cranmer himself was already secretly married to a niece of A. Osiander.

stance that Anabaptists had made their appearance in England (Wilkins III 836) and a certain preacher named Lambert had endeavoured to propagate Zwingli's Eucharistic doctrine. Cranmer's position now became dangerous. He took part in the refutation of the Anabaptists and the condemnation of the obstinate, who were handed over to the secular arm and burnt; also in the theological struggle against Lambert, in which the theologians contended with the crowned theologian and in his royal presence, in this case united with Gardiner, although Cranmer himself had given up the belief in transubstantiation; he was obliged to assent to Henry's death sentence upon the heretic.[1] Intimidated by the despotic King, he was even obliged, after some resistance, to agree to the Articles of Blood (which attacked himself). He sent his wife temporarily to Germany. The prisons became full, although, until the fall of Cromwell (1540) no executions were carried out in accordance with the Statute. Many persons now quitted their native land, the evangelical party was greatly intimidated. Cromwell[2] was executed in the summer of 1540, on the pretext that he had corresponded with the German princes without the knowledge of the King, but in reality because the marriage with Anne of Cleves, which he had brought about after the death in childbed of Jane Seymour (mother of Edward VI),[3] did not meet the King's taste. Immediately afterwards, he was captivated by the charms of Catharine Howard, who was introduced to him by the Catholic party.

In ecclesiastical matters, this **hybrid condition of things** lasted until Henry's death; on the one hand, a preponderance of Catholic tendencies in the persecution of those who held evangelical views (Bonner, Bishop of London, hitherto Cromwell's greatest flatterer, especially distinguished himself[4]), in the restoration of a number of Romish ceremonies that had already disappeared, also in Gardiner's attempt to overthrow Cranmer, which was frustrated by the King's favour;[5] further, in stricter measures in regard to the censorship of books and in limiting the reading of the Bible to the houses of persons of distinction. The revised edition of the *Institution of Man* (1543, in which certainly no mention is made of purgatory) as well as the Book of Ceremonies, which made very little alteration in their Romish character, show how little evangelical principles were able to make their way here and how little Cranmer's very

---

[1] Todd I 257 ff.

[2] R. Barnes who had been employed by him in diplomatic missions had already been executed as "a heretic."

[3] Cromwell's idea in this had certainly been to bring the King into closer relations with the German princes. This marriage was declared null and void by convocation on the ground of an earlier betrothal of Anne.

[4] The torture and execution of Anne Askew (1546) for refusing to believe the doctrine of transubstantiation caused a great sensation.

[5] Cranmer confessed his secret marriage, but also pointed to the fact that he had sent his wife away.

modest attempts succeeded in effecting. To this must be added, that Henry had been drawing closer to the Emperor since 1543 (against France), in connection with which he declared his daughter Mary (she came after Edward and before Elizabeth) capable of succeeding to the throne, promised to take measures against heretical writings and to abstain from all further innovation, in return for which Charles was to promise not to allow any resolution to be passed against him in the coming Council. On the other hand, the Reform party at length found a patroness in Catharine Parr (the widow of Lord Latimer), when she was elevated to the dignity of wife of the King after the execution of Catharine Howard (1542). During Henry's last years, it was a fact of the greatest importance that Bishop Gardiner, who had hitherto been the most influential man of the Romish party, fell into disgrace, and the Seymours, the nearest maternal relatives of Edward the heir to the throne, became the rising stars at Court, while the Howards (at their head the Duke of Norfolk and his son Count Surrey) excited the King's suspicion. Both having become implicated in a trial for high treason, Surrey was executed and Norfolk only saved from a like fate by the King's death (January 28th, 1547).

3. Evangelical Reforms under Edward VI.

Sources (cont.): Edited by the PARKER Society. N. RIDLEY, *Works*. Cambridge, 1841. J. HOOPER, *Early Writings*. Cambridge, 1843. *Original letters relating to the English Reformation*. Cambridge, 1846. CRANMER, *Miscellaneous Writings*. Cambridge, 1846. *The two Liturgies*, 1549 and 1542, edited by Ketley. Cambridge, 1845. *King Edward VI. on the Supremacy*, edited by R. Potts. Cambridge, 1874. M. BUCER, *Scripta Anglicana*. Basil, 1577.

Literature: GASQUETT and BISHOP, *Edward VI. and the Book of Common Prayer*. London, 1890. BELLESHEIM in Kath. 1891, Jan. DALTON, *John a Lasco*. Gotha, 1881. BENRATH, *Ochino*. ²Braunschw. 1892; the same, in DevBl XVIII 306 ff. (*Ochinos Tragödie*). F. PIJPER, *Jan Utenhove*. Leiden, 1882.

As Edward VI. (1547-1553), who was brought up under Cranmer's guidance, was only ten years old, the affairs of the kingdom were managed by a council of regency, the head of which was the King's uncle, the evangelically-disposed **Duke of Somerset** (Earl of Hertford), and from which the Duke of Norfolk and Gardiner were excluded. Under the Protector's leadership, the Reform party immediately succeeded in obtaining the ascendency. Cranmer now commenced the work of Reformation as he understood it, *i.e.*, the purification of the existing order of things in the name of the royal ecclesiastical power, without breaking through the connection with the past.

Even at the Coronation, he reminded the young King of the example of the youthful Josiah, who freed the land from the worship of images and fostered the true adoration of God. Erasmus's paraphrases of the New Testament were translated; Cranmer, with Ridley, Latimer and others, produced a *Book of Homilies*, in which the principles of Scripture and Justification by Faith found expression; passages from this were to be regularly read in all the churches. Only those who received special permission were to be allowed to preach. A visitation administered the oath of supremacy everywhere to a number of householders in addition to the clergy.[1] Images were done away with, processions were discontinued, the Litany was to be read in the English language; a resolution of Parliament then introduced the Communion in both kinds, and soon afterwards also allowed priests to marry, although celibacy was still indicated as the more suitable practice.

The laws against heretics, which had been in force since the time of the Lollards, were repealed, ecclesiastical bequests, especially those for private masses, were confiscated, in which case, to Cranmer's indignation, the greater part of the property (as in the case of the monasteries) fell into the pockets of the hangers on of the Court. Bishops Bonner (of London) and Gardiner opposed all this. The former, however, submitted as soon as he had been imprisoned; Gardiner, in spite of incarceration and threats, continued refractory,—inconsistently, since he had himself previously (1535) during the reign of Henry, preached unconditional obedience to the royal commands.[2] Cranmer also immediately set to work on a reorganisation of the Liturgy: an *Order of the Communion*[3] (March 8th, 1548) formed the commencement: the *Book of the Common Prayer and Administration of the Sacraments* followed in March, 1549. While adhering as closely as possible to traditional Catholic forms (in the Morning and Evening Prayer [Matins and Vespers] in which the *Breviarium nuper reformatum* of the Spanish Franciscan Quignon (1535) was used) it shows an appreciation of the mass arrangements of the Lutheran Reformation (especially the liturgy of the Cologne Reformation: see p. 148).

But, by the side of the influence of the Lutheran Reformation, which had hitherto by preference affected the evangelically-minded

---

[1] "I from henceforth shall utterly renounce, refuse, relinquish and forsake the Bishop of Rome and his authority, power and jurisdiction. And I shall never consent nor agree that the Bishop of Rome shall practise, exercise or have any manner of authority, jurisdiction or power within this realm or any other of the King's dominions, etc."—KETLEY, *Two Liturgies*, p. 338. Edward VI. in 1549 himself tried his hand as a writer against the primacy of the Pope.

[2] *De vera obedientia*, in E. BROWN, *Fasciculus rerum expetendarum*: London, 1690, II. 800 ff. Cp. *Dictionary of National Biography*, XX. 420 f. 424.

[3] WILKINS IV 11 ff.

circles,[1] that of the **Swiss** began to make itself felt: after the year 1547, writings of Zwingli, Bullinger and Calvin appeared in English translations by the side of numerous writings by Lutherans. But, above all, there soon appeared in person (chiefly in consequence of pressing invitations),[2] numerous heralds of the Swiss Reformation: Peter Martyr and Ochino, Tremellius, Dryander, John a Lasco from Emden, and soon Bucer and Fagius from Strasburg. Calvin gave his advice by letter.[3]

With the co-operation of Calvin and Bucer, who took offence at the papal ceremonial,[4] a **revised** edition of the Common Prayer-book was brought out in 1552. In this the consecrated oil, exorcism, signing the cross, prayer for the dead, auricular confession, dedication of the baptismal water, and several other things were done away with; in the case of the Lord's Supper, it was expressly observed that kneeling indicated no adoration of the elements—this would be idolatry, as the latter preserve their true natural substance, but Christ's body and blood are not here, but in Heaven. In like manner, the holy wafers, which were still preserved in the first edition (only larger and thicker, such as could be divided between two communicants) were replaced by ordinary wheaten bread ("such as is usual to be eaten at the table with other meats"). These alterations show the increasing influence of the Swiss views, which change Cranmer's original programme and drive him beyond it. Englishmen like Coverdale, J. Rogers, and J. Hooper, who had fled from the country, returned and strengthened this tendency. Cranmer summoned Martyr to Oxford, Bucer (died 1551) and Fagius (died 1549) to Cambridge, to train a new theological generation and to be the theological representatives of the evangelical doctrine. Ochino, who was actively engaged as minister of the Italians in London, here composed his furious controversial treatise: *A Tragedie or Dialogue of the unjuste usurped primacie of the Bishop of Rome* (1549). But now men also appeared on the scene, who desired to deal **more seriously** with Calvinism in constitution and ritual. The Scotch champion of Swiss Reformation, **John Knox,** who had been kept a prisoner in France on a galley since 1547, but liberated in 1549 (probably in consequence of

---

[1] In 1548, Cranmer had caused the children's sermons, which had been subjoined to the Brandenburg-Nuremberg church order of 1533 and explain **Luther's** small Catechism, to be translated into English from the Latin edition by **Justus Jonas** and thereby circulated **Luther's doctrine of the Eucharist.** (*A Short Instruction into the Christian Religion*). This is the "Catechism of Jonas," for which DALTON, p. 328, has in vain instituted enquiries. Those who favoured the Swiss views took this publication as a proof that Cranmer had given way. Original letters, p. 381.

[2] Melanchthon, who was also invited, was obliged to refuse his co-operation in consequence of the needs of the Saxon churches.

[3] Calvin to Cranmer CR 41, 682; 42, 312; to Edward 41, 669; 42, 30. 38. 341. 494; to Somerset 41, 16. 18. **77.** 528; 42, 155.

[4] *Ex corruptelis papatus audio relictam esse congeriem, quae non obscuret modo, sed propemodum obruat purum et genuinum Dei cultum.* Calvin CR 41, 683.

English intercession), had at once been appointed preacher in England, and, in combination with J. Hooper who had returned from Zürich, fought for the biblical purism of the Swiss and the purifying of the service of God from all "idolatry." (It was at his earnest request that the remark about kneeling had been inserted in the revised edition of the Prayer-book, 1552). In 1550, a community of refugees (Germans, French, Walloons, Netherlanders, Italians) was established under **John a Lasco,** Micronius, and Utenhove, which adopted a strictly Presbyterian ritual, with Calvinistic ecclesiastical discipline, doctrine, and form of worship.[1]

All the same, the English Church upheld the episcopal constitution under royal supremacy, just as, in spite of all purifications, it adhered to the Catholic tradition of worship. But, at the same time, a confession of Faith[2] was drawn up in 1552 in the 42 Articles (by Cranmer and Ridley, Bishop of Rochester). This confession proclaimed with decision the exclusiveness of the principles of Scripture, justification by faith alone, and the Calvinistic doctrine of the Eucharist—consequently deviating from the Catechism of 1548, and also not in complete agreement with the liturgy. This was the origin of a new Catechism (1553, drawn up by Poinet, Bishop of Winchester): the Lord's supper is a "thankful remembrance of the death of Christ": the bread and wine "represent," "stand in place of" the body and blood: as bread and wine nourish the natural body, so the flesh and blood of Christ nourish the soul through faith: faith is the mouth of the soul.[3]

But the carrying out of this Reformation met with great difficulties. Opposition sprang up amongst the people and clergy. The Catholic minded were supported by Mary, who steadfastly continued her resistance to the innovations, and by Bishops Gardiner and Bonner, so that the government again deposed and imprisoned both of them. The peasantry, oppressed by the nobility and suffering from severe economical distress,[4] laid all its social need to the account

---

[1] See the Works of John a Lasco ed. Kuyper II. Amst. 1866, p. 1 ff. The ritual p. 285 ff. The *Compendium doctrinae* 1551, p. 341 ff. Catechism 1551. Also, RICHTER, *Kirchenordnungen* II 99 ff.; WILKINS IV, 64.

[2] *Two Liturgies*, p. 572 ff. NIEMEYER, p. 592 ff. We find predestination without any accentuation of its harshnesses in Art. 17; Art. 29: *Christi corpus in multis et diversis locis eodem tempore praesens esse non potest . . . . non debet quisquam fidelium carnis eius et sanguinis realem et corporalem praesentiam in Euchar. vel credere vel profiteri.* The 42 Articles at the same time make use of the 14 Articles, which the German deputation had drawn up (1538) in consultation with the English theologians (p. 205), and, indirectly through them, frequently of the CA word for word, and also of the Wurtemberg Confession (p. 159). Cp. SCHAFF I 623 ff.

[3] *Two Liturgies*, p. 485 ff.

[4] Cp. PHILIPPSON, *Westeuropa*, p. 46 ff.

of the ecclesiastical innovations and grumbled at the abolition of the monasteries. Deeds of violence and disturbances resulted, the restoration of the mass was demanded and the recall of Cardinal **Pole**, a relative of the royal house, who had been out of the country since 1532 and had worked against Henry in the attempt to win back England to the Pope. Peace had to be maintained by force of arms, especially in Devonshire and Norfolk (1549). Yet the measures of reform were not hereby checked, not even by Somerset's fall in 1549 (he was executed in 1552), who was succeeded by the Earl of Warwick (Duke of Northumberland). For the latter also found himself compelled to follow Edward's wishes in this respect. In order to confirm the new state of things, the ecclesiastical law and constitution had already been reorganised (*Reformatio legum ecclesiasticarum*), in order to suppress all resistance to the Reformation by the power of the authorities, when the death of Edward (when only 15 years of age) brought about a complete change in affairs. It now became evident that the Reformation had not as yet become a national matter.

CHAPTER SIXTH.

The Reformation in Poland, Hungary, Transylvania, and amongst the South Slavs.

1. In Poland.

Sources: A. THEINER, *Vetera Documenta Poloniae et Lithuaniae* II and III. Rom, 1861, 1863. *Fontes rer. Austr.* 2, XIX. Wien, 1859.

Literature: Count VAL. KRASINSKI, *Gesch. d. Ref. in Polen* (German translation by W. A. LINDAU. Leipz., 1841). FISCHER, *Gesch. d. Ref. in Polen;* 2 vols. Grätz, 1856. CHR. HARTKNOCH, *Alt- und Neues Preussen.* Frankf., 1684. H. DALTON (see above, p. 207).

Since 1386, Poland under the Jagellons, by the marriage of the Lithuanian prince Wladislav Jagello (who was at the time still a heathen and was only now baptised) with Hedwig (Vol. II, p. 521), which brought it into personal union with Lithuania, represented a republic of nobles with a royal head. The nobility had attained to great power during the struggles of the fifteenth century, the most distinguished families of which, as Palatines and greater and lesser castellans, together with the two archbishops (of Gresen and Lemberg, who themselves belonged to the nobility) and thirteen bishops formed the senate of the kingdom, on whom the peasant serfs were entirely dependent. By the side of the nobles the **German** population of the towns had gained for themselves a privileged position with German rights. Owing to the fact that a considerable number of the Lithuanian subjects were Greek Catholics, that the Jews, expelled from Germany, had found an asylum in Poland, and that the Hussites also (in spite of the strict prohibition of 1424) had obtained shelter there, the ground was already prepared for a tolerant treatment of various forms of worship existing side by side. Under King **Sigismund I.**[1] reformatory ideas rapidly forced their way in; the towns from Danzig (Jac. Knothe [Knade], cp. TSCHACKERT I 135) to Cracow, as well as the nobles who were jealous of the authority of the bishops, lent a willing ear to them. Certainly, in 1523, Sigismund decided upon an unusually harsh prohibition of Lutheran writings and threatened with death all who possessed copies or circulated them; the synod of Leczic (October, 1523) condemned all heresies, especially those of Luther and Huss, and one of the bishops, Krzycki, attacked Luther in a bitterly abusive lampoon. But such measures were unable to check a movement, which, in consequence of events in Prussia, the land of the Order, the intercourse of the towns with Germany, and the students at Wittenberg received continual support from the young nobles. When the city authority fell, Danzig led the way in the introduction of the Reformation; in the other towns its friends made their appearance more courageously, and even the peasants became restless and began to imitate the example of the Germans by violence.

---

[1] 1506-48.

Then Sigismund roused himself; the diet of Petrikau (1526) voted for measures of force, and Danzig was cruelly punished for its disturbance;[1] the progress of the Reformation was thereby checked for some years, but not with lasting success. The prohibition to attend heretical universities was disregarded by the nobles (cp. THEINER II 527); Wittenberg and Strasburg, then Zürich and Geneva exercised their power of attraction; the writings of the reformers were read in the towns as well as at the residences of the nobles. The King himself certainly desired to be a true son of the Roman Church, but could not make up his mind to consistent severity against the innovators; even in different episcopal sees leanings towards the Reformation were shown. Calvin obtained ever-increasing influence amongst the Polish nobles, as the greater sharpness of the antagonism to Rome was agreeable to the passionate character of the Poles, and French teaching was more congenial to their sensitive national feeling than that which had its origin in Germany, while the burgesses sided with Luther. Many of the Lutheran preachers were ignorant of the language, and hence renounced from the outset the idea of a propaganda amongst the Poles. In addition, even Italian refugees (Blandrata and others) visited the country, who propagated anti-trinitarian doctrines amongst the nobility, and, on the other hand, in 1548, some of the Bohemian Brethren who had been driven from Bohemia, who were settled by the families of Gorka and Ostrorog upon their estates.

Sigismund's son **Sigismund II. Augustus,** who was related through his first wife to the evangelical prince Radziwill and corresponded with Calvin and Melanchthon, allowed the Reformation freer scope, the power of Catholicism visibly disappeared, the towns and the nobility openly declared their adherence to the Gospel.[2] In 1555, there took place, on the one hand, a gathering of the different branches of the evangelicals at Kozminek, at which the zealous Bohemian "Brethren" with their firmly established ecclesiastical institutions induced the others to decide to join them and to accept their ritual: on the other hand, the evangelical nobility, at the diet of Petrikau, demanded a national Council under the presidency of the King, to which also Calvin, Beza, Melanchthon, and their countryman John a Lasco (p. 210) were invited, in order that a confession of faith for Poland might be decided upon: this would have been a severe defeat for Catholicism. The diet, at any rate, gave each nobleman the right of arranging divine service in his house as he thought fit. The King granted various towns (Danzig, Elbing and others) free exercise of religion.

---

[1] Duke Albert of Prussia and the excellent John of Schwarzenburg intervened vigorously in favour of the evagelicals. Cp. STROBEL, *Verm. Beiträge*, p. 3 ff.

[2] In the whole of Samogitia there were hardly six or seven Catholic clergy: Lithuania had become almost entirely Protestant.

Thus the Reformation seemed destined to find a home and legal recognition in Poland.

2. In Hungary and Transylvania.

Sources and *Literature:* G. D. TEUTSCH, *Urkundenb. der erg. Landesk. A. B. in Siebenb. I.* Hermannst. 1862. Various older historical works collected in FABÓ ANDRÁS, *Monumenta Evangelicorum A. C. in Hungaria.* 4 vols. Pest, 1861-1873. F. A. LAMPE, *Hist. eccl. ref. in Hung. et Transylv.* Traj. ad Rh., 1728. BAUHOFER, *Gesch. d. erg. K. in Ungarn.* Berl., 1854. JOH. GRAF MAILÁTH, *Gesch. der Magyaren,* III. Regensb., 1853. J. BORBIS, *die erg.-luth. K. Ungarns.* Nördl., 1861. ST. LINBERGER, *Gesch. des Evg. in Ungarn sammt Siebenb.* Budapest, 1880. Litterae hungaricae ad Bullingerum datae in E. BÖHL, *Confess. Helv. post.* Vindob., 1866, p. 97 ff. SZLÁVIK in ZKG XIV 202 ff.

The feeble Louis II., the husband of Mary, sister of Charles V.,[1] was on the throne of Hungary. Students, especially from the comitat of Zips (a German settlement), who attended the University of Wittenberg, and merchants, who attended Leipzig Fair, introduced Luther's doctrines and writings into the country at an early date. Louis issued impotent prohibitions, and preachers of the Gospel soon appeared openly in Hungary and also in Transylvania. In 1524, Campeggi visited Hungary and advised severer measures; bloody regulations of persecution had already been issued in 1523, and, in particular in 1525, at the diet of Rákosch;[2] only **one** victim, however, was sacrificed, a bookseller in Buda, who had offered reformatory writings for sale. Suppressed in one place, the movement blazed up again in others. A rising of the miners and wood-cutters (1526), which combined the demand for evangelical freedom with amelioration of their social position, led to much more bloodshed and to more serious imperilling of the fortunes of the party of reformation.

Soon afterwards, however, the fatal battle of Mohacz (August 29th, 1526) at one blow altered the condition of affairs in favour of the Protestants. Seven bishops had fallen in battle with the King; East Hungary with Transylvania swore allegiance to **John Zapolya** (1526-1540), the South-West to **Ferdinand** (1526-1564). The former vigorously opposed the Reformation, but was soon obliged to retire to Poland; then the victory of the Reformation was rapidly accomplished, especially owing to the noiseless, but well-directed activity of the learned and pious **John Honter,** who (in 1542) openly introduced Cronstadt and the whole of Bursenland to the Reformation, composed a ritual and promoted public education.

---

[1] When Luther (November 1st, 1526) dedicated his exposition of the four consolatory Psalms (EA 38, 369 ff.) to this queen as a woman who "was favourably disposed to the Gospel and yet was greatly let and hindered by the godless bishops," he mistook her religious attitude.

[2] "Lutherani omnes...capiantur et comburantur."

Hermannstadt followed in 1543, and, in 1545, the evangelical Saxons at a synod at Mediasch entered into a church association. Honter now wrote (1547) the *Reformatio ecclesiarum Saxonicarum in Transilvania*,[1] and the Saxon diet, in 1550, bestowed its legal sanction upon this ordinance. When Zápolya's widow Isabella returned with her son John Sigismund to the land of Transylvania, she found the Reformation so firmly established, that violent opposition appeared fruitless. John Sigismund himself accepted the evangelical confession, and in 1556 the Catholic bishop was driven out of the country. The evangelical established church[2] was organised; an attempt was also made to gain over the Greek-Catholic Wallachians in the country, although it proved unsuccessful.

In Hungary, the irresolution of the government at the same time enabled the Reformation to establish itself with increasing firmness. The towns of Zips and the mountain towns led the way, but also many magnates accepted its doctrines. **Matthias Biro Devay**, Hungary's most prominent reformer, had studied at Wittenberg since 1529, and afterwards (1531) worked in Buda and Kaschau on behalf of the Reformation, both by preaching and writing: he had then been taken as a prisoner to Vienna, where Faber had had him examined;[3] subsequently released, he had resumed his preaching in Zápolya's province, until here also he was condemned to silence by a three years' imprisonment. He now put himself under the protection of one of the evangelically minded magnates (Nádasdy) and continued the fight with his pen, but in 1536 he again visited Germany, where he became friendly with Melanchthon, and afterwards, in Bâle, with Grynaeus. On his return home, he resumed work partly as an itinerant-preacher, partly as head of a school, but especially with his pen—now employing the language of the country; his friend **John Sylvester** translated the New Testament into Hungarian. Again expelled, he proceeded to Wittenberg and on to Switzerland (where, to Luther's indignation [de Wette, V 644], he definitely joined the Swiss), in order finally to devote himself once more in his home (at Debreczin) to the building up of the evangelical church—but now, as it was understood by the Helvetic reformers. Here, evangelical preaching had in the meantime advanced irresistibly: the provost of Zips, Joseph Hervát, and even

---

[1] In Latin and German in TEUTSCH, Urkundenb. I 6ff., 36 ff.

[2] The first German-Lutheran hymn-book (by VAL. WAGNER) appeared about 1554. Cp. Archiv für siebenb. Landeskunde N. F. 22, 26 ff.

[3] See the proceedings of the examination in LAMPE p. 80 ff.

the bishops of Neitra and Weszprim gave up their dignities and professed adherence to evangelical doctrines. In 1545, the evangelical Hungarians assembled at a synod at Erdöd and, in 1546, at Eperies[1]. Defenceless and discouraged, Catholicism was here confronted by its decline. In 1547, Ferdinand demanded a confession: the Upper Hungarians thereupon handed over an extract from the CA in the Confessio Pentapolitana (already accepted at Eperies), whereupon the King left them in peace.

But the germ of discord was already growing up amongst them. The splitting of Protestantism in Germany and Switzerland exercised an injurious effect over the border. On the whole the Hungarians followed the Helvetic, the Germans (and Slavs) the Lutheran trend of doctrine.[2] Hitherto, however, the CA had been accepted by all the synods, but the connection of a number of clergy with Switzerland (Bullinger) produced the result that at first a dispute arose about doing away with the altars, then (1557) part of the Magyars accepted a reformed confession of faith (*Confessio Csengerina*)[3] at **Zenger,** whom the mountain-towns (Kremnitz and others) confronted in 1558 with their Lutheran confession (printed in Borbis p. 22 ff.). Melanchthon, who was solicited by the Transylvanians for his judgment, sent an opinion, which although cautiously worded was Lutheran in tenor, upon the manifold points of difference (CR IX 429 ff.), in consequence of which the synod at Mediasch (1560) excluded certain persons who spoke against the Lutheran doctrine of the Eucharist, but subsequently, in 1564 at Enyed, the **division** of the Transylvanians into a Saxon church which accepted the Confession of Augsburg and a Magyar, which accepted the Helvetic Confession, was openly accomplished. The same division took place in Hungary, where Calvinism made increasing progress, after a prolonged struggle at the synod of Debreczin (1567), at which the Magyars accepted the second Helvetic Confession (see p. 187) and the Lutherans separated from them.

But Unitarianism also had already obtained a firm footing, especially in Transylvania, under the patronage of John Sigismund. Even Anabaptists made

---

[1] The Synod's tenets of confession are lost; hence it is disputed whether their tenor was entirely Lutheran or whether the Swiss type was already prominent. At Eperies, the CA and Melanchthon's Loci were agreed to.

[2] Hence we find, even at the present day, the "Magyar" and "German" beliefs distinguished in the mouth of the people. The Hungarians at the University of Wittenberg (Schola Hungarica) had been greatly influenced by Melanchthon's writings.

[3] NIEMEYER 539 ff. SCHAFF I 589 ff.

their appearance, and the many-sided theological quarrel in Germany, which threw out its shoots as far as Hungary (the adherents of Osiander; his antipodes **Stancaro**, who propagated in person, in Poland and Hungary, his doctrine that our justification is to be attributed to the human nature of Christ alone; the followers of Flacius) checked the development of the life of the youthful evangelical communities and paved the way for the Catholic reaction which was also preparing here.

3. The Gospel amongst the South Slavs.

Literature: W. SILLEM, *Primus Truber*, Erl., 1861. TH. ELZE, P. *Wiener* in Jb d. Gesellsch. f. G. d. Prot. in Oesterr., 1882, 1 ff.; the same in RE XVI 56 ff.

Luther's Gospel also penetrated to the Slav peoples, at first into Carniola, Carinthia and Styria. Its first traces appear at Laibach (in 1530), where the house of the clerk of the court, Khlobner, was the centre of a small circle of evangelicals; in the following year the young priest **Primus Truber** of Carniola was called to the Cathedral of Laibach, where he preached the doctrines of Luther, and, when this was forbidden him, in another church: he also soon found a man of the same views as himself in **Paul Wiener**, a canon of the cathedral.

Notwithstanding many perils, both managed to remain here until 1547. Truber had also been appointed canon in 1542, and was specially entrusted with preaching in the Wendish popular language; then, during the Schmalkaldic War, the bishop took proceedings against both. Truber fled; Wiener was taken, transported to Vienna, and finally allowed to emigrate to Transylvania, where he found a rich field of work at Hermannstadt, and in 1553 became the first superintendent of the evangelical church of Transylvania. In 1548, Truber repaired to Germany and found a post at Rothenburg on the Tauber (and then at Kempten). He now applied himself to the task of his life, that of rendering the Gospel accessible in print to his Wendish countrymen, whose dialect was as yet altogether without literature. Working indefatigably, partly in connection with Vergerio, but especially supported by the Styrian nobleman, Baron Hans Ungnad, who had emigrated to Wurtemberg, he provided them with the Catechism, the New Testament,[1] the Psalms, Confessions of Faith, a book of homilies, hymns, etc., in the form of translations, in part freely adapted from German writings. Most of these works were printed at Tübingen. A younger friend of Truber, Stephen Consul, in his turn transported many of them to Croatia and Illyria. Meanwhile, the evangelical movement made such progress in his native land, that the estates of Carniola were able to summon Truber to be provincial preacher; from 1561-1565 he organised the affairs of the evangelical church (the Slovenian ritual, 1564; an evangelical provincial college). Although he was again expelled in 1565 by the Archduke Charles, he left behind him an organised evangelical church as his work, until, under the Jesuit's pupil, Ferdinand, the counter-reformation (1599) here also destroyed what evangelical belief had created. But, in the meantime, the whole of the Scriptures had been presented to the Slovenians in their own language by **Dalmatin** (1581); Styria, Carinthia and Carniola had defrayed the cost of printing in common.

---

[1] Cp. SCHELHORN, *Ergötzlichkeiten*, III 806 ff.

THIRD DIVISION.

The Restoration of Catholicism.

Preliminary Remarks.

The cry for ecclesiastical reform had made itself heard, loudly and frequently, since the fearful times of the papal schism at the end of the Middle Ages: many attempts were made (councils of Reform, reforms in the monasteries); but the secularisation of the Curia, the predominance of worldly interests over those of the Church had paralysed all reforms. At the end of the Middle Ages a Catholic reform was commenced in the Spanish Church (Vol. II. p. 546), which aimed at Thomism in the teaching, improvement and discipline of the clergy and the monasteries, and at the same time offered satisfaction to more ardent religious longings in the means of devotion provided by mysticism. Had this reform become effective earlier and already advanced further, when Luther appeared upon the scene, the ground would have been cut from under the feet of many most effective accusations and many a need would have been satisfied; Rome would then have been spared the sight of the fearful defection which the early years of the Reformation brought upon her. But this reform came too late: the blindness of the Curia had done everything to assist the Reformation to its first great and victorious campaign. It was not until the year 1540 that, in consequence of the crisis at the Court of Rome and the foundation of the Order of the Jesuits (Spain's gift to the Church), a sudden change took place, from which date the Roman Church opposed the evangelical Reformation with its reforms and organised resistance. It was too late for **an understanding** with Protestantism (a reunion)—too late to allow the voices to be heard which recommended a *rapprochement* and agreement with the religious ideas of the Reformation, but still early enough to bring the Reformation to a standstill and to deprive it again of considerable portions of its sphere and influence. Naturally, this Catholic restoration, as it only met with an abrupt rejection in face of the Reformation, was bound also to suppress the elements in its own midst, which in any way exhibited features akin to the Reformation—such as Augustinianism and the desire for a national church : this Catholicism was bound to ripen into Romanism.

CHAPTER FIRST.

The Catholic Reaction and the Extinction of the Reformation in Italy.

1. Evangelical movements and Catholic Reforms.

Sources and *Literature:* Bibliot. della riforma Ital., 1883 ff. DAN. GERDESIUS, *Specimen Ital. Ref.* Lugd. Bat. 1765; a literary historical account in SCHELHORN, *Amoenitates und Ergötzlichkeiten;* M'CRIE, *History of the progress and suppression of the Reformation in Italy.* Edinb., 1827 (in German, Leipz., 1829); C. CANTU, *Gli Eretici d'Italia,* 3 vols. Turin, 1865-1867. COMBA, *Storia della riforma in Italia,* I. Firenze, 1881; F. DITTRICH in JGG V 319 ff.; VII 1 ff.; the same, *Gasp. Contarini.* Braunsb., 1885; M. PHILIPPSON, *Gesch. Westeuropas im ZA von Philipp II.* Berl., 1882, 1883; W. MAURENBRECHER, *Kath. Reformation I.* For *Renata of Ferrara* see HENKE in HZ 25; BONNET in Revue chrét., 1875; B. FONTANA, *Renata di Ferrara.* I. Roma, 1889. For J. VALDÉS cp. the literature in RE 16, 276 ff.; add WILKENS, *Gesch. d. span. Protest.* Gütersl., 1888, p. 86 ff.; his *Mercur und Charon* in Reformistas antig. españ. IV and in E. BÖHMER, Roman. Stud. 19; his *Considerazioni* in Bibl. Wiffeniana I 63 ff. (in German by BÖHMER. Halle, 1870); add MÖLLER in StKr 1866. For the entire Neapolitan circle, see L. AMABILI, *Il S. Officio della Inquisiz. in Napoli* I. Città di Castello, 1892. For *Gaetano di Tiene* see W. LÜBEN. Regb., 1883; for *Caraffa,* BENRATH in RE XI 332 ff.; Campeggi's opinion in FRIEDENSBURG, Nuntiaturberichte II. BENRATH: Ueber die Quellen der ital. Ref.-Gesch. Bonn., 1876; the same, *Theatinerorden* in RE XV 377 ff. *Consil. de emendanda eccl.* in LE PLAT, Monum. Trid. II 596 ff. SCHELHORN, *De consilio de emend. eccl. auspic. Pauli III. conscripto Tiguri,* 1748. On the establishment of the Inquisition at Rome, see Reusch, Index I 169; Benrath in HZ 44, 460 ff.

The stream of reformatory ideas that flowed through all the countries of Europe showed how violently the power of Rome over men's minds had been shaken in spite of the official victory of the papal system over all previous reformatory tendencies, as celebrated by the Lateran Council (Vol. II, p. 530). For a long time the powers of the Church seemed as it were paralysed in the presence of the new movement, and, above all, through the fault of the Popes themselves. Instead of devoting their most serious attention to the enormous falling away in Germany, they directed it first and foremost to the preservation of their political power in Italy. The papacy missed the chance of saving Catholicism that was threatened on all sides. Even on the soil of Italy, which was connected with Rome by manifold interests, its authority over men's minds was tottering.

In Italy also deeper religious emotions of an evangelical character showed themselves by the side of critical and illuminating tendencies. From a literary, aesthetic and artistic point of view, Italy stood at the head of the secular culture of the age; it sheltered the most accomplished members of high society, whom humanism had elevated with its revival of the antique, its formal emancipation and extension of its sphere of view, and its aesthetic refinement. Art, freed from fixed ecclesiastical traditions, received a powerful impulse, opening its arms to Nature and at the same time to the influences of antiquity. A strongly developed political life with entirely secular, regardlessly egoistical maxims was added to this. This culture of the Renaissance, emancipated internally from ecclesiastical hypotheses, frequently leading to heathenish ideals and conceptions of life, not infrequently combined with moral frivolousness, nevertheless knew how to get on well with the existing churchship on the whole. At the Court of Leo X. irreligion was the open secret of the upper circles; but here, as in Venice and Florence, people had to reckon with the Church and its claim to sovereignty, as with every other given secular power. The authority of the Pope over the whole Church here appears as the interest of Italy. The splendour of the Church, for numbers a matter of pecuniary advantage, is popular and a delight to the people, who approve of just the secular and heathen traits as exhibited in Rome, which set their impress upon their piety.

But, even amongst the educated and nobility of the nation, there is no lack of persons, whose highly-developed culture at the same time longs for deeper religious feeling and renewal. Men, who were subsequently driven in opposite directions by the development of things, still stood side by side in the two first decades of the Reformation, connected by the desire for the resuscitation of extinct religious life. Such was that club consisting of some fifty to sixty clerical members, which was organised at Rome in 1523 under the title of **"The Oratory of Divine Love"** for the purposes of common practices of piety and devotion. Here also, by the side of the tendencies of sincere Catholic devotion and the endeavour to regenerate the clergy morally, biblical-evangelical views showed themselves prominently, without any intention,—without even any idea of the possibility of a conflict with the official church. Sadoleti, Giberti, Caraffa and others belonged to the union, the activity of which extended to Vicenza, Verona, and Venice.[1] The storm of the year 1527 dispersed the confraternity. But active literary intercourse also brought fresh ideas into the country from Germany and Switzerland. The writings of Luther and others were circulated in an Italian translation (partly under

---

[1] KERKER in ThQ 1859, p. 9, has proved that Contarini did not belong to this oratory, as has frequently been asserted.

fictitious names): thus Luther's *An den Christlichen Adel*[1] appeared (in 1533) as *Libro de la emendatione et correctione dil stato Christiano* (probably translated by Bartolomeo Fonzio WA VI 400 f. 632) and Melanchthon's *Loci*[2] as *I principii de la Theologia di Ippofilo da Terra Nigra* (about 1534, CR XXII 654 ff.). The strained relations and struggles between the Emperor Charles and Clement VII., which led to the conquest of Rome in 1527 (p. 71), and political complications in general, extensively promoted criticism of the secular power of the papacy and the secularised church. In Venice, the political feeling of independence in the powerful commercial republic favoured freer impulses, at least to such an extent that there was no inclination to be at the service of Roman demands Here, in 1530, the Italian translation of the New Testament by Brucioli was printed and, in 1532, the whole Bible. Distinguished Venetians followed with lively interest the course of the German reform-negotiations and entered into correspondence with Melanchthon. **Renata (Renée), Duchess of Ferrara,** a French princess, who had married Ercole d'Este in 1527, made the little court of Ferrara the rendezvous of the most distinguished intellects (p. 177): men who had evangelical leanings as well as those who were interested in a Catholic reform entered into friendly intercourse with her—a Calvin as well as a Contarini. In **Modena** a community of zealous adherents of the evangelical doctrine of grace[3] was formed at an early date: it was supported (after 1536) by Bishop Giovanni de **Morone,** a friend of Contarini, even after the Augustinian Fra Serafino had attacked it vigorously in controversial sermons. It was the doctrine of justification by faith in God's mercy and Christ's merit that was here fostered. Even Morone's espousal of papal interests as nuncio in Germany (1536-1538) and then again at the discussion at Worms (1540) did not hinder him from allowing the doctrine perfect liberty: he was of opinion that the authority and system of the Church were compatible with such an evangelical conception. During the thirties one of the chief meeting-places for the evangelically minded of all ranks in the country, who thought to fill up the forms of ecclesiastical life with evangelical matter, was **Naples.** The most important religious personality here was **Juan Valdés,** a Spaniard by birth, brother of the imperial secretary Alfonso, who died in 1532 (p. 71). Juan, a man also of humanistic merits (Dialogo de las lenguas) wrote (in 1528) the keenly satirical dialogue "Mercury and Charon," similar to the dialogue "Lactantius" composed by his brother, only richer in theological reflections. In 1531, he left Spain for Rome, where he was promoted by the Pope to the office of Chamberlain after the former had made peace with the Emperor: but, for the most part, he lived in Naples as the spiritual and intellectual centre of a circle of religiously awakened persons, which at one time reckoned three thousand supporters, who, " without actually attacking the State Church, sought to lay independently the firm foundation of a free Kingdom of God." He translated the Psalms for the widowed Duchess of Trajetto, Julia Gonzaga, whose spiritual director he was, and wrote devotional elucidations of the books of the New Testament in particular: he described the evangelical way of salvation in the *Alfabeto Christiano* and, in the *Cento e dieci divine considerazioni* gave directions for the life of the spiritual man in God. He died in 1541, shortly before the

---

[1] [See p. 25].
[2] [See p. 38].
[3] Cp. Sommario della s. Scrittura; add ThLZ 1877, 671 ff. and above p. 196.

outbreak of the persecution. The best known and most famous work of evangelical Italy, *Del Benefizio di Cristo*, proceeded from the circle which gathered round Valdés; the author of this treatise, which was for a long time attributed to Aonio Paleario, is now known to be **Benedetto da Mantova,** an Augustinian monk of San Severino (Benrath in ZKG I 575 ff.). Amongst other members of the circle may be mentioned Pietro Martire Vermigli, Marcantonio Flaminio, the Franciscan Ochino, and also ecclesiastical dignitaries, such as Cardinal Pole, who had fled from England (p. 211).

Meanwhile the idea of a **Catholic** Reformation had gained wider support and fresh development. The "Oratory" might indeed provide individuals with edification and strengthening of religious feeling, but the accidental, purely private character of the union, the irregularity with which the associates took part in the common efforts prevented its having any far-reaching effects. Then the idea sprang up amongst the members of the Oratory of giving a more permanent form to its objects by the foundation **of an Order** and of exercising a higher influence in the direction of the reform of the Church. Count **Gaetano di Tiene**, with Caraffa and some other members of the Oratory, founded (in 1524) **the Order of the Theatins** (the name was borrowed from Caraffa's see, Theate [Chieti in the Abruzzi]),—an order which, outbidding the mendicant orders in strictness as to lack of personal property, set itself the task of forming a religiously earnest, ecclesiastically trained clerical family, whose duty it should be to enliven the interest of the Catholic people in its worship (more frequent communions, better methods of preaching), to devote itself to tending the sick with regardless self-sacrifice, **to combat heresy in every form.** The Order spread rapidly over the whole of Italy, and with it its watchword: Ecclesiastical Reform and war against heretics! In **Giovanni Pietro Caraffa** the personality in whom these two ideas were most intimately combined here comes into prominence.

A sojourn of several years in Spain had made him acquainted with that strong Catholic current of reform which, while it at the same time harked back to Thomas Aquinas and also to the ecclesiastical normal theologian, strove energetically for improvement of discipline and morals and also for the reconquest of the power and dignity of the Church, such as it had possessed in the brilliant times of the Middle Ages. Under Adrian VI. he had devoted his attention to a scheme of reform for the administration of the Church; under Clement also he had worked zealously for ecclesiastical reforms. After the sack of Rome in 1527, the desire for an unsparing search for and persecution of heretics became more prominently manifested in him. When Paul III. was obliged to approach the question of the summoning of the Council, in order not to lose the Catholic Church in Germany completely, it was a question in Rome of coming to an understanding as to the means which could be adopted to heal the abuses of the Church, even of the Roman Curia itself. In 1536, the Pope nominated a commission, which was to make a list of the abuses of the Church and lay it before himself: Caraffa, Pole, Sadoleti, Contarini, and others belonged to it and worked zealously and sincerely, without sparing the sins of the head. A **Consilium de emendanda ecclesia** (1537), which was also published in 1538 by Luther in German without any idea that in this case a zeal for reform was actually aroused, was the fruit of its work. About the same time, Cardinal Campeggi in combination with his brother handed over a detailed reply to the *gravamina* of the German nation, in which he was obliged to recognise many grievances as well founded and to speak in favour of a reform of the ecclesiastical system. But Paul III. met with opposition in those immediately around him and put off the necessary reform of the Church together with the projected council.

Henceforth, Caraffa appeared at the head of the reactionary party, helped to repress the reform party (Contarini) which was inclined for compromise—the Ratisbon colloquy is the last unsuccessful attempt at a peaceful arrangement with the Protestants—and succeeded in getting Paul III. to reorganise the Inquisition after the Spanish model in the bull "Licet ab initio" (July 21st, 1542) and to establish the "Sant' Uffizio" at Rome under his presidency. (Ignatius Loyola had also co-operated in this.) The principle was, above all, to punish those in high position amongst the evangelically minded; "for thereupon depends the salvation of the lower classes."

That **religious** movement within Romish circles becomes a strictly **ecclesiastical** reaction against every innovation, an obstinate adherence to the foundations of the ecclesiastical system connected with a struggle for life and death against the innovators.

2. The Annihilation of the Italian Reformation Circles.

Literature (continued): For Peter Martyr, see C. SCHMIDT. Elberfeld 1858; RE XVI 356 ff.; for Ochino, BENRATH.[2] Braunschweig 1893; for Paleario, M. YOUNG, 2 vols. Lond. 1860; J. BONNET, German by MERSCHMANN. Hamb. 1862. BENRATH in Gelzer's Monatsbl. 1867. Oct.; RE XI 164 ff.; R. STÄHELIN, *Briefe aus der Ref.-Zeit.* Basel. 1887, p. 27 ff.: Coelius Secundus Curio, in ZhTh 30, 571 ff., 42, 411 ff.; RE III 396 ff.; Olympia Morata, Opp. Basil. 1570; RE X 269 f.; Vitt. Colonna, E. FERRERO and GIUS. MÜLLER, V. C. Carteggio. Torino 1889; Biography by REUMONT. Freib. 1881; add BENRATH in Augsb. Allg. Ztg. 4. Jan. 1882; CAMPORI, Modena 1878; Vergerius: C. H. SIXT, P. P. Verg. Braunschweig 1855; Briefwechsel zwischen Herz. Christoph und P. P. V. (StBlV 124). Tüb. 1875; Nuntiaturberichte I; FERRAI in Archivio stor. Ital. XV and XVI; F. HUBERT, *V.s publicist. Thätigkeit.* Gött. 1893; Spiera: CR XX 613 ff.; RÖNNEKE in ZhTh 44, 71 ff.; Carnesecchi: MANZONI in Miscell. di stor. patr. X. Turin 1870; BENRATH in HTb 6. F. 4, 168 ff.; the same, *Gesch. d. Ref. in Venedig.* Halle 1887; the same, Art. Caraccioli in RE III 142 ff.

Thus began the bloody war of extermination against the evangelical party of Reform in Italy. Many victims fell :[1] many, driven out of the country, found a refuge outside their native land ; but we cannot be surprised that, during this war of persecution, in the case of many who were persecuted a thoughtful and quiet development of evangelical ideas was checked and a radicalism of anti-trinitarian or sceptical stamp, but especially, baptist enthusiasm was aroused. Indeed, the pronounced opposition to the old heathen form of popular Catholicism there prevalent, which was obvious to the evangelicals of Romance origin, already gave an impulse in the direction of Radicalism.

The circle of Valdés was dispersed. **Peter Martyr Vermigli**, the Augustinian canon, a Florentine of noble birth, born in 1500, prior of a monastery at Naples, and then at Lucca (1541), was obliged to abandon all active preaching of the Gospel and to flee from the Inquisition in 1542. He found refuge in Zürich, Bâle, Strasburg, and entered the ranks of the reformatory theologians as an active co-operator, whom we have already met on page 209. **Bernardino Ochino** of Siena, at first a Franciscan Observant,[2] then joined the stricter Capuchins, amongst whom he became a famous itinerant preacher of the Order; appointed "apostolical missionary" by the Pope, introduced to evangelical doctrines by his own study of the Bible and personal contact with Valdés, he was again (in 1541) chosen a second time general of the Order, in spite of the charge that was already hanging over him, but, in the following year, summoned by the Inquisition and warned by Contarini, he was obliged to take to flight like Vermigli; at Geneva, he became minister of a community of refugees that had assembled there, later, in the reign of Edward VI., of a similar community in London. On his return to Switzerland, where he was for some time minister of the evangelical Italians who had been expelled from Locarno (p. 189), he gave himself up more and more to scepticism and subtle investigation of matters of belief and Christian ethics (? polygamy), thereby bringing upon himself a melancholy, restless life (he died in 1565).[3] Incited by Valdés and Vermigli, a nephew of Caraffa, the Marquis **Galeazzo Caraccioli**, also gave up his court-office and brilliant social position in 1551 and repaired to Geneva; in the courage of his belief, he resisted all the efforts of his family, even the promises of his uncle, who had become Pope, to induce him to return home; he vainly endeavoured to persuade his wife to share his exile with him. He died in 1586, a highly esteemed support of the Italian community of refugees. The

---

[1] A list of those who were executed in Rome itself has been put together by DÖLLINGER-REUSCH, *Die Selbstbiogr. Bellarmins*, p. 235 ff. Cp. further the *Compendium processuum* in Arch. della Soc. Rom. di Stor. Patr. III 268 ff., 449 ff.

[2] See Vol. II, p. 540.

[3] He is the characteristic representative of youthful Evangelism in Italy in the haste with which he took up problems with which Protestantism, ecclesiastically consolidated and purified, had long finished. Remembering the discredit which the bigamy of Landgrave Philip and its theological defenders had brought upon the evangelical cause, we can understand the harshness with which Zürich treated **Ochino**. Cp. BOSSERT in ThLZ 1893, 212.

humanist **Aonio Paleario** of Siena, who was indicted in 1542 for a work upon the expiatory death of Christ, was enabled to secure his liberty on this occasion by his masterly self-defence; but after working cautiously in Lucca and then in Milan, he was accused for the second time in 1567; after three years' imprisonment he died the death of a heretic. The humanist **Coelius Secundus Curio**, who had been won over to evangelicalism by the writings of the reformers, was at first seized by the Inquisition at Turin, and only escaped from prison by stratagem; after staying at the Court of Renata, Duchess of Ferrara, where he won over the noble Olympia Morata to evangelical principles, he attempted, as he had done before in Pavia, to influence the University of Lucca in favour of the Reformation, until he arrived in Switzerland as a refugee in the year 1542; there, first at Lausanne and then at Bâle, he actively devoted his services to humanism and a Protestantism understood by him in a latitudinarian spirit, neither sharply Calvinistic nor Lutheran, which accordingly brought upon him the reproach of Pelagianism and even of anti-Trinitarianism. In his *Pasquilli* (1544) he covered the papacy with abundant ridicule.

Even Renata was unable to prevent the Inquisition being introduced into Ferrara in 1545; the evangelical community that had gathered together there was dispersed, individual steadfast professors of the new doctrines were put to death; she herself was imprisoned in 1554 as a suspected person, but submitted, although outwardly only: after her husband's death she returned to France in 1560, where she devoted her energies, until her death in 1575, to protecting the Protestants during the terrible times of the religious wars. The much admired **Olympia Morata**, the classically educated lady companion of Renata's daughter, who first became acquainted with evangelical doctrines through Curio and, after 1548, exchanged frivolous court-life for evangelical earnestness, followed her husband, the German physician Grunthler, to Germany, where she found the protection which her native land refused her (died in 1555). The noble poetess **Vitt. Colonna**, Margravine of Pescara, the friend of Cardinal Reginald Pole and, like him, inclined to an evangelically framed doctrine of justification, did not, however, take the decisive step, which would have severed her from the Romish Church. In **Venice**, to which the Inquisition was at first unable to extend its arm, the connection of the little, evangelically minded community with Germany was kept up in particular by **Balthasar Altieri**, a Neapolitan in the service of the English ambassador. Together with Luther's and Melanchthon's writings, those of the Swiss and Strasburgers were read, as well as the writings of Servetus. The sudden denunciation of **Pietro Paolo Vergerio**, Bishop of Capodistria, as a "Lutheran," must have caused great excitement. Formerly a law lecturer at Padua, then an advocate at Venice, he had turned his attention to the Church in 1530, having lost his wife after a short but happy married life: he became papal secretary, and was very soon appointed papal plenipotentiary in diplomatic missions; in 1533, he was sent by Clement VII as nuncio to Ferdinand's court; in 1535, Paul III. bestowed a similar post upon him. He had fulfilled his office energetically, certainly not without ambition, but also with an incorruptible sense of justice: an enemy of the heretics, but also an outspoken censor of ecclesiastical abuses, undauntedly pressing for ecclesiastical reforms, and, above all, the summoning of the Council. Rewarded with the bishopric of Modrusch in Croatia, then with that of his native town, he returned home in 1536; he made his appearance once again in Germany at the religious discussion at Worms (1540) and worked in promoting the general

Council, by order of Francis I. It is uncertain whether he had a secret mission from the Pope;[1] in any case he was regarded with distrust by the official deputies of the Curia, in his attitude here also a representative of the Catholic reform party. After his return home, while engaged upon an essay "Against the Apostates in Germany" he underwent a profound alteration of mind. At the end of 1544, the monks of Capodistria, enraged at the strict discipline which he maintained amongst the clergy, secretly accused him of sowing the seeds of Lutheran heresy. The trial that subsequently took place before the inquisition tribunal of Venice was a protracted one; still, the suspect was refused a seat at the Council of Trent. This had a decisive influence upon his inner development (Hubert, p. 244 ff.). In 1548, proceedings were again taken against him; on the 3rd of July, 1549, the Pope deprived him of his office and also of his priestly dignity as a heretic; he escaped imprisonment by flight to the Grisons, removed in 1553 as "Councillor" of Duke Christopher to Tübingen, from that time forth leading a restless, wandering life,[2] and only serving the evangelical cause in Italy by numerous, for the most part polemical pamphlets[3] and correspondence with his countrymen. In the year of his flight he published[4] the tragic story of **Francisco Spiera**, an advocate of Cittadella, who, when Venice after the victories of the Emperor could no longer escape the work of the Inquisition, solemnly renounced the evangelical belief in 1548 after repeated examination. Six months later, however, he died in despair, dreadfully tormented by qualms of conscience, feeling guilty of having committed the sin against the Holy Ghost. Vergerio's experiences at his sick bed entirely converted him. Persecutions became still more violent, when the seventy-nine years old Caraffa mounted the papal chair in 1555. "He covered the whole of Italy with a network of inquisitional offices connected with the Holy Office at Rome." Even the worldly-minded, jovial, clever, but personally by no means zealous **Pius IV** (1560-1565) was unable to alter the system. Caraffa's old, gloomy, and fanatical associate, Ghislieri, as **Pius V** completed the work of crushing Italian Protestantism. While he was Pope, the noble **Pietro Carnesecchi,** formerly secretary and protonotary under Clement VII, associate of the Oratory and of the Valdésian circle of friends, afterwards the secret supporter of quiet evangelically-minded circles in Padua, and finally Councillor of Duke Cosimo II. of Florence, also fell a victim to the Inquisition (1567), after it had already twice before vainly stretched out its bloodthirsty hand against him.

The reckless employment of force was able to carry out its horrible work here the sooner, as the reformatory movement found no support either in the princes or in the community. The supporters of the movement continued for the most part to be confined to the limited circles of educated persons: the Romance temperament chiefly clung to the sensual worship offered by Rome. Strong national indignation at Romish oppression was lacking; on

---

[1] Cp. DITTRICH in Braunsb. Index lectionum 1879. R. MOSES, Die Religionsverh. zu Hagenau u. Worms. Jena 1889, p. 91 ff. HUBERT, p. 7 ff. 243 ff.
[2] He died in 1565.
[3] Biblioth. della riforma ital. I and II.
[4] Bibl. della ref. it. II 112 ff. HUBERT p. 264 ff.

the other hand, a thousand various interests were connected with Romish churchdom. To these were soon added strongly divergent views and ecclesiastical ideals,—by the side of an orthodox Protestantism, for the most part of a Swiss complexion, a sober-minded Anabaptism, but also a radically anti-Trinitarian Anabaptist party, which in 1550 was secretly organised at a Council in Venice (see below). Rome owed a considerable portion of her successes to this internal disruption. Switzerland, first and foremost, became the home of those who had fled from the Inquisition in time.

CHAPTER SECOND.

The Order of the Jesuits.

St. Ignatius.

Sources and *Literature*: S. *Ignacio de Loyola*, Cartas. 4 vols. Madrid, 1874-1887; also some letters in ZkTh IX 310 ff.; [Tollenarius] *Imago primi seculi Soc. J.* Antw., 1640. N. ORLANDINO, *Hist. S. J.* Rom., 1614; CRÉTINAU-JOLY (the official panegyrist of the Order), *Hist. de la comp. de J.* 6 vols. Paris, 1844-1846 (in German. Wien, 1845 ff.); J. HUBER, *der Jes.-O.* Berlin, 1873; V. FRINS (S. J.) in KL VI 1374 ff. On Ignatius: CONSALVI (*Acta ex ore Ignatii excepta*) in ASB, July, VII 634 ff.; RIBADENEIRA Neap., 1572; (JOH. PIEN) in ASB, July; VII 409 ff.; GENELLI, Innsbr., 1847; E. GOTHEIN. Halle, 1885; F. GESS in HTb 6 F. 12, 265 ff.; M. RITTER in HZ 34, 305 ff.; H. BAUMGARTEN. Strassb., 1880; VON DRUFFEL, *I. v. L. an der römischen Kurie*. München, 1879. BARTOLI, *Histoire de St. Ignace*: 2 vols. Lille, 1893. For the Camaldolites, see HELYOT, *Hist. des ordres monastiques*. V. 236 ff., 263 ff.; for the Capuchins, BOVERIUS, *Annales Ord. Capuc.* (about 1630); HELYOT VII 164 ff.

The old Orders, in spite of the reforms, which the 15th century had brought them, had not shown themselves able to withstand the onset of the Reformation. The mendicant Orders, in spite of those attempts at reform, owing to their mental torpor and moral depravity had been one of the chief objects of attack for Protestant polemics: on the other hand, good and bad elements from the ranks of the monks had supported the Reformation in large numbers, although quite a number of literary opponents of the latter had arisen from the same circles. The existing orders had been all together sympathetically affected by the great religious movement. The principle was now generally laid down by papal resolutions, that, considering the abundance of already existing orders, the question of new foundations should not be mooted: but the epoch of the Reformation is also characterised as a new epoch of the Church, by the fact that in it the nature of the Order also brings forward **new** formations. It was certainly of less importance, that in the Order of the Camaldolites,[1] owing to the

---

[1] [See Vol. II., p. 192.]

efforts of Paul Giustiniani, a separate congregation was formed which bound itself to the strictest observance of severely ascetic rules; that further, in the Order of the **Franciscans, Matteo de Bassi** brought about the separation of the **Capuchins** in 1528, in the intent to restore the the original rule and manner of life of St. Francis (a pointed hood[1] and long beard) and to revive his spirit. The latter was only the continuation of a movement which had been long in active existence in the Order,—a movement which was regarded by the older parties of the Order with disfavour and by the Curia with a certain amount of anxiety and was checked in its development, while persons like the noble Vittoria Colonna gave it her lively sympathy and support. But, while devoting themselves zealously to popular preaching, they gained a large number of adherents and reconquered for the Order a part of the influence over the Catholic people, which it had possessed in earlier times. It was not until 1619 that they became an independent Order. The importance of the Order of Theatins for the education of a capable and earnest band of clergy has been already mentioned (p. 220). The Order of **Barnabites** founded in Milan in 1530, together with the *Angelicae sorores* under its direction, sought its mission without, in reclaiming those who had become estranged from the Church, but did not meet with widely-extended success. **The characteristic production of the period of the Reformation is the Society of Jesus.**

Don Iñigo (Ignatius) Lopez de Recalde of the house of Loyola, the younger son of a noble and distinguished Basque family, was born in 1491. He was brought up at the Court of Ferdinand, reared on the ideals of chivalry and in knightly reverence for the Church. Having been wounded at the defence of Pampeluna against the French (1521), he occupied his glowing imagination with the heroic deeds of the Saints[2] during his lengthy confinement to a bed of sickness, and asked himself, " What if I did as St. Francis or St. Dominic ? " In an ecstasy of enthusiasm, he tore himself aloof from his earlier life and devoted himself as a Knight of the immaculate virgin—at Montserrat he hung up his arms on the altar of Mary and kept vigil over the standard. In the garb of a hermit he entered the Dominican monastery of Manresa and commenced the strict life of an ascetic in prayer and scourging. Here he subjected himself, by a conscious act of volition, to the despairing horror of self-examination, and again soared into the blessed ecstasies of the visionary, " a conscious fanatic," " the most temperate administrator in the province of his extravagances," who made that which was the absolute aim of others before him the means of spiritual

---

[1] [*Cappuccino.*]
[2] *Vita de los santos en romance* (i.e., in the Spanish language).

discipline. Here, in his own experience, those *exercitia spiritualia*[1] were performed, which he subsequently required from each of his pupils, "the drill regulations of the warlike order." After that, living on charity, he entered (1523) upon his pilgrimage to Jerusalem, whence, however, he was compelled to return by the official representatives of the Christians, the Franciscans. Looking at the matter as a practical man, he at once became convinced that, considering the neglected condition of the Christians there, it was not the time for him as an individual to look for his life's task in those parts. He returned home, where it soon became evident to him that, in order to be able to labour effectively, he must first thoroughly master the culture of the period. Accordingly, the thirty year old pupil took his seat upon the school-bench at Barcelona; two years later, he went to the University of Alcalá, and then to Salamanca, where he studied scholastic philosophy, and at the same time gathered together the early companions with whom he practised the *exercitia spiritualia*. This, however, made him an object of suspicion to the Inquisition, and several times brought him into great danger and into prison. He prudently transferred the place of his studies to Paris in 1528 (he took his Master of Arts in 1534), supported by many gifts received from both male and female friends. Here, exhibiting great cleverness in dealing with and gaining the affections of men, he had already gathered round him a small body of followers, consisting of the poor Savoyard Peter Faber (Le Fèvre), the noble Biscayan Francis Xavier, the Castilians Diego Lainez and Alonzo Salmeron, besides Bobadilla, Rodriguez, and a few others. In 1534, the little band took a vow in the church of Mary at Montmartre to work in Palestine on behalf of the Church and for the benefit of their fellow-men; or, if this should not be practicable, **to place themselves at the disposal of the Pope to be employed in whatever manner he thought fit.** In 1536, the members, who had in the meantime been ordained priests or were consecrated at this time, again assembled in Venice, in order to proceed together to Palestine. There Ignatius and Caraffa met: the refusal of the former to incorporate his associates with the order of Theatins, and the national opposition between Spaniard and Neapolitan laid the foundations of Caraffa's deep dislike for Ignatius. In 1537, the members presented themselves before Paul III at Rome and disclosed to him their plans respecting the Holy Land. Having returned to Venice abundantly equipped for their proposed journey, they took the vow of poverty to the papal nuncio, but found their scheme wrecked by the naval war between Turkey and Venice; they accordingly decided to remain in Europe and devote themselves to the care of the sick, but especially to preaching (in the streets) and the instruction of the young in the catechism. Ignatius again took a journey to Rome, to put himself at the dis-

---

[1] *Exercitia spiritualia S. Ignatii*, first printed in 1548; Dill. 1583; Paris, 1865; cp. HZ 34, 321 ff.; HUBER, p. 14 ff. JANSSEN, IV 375 ff. They are spiritual exercises of four weeks duration, whereby the ascetic is to discipline his spiritual life, under the supervision and at the command of his master of exercises, by meditations upon prescribed subjects which amounted to hallucinations, and by prayers and examination of conscience. For his treatise Ignatius made use of the mystico-ascetic *exercitatorium spirituale* of the Abbe Garcia Cisnero at Manresa (1500: reprinted Regensb. 1856). Every Jesuit had to perform the full course of exercises at least twice in his life: they were shortened every year to 8 or 10 days. Cp. also ASB, July, VII 423 ff.

posal of the Pope; he had by this time also discovered the proper name for the Society,—Compañia de Jesus (Company of Jesus). Paul III received him in a friendly manner; his *exercitia spiritualia* continually gained him new friends in the higher circles in State and Church. Having been at length (November 18th, 1538) finally cleared of the suspicion of heresy by a court appointed by the Pope, he proceeded, together with his friends, to discuss the constitution, for which it was desired to obtain the ratification of the Pope.

The most characteristic feature of this Constitution was that, while the members of the Order were to be unconditionally at the disposal of the Pope, they were on the other hand to be bound by military obedience to the general **who was elected for life**. In spite of the advantage which such a body must have offered the Papacy, the decision in regard to the papal confirmation was for a considerable time in abeyance, as there was no inclination to increase the number of Orders. The request of the King of Portugal, that some of the members should be sent as missionaries to the colonies over seas, accelerated the decision to bestow the papal confirmation. The bull *Regimini militantis ecclesiae* of September 27th, 1540, at length uttered the decisive word, although at first the number of members was limited to sixty; three years later this limitation was abandoned. Preaching and religious instruction (especially of the young) are here indicated as their chief task, together with absolute obedience to the orders of the Pope in the cause of the mission.[1] Ignatius was elected first general on April 4th, 1541. The vow of poverty was only binding upon the persons of the "professed" monks; the Society itself was allowed to possess property in the interests of their common aims. Specifically monastic asceticism retired into the background; the Order was unacquainted with common meeting for prayer. The prevailing aim of the Order was now activity outside—no longer, as originally, monasticism, mortification and contemplation.[2]

---

[1] Still, what Clement XIV. wrote of the Order in 1773 is substantially correct: *Compertum habuimus, cum . . . . ad* **haereticorum** *et maxime infidelium conversionem . . . . fuisse institutum*. Aquaviva had already appointed as a stock subject of discussion for novices: "Concerning heretics and unbelievers, in order to encourage the mind to battle with the sword of the Spirit" (*Institutum Soc. Jesu*, Pragae, 1757, II 329).

[2] "Ignatius desired absolute renunciation, and yet rejected asceticism; he cleverly turned fanaticism to good account and at the same time excluded it from all activity; he put forward the complete servitude of thought and will as an inviolable duty and as imperatively required the most perfect development of every capacity and quality of the soul; he put himself forward,

2. The Society of Jesus.

Sources and *Literature* (continued): *Constitutiones S. J.* Romae, 1583. *Regulae.* Dilingae, 1583. *Corpus Institutorum S. J.* Antw., 1702. *Institutum S. J.*; 2 vols. Prag., 1757; Rom., 1869. PACHTLER, *Ratio studiorum* (in Mon. Germ. paed.); 3 vols. Berlin, 1887-1890. *Instructions pour le noviciat* in Gelzer's Prot. Monatsbl. XXIII, 45 ff. and 129 ff. J. FRIEDRICH, *Beiträge zur Gesch. d. Jes.-O.* in ABA XVI, 87 ff. B. DUHR, *Jesuitenfabeln.* Freiburg, 1891. (*Monita Secreta.* Krakau (?) 1612, and in frequent later editions *e.g.* Romae (?) 1782.) P. DREWS, *P. Canisius.* Halle, 1892. For the school-system of the Jesuits, see the Literature in SCHMIDT, *Gesch. d. Erziehung* III, 1 (by G. MÜLLER); PACHTLER I, p. xlv ff.; A. KLUCKHOHN in ABA XII, 3.

The Order was destined soon to enjoy special patronage from the Popes. Paul III. had already bestowed upon it the unusual privilege of giving itself further constitutions and altering preceding ones, as circumstances required, and therewith a mobility which had not hitherto been granted to any Order; in 1545 it received the general right to preach everywhere, to cause confessions to be heard everywhere by its priests (even to absolve in a number of reserved cases, and to commute vows); other privileges established the free right of the general to control the members; great liberties and prerogatives soon gave it the position of a State in the spiritual State of the Church. In order to tighten the reins of the discipline of the Order, Ignatius transferred the **entire** development of the members to their own colleges.

While Ignatius was still alive, the Order established itself in **Spain**, where the Dominican Melchior Canus indeed issued warnings against him as the precursor of Antichrist, but, in the person of the Viceroy of Catalonia, Francis Borja, Duke of Gandia, a member and an influential patron of the Order was secured. Soon, the Universities and the whole of Spain were in its occupation. In **Italy** the Order extended itself rapidly, but, in Venice, it was the subject of serious accusations as early as 1560. Its success was even more rapid in **Portugal** (a college at the University of Coimbra), as well as in the Portuguese possessions in Brazil and the East Indies (the rapidly thriving college at Goa, founded by **Xavier** in 1542). In **the Netherlands**, it gained a firm foothold in 1562: it was admitted into **France** in 1550 by Henry II., but in 1554 con-

---

more decidedly than anyone else, as an upholder of the inviolable system of the medieval Church, and drew the entire modern humanistic culture into the range of the pursuits of the Order; he indifferently abandoned all the rules, whereby the other religious societies endeavoured to extort an outward similarity, and yet gave it a constitution, the expressed object of which was to make the Jesuits in all countries and peoples a harmonious corporation, carrying out the same exercises. Thus, he methodically and successfully executed one of the highest works of art, which the human mind ever thought of."—GOTHEIN.

demned by the Sorbonne as "dangerous to faith, calculated to disturb the peace of the Church, to overthrow the monastic orders, and better adapted to pull down than to build up"; it was not until 1562 that it obtained conditional admittance. Ignatius himself founded in Rome (1551) the Collegium Romanum as a principal educational institution, and (1552) the Collegium Germanicum for the training of capable German clergy for the struggle against the heretics.[1] In 1540, **Peter Faber** set foot on **German** soil and, in 1543, gained over in the person of **Peter Canisius** (Peter Kanis of Nimwegen) the first German who exercised a lasting influence upon Catholic popular instruction by means of his Catechisms. Duke William IV. summoned the Jesuits to Bavaria, where they first gained a footing in Ingolstadt (Salmeron and Canisius): they entered Austria in 1551. At his death (July 31st, 1556), Ignatius left his Order a society consisting of more than 1,000 members (amongst them, it must be admitted, only 35 "professed" proper, the officers of this army), about 100 colonies, distributed amongst 12 provinces, and extending as far as Brazil, Abyssinia and the East Indies. But the comprehensive correspondence of Ignatius (which has recently become accessible) also shows how the sincere fervour of his piety involuntarily changed into a cunning, tenacious and supple spiritual diplomacy, which was by no means particular in its choice of means.[2] For where, as in this case, the Church and its authority is identified with the Kingdom of God, the advancement of the Order, of its influence, of its unhindered progress, as the means which is to serve the Church, becomes the one thing to which all other considerations must yield.

The Constitution of the Order[3] is a combination of a military dictatorship with an aristocratic element. At the head is the **General**, who not only requires the obedience of his subordinates, but also their sincere assent to his will, the sacrifice of their own understanding to the understanding of him who is set over them.[4] Every member of the Order has to see in him Christ himself. The

---

[1] For the Collegium Germanicum cp. Ignatius's letter of the 30th of July, 1552, in FRIEDLÄNDER, *Beitr. zur Ref.-Gesch.* Berlin, 1837, p. 275 f.

[2] How Ignatius himself trifled with the oath and, by means of a *reservatio mentalis*, was able to swear the opposite of what he meant, is shown by his letter (Cartas I 142); cp. v. DRUFFEL, p. 12, 38.

[3] The *Monita privata Soc. J.* which appeared in 1612 (also called *Monita secreta* in a later recension), is a satire upon the Order, written by the ex-Jesuit **Hieron. Zaorowski** (**Reusch**, Index II 281), an exaggerated attempt to throw the blame of the evil practices resorted to by many Jesuits, in order to obtain reputation and wealth, upon secret instructions. The only thing worth noticing in regard to it is, that the first MS. copy was found in 1611 in the Jesuit college at Prague, and that MSS. of it existed in other Jesuit colleges. **Mariana's** treatise *de regimine societatis*, which was very embarrassing to the Order, and was printed after his death in 1625, brought grave charges against the regulations of the Order and essentially contains the document, which was laid before Clement VIII in 1593. It was in vain declared by the Jesuits to be spurious. (FRIEDRICH 98 ff.; REUSCH, II 281 f.)

[4] *Qui se totum penitus immolare vult Deo, praeter voluntatem intelligentiam quoque (qui tertius et summus gradus obedientiae) offerat necesse est; ut non solum idem velit, sed etiam idem sentiat quod superior eiusque iudicio subiciat suum, quoad potest devota voluntas intelligentiam inflectere* (Epist. Ignatii de obedientia. Regulae 1583, p. 64 f.). *Intelligentia, ne fallatur, ad Superioris intelligentiam conformanda est* (p. 67).

Constitutions demand obedience from the subject *perinde ac si cadaver esset, quod quoquo versus ferri et quacunque ratione tractari se sinit, vel similiter ac senis baculus*.[1] The **general congregation** elects the General for life, but may depose him from office in the case of his offending against the doctrines or manner of life or prejudicing the interests of the Order; he has to reside permanently in Rome; a father-confessor, appointed by the Order, an Admonitor and Assistants (*assistentes*) stand by his side, to watch over and advise him. Provincials are set over the provinces of the Order, who, like the rectors of the educational institutions and the superiors of the houses of the "professed" were as a rule only appointed for three years by the General. In the Order itself different classes and orders are distinguished. First comes the **noviciate** (lasting as a rule two years) which commencing with the *exercitia spiritualia*, is devoted to ascetic exercises and low and burdensome services, and the practice of humility and obedience, to test the novices and detach them from all relations with the outer world.[2] By taking the three (simple) vows, the novices become members of the Order, and those who are to be prepared for the priesthood are promoted to be *scholastici approbati*; amongst these are also reckoned the lay-brethren, who have taken the same vows, but are not yet promoted to be coadjutors. The former now enter a Jesuit **college**, where they first complete the course of humanistic studies; then, after they have as a rule filled the office of teachers at a Jesuit educational institution, they commence a several years' study of theology, after which they may be consecrated priests. Next follows the taking of the three public vows, whereby they become **regular coadjutors**. They are now at the disposal of the General to make use of them as he pleases. If they stand the test, they advance to the rank of **Professed** of the **three** vows (by a *votum solemne*). Only a small number of them (who must be at least 45 years of age) are finally promoted to the ranks of the **Professed** of the **four** vows, and thereby gain admission to the inmost circles of the Society. The fourth vow has reference to obedience to the Pope for missionary purposes amongst the heathen and heretics. They live, when their services are not required, in the houses of the "Professed." No one can leave the Order of his own authority, but the Order can eject members at every stage. The General rules the Order on the basis of a highly-developed report-system: every month, every provincial; every three months, each superior and master of novices; every six months, each consultor (an adviser appointed for the provincials by the General) sends in an accurate report of the members, the houses, &c. By means of a perfect system of observation, surveillance, and information, each member remains under the eyes of his superior, and finally, of the General, who is thus in a position to lay his hands upon the man who is best adapted for each post.

---

[1] The attempt to elicit from the Constitutions VI 5 that the Superior can bind his subordinates to that which is a sin, was a misunderstanding of Catholic terminology. Rather, their obedience is limited to things *in quibus nullum manifestum est peccatum* (Constit. VI. I. 1). Certainly, the subordinate who also sacrifices his **understanding** to his Superior, when confronted by a command involving a sinful act, would be in a difficult position: he has to "convince himself" that all commands that are given him "are right."

[2] *Et ita curandum ei est, ut omnem carnis affectum erga sanguine iunctos exuat. Sanctum est consilium, ut assuescant non dicere, quod parentes vel fratres habeant, sed quod habebant.* (Exam. gener. 4, 7.)

The efficacy of the Order was maintained above all by means of the **Confessional**, the system of **Teaching**, and the **Mission**. In order to reconquer the districts endangered or lost in consequence of the Reformation, it was of supreme importance to re-catholicise the higher orders of the Catholic people and render them serviceable for Church purposes. The people were stimulated to a frequent and regular use of the Confessional, after having been accustomed to confession only once, or at most twice a year; it was only through the efforts of the Jesuits that it attained to its present eminent importance. In like manner the Jesuits (and similarly Philip Neri) permanently introduced more frequent communions in place of the practice of communicating only once a year (at Easter) and dispelled the mistrust existing against laymen who desired the Sacrament several times in the course of the year (cp. KL III 730 ff.). They were very successful in their endeavours to become father-confessors of the princes, the nobility, and the upper and more influential social circles. By these means they naturally obtained an influence also upon politics, the course of which they endeavoured to direct in the interests of Rome and to the struggle against the heretics. The Order worked everywhere with a view to the centralisation of the ecclesiastical constitution, regarding heretics as beyond the pale of the laws and upholding the subordination of the authority of the State to that of the Church. (For their doctrine of State see below). The counter-Reformations, subsequent to the second half of the 16th century, with their deeds of violence, everywhere exhibit a secret or open influence of Jesuitic suggestion. Activity in the Confessional gradually exercised a momentous influence upon the moral teaching of the Order, since, in order to maintain their position, the confessors were impelled to court popularity by indolence and indulgence. (On this point, see further below). While popular education was greatly neglected where they obtained influence, they gained over the youth of the upper classes by their much-famed and much-abused system of instruction and education. In its merits it shares those of the better humanistic institutions,—indeed, the oldest Jesuit teachers were themselves the disciples of humanists—and yet it was enough to paralyse the working of the Protestant humanistic schools and universities: but, by constantly changing its teachers and by the preponderating employment of a young and inexperienced staff, it endangered the soundness of its performances; by turning ambition and denunciation to the best account it injured moral culture; by making a parade of the performances of the pupils it promoted merely a show of learning. The Jesuits themselves have always laid special stress upon their brilliant missionary successes (see below). The attempt of an Englishwoman, Mary Ward, at the commencement of the 17th century, to found a **female** Order modelled upon that of the Jesuits, led to very unsatisfactory results: life without confinement led to so many scandals that the Order was done away with by a brief of Urban VIII (1631).[1] Some of them, however, devoted themselves under the name of " English Nuns" to the instruction of young women and, in this new form, their society was finally approved by the Pope (1703).

---

[1] *Bulla Urbani VIII. de Jesuitissis*, ed. HOORNBEEK. Ultraj. 1653.

CHAPTER THIRD.

The Council of Trent.

1. Its External Course.

Sources: J. LE PLAT, *Monumentorum ad hist. C. T. spect. amplissima collectio;* 7 vols. Lovan, 1781, ff. (Vols. I-VI, a collection of the older authorities; Vol. VII also contains fresh material). MENDHAM, *Memoirs of the Council of Trent* (from an Oxford MS.). London, 1834; the same, *Acta C. Tr. anno 1562 et 1563, a Card. Paleotto descripta.* Lond., 1842. SICKEL, *Zur Gesch. d. C. v. Tr., Actenstücke von 1559-1563.* Wien, 1872. A. THEINER, *Acta genuina Conc. Tr.* (Reports of Massarelli, who drew up the minutes of the proceedings); 2 vols. Agram, 1874. (For the history of this edition see C. HASE, *Reformation und Gegenreformation*, p. 363 f.). DÖLLINGER, *Beiträge* I and III; the same, *Samml. von Urkunden z. Gesch. d. C. v. Tr.;* 2 vols. Nördl., 1876. PLANCK, *Anecdota ad hist. C. Tr. pertin.* Gött., 1791-1818. JAC. LAINEZ, *Disputationes Trid.* ed. Grisar; 2 vols. Innsbruck and Regensb., 1886. VON DRUFFEL, *Monum. Trid.* in ABA 1884 ff.; the same, *Die Sendung des Card. Sfondrato an den Hof Karls V.* ABA XX. CALENZIO. *Documenti inediti.* Roma, 1874. *Canones et decreta C. Tr.* Romae, 1564; edited by AEM. L. RICHTER. Lips., 1853, and many other editions; see also DENZINGER, "p. 178 ff., for the *Dogmatic Decrees*.

Literature: P. SARPI (died 1623), *Istoria del conc. Tr.* Lond., 1619; in Latin, London, 1620; in French, by LE COURAYER, Amst., 1736; in German, by RAMBACH, Halle, 1761 ff.; on the other side, the Jesuit Cardinal Sforza PALLAVICINO (died 1667), *Ist. del C. di Trento.* Roma, 1656-1657; revised edition, 1666; in Latin, 1672; in German, Augsb., 1835. (For the value of both works, see RANKE, *Päpste*, ⁸III Appendix; VON DÖLLINGER, *Sammlung* I, p. vi ff.). SALIG, *Vollst. Hist. d. Tr. C.* Halle, 1741. RANKE, *Päpste*, I; *Deutsche Gesch. im ZA d. Ref.*, V. VON WESSENBERG, *die grossen KVersamml.;* Vols. III and IV. Constanz, 1840. PASTOR, *Reunionsbestr.* Freib., 1879. MAURENBRECHER in HTb 6, F. V, VII, IX. TSCHACKERT in RE XVI 4 ff. DÖLLINGER (and VON DRUFFEL), *Kleinere Schriften.* Stuttg., 1890, p. 228 ff. PREUSS, *das C. v. Tr.* Berl., 1862. M. RITTER, *Deutsche Gesch. im ZA der Gegenref.*, I. Stuttg., 1889, p. 141 ff. For the influence of the Jesuits on the Council, see GRISAR in ZkTh VIII 453 ff. *Die Geschäftsordnung des C. von Tr.* Wien, 1871. (THEINER, Acta I 1 ff.) VERMEULEN, *die Verlegung des Conc. v. Tr.* Regensb., 1890 (written from an ultramontane standpoint far in advance of Janssen's). SCHMID in JGG VI 1 ff. TH. MÜLLER, *Das Conclave Pius' IV., 1559.* Gotha, 1890. R. HINOJOSA, *Felipe II. y el concl. de 1559.* Madrid, 1859 (Rev. hist. 46, 153). W. Voss, *die Verhandlungen Pius' IV mit den katholischen Mächten über die Neuberufung des Tr. C.* Leipz., 1887. B. DEMBINSKI, *Rom und Europa vor d. 3. Abschn. d. Tr. C.* (Polish). Krakau, 1890 (cp. HpBl 107, 631). SICKEL in AÖG 45. REIMANN in FdG VIII 177 ff. H. LÖWE, *Die Stellung Ferd. I. zum Tr. C.* Bonn, 1887.

First Period. (Cp. p. 150 f.). At the end of May, 1545, twenty bishops at last made their appearance in Trent. The Italian episcopal city, situated on the frontier of Germany and belonging to the Empire, had been the utmost concession the Pope would make to the demand for a Council on German soil. He had now nothing to fear from the Germans, neither from the Protestant section, which did not appear but rejected the Council at the Diet of Worms as not being a free one, nor from the Catholic. Three tasks were marked out for the Council in the bull of convocation: the removal of religious discord by doctrinal decisions, the reform of ecclesiastical abuses, and the discussion of a crusade against the unfaithful. The legates Del Monte, Cervino, and Reginald Pole at first delayed the opening of the Council, and thereby prevented all resolutions on matters of dogma, out of consideration for the Emperor, and resolutions of reform, out of consideration for the Pope. According to Charles's categorically expressed desire, in consideration of the still imminent reckoning with the Schmalkaldic League for which he needed the assistance of the evangelical princes, only decrees of reform were to be passed,—such as concerned matters of dogma, not until he should have compelled the Protestants to take part in the Council. The Pope, on the other hand, desired a speedy reckoning with Protestant doctrines and then, the execution of these anathemas in war. But now, as the "recess" of the Diet of Worms had announced a religious discussion and a fresh diet to deal with the German religious question, those assembled demanded with ever increasing impatience the opening of the Council; several again took their departure, and as the Emperor rejected the Pope's proposal for a transference of locality, the latter now decided to proceed vigorously. At last, on the 13th of December, the Council was opened by twenty-five bishops, one of whom was a German.

Now for the first time attention was paid to the question, **how** deliberations should be carried on. The voting "by nations" employed at Constance was not even proposed by any party: this rendered the preponderance of the Italians easier. Besides, the bishops who were only represented by procurators were in most cases deprived of the right of voting by the legates. The poorer Italian bishops received special allowances from the Pope, in order to be able to make their appearance at Trent. Nevertheless, the Pope had not at first a sufficient number of safe votes at his disposal; hence, the further calling up of Italian bishops was regarded as a specially pressing matter. It was agreed that dogmatic and reformatory decrees should be discussed at the same time, a resolution, which the Pope at first (January 21st, 1546) rejected, but subsequently allowed to be carried. The sittings themselves were only used for the formal acceptance and announcement of the resolutions; the real work was in the hands of the three congregations of the Council which sat at the same time under the control of the legates, and amongst which all the members were distributed, in accordance with the sound principle of *divide et impera*.[1] At the same time, the legates reserved for themselves the exclusive right of putting forward proposals for deliberation.

> To all resolutions directed against ecclesiastical abuses was added, "under reserve of the authority of the Pope": consequently, their execution was left to the discretion of the Curia. The question of the legal position of the Council towards the Pope was carefully kept out of sight by the legates: hence also, the designation of the Council as *synodus universam ecclesiam repraesentans* was rejected as reminiscent of Constance;[2] any attempt to lay stress on the ideas of the episcopal system as put forward by the bishops was vehemently censured by the legates.

At last, on the 11th of February, 1546, the discussion of the first dogmatic subject commenced. In order to render the Council still more pliable and afterwards to set it aside altogether, after eight sittings it was, under pretence of an epidemic, contrary to the Emperor's wish, transferred by a majority of the Italian votes to **Bologna** on the 11th of March, 1547, but some of the bishops (the Spanish) by the Emperor's instructions remained at Trent. The fathers of the Council who had repaired to Bologna resolved to put off further work; the Emperor demanded their return to Trent, and finally threatened to summon a new Council to carry out healthy reforms. But the Pope, extremely irritated against the Emperor by the murder of his son Pierluigi (September 20th, 1547), refused to retransfer the Council. Charles then proceeded independently by means of the Interim to the arrangement of ecclesiastical matters for the subject Protestants, and also issued reformatory regulations for the Catholic districts (see above, p. 154). The Pope, who was eager to obtain the duchy of Piacenza for his grandchildren, above all desired that the Emperor should not become too powerful. On the 17th of September, 1549, he dis-

---

[1] The separate deliberations were then all put together at a general congregation and promoted to the dignity of resolutions.
[2] Cp. DÖLLINGER, *Beiträge* I 392.

missed the bishops who were still assembled at Bologna and now endeavoured to escape the continuation of the Council by reformatory conferences in Rome. But the imperial episcopal party still assembled at Trent refused to attend: the French clergy also declined to take part in the proceedings, as reform of the Church was now only to be looked for from the Church itself. But the bishops at Trent, in conformity with the Emperor's will, had abstained from all activity in the Council, in order to avoid a schism. While affairs were in this state of confusion, Paul III. died on the 10th of November, 1549; the Cardinals recognised how greatly he had injured the Church, and pledged themselves in conclave that whoever should be elected should hold the Council as soon as possible and reform the Curia.

Second Period. Julius III. (Cardinal del Monte, p. 158) immediately entered upon a policy friendly to the Emperor and recalled the Council to Trent, where it was opened in May, 1551, under Cardinal Crescentio with two "assistants" Lipomani and Pighino: it commenced its proceedings in the autumn. Its composition was almost entirely new: the Jesuits Lainez and Salmeron appeared as the Pope's theologians: Spain had sent, amongst others, Melchior Cano. France, now arming for a fresh war against Charles, was not represented at all and refused in advance to admit the binding power of the resolutions of the Council. The Emperor had promised the German Protestants, in addition to safe-conduct, that they should be heard on all disputed points,—consequently, also in regard to those already decided. It was evident that his plans were bound to fail in this point (see above p. 159). The evangelical deputies could not recognise the resolutions that had already been taken and were only able to protest against a Council which was so fettered that it was obliged to allow itself to be treated by Crescentio like a number of school-boys. But, as the Emperor found that neither the reunion of the evangelicals nor a satisfactory reformation of the Roman Church resulted, he himself lost the desire for the continuation of the sitting of the Council. The Pope had already drawn up the bull of suspension, when, on the news of the advance of the Elector Maurice, on the 28th of April, 1552, the Council was adjourned for two years.

The two years became ten. In the meanwhile, Germany, by the treaty of Passau and the religious peace of Augsburg, had procured a settlement of ecclesiastical affairs, and consequently no longer had need of the Council. The imperious and passionate **Paul IV** (1555-1559) regarded the Inquisition as far more effective than a Council and desired that reforms should proceed only from Rome without the co-operation of a Council; his war with Philip II. completely held back the plans of a Council. To this was added his enmity to the Emperor Ferdinand, which was partly based on personal grounds and was partly fostered by the fact that he could not forgive him for concluding the religious peace and tolerating Protestant leanings in his son Maximilian. Defiant in his resentment, he refused to recognise the successor of Charles V. who had been agreed upon by the Electors before his sanction was solicited for the abdication of the former and the succession of the latter. The Pope regarded the Protestant Electors as heretics who had forfeited all rights, while Ferdinand was resolved to keep the religious peace honourably. Paul found himself abandoned in this conflict even by France and Spain, but drove the Emperor's counsellors by his behaviour to a theory of constitutional law, which freed the German imperial dignity from ratification by Rome, and to theories in regard to the Church, which remind one of the days of the Council of Bâle.

In the conclave that was held after Paul's death, the Cardinals themselves demanded reconciliation with the Emperor and the summoning of the Council from the future Pope. The former was soon brought about, after some difficulty, by the diplomatic **Pius IV.**, to Ferdinand's very great joy; he recognised Maximilian's succession, and, in the knotty question of the administration of the cup to the laity, in a secret brief (December 10th, 1561) empowered Ferdinand, the layman, to grant the cup in his name to the son at discretion (JGG XIV. 31 f.).[1] The summoning of the Council was certainly not in accordance with the Pope's ideas, but he yielded to the pressure of circumstances. On the 25th of March, 1560, he announced his willingness and opened negotiations with the powers. He decided upon this step not, first and foremost, for the sake of Germany, but particularly for the sake of France, which thought seriously of a national council.

Third Period. On the 29th of November, 1560, Pius announced the Council: on the 18th of January, 1562, it was reopened under the presidency of Gonzaga, Seripando, Hosius, Simonetta and Altemps: the episcopate had a much greater part in it (as many as 270 bishops were present for a time), but there was again a preponderating majority of Italians. At the desire of France and Ferdinand, the Protestants were invited by the nuncios Delfino and Commendone on the occasion of the Naumburg diet of princes, but naturally did not appear: thus, it was at the same time admitted that the Council could only be an assembly for the Catholic world, no longer for Western Christianity. It might be questioned whether the Council was to be regarded as a new one or only as a continuation of the earlier one.

Still, even the earlier resolutions had not been recognised in due form. Hence the Emperor and France insisted upon now treating

---

[1] At first Pius IV. also had refused to recognise Maximilian and wanted to deny the evangelical Electors the right of voting; DÖLLINGER, *Beiträge* I 339.

the Council as a new one, but the Pope, in agreement with Philip
II., decided in favour of styling it a continuation of the earlier one;
thus, the assembly entered upon the full inheritance of the earlier
resolutions. Ferdinand had caused proposals of reform to be
zealously worked at,[1] which certainly brought forward many
salutary ideas for the improvement of the clergy and the removal
of abuses in monastic affairs and demanded the marriage of priests,
the cup for the laity, the alleviation of the commands relating to
fasting with regard for public feeling, but in reference to the
position of the Pope in regard to the Church and in reference to
the reform of the Curia, in view of Ferdinand's horror of conflicts
and his minister Seld's sudden change of mind, every demand
was evaded with feeble words. While France and Frederick now
especially demanded reformation decrees, those connected with
dogma were given the preference as likely to cause fewer conflicts
between the parties concerned, but also the opposition to Protestantism was thereby intensified. In reference to the reforms,
the Pope pursued the clever plan of allowing himself to be pressed
and then at least conceding something. Ferdinand's "Reformation
pamphlet" was handed to the legates instead of the Council and
rendered harmless by them and the Curia. Amongst the bishops
the question of the importance of the episcopal system was again
especially discussed (in particular by the Spaniards, and then also
by the French), and raised to the practical demand for the obligation upon every bishop **to reside**; on this point the Italians upheld
the interests of the Curia against nearly all the non-Italians, by
hindering every formal decision of the question of principle in
regard to the divine right of the episcopate. (Pius conceded that
residence was certainly a matter of divine right, but was of opinion
that to declare it would amount to the destruction of the Romish
Court.) The influence of the powers on the Council was paralysed
by the conflicting tendencies of Ferdinand and Philip II. The
former (supported by Bavaria) was in favour of **Concessions** (administering the cup to the laity and allowing priests to marry)
to check apostasy in Germany and to win over again at least a
part of the Protestants: Philip on the contrary looked with
abhorrence upon every step, which met the wishes of the heretics:
he desired the simple extermination of the latter. Rome also was
at one with Philip on this point. No sitting was held between

---

[1] Cp. SICKEL, p. 69 ff. 252 ff. SCHELHORN, *Amoen. hist. eccl.* II 501.

September, 1562 and July, 1563; disputes of the most varied kind (in particular disputes as to the status of the envoys) and faction amongst the bishops, which caused the legates to apprehend a schism, threatened to stop the continuance of the Council. But then Philip broke the serried ranks of the episcopally-minded opposition, since even the power of the princes felt itself cramped by the episcopal system. Still, it seemed as if the appearance of a large number of French bishops (November, 1562) would again start the demand for reform and the Curia now actually agreed to concessions, but also threatened the governments with a searching reform of the rights exercised by them over the church of their districts, and won over the imperial theologians by bribes; the conflicting interests of the States put an end to further hopes. Lastly Ferdinand (and also France), whom the behaviour of the Curia filled with displeasure, but whose hands were at the same time tied owing to his desire to see his son Maximilian recognised as King of Rome by the Pope, were anxious to see the last of a Council which did not correspond to their wishes. The "reform decrees," which were still being drawn up, were submitted to the Pope for confirmation. The final negotiations were hurried over, and important matters that were left uncompleted were left to the Pope to settle. On the 4th of December, 1563, the last session was opened. The Pope confirmed the decrees, although many in Rome were heard to declare that his authority was not adequately preserved by the Council.

2. The Theological and Ecclesiastical Results of the Council.

Literature (continued): M. CHEMNITZ, *Examen conc. Tr.*, 1566. Berl., 1861, 1862. KÖLLNER, *Symbolik der kath. K.* Hamb., 1844. A. HARNACK, DG III 588 ff. SEEBERG in ZkW XI 546 ff. REUSCH, *Der Index der verbotenen Bücher;* 2 vols. Bonn, 1883, 1885. DIENDORFER in KL VI 650. Breviary: SCHMID in ThQ 66, 451 ff. Vulgata: FRITSCHE in RE VIII 455 ff. DÖLLINGER-REUSCH, *Die Selbstbiographie Bellarmins.* Bonn, 1887, p. 111 ff. COURAYER, *Discours historique sur la réception du conc. de Tr.* Amst. (Appendix to Vol. II. of his translation of Sarpi's work (p. 237), p. 772 ff.)

The dogmatic decrees of the Council are under the influence of the Reformation; in them Catholicism, compelled by the opposing attitude of Protestantism, is driven to declare its own principles. But, at the same time, numerous questions, which were disputed even amongst the fathers of the Council themselves, were unavoidably left unsettled, for it was an established principle not to decide such differences, but to pass them over in silence, and important concessions had to be made to the Augustinian-Thomistic theology, of which the Spaniards were the chief representatives. Hence, the dogmatic decrees of the Council of Trent are no more an adequate picture of the spiritual character of the newer Catholicism than its reform decrees are a just representation of the actual ordinances and organisation of the Church.

The 3rd session (February 4th, 1546) had commenced with the repetition of the *Symbolum Nicaenum;* the momentous 4th session (April 8th, 1546) was devoted to the question of the sources of the faith of the Church. Under the influence of the Reformation the Tridentine fathers avow it to be their aim *ut puritas ipsa evangelii in ecclesia conservetur;* but they turn against Protestantism, preferring the *Canon ecclesiae, i.e.,* the Alexandrine canon, to the *Canon Hebraeorum,* and consequently canonise the Apocrypha as a concession to custom, while further placing by the side of the Scriptures as a second source of revelation the *sine scripto traditiones* (unwritten traditions), *quae ab ipsius Christi ore ab apostolis acceptae aut ab ipsis apostolis, spiritu sancto dictante, quasi per manus traditae, ad nos usque pervenerunt:* which these were was not stated (Bishop Bertano frankly declared: "We accept those we approve, but decisively reject those which do not meet with our approval"). The Vulgate, the corruptions in the text of which are to be removed by the Pope, is declared to be the authentic Bible recension, and the right is assigned to the Church of being the only authentic interpreter of the Scriptures. The 5th and 6th sessions (June 17th, 1546, and January 13th, 1547) issued decrees concerning original sin and justification; herewith they also broke away from the tenets of the Reformation in regard to the doctrine of Salvation, however noticeable the influence of these upon the character of their own doctrine may be. At the same time, the opposition in their own camp between Pelagianising Nominalists and adherents of Thomism compelled compromises of all kinds and a formulating of doctrine couched in the most diplomatic language possible, which might leave room for the most diverse interpretations. It is characteristic, that free will is regarded as only weakened by sin, the process of salvation is consequently treated as a product of divine workings of grace and human performance (even the *meritum de congruo* can be thus interpreted); that the concupiscence that remains behind in one who is baptised is not judged as a sin; that faith is treated essentially as an assent to the divine revelation and, according to this, only as *initium iustificationis;* in like manner, the evangelical conception of the faith that justifies as confidence in the grace that forgives sins, of grace as the divine feeling of love, and of justification as the forgiveness of sins, is expressly rejected; certainty of salvation is denied. Justification is an act of God, which takes place at baptism and then, after each deadly sin, is renewed at the penitential sacrament, and brings about forgiveness of sins and salvation at the same time by means of the inpouring of grace, conditional upon the man showing himself willing to meet it. Faith, *i.e.,* assent in principle to the doctrine of the Church as preached, is the condition. In this justification the man receives *spes* and *caritas* in addition to *fides,* and thus justification goes on as a process *usque ad mortem,* in which the man earns eternal life for himself by good works; yet these *merita* must in like manner be regarded as *dona Dei*. But the pith of the Tridentine resolutions does not lie in this doctrine of justification with its hesitating and ambiguous formulas; the only thing of practical importance in them is, that room is left for meritorious good works. The subsequent sessions are far more important for the tendency which dominates Tridentine Catholicism. Of these, the 7th and 8th belong to the *first* period of the Council; the 9th and 10th to the time of transference to Bologna; the 11th to the 16th session were held during the *second* period at Trent, 1551-1552; the 17th to the 25th at the time of the *third* assembly at Trent, 1562-1563. The Church is a sacramental institution; the seven sacraments instituted by Christ,[1] the *intentio* of the *minister sacramenti—faciendi quod Ecclesia facit*—being assumed, act *ex opere operato* as a vehicle of grace in all those *non ponentibus obicem*.

In reference to the Lord's Supper, transubstantiation and concomitance, and the presence of Christ substantially in the transformed elements *ante vel post usum* are maintained, and hence the adoration of the host and Corpus Christi Day are insisted upon; the right of refusing the cup to the laity is dogmatically established; but a condemnation of the practice of administering it to them was omitted out of politic respect for certain princes and public opinion in Germany; finally (at the 21st session) it was decided that the Pope should be at liberty to administer it in special circumstances. The declarations concerning the mass (22nd session) are dogmatically uncertain and full of contradiction; but the practical tendency to preserve the evil practice of the mass in its entirety is clear (for the living—*pro peccatis, poenis, satisfactionibus et* **aliis necessitatibus**—and dead, *in honorem sanctorum;* the use of the language of the country is excluded: the *canon missae* entirely approved.

In reference to the doctrine of **penitence**, a step in advance is recognisable: those who defended *attritio*, as being sufficient for the reception of the Sacramental grace, submitted and *contritio* was required. But, while *attritio* was still conceded to the "attritionists" as *contritio imperfecta* and a salutary preparation, the new "attritionism" of the Jesuits was able, under the protection of these principles, to claim the rights of citizenship in the Romish Church (see below). In the sacrament of penitence the priests perform the functions of *iudices, ad quos omnia mortalia crimina deferantur:* they not only pronounce, but also administer absolution. As, after forgiveness, the *poena peccati* still remains, room is left for the *satisfactiones*[2] of the sinner; room is thereby also left for indulgences, as to which, while no dogmatic theory is developed, it is readily admitted that they have been greatly misused, but at the same time, they are defended as a salutary ecclesiastical institution in the face of all opposition. Purgatory and the adoration of the saints (25th session) and the worship of images and relics are upheld in carefully expressed language without any dogmatically exact statements; the existence of abuses is also admitted in this case, and orders are issued against such. The marriage of priests is anathema.

In its dogmatic aspect, the Council denotes the exclusion of the Reformation,

---

[1] The number seven had been firmly established as the doctrine of the Romish Church since the Council of Florence, 1439; MANSI, Conc. XXXI 1054. RAYNALDI Ann. 1439 XV.

[2] [Penalties for sin imposed on the offender by himself or by the priest in order to avert its temporal consequence].

and, conformably to this, of the endeavour to come to an **understanding** with Protestantism; henceforth, it was only a question of the attempt to **subject** the Protestants to these canons.

The **reform** decrees of the Council introduce a number of organising regulations dealing with the superintendence and theological training of the clergy, the institution of clerical seminaries, the election of bishops, reform of the visitations of the cathedral chapter, synods; in short, for the training of the clergy and people from a moral and intellectual point of view. The duty of episcopal residence was proclaimed, but at the same time, a back-door was opened for the Pope, so that he could make exceptions when he thought fit. The ecclesiastical form of the celebration of marriage was also regulated: declaration of consent before the parish priest and two or three witnesses.

To assist this concise epitome of the powers of the Church from the letter of the law to actual life, was henceforth the conscious aim of the Order of the Jesuits. A new period of mighty development dates from the Council of Trent. A lofty enthusiasm for the Catholic cause revives: a propaganda is carried on in its behalf, which is carried out, often with harshness and cruelty, but still also from a strong conviction. The principle of freedom from human authorities and the individual religious conscience were confronted by the principle of vigorous ecclesiastical authority with fresh power, which also, together with much external attachment to the Church, brings into prominence numerous personalities, ready to risk and sacrifice everything for it. From this time, Protestantism was no longer able to wrest greater successes from this regenerated Catholicism, but was obliged to restore a considerable part of its conquests.

The Pope ratified the Council on the 26th of January, 1564 (*Benedictus Deus*) and declared himself the authentic interpreter of its decrees[1]; he subsequently asserted the legal obligation of the reform decrees as valid from the 1st of May of the current year, and established a college of Cardinals, to superintend their execution. But only Italy (with Venice), Poland and Portugal willingly accepted the new laws of the Church at once. In Spain, Philip II. certainly accepted the decrees, but reserved to himself the right of modifying their execution in accordance with the law of the State; the same declaration was made for the Netherlands and Naples. In France, assent was indeed given to the dogmas of the Council, but the reform decrees were looked upon as a curtailing of the liberties of the Gallican Church and the royal rights; hence that

---

[1] *Nos difficultates et controversias, si quae ex eis decretis ortae fuerint, nobis declarandas et decidendas . . . . reservamus.*

country refused to publish the resolutions, although clerical synods accepted the decrees. In Germany, the Pope prevailed upon Ferdinand and Maximilian to accept the Council, by conceding the cup to the laity, but it never became a law of the Empire : matters stopped short at a tacit acceptance, the right of modifications by the legislation of the country being reserved. The same was the case in Hungary.

To complete the restoration of the Church, certain important works were added to those of the Council,—works which were partly from the outset left by the Council for settlement by the Pope, and partly were obliged to be finally left over to him owing to the termination of the sessions. In 1563, the plan had been conceived, of causing a confession of faith to be proclaimed by the Council, which should be sworn to not only by the clergy but also by all civil officials; but the deputies of the States protested against this interference with the rights of the princes. Accordingly, such obligation of confession was decided (24th session) to be necessary only for those who were to be promoted to clerical offices and for teachers in the University, and Pius IV. interpreted this resolution by proclaiming, through the bulls of November 13th, 1564 (*In sacrosancta* and *Iniunctum nobis*) in the so-called **Professio fidei Tridentinae** the formula for this religious oath as *Forma professionis fidei Catholicae;* this contains the Nicaea-Constance symbol, a summary of the Tridentine decrees of belief, and an additional article upon the primacy of the Pope (*e.g.*, *Romanam ecclesiam omnium ecclesiarum matrem et magistram agnosco.*)[1] As the Pope in this case, in the interest of the papal system, went beyond what had been left unfinished by the Council, so also did he in the **Catechismus Romanus**, which had been prepared by the Council, but finally left to the Pope for completion. (25th session.) In January, 1562, the Council had arranged for a committee for this work, but it had never been formed. Subsequently, Pius IV. handed over the work to the Bishops Marini, Foscarari, Calini, and the Portuguese theologian Fureiro, (three of these were Dominicans). But Pius died before the revision of the language was completed; Pius V. did not take the step of publication until 1566, after repeated revision. The Catechismus Romanus is a collection of pastoral instructions for pastors and catechists: a popular, practical system of dogma, treating continuously of the Apostles' Creed, the Sacraments, the Ten Commandments and Lord's Prayer, something essentially different from what had been planned at Trent. In this the Pope is designated not only *caput universi fidelium generis*, but also universal **Pastor**. On the other hand, owing to the influence of the Dominicans Thomism was able to express itself more freely and clearly than at Trent ; hence, the symbolic reputation of the Catechismus Romanus was contested in the later dispute concerning the doctrine of grace, as being a private work and written in a party spirit.

Other important works decided upon by the Council and carried out at Rome were: the drawing up of the **Index librorum prohibitorum** (after 1562 ; cp. sessions 18 and 25),[2] for the continuation of which under Pius V. 1571 the

---

[1] From that time also frequently used as an oath by converts.

[2] The Index drawn up at Trent was published by Pius IV. in 1564. Bible reading in the language of the people is only allowed to those who receive written permission from the bishop and inquisitor on the advice of the confessor.

congregatio indicis was appointed: further, the regulating of public worship and rendering it uniform by the issue of the **Breviarium** *Romanum* 1568 f., of the **Missale** 1570 etc., whereby the *usus* of the Roman Church was maintained against the traditions of individual countries and provinces which were frequently divergent. Lastly, we may mention the restoration of the authentic recension of the **Vulgate** which had been left by the Council (4th session) to Rome. It was Sixtus V. who first started this work: a congregation appointed by him commenced its preliminary labours in the criticism of the text in 1588, and in 1590, the authentic edition (omitting the third and fourth books of Esdras, the third book of the Maccabees, and the Prayer of Manasseh) appeared under the personal, less fortunate co-operation of the Pope; but after his death (which took place in the same year) this version was so violently attacked by the Jesuit Bellarmine, who had a personal grudge against the Pope,—and certainly errata afforded a convenient handle for criticism—that Gregory XIV. instituted a fresh commission, and Clement VIII. bought up the copies. This commission caused the edition of Sixtus to disappear almost completely,[1] and, in 1592, issued a new edition (the *Editio Clementina*): in this the third and fourth books of Esdras and the Prayer of Manasseh are added. The weighty claim to authenticity also in this case contrasted singularly with the quantity of errata; and as, in a very large number of passages,[2] it varied from the Sixtine edition, the adversaries of Rome had a welcome opportunity of throwing light upon the *concordia discors* of the two papal editions. But the most instructive thing was, that a later Pope immediately corrected, with so unsparing a hand, a work which had been issued with an appeal to the **infallibility** promised by God to the successor of Peter. This edition of the Vulgate is founded upon the form of text circulated in the Middle Ages by the Paris theologians (**Denifle** ALKM IV 284).

---

[1] Reprinted at Antwerp, 1630.
[2] JAMES (*Bellum papale*, Lond., 1600) enumerates 1207 passages.

CHAPTER FOURTH

The Popes of the restored Catholicism.

Literature: RANKE, *Die römischen Päpste in der letzten 4 Jahrh.* "Werke 37-39. M. BROSCH, *Gesch. des Kirchenstaates.* I. Gotha 1880. B. HILLIGER, *Die Wahl Pius V. zum Papste.* Leipz. 1891. LORENTZ, *Sixtus V. und seine Zeit.* Mainz, 1852. *Nuntiaturberichte.* Dritte Abtheilung. I. Berlin. 1892. DRERINGER, *Der heilige Carl Borromäus.* Cöln 1846. For the dispute about the Calendar see F. STIEVE in ABA XV 3; KALTENBRUNNER in SDWA 82, 289 ff.; 87, 485 ff.; J. SCHMID in JGG III and V: MIÖG XII 639. Sarpi: *Opere,* Venez. 1677, Helmst. 1761 ff. FULG. MICANZIO *Vita del Padre Paolo.* Leyden 1646. E. MÜNCH, *Fra P. Sarpi.* Karlsr. 1838. G. CAPASSO, *Fra P. S. e l' Interdetto di Ven.* Firenze 1880; NÜRNBERGER in JGG IV 188 ff.; the same, in RQ II 64 ff.; 248 ff.; REUSCH, Index II 319 ff.; Galilei: K. v. GEBLER, *Gal. Galilei und die röm. Kurie.* Stuttg. 1876; REUSCH, *Der Process Gal.s und die Jesuiten.* Bonn 1879; GRISAR, *Gal.-Studien.* Regensb. 1882; FUNK in ThQ 1883, 405; SCHANZ in JGG III 163 ff.; the same, in KL V 18 ff.

The crisis, which had been consummated by Caraffa, also exercised its influence upon the Curia and the occupants of Peter's chair. This, first and foremost, remained a matter that concerned Italy, and its high offices were posts for the support of the Italian nobles. But the frivolity and profane ideas of the Renaissance were forced to yield, though tardily, to a new religiosity; the restoration of Catholic sympathies exhibited itself in many respects also as a reform of morals. The morals of the Popes were in part austerely strict, dynastic interests gave way to ecclesiastical considerations. Nevertheless, nepotism does not disappear, and the Curia still remains the arena of the intrigues of ambitious Cardinals. It is, however significant that it was just at this time that a Palestrina (died 1594) brought polyphonous vocal music to its purest and loftiest perfection, and thereby not only protected this music from the interdiction threatened by the commission appointed by the Council of Trent, but also formed a school and introduced a classical period of Catholic church music (Orlandus Lassus at München, died 1595; Vittoria Allegri, died 1652). Caraffa, elevated to the papal chair (1555-1559) in his 79th year as **Paul IV.**, harsh and passionate, hated by the people, injured the cause which he so zealously represented by his hostility to the Habsburgs and his French policy, which involved him in a war (which turned out unluckily for him) with Philip II. about Naples;[1] he did equal harm by his nepotism, which he employed in the case of persons so unworthy that he himself was obliged to pronounce sentence of deprivation of office and banishment upon them. The *Consilium de emendanda ecclesia* (see above, p. 223) which he himself had formerly drawn up as Cardinal was placed by him on the index, when Pope, in 1559 (see **Reusch**, Der Index I 396 ff.). What Protestantism had to expect from the restored papacy, he showed in the bull *Cum ex apostolatus officio* (1559) in which, by virtue of his *plenitudo potestatis super gentes et regna*, he declared all apostates, whether clerical or lay, princes or subjects, deprived of all dignities and rights, and gave every Catholic full powers to levy execution on their possessions. Heretic princes are *eo ipso regnis et imperio penitus et in totum perpetuo privati et ad illa de cetero inhabiles et incapaces* (BM VI 551 ff.). **Pius IV.** (Cardinal Medici,[2] 1559-1565) completed the work which had been broken off by the Council (see above, p. 240), and by clever diplomacy in his dealings with the secular powers gained more than Paul IV. by his harshness. His nepotism elevated his young nephew, **Carlo Borromeo**,[3] who was in the hands of the Jesuits, to the highest dignities, and also gave him authority and opportunity, both as Cardinal and Archbishop of Milan, to employ his stringent zeal upon the reform of priests and monasteries as well as the extermination of evangelical movements. A dark stain upon his administration is his bloody persecution of the house of Caraffa, to which, however, he owed his election, and he again carried on a profitable business with the high offices of the Church. **Pius V.** (1565-1572), the Dominican Ghislieri, honourable in his monastic holiness, carried on the works (see above, p. 247) which had been left unsettled by the Council, renewed Paul IV's. bull of deposition, revived with greater stringency the old bull of Maundy Thursday In coena Domini (Vol II., p. 312) against the errors of the Reformation, pronounced

---

[1] For the bull of deposition and excommunication issued against Philip see DÖLLINGER, *Beiträge* I 218 ff.

[2] An upstart, who gave himself out a connexion of the Florentine princely house.

[3] See HILLIGER, p. 33 ff.

sentence of deposition upon Elizabeth of England (BM VII 810 ff.),[1] and celebrated the naval victory of the Spanish, Venetian, and papal arms over the Turks at Lepanto (1571) as a triumph of the prayers of the rosary. He enjoined upon all Catholic physicians as a duty, that they should above all admonish their patients to call in a Catholic confessor, and to refuse to attend upon them, if this demand were not fulfilled within three days (BM VII 430). **Gregory XIII.** (1572-1585), who made his son and nephew Cardinals, is of the highest importance in consequence of the energy, conscious of its aim, with which he placed every means at the service of the counter-Reformation and, in particular, endeavoured to bring about the reconquest of Germany. By the side of the already existing nunciature of Vienna he established a similar one at Münich in 1573 for South Germany, in 1580 another for Styria, and, above all, in 1584, one for North-west Germany and the Netherlands at Cologne. The Massacre of St. Bartholomew was his delight. The existence of the Collegium Germanicum was assured by him, the Collegium Romanum was considerably enlarged. He hoped, with the aid of his revision of the Calendar in 1582 (the bull *Inter gravissimas*), to prove himself the *de facto* head of Christendom by means of the expected adhesion of the East and the Protestants. But the Patriarch of Constantinople could not be persuaded to accept it, and the Protestants treated the matter from the point of view of their confessions of faith; in places, where there was a mixed population (such as Vienna and Augsburg) violent conflicts ensued, and it was only gradually (in the 18th century, in Germany in 1700, in England in 1752, in Sweden in 1753) that the Evangelicals, in recognition of the real improvements effected by the new arrangement of the Calendar, abandoned their attitude of refusal. With Gregory XIII. the so-called **lesser** nepotism commences at the Curia: it is no longer a question of installing members of the family in the possession of Italian principalities: it is deemed enough to endow the family abundantly and to place it on a par with the most distinguished patricians by elevation of rank. Up to the death of Alexander VIII. (1691) nepotism carries on its existence in this altered form.[2]

---

[1] "*Flagitiorum serva Elizabeth,* **praetensa** *Angliae regina.*" "*Praecipimus et interdicimus universis et singulis proceribus, subditis, populis . . . ne illi eiusve monitis, mandatis et legibus audeant obedire. Qui secus egerint, eos simili anathematis sententia innodamus.*"

[2] Döllinger, *Kirche und Kirchen.* München, 1861, p. 528.

The Franciscan **Sixtus V.** (1585-1590), a man with high endowments for his office, but at the same time a visionary, proceeded with bloodthirsty severity against the nuisance of banditti in the States of the Church, and materially contributed to the improvement of the condition of affairs at Rome and in the country. By no means favourably disposed towards the Jesuits, unfortunate in his league with Spain against England, hesitating in his anti-French policy between Catholic interests and the fear of Spanish superior force, he attained little; the Roman people thanked him for the strictness of his rule with the legend that the devil finally carried off his soul in a storm. The succeeding Popes (Gregory XIV., Innocent IX., Clement VIII.) were especially engaged by the disturbances in France: they took the side of the league and thereby lent their sanction to the revolt against Henry IV. It was not until the latter went over to the Catholic Church that Clement VIII. gradually gave in and was now enabled, with the assistance of France, to acquire Ferrara in 1597 as a papal fief. **Paul V.** (1605-1621) became involved in a dispute with the republic of Venice, in which the interdict was employed for the last time by the medieval method of exerting pressure.

Under the doge Marino Grimani Venice had issued laws which set limits to the acquisition of property by the clergy, and made the founding of new churches and monasteries dependent upon the permission of the State. In this lay the real cause of the conflict. The occasion, however, was afforded by the imprisonment of two clerics for great offences, such as indecent assault: the Pope demanded their surrender together with the revocation of the laws: but the public refused both. The dispute reached a crisis on the question of the superiority of ecclesiastical or clerical authority; this accounts for the interest taken in its course by all the secular powers, and Venice also did not hesitate to accentuate this important point of principle. **Paolo Sarpi**, the provincial of the Servites, wielded his pen as a keen opponent of the Jesuits and of a papacy that was led by them and also in a spirit of vigorous patriotism, in order to defend the good cause of the Republic against the Curia. The Republic treated the papal interdict (1606) with contempt: the Jesuits, Capuchins, and Theatins were obliged to give way; the clergy were induced to continue divine worship. Only Philip III. of Spain took the side of the Pope, Henry IV., formally neutral, stood by Venice, Rudolph II. endeavoured to intervene, England offered the Republic an armed defensive alliance. At last, through the intervention of France and Spain, an agreement was arrived at: Venice delivered up the captives to the ecclesiastical court and promised not to put the offensive laws into operation; but, on the other hand, neither sought absolution from the interdict, nor recalled the Jesuits. The political state of affairs compelled both parties not to push matters to extremes. "Any idea of a real victory of the Pope is out of the question" (Funk). Sarpi experienced the deadly hatred of his adversaries in a murderous attempt which has made the "*stilus*" *Romanae curiae* proverbial.

After the brief rule of **Gregory XV.** (1621-1623), to whom the Church is indebted for the canonisation of the first Saints of the Jesuit Order, Ignatius and Francis Xavier, Cardinal Barberini succeeded as **Urban VIII.** (1623-1644). He created the Congregation of Immunities for the special purpose of keeping a watchful eye upon all attacks by the princes upon the rights of the Church. The great religious war strengthened the feeling of the community of interests of the Catholic States and the Papacy. Nevertheless, this solidarity of interests in favour of Urban was thwarted by the opposition to the Spanish-Austrian power, so that he was able to pose, in his hesitating policy, as a friend of the Franco-Swedish alliance against the Habsburgs, and it was said of him, as was bound to be the case, that he rejoiced at the victories of the Swedes. His reign has obtained a melancholy notoriety in consequence of the issue of the process against Galileo and the condemnation of the Copernican system.

Galileo's letter of December 21st, 1613, is theologically interesting. He expressed his willingness to render his unconditional submission to the Bible in the matter of salvation, but in the matter of the knowledge of nature he wanted the Bible, which adheres to the popular method of expression, explained in accordance with the results of certain scientific demonstrations. In order to put an end to a continuance of suspicions, he himself pressed for an ecclesiastical decision. The Holy Office, called upon by the Dominicans, in 1616 declared the Copernican propositions :[1] that the sun is the centre of the world and consequently without local motion ; and that the earth is not the centre and moves, as philosophically absurd and theologically heretical: after this, Galileo was ordered to abandon these opinions under pain of incarceration. He submitted, and on the 5th of March, 1616, the Copernican theory was formally **forbidden.** In 1630, Galileo again ventured to discuss the arguments for and against the different systems in the interest of the Copernican, received permission to print his work at Rome and published it in 1632. In regard to this, a new process was entered upon at the request of the Congregation of the Index, aided by the efforts of the Jesuits as Aristotelians. The accused, who was nearly 70 years of age, took refuge in several feeble evasions: even under threat of torture[2] he persisted that, since 1616, he had ceased to share the view of Copernicus and had only countenanced this theory from ambition and heedlessness: he subsequently solemnly abjured it and was condemned to imprisonment : the sentence, however, was commuted for banishment by the Pope. He died in 1642 a Catholic Christian. It was not until 1820 that the Curia abandoned

---

[1] These had already been expressed in 1543 in the treatise *De revolutionibus orbium coelestium* but remained without censure, since, according to A. Osiander's preface, they were only put forward as hypotheses in order to facilitate the calculation of the course of the stars.

[2] This appears to have been only a *territio verbalis*, which did not proceed to the rack itself.

its attitude towards the Copernican system; it was not until 1835 that the prohibition of the writings of Copernicus disappeared from the Roman Index Expurgatorius.

The enlargement of the Papal States by Urban (he acquired Urbino, but fought unsuccessfully against Parma), and the exorbitant enrichment of his relatives (Barberini) show how Urban understood his papacy. During his rule, in 1627, the bull dealing with the Eucharist received its definitive form as Rome's curse upon the Reformation: *Excommunicamus et anathematizamus quoscunque Hussitas, Wichlephitas, Lutheranos, Zwinglianos, Calvinistas, Ugonottos, Anabaptistas, Trinitarios . . . . eorumque receptatores, fautores, et generaliter quoslibet illorum defensores, ac eorundem libros haeresim continentes . . . .*, a sentence, from which only the Pope himself may grant absolution (BM XIII 530 ff.).

With the conclusion of peace at Osnabrück and Münster which took place under **Innocent X.** (1644-1655), who vainly protested against it, the interest of the Catholic princes in and their union with the Curia disappeared: all the States strove after internal solidity and independence; the tendency to withdraw from papal interference also increased. The time of the medieval aspirations of the Papacy was past. And Innocent himself, who lived in unworthy dependence upon the avaricious, heartless Donna Olympia Maidalchini, who regarded all matters of administration from the point of view of money-getting, forsaken by all on his deathbed, so that no one was found willing to pay the expense of his burial, presents an inglorious final tableau at this period of papal history.

CHAPTER FIFTH.

The Intellectual Currents and Forces in post-Tridentine Catholicism.

1. Catholic Learning in the Service of the Counter-Reformation.

Literature: A. HURTER, *Nomenclator liter. recent. theol. cath.* I (1564-1663).[2] Innsbruck, 1892. H. LÄMMER, *Die vortrident. kath. Theologie*, Berlin, 1858; K. WERNER, *G. d. apol. u. polem. Lit.* IV. For Melchior Canus see HUNDHAUSEN in KL II 1804 ff. (after F. CABALLERO, *Vida*, Madrid, 1871); for Baronius, NICERON, Nachr. XXI 328 ff.; R. BAUER in KL I 2038 ff.; Bellarmine: Autobiography, edited by DÖLLINGER and REUSCH, Bonn, 1887; J. B. COUDERC, *Le Vénérable Card. Bell.*, 2 vols., Paris, 1893 (ThLZ, 1893, 380 ff.); HEFELE in KL II 285 ff. J. F. MAYER, *De fide Baronii et Bellarmini*, Amst., 1697. Cajetan: JÄGER in ZhTh 28, 431 ff. Petavius: NICERON, Nachr. I. 139-264; WAGENMANN in RE XI 496 ff. Maldonatus: NICERON, Nachr. XXI 188 ff.; MANGOLD in RE IX 170 ff.; RAICH in KL VIII 547 ff. Estius: MAIER in KL IV 930 f.; C. a Lapide: ALZOG in KL VII 1428 f. Bolland: KL II 986 ff.

In the first decades of the Reformation Catholic theology clearly showed traces of the shock, which had fallen upon the Church. The younger and more vigorous forces had been appropriated by Luther's preaching, the older saw the wisdom, which the Middle Ages had consolidated in Scholasticism, suddenly abandoned to contempt. The new methods of formulating questions and the triumphant tone, with which the new teaching made its appearance, caused bewilderment. The first defenders of the old system, who ventured to show themselves, were for the most part rudely rebuffed by Luther himself or his associates; the most zealous and capable of them laboured under the disadvantage that their writings were rarely purchased, and their efforts met with insufficient support and recognition from the prelates of the Church. Strength was wasted in the petty war of polemical writings, the tone of which on both sides was coarse and insulting. John Eck's *Enchiridion locorum communium* (1525) fell flat before the youthfully exuberant treatise of Melanchthon. Others, such as the well-read and active G. Witzel, were so completely under the influence of the charges made by the Reformation, that they could only support a reformed Catholicism which abandoned Scholasticism and the Protean superstition of the Church and in positive ideas placed its reliance upon Erasmus. Others, again, such as H. Emser and J. Dietenberger, borrowed what was best in them directly from Luther's work; they copied his translation of the Bible, the latter also his catechetical works. Cardinal Cajetan, who had experienced the superiority of the evangelicals in treating of the Holy Scriptures, resolutely applied himself to exegesis that had been long neglected; but, while choosing partly Erasmus and partly Jerome for his guides, he himself became involved in various conflicts with the prevailing views (the Epistle to the Hebrews is not by Paul; divorce for the purpose of adultery is permissible, etc.), and drew upon himself the censure of the Sorbonne.[1]

But the gathering together of the forces of Catholicism was accompanied by a renovation of its theology. The first important work was composed by the Spanish Dominican **Melchior Cano** (died 1560). His *De locis theologicis libri XII*[2] is an energetic attempt to re-establish, in the face of Protestantism, the theological theory of authorities and knowledge as understood by Scholasticism. Theology is distinguished from all other sciences by the fact that it is built up upon authority. *Auctoritas primas in theologia partes obtinet, ratio postremas.* Where these authorities are to be found is the main subject of his controversy with Lutheranism. The authority of the Scriptures depends upon the *approbatio Ecclesiae,* which alone distinguishes canonical from non-canonical writings: *ad summum Pontificem de libris canonicis iudicium pertinet.* The preaching of Paul would have had no validity in the Church, *nisi Petri auctoritate fuisset roboratum.* The Vulgate is accepted by the Latin Church, and is therefore authoritative *in fide et moribus: non est nunc ad Hebraeos Graecosve recurrendum.* But, as not nearly all that pertains to Christian doctrine is revealed in the Canonical Scriptures, as a necessary supplement there was need of the further unfolding of the truth by means of the traditions of the Church. Every scientific controversy with the Lutherans is further *vana et futilis disputatio,* since such controversies *omnia theologiae principia tollunt.*[3] What Cano did towards laying the foundations of Catholic dogmatic theology as opposed to Protestantism, was continued by the Jesuit Cardinal **Robert Bellarmine** (1542-1621) in his *Disputationes de controversiis Christianae fidei adversus huius temporis haereticos,*[4] delivered (1576-. 1589) in the Roman Jesuit college and frequently printed; in these he supports, learnedly and acutely, the whole dogmatic system of teaching in combating Protestantism and defending the Tridentine dogmatics, so that the evangelical dogmatists of the next decade

---

[1] Opera. Lugduni, 1639.

[2] Opera. Paris 1668 p. 1 ff.

[3] Considering Cano's hostility to the Jesuit Order (cp. Opera. p. 185) and his occasional polemics against the excrescences of Scholasticism, we cannot regard him as a liberal-minded theologian; he is the characteristic representative of the dogmatic theology of the Restoration.

[4] Ingolst., 1581-1592, in 3 Fol.

(especially Joh. Gerhard) were forced to answer him uninterruptedly and meet his reasonings. But Flacius had also forced Catholicism, by his Magdeburg Centuries (see Vol. I, p. 9) to defend itself from attack in the province of **history**. The learned member of the Oratory, **Caesar Baronius** (1538-1607), took part in this struggle; from 1588-1607 twelve volumes of his *Annales ecclesiastici* appeared, extending to the year 1198, in which, although they exhibit much uncritical credulity and reliance upon false documents, and, especially in the history of the East, are open to the reproach of many chronological blunders, a wealth of MS. material has nevertheless been brought to light.[1] A masterpiece of learned industry in the collection of materials and critical thoroughness was commenced by the Antwerp Jesuits (**John Bolland** and others) in the *Acta Sanctorum* (1643-1770, 50 vols.; up to 1794, 2 vols., continued since 1837). In the same manner, Flacius also specially forced them to undertake **liturgical** investigations (cp. RE XIV 215), in order to be able to prove the antiquity of the Roman mass. The archaeologist **A. Bosio** in his *Roma Sotterranea* opened up an entirely new field of enquiry, in which Rome thought she had found the testimony of the martyrs of the first centuries in favour of the antiquity of her dogmas and rites. It was of still greater importance that the learned French Jesuit **Dionysius Petavius** (1583-1652), after having produced several patristic, philological and chronological works, turned his attention to the history of dogma, and in his work *De theologicis dogmatibus* (Paris, 1644-1650, 5 vols.) brought together a wealth of material from the authorities of the ancient church—a work, the importance of which was not recognised by the Catholic theological world, until it was forced upon their attention by evangelical contemporaries. But exegesis also was again taken in hand. The patristically learned and versatile Jesuit **Maldonatus** wrote commentaries (especially upon the four Gospels, 1596, 1597), in which are to be found the elements of the textual criticism of the New Testament, philological tact, a return to the dispassionate exegesis of Chrysostom and skilful treatment of the controversy with the evangelical interpreters of the Scriptures. **Wilhelmus Estius** of Douai did the same for the Epistles of the New Testament (1614 f.).

---

[1] The best edition, with the critical notes of the Franciscan Ant. PAGI inserted, is by J. D. MANSI, 1738-1759; reprint by A. THEINER, Bar le Duc, 1864 ff. The continuation by Oderic RAYNALDUS of the Oratory in 9 vols. (for 1198-1566), Rome, 1646-1677, was valuable; see Vol. I, p. 9.

On the other hand, the verbose but widely circulated commentaries of the Jesuit **Cornelius a Lapide** (died 1637) exhibit, together with a wealth of patristic material, a relapse into the arbitrariness and whimsicalities of the fourfold interpretation of Scripture. "The chief supporters of the post-Tridentine struggle against Protestantism were and continued to be **the Jesuits**, who also did most to foster learned and devotional theology, and consequently were the real upholders of Catholic belief and consciousness." (**K. Werner.**)

2. The Decline of Augustinianism.

Literature: BAJI *Opp.* Col. 1696. DU CHESNE, *Hist. du Bajanisme.* Douay, 1731. LINSENMANN, *M.B.* Tüb. 1867. MÖLLER in RE II 66 ff.; MOLINA, *Liberi arbitrii cum gratiae donis concordia.* Lisb. 1588. LE BLANC (the Dominican Serry), *Hist. Congregationum de auxiliis divinae gratiae.* Lovan. 1700; on the other side, ELEUTHERIUS (the Jesuit de Meyer), *Hist. controversiarum de div. grat. auxiliis.* Antw. 1705. TH. DE LEMOS (Dominican), *Hist. congr. de aux.* Lov. 1702. G. SCHNEEMANN (S. J.), *Entstehung und weitere Entwicklung der thomistisch-molinist. Controv.* 2 vols. Freibg. 1879-1880, p. 253 ff.; RE X 153 ff. DÖLLINGER-REUSCH, *Selbstbiogr. Bellarmins.* Bonn, 1887. JANSEN, *Augustinus s. doctrina Augustini de humanae naturae sanitate, etc.* Lovan. 1640, and frequent editions: *Discours de la réform. de l'homme intérieur.* Par. 1727. VANDENPEREBOM, *C. Jansenius.* Bruges, 1883. HARNACK, DG III 628 ff. J. KLEIN, *De Jansenismi origine I.* Vratisl. 1863. H. REUCHLIN, *Gesch. v. Port-Royal,* I 301 ff. REUSCH, *Index* II 298 ff.

Although Thomistic Augustinianism still held the field,[1] the peculiar theological tendencies, which developed themselves in necessary connection with those of the Jesuit Order, pressed forward upon other paths. Ignatius had in the main adhered to the **Thomistic** theology that prevailed in Spain. But Lainez, and in a greater degree Aquaviva opposed it. The Constitutions certainly prescribed the *Summa* of Thomas [Aquinas] as a text-book, but with the reservation that it might be replaced by "a more useful author" or a "Summa more in conformity with the needs of the time"; this greatly offended the Dominicans. The Augustinian element in Thomism strove against the spirit of the Order, which tended to the reduction of the Church to a purely mechanical organisation, and was obliged to make further concessions to free will and the natural powers of the human being. A contest was unavoidable; the internal tendencies of Catholicism offered resistance, and the driving back of the other Orders (especially the Dominicans) by the Jesuits, intensified the opposition.

In **Louvain,** where the theological faculty had advanced from Thomism to decided Augustinianism and had not allowed itself to be turned away from this tendency even by the lenient condemnation of the Augustinian doctrines of **Michael Bajus** by Pius V. (1567),[2] a struggle broke out with the Jesuits **Less** and **Hamel.** This assumed

---

[1] In the *Catechismus Romanus.*

[2] "Ex omnibus afflictionibus" in DENZINGER. ⁶p. 242 ff.; repeated and confirmed by Gregory XIII., 1579 ("Provisionis nostrae"). Cp. also LINSENMANN, p. 266 ff.

greater dimensions in consequence of the semi-Pelagian doctrines of the Jesuit **L. Molina**, Professor at the Portuguese University of Evora (1588,[2] Antv. 1595), in which the infallibility of effective grace, in order to allow the existence of human freedom, is regarded as introduced by a divine " scientia media," whereby the centre of gravity of the process of salvation is transferred to the human side, which receives only support from God, and the *gratia irresistibilis* is only taught in words,—doctrines, which not only called forth the opposition of the Dominicans, but also aroused discontent amongst the older Spanish section of the Jesuits. The Inquisition had already been set in motion against individual Jesuits (for false doctrine, but also for sexual offences at the confessional), when Clement VIII. transferred the controversy to Rome and appointed a congregation (*de auxiliis gratiae*) to decide it. It already seemed as if the verdict would be given against the Jesuits (the supporters of Molina) at the instigation of the Dominicans, but the Order was still too powerful an instrument to be treated in such a manner; besides, France sided with the Jesuits, as Spain with the Dominicans. The matter was the subject of frequent disputations (since 1602); Clement VIII. died in 1605, when he had almost made up his mind to decide against the Jesuits, as Bellarmine had predicted; finally, after the world had waited expectantly for nine years,— without any final decision being reached and only since the Jesuits triumphed too loudly—further dispute as to the *auxilia gratiae* was forbidden (1611). As a matter of fact, semi-Pelagianism had thereby gained a victory.

The beginnings of the Jansenist dispute also belong to our period, —the first act, which was played on the soil of the Netherlands. **Cornelius Jansen,** Professor of theology at Louvain from 1630, and Bishop of Ypres from 1636, had committed to writing the fruit of his years-long studies of Augustine in a work dealing with the latter, which, in accordance with his will, was published by his friends in 1640 after his death, which took place in 1638.

Jansen sees in Scholasticism an erroneous development of theology, an excessive exaltation of human intelligence, a defilement of theology by Aristotelian philosophy. The over-estimation of the power of knowledge arises from the under-estimation of sinful corruption. Like a strict Augustinian, he teaches the impotence of fallen man for good and a predestination conceived from an infra-lapsarian point of view: at the same time, his teaching as to the Church and its authority is Catholic and Augustinian. Augustine is for him **the genuine Catholic tradition**; every attempt to go beyond him leads to error. The doctrine that mere *attrition* combined with the Sacrament is not sufficient for justification and reconciliation, was a special interference with the practice of the Church. At Louvain, Jansen had already assumed the anti-Jesuit attitude of this University and become intimate with Duvergier, the famous Abbot of St. Cyran. The two united in their efforts to secure ecclesiastical reform, deeper and more earnest religious feeling within the limits of the Catholic Church. Jansen's relation to France was of momentous importance for him. In the difficult, apparently indefensible position of the Spanish Netherlands between Holland and France he had, in his *Mars Gallicus* (1635),[1] sharply opposed French policy, which supported the Dutch and Germans against Spain. Subsequently, he thereby compromised his friends in France, while the Jesuits obtained a suitable opportunity of setting Louis XIV. against the Jansenists; in his own country this political treatise procured for him the bishopric of Ypres.

The Jesuits now at once attacked the posthumous work, supported by the condemnation of Bajanism by Pius V. and Gregory XIII. Jansen, who had himself felt this difficulty, had calmed himself with the reflection, that the rejection of Augustinian tenets by these Popes was due more to the desire of putting down disputes than to any wish to come to a real decision: he had also in his will expressly submitted to the judgment of the Church. The "Index-congregation" had already prohibited his book in 1641—but also the Jesuit counter-treatise. In the same manner the bull of Urban VIII. (In eminenti, 1642) referred to the earlier decision which prescribed silence, but at the same time censured Jansen for having reproduced doctrines, which had already been rejected by Rome. The opposition of the higher clergy of the Netherlands, and especially of the University of Louvain, together with the objections that doctrines taken word for word from Augustine were here condemned, were soon silenced, when the Spanish Government also went over to the side of the Pope (since 1647). But now a serious after-piece was played in France (see later).

Gallicanism and its Opponents. The Jesuit doctrine of the State.

Literature: Dupin, *Manuel du droit public ecclés. franç.* Paris, 1844; the same, *Les libertés de l'Égl. gallic.* Paris, 1824; S. J. Baumgarten, *Von den Freiheiten der K. v. Frankr.* Halle, 1752. Article "*Gallic. Freiheiten*" in KL V 66 ff. Baillet, *La vie d'Edm. Richer.* Amst., 1715. Puyol, *Edm. R.* Paris, 1877. L. v. Ranke, *Die Idee der Volkssouveränetät in den Schriften der Jesuiten.* Hp. II. 606 ff. O. Gierke, *Joh. Althusius.* Bresl., 1880 (Untersuchungen zur deutschen Staats-u. Rechtsgesch. VII), p. 65 ff. Reusch, *Der Index* II 341 ff. 327 ff. Ellendorf, *Die Moral u. Politik der Jesuiten.*

In opposition to the medieval subordination of the State to the Church, the idea of the independent authority of the State had

---
[1] See Reuchlin I 333 ff.

become powerful even amongst the Catholic princes and showed itself as a monarchical absolutism, which now on its side desired to bring the church of its district into a state of dependence, in a manner analogous to the ecclesiastical authority of the Protestant princes of the various districts. Thus the episcopate found itself between two powers. If, at Rome, in consequence of rigid centralisation, the tendency of papal absolutism, and frequently also the abuse of the papal authority, it had to apprehend the repression of its rights, the loss of its independence, the thwarting of its jurisdiction by the nuncios, and also pecuniary losses, and accordingly hoped for protection from connection with the national State authority—on the other hand the encroachment of the much nearer State executive, equipped with secular means of power, was no less threatening to the episcopal position. This explains the fact that the episcopate preferred to seek support against the encroachments of the State from the Pope. Thus placed between two stronger powers, the old episcopal consciousness, however powerfully it bestirred itself from time to time, could never lastingly penetrate the episcopate; for, so far as the bishops resisted the claims of the Pope, they ran the risk of losing to the absolutist State what they had gained there. That consciousness was most powerfully stirred in **France.**

Here, the remembrance of the great councils and the theological opposition to papalism had never died out. The Pragmatic Sanction of Bourges (Vol. II, p. 516) had established (in 1438) episcopalian principles for the French church and by the *appellatio ab abusu* to King and Parliament had conceded an important influence to these courts. The Concordat of 1516 (Vol. II, p. 530) had divided the liberties of the Gallican Church between Pope and King; the principles of episcopalianism were sacrificed to the Pope, but the latter had granted the King considerable revenues, and a practically unlimited right of nomination to all prelacies. Thus, the entire hierarchical organism was essentially under the control of the King. In French theology and amongst the clergy there remained an at least very lukewarm feeling in regard to the claims of the Pope; the old episcopalian views were tenaciously propagated. In the face of French Protestantism the high clergy thought the best thing would be a close connection with the throne; thus, on the whole, a strong national church feeling also remained. This feeling, however, certainly changed during the period of the politico-religious struggles, owing to the papally inclined party of the Guises. But, after Henry IV. went over to the Catholic Church, the national church tendency, the stress laid upon the liberties and rights of the Gallican Church, again asserted themselves. The acceptance of the Tridentine reformatory resolutions had been rejected in France by the State Council and Parliament (against the bishops and Guises). When, in 1593, during the contest of the league with the still Protestant Henry IV., the bishops, at the Assemblée generale, endeavoured to get them accepted, **Le Maistre,** the President of the Parliament, showed by a comparison of the various decrees, how the

Council of Trent had damaged the authority of the crown, by the extension partly of episcopal, partly of papal rights; and the matter was allowed to drop. Several repetitions of the attempt (especially in 1614 and 1615) remained equally unsuccessful. In spite of the opposition of the Pope, Henry IV. was recognised as King and the fact was thereby accentuated, that the Pope had no power of decision in the matter. At that time the parliamentary advocate **Pierre Pithou** wrote his "Libertez de l'église gallicane" (1594)[1] in 83 articles, which show that, in these so-called Gallican strivings, the lively feeling of **national** independence held the chief place and that the **episcopal** self-consciousness was obliged to be subservient to it. The main principles of these articles are:[2] The Pope has no share in the management of secular political matters. In spiritual matters a "suzerain" is certainly admitted, but his authority is limited by the canons of the older synods recognised in France. He is bound by the resolutions of the general councils as by valid ecclesiastical laws, although councils cannot be held without him. His bulls and citations need the placet of the King, etc. After the assassination of Henry IV. the widow-regent Maria of Medici ranged herself on the side of curialistic principles; but Gallicanism was defended by the Parliament and a great part of the clergy, in particular against the Jesuits, who now fought for Curialism. The Jesuit theories in regard to regicide (see below), illustrated by the assassination of Henry III. and Henry IV., called forth the more powerfully as a reaction the national accentuation of the rights of the King independent of ecclesiastical authority. The Sorbonne also ranged itself on this side. While at that time **Paolo Sarpi** in Venice upheld the cause of the Republic against the Pope (see p. 252), in France, **Edmond Richer,** Syndic of the Sorbonne, most vigorously supported Gallican principles[3] against certain theses, which the Dominicans had proposed for disputation in 1611 (1. The Pope cannot err *in fide et moribus;* 2. The Council is *in nullo casu* above the Pope; 3. The Pope has the right of laying what is doubtful before the Council, of confirming or rejecting its decisions, of imposing perpetual silence upon the parties).[4] Richer forbade the disputation on these points; the Dominicans now declared that their propositions were only put forward as problematical; the Gallican theologians protested that the French Church taught the opposite of those tenets. The disputation was then brought about by the nuncio. The papal party, at the head of which was Cardinal Duperron, Archbishop of Sens, succeeded in forcing Richer to resign his syndicate and "Richerism" was branded as a heretical title. For a time the papal point of view now had the upper hand amongst the clergy, but with the restriction that, even in the declaration to Urban VIII (1625),[5] which went to the greatest length, a downright assertion of infallibility and of the right of the Pope to depose Kings was avoided. The course of action followed by the Crown (Richelieu) was guided by the needs of high policy. Thus the adhesion

---

[1] Reprinted in Dupin, *Manuel*, p. 1 ff. Later, Dupuy (Puteanus) wrote a commentary upon it (Paris, 1652).

[2] On the internal ambiguity of the episcopalian theory, cp. Harnack, *DG* III. 619.

[3] *De ecclesiastica et politica potestate*, 1611, enlarged 1629; in *Collectio Tractatuum*, p. 1 ff.: also, his *Defensio*, recently reprinted in the same collection.

[4] *Collectio Tractatuum*, p. XV.

[5] See Gieseler III. 2, 591 note.

of the Pope to France in the Thirty Years' War caused a temporary persecution of Richerism. Richer was violently compelled to recant (he died 1631). In like manner, Richelieu caused the French bishops to reject the writings of Dupuy (1639). Meanwhile, there was no lack of representatives of Gallican principles,[1] and the interest of the executive power again tended in the direction of asserting the independence of the State in regard to the Pope and of appealing in the matter to Gallican principles, which were of greater service to established churchdom than to the bishops. They could also be used as political scarecrows. Accordingly, Richelieu caused the idea to be circulated that France would perhaps establish a patriarchate of her own and entirely break away from Rome. However, he soon again altered his tone, owing to the sensation caused by this idea.

Jesuit proficiency in polemical literature furnished the papacy with skilful defenders, above all Cardinal **Bellarmine** with his tractate *De potestate summi Pontificis in temporalibus* (1610).[2]

In this, the medieval claims of the supreme power of the Pope in secular matters also are defended against the Gallicans; the reverse of this is the theory of the **profane** origin of the secular authority. In opposition to the Reformation, a purely secular construction of the State and of the authority of the ruler is given, in order to deduce the necessity of the subordination of this work of man to the divinely established spiritual power of the Church. In so far as relations to the Church were left out of the question, a modern secular doctrine of the State was the result. Certainly the executive power also, considered generally, is derived from God, but in its totality (*multitudo*) it is laid down and handed over (*iure naturae*) to definite persons; the special form is decided by the *ius gentium, deductum ex iure naturae per humanum discursum*. It depends upon the will of the totality, whether it is in the form of republican or monarchical authority. If legitimate reasons exist, the multitude can change monarchy into aristocracy or democracy. Even if the Pope is not directly secular lord of all lands,[3] yet, for spiritual purposes, he possesses the supreme right of disposal of the temporal property of all Christians. Even if he is not *ordinarius iudex* of the princes, he can *regna mutare*, if it is necessary for the salvation of souls. If he cannot make laws in a regular manner, when the salvation of souls is in question, he can annul or sanction laws.

Other Jesuits (*e.g.* **Mart. Becanus**, *Controversia Anglicana*, Mainz, 1612) defended similar principles with much less reserve, especially the proposition that the political authority vested in the people could be taken from an unjust prince and that no faith was to be

---

[1] De Marca, *De concordia sacerdotii et imperii*, 1641.

[2] See also his instructive letter on the infallibility of the Pope in Döllinger, *Beiträge zur polit* .... *Gesch.* III 84 ff. and, in addition, GGA 1884, 582.

[3] The disputing of the proposition *Papam esse dominum directum totius mundi*, which he had already brought forward in the first volume of his *Controversia*, met with such disapproval at Rome, that Sextus V. placed this work on the Index of 1590; but the next edition again erased his name.

kept with a heretic prince, according to the command of the Vicar of Christ; consequently, it was a popular sovereignty subordinate to the nod of the Pope;[1] further (**Mariana**, *de rege et regis institutione*, 1599; Mainz, 1611, p. 51 ff), that the murder of tyrants is lawful. These doctrines had their origin in the rising of the French league (the majority of the French Jesuits had since 1576 supported the league against the King) and had very practical heads (Elizabeth of England, Henry III.[2] and Henry IV. of France). Light is thrown upon the importance of this doctrine at the time by the fact that Mariana's book was burnt in Paris in 1610 by order of the Parliament, on the ground that the doctrine of the Jesuits was responsible for Ravaillac's act, and Bellarmine's *De potestate summi Pontificis* was prohibited in France in the same year and became the subject of a lively literary quarrel. Aquaviva found himself compelled to forbid, as a matter of form, the theory of the lawfulness of the murder of a tyrant for the members of the Order (*ut nemo audeat asserere*, **cuicunque** *licitum esse sub* **quocunque** *tyrannidis praetextu reges et principes occidere*); in reality, it was quietly proclaimed under his eyes. Mariana's work was not placed upon the Index.[3]

But, in England, those doctrines were of momentous import for the position of the Catholics in that country. After Elizabeth had been excommunicated by the Pope in 1570 and declared deposed, the Catholic party endeavoured to set on foot the most desperately energetic agitations, in order to regain the country for Catholicism; England replied with the most severe edicts of persecution against Catholic priests. After the discovery of the Gunpowder Plot an "oath of allegiance" was required from the English Catholics (1606), in which they were obliged to testify that the Pope had no authority to depose James, the lawful King, or to absolve his subjects from the oath of allegiance;

---

[1] "The Pope is the shepherd set by Christ over the whole Church. To the dogs of this shepherd also belong Emperors and Kings; lazy and worthless dogs are to be at once removed by the shepherd." Becanus in REUSCH II 346.

[2] Mariana expressly justified the assassination of Henry III. (*monumentum nobile*); the perpetrator is regarded by him as *aeternum Galliae decus*. The Jesuit Guignard was executed on pretence of his having been concerned in Chatel's attempt to assassinate Henry IV. (1595); the Order was within a little of being banished from France in 1598.

[3] ELLENDORF, p. 408 ff. HUBER, p. 266 ff. For Mariana's doctrines see also M. KIRCHNER in *Deutsche Blätter*, 1874, p. 542 ff. If Melanchthon, in an excited expression in a letter (CR III 1076) expressed a desire for some one to take the life of the tyrant Henry VIII., we must set against this his own clearly stated **theory** (CR XVI 440) of the absolute detestableness of the murder of tyrants. The essay *Denonciation des Jésuites* (Paris, 1727) collects many political expressions of opinion in regard to the deposition of princes and the assassination of tyrants (p. 201-206).

they were further obliged to abjure the doctrine of the lawfulness of putting a tyrant to death as heretical. The Jesuits (Bellarmine and others) declared this oath inadmissible, and it was condemned by Paul V. in 1606 and again in 1607. Nevertheless, the doctors of the Sorbonne now declared the oath to be admissible, and many Catholics took it; but Urban VIII. and Innocent X. reconfirmed the verdict of condemnation. When, in 1648, English theologians again declared against the power of the Pope to depose, their declaration was condemned in Rome as heretical, although the decree was not published. It was not until later that Rome became more cautious in this respect.

4. The Corruption of Moral Teaching by the Jesuits.

Literature: DÖLLINGER-REUSCH, *Gesch. d. Moralstreitigkeiten in der röm.-kath. K.*; 2 vols. Nördl., 1889. ELLENDORF (p. 260); HUBER (p. 228); REUSCH, Index II 309 ff.

In the interest of the authority of the confessional, the Jesuits applied themselves with special zeal to moral instruction in the form of casuistry, just as Franciscans and Dominicans, as the most eminent confessors of the people, had fostered this science in the Middle Ages. A large number of moralists (especially Spaniards, but also Belgians and Germans) built up this branch of knowledge with unwearied energy and hair-splitting dialectic; **Fr. Toletus** (died 1596; *Summa casuum conscientiae*. Rom., 1568), **Eman. Sa** (died 1596), **Thom. Sanchez** (died 1610, *de sacram. matrim.* Genua, 1592), **Fr. Suarez** (died 1617), **Filliucius;** somewhat later **Tamburini** (*Explicatio decalogi*, 1654; *Methodus expeditae confessionis*, 1647), **Laymann** (*Theol. moralis*. München, 1625), **Busenbaum** (*Medulla theol. mor.*, from 1645 to 1675 in 45, to 1776 in over 200 edd.), **Escobar**[1] (died 1669, *Liber theol. mor.*), the Belgian **Less**, the Englishman **A. Terillus** (died 1676), and others. If the confessor is judge in the confessional, he has to consider the magnitude of the offence confessed to him, to listen to accusation and **defence.** Since the Jesuit casuists, certainly in part misled only by the dialectical problem, became more and more the advocates of the sinner, their morality became a methodical guide to quieting the conscience. But this trend of their moral teaching is closely connected with the ecclesiastical tendency of the Order and with the semi-Pelagianism of their theology. If the Church is the end to which all is to be subordinated, this end which dominates

---

[1] It was said of him that he bought heaven dearly for himself, but sold it to others cheaper. The words *escobarder*, *escobarderie* (to equivocate, shuffle) are derived from his name.

everything drives back all uneasy moral considerations and scruples. This end excuses and justifies the means.[1] And the tendency to the subjection of the laity to ecclesiastical guidance brings down the moral claims of the confessors to the level of a lax secular morality. If the man was assured of his salvation by the fact that he subordinated himself to the Church and made use of its Sacraments, there was no need of moral elevation, of heightening the feeling of sin, of the impulse to personal sanctification; to come to terms with the life of the world commended itself as the best way to make the yoke of the Church as easy as possible for the multitude. This idea of the Jesuits is not an entirely new one; they only follow the tendency inherent in the institution of the confessional (inclusive indulgence) and exhibit its results, just as their casuistry was only a continuation of the *Summae* of the Middle Ages and perhaps not a single one of their propositions that have given offence was originally drawn up by them.

As essentially prominent characteristics may be noticed: 1. **The dialectic pulverising of the idea of sin generally,** whereby many things ceased to be regarded as sins: "deadly" sins are reduced to "venial" ones. Instead of measuring the moral condition as a whole by the objective law of God, they proceed by the subjective judgment passed upon the individual act considered by itself alone. Sin in the full meaning of the word only exists where an act is performed in full consciousness and with a free will; consequently, a deadly sin that abolishes the state of grace is only present where the understanding recognises perfectly and clearly the bad in an action, and where the will fully and freely agrees (distinction between philosophical and theological sin). What a scope for *ignorantia invincibilis* and *inadvertentia invincibilis* in exculpation of the sinner! All the affections and passions in this case become so many reasons for exoneration. 2. The undermining of the moral consciousness is further assisted by the **Probabilism** (*si est opinio probabilis, licitum est eam sequi,* **licet opposita sit probabilior**), first formulated by the Dominican Barth. de Medina (1577), but soon accepted by the Spanish Jesuits and systematically developed in the Order: this doctrine reduces the voice of conscience to silence, by allowing it to be sufficient for decision on a point of morality, if probable authorities are adduced, even though the opposite course of action appears safer to the conscience: consequently, a man's own conscience is suspended in favour of someone else's. The authority of only **one** respected teacher can render an opinion probable. Tamburini says in the strongest language: *Absolute puto cum Salas, Vasquez, Sanchez, etc., satis esse in omnibus casibus conscientiae probabiliter opinionem esse probabilem.* While this probabilism at first met with opposition in the Order itself (Bellarmine and others), it became its ruling

---

[1] The Order did not express the principle, that "the end sanctifies the means" in so many words, but as a matter of fact defended it; cp., *e.g.*, BUSENBAUM, *Medulla*, IV 3, dub. 7 art. 2 res. 3: *Si finis est licitus, etiam media sunt licita.* VI Tract. 6 c. 2: *Cui licitus est finis, etiam licent media.*

doctrine in the first half of the 17th century. 3. The *methodus dirigendae intentionis:* that a man can commit, without burdening his conscience, an act which is otherwise forbidden, if the intention is directed towards the attainment of a praiseworthy aim : the subjective motive consequently deprives the means of its sinful character. 4. The *restrictio* or *reservatio mentalis :* that, for the sake of a good or lawful aim, it is permissible to limit one's language, promise, or oath arbitrarily to a narrower sense than the tenor of the words gives him to whom they are addressed to understand; that is to say, it is lawful to **deceive** another with words, which are intended in a different sense from their natural one. With this also is connected the principle of Amphibolia, the intentional use of ambiguous expressions.[1] 5. The **weakening of the earnestness of penitence** corresponds to this decomposition of the moral consciousness. According to the precedent of the medieval doctrine of indulgence, it was taught that not *contritio*, but only *attritio formidolosa*, a *dolor imperfectus de peccato* was requisite; according to some, even the fear of the temporal punishments of sin is sufficient (in contradiction to Conc. Trid. Sess. XIV. c. 4, where an entirely different *attritio* was recognised as the preliminary step to true repentence). 6. In like manner, **the examination of the conscience**,—which, in order to be able to confess completely, must examine the past life most carefully,—was degraded to " moderate diligence " by the practice of frequent confessions : in this case also, consciences are not sharpened by suitable counsels, but quieted. It was even taught what reasons can justify a man in remaining silent about sin, without his being deprived of lawful absolution. It was also taught by some, that a person could confess and receive absolution by letter or through a messenger. We may here also mention the discussions in regard to the question. how often and when we are bound to love God above all, and the distinction between " effective " and " affective " love of God.

The wonder of the Jesuits at God having made the way to salvation so exceedingly convenient occasionally finds naïve expression : they are proud of having brought this facility to light. "At the present time sins are expiated much more speedily and zealously than they were formerly committed : nothing is more usual than monthly or weekly confession ; most people can scarcely commit sins faster than they confess." (*Imago primi saec.* III 8.) They prided themselves on having brought morality to a complete development, as the Schoolman boasted in regard to dogmatics. But they had thereby accommodated themselves to the spirit of the Catholic people, especially to the higher circles, and thus created that comfortable combination of clerical devotion and secular enjoyment of life which was characteristic of Catholic society, especially that of France.[2]

---

[1] During the persecution of the Catholics by Elizabeth, a text-book, approved by the Jesuits, appeared, which contained instructions when and in what manner subterfuges might be employed in presence of the authorities. DÖLLINGER-REUSCH, *Die Selbstbiogr. Bellarmins*, p. 206.

[2] Cp. *La dévotion aisée* (1652), by the Jesuit LEMOINE : ELLENDORF, p. 336 ff.; HUBER, p. 312 f.

The more religion was unspiritualised, the more natural was it, that all its factors **that were concerned with the senses** should grow in importance. The Jesuits soon took over the lead in the sensually directed worship of Mary: after hesitating at first, they decidedly took the part of the Franciscans in the dispute about the *conceptio immaculata;* they were inexhaustible in the invention of special devotions, pilgrimages, the erection of wonder-working images and the like, as well as in the formation of brotherhoods for the special exercise of devotion.

A violent reaction against the spirit that gathered strength here first took place about the middle of the 17th century in French Jansenism.

5. The Cultivation of Mysticism.

Literature: HEPPE, *Gesch. der quietist. Mystik.* Berlin, 1875. ZÖCKLER in ZlTh 1864 ff. NIPPOLD in JprTh 1877. A. RITSCHL, *Gesch. des Pietismus.* I 467 ff. Teresa: WILKENS in ZwTh 1862; E. GENONVILLE, *S. Thérèse et son Mysticisme.* Montauban, 1893. Abundant literary information in ZÖCKLER in RE XV 313 ff. J. A. FROUDE, *The Story of the Spanish Armada.* Leipz. 1892, p. 165 ff. L. de Leon: Biography by WILKENS. Halle, 1866; REUSCH. Bonn, 1873. Alumbrados: BLUNT, *Dictionary of Heresies.* Lond. 1874; ZÖCKLER in RE I 305 ff. Fr. de Sales: Oeuvres, 1641. Paris, 4 vols., 1836; German by Schaffh. 1846 ff. Biography by MARSOLLIER. Paris, 1747; RENSING, Paderb. 1818; BOULANGÉ. Mons. 1847.

In the post-Tridentine Church also a strong current of mystical ideas and feelings, starting from medieval phenomena (in particular, Franciscan mysticism), went on its course as an important supplement of the piety that concentrated its attention upon clerical correctness and activity in works, and now served the purpose of the monastic counter-reformation. Corresponding to the ideal of bliss formerly indicated by Duns Scotus, as that of a resting of the will in the love of God, the elevation of speculation to a vision is not so much striven after in this case, as the passivity of **rest** in pure love and tranquillity of will; God's will becomes effective where all egotistical selfwill has ceased. But then, as not unfrequently happens, partly owing to the influence of Jesuit confessors, refined asceticism (especially flagellation) was combined with this **Quietism**: and thus, in this case also, mystic tranquillity passed into ecstatic conditions. Then an overexcited nervous life began to play its part. But its first aim is only the giving up of all that belongs to us to the attainment of direct union with God, in order to attain to the life of God in ourselves. **Spain** is the home of this mysticism, but in the 17th century it also spread considerably in **France.**

The characteristics of this mysticism (*oratio mentalis*) had already been developed in the Franciscan **Petrus of Alcantara** (died 1562, *De oratione et meditatione*) and in **Francis of Osuna** (*Abecedario espiritual*). Connected with them is **Teresa de Jesus** of Avila, a female reformer of the Carmelite Order (died 1582), and her spiritual friend[1] **Juan de la Cruz**, the reformer of the Carmelites (died 1592); they practise silent prayer, from which after self-torture proceed ecstasy and vision. Here also should be mentioned the inspired Dominican preacher **Luis de Leon** and especially, Father **Gregory Lopez**, a recluse of Mexico, whose life was an unbroken internal prayer, a single continuous act of bare faith (*i.e.*, a faith which neither entered into intelligent reflections, nor depended upon subjective conditions of greater or less movements of feeling). In all these religious subjectivity showed itself relatively independent in reference to ecclesiastical precepts, but yet in strict dependence upon the Church, dominated by the monastico-ascetic character of ecclesiastical piety. On the other hand, this piety had taken a direction **hostile to** the Church in the **Alumbrados** (Illuminati) who sprung up in Spain soon after 1520; in their case the prayers of the Church were depreciated by the prayers of the heart: the Soul, elevated above mere belief to essential union with God and perfection, no longer needed the intervention of salvation by sacraments and good works, as it is no longer in a position to commit real sins. About the year 1575, the Inquisition suppressed this mystic sect, but was unable, however, to exterminate it completely. Traces of them are to be found still later in Spain, as in the north and south of France.

This clerical mysticism survived on **French** soil in the person of the celebrated **Francis de Sales**, the zealous converter of Protestants, from 1632 Catholic bishop of Geneva (Annecy), **Madame de Chantal**, who was under his spiritual guidance, with whom he founded the Order of **Salesian** women (Visitants, Order of the Visitation of Mary) in 1610, and pushed mortification and agreement with the will of God to "love without reward," to "disinterested" love of God, to holy indifference. By the side of decided adherence to the Church, its belief and exercise of obedience, the idea of a perfection, no longer needing the purification of purgatory, is vaguely present in this case.

This mystic piety, directed to perfection, spread widely in the 17th century, particularly in the Romance countries. The writings of the Mystics as they were called, approved by the authorities of the Church, found countless readers; the reformed Carmelites, the Salesian women and other societies afforded opportunities for the cultivation of this mysticism. The Church pronounced the most prominent of these older mystics holy or blessed, and recognised the value of this movement as a counterpoise to evangelical piety. Numerous ascetic writers fostered—although not specially the quietest characteristic— the spiritual life mystically understood, perfection in self-renunciation, godlike tranquillity, love of God, *transformatio in Deum*. In France, monasteries of the Theresian congregation increased; two active literary supporters were **Francis Malaval** and **Jean de Bernières**-Louvigny (died 1659: *Le Chrétien intérieur*); the latter was a man who, pursuing a secular calling and without

---

[1] Such friendships of souls are characteristic of the whole of this tendency of thought.

becoming a monk, gathered together the pious circles of northern France. But his writings exercised an influence beyond his own confession (translated by Tersteegen into German), although this mysticism always has something inter-confessional in itself. There were circles in France, by which Bernières' ideas were admired as a new form of the Gospel, as the uncovering of the kernel hidden by the shell of ecclesiastical dogmatism.

6. Orders and Congregations at the Service of the Counter-Reformation.

Literature: For the Oratorians see RE X 478 ff.; M. TABARAUD, *Hist. de Pierre de Bérulle.* 2 vols., Paris, 1817. REUCHLIN in ZhTh 29, 142 ff.; A. PERRAUD, *L'Oratoire de France au XVIIe et au XIXe siècle,* ²Paris, 1866; ThQu 1835. Vincent: Biography by ABELLY; Paris, 1664; L. Count STOLBERG, Münster, 1818. MAGNARD: 4 vols., Paris, 1860-1878. WILSON. Lond., 1874. E. de MARGERIE, *La Société de St. V. de P.*, 2 vols., 1874; UHLHORN, *Christl. Liebesthätigkeit.* III 210 ff.; KL III 922 ff. BUSS, *Der Orden der baumherz. Schw.* Schafth., 1847. LECHNER, *Leben d. h. Joh. v. Gott.* München, 1857.

The newly-kindled ecclesiastical life within the Romish Church showed itself in numerous new foundations and unions for purposes of common life and work. Four points are of most prominent importance. (1) The place of the old ideals of monastic perfection and avoidance of the world was taken by the idea of union for the purpose of **practically ecclesiastical** objects: the training and promotion of the clergy, and the deepening of their religious life; co-operation in the religious education of the people in the confessional, by preaching and missions among the people; the education of youth, nursing of the sick and the like. (2) In conformity with this, the more movable and freer form of the **Congregation** is now frequently preferred to the life proper of an Order; in place of *vota solennia* and the strict seclusion of nunneries we find *vota simplicia* (*congregationes religiosae,* or *piae,* according as the approval of the Pope has been obtained or is still withheld), or no vows are taken at all, or only for a definite time, or not all three are taken (*congregationes seculares*). In these laxer forms it became possible to put the **female** sex in motion to co-operate on behalf of the tasks of the Church. (3) The leadership, which the Spaniards held in the first half of the 16th century in the elevation of religious life, gradually yields to that of France. (4) All these new foundations are at the service of the counter-Reformation, in that they not only firmly reunite the Catholic people to its church, but at the same time carry on **propaganda** by means of their practical activities, and endeavour practically to overcome heretics. Of a number of foundations we may especially mention the following:

1. The Florentine **Philip Neri**, in whom, together with a mystical, ecstatic devotional fervour, a humorous, worldly jovial temperament reacted against the dark and gloomy spirit of official Romish piety, gathered together in Rome a congregation of secular priests (approved 1574) who, besides praying, were to preach and administer the Sacrament, for which duties they were to be thoroughly trained; in their prayer-hall (Oratorium, hence the name **Oratorians**), prayer meetings were held every evening for every man, at which, together with instructive and edifying discourses, a more cheerful form of church music with instrumental accompaniment (Oratorios) was used. The ecclesiastical historians, Baronius and Raynaldus (p. 257), belonged to this union.
2. A focus of specially **learned** studies was the **French Oratory** founded in 1611 by Cardinal de **Berulle**, a congregation of priests without any vow of an Order, subordinate to the bishops, founded for the purpose of common life, learned conversation and support of the parish clergy in the confessional and the care of souls. Soon, suspected of Jansenism, Cartesianism, and then of the philosophy of "enlightenment," distinguished by learned men like Thomassin and Richard Simon, the philosopher Malebranche, the pulpit-orator Massillon, and others, the congregation subsequently furnished the Revolution with many adherents. In 1792 it disappeared; in 1864 Pius IX. revived it. 3. The Portuguese **Johann Ciudad** (Di Dio), after having led a wild life, was roused by a penitential sermon of Juan de la Cruz (p. 269). and commenced to tend the sick and poor in Granada in 1540; a union of associates in this work gathered round him, but after his death (1550) was soon changed from a secular congregation into the **Order of the Brothers of Charity**. 4. Of still greater importance were the foundations of **St. Vincent de Paul**. The son of a Gascon peasant[1] (born 1576, died 1660, canonised 1737), who, in the course of an eventful life, ripened into an earnest pastor and friend of the people, he created, to meet the varied needs of the time, quite a number of new organisations, in a sincere spirit of sympathy combined with inventive charity and wonderful practical discretion. His insight into the spiritual neglect of the rural population determined him to gather together the society of the **Priests of the Mission** (also called Lazarists from St. Lazare in Paris)—the Oratorians were less serviceable in dealing with the ordinary man—in order to re-awaken, by means of missions, a Christian and spiritual life, especially in the rural communities. With these societies were combined spiritual exercises for candidates for ordination, intended to deepen the religious convictions of the priestly order, and further, conferences of the clergy to discuss ecclesiastical and spiritual questions; also *retraites spirituelles* were formed for the laity. His appeal to the community of Chatillon, where he for a time officiated, to assist a poor family in its need, obtained such ample success, that he was obliged to draw up regulations for the relief of the poor and the distribution of charitable gifts. He accordingly instituted unions of married and unmarried women (*confréries de la charité*) to administer local relief to the sick and poor. The contingent and hence uncertain efficiency of these unions further led him

---

[1] Spain has recently (but in vain) claimed the honour of having been his birthplace.

to call upon specially adapted forces for steadily and continuously carrying on the work of charity, and to make the relief of the sick and poor **the professional duty of women.** Thus, at the instigation and with the co-operation of the pious widow Le Gras his society of the **Sisters of Charity** (*filles de charité, soeurs grises*, confirmed by the Pope in 1668) was started in Paris in 1633.

Here common life only serves as a preparatory training for a profession and as a base of operations for the work of charity to others, only where it was needed. The "mother-house" took the place of the cloister with its life of seclusion; the "active" life asserts its nobility against the glory of perfection, which the "contemplative" had hitherto claimed. Simple vows to be repeated every year take the place of the vows of the cloister; but use is only rarely made of the permission to leave the "mother-house." The sister who serves Christ in the person of the poor in the midst of the world replaces the world-shunning nun who seeks her own perfection. Thereby Vincent called upon women to co-operate in the service of the Church, for their work is not only intended to serve to alleviate bodily necessity but at the same time to minister to the souls of the sufferers; nay, it enters directly into the service of the counter-Reformation, in so far as the conversion of heretics appears the highest task which they are called upon to accomplish, not only to Vincent, but to all his sisters.

CHAPTER SIXTH.

The Missionary Conquests of Catholicism.

Literature: HENRION, *Allg. G. d. kath. Missionen;* 4 vols. Schaff. 1847-1852. H. HAHN, *Gesch. d. kath. Missionen;* 5 vols. Köln, 1857-1865. MARSCHALL, *Die christl. Mission.;* 3 vols. Mainz. 1863. KALKAR, *Gesch. d. röm.-kath. Mission.* (from the Danish). Erl., 1867. For Las Casas, see BENRATH in RE VIII 424, add WEISE in ZhTh 4, 166 ff.; 8, 1, 136 ff. Francis Xavier: REITHMEIER. Schaff. 1846. VENN-HOFFMANN (from the English). Wiesb., 1869. N. GREFF. Eins. 1885. M. MÜLLBAUER, *Gesch. d. kath. Miss. in Ostindien.* Münch., 1851. Paraguay: E. GOTHEIN, *Der christl. soc. Staat der Jes. in Paraguay.* Leipz., 1883 (Staats-und social-wiss. Forsch. IV, 4). J. PFOTENHAUER, *Die Missionen der Jes. in Parag.;* 3 vols. Gütersl., 1891-1893. Propaganda: O. MEJER, *Die Prop.;* 2 vols. Gött., 1852-1853; the same in RE XII 242 ff.; HpBl 10, 84 ff.

The extensive losses, which Catholicism suffered in Europe, were in a measure counterbalanced in the new countries which Spanish, Portuguese, and also French conquerors opened up in North and South America, as well as the East Indies. The conquerors and adventurers were followed by missionaries, especially Franciscans and Dominicans; vigorous proselytism was carried on. Alexander VI. had divided the new world between Spain and Portugal; naturally, it was intended that the Cross should here supplant heathenism. Certainly the mission met with great difficulties, due to the inhumanity and brutal greed of the conquerors. In place of tribute, the Spaniards caused the natives to be told off to them as labourers (*repartimientos*); this developed into actual slavery, and the promise that the native labourers should receive Christian instruction was withdrawn on the contemptible plea that they were not fit for conversion. High praise is due to the constant efforts of the pious Spaniard **Bart. de las Casas,** who devoted more than fifty years to prove the capacity of the Indians for becoming Christians,[1] and to obtain a mitigation of the cruel treatment to which they exposed (he especially attacked the *Democrates secundus* (1552) of **Sepulveda,** who ventured to defend the violent deeds of the Spaniards on the ground of divine and secular right). The *repartimientos* themselves continued to exist as a necessity, but he had not laboured in vain for a more humane treatment of them, being powerfully supported in this by the Dominicans in particular.[2] The American missions could record large numbers of converts; thus, in

---

[1] In 1537 Paul III. was obliged to decide: *Indos ipsos utpote veros homines non solum fidei catholicae, sed etiam sacramentorum capaces existere decernimus et declaramus.*—PFOTENHAUER I 75.

[2] He has been erroneously made responsible for the introduction of negro slaves into America; the trade in negroes had been in existence since 1506.

1535, the Franciscans could boast of having converted 1,200,000 Indians (JGG XIII 195). Soon the Jesuits entered upon a successful rivalry. In 1542, **Francis Xavier** set foot on the soil of Hindostan, at Portuguese Goa, where it is asserted that he baptised hundreds of thousands, living a life of stormy, restless activity but also one of self-sacrificing love in the cause of the heathen, without possessing any knowledge of their language or lasting patience.[1] His chief success was his influence on the degenerate Europeans, whose conscience he roused in regard to the heathen. In 1549 he went on to Japan; here also his ignorance of the language hindered his efforts from being thoroughly effective, but he was successful in opening the door for the Jesuit mission for a considerable period. On his way to China, he was suddenly overtaken by death (1552). It was in China that, in 1573, the Jesuit **Matth. Ricci** commenced missionary work, but in quite a peculiar manner. Adopting the dress of a mandarin, he endeavoured to procure an entrance by a display of mathematical and astronomical knowledge; by adapting himself to Chinese popular customs and religious ideas (*e.g.*, the worship of ancestors) he sought to make the Christian religion acceptable to them. By so doing, he really confirmed his reputation, gathered numerous helpers round him, and founded a gradually increasing Catholic Chinese Church. After 1610, **Joh. Adam Schall** carried on Ricci's work. But when, after 1630, other Orders, especially Franciscans and Dominicans, took up the same work, they brought the most serious charges against the worldly wise practices of the mission; and now the years of long, embittered controversy about the Chinese rites began. The behaviour of the Jesuit **Rob. Nobili** on the coast of Malabar (1606) gave still greater offence; he appeared as a Brahmin, preserved, at least for a time, the regulations of caste, caused heathen customs to be kept up, and, at the celebration of the Holy Communion, refused to recognise the equality of the despised caste of the Pariahs. The hopes, which he and his successors placed upon this system of accommodation, were disappointed, in that members of the higher castes were only gained over in small numbers. In this case it was the Capuchins who led the campaign against these "Malabar rites." They were finally successful, in spite of the hesitation of the Popes[2] and the most obstinate resistance of the Jesuits in both mission districts, to whom they were finally able to oppose the sentence of the Pope. It was not until 1742 that their resistance was broken. In 1549, the Order had also commenced successful operations in Brazil and gained the confidence of the Indians. Summoned from here in 1586 to **Paraguay,** they obtained leave from Spain (1610) to establish an independent Indian state under Spanish supremacy.[3] By strictly isolating all foreigners, even the Spanish officials (the Spanish language was forbidden for natives), they succeeded in setting up an efficient patriarchal government over their "reductions."[4]

---

[1] Cerri, the secretary of the Propaganda, officially informs Innocent XI. that the Jesuits are in the habit of "never writing to the congregation, without speaking of thousands of persons whom they have converted, a fact which makes us give little credit to what they say." *État présent de l' égl. rom.* Amst., 1716, p. 113.

[2] In 1623, Gregory XV. practically decided in favour of the Jesuits.

[3] GOTHEIN has drawn attention to the similarity of the plan of constitution here followed by the Jesuits to the Utopian "Sun State" of the Dominican Th. Campanella.

[4] *i.e.*, the converted Indians.

after the model of a socialistically disposed trades union, in which the natives, as "children with beards," were systematically kept upon the footing of children of human society by life-long paternal education and tutelage, and were trained to subjection to the Church and the fathers. The great perfection of their capabilities, as well as the fateful limitations of their system are here apparent with equal clearness; they had not been able to educate men to freedom—hence, when their model state fell to pieces after 1750, no results of their introduction to Christianity remained. The task of teaching Christianity and civilisation to the natives without slavery, was as yet only solved in an unsatisfactory manner.

The Cardinals' congregation **De propaganda fide**,[1] which places the mission priests appointed by Orders or national colleges under *Praefecti apostolici* served the purpose of centralisation and the ecclesiastical direction of the extended Catholic missionary undertakings from the year 1622; on the success of the mission, the praefectures develop into apostolic vicarships, and the latter finally into new bishoprics. (Even the districts occupied by Protestantism were regarded as *Terra missionis* and hence subjected to the Propaganda). In 1627, Urban VIII. added the **College** (*Collegium Urbanum*) to the Congregation of the Propaganda,—a seminary, in which the young of all nations of the world were to be brought up as missionaries.

---

[1] Instituted by G regory XV.

FOURTH DIVISION.

The Disruption and confessional Separation of German Protestantism.

CHAPTER FIRST.
Dogmatic Controversies in Lutheranism.

Literature: HEPPE, *Gesch. des deutschen Protestantismus* (1555-1581). 4 vols. Marb. 1852-1859; the same, *Entstehung und Fortbildung des Lutherthums und die kirchlichen Bekenntnissschriften desselben von* 1548-1576. Cassel 1863. FRANK, *Theologie der Conc.-Form.* 4 parts. Erl. 1858-1865. HERRLINGER, *die Theologie Mel.s.* Gotha 1879. PREGER, *M. Flacius.* 2 vols. Erl. 1859-1861. MÖLLER, *A. Osiander.* Elberf. 1870. J. VOIGT, *Herzog Albrecht und das gelehrte Wesen seiner Zeit.* HTb II 253 ff. G. WOLF. *Zur Gesch. d. deutschen Protestanten*, 1555 to 1559. Berl. 1888. A. BECK, *Joh. Friedrich der Mittlere.* 2 vols, Weim. 1858. LOOFS [3]406 ff.

Amongst the different tendencies, which showed themselves prominently in the German Reformation, the fanatical and anti-Trinitarian (see below) were so completely crushed, that they were only able to produce trifling disturbances in isolated instances, but could no longer direct or settle the direction in which Protestantism continued moving. On the contrary, Luther's opposition to Zwingli was and continued of momentous importance; the influence of the two men had come into conflict in South Germany and had led to lengthy struggles. But further, the intensifying and modification of the Swiss Reformation by Calvin had not succeeded in bringing about an arrangement with Lutheranism, in spite of an approximation in points of dogma. In addition, differences had arisen between Luther and Melanchthon, which were intensified by their followers to embittered hostility. In this, a peculiar condition of things resulted: Melanchthonianism, in the question of the Eucharist, came into close contact with Calvinism, while, on the contrary, in the doctrine of free will and predestination, it was further removed from it than the so-called Gnesio-Lutheranism. But now, after the external hierarchico-ecclesiastical unity had come to an end, Protestantism sought its unity more and more in a purified doctrinal theology: "pure doctrine," in its dogmatico-theological meaning, was placed in the foreground as the bond of religious companionship. Hence, even apart from those different tendencies, every dogmatic departure and separate opinion of a theologian was bound to exercise its influence at once out of the theological arena upon the life of the Church. Melanchthon, more than anyone else, promoted this development by his definition of the Church as a *coetus visibilis, similis scholastico coetui*, the foundation of which is the *cognitio incorrupta omnium articulorum fidei* and the exclusion of all *cultus idolorum*, and the members of which are those *qui consentiunt de vera doctrina* and upon whom *iure divino obedientia* to the ministry that introduces pure doctrine is incumbent (CR XXI 833 ff.). It was necessary that a church, which defined itself as the school of pure doctrine, should be able to make every question of doctrine a question of existence and only to find the safeguard of its stability in continually sharper formulations of confession. A universal symbolical fixation of its doctrine was hence a condition of existence for it.

1. The Points of Difference between Melanchthon and Luther.

Literature: G. KAWERAU, *J. Agricola*. Berl. 1881. R. A. LIPSIUS, *Luthers Lehre von der Busse*. Braunschw. 1892. J. C. SEIDEMANN, *J. Schenk*. Leipz. 1875. G. MÜLLER, *P. Lindenau*. Leipz. 1880; the same in ADB 31, 49 ff. P. VETTER in NA f. sächs. Gesch. XII 247 ff. L. GÖTZE in XIV Jahresb. d. Altmärk. Vereins. Salzw. 1864, p. 69 ff. KOLDE, *M. Luther II*.

Melanchthon had at first closely attached himself to Luther, for it was under his powerful influence that the humanist had been driven into theology. Averse to theological disputes, he would have preferred to withdraw to his humanistic and generally scientific efforts, but Luther and the pressing need of the evangelical cause held him fast to theology; he was obliged to make his appearance wherever it was a question of carrying on discussions dealing with questions of dogma, or of finding the purified formulas necessary for *doctrina publica*. To this must be added his eminent importance for the generally scientific and also theological training of the younger Protestant generation, which reverenced in him the *praeceptor Germaniae*. His way of thinking, determined by humanism, which in the matter of dogma on every occasion followed what most readily attached itself to the general religious ideas of humanism, and shrank back from Luther's deep paradoxes and the passionate manner of his trend of belief, and his horror of all *inanes disputationes* gradually asserted itself also in actual divergences. With the revision of the loci theologici in 1535 this peculiar manner of doctrine is essentially complete in the case of Melanchthon.

(a) Since 1527, Melanchthon had abandoned the deterministic bent of the Reformation and supported the idea of a **Synergism**, which should keep the causality of sin aloof from God and assert the feeling of man's responsibility.

Man's salvation can only be accomplished with the aid of a co-operative decision of his own will, without any mention of merit on his part being admissible. Hence Melanchthon maintains, partly a certain freedom of fallen man for *iustitia civilis*, partly a self-uplifting of the will brought about by grace itself (that it does not reject the offered promise, fights against its own weakness, etc.). An inalienable practically ecclesiastical ethical interest in this case endeavours to obtain recognition in a dogmatically contestable form.

(*b*) A similar interest leads him to lay stress upon **the necessity of good works** for believers in the face of the false, indolent, fleshly abuse of the doctrine of justification by faith. We find this already in the Visitation articles, but especially in the loci theologici of 1535, in which occurs the expression: *bona opera necessaria sunt ad vitam aeternam, quia sequi reconciliationem necessario debent* (CR XXI 429)[1]—and *bona opera* **merentur** *praemia corporalia et spiritualia* (CR XXI 433).

(*c*) In the Eucharistic controversy, although Melanchthon was at first entirely on Luther's side and bluntly rejected union with the Swiss, yet he had no sympathy either with the doctrine of ubiquity or the *manducatio oralis*. Then Oecolampadius's *Dialogus* of 1530 taught him that some of the fathers of the Church testify in favour of the symbolical interpretation of the sacramental words: from that time he abandoned Luther's understanding of these words. Bucer's efforts at mediation (the colloquy at Cassel, 1534), at which Melanchthon already felt himself *nuntius alienae sententiae*)[2] made a further impression upon him, and induced him to fall back upon what in his judgment was alone essential, the self-communication of Christ to believers and the inner spiritual union with him as a guarantee of the *res in evangelio promissae*, i.e., *remissio peccatorum et iustificatio propter Christum*. Not *in pane*, but *cum pane: cibus animae*, a spiritual enjoyment, as a self-communication of the God incarnate with the believing soul, resting upon a personal act of will on the part of Christ. In conformity with this Melanchthon in 1540 altered the Latin text of the CA in Article X.: *quod corpus et sanguis Christi vere adsint et distribuantur vescentibus* into *cum pane et vino vere exhibeantur corpus et sanguis Christi vescentibus* and struck out the words *et improbant secus docentes*.

The extent of these divergences was not clearly made manifest during Luther's lifetime, partly owing to Melanchthon's prudence, partly to Luther's confidence in his comrade:[3] trifling disturbances, due to various accusations,

---

[1] In the previous sentence we find, quite after the Lutheran manner: *donatio vitae aeternae coniuncta est cum iustificatione*, i.e., *cum remissione peccatorum et reconciliatione, quae fide contingit*. Here also the more accurate definition must not be overlooked: *illa obedientia est iustitia non quia legi satisfacit, sed* **quia iam personae placent.**

[2] See above, p. 124; add ZhTh 44, 123 ff.

[3] Although Luther did not approve the alteration in the Confession of the Church—as early as 1537 Melanchthon had been denounced to the Elector for "toning down" the text, CR III 366—yet, in 1541, he testifies to his master Philip that he and the other Wittenbergers had adhered to the Confession (de Wette V 357). Brenz also writes, in reference to this *posterior editio*: *scio Philippum citra iudicium nil temere mutare* (CR IV 737). Selnecker even asserted subsequently that this *confessio posterior* was *relegente et approbante Luthero recognita* (Catalogus conciliorum. Francof. 1751, p. 97).

had been arranged from time to time; his indignation at the Eucharist doctrine of the Cologne Reformation was, however, directed rather against Bucer than Melanchthon (de W. V 703 f.). But these relations render it psychologically comprehensible how, the longer Melanchthon was intimate with Luther, the more confined and oppressed he felt.[1]

When **John Agricola**, in 1527, attacked Melanchthon's theory of the importance of the law for the penitence of the Christian and of the superiority of the preaching of the law to the preaching of faith, his attack was aimed at Melanchthon (see above, p. 78); at that time Luther had taken Melanchthon under his protection and Agricola had half beaten a retreat. When then, ten years later, Agricola again asserted his antinomianism in Wittenberg itself, distinguished " pure " and " impure " passages in the writings of the Wittenbergers, wanted to do away with the preaching of the law altogether and contested the theory that the Gospel belongs to those hearts which have been stirred to repentance by the law, he was now naturally obliged to turn against Luther himself, who, being in fact personally embittered against the vain and secretly agitating behaviour of his old friend, first reduced him to silence and then made him recant; Agricola, enraged against the Wittenbergers, escaped to Electoral Brandenberg. Under a similar reproach of having taught the antinomian doctrine.—" do what you will, only believe, so you will be blessed " (which, however, finds no adequate confirmation in his **writings**), **James Schenk**[2] was driven from his post as Court preacher to Duke Henry of Saxony in 1538, and, when he endeavoured to find employment at the University of Leipzig as professor and preacher, he was here also looked upon with suspicion, chiefly owing to Pfeffinger's zeal, and, finally, like Agricola, he retired in 1543 to Brandenburg. Here his arbitrary and idle behaviour had chiefly met with an opposition, which made use of the reproach of antinomianism and other doctrinal divergences only as a convenient handle against the gifted, but also troublesome man, to whom order was repugnant.

Conrad Cordatus had also turned against Melanchthon, violently attacking (1536) his pupil **Cruciger** for the doctrine that Christ is the *causa propter quam*, but that *nostra contritio et noster conatus* are the *causae iustificationis* **sine quibus non** (CR III 350): it was a question of the philologists of Wittenberg, "who prefer to read the dead Erasmus, than to listen to the living Luther" (CR III 159). Melanchthon took up Cruciger's cause; Cordatus now extended his accusations to the revision of the *loci*, and wanted to have the matter decided before the theological faculty; but in this case also Luther played the part of peacemaker, and protected the harassed Melanchthon with his friendship. But the sultriness of a storm of dissent, already present and felt, although it did not as yet lead to an open formation of parties, brooded over Wittenberg: mistrust grew up luxuriantly.

---

[1] Cp. e.g., Melanchthon's complaint of Luther: πολλάκις σημαίνει τὴν παλαιὰν ὀργὴν et haec erumpet (CR III 595).

[2] He had already brought himself unpleasantly into notice in 1537 by his denunciation of Melanchthon to the Electoral Chancellor Brück for conniving at Catholicism.

2. The Controversies after Luther's Death.

Literature (continued); SCHLÜSSELBURG, *Haereticorum inde a temp. Lutheri catalogus.* Frcf. 1597. SPIEKER, *A. Musculus.* Frankf. a. O. 1858. G. L. SCHMIDT, *J. Menius.* II. Gotha, 1867. SEEHAWER, *Zur Lehre vom Gebrauch des Gesetzes und zur Geschichte d. späteren Antinomism.* Rostock, 1887. WILKENS, *Zur Brem. KG* in Brem. Jb. III 42 ff. GERDESIUS, *Hist. motuum ecclesiast. in civitate Brem. temp. Hardenbergii suscitatorum.* Gron. 1756. STROBEL in Beitr. zur Lit. II 109 ff.; W. MÖLLER, *A. Osiander.* Elberf. 1870. C. A. HASE, *Herzog Albrecht und sein Hofpred.* Leipz. 1879. For the Rostock Eucharistic controversy, see J. WIGGERS in ZhTh 18, 613 ff.

After Luther's death, (*a*) the Interim first afforded the opportunity of revealing the difference between the Philippist manner of thought and that familiar in Luther: in the **interimistic or adiaphoristic controversy.** Under pressure of political necessity, Melanchthon had offered his assistance in drawing up the so-called **Leipzig Interim,** in which **Flacius** and his associates saw not only a dangerous blunting of the specifically Protestant doctrine, but also a bargaining with detested papist institutions; in the defence of such usages that were again permitted as *adiaphora* they saw a denial of the duty of a confession of faith. The greater the services these Gnesio-Lutherans had rendered, during the momentous days of the Interim, towards strengthening the faith of the evangelicals by their audacious and defiant pamphlets (p. 158), the more Melanchthon felt the attack, which he had to submit to at the hands of these same men and partly in the same writings. After the conclusion of the struggle, Melanchthon agreed to insert in his *Examen ordinandorum* (1552) an express rejection of the Interim and the recognition of the duty of a confession of faith in reference to the ceremonies (CR XXIII, LXX).

This controversy was immediately connected with (*b*) The **Majoristic** controversy. **George Major** of Wittenberg (died 1574) found himself attacked by **Amsdorf** in 1552 for his assertion of the necessity of good works for salvation; Amsdorf further had the presumption to make the far more objectionable assertion, that they were injurious to salvation: similarly, A. Musculus of Frankfort on the Oder declared, against Abdias (Gottschalk) Praetorius: "they are all of the devil, who teach so: *nova obedientia est necessaria.*" This controversy afforded Melanchthon the opportunity of more closely defining the sense, in which a necessity was spoken of, so that all the meritoriousness of good works is kept at a distance (cp. CR VIII 410 ff). Major gave in in 1558, Praetorius left the March. Justus Menius, whom Amsdorf had drawn into the dispute, in 1556 performed a sort of act of recantation, which however did not satisfy Amsdorf: Menius, in the face of the hostility exhibited towards him, retired to Leipzig, but even here was pursued by the attacks of Flacius and Amsdorf (he died in 1558). In a more limited circle the Majoristic gave rise to a fresh **antinomian** controversy, in which the *tertius usus legis* was discussed, in regard to the question whether in the case of one who was born again the law was still to be regarded as the obligatory norm of the divine will and as the rule of life. In the cause of the rejection of Majorism, individual Gnesio-Lutherans (Poach and Anton. Otho in Nordhausen) disputed any relation of the justified man to the law, since the law produced punishment but not good works, and justified man, illuminated by the spirit, **of himself** does what is good. Others, like Mörlin and Wigand, attacked this doctrine as a suspicious kind of mysticism.

(c) When then, in the Sacramental controversy (that was kindled afresh in 1552) of the Lutherans with Calvin, Peter Martyr, and against the *Consensus Tigurinus*, **Joachim Westphal** of Hamburg accused Melanchthon of an understanding with Calvin, and the latter expressly appealed to Melanchthon, who wrapped himself in silence, the Philippists were accused by the Gnesio-Lutherans as **Crypto-Calvinists** (p. 185). Also, in the violent dispute, which the Bremen preacher, **John Timann**, commenced with his colleague, **A. Hardenberg** (who held the same views as Melanchthon), in regard to the Eucharistic doctrine (in which Timann treated ubiquity as a firmly-established dogma of the Lutherans,[1] and Hardenberg protested against it, in 1548, 1552 and 1555 and subsequently), Melanchthon certainly gave the advice to be prudently evasive (oro, ut multa dissimules CR VIII 736), and the Wittenberg judgment (CR IX 15 ff.) fell back upon biblical phrases, but through the course of the disputes he only strengthened the suspicion that he sided with Calvin.

(d) A **synergistic** controversy (a continuation of the Majoristic) was called forth by the *Propositiones de libero arbitrio*, which **J. Pfeffinger** of Leipzig had composed from Melanchthon's point of view. **Amsdorf** attacked this treatise in 1558, and **Flacius** made use of this dispute in order to attack Melanchthon's Synergismus, especially the definition adopted by him from Erasmus in the edition of the *loci theologici* of 1548: *liberum arbitrium est facultas applicandi se ad gratiam* (CR XXI 659).

(e) Without exciting wider circles, a Eucharistic controversy took place between the Lutheran pastors of Lübeck and Rostock. It was a question of clearing up the Lutheran idea of **consecration:** whether the body and blood of Christ are present before eating and drinking; whether there is need of renewed consecration, on replenishing the elements; where the "moment," the *momentum praesentiae corporis et sanguinis Christi* is to be placed; how the remains of the Lord's Supper are to be treated. In this case, Catholic traditions contended with the evangelical principle: *Extra usum nihil est sacramentum* (de Wette V 777). In vain Chemnitz and Chytraeus endeavoured to reconcile the contending parties; the chief spokesman of the Catholically inclined party, John Saliger, was dismissed from office (1569), but the question in dispute cropped up again several times in the Mecklenburg communities up to the end of the century. Joachim II. drove a clergyman from the country for spilling the consecrated wine and was even inclined to punish him more severely (ZhTh 19, 488 ff.); and Sarcerius advised that the fragments of the holy wafers that had fallen to the ground should *erasa terra comburi* (CR IX 962).[2]

It was natural that **Flacius** and his following should especially gain supremacy, where the Interim had been met with resolute opposition—in Magdeburg, Ernestine Saxony (Weimar, Jena) and North Germany; the new University of Jena in particular, since Flacius had been called thither (1557), became the stronghold of pure Lutheranism. On the other hand, the Philippists dominated Electoral Saxony. Pomerania, Hesse and South Germany still

---

[1] Farrago sententiarum consentientium in vera et cath. doctrina de coena domini. Francof., 1555.

[2] Cp. Luther's angry letter against a clergyman, who had ventured *hostias consecratas ac non consecratas pro eodem habere*. De Wette V 776 f. and the Chronicle of John Oldekop (StBl V 190), p. 225 f., 411.

remained fairly unprejudiced spectators, since, generally speaking, the high reputation of Melanchthon and his writings had not yet been shaken at first by all this.

Apart from these philippistic disputes, stands the extraordinarily embittered **Osiandric** controversy, which disorganised the **Prussian** national church. Andrew Osiander had left Nuremberg on account of the Interim and was received at the court of his old patron Duke Albert of Königsberg. In 1550, he confronted the doctrine of imputative justification (which in fact was frequently put forward very extrinsically and without the religious authority of the Lutheran idea of belief), as being a doctrine colder than ice, with the doctrine of the **essential divine justification,** *i.e.*, the real indwelling of Christ who becomes ours by faith, who makes man really just. He thereby intended mainly to fight for the true Luther against the Philippists, whom he also hated on account of the Interim and their Eucharistic doctrine, but he was obliged to undergo the experience of finding out that Flacius and his party were quite as powerful opponents as Melanchthon. J. Brenz, whose services were requisitioned by the Duke, failed in his attempts at mediation. Osiander died in the autumn of 1552. The controversy continued, but assumed a different character, so that the court preacher **Funck,** the supporter of Osiander, was now able to side with the Philippists; the resentment of the country against the favoured camarilla at last succeeded, with the assistance of Poland, in bringing the hated advisers of the old and feeble Duke to trial. Funck was executed in 1566.

CHAPTER SECOND.

Philippists and Gnesio-Lutherans.

Literature (continued): HOENN, *Hist. d. zu. Naumb. gehalt. Convents*, Frankf., 1704; GELBKE, *der Naumb. Fürstentag.* Leipz. 1793; CALINICH, *D. N. Fürstent.* Gotha 1870; WAGENMANN in RE X 437 ff.; A. KLUCKHOHN, *Friedr. d. Fromme.* Nördl. 1877; KUGLER, *Herz. Christoph.*, 2 vols., Stuttg., 1868-1872. SCHNEIDER in Th. Stud. aus Württ., 1882, 267 ff. WAGENMANN in RE XIV, 793 ff.; WALTE in ZhTh 34. 28 ff.; SPIEGEL, *A. R. Hardenberg.* Brem. 1869 (Brem. Jb IV); ROTTLÄNDER, *Dan. v. Büren*, Gött. 1893; K. MÜLLER in Pr Jb 63, 121 ff.; GILLETT, *Crato v. Crafftheim.*, 2 vols., Frankf. 1860; H. REMBE, *Der. Briefwechsel d. M. C. Spangenberg.* I., Dresd. 1888. WILKENS, *Til. Heshusen*, Leipz. 1860.

The most distinguished Protestant princes felt the dangerous and disturbing character of this theological spirit of disputation, especially after it had broken up the religious Colloquy of Worms (see below) and they endeavoured, in the **Frankfort Recess 1558** (**Wolf**, p. 110 ff.), to calm it by means of a discreet explanation and to work for the maintenance of unity. Owing to an opinion expressed by Melanchthon (CR IX 463 ff.)—the Wurtembergers also had given a similar verdict (**Wolf**, p. 389 ff.)—the idea of settling all disputed points of doctrine by means of a **synod** was abandoned, and Electoral Saxony, Brandenburg, the Palatinate, Wurtemburg, Hesse, Palatine-Zweibrücken and Baden-Durlach, expressly acknowledging the three chief symbols, the CA and the Apologia, agreed upon the following declarations (CR IX 489 ff.), making use of Melanchthon's Essay (CR IX 403 ff.):

(1) Acknowledgment of the *sola fide*, and justification by *iustitia imputata propter Christum*, not on account of the "new life" that had begun; (2) *nova obedientia est necessaria* on account of God's unchangeable order and as the internally necessary consequence:[1] yet the clause *necessaria ad salutem* must not be added, in order to avoid all *meritum*; (3) at the Lord's Supper Christ is present truly, really, and living, and with bread and wine gives his body and blood to be partaken of; transubstantiation, as well as the Zwinglian theory, is rejected; the *manducatio* of unbelievers is passed over in silence; (4) In times of persecution and when the pure doctrine is in danger, Adiaphora cease to be Adiaphora. Measures against "quarrelling and strife" tending to the preservation of peace and unity form the subject of the resolution.

---

[1] Of justification.

But this union was unable to banish the spirit of strife. **John Frederick** *der Mittlere*[1] of Saxony would not accept the Recess (Flacius called it the "Samaritan Interim"), but commissioned his theologians to prepare the **Confutation of Weimar** (1559) directed against all heresies that had recently cropped up, in which everything Philippistic is treated with special irritation. It was at once introduced according to law in the Duchy of Saxony as the norm of instruction. In consequence of this, however, in Jena itself the dispute arose with **Victorinus Strigel**, a pupil of Melanchthon, who in the cause of the Synergistic method of instruction raised objections against the book of Confutation, was subsequently imprisoned and brutally treated, but released after some months. In the course of the Synergistic controversy **Flacius**, in a disputation with Strigel (Weimar, August, 1560)[2] proceeded to the assertion that in consequence of the corruption due to Adam, whereby man was changed into the image of Satan, original sin had become the substance (*substantia formalis*) of fallen human nature. He thereby introduced the germ of dissension into Jena itself, as was soon to become evident. At the **Naumburg Diet of Princes** (1561) summoned by the Elector Augustus, in order to bring about a fresh interpretation of the CA of 1530 (p. 241) to attest the Protestant unanimity in the face of the Council of Trent, a dispute arose upon the question, which copy of it should be subscribed to. The two Electors of the Palatinate and Saxony desired subscription to the edition of 1540, which, while not differing in substance from the first, was composed with greater "clearness and dexterity," while the others insisted upon the earlier copy of 1530.[3] The Ernestine and Rostock theologians expressly issued warnings against Melanchthon's "corruptions" that had made their way into later editions. John Frederick also desired express recognition of the Schmalkaldic articles drawn up by Luther as a common confession of faith: in another quarter the setting up of the Frankfort Recess and the Confessio Saxonica (see above, p. 158) was desired: but there was a unanimous feeling that, besides the CA, only the Apologia should be mentioned. A laborious comparison of the different editions

---

[1] *i.e.*, "the middle," so called to distinguish him from his father and brother.

[2] *Disputatio inter Flac. et Strigel. Vinariae habita;* ed. S. Musaeus. 1562. This contains Flacius's tractate: *Quod homo sit corruptus ac mutatus in primo lapsu non tantum in accidentibus, sed etiam in substantia.* (See further in the *Clavis Scriptur. sacrae* (1567): *De peccati originalis essentia,* see below.

[3] Against this Frederick III. urged, amongst other things, that the Romish doctrine was avowedly not excluded in this in Art. X.

was entered upon, and now for the first time the serious confusion introduced into the text by Melanchthon's continued attempts at emendation was perceived. Finally, it was agreed to subscribe to the edition of 1531, but to designate (in a Preface) that of 1540 as the "more stately and detailed explanation and augmentation" of the original edition,[1] and (out of courtesy to the Elector of the Palatinate), to add a protest against transubstantiation and the mass, with the remark that "the Sacrament nihil esse extra *usum* (Brauch der Niessung.") But now John Frederick and Ulric of Mecklenburg (backed up by the Rostock theologian **David Chytraeus**), to whom an explicit condemnation of the Sacramentarians (*i.e.*, the Philippists at the time) was denied, refused to subscribe : others followed their example: the former secretly left the diet with a protest against the Preface: the work of union was destroyed. The Preface also subsequently met with objections from another quarter (the assembly of the States of the lower Saxon circle at Lüneberg, August, 1561): the **rift** was plain for all to see.

Certain events in the Palatinate, to which John Frederick expressly referred, had influenced this irritation on the Lutheran side. Here, where, since 1533, Frederick II had paved the way for the Reformation with the co-operation of Melanchthon, which Otto Henry had carried through in 1556, choosing Melanchthon's *Examen Ordinandorum* as the foundation of instruction, but the Wurtemburg ritual as the model for divine service, **Tilemann Hesshus**, whom Melanchthon himself had recommended to Heidelberg, commenced a Eucharistic controversy with his deacon William Klebitz. **Frederick III.**, who succeeded Otho in 1559, was obliged to deprive both of their office, in order to secure quiet. Melanchthon,, in an opinion delivered by him (Nov. 1st, 1559, CR IX 960)[2] exhorted the Elector to prevent all useless disputation (including that upon the "monstrous" theory of ubiquity), that the people might not be roused to excitement by them. Frederick thereupon prescribed the simple form of doctrine, that Christ's body was received with the bread. He now also summoned theologians who held Catholic views to Heidelberg, and was rightly regarded as a Crypto-Calvinist. In the face of this movement in the Palatinate, Duke **Christopher** convened a synod at Stuttgart which, under the guidance of

---

[1] In regard to the **wording**, its relation to the Invariata is looked upon as that of the interpretation to the text, not as a recognition of the Melanchthonian type **by the side of** the Lutheran (Heppe, Kluckhohn), but not so that the *variata* should be tolerated (Calinich, Zöckler) as a harmless by-form of the *invariata*, which alone sets the standard. How far the subscribers were clear about the question is another matter. John Frederick's theologians quite correctly recognised the significance of the preface for them; in their eyes the *variata* was only an interpolated private work of Melanchthon.

[2] This characteristically commences, *Non difficile, sed periculosum est respondere*.

Brenz (Dec. 1559), accepted the Lutheran Eucharistic doctrine, including the theory of ubiquity based upon the *communicatio idiomatum*. Melanchthon scoffed at it as "Hechingen Latin" (CR IX 1034), and also issued a warning against the inevitable confusion, but in vain. On April 19th, 1560, he was removed from all earthly strife.

In **Bremen** the Sacramental controversy with A. Hardenberg was continued after Timann's death (1557). By his refusal to subscribe to the CA (even to the *Variata*), as he was pledged to the Scriptures alone, Hardenberg had assumed a readily assailable position and excluded himself from the religious peace; but his acceptance of the Frankfort Recess made him safe again for a time. The controversy was however immediately resumed by T. Hesshus who was summoned to Bremen in 1559; the latter removed in the following year to Magdeburg, but carried on the contest from there until, in 1561, he was removed by the Low Saxon Municipal League, before which the new (evangelical) Archbishop of Bremen, Duke George of Brunswick-Lüneberg had brought the matter, by a resolution of the dietine issued from Bremen, in order to restore tranquillity. (He subsequently found scope for his activity in the community of Emden, which was inclined to reformatory views.) Hesshus, like the strict Lutherans of Jena, belonged to the controversial theologians, who, in the cause of the pure doctrine, imposed upon the clergy as its guardians the duty of excommunicating the adherents of impure doctrine by virtue of the power of the keys. The administration of this ban caused many scandals. Even John Frederick *der Mittlere* found himself compelled to take proceedings against such sovereign authority of the pastors. For Flacius and Musaeus, supported (since 1560) by John Wigand and Judex, now endeavoured, with the assistance of the town clergy, to maintain of their own authority the orthodoxy of their book of Confutation **on the line of ecclesiastical discipline** and thereby to establish a theological authority of conscience. Thus, the distinguished jurist Wesenbeck, for refusing to assent to the Confutation, although he acknowledged the CA, Apologia and Schmalkaldic Articles, was, at their instigation, debarred from acting as sponsor by a clergyman. By similar acts and their violence against V. Strigel the Flacians roused up against themselves a **Lutheran moderate party**, which also represented the government of the Church by the ruler of the country against the autonomous authority of the pastors and thereby obtained influence at Court. John Frederick deprived the clergy of the right of excommunication and transferred the censorship of books to a consistory at Weimar (1561). When the Flacians passionately resisted this procedure as an arbitrary alteration of the constitution of the Church and demanded self-government (*i.e.*, the rule of the pastors), he resolved (December 10th, 1561) to **deprive** Flacius and Wigand **of their office,** together with forty pastors, who refused to acknowledge Strigel's reassuring declarations and the *Declaratio confessionis Strigelii* (1562),[1] drawn up by **James Andreä,** who had been summoned from Wurtemberg. The place of these professors was now taken by Wittenbergers, Stössel, after a few years Selnecker and others. Hesshus also, who finally laid the whole council of Magdeburg under the ban, thereby again brought expulsion upon himself (1562). A similar

---

[1] This *declaratie* is the origin of the dislike of the whole body of Flacians to the "aulicus" Andreä. Cp. the interesting communications of the Flacian Bresnitzer in ZlTh 16, 695 ff.

revulsion took place in Bremen. Here, Musaeus who had been driven from Jena, had been appointed superintendent, and endeavoured to carry through a new ecclesiastical order, intended to secure for pastors the freest use of the ban, in order thereby to be able to meet effectually "the blasphemies of the Sacramentarians." Thus, the Eucharist controversy here produced a conflict with the council about the ban, at which the citizens vigorously espoused the cause of Hardenberg's friend, the burgomaster Daniel von Büren, and prevented his exclusion from the council; Musaeus and a number of preachers were obliged to withdraw, and many members of the council who held the views of Flacius fled from the town. On the 3rd of March, 1568, an arrangement was agreed to at Verden, in accordance with which the fugitives returned and Bremen acknowledged the CA, the Apologia, the Lutheran Catechism, the Church Order, and the **Frankfort Recess.**

In Wittenberg and the whole of Electoral Saxony the Philippistic was the prevailing direction of thought; the Elector Augustus, Maurice's successor, considering Melanchthon's close intimacy with Luther, felt confident of preserving the genuine Lutheranism. In fact, Melanchthon's writings, his academical activity and his participation in the most momentous religious negotiations had been of fundamental importance; he had formed and trained the Protestant clergy—even his subsequent opponents. Immediately after his death the **Corpus doctrinae Christianae** (Leipzig, 1560), appeared, which, besides the three old symbols, contained writings composed only by Melanchthon, the CA, the Apologia (both editions 1542), the Confessio Saxonica, the Loci theologici (recension of 1556), the Examen ordinandorum and Responsiones ad impios articulos Bavariae inquisitionis (see below). The Leipzig consistory secured the introduction of this **Misnicum** or **Philippicum Corpus** as a confession of doctrine in all the churches. In opposition to this, other churches now drew up strictly Lutheran Corpora doctrinae, and numerous **separate collections of Confessions** were the result. In this case it was a principle, to accept only **Lutheran** writings besides the oecumenical symbols and the CA together with the Apologia but in a varied selection, extracts from his polemical writings and the like being admitted in addition to both Catechisms and the Schmalkaldic articles. Amongst these Corpora may be mentioned those of the city of Brunswick (1563), Prussia (1567), Brunswick-Wolfenbüttel (1569, in which first occurs the selection which subsequently reappears in the Book of Concord, and 1576, Corpus Julium), the Duchy of Saxony (1570), Brandenburg (1572), Brunswick-Lüneburg (Corpus Wilhelminum, 1576).[1]

---

[1] For Nuremberg and the Margraviate of Brandenburg, which Luther and Melanchthon endeavoured to unite in their "Standard books," see STROBEL, *Beitr. zur Lit.* I 263 ff.

Melanchthon's son-in-law, **Caspar Peucer**, physician in ordinary to the Elector, exercised considerable influence upon his master. The Philippists were impregnated with the idea that their conception of things, which was in fact essentially that of Melanchthon himself, was justified within the limits of the German Reformation, and that no innovation ought now to be introduced, although the younger generation naturally fell more and more decidedly under the influence of Calvinistic theology; but they also concealed the fact that, in regard to the Eucharistic doctrine and Christology, they found themselves by no means in agreement with Zwingli, but essentially so with Calvin. To the Elector they represented themselves as Lutherans, who only guarded themselves against extremes (the doctrines of Flacius and the theory of omnipresence), and this did not escape the reproach of underhandedness from the side of the Calvinists. To the middle of the sixties they were at the height of their reputation. But a rapid and complete change took place, originating at first in the Duchy of Saxony. John Frederick *der Mittlere*, relying implicitly upon the revelations of a visionary and hoping, with the aid of French gold, to be able to recover the lands that had been lost to the Ernestine house and the electoral dignity, allowed himself to be drawn (in 1563) by the restless Frankish nobleman **William of Grumbach** into his seditious enterprises against the Bishop of Würzburg[1] (who had confiscated Grumbach's property) and then afforded protection to the outlaw. At length, the Emperor Maximilian, on the 12th of December, 1566, proscribed Frederick; the Elector Augustus, who was charged to carry out the sentence, besieged him and Grumbach at Gotha; a mutiny of his troops compelled capitulation, after which Grumbach, Chancellor Brück (the younger) and the Duke's prophet were executed (quartered): John Frederick was declared to have forfeited his authority and sentenced to imprisonment for life (1567). He was succeeded by his brother **John William**, who, although on friendly terms with the Elector Augustus, again threw open Jena to the strictly Lutheran theologians Wigand, Coelestinus, Tim. Kirchner, and Til. Hesshus (but not Flacius). This occasioned a colloquy between the Electoral Saxony and Ernestine theologians at Altenburg (the autumn of 1568 to the spring of 1569),[2] which, however, only further embittered the opposing parties and at first strengthened the authority of the Philippists in Electoral Saxony. The Elector required from all the clergy an engagement to adhere to the Corpus Philippicum and expressly reject Flacianism. **Flacius**, undoubtedly the most important of the "Gnesio-Lutherans," had in the meantime brought forward in detail his doctrine of original sin (see above p. 284) as one of high importance and thereby introduced discord into his own camp, since only a few such as Cyriacus Spangenberg of Mansfeld, later in Austria, Chr. Irenaeus, court preacher at Weimar) agreed with him, while the majority (such as Wigand, Hesshus, Conrad Schlüsselburg) became his bitter opponents and fought against his doctrine as a new Manichaeism.

---

[1] These adventurous schemes had been projected since 1557.
[2] The Acts of the Colloquy: Jena 1570; Wittb. 1570; Lips. 1870.

CHAPTER THIRD.

The Work of Concord.

Literature (continued): R. HOSPINIANUS, *Conc. disc.* Tig. 1607; in *Opp.* t. V; L. HUTTER, *Conc. concors.* Vit. 1614; HEPPE and FRANK above p. 276; UN 1718, 188 ff.; Dän. Bibl. IV 212 ff., V 355 ff., VIII 334 ff., IX 1 ff.; TH. PRESSEL in ZhTh 37, 3 ff., 268 ff., 445 ff., 473 ff.; the same in Jd Th 22, 1 ff., 207 ff. For the writings of the Flacianists against Andreä see M. VOLMAR, *Vom neuen Samarit. Interim D. Jac. Andreä* 1578. SCHAFF I 258 ff.; JOHANNSEN in ZhTh 17, 1 ff.; 20, 368 ff.; 23, 344 ff.; 31, 461 ff.; BESTE, *Gesch. d. Braunschw. Landes-Kirche.* Wolfb. 1889; CALINICH, *Kampf und Untergang des Melanchthonianismus in Kursachsen* 1570-1574. Leipz. 1866: KLUCKHOHN in HZ 18, 77 ff.; PEUCER, *Hist. Carcerum.*, Tig. 1604. HACHFELD in ZhTh 36, 230 ff.; PRESSEL in JdTh 11, 640 ff.; J. H. BALTHASAR, *Hist. d. Torg. Buchs.* 1741-1756; HEPPE, *Der Text d. Berg. Conc.-F.* Marb. 1857; the same in ZhTh 22, 283 ff.; 27, 465 ff.; LENTZ in ZhTh 18, 265 ff.; H. G. HASSE in ZhTh 18, 315 ff.; RICHARD, *Der kurf. sächs. Kanzler Krell.* 2 vols. Dresd. 1859; F. BRANDES, *Der Kanzler Krell.* Leipz. 1873.

1. The First Attempt and the Overthrow of the Philippists in Saxony.

Wurtemberg, where Duke Christopher had a warm interest in the restoration of harmony, now became the head-quarters of repeated efforts, to find ways and means for this purpose. **James Andreä** in particular, chancellor of the University of Tübingen (the son of a smith, hence called also Schmidlein, Schmidjakob), took this upon him as the task of his life. **Julius,** Duke of Brunswick, whose theologians (M. Chemnitz and Nic. Selnecker) represented a more moderate doctrine of omnipresence (*omnivolipraesentia*)[1] than the Wurtembergers, when Andreä (in 1568, and again in 1569) assisted him in the re-establishment of his national church, as well as William Landgrave of Hesse (eldest son of Landgrave Philip, who died in 1567), showed themselves favourably disposed to the plan. After 1569, Andreä approached the Wittenbergers with his proposals,

---

[1] An *omnipraesentia voluntaria et potentialis*, not *naturalis vel essentialis*, of the body of Christ. Compare, in addition to the loci theologici of Chemnitz, his tractate *De duabus naturis in Christo* (1570).

without sacrificing the doctrine of omnipresence, which he himself had defended at the Maulbronn Colloquy (see below) against the "reformatory" inhabitants of the Palatinate. If only an agreement could be come to with the latter, it was bound to be of the greatest importance for the whole of Lutheran Germany, as some of the national churches (Pomerania, Hesse) had hitherto taken no part in the dogmatic controversies) and the clergy everywhere were still under the continuously operating influence of the Melanchthonian dogmatic writings, so that it appeared possible to put a check upon the advance of the exclusive Lutheranism, which was zealously supported, not only in Jena, but also in Lower Saxony and partly in Brandenburg (Musculus). The people of Jena immediately declared against Andreä's proposals, since they missed the explicit condemnation of the heretics; at Wittenberg, offence was taken at the doctrine of omnipresence and the recognition of the Corpus Philippicum was also demanded. The proceedings of the **Convention of Zerbst**, May, 1570, turned especially upon the latter point, all Andreä's dexterity was unable to prevent the laboriously attained result of this meeting being immediately rendered useless, when, on his own authority, he published the Recess of Zerbst. Landgrave William, disappointed, refused to have anything further to do with the matter.

When the Wittenbergers were accused before the Elector by Duke Julius in consequence of their rejection of the doctrine of omnipresence, on the occasion of a disputation at Wittenberg, for which the younger Cruciger had composed theses written in a vigorously polemical tone against the Christology of the Wurtembergers),[1] they endeavoured to justify themselves in the cautiously worded "brief, plain and simple confession" (July 31st, 1570). In the following year Peucer and Pezel came forward more boldly in the Wittenberg Catechism (*Catechesis . . . . contexta ex Corpore doctr . . . . accommodata ad usum scholar. pueril.*),[2] and with the doctrine of Christ's body locally circumscribed in heaven excited the violent opposition of the Lutherans, to which they retaliated with a vigorous defence (the so-called "Wittenberg foundation").[3] The Elector Augustus, who had become suspicious was again tranquillised by the so-called *Consensus Dresdensis* (October, 1571). For when the Heidelberg theologians declared that it was indeed **their** doctrine, **Stössel** backed out of it so cleverly,

---

[1] See the defiant thesis (No. 30) in Heppe, *Gesch. d. Prot.* II 312.

[2] It was intended to form the intermediate stage of instruction between Luther's small Catechism and the Loci theologici at schools and colleges.

[3] Von der Person und Menschwerdung unseres HErrn J. Chr. Der wahren Christl. Kirchen Grundfest wider die newen Marcioniten [Of the Person and Incarnation of our Lord Jesus Christ. The foundation of the true Christian Church against the new Marcionites] Wittenb., 1571.

that he again convinced the Elector of the disagreement of his theologians with the Calvinists; but in this dishonourable game ruin was preparing. After Duke John William's death, when Augustus received the tutelary government of Ernestine Saxony, the zealots **Wigand** and **Hesshus** were banished (1573), and many of the clergy who belonged to their party were obliged to withdraw. In 1574, the *Exegesis perpetua controversiae de coena domini* (German version, Heidelberg, 1575; reprint by Scheffer, Marburg, 1853)[1] appeared anonymously in 1574 at Leipzig (Vögelin) but with a Genevese imprint; its author was the physician John Cureus (died 1573) of Glogau, who, like the imperial physician in ordinary, Crato von Crafftheim of Breslau had zealously promoted the spread of Philippism in Silesia. Here, the Melanchthonio-Calvinistic doctrine of the Eucharist was openly expressed, the *manducatio oralis* and the partaking of the body of Christ on the part of unbelievers rejected. Although the Wittenbergers had nothing to do with this treatise, different Lutheran princes now assailed the Elector: a confidential letter from Stössel to Schütz, which, treacherously given up, was handed to the Elector, opened the eyes of the latter, and brought about the "great and divine marvel" that, terribly enraged at the attempt to misuse his influence for the purpose of smuggling in Calvinism, he caused the chiefs of the Philippist party to be imprisoned: Peucer (till 1586), the privy councillor Cracow, against whom even the torture was used (HZ 18, 81.110 ff.), the court preacher Stössel (both died in prison) and Schütz. The party (that had long been in existence) of the theologically inclined Electress and the Dresden court preacher, supported by the dislike of the country to Cracow who represented princely absolutism in opposition to the cities, now triumphed. The articles that were immediately drawn up at the diet of Torgau (May 1574) adhered to the supposition that Luther and Melanchthon were agreed, and hence to the *Corpus Philippicum* and the *Consensus Dresdensis*. It was assumed that Lutheranism had always been taught in the country and as if, now, only a few Crypto-Calvinists had been discovered: if the theory of omnipresence also was rejected, on the other hand, Luther's conception of the Eucharist was represented with explicit rejection of Calvinism. The successful overthrow of unmasked Calvinism was celebrated by a solemn thanksgiving service and a commemorative medal. Theologians and clergy were obliged to subscribe, those who refused subscription were banished. Widebram and Pezel betook themselves to Nassau, the younger Cruciger to Hesse. (From this time onwards we can observe how these Philippists followed Calvin's theology also in the doctrine of predestination).[2]

2. The Concord.

Although the overthrow of Philippism, as the rejection of the theory of omnipresence shows, certainly did not yet satisfy the strictly Lutheran claims, yet it ushered in the victory of rigid Lutheranism, while indicating to the Wurtemberg efforts for agreement the tendency, which finally prevailed in the Formula of Concord: the tendency to a decided exclusion of Philippism.

---

[1] Cp. HEPPE, *Gesch.* II 467 ff. for the author and tendency of the exegesis.
[2] Cp. GILLET II 239.

From his six sermons on the errors of doctrine that had made their appearance since 1548,[1] which he had sent to Duke Julius, M. Chemnitz of Brunswick, Chytraeus of Rostock, and others (1573), Andreä, at the request of the latter, prepared an Epitome of dogmatic statements, which he completed in the so-called **Book of Tübingen** or the **Swabian Concord** (1574).[2] The insertion of the exhaustive discussions which had taken place in the Lower Saxon consultations (especially the Lord's Supper and Free Will) under **Chemnitz's** direction originated the comprehensive **Swabio-Saxon Concord**,[3] in which Andreä could find nothing to criticise as far as the substance of the doctrine put forth was concerned, but blamed the prolixity of the theological discussions, the repetitions and introduction of dogmatic termini. Since, further, difficulties had been raised in various national churches (Brandenberg, Prussia), the support of which had been reckoned upon, the work appeared to be again at a standstill. Meanwhile, at the instigation of the Elector Augustus and through the mediation of Count George Ernest of Henneberg, Louis Duke of Wurtemberg and Charles Margrave of Baden were induced to have a "formula of Concord" drawn up by theologians from Wurtemberg (the court preacher Luc. Osiander and Provost B. Bidembach), Baden and Henneberg, which was subscribed by the latter on the 19th of January, 1576, at the monastery of Maulbronn. This **Maulbronn Formula** (JdTh 11, 640 ff.), which, while practically agreeing in the norm and substance of its doctrine, followed a different arrangement (adhering to the CA), like the Swabio-Saxon Concord, was communicated to the Elector **Augustus,** who now caused further steps to be taken. A meeting of his theologians at **Lichtenberg** (February, 1576) was prepared, by a majority of votes, to drop the Corpus Philippicum in favour of a formula of Concord to be drawn up and a book of Concord. Andreä, summoned to Electoral Saxony, now set to work at the **Torgau Convention** (May 28th to June 7th, 1576), in co-operation with the theologians of the Electorate (especially Selnecker), with Chemnitz and Chytraeus, besides the theologians of the Electorate of Brandenburg, the general-superintendent A. Musculus and Professor Christopher Körner (Cornerus) of Frankfort-on-the-Oder. The Swabio-Saxon Concord was taken as the foundation, but subjected to considerable revision (the honourable mention of Melanchthon disappeared!) and in addition some peculiar features of the Maulbronn formula were admitted. This was the origin of the **Book of Torgau,** which was then sent to the different evangelical States for their opinion and approval. The answers received were of a very different nature. On the one side (the Brunswickers and the Lübeckers assembled at the Mölln Convention, the Hamburgers and Lüneburgers) explicit condemnation of the errors of Philippism was demanded—Hesshus and Wigand (now in Prussia) even required **special** condemnation of all heretics **by name,** Melanchthon as well as Flacius—on the other hand greater gentleness was demanded in dealing with the Philippistic method of teaching; Pomerania, Anhalt and Magdeburg protested more or less vigorously against the attempt "to tear Luther and Philip asunder" (in the words of Joachim Ernest of Anhalt).

[1] Printed in HEPPE III, *Beilage* p. 1-75.
[2] ZhTh 36, 230 ff.
[3] HEPPE III, *Beil.* p. 166-325.

With due regard to these criticisms, the final revision was carried out at the **Monastery of Bergen** near Madgeburg (March-May 1577) by Andreä, Chemnitz and Selnecker, assisted by Chytraeus, Cornerus and Musculus: the result was **The Book of Bergen**. This is the *solida declaratio* of the Formula of Concord. At the same time, the theologians revised the brief abstract (the Epitome) that had been prepared in the meantime by Andreä from the Torgau Book, and approved it. The Book of Bergen eliminated still more decidedly the traces of the Melanchthonian teaching which had still lingered in the Swabio-Saxon Concordia and even in the Torgau Book as a reminder of the fact that Chemnitz, Selnecker and Chytraeus themselves had come from Melanchthon's school; they had also nearly admitted Synergistic views and at least Selnecker and Chemnitz represent the halfway view of the omnipresence of Christ. But the result of continuous development along the dogmatic path entered upon with the essential co-operation of Melanchthon now gave the preponderance to the strictly Lutheran conception, although the doctrine of omnipresence was not expressed unhesitatingly in the absolute sense in which it was understood by the Wurtembergers. At Bergen, the demand for a **general synod** with a view to a final decision was agreed to, but anything of the kind still appeared too dangerous to the promoters of the work; they accordingly countermanded the proposed synod (May 28th, 1577), preferring to collect the signatures of the States first, after which a synod would no longer cause discord. Accordingly, in June, 1577, the work of collecting signatures, carried on hastily and with all kinds of artifices of suppression, commenced under the direction of Andreä, Selnecker and Polyc. Leyser, at first in Electoral Saxony. At the same time the Electors of Saxony and Brandenburg sent copies of the Book of Bergen to the States, whose assent was hoped for.

Those who were more closely allied to the reformed party in vain attempted to prevent the "Concord," which was bound to make the split final. In the Palatinate, after the death of Frederick III in 1576, Lutheranism was restored by Louis VI. However, out of regard for his brother, the Count Palatine John Casimir, who steadfastly adhered to the reformed Confession, and the reformed Convention of Frankfort (Sept. 1577), he expressed a wish for some slight modifications, in order to be able to assent to the "Concord." But, as the book had already been accepted in many German territories (Saxony, Brandenburg, Brunswick, Lüneberg, Mecklenburg, Wurtemberg, the Lower Saxon cities and others), it was now only through the **Preface** (which, after the fruitless Convention at Tangermünde, having been resolved upon at that of **Schmalkalden**

(1578), drawn up by Andreä and put forward at Jüterbogk, was finally accepted by Louis, after manifold discussions and revisions, that allowance could be made for his scruples to a certain extent.[1] A second Preface "*Bericht der Theologen auf etliche fürgewendete Bedenken*" (printed in JdTh 11, 711 ff.) was entirely set aside on Louis's protest. In the meantime, at the Convention of Cassel, 1579, the Melanchthonians (Hesse, Anhalt, Nuremberg) combined in a closer union, in order to offer resistance to the pressing advance of exclusive Lutheranism, and protested both against the tenor of the Formula of Concord and the manner of its establishment. (For the declaration of the people of Anhalt see Niemeyer, p. 612 ff.)

Fifty years after the delivery of the CA, on the 25th of June, 1580, **the Book of Concord**, *i.e.*, the **Corpus of the Lutheran Confessional Symbols** (now completed by the Formula of Concord) in which they had already been printed since 1578, was published at Dresden, at first only in the **German** language.

After L. Osiander (1580) and Selnecker (1582) had made Latin translations, the one which was finally settled at a convention held under Chemnitz at Quedlinburg became the officially recognised Latin text of the Formula of Concord (Leipzig, 1584). The selection of the confessional writings here combined is that which was first made in 1569 by Chemnitz and Andreä in the Corpus doctrinae for Brunswick-Wolfenbüttel. Andreä, denounced by his personally-mortified co-operator Selnecker to the Elector Augustus, was finally dismissed in disgrace. It was a splendid success, this Concordia signed by 86 evangelical imperial States (51 Princes and Lords, amongst them three Electors [Saxony, Brandenburg, Palatinate] and 35 cities) and about 8,000-9,000 theologians; as little can the high dogmatic importance of this fundamental work be contested, which shrewdly drew conclusions in the direction of Lutheranism formerly taken by the sons and descendants of the Reformation, and at the same time by means of dialectic distinctions steered between the cliffs openly as errors of recognised positions. Just as, in the dogmatic contests of the old Church, a formula in itself completely free from inconsistency was never really attained to, but only a combination of postulates opposed to each other as equally

---

[1] The Palatine saw his more important demands (recognition of the Naumburg Resolutions and the writings of Melanchthon, the removal of the "Damnamus") only partly carried through. The expression "invariata" was struck out and only a prima and altera editio were spoken of; now at least Melanchthon's scripta utilia were mentioned; Damnamus was struck out and Rejicimus deemed sufficient. Cp. the text of the Praefatio ZhTh 37, 304 ff. and in the Libr. symb.

recognised as essential, to the exclusion of the contrasted one-sided views, the same was the case in the Formula of Concord.

Thus in Art. I and II both Synergists and Flacians, in Art. IV both Major's and Amsdorf's theses are rejected: in Art. X, in regard to the question of predestination, the universalism of God's will to save mankind, at the same time predestination as the ground of eternal happiness, and unbelief as the ground of condemnation, are affirmed, without an arrangement of the difficulties being arrived at. In regard to the Eucharistic doctrine, the statements hesitate between the absolute omnipresence[1] of Luther and Andreä and the Multivolipraesentia of Chemnitz.[2] But the drawbacks of this achievement are also great. According to it, the Reformation was the purification of the **doctrine** *de praecipuis Christianae religionis formulis;* the propagation and defence of this *formula purioris doctrinae* is the chief duty of the Lutheran Church; it is the doctrine in which *boni omnes* agree, although there are pious men in other churches, who are without knowing it members of the true Church, since in their simplicity *negotium ipsum non probe intelligunt.* Evangelium **doctrina** *est quae docet,* **quid** *peccator* **credere debeat,** *ut remissionem peccatorum apud Deum obtineat* (714, 20): this theory most clearly shows the alteration, which had taken place in Luther's doctrine of belief. The juristico-dogmatic trend of Protestantism was sealed or attained the ascendency: a new scholastic system of dogma overgrew the old simple evangelical confession of the community: a period of prosperity was introduced, but one of momentous importance for the Church of the theologians.

Protestantism was now definitely split up: even Calvinism was opposed to it as a foreign confession of faith, a hostile antagonistic principle. Melanchthonianism, which might have formed a connecting link, was expelled and in great part driven over to Calvinism. Certainly, its expulsion was not universal. A great part of the clergy persisted in thankful remembrance of their teacher Melanchthon; but certainly the one-sided and blunter, though more vigorous and defined spirit of the Lutheranism of the Formula of Concord now obtained (after the manner of extreme trends of thought) the upper hand, as far as the authorities assisted to spread it. But yet all the national churches of the Reformation were not really united under this formula. A still considerable number refused to accept it without renouncing their character as belonging to the Lutheran Churches.

In **Schleswig-Holstein,** it was especially the influence of Paul von Eitzen, Superintendent of Gottorp, who was on friendly terms with Melanchthon, combined with the character of the country which was less accessible to dogmatic

---

[1] 784, 81: **omnia** *plena sunt Christi iuxta humanitatem.*

[2] 768, 29: *homo Christus* **iuxta verba testamenti sui** *corpore et sanguine suo in sacra coena praesens esse* **potest** *et revera est.*

strife, which had this success; similarly, in the Hadersleben dominion, Provost Petraeus.[1] Frederick II. of Denmark also rejected the Concord and forbade the Formula in his country; he even threw the latter with his own hands into the fire (ZhTh 20, 662). In **Hesse** the strict Lutheran Upper Hessians stood opposed to the Lower Hessians who were averse to the Formula. The latter (Landgrave William)[2] finally succeeded in getting the four Landgraves to refuse their assent to it: Pomerania, Anhalt, Palatine-Zweibrücken did the same; Silesia took no part in the negotiations, owing to its relation to the Emperor. In 1573, Nuremberg, together with the Margrave of Anspach, had drawn up an essentially Philippistic Corpus doctrinae, and in 1576 founded the University of Altdorf, at which the same spirit prevailed. Thus the Formula of Concord was also rejected. The same thing happened in Frankfort on the Main, Spires, Worms, the city of Magdeburg (the archiep. clergy under Brandenburg administration were obliged to subscribe), Nordhausen and Strasburg, owing to its connection with the Swiss (violent controversy of the theologian John Pappus with the Philippist Rector John Sturm—it was not until 1597 that the strictly Lutheran party and with it the FC gained the day. But the most striking thing was, that one of the chief promoters of the work of Concord, Julius Duke of Brunswick, now refused to have anything to do with it—for a very ignoble reason.[3] He was angry with Chemnitz, since the latter had stoutly protested on the other hand, that the Lutheran prince was endeavouring to secure for his son Henry Julius papal confirmation and enthronisation as Bishop of Halberstadt, and caused the two other princes to be shaven, in order to obtain canonical offices for them, a course of procedure running directly contrary to the doctrine of the Formula of Concord *de adiaphoris :* but Hesshus, who was now his theologian, could not tolerate Chemnitz. Brunswick accordingly returned simply to his Corpus Julium. The effect of this state of affairs was, that the University of **Helmstedt** was able to become the home of an independent and original theology. The opponents of the Formula of Concord were apprehensive that Saxony or Wurtemberg would now do their utmost with the Emperor to get the Formula of Concord authorised **by order of the Empire**, but this idea, in spite of the inclination for it, was not realised. (See von Bezold, Briefe des Pfalzgrafen Johann Casimir I 561.)

3. The Downfall of Crypto-Calvinism in Saxony.

Nor were dogmatic controversies ended by the Formula of Concord. At first strife broke out over the Formula itself. Numerous rejoinders appeared: by Ambrose Wolf [i.e., Christopher Herdessianus of Nuremberg] at Neustadt on the Haardt, a " History of the Augsburg Confession"; the "Neustadt admonition" of the Count-Palatine's theologian John Casimir (Ursinus, 1581), polemical writings of the theologians of Bremen and Anhalt; on the other side it was

---

[1] The Formula of Concord was not recognised as a symbolical book in the regal part of the country until 1647, in the grand-ducal until 1734, but, after 1784, was once more bound to the Invariata.

[2] Cp. his characteristic letter to Coelestin on the "Great Book of Discord and Dilaceratio Ecclesiarum " in STROBEL, *Beitr. zur Lit.* II 162.

[3] Cp. also, however, the account in HUMMEL, *Epp. semicenturia*, p. 84 f. The city of Brunswick on the other hand accepted the Formula of Concord.

attacked by the Flacian Irenaeus (*Examen libri concordiae*). This caused the three Electors to get rejoinders written by Kirchner, Selnecker and Chemnitz, as to which, with the assistance of several States, an agreement was come to at Erfurt in 1581 and then in Brunswick. Thus, amongst other writings, the "Erfurt Apology" (Magd., 1582) and the "True History of the Augsburg Confession" (against A. Wolff, Leipz., 1584). The former, with its description of omnipresence, gave fresh occasion for a controversy with Hesshus and led to violent discussions in the Colloquy of Quedlinburg (1582).

And, in spite of the Formula of Concord, the spirit of Philippism was destined to come to life once again, although very late in the day, in Electoral Saxony. Augustus thought that he had now brought complete tranquillity into churches and schools; but after his death (1586) things changed. Christian I., educated by the court preacher Schütz, was averse to such exclusiveness, and, besides this, had closer relations with his brother-in-law, John Casimir the Count-Palatine. With the eye of the statesman, he saw in the Formula of Concord a hindrance to the invigoration of Protestantism. At his side stood the capable lawyer **Nic. Krell**, whom the Elector Augustus had given him as counsellor and whom he now raised to the Chancellorship, not the originator of the feeling of opposition already existing at the Court against the Formula of Concord, but only its organ.

On the ground of a Confession proposed by the latter, he was excused signing the Formula of Concord. In 1588, Krell caused a mandate to be renewed, which Augustus had formerly issued in 1566, forbidding unnecessary quarrelling amongst preachers. Some zealots lost their position, e.g., the court preacher Mirus, who had attacked the Elector in the pulpit: and no attempt was made to stop Polyc. Leyser, when he received a call to Brunswick. The seceders were replaced by those who held the views of the Philippists. An annotated Bible, brought out by the court preacher Salmuth and Urban Pierius at the expense of the Elector (only finished as far as Chronicles II.) purposely combated the theory of omnipresence in the notes; an edition of the small Catechism, which explained it only by passages of the Bible, came equally under the suspicion of favouring Calvinistic views. The abolition of exorcism in Baptism which was ordered in 1591 aroused the passions of the people.[1] Christian himself had one of his children baptised without it. Although all the consistories had proposed this omission and the majority of the pastors had agreed (at the wish of the communities as was pretended), yet the carrying through of this measure stirred up the people to an extraordinary extent. Then, Christian died on the 25th of September, 1591, and Duke Frederick William of the Ernestine line was appointed guardian of the minor Christian II.; his influence and that of the widowed Electress Sophia brought on the reaction. Krell had the nobility against him in consequence of

---

[1] Further, the second edition of the Book of Concord, out of consideration for Louis, Elector of the Palatinate, had been obliged to omit Luther's "Little Book of Baptism." Cp. ZhTh 37, 594 ff.

the limitation of hunting privileges. Krell, Salmuth and others were imprisoned. Four *articuli visitatorii*[1] were now drawn up against Philippism with sharply-defined antitheses against the reformed party and, at a church visitation held by Hunnius, Mirus, Selnecker and Mylius, were laid before all the clergy and also the professors and patrons for subscription: those who refused to sign were deprived of office and driven from the country (amongst them seven Wittenberg and eight Leipzig professors); the Ramistic and anti-Aristotelian philosophy was forbidden as the promoter of Calvinism. The people were so irritated against actual or supposed Calvinists, and such passionate outbreaks occurred, that, in 1592, the administrator was obliged to issue a mandate against the irritation of the people by the preachers. In the long dragged out suit against Krell, in addition to the charge that he had endeavoured to seduce the Elector to Calvinism, it was also suggested that he had advised a connection with France to the Emperor's prejudice. (Christian, like other princes, had supported Henry IV. of Navarre in his struggles for the French crown). This point was destined to make an impression at the imperial Court. For it was in the interest of Austria to prevent the introduction of reformatory ideas into Germany, as it denoted a strengthening of the French Huguenot party, whereas strict Lutheranism was more accessible to the imperial policy. Evading the Imperial Chamber, the Emperor charged the Court of Appeal at Prague with the sentence, which said nothing about the point of religion, but condemned him to death for his "intrigues with a foreign power." Krell protested in vain; the clergymen, who visited the prisoner, did their utmost to elicit from him a confession of sin before God as an admission of his guilt before an earthly judge. He was beheaded on the 9th of October, 1601.

The good Lutheran watch-word of that time, "Rather Catholic than Calvinist,"[2] throws a lurid light upon the mutual hostility which divided the ranks of the Evangelicals: but it must not be forgotten that the policy by which Calvinism had crept into Lutheran Churches and the haughtiness with which it looked down upon the Lutherans as persons who had stuck fast in the slough of Popery were in great measure to blame for this irritation. In addition to this, a **political** antipathy became more and more combined with dogmatic dissent. The Calvinists were regarded by the Lutherans as the foes of political order; the struggles of the French as well as the Dutch Calvinists were, in the eyes of their opponents, a rebellion against the authority of the State,—a revolt hostile to God.[3]

[1] See *Corpus iuris eccl. Sax.*, Dresd., 1773, p. 256, in HASE, *Ausgabe der symb. Bücher*, p. 862 ff. SCHAFF I 345 ff.

[2] See e.g. in VON BEZOLD, *Briefe des Pfalzgrafen Joh. Casimir* II 207. *Hostilioribus animis persequuntur Calvinistas quam Pontificios*, writes Rehdiger, 1575, GILLET II 87. See a truly frightful description of a Calvinist from the pen of a Lutheran in GILLET II 397 f. In 1564, at Oettingen, a pastor suspected of Calvinism was asked by the Lutheran Consistory, "whether he believed that the Calvinists were saved," ZfTh 16, 707. See a travesty of the 2nd Psalm in ridicule of the Calvinists in STROBEL, *Neue Beiträge* V 401.

[3] Cp. Andreä in HUTTER, *Concordia concors*, 1614, Fol. 151.

CHAPTER FOURTH.

The Advance of Calvinism in Germany.[1]

Philippism, which at first was akin to Calvinism only in the Eucharistic doctrine, while in other respects further removed from it than the strict Lutheranism which repelled it, found itself more and more compelled, by the need of connection with some other party, to go over to the camp of the Calvinists: owing to its greater weakness and indefiniteness in the matter of dogma it showed itself accessible to the further influence of Calvinism in the matter of dogma. A number of Lutheran established churches completed their desertion to Calvinism, which, however, they looked upon not as a change of confession, but only as a more consistent carrying-out,—a completion of Luther's Reformation. They considered themselves, both before and after, as kinsmen of the CA, but, in spite of the fact that they appealed by preference to Luther, were regarded by the Lutherans as Calvinists, since as a matter of fact Calvin, and especially Bullinger, also theologically exercise the strongest influence upon them. In Germany, in regard to the constitution of the Church, the (Lutheran) established churchdom operated subsequently with the influence of the authori-

---

[1] The name "Reformed" was not developed until the period subsequent to the Formula of Concord. In the latter (633, 5 and often) the *Romanenses* are contrasted simply with *reformatae nostrae ecclesiae;* the Knights of Anhalt, as late as 1598, by the words "our reformed Church" indicate the Lutheran character of the same. At first, "Lutherans," in the mouth of Romish opponents, was the usual name for all supporters of the Reformation, not a sharply defined denotation of a confession of faith. After Calvinism was introduced into the Palatinate, the terms used were Lutherani and Calvinistae, that is to say Helvetii,—in a polemical spirit, theologi ubiquitatis or Pseudo-lutherani on the one hand, and Sacramentarians on the other. But now, the Calvinists readily denoted their remodelling of the **Lutheran** Church-system as *reformare ecclesias* (GILLET II 51) and boasted of their "true **really reformed** religion" in contrast to that of the Lutherans (GILLET II 422). It was not until the name turned its point **against Lutheranism,** that it became the name of a separate confession of faith. (Cp. also HEPPE, *Urspr. u. Gesch. d. Bezeichnung ref. und luth. Conf.* 1859.)

ties upon the administration of the Church, and hence the Calvinistic church-constitution only obtained a feeble influence and the theocratic character of Calvinism did not attain development: from this cause these ecclesiastical bodies formed **an intermediate stage** between pure Calvinism and pure Lutheranism.

Immediately after Melanchthon's death, Calvin's spirit carried on an increasingly perceptible propaganda in Germany: as early as 1561 the acute Canisius wrote to Hosius: *Calvinus Lutherum suppressurus videtur non solum in Gallia, sed etiam in Germania*.[1] The University of Geneva exercised increasing power of attraction. The fact that in that city a far stricter discipline prevailed than in the German colleges, came to be regarded by earnest minds as a by no means contemptible recommendation of Calvinism itself.[2] In addition, it will be observed that Calvinism found a soil, chiefly and at first, in that part of Germany which was most developed in the matter of culture, namely, the West; its propaganda in the East was limited preponderatingly to definite strata of the higher classes (court circles, higher officialdom, the Humanists), to which it partly forced its way together with the preference shown for the French language and to which it recommended itself as something finer and imported in contrast to the coarser Lutheranism.

1. The Electoral Palatinate.

Literature: ALTING, *Hist. eccl. Palatinae in* MIEG, *Monumenta pietatis et literaria.* Fref. 1701. STRUVE, *Pfältz. KHistorie.* Frkf. 1721. VIERORDT, *Gesch. d. Ref. in Baden.* Karlsr. 1847, p. 457 ff. A. KLUCKHOHN (see above, p. 283); the same, *Briefe Friedr. d. Fr.* 2 vols. Braunschw. 1868-1872. FALK in JGG X 47 ff., XII 37 ff. SUDHOFF, *Olevian und Ursin*. Elberf. 1857; Letters of Ursinus in ThArb. rh. Pr. Ver. VIII/IX 79 ff.; GILLET II 97 ff.; H. BASSERMANN, *Gesch. d. Gottesdienstordn. in d. bad. Landen.* Stuttg. 1891; p. 60 ff. *Heidelb. Kat.*; NIEMEYER, p. 390 ff.; A. WOLTERS, *Der H. K. in seiner ursprünglichen Gestalt.* Bonn, 1864; SCHAFF I 529 ff., III 307 ff.; the same in ZhTh 37, 113 ff.; M. A. GOOSZEN, *De H. C.* Leiden, 1890; *Das Büchlein vom Brotbrechen*, 1563; new edition by Doedes. Utrecht, 1891; St Kr 1893, 615 ff. Maulbronn: KLUNZINGER in ZhTh 19, 166; additional literature in Kluckhohn *Briefe* I 505 f. GILLET in HZ 19, 42 ff. H. HAGEN, *Briefe v. Heid. Prof. u. Studien* (1561-1589). Heidelberg, 1889. For Neuser, see G. E. LESSING, Werke (Hempel) XV 23 ff.; VEESENMEYER in St Kr 1829, 553 ff. For Silvanus see SCHELHORN, *Ergötzlichk.* I 571 ff. VON BEZOLD, *Briefe des Pfalzgr. Joh. Casimir*, 2 vols. München, 1882-1884.

The excellent Elector **Frederick III.**, a thorough biblical student, who in all his reforming activity as well as his violent interference with Catholic ritual and the like was guided by the religious

---

[1] Cp. also DÖLLINGER, *Beiträge* I 514.

[2] Cp. the letter in GILLET II 87, which refers the hatred of the Lutherans for Geneva to the *sanctior vivendi ratio, quam Genevenses maxime omnium ac honestissime tenent*. (See further KRAFFT in ThArb. rh. Pr. Ver. I 16 ff.

motive of theocratic zeal against all **idolatry,** after the expulsion of Hesshus (1559; see above, p. 285) had been still more strongly confirmed in his dislike of exclusive Lutheranism by a disputation that took place at Heidelberg between the Calvinistically inclined Professor Boquin and others and some Saxon theologians. After he had fruitlessly striven at Naumburg (1561) to bring about the union of the evangelical States on the basis of the Variata, he caused a new ritual and the famous **Heidelberg Catechism** (1563) to be drawn up, in particular by **Caspar Olevianus** (a pupil of Calvin and a native of Treves) and **Zacharias Ursinus** (a pupil of Melanchthon).[1] This work, distinguished by preciseness of expression, earnestness of feeling and dogmatic cautiousness, most closely approximates, in the Eucharistic doctrine, to the Melanchthonian method of teaching, while, in regard to the doctrine of predestination, it is silent (although both its authors held decidedly predestinarian ideas). An ecclesiastical council, composed of three clerical and three lay members, was to direct the affairs of the Church. This procedure on the part of Frederick called forth great excitement, especially in Lutheran Wurtemberg (Brenz). Duke **Christopher,** in the hope of bringing back Frederick to the Lutherans, agreed to his proposal to arrange a discussion at **Maulbronn** (1564) between the Palatiners (Boquin, **Olevianus**, Ursinus and others) and the Wurtemberg theologians (Brenz, **J. Andreä,** Th. Schnepp and others), at which the question of the Eucharist took a prominent place and the Wurtembergers laid great stress upon the theory of omnipresence; but it led to no results. But an accusation, which the Emperor Maximilian, pressed by the Pope, brought against Frederick at the Augsburg diet (1566)—of violating the religious peace by the introduction of Calvinism—and which individual Lutheran States (especially Frederick's cousin, Wolfgang of Zweibrücken) seemed disposed to support, did not succeed in face of the manliness of his attitude and, lastly, of

---

[1] The intensifying of the 80th question in the second and still more in the third edition ("And therefore the mass is fundamentally nothing else than a denial of the one sacrifice and suffering of Jesus Christ and an accursed idolatry") was the result of Olevianus's request put forward by the special order of Frederick, CR 47, 683 f. Bullinger's Zürich Catechism was also specially made use of for the Catechism. "The little book, by the unanimous approval, which it met with amongst the members of the German Reformed Church, knit together their hitherto isolated circles even more than the CA had done in earlier times, so that they suddenly appeared more united than the Lutherans separated into their two camps." WOLTERS, *Ref.-Gesch. von Wesel*, p. 254.

the political insight of the Lutherans. He was able to appeal to the fact that he took his stand throughout on the Confession of the Naumburg diet. But his experiences at that diet made him by no means disinclined to the idea of an armed defence of the Gospel and, from that time forth, an advocate of a **warlike policy of union**.[1] Further, in conformity with the wishes of his theologians, he endeavoured to make room for Calvinistic discipline in the Palatinate by the introduction of presbyteries. On this point, the Zwinglian **Erastus** (a physician and electoral councillor) fell out with the Calvinist Olevianus: the former especially championed the maintenance of the ecclesiastical ban and fought for a State-church system, which should place discipline in the hands of the police and a secular penal court.[2]

After Frederick's death in 1576,[3] his son **Louis VI.** (previously governor in the preponderatingly Lutheran Upper Palatinate) brought the Palatinate back to Lutheranism. Olevianus was deprived of office, those who had hitherto been most influential removed, reformed pastors and teachers (more than 500) set aside, Lutheran forms of worship restored at Baptism and the Sacrament. The educational institutions founded by Frederick III. (the Collegium sapientiae) were obliged to become Lutheran. The University was, comparatively speaking, spared, but Boquin, Zanchius and Tremellius were dismissed. After Louis's sympathy with the Formula of Concord was obtained by certain concessions (see p. 293), his demand that this confession should be recognised caused further measures to be taken, especially against the refractory University of Heidelberg. But in the country also considerable resistance manifested itself: and Louis, who was at heart by no means inclined to violent measures, at last showed signs of a change of mind.

During his reign, the decidedly Calvinistic elements had gathered round his brother, the Count-Palatine **John Casimir**,[4] who had

[1] For the violent introduction of Calvinism into the Lutheran-minded Upper Palatinate cp. WITTMANN, *Gesch. d. Ref. in der Oberpfalz*. Augsbg., 1847, p. 28 ff.

[2] With this dispute is connected the action of certain clergy trained by the Church authorities, who now not only became reconciled to anti-Trinitarian ideas, but designed a complete apostasy from Christianity. With Calvinistic Old Testament severity Olevianus and his supporters declared them worthy of death in accordance with the Mosaic law: Neuser fled, Silvanus was executed in 1572.

[3] See his testamentary **Confession** in HEPPE, *Die Bek.-Schriften der ref. Kirchen Deutschlands*. Elberf., 1860, p. 1 ff.

[4] For the agreement between the two brothers to leave each other alone in ecclesiastical questions but in other things to render each other mutual assistance, since "both of them acknowledge the Holy Scriptures, the CA and its Apology in right understanding in accordance with the guidance of the Word of God, recognise **one** Saviour and consequently are united against the Pope and his false Church" (January 27th, 1578) see VON BEZOLD I 291.

received Kaisers-Lautern, Neustadt an der Haardt, together with Bockelhein as his inheritance. Those who had been driven from Heidelberg found a refuge at the college founded by him at **Neustadt**; and thus, the little place for a short time attained great importance, since students gathered together there from all parts of Germany, France and other countries. After Louis's death, John Casimir, basing his claim upon the arrangements of the Palatinate house, in the capacity of guardian by rights of kinship of his son who was still under age, asserted himself in the Palatinate, although Louis had attempted, in the interests of Lutheranism, to appoint assistant guardians of Lutheran tendencies (Duke Louis of Wurtemberg, Louis Landgrave of Hesse and George Frederick of Baden).

He first claimed a church for the "reformed" in Heidelberg, forbade accusations of heresy in the pulpit, and urged a friendly understanding through the medium of a religious discussion. But the Lutheran preachers refused to allow the right of *elenchus* to be taken from them. He then demanded—which is characteristic of the view of the essential unity of the Lutherans and "the reformed" by which he was dominated—that, at the fresh elections for the Heidelberg presbytery, men of reformed ideas should also be chosen; subsequently, on the 15th of January, 1584, he deprived all the ecclesiastical councillors of office for insubordination, and nominated a reformed ecclesiastical council. However, the pointless comedy of a religious discussion was performed in the presence of the Court, the University, and a number of visitors (April 4-13, 1584).[1] The "reformed" Grynaeus of Bâle and Zanchius of Neustadt an der Haardt were opposed by the Lutheran John Marbach. Chancellor Ehem pronounced in favour of Grynaeus, but the students laughed at him. John Casimir now proceeded to severer measures. Grynaeus, Francis Junius, Tremellius and others appeared at the College of Heidelberg, and the five Lutheran city clergymen were dismissed; about 400 Lutheran clergy lost their offices; violent attacks were made, especially by the Wurtemberg theologians (Luc. Osiander, then Jac. Andreä) upon the peacefully disposed Pareus and others. When John Casimir died in 1592, the eighteen years old **Frederick IV.**—in spite of the counter-efforts of his Lutheran uncle, Count Palatine Richard von Simmern—succeeded in obtaining independent authority. Reformed churchdom was carried through and confirmed by him. But at the same time, correctly recognising the perilous situation of German Protestantism in the face of the Catholic policy of restoration, he attached great importance to the union of the Protestants, and, on this account, to a reconciliation of the opposing sister-confessions; hence, efforts in this direction in his case went side by side with strivings after political union. The theologian **David Pareus** in particular earnestly upheld this "irenic" attitude (see below). In the time of John Casimir, he had already brought out an edition of Luther's Bible, omitting or rather abbreviating the glosses (this was attacked by J. Andreä as "a right devilish piece of villainy)."

---

[1] For the literature, see VON BEZOLD II 205.

2. Nassau.

Literature : STEUBING, *Kirchen- u. Ref.-Gesch. der Oranien-Nassauischen Lande.* Hadamar, 1804. For Sarcerius, see ENGELHARDT in ZhTh 20, 79 ff. RÖSELMÜLLER, *Ev. S.* Annab. 1888. For Piscator : STEUBING in ZhTh 11, 4, 98 ff.; the same, *G. der hohen Schule Herborn.* Hadamar, 1823.

The theologians Widebram and Pezel (p. 291) who had been driven from Wittenberg on the downfall of Philippism in 1574 were employed (after 1577) by Count John VI. of **Nassau-Dillenburg** in carrying out reformatory ordinances.

Here, in the countries of the Othonian line (Siegen, Dillenburg, Hadamar and elsewhere), the work of reformation had been carried out by Count William the Rich, who, after an ecclesiastical ordinance of 1534 (in which year he had also joined the Schmalkaldic league), which at first only attacked practical church abuses, had introduced the Brandenburg-Nuremberg ecclesiastical order.[1] The Saxon theologian Erasmus **Sarcerius** had, as superintendent and visitor since 1538, completed the new order of things. **Synods** of the clergy were formed at an early period, as a court of judicature in regard to the manner of life led by the clergy and their administration of office.[2] Melanchthon's Loci were regarded as the textbook; learned schools were established at Dillenburg, Herborn, Siegen, and Hadamar. At the time of the Interim, which the Emperor desired should be carried out, Sarcerius resigned his post; after a brief period of unrest, during which the Archbishops of Treves and Mainz had endeavoured to regain their jurisdiction in the country, the synod was restored after the treaty of Passau. In like manner, in Nassau-**Weilburg** (and Usingen), in the time of Count **Philip III.**, where **Erh. Schnepf** had already preached evangelical doctrines in 1528, before he was called to Marburg, an evangelical order was introduced after 1546, chiefly through the instrumentality of the learned Tyrolese, Dr. Caspar **Goltwurm**; he had certainly been obliged to retreat before the Interim, but after the treaty of Passau had resumed his work and firmly established the reformation of the country. The son of Count William of Nassau-Dillenburg, John VI. (brother of William of Orange), in 1570 had appointed the Lutheran **D. Maxim Mörlin** (brother of the better known Joachim Mörlin) court chaplain and superintendent. But, when M. endeavoured to introduce strictly Lutheran views by means of church visitation, he met with little sympathy in the country, as relations with the Netherlands and the Count's own inclinations pointed another way. In 1572, Mörlin resigned his office and returned to Coburg. In the Eucharistic controversy, Eoban Geldenhauer (**Noviomagus**), together with the majority of the clergy, favoured more and more the attitude taken up by Frederick III. of the Palatinate, a Calvinising Philippism, which however refused to give up its membership of the CA.

---

[1] RICHTER, KOO I 173 ff. 277. However, his dispute with Landgrave Philip about Katzenellenbogen hindered the practical results of his membership: this was, again, of service to him at the end of the Schmalkaldic War. According to ARNOLDI, *Geschichte der Oranien-Nassauischen Lande*, III (Hadamar. 1801), pp. 178 and 190, the Nuremberg order was accepted in 1533 or 1534, and William entered the Schmalkaldic league at Christmas, 1535.

[2] Cp. SARCERIUS, *Von Synodis und Priesterlichen Versamlungen*, Leipz. 1553.

With the co-operation of the Philippists who had been expelled from Wittenberg, whose numbers were swelled by Palatinate preachers who had been driven out by Louis VI., Nassau-Dillenburg was led decidedly to reformed church government; the Confession of the **Dillenburg Synod** of 1578[1] (which vigorously combated the doctrine of omnipresence, appealed to the Variata as the authentic rectification of the Invariata and advocated energetic reform in worship according to a reformatory model) was accepted throughout the country. The introduction of regulations affecting Church discipline and presbyteries followed in the same year: in 1581, the use of the Heidelberg Catechism was approved. Caspar Olevianus (who, since his removal from Heidelberg, had been tutor to the children of Count Wittgenstein at Berleburg) was summoned in 1582 to **Herborn** where, in 1584, a reformed University was founded, to the flourishing condition of which, in addition to Olevianus, Ursinus and John **Piscator** materially contributed as its theologians. The neighbouring counties of Wittgenstein, Solms-Braunfels, Sayn, Isenburg and Wied joined this development, which found its completion at the **General Synod of Herborn** in 1586;[2] the acceptance of the resolutions of the Synod of Middelburg of 1581 brought about a leaning to the **Dutch** ecclesiastical order. Nassau-Weilburg, on the other hand, remained Lutheran.

3. Bremen.

Literature: J. H. DUNTZE, *Gesch. der freien Stadt Bremen* III. Bremen, 1848. WALTE in ZhTh 36, 339 ff.; 42, 50 ff.; 448 ff.; 546 ff.; 43, 163 ff. IKEN in Brem. Jb IX 1 ff. MALLET in RE XI 551 ff.

In **Bremen** also, the antipathy to exclusive Lutheranism and the Formula of Concord that had been for a long time in existence led through Philippism to the victory of Calvinism. Jodocus **Glanaeus,** pastor of St. Ansgar, as an adherent of strict Lutheranism, opposed his Philippistic superintendent **Mening,** who, in 1572, had introduced a "declaration" (or "a more simple and more unanimous understanding of the chief articles of Christian doctrine, in particular the Last Supper of the Lord"). The Council in 1580 called in **Widebram** and **Pezel,** with whom Glanaeus at the outset refused to negotiate as suspected persons. Pezel was then definitively won over to the Church of Bremen; Glanaeus was deprived of office and Pezel appointed pastor of St. Ansgar in his place; after the death of Mening in 1584, he became superintendent of the churches and schools, and at the same time Professor of theology at the Lyceum

---

[1] STEUBING p. 107 ff. HEPPE, *Bek.-Schriften der ref. Kirchen Deutschlands,* p. 68 ff.

[2] See its resolutions in RICHTER KOO II 473 ff.

founded by Daniel von Büren. He introduced a catechism drawn up by himself, which, known as the "Bremen Catechism," remained in use together with the Heidelb. Cat. (accepted later) till the last century; breaking of bread was adopted in place of the sacramental wafers; exorcism at baptism, "idols and images" were done away with. Yet, in 1590, Bremen refused the title of "Calvinist" as unauthorised; but the strictly predestinarian Consensus ministerii Bremensis ecclesiae of 1595[1] shows that in reality the Calvinistic view of the Philippists had gained the mastery, as Bremen, pursued with hostility by its Lutheran archbishops, whose rights over the city were doubtful, and by Lutheran neighbours, openly declared itself as Calvinist and as such sent representatives to the Synod of Dort.[2] The by no means inconsiderable number of citizens who had remained Lutheran, until then obliged to attend foreign churches, at last found an ecclesiastical centre at the Cathedral, which had been shut after Hardenberg's dismissal but was thrown open by the Danish prince Archbishop Frederick to the Lutheran form of worship in 1638.

4. Anhalt.

Literature: JOHANNSEN, *!Der freie Protestantismus in Anhalt.* ZhTh 16, 269 ff. G. SCHUBRING in ZlTh 1848, 8 ff. G. ALLIHN, *Die ref. Kirche in Anhalt.* Cöthen, 1874. A. ZAHN, *Das gute Recht des ref. Bekenntnisses in Anhalt.* Elberf., 1866. H. DUNCKER, *Anhalts Bekenntnissstand von 1570-1606.* Dessau, 1892; the same, *Nachwort.* Dessau, 1892.

The dislike to the Formula of Concord and the generally prevalent Philippism found support in **John George I.**, who was sole regent from 1587 to 1603 for his brother, who was under age. **Peucer**, having been released from prison (see p. 291) in 1586 at the request of the Electress of Saxony, a princess of Anhalt, lived in Dessau as physician in ordinary and theological adviser. In the time of **Joachim Ernest**, John George's father, all the declarations of the Anhalt theologians, whose spokesman was the superintendent of Zerbst, M. Wolfgang **Amling**, had adhered throughout to the Philippist standpoint in the negotiations concerning the Formula of Concord: indeed, in the "Confession of the Holy Eucharist" of the four superintendents (1585), which was subscribed by all the clergy, an attempt was made to bring about as close an approximation as possible to the Lutheran churches. John George, on the contrary, commenced in 1589 with the abolition of exorcism—John Arndt of Badeborn had to retire from Anhalt in consequence of his opposition—without at first intending an alteration of the confessional status; it was only after his marriage to a daughter of the Count Palatine John Casimir (in 1595) that he went further, prescribing more extensive reforms (of a Calvinistic tendency) in public worship, which met with vigorous opposition in the congregations; a ritual after the Palatine model, and a new Catechism remained in an unfinished state;[3] the "recess" of the diet

---

[1] HEPPE, *Die Bek.-Schriften der reform. Kirchen Deutschlands*, 1860, p. 147 ff. IKEN in Brem. Jb X 84 ff.

[2] IKEN in Brem. Jb X 11 ff.

[3] The twenty-eight Articles of 1597, subscription to which was to introduce Calvinism in doctrine and worship (first printed in LENZ, *Historisch-geneal. Fürstellung des Hochfürstl. Hauses Anhalt.* Cöthen, 1757, p. 369 ff.), are apocryphal: cp. DUNCKER, p. 102 ff.

of 1603 declared yet again that no alteration had been made in the acknowledgment of the CA by the Church. When the principality was divided in 1606, the princely brothers decided to adhere as far as possible to the Church of the Palatinate. In 1616, the Palatine ritual was introduced at Bernburg by the side of the Heidelberg Catechism; the latter was also much in use elsewhere. However, Anhalt was not invited to the synod of Dort and took no part in it. In spite of the repeated acknowledgment of the CA (according to the Variata) by the princes in 1647, their country had as a matter of fact become Calvinistic: only Anhalt-Zerbst restored Lutheranism after 1644.

5. Baden.

The transitory encouragement of Crypto-Calvinism in Electoral Saxony and its sudden end has been mentioned above (p. 287 ff.). The attempt of the Margrave **Ernest Frederick** (brother of the Margrave James, who had turned Catholic, see below) to introduce Calvinistic reforms in the **Baden lowlands** (Durlach-Pforzheim) was also transitory. He renounced the Formula of Concord, which had been accepted under Lutheran guardianship, and gave the preachers an order of instruction. "A short and simple Confession, according to which the church and school beadles of the margraviate of Baden were to conform to doctrine," Staffort (a castle and village belonging to the margrave near Durlach), 1599. To justify his step and fundamentally combat the Formula of Concord he subsequently produced the so-called "Book of Staffort." "The Christian scruples and important and well-founded reasons which have hitherto caused Lord Ernest Frederick, the illustrious Margrave of Baden, to abstain from subscribing the Formula of Concord . . ." Staffort, 1599, one of the most prominent treatises issued against the Formula. But his efforts met with resistance in the country, and his death in 1604 put an end to the matter.

6. Hesse and Lippe.

Literature: HEPPE, *KGesch. beider Hessen;* 2 vols. Marb., 1876; the same, *Gesch. der Hess. Generalsynoden von* 1568-1582; 2 vols. Kassel, 1847; the same, *Die Einführung der Verbesserungspunkte,* 1604-1610. Marb., 1853. W. MÜNSCHER, *Versuch einer Gesch. der Hess. ref. Kirche.* Kassel, 1850. For Hyperius, see MANGOLD in RE VI 408 ff.

The attitude of Hesse, in the time of Philip, had never been exclusively Lutheran, but had always remained open to relations with Strasburg, and, through the latter, with Switzerland. One of the most prominent Marburg professors, **Andrew Hyperius**, exhibits partly Melanchthonian, partly Calvinistic traits. In 1564, at the Marburg graduations allegiance was taken to the Variata (ZhTh 24, 155 ff.); the church ritual of 1566 bears a Melanchthonian character. In regard to the Eucharistic question, Philip in his will referred to the arrangements of the Wittenberg Concord of 1536. After Philip's death in 1567 the territories were divided, but at first held together, although, even at this early date, in Lower Hesse a decided leaning towards the reformed, in Upper Hesse (Aegidius Hunnius) towards the Lutheran type manifested itself. Under the influence of William IV., Landgrave of Lower Hesse, the Formula of Concord was rejected, while a part of Upper Hesse subscribed to it. Hence, at the general synods held in common during these years until 1582 much uncertainty prevailed, and the differences between both tendencies of thought increased, so that finally it was found necessary to renounce the idea of again assembling the representatives of the clergy of the whole of Hesse. In Lower Hesse (Cassel) the learned theologian, the Calvinistically inclined Landgrave Maurice took a further decisive step in the so-called " Verbesserungspunkte" (1605), after a portion of Upper Hesse also had fallen to his share in 1604 in consequence of the death of the Landgrave Louis.

> These "points" declare (1) against the dangerous and unedifying disputations about the person of Christ and the theory of omnipresence; (2) in favour of the reformed arrangement of the commandments and the abolition of images (2nd commandment!); (3) in favour of the rite of breaking of bread at the Lord's Supper. By appealing to the earlier confessional status and the resolutions of earlier general synods, Maurice was able to assert that this involved no alteration in religion. But the matter stirred up the most violent struggles in the country and called forth active and passive resistance, while the recklessness of the Landgrave inflicted severe wounds upon the ecclesiastical life of the land;[1] the Lutheran theologians at Marburg were dismissed and replaced by Philippistic. The confession of the general synod of 1607,[2] while in the main essentially Philippistic, nevertheless, in accordance with the state of things, and in spite of the appeal to Luther, the CA, and the Apologia, denotes the adhesion of the Church of Hesse-Cassel to the **reformed** Churches. (In opposition to Marburg the Lutheran Landgrave Louis V. of Hesse-Darmstadt now founded the University of **Giessen**). Yet the Marburg theologians themselves advised against the introduction of the Heidelberg Catechism into the Marburg Paedagogium, although it was the best, since indeed the idea was firmly held that Lower Hesse had not carried out a change of confession properly so-called. As a matter of fact, the above Catechism came more and more generally into use. At the Leipzig Colloquy of 1631 we find Hesse-Cassel also on the reformed side. During the complications of the Thirty Years' War, Maurice was deprived of that part of Upper Hesse, which he had obtained, by sentence of the Imperial Privy Council, in consequence of the change of religion which was contrary to the will of Louis IV.; this portion of territory was temporarily included in Hesse-Darmstadt, in consequence of which

---

[1] "In his fatal blindness, he was firmly resolved to lay low every obstacle which stood in the way of his object with the might of his princely arm." HEPPE, *Verbesserungspunkte*, p. 99.

[2] See HEPPE, *Verbesserungspunkte*, p. 71 ff., and VILMAR, *Gesch. des Confessionsbestandes der evg. Kirche in Hessen.* ²Frankf., 1868.

Lutheranism was restored in it. Cassel now took the Swedish, Darmstadt the imperial side. After the peace of Westphalia, Hesse-Cassel (the Landgravine Amelia) certainly recovered a part of Upper Hesse; but Lutheranism, which had in the meantime, been firmly established here, was no longer fought against.

In the County of **Lippe**, also, in 1602, in the time of Count Simon VI. the reformed ritual drove out the Lutheran; however, the city of Lemgo offered an obstinate resistance and, under Simon VII., obtained the concession of practising the Lutheran religion.

7. Electoral Brandenburg.

Literature: HERING, *Hist. Nachricht v. d. ersten Anf. der evg. ref. Kirche in Brandenburg.* Halle, 1778; the same, *Beiträge zur Gesch. der evg. ref. K. in den preuss. Ländern.* Breslau, 1784. J. SCHMIDT, *Zur Gesch. des Kurf. Joh. Sig.* Schweidnitz, 1862, 1866. MÜHLER, *Gesch. d. KVerfassung in d. Mark Brandenb.* Weimar, 1846. M. KRENKEL, *Wie wurden Preussens Fürsten ref.?* Leipz., 1873. G. KAWERAU in RE XIV 227 ff. WANGEMANN, *Joh. Sig. u. P. Gerhardt.* Berlin, 1884.

Lastly, the conversion of the Elector **John Sigismund of Brandenburg** was of quite special importance. When a young prince, during the time of John George, 1593, he had been obliged to give a written promise of his readiness to abide by Lutheranism and the Formula of Concord. But during the time of his father Joachim Frederick (1598-1608), the unbending attitude of the grandfather had already been abandoned; the common interests of Protestantism in Germany were considered, blind hatred of the Calvinists abated. Nevertheless, even in 1602 he had sanctioned the Formula of Concord anew, and John Sigismund had entered into this promise. The latter, however, in consequence of a stay at Strasburg, his connection with the Elector Frederick IV of the Palatinate—his son George William wedded a Palatine princess—the study of the *Concordia discors* of Hospinianus and his relations with the Landgrave Maurice of Hesse, who stayed in Berlin in the year 1613, became strengthened in this more liberal attitude and accessible to reformatory influences. In his *entourage* there was no lack of theologians (Solomon Fink),[1] who had advanced from Philippism to Calvinistic leanings. Even before his accession to the throne,

---

[1] In 1614, Fink, in his "Sakraments-Spiegel" [Mirror of the Sacrament], delivered an incredibly coarse polemic against the Lutheran doctrine and practice of the Eucharist (cp. Unsch. Nachr. 1729, p. 217), and the Lutheran zealots in general, whose excesses have been frequently noted; the Calvinistic Hotspurs, who exhibited equal intolerance and abuse of their opponents, must not be forgotten.

he had been at heart won over to Calvinism; the conversion of his brother Ernest and the complaint of the Berlin clergy against his doctrine of the Eucharist and of the State against Fink compelled him to come forward **openly** with his confession.[1]

On the 25th of December, 1613, he caused the reformed Sacrament to be administered to himself in the Cathedral, after he had declared to the clergy, that he had no authority over the conscience in view, but that the authorities also had the right to order preaching according to their conscience. Considering the great excitement in the country, which was the more intelligible, as hitherto change of religion on the part of the authorities had always been followed by a change on the part of the country, the Elector contented himself with forbidding, by a mandate of the 24th of February, 1614, abuse from the pulpits; his initial attempts to impose the Variata upon the country as the foundation of doctrine, were abandoned; the Lutheran theologians of the country withdrew from a disputation with the Court theologians and the Heidelberg Professor Abraham Scultetus, after their spokesman Gedicke, formerly the Elector's tutor, had taken to flight for fear of personal danger. But, in the meantime, Sigismund had published his confession (Confessio Sigismundi, May, 1614),[2] which claims to be that of the improved CA and of the purifying of Lutheranism from the "papist superstition." Predestination is taught in it, but its logical results are at the same time rejected.[3] He hoped for the voluntary adhesion of the Church of his country and would gladly have re-formed it on the basis of the state of things previous to the Formula of Concord: he accordingly did away with all obligation to observe the latter. He was supported by individual theologians, above all, by Chr. **Pelargus**,[4] superintendent and Professor at Frankfort-on-the-Oder. But, in view of the irritation of parties, he was unable to carry out his ideas of union to a greater extent, and he was prudent enough not to yield to the instigations of his Calvinistic *entourage*, to desist from all employment of force, and also to draw up for the States a pacifying written promise (the 5th of February, 1615), according to which he, for instance, declared that he would never force upon any of the communities against their will a preacher whom they regarded with suspicion in places where the ruler of the country exercised patronage. As he would have been legally justified in "introducing religion as the highest royal prerogative free and without limitation," he naturally made efforts of various kinds to circulate his views and to protect those who were willing to meet them: for instance, he gave instructions to the theological faculty of Frankfort-on-the-Oder, which excluded exclusive Lutheranism. In consequence of this, this faculty was regarded by the country as reformed, and accordingly the clergy sought their preparatory training at Wittenberg. But, on the whole, the

---

[1] The view of things which would attribute his conversion to political considerations (the Jülich heritage, regard for the Netherlands) is unfounded. See on the point WANGEMANN, p. 14 ff.

[2] The theologian who composed it cannot be identified with certainty. It is printed in NIEMEYER, p. 642 ff. Cp. SCHAFF I 554 ff.

[3] The Elector, who was also personally a universalist, refused to send representatives to the Synod of Dort: cp. WANGEMANN, p. 59.

[4] See GASS, *Gesch. der prot. Dogmatik* I 301.

Lutheran established Church remained uninjured; Sigismund was content to procure free exercise of their religion to the Reformed and equal recognition **by the side of** the Lutherans. Individual small reformed communities were formed almost entirely in connection with places where there was an electoral Court (court-chaplains). Although all this did not take place without friction, mistrust and dispute, yet here the territorial idea was successfully broken through in favour of that of religious equality, but at the same time the foundation was laid of the **Unionist policy of the Hohenzollerns**. But the first result was hostility between Saxony and Brandenburg, which materially contributed to the weakening of Protestantism during the Thirty Years' War.

In **Silesia** also Philippism had found numerous friends; Breslau held firmly to the Corpus Philippicum, and in the duchies of Brieg and Liegnitz the same was the recognised text-book as late as 1601. But, on the one hand, strict Lutheranism made progress; on the other, the Melanchthonians made further advances in the direction of Calvinism; at the commencement of the Bohemian War Duke John Christian of Brieg openly went over to Calvinism (1619) and in Breslau the Reformed obtained (March 5th, 1620) from Frederick, the new King of Bohemia, permission " to practise the reformed religion freely,"—a liberty, which, however, they soon lost through the vicissitudes of war.

8. The Lower-Rhenish Church.

Lit.: M. GÖBEL, *Gesch. d. christl. Lebens in der rhein.-westf. Kirche.* I. Koblenz 1849. A. WOLTERS, *Ref.-Gesch. d. Stadt Wesel.* Bonn 1868. KRAFFT, *Ueber die Quellen der Gesch. der evg. Bewegungen am Niederrhein* in Th Arbrh Pr V I 1 ff.; the same, IV 107 ff. L. KELLER, *Die Gegenref. in Westf. u. am Niederrhein*, 2 vols., Leipz. 1881; the same, Pr Jb 1881. J. HEIDEMANN, in Weseler Gymn. Progr. 1853 and 1858. M. LOSSEN, *Briefe von Andr. Masius und seinen Freunden*, 1538-1573. Leipz. 1886. For Monheim, see KRAFFT in RE X 221 ff.; for Buscoduc.: KRAFFT in Z. berg. Gesch.-Ver. 26, 213 ff.; for Bommel: KRAFFT in Monatsschr. f. rhein.-westf. Gesch.-Forsch. II 224 ff.; VAN MÉER, *De Synode te Emden* 1571. 's Hage 1892.

The course of events was quite different in regard to the origin of the reformed Church on the **Lower Rhine** (Cleves). The " Erasmian " efforts of John III. and William IV.,—assisted by the Humanist Conrad Heresbach,—in the direction of reform have already been spoken of (pp. 120 and 148). We must also mention the able schoolman, John **Monheim**, who since 1545 had brought the learned Düsseldorf school into great repute, and whose Catechism (republished by H. Sack, 1847) represented an essentially evangelical (Calvinistic) standpoint; this work, however, was forbidden at the instigation of the Jews settled in Cologne. That half-hearted reform in the national Church, after it had again applied itself more decisively in 1558 to evangelical reforms, succumbed in 1570 to the counter-Reformation brought about by the Jesuits, the more easily as the national Church had always claimed to be Catholic.

On the other hand, vigorous germs existed in the independent evangelical communities, which laboriously asserted their existence. After the fall of the Anabaptists, the unfortunate issue of the Gueldres war (1543) and the ill-fated Cologne reformation, the evangelical cause found its support amongst a large number of the Lower Rhenish nobility, and especially, at the city of **Wesel**. Here also at first **Lutheran** views had exercised influence (in 1543, prohibition of the mass by the Council, the appointment of clergy of Lutheran views [Nic. Buscoducensis]; the authorisation of the CA and the "Cologne reformation," consequently somewhat after the views of **Melanchthon** and Bucer). When, in 1545, the first Dutch (Walloon) fugitives, fleeing from the bloody edicts of Charles V., found a welcome in Wesel, they were obliged to subscribe to a mildly Lutheran confession, rejecting the Sacramentarians (Wolters, p. 455). "At that time no one suspected that the future of the evangelical church of the Lower Rhine depended upon this poor crowd of cloth-weavers, on the fugitive community which was formed from them." After the Schmalkaldic war all the evangelical teachers in Wesel (Soest and Lippstadt) were driven out, and the Catholic doctrine and ritual re-established. But the citizens remained faithful to the evangelical doctrine, and became more and more imbued with an anti-papistical spirit. In 1554, some of the London fugitives (Walloon, French and English), who had been driven out by Catholic Mary, found a welcome in Wesel and assisted the city to industrial and commercial development. The strangers, however, were refused self-dependent existence as an independent community as well as union with the existing Walloon community; but the Council, in accordance with the traditional Lutheran views of the duty of the authorities, demanded union with the existing Lutheran Church. This occasioned continual friction, examinations of belief and the like, here and wherever they were received. In Wesel, the Council and the clergy, who had been in the meantime won over to a more sharply-defined Lutheranism, in view of the Heidelberg Eucharistic controversy (1559) and the victory of the reformed church-constitution in the Palatinate, now endeavoured to keep the citizens, who were strongly influenced by this, to Lutheranism, and, in 1561, required them to bind themselves to a new, strictly Lutheran confession (*confessio Wesaliensis*).[1]

Not only, however, did the strangers decidedly refuse, but, in consequence of their growing influence and the co-operation of events in the Palatinate, a complete change became noticeable in some of the clergy and amongst the citizens (1564). Exorcism at

[1] GÖBEL I 405 ff. WOLTERS, p. 456 ff.

baptism was first left optional, in opposition to the strictly Lutheran Plateanus, and then the Heidelberg Catechism, which Hesshus, who was staying in Wesel, had violently resisted, was successfully introduced by **Nicolas Rollius**,[1] and the ground was thereby laid for going over to the reformed confession. In 1567, the last great immigration from the Netherlands into all the large and small towns of the Rhine district took place by thousands. In 1566, the first constituent synod of the Dutch churches—chiefly attended by Belgian communities—had been just held in Antwerp, when the whole of this church, which was preponderatingly Walloon, was driven out by Alba and sought refuge in West Germany (from the Palatinate as far as Wesel and Emden). These communities, "which sit under the Cross and are dispersed through Germany and East Friesland," **held firmly to their independence**, although they now found a reformed church constitution in existence both in Wesel and in the county of Mörs (where Count Hermann had caused reforms to be introduced since 1560, especially by Henry Bommel, the author of the Oeconomia Christiana [p. 196], who had been driven from Wesel; they even brought their communal constitution with them, and, at their reorganisation in 1568, held their **national meeting at Wesel**,[2] and in 1571 their **Synod at Emden**[3] (in both of which Peter Dathenus of Ypres, court-chaplain of Frederick III., who had been asked for from the Palatinate, took part). This was of the highest importance for the formation of ecclesiastical life on the Lower Rhine. For, while in many places the fugitive communities were soon driven out again (in Aix-la-Chapelle and Cologne by the Catholics, and in Frankfort-on-the-Main by the Lutherans in 1561), in other places (Emden, Emmerich, Cleves) they were tolerated; nay, in Wesel and on the entire Lower Rhine their views in regard to the still existent Lutheranism prevailed, and therewith at the same time their ecclesiastical constitution came into vogue.

According to the Emden resolutions, the exiled communities are divided into three: the German and East Friesian, those "under the cross" (Belgian-Dutch), and the English, which were still to be organised. It is not a national churchship, but a free union of communities which are held together by a common confession (Confessio Belgica and Gallica; the Genevese, or, in other

---

[1] Teschenmacher has erroneously made him Duke William's court-chaplain. Cp. Monatsschr. für rhein.-westf. Gesch.-Forsch. II 226.
[2] RICHTER, KOO II 310 ff.; more fully in WOLTERS, p. 335 ff.
[3] RICHTER, II 339 ff.

words, Heidelberg Catechism), by the ecclesiastical discipline of the presbyteries and by synods; a state of things strongly in contrast to the form of Protestant churchdom elsewhere on German soil. The **German** community of the town of Wesel, led by its pastor Heitfeld, now at first **gave its adherence** to the Dutch-Cleves synod (1579); the remaining Lower Rhenish reformed communities followed suit and, after this example, entered into the organism of the Dutch Church. Since, about this time, the political revolution in the Netherlands made it possible for the exiles to return, and a great part of them actually did return, the German element obtained the preponderance amongst those who remained behind, and their synod at last consisted more of native German than of Dutch communities of exiles. Accordingly, when the synod of Cleves, after a long interruption (due to the occupation of the country by the Spaniards during the Jülich-Cleves controversy of succession) again met in 1603, it no longer employed the Dutch, but the German language; however, it remained in its organism connected with the Church of the Netherlands, sent representatives to its synods and recognised the church orders drawn up at the synods of Dort (1578) and Middleburg (1581).

The synod of **Cleves** was soon supplemented by a synod of **Jülich**. Dutch elements, scattered about the cities, in this case also form the starting-point (Aix-la-Chapelle and Cologne). But organisation was brought about by the entry of the county of Mörs. Under the protection of Count Adolf of Nüenar-Mörs the first class-assembly of the districts of Aix-la-Chapelle, Jülich, Düren, Cologne and Neuss took place in Bedbur (Bedburreiferscheid) in 1571. In the first provincial synod of Jülich (1572) the **Berg** communities also took part, together with "private" communities, communities of "voluntary Christians," which maintained themselves in spite of continuous oppression, being quietly provided for by travelling preachers or enlightened brethren, united by the Heidelberg Catechism as their confession, and throughout their persecution protected by influential patrons. After the end of the century[1] these Berg communities had constituted themselves a Berg provincial synod and soon afterwards accepted the Emden resolutions. They were at first frequently obliged to hold their meetings secretly. In 1610, these (Jülich-Cleves-Berg) communities broke away from the connection (now become unnatural) with the Netherlands and held the first general synod of their own.

The state of affairs in the **March of Westphalia** and the neighbouring countries assumed a peculiar aspect. Here the reformation on the **Lutheran** model proceeded from the citizen communities of the towns, the magistrates of which took ecclesiastical affairs in hand. The state of the Church in the influential city of Soest became the standard for wider circles; the adhesion of this city to the Concord was decisive in favour of Lutheranism. Here, on the whole, the Lutheranism of the Lower Saxon Churches was adopted. Meanwhile, in the March, individual reformed communities were formed under great difficulties, which then endeavoured to join the reformed churches in Jülich, Cleves, and Berg.

---

[1] The first Berg synod took place at Neviges in 1589 (five communities).

FIFTH DIVISION.

The Struggle between Reformation and Counter-Reformation.

CHAPTER FIRST.

The Counter-Reformation in Spain and the Netherlands.

1. The Extinction of Evangelical Movements in Spain.

Sources and *Literature:* *Obras antiguas de los Espanoles reformados;* 20 vols. 1847-1870. Biblioth. Wiffeniana. *Spanish Reformers*, described by E. BÖHMER; 2 vols. Strassb. and London, 1874-1883. Review of the Literature by C. A. WILKENS in ZKG IX and X. A. LLORENTE, *Krit. Gesch. d. span. Ref.* (German tr. by Höck). Gmünd, 1819. A. DE CASTRO, *Hist. de los Protest. Espagnoles*, Cadiz, 1851 (German tr. by H. Hertz). Frankf., 1866. TH. M'CRIE, *Gesch. d. Ausbreit. u. Unterdrück. d. Ref. in Spanien* (German tr. by Plieninger). Stuttg., 1835. M. MENENDEZ Y PELAYO, *Hist. de los Heterodoxos Espanoles.* Madrid, 3 vols., 1880-1882. WILKENS, *Gesch. d. span. Protestantism.* Gütersl., 1888 (the best compilation of material). E. BÖHMER, *Franzisca Hernandez u. Frai Franz. Ortiz.* Leipz., 1865. For Enzinas. see STROBEL, *Neue Beitr.* V 213 ff.; ZKG XIII 338 ff., 346 ff.; ZhTh 40, 387; his *Denkwürdigkeiten vom Zustande der Niederl.* etc., in German by H. BÖHMER. For Carranza, H. LAUGWITZ, *B. Carr.* Kempten, 1870. GAMS, *KG in Spanien* III 198 ff. For Luis de Leon, see above, p. 269. BENRATH, Articles Ximenes, Carranza, Inquisition in RE; MAURENBRECHER, *Studien und Skizzen.* Leipz., 1874. *Gesch. d. kath. Ref.* I 37 ff.; the same, *Die Lehrjahre Philipps II.* HVb 6; F 2, 271 ff. E. MARCKS, *Ph. II.* in PrJb 73, 193 ff. H. CH. LEA in ZKG XIV 193 ff.

Spain, which Ferdinand and Isabella had made a united monarchy, owed its newly aspiring power to the very close connection between political measures and ecclesiastical ideas; a strictly Catholic regal church government successfully guarded the prerogatives of the Crown in opposition to the Pope in the same manner as it endeavoured to unite the whole country in the Catholic faith and devoutness. The Inquisition combined the resources of State and Church to keep the country free from Moors, Jews and heretics. Considerable efforts were made to renovate the clergy inwardly on Catholic principles and to bring about a religious regeneration of the Church. The monasteries were reformed, the clergy brought under discipline. Cardinal **Mendoza** and Francis **Ximenes**, his successor in the Archbishopric of Toledo, were especially prominent. The Universities of Salamanca, Alcala, Seville and Toledo flourished exceedingly. Thus Catholicism experienced a development, which afforded it greater powers of resistance against the evangelical elements which even here penetrated sporadically; but the result of these vital powers being destroyed by reckless violence was, that spiritual life was benumbed in the midst of Catholic forms.

Spain also had had its humanism, which was enthusiastic about Erasmus, and criticised, after its manner, monastic coarseness and ignorance; the imperial secretary, Alfonso Valdés, represented this trend of thought at the Court of Charles V., but his lampoon (see p. 71) called forth in Spain extreme measures on the part of the Inquisition against all the Erasmians. But already, subsequently to 1521, Luther's writings also made their way over the Pyrenees, and Spaniards studying abroad came into still closer contact with the evangelical movement. Amongst the clergy and upper classes Lutheranising tendencies were active during Charles's reign. The layman **Rodrigo de Valer** began to preach God's grace in the streets of Seville and violently attacked the corruption of the Church; he was looked upon as a harmless fool. But Canon **Juan Gil** (Egidius) received a wholesome impulse from him and became a preacher of self-experienced salvation. He was supported by Constantino **Ponce de la Fuente**, preacher at the Cathedral (Bibl. Wiff. II 1 ff.), who, by his preached, as well as his written, word (especially la confession de un pecador penitente, 1544) exercised an important influence and was left undisturbed as long as he preached sincerity and earnestness after the manner of the mystic theology without attacking the Church. In 1552 Gil was denounced, craftily forced to recant, and condemned to imprisonment. Fuente, however, was promoted to his place. Juan **Perez** (Bibl. Wiff. II 55 ff.) fled from Seville to Geneva, where, in 1556, he had his Spanish New Testament printed; a Catechism and a translation of the Psalms followed. But, together with these works, others that were violently polemical found their way to Spain; their discovery set the Inquisition to work.[1] Accordingly, **Cassiodoro** de Reina (Bibl. Wiff. II 163 ff.) now also fled to Switzerland, where his Spanish Bible appeared in 1569.

Other Spaniards first came into contact with the Reformation in foreign parts; John **Diaz** (see p. 152), who was murdered in 1546 at Neuburg on the Danube by the contrivance of his own brother; Francis **Enzinas** (Dryander) of Burgos, who, having at an early date visited the Netherlands, went to Wittenberg, where he made a translation of the New Testament into Spanish in Melanchthon's house (1543), which he had printed at Antwerp. This brought upon him the Inquisition and imprisonment; he managed, however, to escape, and lived an unsettled life in Wittenberg, Strasburg, Switzerland, England, and, lastly, Strasburg, until his death in 1552 (Bibl. Wiff. I 131 ff.).

During the lifetime of Charles V., whose attention was taken up by German affairs and the wars with France, matters were to a certain extent allowed to drift; small communities were able to assemble in Seville, Valladolid and other places, which led a secret conventicle-life and found edification in the evangelical writings that they managed to smuggle in; but in this case also

---

[1] The Index of the Inquisitor-general Quiroza (1583), printed in Castro's history (German edition, p. 305 ff.) gives a synopsis of the Spanish literature, which the Inquisition ordered to be destroyed.

the lower orders displayed little sympathy. It was **Philip II.** (1556-1598) who first ruthlessly carried out the extirpation of the heretics. The Inquisition introduced severer measures; Paul IV. supported the pious work. Not only were backsliders to be handed over to the "secular arm," *i.e.*, doomed to death, but those abjurers, whose recantation was suspicious, were only to be crushed by fear. Their property was confiscated, the informers received the fourth part of the confiscated property; the confessional, by refusing absolution, was also intended to extort full confessions (*e.g.*, the betrayal of guilty persons). In 1559 appeared the first *Index librorum prohibitorum* in Spain. The means at the disposal of the spiritual court of justice were strengthened. Executions, in order to intensify the impression, became public solemnities, autos de fé (*Actus fidei*) horrible public festivals of religion and patriotism at the same time, the Court even taking part in the ecclesiastical part of the Act.[1] Words and thoughts were strictly watched; even the highest dignitaries were not safe from the prying gaze of the Inquisition.

The Dominican, Bart. **Carranza,** a zealous persecutor of the heretics, who was raised to the archbishopric of Toledo in 1558, in consequence of a commentary on the Catechism which appeared in the same year at Antwerp, fell under the suspicion of having propounded the Lutheran doctrine of justification. The action which was brought against him lasted for seventeen years; Philip, in the cause of his Spanish inquisition, contended with the Pope for the prerogative of judging the first Spanish prelate. The Council of Trent supported his cause and declared his Catechism to be unassailable. Pius V., himself a Dominican, transferred the case to Rome; finally, under Gregory XIII., Carranza was condemned to abjure sixteen heretical propositions, to suspension and the usual penances (1576), but died a few days after. **Augustin Cazalla,** formerly the Emperor's Confessor, who, being secretly a Lutheran, had made his mother's house in Valladolid the meeting-place of a small community, was his pupil. In 1559, he was burnt in Valladolid at the first greater Auto de fé together with his brothers and sisters, the body of his mother (already deceased) and other comrades. At Seville (see p. 316) **Const. Fuente** now fell into the hands of the Inquisition, his desperate resolve to join the Order of the Jesuits being unable to save him; nothing but death from fever (1560) in prison saved him from perishing in the flames. The learned Augustinian **Luis de Leon,** Professor at Salamanca, who was prominent as a poet, was obliged to spend five years in prison on a trifling suspicion, *e.g.*, of having declared the Vulgate to be capable of improvement.

---

[1] Reg. Gons. **Montes** describes the terrorism and the artifices employed by the Inquisition in his *Sanctae inquisit. Hispan. artes*, 1567. Cp. WILKENS, p. 183 ff., 234 ff. LLORENTE's figures, where they can be tested, can be shown to be exaggerated.

The Autos de fé of 1559 and 1560 practically completed the work of terror; the succeeding years could only glean. Protestantism was annihilated, before it had taken root in the life of the people. Spain was certainly spared the troubles of a religious war; but this speedy victory over the Reformation was for a long time the ruin of Church and Nation.

2. The Religious Struggles in the Netherlands.

Sources: Archives ou corresp. inédite de la maison d'Orange-Nassau, by GROEN V. PRINSTERER, 1835, ff. Corresp. de Philippe II sur les affaires des Pays-Bas, by GACHARD. 2 vols. Brux., 1848, 1851.

Literature: see above, p. 196; CUNO, Fr. Junius d. Aelt. Amst., 1891. J. REITSMA, Oostergo. Leeuwarden, 1888; F. NIPPOLD, Die römisch-kath. K. im Königreich der Niederl. Leipz., 1877. H. v. TREITSCHKE, Die Rep. d. verein. Niederl. in Pr Jb 24. W. P. C. KNUTTEL, De toestand der nederl. Katholieken ten tijde der Republiek. s'Gravenh., 1892.

In the year 1554, when Philip II. left the Netherlands (p. 198), fourteen new bishoprics were created,[1]—a measure, the original object of which was to separate the Netherlands completely from France and Germany by the development of an ecclesiastical polity of their own: but it met with a very chilling reception as being a strengthening of the hierarchy and an alleviation of ecclesiastical measures of force, as well as an encroachment upon special rights and liberties. (Hitherto, of the bishoprics which were only four in number, Cambray, Arras and Tournay were under Rheims, Utrecht under Cologne; now, the three archbishoprics of **Mecheln** with Antwerp, Ghent, Bruges, Ypres, Herzogenbusch, Roremunde; **Cambray** with Arras, Tournay, St. Omer, Namur; **Utrecht** with Haarlem, Deventer, Leeuwarden, Middleburg, Groningen.) While Philip left his half-sister **Margaret of Parma** behind as Stadtholder, he appointed a privy council to assist her under the direction of **Anton Perennot Granvella** (son of Charles V.'s Chancellor), Bishop of Arras, upon whom the newly-founded archbishopric of Mecheln was conferred, and who, up to 1564, when he was recalled at the entreaty of the nobility, carried out Philip's ideas in church and state policy. Struggles for the liberation of the Netherlands commenced. Until the recall of Granvella, it was not antagonistic church principles that occupied a prominent place, but the conflicts of the Spanish Government with the States of the country, the nobles' hatred of Granvella, and the attitude of the States towards the relations between Spain and France. It was not until after his fall that the ecclesiastico-political struggle with the bishops, the mighty growth of the reformed communities, and the attempts to combine with the German and French Protestants commenced. In 1564, Philip uncompromisingly demanded the acceptance of the resolutions of the Council of Trent and the passing of the laws against heretics.

Then, in 1566, at the entreaty of the Calvinistic preacher,

---

[1] RAYNALDUS, Ann. 1559. n. 33 ff. DÖLLINGER, Beiträge I 248.

Francis Junius, a number of noblemen[1] entered into a "league of the nobility," adopting as their programme the so-called "Compromiss" drawn up by Philip of Marnix, to resist the introduction of the Inquisition to the uttermost and demanded the removal of the edicts against heretics and the convocation of the States-General. At the same time the "Union of the Consistories" held a meeting at Antwerp, and began with the organisation of the Calvinistic denominational Church. The adherents of the new doctrine now came forward at excited meetings, and when Philip's answer to the Regent's totally inadequate proposals for moderation arrived, which certainly did away with the Inquisition but contained a demand for the dissolution of the nobility and the violent suppression of evangelical sermons, excesses followed, attacks upon churches and images, plundering of monasteries (no blood, however, being shed) —the elementary expression of long pent-up popular feeling, which was not intended either by the league of the nobility or the consistories of the community, although violently stirred up by preaching against the "pollution" of the worship of images. Four Seigneurs devoted themselves to calming men's minds and restoring order, **William of Orange** (who had been brought up as a Protestant, but at that time had not as yet espoused the cause of the Reformation) only on the basis that toleration should be meted out to the Calvinists. William saw that Philip would now bring about a ruthless reaction, but he could not succeed in persuading the other Seigneurs to a common national resistance.

On the 1st of December, 1566, the league of the nobility was reorganised in combination with the "Consistorials" under Brederode and Marnix for the defence of the Christian faith. But Margaret's troops speedily put down the first resistance, the league of the nobility was dispersed, the Calvinists fled in crowds before the cruel reaction. Then, in 1567, the Duke of **Alba** appeared, to carry out at one and the same time the annihilation of heresy and the restoration of absolute Spanish authority at the expense of the rights of the States. The imprisonment of Egmont and Horn, the two representatives of the higher nobility, was followed by the establishment of the "Council of Disturbances,"

---

[1] They were called Gueux, since one of the Regent's councillors called out to her that she need not be alarmed by these beggars. The Evangelicals in the country style themselves those who have devoted themselves, "tot de gereformeeder religie" (1566, CUYPERS VAN VELTHOVEN, *Bois-le-Duc*, Brüssel, 1858, I, p. 118, 125 and often.

"the Council of Blood," which now persecuted all heresy as **high treason**. The fugitives gathered round William of Orange, who did not himself abandon Catholicism until 1573. Alba's tyranny, exercising an effect far beyond the circles of the religious parties interested, brought about **a rising of the nation**. But Lutheran Germany looked on idly in its confessional prejudice and political embitterment: Eric of Brunswick even fought on Alba's side against the "Sacramentarians." In 1573, Alba left the country in which he had pronounced 18,000 sentences of death to no purpose. The command in the struggle for liberty fell to Orange. During this struggle, the Walloon provinces,—which were rapidly inflamed but as rapidly discouraged, and in which, after the expulsion or annihilation of the Reformed, Catholic tendencies revived under the influence of the nobility,—separated themselves more and more from the democratic and reformed North, which was awakened more slowly, but then obstinately stood firm. At the **Agreement of Ghent** (1576) these Walloon provinces stipulated that the Catholic Church should be left untouched; and after the seizure of the unreliable Duke of Aerschot in 1577 the Catholic insurgents again approached the Spanish Government. The connection between Belgium and the Batavian country was broken up (Treaty of Arras, 1579). In 1581-1585, **Alexander of Parma** conquered Ghent, Brussels, Vilvorden, and Antwerp: the Protestant Belgians abandoned their home in thousands, in Flanders whole tracts of land became desolate. Thus, Belgium remained under the influence of Southern Europe without attaining to independent development,—**a spoil of the Counter-Reformation**. The emigrants were for the most part of Germanic descent; Neo-Latin peoples advanced into the desolate tracts of land. The Jesuits immediately invaded Antwerp and spread themselves over the whole of Belgium. But Spain inspired the nobility with its pride and the people with a fiery hatred of the Protestants. The development of the land was visibly retarded; more than half the property came into the possession of the Church.

It was otherwise in the North. "Here, through unspeakable suffering and wonderful victories, the foundation was laid for a new nationality." Here, on the 10th of January, 1579, the majority of the northern States, in the **Union of Utrecht**, bound themselves by a perpetual alliance to common resistance to intolerance; the more immediate regulation of religious matters was left to the provinces. In 1581, it was declared that the King of Spain had forfeited his authority and the freedom of the country was upheld during the life of William of Orange, who protected the liberty of the land against the Spaniards and the lower classes against the ambition of the town-councillors, and, after his assassination (1584), which prevented his being elected sole ruler, by his son Maurice. In 1609, a twelve years' cessation of hostilities was obtained from Spain—a deep humiliation of the haughty Spanish power—which, after the contest had broken out once again in 1621, at the Peace of Westphalia became a final recognition of independence. The reformed Church, during the struggles for freedom, had already attained an extraordinary development. Its educational institutions, Leyden (in 1575, to reward the heroic defence of the city against the Spaniards, it was given the choice of exemption from taxes for several years or a University, and chose the latter), Franeker (1585), Groningen (1612), Utrecht (1636), Harderwyk (1648), give evidence of the earnestness with which theology was cultivated.

In regard to the position of ecclesiastical affairs, we must consider:

1. **The relation of the Reformed to the Catholic Church.** The latter had not disappeared in the States-General, but at first even still formed the (gradually decreasing) majority. Notwithstanding, the compact Calvinist minority reduced the Catholics to the condition of citizens without rights—a remarkable testimony to the political power of Calvinism. Although it was indeed the Netherlands that, in consequence of their history, became the home of the principle of religious liberty, yet, after all the religious struggles, men's passions (especially amongst the lower orders of the people) were still too powerful to permit of such liberty being conceded equably to others by those who placed their own trust in the right of freedom of religious belief. The age could not conceive a state without a national church, and the Catholics were under suspicion, as having Spanish leanings. Public worship, as well as admission to public offices, remained forbidden to Catholics (until the French Revolution). Spain, in spite of all her efforts, had not been able to secure the right of public exercise of the Catholic form of worship at the armistice of 1609. People were afraid of the "serpent in their own bosom." Calvinism also showed itself exclusive in its attitude towards both Lutherans and Anabaptists; certainly a home and liberty of conscience (not without the influence of mercantile interests) were conceded to them, but they were prevented from propagating their doctrines.

2. **The relation of the Reformed Church to the State.** In the times of persecution, the communities of the northern provinces—those of the southern had for the most part fled to East Friesland, the Lower Rhine (Wesel), and the Palatinate—had naturally organised themselves in complete independence of the executive power, in presbyterial self-government in the sense of the *Confessio Belgica* and the church regulations drawn up at the Synod of Antwerp in 1564 and 1566. On the other hand, in the Netherlands that were gaining their freedom, as may easily be conceived, an inclination to bring ecclesiastical matters under their influence showed itself amongst the authorities both of the States and cities: in this the champions of political interests, in their attitude

towards the strict Calvinism of the clergy and of ecclesiastical circles were dogmatically more liberal-minded, and not seldom religiously indifferent. This State-church tendency found support in the so-called **Erastianism** (Erastus [the Graecised form of Lieber], Professor of Medicine at Bâle, who died in 1583), who upheld the right of the secular authorities to control church affairs, in the sense of dogmatic liberal-mindedness, and thereby set himself in opposition to the exclusive spirit of Calvinistic orthodoxy, developed in self-government, which repelled all Lutheran, Melanchthonian or Erasmian elements. The State-church tendency, which subordinated the Church to the provincial States, was expressed in the rough drafts of an ecclesiastical system drawn up in 1576 under the authority of William of Orange, which recommended presbyterial organisation of the communities, but appointment of the preachers, elders, and deacons by the city magistrates. The presbyterian spirit of independence remonstrated against this at the Synod of Dort, 1578 (the first Dutch national synod), but could not prevail in face of the States. The negotiations, which were protracted for a considerable time and accompanied by zealous theological disputation, at that time led to no common result—the assassination of William arrested all progress: the regulation of the constitution remained the business of the individual provinces. Oldenbarneveld adopted the middle course in the State-church order of 1591, which allowed a presbyterial and synodal constitution, but insured the States the right of sending as many deputies as they pleased to the provincial synods, and thereby securing a majority on every occasion—an expedient which satisfied no party. Also at the Synod of Dort (1618-1619), after questions of dogma had been settled, the question of the constitution of the native church was discussed with the deputies of foreign churches. The fact that this synod met was a concession to the spirit of the strictly Calvinistic, free church party, which was now vigorously bestirring itself. But here, dogmatic and constitutional struggles co-operated in a peculiar manner with the purely political constellation. The appearance of **Arminianism** had given occasion to the synod. For this and the course of events at the synod see below.

CHAPTER SECOND.

The Religious Struggles in France.

Literature (continued from p. 190). Poissy: H. KLIPFFEL, *Le colloque de Poissy*. Paris, 1867. BAUM, *Th. Beza II*. The Wars: LACRETELLE, *Hist. de France pendant les guerres de religion*. 2 vols. Paris, 1814. E. MARCKS, *Coligny und die Ermordung Franz v. G.*s in HZ 62, 42 ff.; The Massacre of St. Bartholomew: *Correspondance du roi Charles IX. 1572*. Paris, 1830; L. WACHLER, *Die Pariser Bluthochzeit*. Leipz., 1826. SOLDAN, *Frankreich und die Bartholomäusnacht* in HTb 3. F. 5, 75 ff.: H. BAUMGARTEN, *Vor der Bartholomäusnacht*. Strassb., 1882 (against WUTTKE, *Zur Vorgesch. der Bartholomäusnacht*. Leipz., 1879, and BORDIER, *La St. Barthél*. Geneva, 1879): TH. SCHOTT in ThLZ 1882, Sp. 231 ff. PHILIPPSON, *Westeuropa*, p. 225 ff.; the same, *Die röm. Curie und die Bartholomäusnacht* in DZG VII 108 ff.; DE LA FERRIÈRE, *Lettres de Catherine de Méd*. Paris, 1891; the same, *La St. Barth*. Paris, 1892. The meeting at Bayonne: COMBES, *L'entrevue de Bayonne*. Paris, 1882. E. MARCKS, *Die Zusammenkunft von B*. Strassb., 1889; HILLIGER in HTb 6. F. 11, 239 ff. PHILIPPSON, *Westeuropa*, p. 121; KLUCKHOHN in ABA IX 1, 151 ff. and 2, 179 ff.—SAYONS, *Études littéraires sur les écrivains français de la réformation. II.*—ARMSTRONG, *The political theory of the Huguenots* in English Historical Review XIII, 13 ff. TREITZSCHKE, *Hub. Languets Vindiciae*. 1846.—CH. LABITTE, *De la Démocratie chez les Prédicateurs de la Ligue*. ²Paris, 1866. HAFERKORN, *Die Hauptprediger der Ligue*. Dresden, 1892. M. PHILIPPSON in HZ XXI 73 ff, E. STÄHELIN, *Der Uebertritt Heinrichs IV*. Basel, 1856. (BENOIST) *Hist. de l'édit de Nantes*. 5 vols. Delft, 1693.

1. The Massacre of St. Bartholomew.

The shrewd, but at the same time irresolute Italian Catharine took over the regency on behalf of Charles IX. (1560-1574), the ten-year-old brother of Francis II. At first she attempted to play the different parties off against each other and to keep them in check: hence, concessions were made on both sides. The petition of the Protestants for religious liberty created an impression; an amnesty was agreed to, the edict against heretics mitigated, Condé liberated, searching ecclesiastical reforms proposed (assembly of the prelates at Poissy). Catharine appointed Antony of Navarre lieutenant-general. The Catholic party, aghast at this policy, began to negotiate with Philip II. In September, 1561, a **religious discussion** (which lasted till October 13th) took place at **Poissy** (*disputatio Pussicena*), in which Beza and Catharine's countryman Peter Martyr

(Pietro Martire) of Zürich took part.[1] Theological strength was undoubtedly (at least at first) on the side of Beza,[2] until the opposite party was reinforced by Lainez and Muret. The points discussed were the doctrine of the Eucharist and the jurisdiction of the Church. Charles of Lorraine hoped, in regard to the latter point, to elicit the internal dissension among the Protestants; but Calvin had warned them by letter not to take upon themselves the responsibility of the CA (although he himself had previously subscribed to it). A similar tendency is attributed to the invitation of German Lutherans to the conference recommended by Christopher Duke of Wurtemberg; but they (Jac. Andreä) came too late for the difference to have shown itself. A clausular formula dealing with Christ's presence at the Eucharist, so far as could be conceded according to Calvin's ideas,[3] upon which Catholics and Reformed came to an agreement after several conferences, was practically without result; the Sorbonnists at once declared it inadequate and heretical. Nevertheless, the discussion raised the courage and self-consciousness of the Huguenots. They met together everywhere, and now and again proceeded to violent measures, taking forcible possession of churches, which however in many places were voluntarily abandoned to them for undenominational use. At an Extraordinary Council of the Empire, on the proposal of the able Chancellor l'Hospital an edict was promulgated (January 17th, 1562) which granted the Reformed **restricted religious liberty.** They were certainly ordered to restore all churches and clerical revenues taken from the Catholics, but decrees of punishment against services **outside the towns,** which were placed under police supervision, were now abolished; synods and consistories were only to be held with the approval of the authorities. In spite of the scantiness of the concessions made, the Huguenots on the whole accepted the edict with joy; Beza exerted himself to allay possible discontent, but on the other side it met with obstinate resistance. Many parliaments refused to recognise it, the unprincipled Antony of Navarre went over to the Catholic party, while Francis of Guise declared that he would hew the edict in pieces with the sword. At first, he certainly took part in a meeting with Duke Christopher and his theologian Brenz at Zabern, at which the Cardinal of Lorraine gave his assent to the Lutheran doctrine of the Sacrament. But while Christopher gave himself up to the hope that he had obtained a great success, Francis, on his journey home, on the 1st of March accidentally came upon a Huguenot congregation engaged in the act of worship at the little town **of Vassy** in Champagne; he ordered a **massacre,** which gave the signal for the fateful **civil** and **religious** wars.

The **first** of these, in which Condé had been driven to take up arms by Catharine herself, concluded with the murder of Francis of Guise, a religious vendetta, which Coligny called a fortunate event for France (although he was able to repudiate its authorship), and the **Peace of Amboise** (March 19th, 1563), which was so far behind the edict of 1562, in that it guaranteed freedom of religious service only for a definite number of towns (inside the same). The

---

[1] Vergerius in vain endeavoured to get himself invited. See Briefwechsel Christophs und Verg., p. 285 ff.

[2] "Would to God this man were dumb or we ourselves deaf!" sighed the Cardinal of Lorraine.

[3] In SOLDAN I 511. BAUM II 344.

second war, which was commenced by the Huguenots (1567 to 1568), was terminated by the **Peace of Longjumeau**, at which pretty much the same written promises were given. In August, 1568, however, war was kindled for the **third** time; the **Peace of St. Germain-en-Laye** (1570), which was extorted from the Court by the power of the Protestants and its own need of money, granted an amnesty, complete liberty of conscience, a carefully defined freedom of worship for the nobles, and two places in every district for the reformed service; the Huguenots received as security four strongholds (La Rochelle, Montauban, Cognac and La Charité), which were to be restored to the King after two years—momentously characteristic of the false position of a State within the State which fell as a burden not only upon the Huguenots.

Peace now seemed assured, especially as Coligny was summoned to Court and began to acquire influence over Charles IX. In addition, foreign policy underwent a change; France withdrew from Spanish and papal influence, determined to support the Dutch in their struggle for freedom, in the hope of at the same time gaining Flanders. The internal reconciliation was to be sealed by the marriage of the youthful Henry of Navarre (son of the wavering Antony and the decidedly Protestant Jeanne d'Albret) to Margaret of Valois, sister of Charles IX.; on April 11th, 1572, the marriage contract was concluded, in spite of the refusal of the Pope to grant a dispensation. On the occasion of this marriage on the 24th of August, during the night before **St. Bartholomew**, the hatred of the Guises discharged itself upon the Huguenots—with the co-operation of Catharine, who now saw her influence over her son threatened—in the horrors of a terrible massacre. The defeat of the French in the Netherlands (July 17th) brought on the catastrophe, as Catharine was now enabled to counteract Coligny's influence with Charles. An attempt upon the life of Coligny (August 22nd), ordered by Catharine, failed, and he was only wounded; Catharine, in agreement with her son Henry of Anjou, now for the first time fighting seriously for her influence (which seemed threatened by the sympathy of the King for the wounded man) and in order to forestall the vengeance of the Huguenots, succeeded in convincing Charles of the danger which threatened him and of the necessity of making use of the favourable moment. With the assistance of the fanatical temper of the Parisian citizens, the cruel deed was carried out by 20,000 city militia under the command of the Guises. Coligny and many noble and distinguished leaders of the party fell; the bloodshed spread to the provinces. (The estimate of the number of the victims differs extraordinarily: in Paris, 1,000-10,000; in France, 12,000-100,000.)

The deed, although it had not been long premeditated,[1] was not merely the inspiration of the moment. Fanaticism and mixing up in the rivalry of political parties afforded the inflammable material; plans of murder had been long since suggested to the Court by Spain and the Pope, and had been meditated by Catherine for years past. At the Roman and Spanish Courts, where approval was regarded as certain, French diplomacy represented the matter as *acte prémédité*, to the Emperor as the fault of the Guises, and then as a matter of desperate self-defence. But the Cardinal of Lorraine immediately caused it to be spread abroad that the massacre was the final step in a policy which had been carried on for years with the object of putting obstacles in the way of the crown returning to a more conciliatory policy. Gregory XIII. certainly knew nothing of the affair beforehand, and appears to have been shocked at first, but subsequently congratulated the King, ordered illuminations in Rome, caused guns to be fired, a procession to be arranged, a Te Deum to be sung, and a medal commemorative of the *Ugonottorum strages* to be struck. (Charles's commemorative medal bears the inscription: *Pietas excitavit iustitiam!*)

2. The Edict of Nantes.

The atrocity of St. Bartholomew became the signal for fresh, embittered wars during the reign of Charles IX. (died 1574) and the shamelessly vicious and at the same time bigoted **Henry III.** (died 1589). The Huguenot movement, hitherto politically ambiguous, directed rather against persons than against principles, **now became a fundamental political opposition**, which also sought for a theoretical confirmation. The *Francogallia* (1573) of **Francis Hotman** (the biographer of Coligny) and the pseudonymous (**Herbert Languet's**) *Vindiciae contra tyrannos* (1579) justified the theory, the former especially, that female government was illegal in France and that the royal authority was limited by the will of the people, while the latter upheld revolt in case of misuse of the same authority.[2]

The **fourth** religious war was ended in 1573 by the **Peace of Boulogne**, which left the Huguenots only a miserable remnant of their hardly won liberties; the **fifth** (1574-1576), the **sixth** (1577), the **seventh** (1580) obtained fresh assurance of

---

[1] It has been erroneously attempted to attribute it to the meeting of Catharine with her daughter Elizabeth, the wife of Philip II., and Alba, at Bayonne in 1565; the only connection between the two events was the fact that that meeting had aroused the suspicion of the Huguenots and thus hastened the outbreak of the second religious war (p. 325).

[2] Here we find the questions: An subditi teneantur Principibus obedire, si quid contra legem Dei imperent. An liceat resistere Principi legem Dei abrogare volenti etc. An et quatenus Principi Rempublicam aut opprimenti aut perdenti resistere liceat. An iure possint aut debeant vicini Principes auxilium ferre aliorum Principum subditis, Religionis purae causa afflictis aut manifesta Tyrannide oppressis. The treatise *Réveille-matin des Français* went still further.

a certain amount of toleration.¹ Henry of Navarre, who, after the massacre, like Condé, had abjured the Protestant faith and fought against the Huguenots, and who had lived a life as unchaste as that of his brothers-in-law, which at that time was almost looked upon as the custom of the Court,—his wife who was guilty of incestuous practices almost outdid him in this—again took the side of the Reformed in 1576 against Henry III. and Henry of Guise. In 1576, the latter put himself at the head of the **league** supported by Spain (Philip II.) and the Pope, a party combination for the energetic promotion of Catholic interests (in certain eventualities even against the King) and the complete restoration of the Catholic religion in France; at the same time, it served Guise's ambition, and endeavoured to set the King aside.² At first of trifling importance, it subsequently, relying upon the religious hatred fostered by it and especially upon the fact that by the death of the King's youngest brother (Duke of Anjou, formerly of Alençon) a prospect of succession to the throne was opened to Henry of Navarre, obtained the most decided ascendency over the King. After the **eighth** war, it extorted from the King the **Treaty of Nemours** in 1585 (the Edict of June or Edict of Union), which "brought three times as many Huguenots to mass as the Massacre of St. Bartholomew": all previous concessions were hereby revoked. Sixtus V. excommunicated Condé and Henry of Navarre, declared them and their descendants deprived of their dignities, "especially their claim to the throne of France."³ The **ninth** war (that of the three Henrys) was successful as far as Henry of Navarre was concerned, but the King still vainly endeavoured to free himself from the terrorism of the Guises; he allowed the second Edict of Union to be wrung from him, which contained his promise upon oath not to lay down his arms before the last heretic was exterminated, commanded his subjects to do the like and never to recognise a non-Catholic prince as King. At the assembly of the States of the Empire at Blois this edict was confirmed by oath and made into a statute. On the 4th of December, 1588, the solemn reconciliation of the King to Henry of Guise (obtained by compulsion) took place; but a few days later (December 23rd and 24th) Henry III. got rid of his tyrants by causing Henry of Guise and his brother Charles the Cardinal to be assassinated. The third brother, the Duke of Mayenne, escaped a similar fate, and, having placed himself at the head of the League, and being supported by the indignation of the Catholic majority, so harassed the King, that he sought refuge with Henry of Navarre and threw himself into his arms, This proved the salvation of the monarchy; but Henry III., who had now been summoned to Rome by Sixtus V. under threat of excommunication, was murdered (1589) in the camp of St. Cloud by the fanatical Dominican Jacques Clément.

Henry of Navarre, now **Henry IV.** (1589-1610), found himself in

---

¹ After 1576 we find the expression "la religion prétendue réformée.."

² During the course of events, the democratic, the anti-monarchical tendency continually gained strength in this Catholic party.

³ *Mémoires de la Ligue* I 214. At that time Bellarmine also published an essay under a false name, in which he defended the bull of Sixtus V. and declared that Henry had forfeited the right of succession to the throne. (See DÖLLINGER-REUSCH, *Die Selbstbiographie Bellarmins*, p. 88 ff.

an extraordinarily difficult position in the struggle with the League,[1] which was supported by Spain and the Pope. Accordingly, after considerable hesitation, he found himself compelled again to abjure the reformed faith in 1593,—a step which political considerations showed him was indispensable for pacifying the country and securing the crown. At the same time this step freed him from the troublesome fetters of the reformed ecclesiastical discipline. Notwithstanding, Clement VIII. refused him recognition as King of France, and called upon the subjects to continue their resistance. It was not until 1595 that the Pope gave in after Henry's successes. His previous co-religionists, deprived of their leader and exposed to numerous acts of violence, were compelled to reorganise themselves as a political party (*Conseil général*). After lengthy negotiations the **Edict of Nantes** was finally issued April 13th, 1598, to secure the position of the Reformed.

> The Catholic religion is that which prevails in the State, hence their feast days are before all to be observed: but the Reformed are no longer to be persecuted for the sake of their religion. In Paris and five miles round, Rheims, Toulouse, Dijon, as well as in the army (the quarters of the reformed commanders excepted), no Reformed service was allowed to be held. Obligation to pay tithes and subordination to the Catholic laws of marriage continued in force. But the Reformed were to be admissible to all offices of State; in the Paris and other Parliaments there were special commissions to deal with their affairs, half of the members of which were to be chosen from the Reformed. Calvinistic service was allowed, wherever it had existed up to 1597; special buildings were granted for the purpose; the restoration of those of which they had been deprived was promised. Their children were not to be forcibly taken from them to be brought up as Catholics. They were to retain for eight years their fortresses and strongholds as security. The Catholics were allowed the free exercise of their religion throughout France; they were in consequence enabled to restore their form of worship in 250 towns and 2,000 villages. The germs of conflict in this edict consisted in its contradiction of the traditional view, that the Catholic Church could tolerate no other form of worship by the side of its own, and of the canonical condemnation of heresy: further, in the position of the Reformed as an armed corporation in the State. The opposition of the University of Paris, of the Parliament, and of the bishops to the edict was only with difficulty overcome by Henry IV.

The interval between 1598 and the Edict of Grace (Nîmes) 1629 is the period of the **political** power of French Calvinism as a State within the State. The consolidation of the position of its Church now also took place; new educational institutions flourished; at

---

[1] BOUCHER, *De iusta Henrici III. abdicatione.* Lugd., 1591; G. ROSSAEUS, *De iusta Reipubl. Christ. in Reges impios et haeret. authoritate.* 1590 (both written for the League and against Kingship).

Sedan (founded in 1580 by Duke Henry of Bouillon), Saumur (in 1604, by Duplessis-Mornay), Montpellier, Montauban, Nîmes, Pau (in Béarn), besides several gymnasia. The example set by Henry IV. and his expressed wish certainly enticed several back to Catholicism; the Jesuits who had been expelled in consequence of the act of Clement and their defence of it, as well as of a murderous attack upon Henry IV. laid to their charge, returned in 1603 and commenced their work of conversion. Yet Henry, up to the time of his death by Ravaillac's murderous hand, continued to show favour to the Reformed.

The government by women and the intrigues after his death during the minority of **Louis XIII.** promoted, amongst the Huguenot nobles as well as in the democratic towns, the spirit of independence which had been awakened by the political rights bestowed upon them; in the organised league of the Huguenots even the ideas of a Huguenot free and federal state, or of a foreign protectorate were entertained, but repressed by divergent interests and internal differences, as well as by the influence of thoughtful men like Sully and Duplessis-Mornay. But it was a matter of supreme importance that Louis XIII., on the declaration of his majority, restored the mass by force of arms (1620) in the district of Béarn, the mother-country of French Protestantism, and effected a regular counter-Reformation. The flames of religious and civil war broke out afresh. After the Huguenots found that the conditions of the Peace of Montpellier (1622) were not kept, they sought the support of England; on the other hand, the development of the French State proceeded under Richelieu's guidance to the bringing about of a monarchy in opposition to the aristocracy generally and the Huguenot league in particular, the political existence of which it was decided must be annihilated. The fall of La Rochelle (1628), which heroically defended itself after being abandoned by the English, and the final subjection of the last Huguenot leader, the Duc de Rohan, was followed by the **Edict of Grace of Nimes** (1629), which brought about the decisive change that, while the ecclesiastical and civil rights granted by the Edict of Nantes were confirmed, political independence was lost, and thus the **political corporation** of the Huguenots ceased to exist.

CHAPTER THIRD.

The Struggles in England and Scotland.

1. Bloody Mary.

Sources and *Literature* (continued from p. 207): *Examinations and writings of* J. PHILPOT. Camb., 1842. *Writings of* J. BRADFORD. Camb., 1848. MICHELANG. FLORIO, *Hist. de la vita e de la morte de l'Ill. Sign. Giov. Graia*, 1607; R. DIXON (Anglican), *History of the Church of England.* IV. Lond., 1891; A. ZIMMERMANN (S. J.), *Maria d. Kathol.* Freib., 1891 (a vindication).

The powerful and arbitrary Duke of Northumberland had persuaded Edward VI., when his health began to fail, to consent to the perverse arrangement, whereby his (Northumberland's) daughter-in-law **Jane Gray**, great granddaughter of the sister of Henry VIII., was declared heiress-apparent (Elizabeth's illegitimacy had not yet been removed by a resolution of Parliament). But hostility to Northumberland brought about the elevation of **Mary** (1553-1558), who was recognised as queen a few days after Lady Jane's accession had been proclaimed. This introduced a complete revolution in the state of affairs.

The foreign theologians fled, Gardiner and Bonner were restored to posts of honour, and the former became Mary's right hand; Northumberland was condemned as guilty of high treason, Edward buried in accordance with the old Catholic ritual, liberty of preaching and the press limited. Soon the prominent clergy, the supporters of innovation, were imprisoned. Parliament, which opened with the celebration of a mass, was obliged to recognise the validity of Henry's marriage to Mary's mother, and, in spite of its reluctance, to annul all Edward's religious ordinances. It became evident how strong a hold the old Church still had upon the people, who were unwilling to abandon the old worship. Mary contented the nobles by handing over to them the confiscated church property. Romish sympathies revived amongst the clergy. After the dissolution of Parliament, Mary had a freer hand with Gardiner; large numbers of married clergymen were reduced to beggary with their wives and children: divine service in English was forbidden. The next step, the arrangements for her marriage with **Philip II.** certainly excited violent opposition in the country and for a time shook her position. But she overcame the resistance and behaved with greater harshness. Jane Gray died on the scaffold. Persecution (now as much political as religious) began with fresh violence. In the summer of 1554, Mary was married to Philip (eleven years younger than herself), who brought Spanish theologians (Soto and Carranza) with him into the country: thousands of foreigners were obliged to leave England, and large numbers of natives were compelled to flee (amongst them Knox). The royal supremacy was abolished and again made dependent upon the Pope. Cardinal **Pole** (who personally held much milder views than the Queen) appeared in November, 1554, again received England into the bosom of the Romish Church (Wilkins IV 91 ff., 110 ff.), and was appointed Archbishop of Canterbury and Chancellor of Oxford and Cambridge. When his hope of issue, and with it that of succession to the throne of England was disappointed, Philip left the country (1555). The persecution assumed a bloody character; after Gardiner's death (Nov. 1555), Bonner became the willing instrument to carry out a bloody butchery. Two or three hundred executions followed, all the important leaders being singled out,—the baptism of blood of the English Church. The three most distinguished heads of the reformed clergy, **Cranmer, Ridley** Bishop of London, and **Hugh Latimer** Bishop of Worcester had already been thrown into prison (1553). The two last were burnt at Oxford in 1555; Cranmer, deprived of office by the Pope[1] and exhausted by prolonged tortures, made a kind of recantation, which he subsequently retracted: this brought him to the stake in 1556. The bodies of Bucer and Fagius were disinterred and burnt together with their writings. Mary died childless on the 17th of November, 1558, Pole on the following day.

During the harsh oppression of this reign a total revolution took place in the feelings of the nation; the excesses of their bloody reaction did more towards making England Protestant than all the efforts of Edward's reign. On the other hand, the result of the reign of Mary was, that the Catholic party has never entirely disappeared in England, as was the case in Scandinavia.

2. Elizabeth.

Sources and *Literature: Correspondence of* MATTHEW PARKER, *1535-1575.* Camb. 1853. JOHN STRYPE, *Annales of the Reformation during Elizabeth's reign.* ²Oxf. 1824. *De persecutione anglicana libellus* (a Jesuit account). Romae, 1582. *Martyrium R. P. Edm. Campiani, 1581.* Lov. 1582. SPILLMANN (S. J.), *Die engl. Märtyrer unter Elis. bis* 1583. *Maria-Laacher Ergänzungsheft* 39/40. BRIDGETT and KNOX, *The true story of the Cath. Hierarchy deposed by Queen Elizabeth.* Lond. 1889 (HpBl 105, 278 ff.). E. BEKKER, *Elis. u. Leicester (1560-1562).* Giessen, 1890. F. KNOX, *Records of the English Catholics under the penal laws.* Lond. 1878 (HpBl 82, 39 ff.). TH. G. LAW, *A hist. sketch of the conflicts between Jesuits and seculars.* 1890. BELLESHEIM, *Card. Allen u. die engl. Seminare auf dem Festlande.* Mainz, 1885. S. HOPKINS, *The Puritans and Queen Eliz.* 3 vols. New York, 1875.

Elizabeth (1558-1603), by birth and education (she was brought up by Cranmer) the antipodes of Mary, had endeavoured, during

---

[1] WILKINS IV 132 ff.

the reign of the latter, to secure her life by a politically shrewd acceptance of Catholic forms, had been imprisoned for a time and threatened with death, and, finally, was entreated by the dying Queen to uphold the Catholic religion. At first, she behaved with discretion and in a conciliatory manner, favoured by Spain, which from hostility to her would have furthered the cause of Mary Stuart, and, consequently, of France; hence the English Catholics also did homage to her with a good grace.[1] But, in consequence of her birth—she was declared illegitimate by Rome—and the behaviour of her opponents, she was led into the path of ecclesiastical reform and the restoration of the royal supremacy.

Pope Paul IV. declared her accession to be illegal; upon this Mary Stuart, as the granddaughter of the sister of Henry VIII., based her claims, on the advice of the Guises styled herself Queen of England, and remained a menacing pretender, supported at first by France and the Pope, and then by Spain. The Parliament of 1559 (opened with mass and an evangelical sermon at the same time) recognised Elizabeth's right of succession, and declared that any expression of doubt on the point should be punished by confiscation of property and all opposition regarded as high treason. The same Parliament restored to her the highest ecclesiastical authority (not indeed as its head, but as "supreme governor" of the Church); this authority was to be exercised by a board to be appointed by the Crown (a court of high commission). The Oath of Supremacy was restored: only 183 Catholic clergymen out of about 900 refused to take it. (This oath was subsequently prescribed also for the members of the Lower House and for all who did not take part in public worship, but in practice it was not carried out, although it thus became possible to take measures against suspected persons).

In June 1559, the **Act of Uniformity** followed. Elizabeth had handed over Edward's Liturgy (p. 208) to a mixed commission for revision; the Act now introduced this liturgy with certain alterations.[2] A relapse into Romanism was threatened with severe punishments; yet the penal laws were at first administered with mildness. The opposition to this innovation, which was raised in

---

[1] The statement that, as early as 1559, it was intended that Calvin should be invited to England by Elizabeth, is quite improbable.—*Calendar of State Papers, Spanish, 1558-1567*, p. 39.

[2] The prayer against the Pope (From all sedition and privy conspiracy, from the tyranny of the Bishop of Rome and all his detestable enormities . . . Good Lord, deliver us. KETLEY p. 233) was struck out, as well as the declaration that kneeling at the Lord's Supper was not intended as adoration (restored in 1662); images, crucifixes, congregational singing and music, as well as the vestments of the priests were to be retained (in 1552 a table, covered during the Communion with a white linen cloth, was ordered to be placed in the body of the Church, on the north side of which the priest was to stand).

convocation, was finally disregarded. All the bishops but one, whose number had diminished of late years from twenty-three to sixteen, now refused to take the oath of supremacy and were obliged to retire,[1] together with a number of the higher canons, but only a few ministers. **Matthew Parker**, formerly the chaplain and friend of Elizabeth's mother, who had subsequently retired into subordinate positions and devoted his life to learned studies, was now drawn out of his retirement by the Queen and promoted to the archbishopric of Canterbury. When the fifteen bishops refused to consecrate him, the ceremony was carried out with the assistance of three bishops who had been driven out in the reign of Mary. The consecration of the new Anglican episcopate started again from him, so that the validity of the episcopal succession asserted by this Church, and disputed by Rome, especially the Jesuits, is to be dated back to him (Wilkins IV 198 f.). For the purpose of a confession of faith, recourse was had to Edward's 42 articles, which, modified by Brenz with the aid of the Confessio Wirtenbergica, were accepted by Convocation (1563) as the **Thirty-nine Articles of the Anglican Church.**[2]

The doctrine of the Eucharist is less abruptly reformed, the direct denial of the real presence of Christ being changed into a presence of Christ (*tantum coelesti et spirituali ratione*) in which faith is the medium of reception; it is not asserted, as before, that *Rex Angliae est supremum caput in terris post Christum ecclesiae Anglicanae et Hibernicae*, but only the highest power *in ecclesiasticis et politicis* is adjudged to him, and a *ministerium* of the Word and Sacrament expressly rejected; he only possesses the prerogative which God according to the Scriptures has bestowed upon all pious princes. Any opposition to these articles is threatened with severe punishment. Parliament confirmed them in 1571, when it recognised the previous resolutions in religious matters in the face of the ban hurled by Pius V. against Elizabeth.

The creation of the Anglican State Church in its peculiar adjustment of the demands of the Reformation and the traditions of the old Church was now attacked on two sides.

Above all, by a **Romish agitation.** In 1560, Pius IV. had at first endeavoured to keep Elizabeth in the faith by means of concessions (confirmation of the English liturgy, administering of the cup to the laity, recognition of her succession), offered through a nuncio, but in vain. A second nuncio was refused an audience. In 1561 a conspiracy against Elizabeth was discovered, in consequence of which Parliament demanded further extension of the oath of supremacy. Papist pamphlets and wandering priests in disguise agitated on behalf of the old faith. A conspiracy supporting the claim of Mary of Scotland

---

[1] On the fates of some individual bishops, see Hp Bl 80, 863 ff.
[2] WILKINS IV 233 ff. NIEMEYER p. 601 ff. SCHAFF I 615 ff., III 486 ff.

(who had fled to England in 1568) to the throne, in which some of the nobles took part, broke out into a rebellion in 1569; at the instigation of the defeated Catholic Lords the papal ban was issued (Wilkins IV 260 ff.), and Pius V. did not scruple to support conspiracies against Elizabeth's life.[1]

Parliament now endeavoured (1571) to protect the Queen by a number of severe enactments (against attacks on her person, her orthodoxy and her right to the throne, against the introduction of papal bulls; all officials were bound to the XXXIX Articles). On the other hand, English colleges were established abroad in the cause of Rome (first at the instigation of William Allen, the College at Douai [later at Rheims] by Philip II.; next, that at Rome under Jesuit management by Gregory XIII., followed by several others in Belgium and Spain). Up to the year 1585, about 300 priests were secretly sent over to England from Rome and Douai, who had been exhorted by the Pope himself, "to remove the impious Jezebel" (Froude XI 304); the agitation on behalf of the Romish Church is closely connected with that on behalf of Mary Stuart. The result was repeated revolts, followed by still severer laws; between 1580 and 1590 numerous Roman priests were executed. Staying away from the Anglican service and secretly taking part in the mass were punished with heavy fines. Several risings in favour of Mary Stuart, which however were frustrated by discovery, disturbed the country until she herself fell a victim (1587) to State reasons, and Philip's Armada was defeated and annihilated, all danger from Spain being thereby removed.

But the **Protestant opposition** of the distinctly Presbyterian party was also aroused. This party had successfully fought the battle against Rome in Scotland in 1560; the majority of those who had been driven from England during the reign of Mary had adopted decidedly Calvinistic views abroad, and became acquainted with Calvinistic ritual, ecclesiastical discipline and congregational constitution. Now, the Anglican Church system appeared to them thoroughly leavened with papal and worldly leaven. They took offence (1) at the **Form of Worship** with its liturgy translated from the Popish liturgy, with its pomp, organ, crucifix, vestments, rite of baptism, priests' garments, &c.; and also (2) at the **Constitution**, the royal supremacy and the rule of the State in the Church, as well as the hierarchical structure, the episcopal constitution, the different ecclesiastical grades, the close connection of the episcopate with worldly possession and political status. Lastly (3) they also missed the **discipline**, that *nervus ecclesiae*, especially a strict Sabbath-law, and were scandalised at the traditional worldly Sunday amusements. The opposition of this tendency (known since 1564 by the name of **Puritanism** was **at first** aroused in reference to matters of ritual, especially the priests' vestments;[2]

---

[1] DÖLLINGER-REUSCH, *Die Selbstbiographie Bellarmins*, p. 308 ff.

[2] John Hooper, Bullinger's friend, during the reign of Edward for a long time refused the bishopric of Gloucester that was offered him, since he could not reconcile himself to the episcopal robes.

constitutional questions did not stand in the forefront as in Scotland. Elizabeth opposed demands of this kind with her efforts after uniformity. But, by a logical sequence, the condemnation of unscriptural usages was connected with the question whether the authorities had any power in the matter, without the assent of the congregations. First, as **a party within** the Anglican Church (consequently still recognising the supremacy) and externally more or less acquiescing in conformity, it advanced, with increasing strictness towards the clergy of its views (Nonconformists), until, after 1567, those who held more decided views **left** the established Church, since preaching and the administration of the Sacrament were not permitted them without an alloy of idolatry. Meetings began to be held in private houses; separate communities (first at Wandsworth in 1572) were organised, in which a presbyterian constitution and independence of the congregations in opposition to a hierarchical and State church tutelage were brought about. Thomas Cartwright, a Cambridge professor, an exile since 1570, is a prominent representative of this tendency.

But the spirit of Puritanism exercised a far-reaching effect over the not very numerous separated communities; many of the clergy and laity of the State Church shared it, without outwardly abandoning the latter; and it was just the most capable, who were most deeply attracted by the evangelical cause, who had inclinations in this direction, while at the same time there were many secret Catholics and many unworthy hirelings amongst the officials of the State church. Also a stricter Calvinistic dogmatism, which the XXXIX Articles did not thoroughly satisfy, was combined with puritanical tendencies.

The puritanical piety of the laity at first wove its web in house and family, avoided public worship and in particular withdrew from the lower order of clergy, which was frequently uneducated and worldly. But it was persecuted by the State Church with increasing severity (especially under Archbishop Whitgift 1583-1604).[1] The

---

[1] In his time it seemed as if the English Church (in matters of dogma) was destined to assume a more sharply Calvinistic character. At Cambridge a dispute arose between the Calvinistically inclined professors (especially W. Whitaker) and their Arminian colleague Peter Baron (Baro). In consequence of this, in 1595, the doctrine of predestination was accepted by Whitgift and other theologians in the so-called nine **Lambeth Articles**; but Elizabeth immediately suppressed them, and when, in 1604, during the discussions between Episcopalians and Puritans the latter appealed to the Lambeth Articles, they met with violent opposition from the former. Richard Bancroft, Bishop of London, attacked the doctrine of predestination as a horrible one, leading to despair (SCHAFF I 658 ff., III 523 ff.).

clergy were compelled to declare the supremacy of the Queen, the conformity of the Common Prayer Book and the XXXIX Articles to Scripture. Two Puritan clergymen, who refused to take the Oath of Supremacy, were executed in 1583; all opposition to the established form of worship was punished as a violation of allegiance. After the Act of Parliament of 1592, all who obstinately refused to take part in public worship were imprisoned, and, if they persisted in their obstinacy, were expelled the country after three months. Although it is calculated that, towards the end of Elizabeth's reign, about a third of the clergy were removed from office, yet all the oppression of the State Church was unable to stifle these tendencies even in the Church itself.

3. Ireland.

Sources and *Literature:* *Calendar of State Papers, Ireland,* ed. H. C. Hamilton. R. MANT, *History of the Church of Ireland* (1535-1690). London, 1840 (written from the Anglican point of view). A. BELLESHEIM, *Geschichte der kath. Kirche in Irland.* II. Mainz, 1890. *Katholik* 1888. I 197 ff.

Ireland, during the reign of Henry VIII., only nominally subject to the English crown in its larger Western part, still possessed old Irish princes; in the East (the pale), English settlers exploited the people. Henry's attempts to extend his ecclesiastical supremacy to Ireland encountered a resistance from the Church (which was not as yet very pronounced) as well as from the nation. George Browne, who had been appointed Archbishop of Dublin through Cranmer in 1536, with the assistance of a kind of Parliament composed of English colonists, secured the acceptance of the supremacy of the Crown and its severance from the Pope. The clergy acquiesced, monasteries were dissolved, the Irish nobles (the princes) were won over by gifts of church and monastic property. Matters of belief were not touched, hence, in Ireland, the revolution which at the same time confirmed England's power, was carried out in a comparatively peaceful manner. On the other hand, stronger resistance was shown to Edward VI.'s ecclesiastical legislation, when it was sought to impose the **English** liturgy (as a means of anglicising the country) upon the Irish. The resistance was encouraged from France and Rome; nationality and politics helped to keep it up. Some of the higher clergy now fled, a new regal hierarchy was established, while the people and the lower clergy clung firmly to the old worship. After the latter had been restored during the reign of Mary in 1556 by an Act of Parliament, in which, however, they admitted that the rights of the Crown were left intact, Ireland was again obliged to acquiesce during the reign of Elizabeth. The Parliament of 1560 declared that the Irish Church should be reformed on the model of the English. This, however, was only gradually accomplished, in proportion as Ireland came into the hands of English colonists and landowners, together with whom the Anglican hierarchy was put in possession of church property; the people became impoverished, but clung to its Church, being especially strengthened in its resistance by mendicant friars. Ireland remained the thorn in England's flesh; it always kicked at the yoke which was imposed upon it.

4. Scotland.

Sources and *Literature:* J. KNOX, *The history of the reformation of religion within the realm of Scotland.* Edinb. 1732. G. BUCHANAN, *Rerum Scotic. hist.* Edinb. 1583. D. CALDERWOOD, *The history of the Kirk of Scotland,* ed. Thomson. 8 vols. Edinb. 1842-1849. P. HEYLYN, *Aërius Redivivus or the history of the Presbyterians* [1536-1647]. Lond. ²1672 (written with an Anglican bias). VON RUDLOFF, *Gesch. d. Ref. in Schottl.* 2 vols. Berl. 1847. 1849. J. KÖSTLIN, *Die schott. Kirche von d. Ref. bis auf die Gegenwart.* Hamb. and Gotha 1852. BURTON, *The history of Scotland.* ²Lond.-Edinb. 1873. III. BELLESHEIM, *Gesch. d. kath. Kirche in Schottl.* Mainz. 1883. For Hamilton, see P. LORIMER, Lond. 1858; KÖSTLIN in DZ chr. WL 1857; COLLMANN in Zh Th 34, 205; MACKAY in Dict. of Nat. Biogr. XXIV 201 ff. KNOX: Works, 6 vols, Edinb. 1864; biography by M'Crie, Edinb. 1811, London 1874. MACKAY in Dict. of Nat. Biogr. XXXI 308 ff.; for J. Craig, see MACKAY in the same, XII 446.

In Scotland also, in spite of the generally defective state of education, Luther's ideas had early found a welcome. As early as 1525, the introduction of Lutheran works was forbidden, under pain of severe punishment; about this time Tyndale's English New Testament had also found its way to Edinburgh and St. Andrews. At the same time humanistic influences now made themselves prominent, and efforts were made for the improvement of education; a national poetry also began to flourish. Public affairs were as yet still but little developed; the highland clans were practically independent of the King, and the higher nobility of the lowlands enjoyed a large measure of self-dependence. The royal authority relied for its support against the nobles upon the clergy who were provided with large property (nearly half the landed estates) and who, dependent upon the King and employed by him almost exclusively in State affairs, were in addition extremely worldly and, on the whole, ill-educated. The rivalry between prelates and nobles became an important factor in the course of the history of the Reformation.

The first evangelical movements began during the reign of James V., who took over the government in 1524 (his affairs had been managed by a regency from 1513). **Patrick Hamilton** was the first martyr to the evangelical cause. Related to the highest families, he had studied at Paris and Louvain, where he had become a convert to Erasmianism, but soon, however, was enlightened by evangelical principles. In 1527, he fled from the persecution of John Beaton, Archbishop of St. Andrews, to Germany, studied at Wittenburg and Marburg (whither he had been attracted with Tyndale, especially by Francis Lambert), and returned to England in 1528, when he was again seized by the Archbishop, and burnt as a heretic, before he was 24 years old. Evangelical sympathies manifested themselves not only amongst the higher nobility, but also amongst the Augustinians (Alexander Alane [Alesius], stirred up by Patrick Hamilton) and Dominicans. The nobles and landed proprietors in Ayrshire also entered into connection with Lollardism. A mighty movement also made itself felt amongst the citizens; however, especially under Beaton's influence, all attempts at innovation were violently suppressed. Henry VIII. endeavoured (after 1535) to persuade King James to follow the path of his church policy, but the latter, to whom the bishops handed over large sums of money to escape the confiscation of Church property, considered it safer to continue to place his reliance upon the clergy. When James attached himself to the policy of France in opposition to Henry, the result was a war with England, in which a large number of the nobles, although persecution was now stayed, left the King in the lurch. James, defeated by Henry at Solway, died in 1542 out of his mind. A few days before, his wife Mary of Guise had borne him a daughter (Mary Stuart).

During the subsequent minority of the heiress to the throne (1542 to 1560) James Hamilton, Earl of Arran, who at first fulfilled the duties of regent, was under English influence; the reading of the Bible in the English and Scotch languages was allowed. But this influence, especially after the agreement of 1543, which was favourable to England, provoked a reaction, which brought the French-Catholic party to the helm—Queen Mary of Guise, who kept up a close intimacy with her brothers and Catherine de' Medici and Cardinal David Beaton, nephew and successor of J. Beaton. The Earl of Arran was obliged to acquiesce in this influence and to abjure his previous adherence to Luther. Under stress of persecution, the evangelical party now began to unite in an energetic, political party of opposition, which found its basis of support in the nobility, but soon also in the people. But at the same time the connection with Wittenberg ceased,[1] and the party assumed a **Calvinistic** character. After 1545, executions of the evangelicals again took place; Beaton went through the country holding investigations. The evangelical sermons of G. Wishart, who returned from England in 1544, made a special impression; in 1546 he was burnt in the presence of Beaton, whose speedy end he prophesied. Soon after, the latter was murdered by sixteen conspirators with the cognisance of Henry (May, 1546). The nobles, who were hostile to him, occupied the fortress of St. Andrews, and appointed the impetuous **John Knox**, who had been tutor to a nobleman's son, their preacher. He violently attacked the anti-Christian papacy and the idolatry of the Romish worship, and testified on their behalf to the justice of their treatment of Beaton,[2] until the regency, with the help of the French, compelled the fortress to surrender and sent the prisoners (amongst them Knox) to France in French galleys (cp. p. 209). The subsequent fate of the ecclesiastical movement was determined by political conditions, in accordance with its relations to England and France. The effect of the war energetically carried on by Somerset against Scotland during the reign of Edward VI. was that the Queen-mother was able to dispose the regent and a large number of the nobles in favour of France. The six years old Mary Stuart was betrothed to the Dauphin of France and sent to the French Court to be educated. **Archbishop Hamilton** now endeavoured to prevent secession from the Church by means of a Catechism written in the language of the country, which made no mention of the Pope and proposed an evangelically worded doctrine of justification by the side of a rigorous Mariolatry.[3] Measures against the Protestants, which once more led to the stake, were soon checked again by other considerations. Mary Guise, in order to remove the regent, which she succeeded in doing in 1554, and to take his place, was obliged to get in touch with the Protestant nobility. In addition, the opposition to the Anglo-**Spanish** power under

---

[1] From 1519-1544 nine Scotchmen were entered in the Wittenberg Register; since that date, none.

[2] The deed of the conspirators is called "The godly fact," in KNOX, History; but compare also KÖSTLIN, p. 36.

[3] The Catechism of J. Hamilton 1552. Oxf. 1884.

Catholic Mary must be borne in mind. Scotland accordingly now received the fugitive English Protestants.

Knox also returned, the same irreconcileable enemy of the papacy and every kind of hierarchy and papal "idolatry," convinced that force was permissible against "deadly sinners," and at the same time holding more earnest theological views owing to his contact with Calvin. For, fleeing from bloody Mary (p. 331), he had betaken himself to the Continent, where he became intimate with Calvin (and Bullinger), adopted his theological views (even the doctrine of predestination) and learned to value the moral discipline of Geneva. For a time he was minister to a congregation of French and English emigrants at Frankfort-on-the-Main, but had disagreed with it in regard to "unnecessary" ceremonies. In the autumn of 1555, he appeared in Edinburgh, called upon all who held his views to break openly with Catholicism and administered the Sacrament here and there in the reformed manner. Summoned before the spiritual court at Edinburgh, he appeared with so large a following that it was thought advisable to adjourn the case. A letter which he wrote to Mary of Guise was without result. From Geneva also, whither he returned at first as preacher to the English congregation, he exercised a wider influence, proclaiming the theocratic doctrine of the Old Testament,[1] that the authorities are bound, in accordance with the law of God, to do away with and severely punish idolatry (*i.e.*, Catholicism); if they did not do so but rather strengthened it, the nobles and people would not only have the right but would be bound to resist the Queen, even to punish her with death; that the zealot-right of the individual servant of God was in eventualities valid.[2] A number

---

[1] He regards the Gospel as the new law of God, the Church as the external fulfilment and representation of the divine statutory will by a nation which devotes itself to the people of God and thereby enters upon the rights and obligations of Israel.

[2] These views find their analogy in the doctrine developed by Romish theologians and also put forward by Knox's Glasgow tutor, the schoolman John Mayor—that of the right of resistance to princes in the name of the sovereignty of the people (KÖSTLIN, p. 27), and, on the other hand, in the right claimed by the Popes, to dispose of the throne. But in Scotland such theories found an echo among a nobility which from olden times had never respected the tyrannical power of princes. (Of the seven first kings of the Stuart dynasty four had come to a violent end.) Cp. BUCHANAN Bl. 212 b, and the tractate appended to his history, *De iure regni apud Scotos*, in order to instruct the youthful James VI. in his *officium erga cives*. F. G. LAW in the Scottish Review XIX has most ably proved that J. Mayor must not be regarded as the "precursor" of the Scottish Reformation.

of Protestant barons and nobles, with Lord Erskine of Dun and James Stuart (Murray) at their head, in December, 1557, concluded a **Covenant** before the majesty of God and his congregation: "that we by his grace sall, with all diligence, continuallie apply our whole power, substance and our verie lives to mainteane, sett forward and establishe this most blessed Word of God and his congregatioun . . . Unto the which holie Word and Congregatioun we doe joyne ourselves, and doe forsake and renounce the congregatioun of Satan with all the superstitions, abominations and idolatrie thereof."[1] Next to the Holy Scriptures, it was determined to adhere to the English Common Prayer Book. Meetings for purposes of worship were to be held at first in private houses and, in the absence of clergy, by God-fearing laymen. This opposition on the part of the nobles was strengthened by the anxiety called forth by the marriage of Mary Stuart to Francis II.; the incorporation of Scotland with France was apprehended. But Catholic tendencies now showed themselves strongly in the regent, in view of Elizabeth's approaching accession and her doubtful right of succession. The burning of the eighty-two years old evangelical priest Walter Mill excited a feeling of great bitterness. The demand of the Lords of the Congregation for the restoration of the service of the original Christian Church, for the election of ministers by the congregation, was rejected by a provincial council of the clergy in agreement with the regent and severe repression of innovations decided upon. Then the storm broke out. In May, 1559, John Knox re-appeared in Scotland and commenced to preach recklessly against the idolatry of the mass in Perth. Monasteries and abbeys were destroyed all over the country, congregations that resisted were dispersed, the congregation took up arms. A second more extensive Covenant was concluded; the nobles grasped at the property of the churches and monasteries. In spite of the scruples of the strictly monarchically inclined Elizabeth the help of England was obtained, which the regent needed against the French auxiliary troops, "the nobles and commons of the Protestant Church of Scotland declared the regent deposed"; she died during the struggle (June 11th, 1560). France, which was itself in difficulties, on the 8th of July, 1560, agreed to the **Treaty of Edinburgh,** in accordance with which the Congregationalists were granted an amnesty and the French

---

[1] CALDERWOOD I 326 f.

troops removed. Mary Stuart and her husband resigned the English royal title. The Scotch Parliament was to give a decision on the religious question. Francis II. and Mary certainly refused to ratify the resolutions, but Francis died on the 5th of December, 1560, and Mary was unable to prevent the Catholic form of worship being abolished by the Parliament. The bishops in Parliament did not venture any opposition. The Confession drawn up by Knox and others (*Confessio Scoticana*) was accepted.[1]

This Confession is essentially Calvinistic, without any more decided imprint of the doctrine of predestination. The true Church has three *notae* or tokens: pure preaching of the Word, pure administration of the Sacrament, and *disciplina ecclesiastica recte administrata sicut Dei verbum praescribit*. The chief duty of the authorities is *religionis purgatio et conservatio*, the suppression of all *idololatria et superstitio* after the example of the pious Kings of Israel.

With a view to the internal organisation of the Church Knox and others composed the Book of Discipline. In December, 1560, a meeting of supporters of the Church (more or less irregular in consequence of the want of clerical support) which was considered to be the " first general assembly," took place, agreed to this book and made regulations in regard to the appointment of preachers, elders and deacons, as well as marriage legislation. The strict ecclesiastical ordinances of the Book of Discipline met with resistance on the part of some of the nobles, a large number of whom, however, accepted it in January, 1561, and bound themselves to do their best to introduce it. Explicit recognition on the part of the State did not however follow until later.

The main principles of this work are: (*a*) **Constitution**: Each congregation has a minister, elders and deacons (those that are too small can have elders and deacons in common): the clergy are chosen by the congregation of communicants; and in like manner the elders and deacons on the basis of a proposed list.[2] The elders, in conjunction with the pastor, carry out ecclesiastical discipline, but at the same time possess a right of supervision over him; the deacons manage the revenues and charities of the community. In case of lack of ministers, there is the auxiliary institution of "readers and exhorters." Clergy, elders and deacons together form the Kirk-session (like the French *consistoire*); the union of the clergy and elders of several congregations forms presbyteries, over which are provincial synods and lastly the general assembly. The apparently foreign element (**the Superintendents**), due to practical need, is peculiar. Immediately after the treaty of peace the few existing evangelical clergy were distributed, and five of them appointed as travelling preachers over larger districts. Ten such superintendents were now appointed, who gradually had to see about the establishment of single churches in their parishes. They were appointed for the first time by the Lords of the Privy Council, the congregations being only allowed a right of veto. (*b*) **Divine Service** was regulated on the lines of the Geneva ritual, *i.e.*, that of the English foreign congregation, which was formed on the model of the Calvinistic and closely

---

[1] NIEMEYER p. 340 ff. SCHAFF I 680 ff., III 437 ff.

[2] Subsequently, cooptation was substituted for election by the congregation; the office of elder was for life.

related to the Frankfort foreign congregation.[1] The liturgical formularies of this ritual were permitted, but there was no compulsion, which prevented any possibility of bigotry; the minister was allowed to use other similar forms of prayer. The radically "reformed" character of the ritual is clearly seen from **the abolition of every festal observance** except that of the Sabbath, and in the removal of organs, altars, crosses, images, candles, and everything symbolical. For the celebration of the Communion, which is received sitting, the first Sundays in March, June, September and December were appointed. At the weekly "prophesying" the Scriptures are explained, in which the laity also take part. (c) The Kirk-session administers **ecclesiastical discipline** to the extent of excommunication, which carries with it exclusion from ordinary communication and intercourse with members of the congregation and can only be removed by public penance.

However, these principles of the Scotch Church lacked judicial security. Mary Stuart, who met with a friendly reception from the people, returned to Scotland in 1561. She was sincerely devoted to Catholicism and, brought up amidst the refined, but at the same time loose, morals of the French Court, was opposed to the strict morality of the Scotch Calvinists, who now came forward in the name of God as censors of her life. She was certainly obliged to **tolerate** Protestantism, but avoided confirming it in due form, although, to quiet the nobles, she declared that no alteration would be made by her in the existing state of religion. To the indignation of the Protestant leaders, and also of the people, she celebrated mass in her chapel royal and exercised a bewitching personal influence over some of the nobility; in addition to this, the selfishness of the nobles was satisfied by the prospect of ecclesiastical property which was left to them.[2]

The ratification of the Edinburgh agreement was obstinately refused by Mary. Knox and his followers vigorously denounced the toleration of idolatry, the fickleness of the nobles, the morals of the Court, and upheld the right of opposition to idolatrous authorities; none of Mary's feminine wiles were able to obtain any influence over the unbending zealot in the cause of God's honour. Her attitude rather aggravated the spirit of opposition.

---

[1] RICHTER II 149.

[2] Two-thirds of the income of the Church were to be left to the previous owners, who accordingly, without further ecclesiastical work, enjoyed the emoluments of their benefice and formed an influential court for clerical reaction; another third was to be distributed between crown and church and school. But the nobles managed so well that, after the death of the holder of the benefice, the two-thirds above mentioned came into their possession.

At first her half-brother James Stuart (Murray) interposed. After various plans of marriage, which came to nothing (with Don Carlos, Archduke Charles),[1] Lord Dudley [Leicester], she married the young, unprincipled Lord Darley (or Darnley), a Stuart, who now assumed the royal title, while James took up arms as an opponent of the marriage, but was defeated and obliged to flee to England. Darley had hitherto, at least publicly, kept to the reformed religion; after a brief hesitation he abandoned it and drew others of the nobility with him. Mary's intimate relations with Spain must in addition be considered, where plans were forged (as well as by France and the Pope) for the restoration of Catholicism; the Pope's agent was her private secretary and favourite, the Italian David Rizzio. Darley knew that he confirmed Mary in her resolve not to concede him independent royal power, but to keep power in her own hand; hence he approached the Protestant Lords who hated in the person of Rizzio the soul of papist intrigues, and promised them he would return to Calvinism. With Darley's assent—it is not proved for certain that Knox was privy to it[2]—Rizzio was murdered in Mary's presence in 1566. The Catholic plans were thereby thwarted, but Mary's cunning still proved successful over the conspirators. After an apparent reconciliation with Darley, the latter was suddenly assassinated in February, 1567, and his house blown up; Mary did what seemed incredible[3]—gave her hand to one of the murderers, the ambitious James Bothwell, who speedily undid his former marriage.[4] A fresh combination of the nobility now took up arms against Mary and compelled her to abdicate (in 1567) in favour of her one year old son James. Her half-brother Murray carried on the regency. Knox, in his sermon on the coronation of the youthful King, demanded Mary's execution on the ground of adultery and the murder of her husband.[5] Once again she endeavoured to get possession of power with the aid of a favourite, but was defeated by Murray and fled to England (1568), where she met with a friendly reception, but was kept in semi-imprisonment and finally executed (1587; see p. 334).

An Act of Parliament in the name of the King (1567) was connected with the fall of Mary, which bestowed full legal recognition upon the reformed Church; it is "the only true and holy Church of Jesus Christ within this realm." Accordingly, it was now constitutionally "established" for Scotland. The resolutions of

---

[1] Either of these marriages would have been the signal for the Catholic crusade against England; cp. Granvella to Philip II., Sept. 14th, 1563. Papiers d'État VIII 212 ff.

[2] Cp. KÖSTLIN in RE VIII 94 f. Calendar of State Papers, Foreign Series, 1566-1568, p. 35, where, amongst the list of those who were accessory to the plot, the names of "John Knox and John Craig, preachers," are to be found.

[3] Cp. the statement of the Spanish ambassador: It really seems improbable, she being a Catholic as she is, and the divorce for such a reason as that alleged, etc. Calendar of State Papers, Spanish, 1558-1567, p. 635.

[4] Although Edinburgh was in the hands of Bothwell's people, John Craig bravely refused to publish the bans, and only did so under protest.

[5] Cp. Calendar of State Papers, Foreign Series, 1566-1568, pp. 291, 293.

1560 were confirmed, papacy and idolatry forbidden, no other ecclesiastical jurisdiction was any longer to be valid. The internal independence of the Church in reference to the State was maintained, although the right of patronage (of the crown and other patrons) is recognised; the superintendents (in case of eventualities, the synod) are to decide whether those presented by the patrons are fit and proper persons.

But still, **Presbyterianism**, that had here attained the mastery, had to defend itself against certain episcopalian attempts. The bishops were still in possession of benefices, but, as they died out, it was desired to retain their dignity, which as an estate of the realm formed an essential part of the state-constitution, in such a manner that, while the nobles received the emoluments, a clergyman took over the episcopal **dignity**—without any internal hierarchical quality—for which a certain assent of the Church was obtained for some time. But the reformed Church, whose most prominent leader after Knox's death (1572) was Andrew Melville, stamped presbyterian principles most decidedly upon the so-called **Second Book of Discipline**, and asserted them in a manner most disagreeable to the Government in opposition to the bishops and consequently, to the Government. James VI., after he was declared of age, certainly consented in 1581 to sign a national covenant in defence of a true religion, which was subsequently in like manner subscribed by persons of all ranks,[1] a most vigorous declaration against everything papistic, against the *autoritas Romani Antichristi*, and the *erronea et sanguinolenta Tridentini Concilii decreta;* but the split between the Church and the regal authority was unavoidable. In 1584, James carried the so-called "black acts" through Parliament; for he desired to maintain the royal power also in ecclesiastical matters (by the help of the episcopate) in face of the reckless presbyterian spirit of independence. Thus Parliament accorded him a supremacy over the Church also, which was not allowed to hold any meeting without his leave, and commissioned the **bishops** to regulate ecclesiastical affairs in their dioceses. The result of this was an open conflict with the Church; many of the clergy fled, others were thrown into prison. But these provisions, which were entirely opposed to the ideas of the Scotch, under altered political circumstances which compelled James to look for support to ecclesiastical circles, soon made room for **the downright recognition of Presbyterianism** (1592); the Act of 1584 was expressly revoked, the entire presbyterian ecclesiastical system with its ecclesiastical government and exercise of discipline (only under limited continuance of the right of patronage) was confirmed (only without explicit recognition of the individual provisions of the second book of discipline). However, it soon became evident that James's wishes tended in quite a different direction. He took offence at the free and disrespectful right of judgment, which the presbyterian preachers claimed in the face of royal measures, and again attempted to introduce bishops dependent upon the Crown. The Parliament of 1592, sympathising with the Church's independence of political intrigue, had determined that henceforth no representatives of the

---

[1] The so-called *Confessio Scoticana posterior*, NIEMEYER, p. 357-359. SCHAFF, *Bibl. symb.* 1 686 ff.; III 480 ff.

Church should have a seat in Parliament after the manner of the bishops. But James now gained the consent, first of an assembly, then also of a Parliament (1597), whereby—certainly at first with prudent precautions—ministers, who were sent into Parliament by the Crown, were to vote together with the earlier prelates as "parliamentary commissioners of the Church." In 1600 James nominated the first three and also bestowed upon them three old bishoprics. A voice had rightly declared that the horns of the episcopal mitre were still to be recognised under the disguise! More decided steps in this direction followed, after James VI., as the successor of Elizabeth, united the English and the Scotch crowns.

5. England and Scotland under James I.

Literature: F. C. DAHLMANN, *Gesch. d. engl. Revol.* ³Leipzig, 1844. S. R. GARDINER, *The Fall of the Monarchy of Charles I.;* 2 vols. Lond., 1882. H. WEINGARTEN, *Die Revolutionskirchen Englands.* Leipz., 1868. A. STERN, *Milton und seine Zeit.* Leipz., 1877. Books I and II; the same, *Gesch. der Revolution in England.* Berlin, 1881. M. BROSCH, *Zur Gesch. der purit. Revol.* in HZ 51, 1 ff.; the same, *Gesch. von England*, VII. Gotha, 1892.

It now began to be clear how reluctantly James had put up with the censorious, obstinate Presbyterianism of the Scotch, and how greatly the English Puritans were deceived in hoping for greater consideration at his hands. He had himself received a theological training and hence, in his monarchical and theological self-consciousness, he saw in the English established episcopal Church essentially the right mean between ecclesiastical extremes and at the same time the form that best corresponded to his own exaggerated ideas of monarchical power.[1] It was intended that the episcopate, subject to the crown, should overcome the factious, restless spirit of liberty and equality by means of regulations dictated by the King.

In regard to the **Catholics,** he expressed himself very mildly in his first speech in Parliament (March 19th, 1604), held out hopes to them of a more lenient application of the laws, so far as it was a question of peaceful laymen (in fact, the previous exaction of fines on a large scale for non-attendance at the Anglican service almost entirely ceased), and only vigorously rejected the doctrine that the Pope should claim authority even over princes, together with the Jesuit theory in regard to the murder of tyrants, which at that time was creating great excitement (p. 264). But the English Catholics hoped for more from the son of Mary Stuart,[2] and came forward boldly, the more so as the

---

[1] "God has created you a little god, as people are accustomed to say, to sit upon his throne;" so he teaches his son in his treatise $\beta\alpha\sigma\iota\lambda\iota\kappa\grave{o}\nu$ $\delta\hat{\omega}\rho o\nu$ (1598). Compare KÖSTLIN, p. 114 f.

[2] Clement VIII. called upon him (1602) to become a Catholic: it was not until 1605 that he answered with a refusal.

sympathies of the Queen (Anne of Denmark) in favour of Catholicism were well known.[1] But they found themselves deceived, and as James was compelled by his difficult position in regard to the zealously Protestant Parliament to put the laws of Uniformity, which he employed against the Puritans, in force also against the Catholics, the result was **The Gunpowder Plot**[2] (1605), the discovery of which, on the eve of its execution, only served to bring out for a long time the religious opposition of the nation as an uncompromising one. The laws against the Catholics were made more severe in 1606, although the great majority of them had taken no part in the conspiracy; the recusants were to be excluded from the Court and the capital, to be searched by the police at any moment: marriages and the baptism of their children were only to be valid, if performed by Anglican clergy. The **oath of allegiance** pressed with especial harshness upon them, in which they had to recognise James as their lawful lord and master and to admit that the Pope was not competent, either of himself or by virtue of any ecclesiastical authority, to depose the King, to release his subjects from obedience or permit them to offer armed resistance. They had to promise solemnly that they would not allow themselves to be released from the oath of allegiance by any papal dispensation or absolution, that they would give information of all conspiracies that might become known to them, and were forced to declare that they abhorred the theory of the murder of tyrants. This oath (which in other respects was no ecclesiastical oath of supremacy, but rather left the special position of the King in reference to the English Church untouched and only opposed the exaggerated doctrines of the authority of the Pope over princes) excited violent strife. However, the majority of the English Catholics took the oath and thus at least secured for themselves toleration. A marriage scheme, the object of which was to unite the successor to the throne to a Spanish princess and thereby to secure greater freedom in the country to the Catholics, subsequently reawoke the mistrust of the English people.

The more decided became the opposition between the Crown and the **puritan** tendency. In this case also, the opposition assumed at the same time a political character as a counter-blast to the exaggerated ideas of the absolutism of the royal authority[3] (which were soon fostered by a part of the episcopalians), to which they opposed the right of violent resistance to tyranny. The opposition of the King as well as of part of the episcopalians to the Puritans became continually more pronounced. If James had at first still

---

[1] The Scottish Jesuit Abercromby even succeeded in converting her (Brief of Clement VIII. to Anne, January 28th, 1605). But Paul V. already looked upon her as only a very unstable Catholic, in whom no hopes were to be placed.

[2] The innocence of the Jesuits is affirmed by Katholik 1889 II 253 ff. In any case their Superior, Garnet, had previous knowledge of the affair through the confessional. Cp. DÖLLINGER-REUSCH, *Die Selbstbiographie Bellarmins*, p. 201 ff.

[3] These had been also zealously fostered by the Church in England since the time of the royal supremacy, *e.g.*, by the collection of homilies approved by Elizabeth. Cp. KÖSTLIN, p. 126.

laid stress upon the fact that, between the two tendencies of the Protestants, there was unity in regard to the foundation of belief, yet at the Synod of Dort the English theologians took up a more or less reserved attitude, the resolutions of the synod were not accepted in England, and discussions on predestination were forbidden. By order of James (1622) these difficult questions were only to be argued by bishops and deans in the pulpit (**Wilkins** IV 465). Already, owing to the after-effect of earlier currents and under the influence of Dutch Arminianism, the later so-called **Latitudinarianism** began to develop itself,[1] at first as a dogmatic liberal-mindedness and vagueness, as in **William Laud** and **John Hales**, the King's plenipotentiary at Dort, who was there gained over to Arminianism. Soon the "Arminians" were those appointed by preference to the bishoprics. To this must be added the rejection of the austere legal standpoint of the Puritans, as shown, *e.g.*, in the recommendation of Sunday amusements,[2] while Scotland led the way in treating Sunday as the **Sabbath** of the New Testament,[3] and soon also the Puritans of England adopted this view.[4]

The restoration of the Episcopate in Scotland in 1610 (at which English bishops performed the ceremony of consecration) only aggravated the opposition, although the "General Assembly" remained the highest ecclesiastical authority. Measures to that effect had commenced in England immediately after James's accession. He had gained over a party to support him; the Scotch Parliament of 1606 already agreed to the institution of 17 prelacies, bribery (in the form of money-allowances) was resorted to without scruple, his chief opponent, Melville, was enticed to London and imprisoned. Thus James was enabled to carry out his will by the assembly of 1610. Without consulting the Church, he appointed

---

[1] The name was first used in 1660.

[2] Cp. The Book of Sports, issued by the King in 1618, to be read aloud by the clergy, which enumerated the Sunday amusements that were allowed.

[3] Knox brought the name "Sabbath" into use: the first Book of Discipline (p. 341) requires strict observance of the Sabbath, the fourth General Assembly (1562) demands the punishment by the authorities of every transgression of the Sabbath as "ordered by the law of God." Cp. SCHAFF I 776.

[4] N. BOWND (a Norton clergyman), *The Doctrine of the Sabbath*. Cambridge, 1595. 2nd edition. *Sabbathum Veteris et Novi Testamenti*. Lond. 1606. The seventh part of our time belongs to the service of God: the Sabbath of the Christians must be as much a day of rest as the Sabbath of the Jews; popular amusements are to be forbidden, an exception only being allowed in the case of "noblemen" and "great personages." This work produced the first split in the matter of doctrine between the High Church party and the Puritans; the bishops at first vigorously opposed the new doctrine, but just by so doing promoted the rapid spread of the new Sabbatarianism. Cp. SCHAFF I 777 f. Dict. of National Biography, VI 74 f.

two Courts of high commission for Scotland, in which the Archbishops, with other prelates and noblemen, were to perform the functions of an ecclesiastical high court. Finally, in 1618, he obtained from the assembly at Perth the acceptance of five articles, whereby kneeling at Communion, the Communion of the Sick, Private Baptism, Confirmation by the bishops and a number of festivals were reintroduced.[1] Thus, already during the reign of James, an ecclesiastical fermentation arose, which assumed a strongly political character.

6. The Struggle of Catholicising Episcopalianism with Puritanism.

Literature (continued): For Laud, see his works, 7 vols. Oxford, 1847-1860. P. HEYLYN, *Cyprianus Anglicus*. Lond. 1671; S. R. GARDINER in Dict. of Nat. Biogr. XXXII. 185 ff. Westminster Assembly: SCHAFF I 727 ff., III 598 ff.; the same in RE XVI 854 ff.; VON RUDLOFF in ZhTh 20, 238 ff.; NIEMEYER, Anhang.

The fermentation was only increased by **Charles I.**, in whom the episcopal and ecclesiastical, absolutist and monarchical tendencies were closely combined.[2] "No bishop, no King; no bishop, no Church." A theory of the absolutism of the royal power is fostered, according to which the latter is bound by no rights and privileges, all resistance to it is a sin, and only passive obedience remains,[3] a theory doubly dangerous in the case of a King who was politically so lacking in shrewdness and dealt so lightly with the truth. This theory is combined with a **catholicising Episcopalianism**.

If the episcopal office had originally been founded upon a valid ecclesiastical order and recommended from reasons of history and expediency,[4] it is now spoken of as the truly Catholic and Apostolic constitution of the Church whereby the continuity of the latter is guaranteed. Great importance is

---

[1] Christmas, Good Friday, Easter, Ascension, Whitsun.

[2] The connection of the High Church party with the Crown is aptly expressed by the words of Robert Montague: "Do you protect me with the sword: I will protect you with the pen." STERN, *Milton* I 132.

[3] In 1607, Cowell taught that the King stood "absolutely above the law"; the canons of the Convocation of 1606 laid down the principle of passive obedience in all cases. For other examples see KÖSTLIN, p. 147; STERN, *Milton* I 131; Calendar of State Papers, Domestic Ser. 1628-1629, p. 88, where Laud instructs the King that the right of the Crown extends beyond "all oaths and promises exacted from a sovereign," and declares the property and personal freedom of the subjects to be "deprivable of them upon juste cause and so fiscal."

[4] Richard Hooker (died 1600) had already endeavoured to show that the episcopal office had its origin in the time of the Apostles and Bancroft, in 1588, had taught that the precedence of the bishops to the priests existed *iure divino*, but each had met with varied opposition (Cp. SCHAFF I 605); the episcopacy was at first defended as necessary for the well-being, but not for the being of the Church.

attached to the unbroken succession from Peter. The episcopal Church is the only correct mean between Presbyterianism or Puritanism. This, together with its uniformity, must consequently be introduced by the King in all the three kingdoms, of which however Ireland was essentially Catholic and Scotland presbyterian, while in England a vigorous anti-episcopal party offered resistance. Naturally, this episcopalianism was at once combined with an increased appreciation of the sensual, symbolical forms of worship (the restoration of images, crosses and altars) as well as a tendency to secular custom and a civilian position of the clergy (ministers as justices of the peace),—all in downright opposition to puritan tendencies. This high-church proclivity is represented by **William Laud**, who, when a tutor at Oxford, had already given offence by laying stress upon the necessity of baptism for regeneration and the necessity of the episcopate for the Church.[1] During the reign of James, whom he had accompanied on a journey to Scotland and encouraged in the plan of a union of the English and Scotch Churches, having been elevated to the see of St. David's, he took the lead as the champion of " the beauty of holiness " with reforms in the matter of ritual, in which all the traditional church ornaments, except such as appeared expressly forbidden, were again brought out; antiquarian and aesthetic tendencies sought satisfaction. According to him, the standpoint of the Anglican Church is that of the primitive Church of the first four centuries. In the matter of dogma, he passes from the XXXIX Articles to Arminianism, yet even more to Catholicism: in the doctrine of universal grace, the importance of good works for justification, in the Catholic idea of the Sacrament and the *ius divinum* of the episcopal constitution.[2] The Anglican Church is the genuine offshoot of the Catholic, the Romish a sickly branch of the same. " The religion of the Church of Rome and ours is all one." In the reign of Charles I. he speedily became Bishop of Bath and Wells, then of London, and finally (1633), Archbishop of Canterbury; he was a convinced and personally sincere zealot in the cause of his ideals, the soul of church politics, who only promoted those who held episcopalian views, and, with Buckingham and afterwards with Strafford, furthered recklessly absolutist tendencies,—hence the object of increasing popular hatred. The most important offices in State and Church were heaped upon him. The Catholic queen (Henry IV.'s daughter), the presence of Catholic priests in her entourage, the occasionally milder administration of the penal laws against the papists, and, in addition, the Catholicising tendencies of theologians so closely connected with the Court,—all this excited the suspicion of the Puritan circles of the people.[3]

---

[1] " That there could be no true Church without diocesan bishops."

[2] Cp. also JOSEPH HALL, *Episcopacy by divine right* (1637) written at Laud's instigation and revised by him (Dict. of Nat. Biogr. XXIV 77 f.).

[3] However, Laud has been unjustly suspected of having actually worked in the interest of Rome; he refused the Cardinal's hat, with which Rome endeavoured to entice him, and in like manner Charles I. declared to the agent of the Pope " You will never make me a papist." But Laud brought the suspicion upon himself and thereby made the Puritan revolution unavoidable. " Opposition to the Romish Church was for him one neither of principle nor of religion."

Parliament was no longer summoned by the King: royal edicts took the place of the laws. The highest courts of justice in State and Church proceeded with increased violence. In the interests of uniformity the Dissenters were tracked out, the masses were to be kept to their obedience by fear. The attempts of James to unite the English and Scotch Churches were now violently continued; the position of prelates was bestowed upon the Scotch bishops, and Laud wished simply to introduce the English church order and service, but the clergy resisted. In 1635, canons were forced upon the Scotch Church, which imposed the royal supremacy and an almost Catholic ceremonial. Laud revised the English liturgy for it, so that it received an almost Romish formula of consecration, baptismal water consecration, intercessory prayers for the dead, and the like.

Disturbances arose about this at first in Edinburgh itself; soon the whole people rose up to fight the Papism in Anglicanism and, in 1638, concluded a **fresh Covenant** on behalf of Presbyterianism (Schaff I 687). The general assembly at Glasgow (autumn, 1638), from which Charles expected support, went over entirely to the Covenant, charged the Scotch bishops with heresy, simony and all possible vices, and refused to allow itself to be broken up by the King's commissioners, declaring the bishops, the court of high commission, the canons and the new liturgy abolished, and thereby arousing in England also opposition to the royal church policy. The King now had need of Parliament, in order to obtain means against rebellious Scotland, but after three weeks was obliged to dissolve the refractory (**Short Parliament**) in May, 1640. Contrary to all precedent, he caused the convocation of the clergy to be still further deferred and seventeen canons[1] to be accepted, which declared the absolute power of the Crown as founded upon the commandment of God and natural right, the unconditional right of disposal of the property of the subject and the high church doctrine of the episcopal church, and imposed upon the clergy the so-called Etcetera-oath, that is to say the promise, never to consent by word or deed to alter the goverment of this Church by archbishops, deans and archdeacons, etc.[2] This oath made Laud the laughing-stock of the people, since here fidelity to a hierarchy, the details of which people had neither been capable nor desirous

---

[1] HEYLYN, *Cypr. Anglic.*, p. 404 ff.
[2] In HEYLYN, *Cypr. Anglicus*, p. 406.

of enumerating was commended. The Scottish Covenanters now found their confederates in English Puritanism. Hate and scorn were directed against the English bishops, above all against Laud himself. The King was obliged to suspend the Etcetera-oath and on the advance of the rebellious Scots, to summon Parliament again on the 3rd of November, 1640 (**Long Parliament**). The latter was determined to carry on the struggle to the uttermost against both Church and State absolutism. The Earl of Strafford (Thomas Wentworth, at that time the King's representative in Ireland, in the eyes of the people the chief representative of absolutist tendencies) and Laud were impeached. The former was executed in May, 1641, as "a traitor" (not without formal violation of justice); Laud, after having been kept in prison for several years, was finally "mercifully condemned" to be executed as a traitor on the 10th of January, 1645. A petition signed by 15,000 citizens of London demanded the thorough reform of the Church, and the entire abolition of episcopal government; on the other hand, seven hundred clergy petitioned for the reformation of the episcopate. In February, 1641, a bill was introduced to abolish superstition and idolatry. The House of Commons wanted to exclude the bishops (a proposal at first resisted by the Lords) but when the prelates saw themselves threatened by popular feeling and the mob and the Archbishop of York with eleven other bishops presented a protest (declaring that all assemblies of Parliament were null and void since they could not take part in them without personal danger), the prelates were themselves imprisoned at the end of 1641. On the one hand, encroachments on the part of Parliament, which knew it was supported by the sympathy of the country, and on the other hand on the part of the King, finally led (August, 1642) to the **Civil War**, in which the King was supported by the upper and some of the lower nobles and the higher clergy: the Parliament by the landed proprietors and the city populace,—and, from a church point of view, by the Puritans and all the Nonconformists. During the war, the Parliament, which had abolished the episcopal constitution, summoned an **ecclesiastical Assembly** "for settling the government and liturgy of the Church of England, and for vindicating and clearing the doctrine of the said Church from false aspersions and interpretations,"—the **Westminster Assembly**, an attempt to unite the English Church with the Scotch and the "reformed" of the Continent.

It consisted of 151 members, that is to say, 30 non-clerical (10 from the Lords and 20 from the Commons, amongst them J. Selden and Prym), and 121 clerical from the most different counties, amongst them certain bishops (such as the learned **Usher**, Archbishop of Armagh, who had left Ireland shortly before the Irish massacres, had been raised by the King to the bishopric of Carlisle, and was the representative of a very moderate episcopalianism), and some doctors of theology, who, however, with one exception, took no part in the discussions. (The reason of this was that they were bound to the oath of supremacy and prevented by a royal prohibition; besides, the spirit of the assembly was repugnant to them, since it had not been chosen by the clergy and contained laymen.) The majority of those assembled, although for the most part educated at Oxford and Cambridge and ordained in the episcopal church, held puritan views, and were, in regard to the question of constitution, **presbyterian;** individual members were in favour of Independentism (see below), some also of Erastianism (see p. 322). It was no synod duly elected, but **an ecclesiastical assembly of notables** summoned by Parliament, but of respectable importance. In spite of the King's prohibition, it met on the 1st of July, 1643, and sat till 1647.

Parliament and the Westminster Assembly had turned to the Scotch States and the general assembly, for purposes of entering into a combination with them. From the English point of view the political alliance (in the struggle against the King) stood in the foreground, while the Scotch made community of religion the condition of common political action. In Scotland **The Solemn League and Covenant**[1] was drawn up—a solemn brotherhood and obligation to **uphold** the reformed church in Scotland against common enemies, to **reform** religion in England and Ireland in doctrine, divine worship, discipline and constitution, in conformity with the Word of God and the model of the "best" reformed churches, to secure the closest "conjunction" and **uniformity** of the churches in the three kingdoms; further, to extirpate all popery and prelacy, all superstition, heresy and so forth. It is further their wish to defend the rights and privileges of Parliament and the liberties of the kingdoms, but also the person and authority of the King, and to strive after lasting peace; this remarkable document concludes with an earnest confession of sins. The Scotch delegates brought it to England, the Westminster Assembly discussed it, and, with trifling modifications, it was confirmed by the House of Commons and the Assembly on the 25th of September, 1643, and soon afterwards by the House of Lords. In like manner, at the request of Parliament, wherever its authority prevailed, it was accepted by the civil and ecclesiastical officials, although Charles issued a proclamation against it as a treacherous conspiracy; in Scotland also, "a general swearing to the Covenant" for months together took place. The Westminster Assembly also applied to the foreign reformed churches and received for the most part favourable answers; only Hesse sent a warning not to do away with the episcopal constitution.

---

[1] Printed in SCHAFF I 690 f.

The Works of the Westminster Assembly.

1. **The Westminster Confession.**[1]—At first only a revision, of a more decided Calvinistic stamp, of the XXXIX Articles was originally intended, but, after some time had been spent on the work, under the influence of the Scotch, an entirely new confession, taken directly from the Scriptures, was drawn up in outline, completed in 1646 and approved by Parliament. This work, with its clear, vigorous articles of doctrine, in each case supported by Scriptural authority, obtained the importance of the **Confession of Uniformity** of all the **presbyterian** churches and drove out the Confessio Scoticana.[2]

2. **Two Catechisms** (a larger and a smaller) were drawn up, of which the smaller still exists as the widespread Presbyterian Catechism.

3. Divine worship is regulated by the Directory for the Public Worship of God. After images, altars and organs had been abolished at the commencement (October, 1643), **an introduction** to divine service was issued (January, 1645), but without definite set forms, which were left to the preachers' discretion within the limits of certain prescribed regulations.

4. An ecclesiastical constitution was also established: Form of Presbyterial Church and of Ordination of Ministers. At first, in many cases opposition to the royal episcopalianism had only gone so far that a desire had been expressed that all that was properly speaking hierarchical (and absolutist) should be got rid of, and **Usher's** attempt at mediation, which would have reduced the rank of the bishops to that of superintendents and synodal presidents, at the outset did not appear hopeless, especially as it was thought highly of by the Puritans. English Puritanism had not, like the Scotch, a definite constitutional system. But the intensification of the opposition to the bishops who were allied with the absolutism of royalty, and further, the growing influence of the Scotch, exerted against the Independents who zealously bestirred themselves under Godwin's leadership and the State-Church Erastians, assisted **pure Presbyterianism** to gain a victory—a victory which however at once brought into notice the aspirations of an entirely different and much more popular trend of opinion, which opposed quite a different ecclesiastical ideal to (Scotch) Presbyterianism, which in England had become more and more a matter for the clergy only. It was only by way of experiment that Parliament accepted this ecclesiastical order. The synods only carried it out with hesitation and with a small attendance of those who were invited. In the meantime, English Puritanism had developed into **Independency.**

---

[1] In this the **Scotch doctrine of the Sabbath** obtains a complete victory and thereby becomes the characteristic of collective Anglo-American Christianity. Cap. 21. *Deus speciatim e septenis quibusque diebus diem unum in Sabbatum designavit, sancte sibi observandum.* This day, since the Resurrection of Christ, has been changed from the seventh to the first day, *estque perpetuo ad finem mundi tanquam Sabbatum Christianum celebrandus.* It is celebrated by complete abstinence from worldly things, also from all *recreationibus ludicris,* and is to be spent in public and private worship, works of duty, necessity and charity.

[2] With modifications in America in a spirit of complete independence of the State.

7. Independency.

Literature (continued): For Browne, see A. JESSOP in Dict. of Nat. Biography VII, 57 ff. For Johnson, A. GORDON, *ib.* XXX 9 ff.; for Ainsworth, AXON, *ib.* I 191 ff.

As early as the end of the 16th century a novelty had shown itself. **Robert Browne,**[1] educated at Cambridge, who, as an enthusiastic and gifted preacher, had at first opposed the necessity of an episcopal license to preach, had entered into connection with the **Dutch Baptists**, who had fled before Alba to Norfolk, and thus conceived a repugnance against every form of ecclesiastical government that received its authority from the secular authorities. The Kingdom of Christ is a community of believers, who by voluntary agreement with God have bound themselves to obey God and Christ. State churchship is anti-Christianity; but presbyterian ecclesiastical government would also be a wrong to the congregation; the will of the latter must be able to find expression unhindered. Accordingly, he and his followers are fundamentally separated from the Anglican Church: in 1581, he founds a congregation of his own, which, however, only lasted for a short time, in Middelburg and Zealand, where Cartwright (see p. 335) was already managing the Puritan colony. He himself, unstable and greatly afraid of suffering, subsequently again conformed to the State church (he died in 1632), but his ideas had a wider influence; in 1592, there were already 20,000 **Brownists** in England. They were soon persecuted and compelled to propagate their doctrines secretly, while many fled to Holland, where they published their first Confessions: in 1596, A true Confession of faith and humble acknowledgement of the Alegeance which her Majestie's subjects, falsely called Brownists, do hould (by Ainsworth); in 1598, Confession of faith of certain Englich people, living in the Low Countries, exiled.

The man who developed passionately polemical Brownism into **Congregationalism** was **John Robinson**, who, having been driven out in 1608 with his congregation, found a refuge for it, first in Amsterdam and afterwards in Leyden: before (1596) and contemporary with him, **Francis Johnson** and **Ainsworth**, the leaders of the Amsterdam congregation. The new constitutional ideas are the **autonomy** of each individual congregation[1] and its absolute **independence** of the State. Hence they call themselves "Congregationalists," while the name "Independents," which was bestowed upon them in the middle of the 17th century by their opponents is rejected by them at the outset as incorrect, "for no true church is independent," but gradually comes to be accepted by them as expressing "their total freedom from exterior control." In a petition to James (1616) they claim their "right to self-administration and self-government, by the common and free consent of the people, independently and immediately under Christ."

---

[1] In Tyndale's translation of the Bible, this word is used instead of Church, as reminiscent of Catholicism.

The holder of the power of the keys is neither Pope nor episcopate nor presbytery, but the **whole congregation:** the latter exists, where two or three who have become faithful, cut themselves off from the world and unite in the community of the Gospel. Such individual communities or congregations, although certainly they may enter into agreements amongst themselves, can never do so in regard to positions of superiority or inferiority: a presbyterial or synodal ecclesiastical government is no more valid for them than an episcopal one. Certainly the "consociation of congregations" may find expression in a national synod, but never as a court exercising authority over the congregations, which are under the spiritual authority of Christ alone, *i.e.*, of the Holy Scriptures. The universal (catholic) Church is an ideal that will not be realised until Christ's second coming; now, the unity is only that of an invisible community of the faithful, the visible church appears as an unorganised total of individual congregations. Consequently, all historical development and dependence of the religious life of the individual upon the latter is in this case left out of consideration,—an individualism, to which the community of the Church is only the sum total of equivalent religious individualities. But the foundation of it is the (Augustinian-Wicliffian) idea of the Church as the *Congregati praedestinatorum*, carried to such a point under the baptist influence, that the elect and those who are born again must be able to show **signs** and **proofs** of their election and only such are admissible to the congregation. Equality of election does away with every privilege or position of authority within the congregation, and requires complete equality of all the members: hence, the right of "prophesy" enters by the side of the spiritual office.[1] From the "reformed" ideas they adopt the dignity of elder (elected by the congregation), but vigorously resist the congregational aristocracy developed therefrom in Calvinism, which, according to Calvin's interpretation, understands by ἐκκλησία the college of presbyters and hence hands ecclesiastical discipline over to the latter; in his contest with Johnson, whose views were presbyterian, Ainsworth successfully claims such disciplinary power for the whole congregation;[2] the hierarchy of the elders is rejected and their resolutions are subject to the assent of the people. Even the elders are not essential, as if there were no Church without them. With this abstract individualism is combined a cold supranaturalism, which is unable to conceive the divine forces as working in human agencies that have become historical. Hence the zeal displayed against all obligatory attachment to external forms: liturgical forms (particularly of prayer) would bind the Holy Spirit to the foam of our lips.[3] Even Our Father is intended by

---

[1] "In the Assemblies of the Saincts ... all men have not onely liberty, but are exhorted to desire that they may prophesie, that is, speak unto the Church, to edefying, to exhortation and to comfort; ... a woman in regard of her sex may not speak or teach in the church: yet with other women and in her private familie she openeth her mouth in wisdom ... the Lord in their dayes had furnished holy women with the gift of prophesie." AINSWORTH, *The Communion of Saincts* (before 1615), ed. Amsterd. 1640 p. 233.

[2] Hence the Amsterdam community split into Ainsworthian and Franciscan Brownists, until Johnson retired to Emden with his presbyterian following.

[3] Cp. MILTON, *Iconoclastes* 1609 in G. WEBER in HTb. 3. F. 4, p. 48 ff. Ainsworth reckons amongst the Romish idolatry of the Anglicans their reading and singing their prayers upon a book. *An arrow against Idolatria* (1611) ed. 1640 p. 95.

Christ only as a specimen, not as a model of a prayer. All standing feast-days are rejected, while on the other hand they are observed on each special occasion, in all important public affairs. The peculiarities described make it intelligible that, within this congregation, which in other respects theologically belonged to Calvinism, a protest was made against all fixed formulating of confessions of faith; in this case the idea of a progressive reformation is aroused. God reveals himself also in the present, consequently the spirit can lead still further—while the Lutherans desired to abide by Luther, the Calvinists by Calvin.[1]

Even before Robinson's death (1625) this Independency sought a new home for itself in America. Subsequently to 1620, English pilgrims crossed over from their place of refuge in Holland to New England (New Portsmouth) partly moved by missionary ideas, partly in order to be able to preserve their English nationality better. Massachusetts became the centre of their colonies where they were able to carry out their theocratic idea of a state together with their ecclesiastical ideas. Decidedly democratically liberal Independency here soon took a turn in the direction of strict conformity to law and narrow-mindedness. The right of the authorities to punish blasphemy, heresy and the circulation of pernicious ideas is exercised with as great severity as by Presbyterianism at home.[2] Thus, in Boston, citizens were put in irons and condemned to life-long slavery, because they rejected the Word and the Sacrament, denied the existence of angels and devils, and had taught "a gross kind of union with Christ,"—consequently, were mystico-anabaptist fanatics. Roger Williams, who came to them as preacher in 1631, demanded in the interests of religion **absolute religious freedom** and complete **separation of State and Church**, a commonwealth, in which Jews and heretics should have equal rights. Having been driven out, he founded Providence, where baptist fugitives found a welcome: he himself went over to this community in 1639, but soon left it, and waited for a fresh revelation of God,—a prophet of Quakerism.

During the activity of the Long Parliament, in the midst of the Civil War, the Independency hitherto unimportant in England rapidly sprung up into a religious and political power. Hitherto regarded with contempt as "New England Way," it now received reinforcements in the shape of thousands of Nonconformists who

---

[1] Cp. Robinson's words in Weingarten p. 33.
[2] See the description of a State authority agreeable to God in AINSWORTH, Comm. of Saincts, p. 223 f.

returned to England from Holland and America. At first, common opposition to episcopalianism still concealed the deep-seated difference between this Independency and the older Puritanism, akin to Scotch Presbyterianism; also in the strictly "reformed" insistence upon moral discipline members felt themselves united and saw in the various opinions expressed in regard to the question of constitution only a trifling difference. But soon the deep-seated difference of mind asserted itself. The attempts of the Westminster Assembly to carry the presbyterial constitution through, met with the strongest resistance in English national feeling. Certainly, the vigorous opposition of the small Independent minority in the assembly itself was repressed, and the repugnance of Parliament to an intolerant aristocracy of presbyteries which emancipated itself from secular authority was so far overcome out of regard for the Scotch, that the attempt to introduce it was agreed to (1647). But affairs had already taken a most decisive turn. The national spirit of independence reacted upon the Scotch institution with its claim to a new uniformity of the "true" Church. As **Oliver Cromwell's** parliamentary army decidedly interfered and drove back the influence of the Scotch, the prospects of Presbyterianism gave way in favour of the Independency of the "Saints." In 1646, the King was obliged to flee before this army to the Scotch camp, was handed over in 1647 to the English Parliament. This body, now pressed by the Independents and purified from opposing elements (December, 1648), pronounced sentence of death upon Charles I. and carried it out on January 30th, 1649. Independency had gained the victory.

CHAPTER FOURTH.

The Struggle with the Counter-Reformation in Sweden, Poland and Hungarian Transylvania.

1. Sweden.

Literature (see p. 168): K. HILDEBRAND, *Undersökningar till Uppsala Mötes Historia* in HTidskrift, 1893, 89 ff.; *das. Öfversikter*, p. 28 ff.; Litteratur om Uppsala möte.

Eric XIV. (1560-1568), the son of Gustavus, who had for a time lost his reason, being personally inclined to Calvinism, began to make further reforms in matters of ceremonial; hopes were already entertained in Calvinistic circles of being able to obtain a footing here,[1] but his mental unsteadiness and subsequent dethronement[2] by his brothers John and Charles rendered these hopes vain. His brother and successor, the theologian **John III.** (1568-1592), influenced by his wife Catharine, a Polish princess, and by the prospect of ascending the throne, endeavoured for a time to restore a modified Catholicism after the fashion of George Cassander (see below), especially as the numerous Catholic usages that still existed afforded a stepping-stone to it. After the death of the Archbishop Laurence Peterson, under whom the country had received its first ecclesiastical order in 1571, on which the King had exercised a Catholicising influence in certain places but which still bore an essentially Lutheran character, he found in his successor Laurence Peterson Gothus a man accessible for the purposes of his middle course. Gothus declared in favour of the monasteries, invocation of the saints, prayers for the dead and the restoration of Catholic rites. Favoured by the Queen, **Stanislaus Hosius** (p. 360) began to work by correspondence; in 1576, two Jesuits appeared under the mask of Lutheran theologians, and began a course of lectures in Stockholm, which the clergy were obliged to attend. Swedes were educated in foreign parts—Rome, Braunsberg and elsewhere—for service in their native church; Luther's catechism was exchanged in the schools for that of Canisius; an almost entirely Catholic liturgy modelled on the Missale Romanum ("the Red book") was rendered compulsory in 1576.[3] Only South Ermanland under Duke Charles

---

[1] In the last year of Gustavus Vasa Calvin had already attempted to approach him and his successor with a dedication. CR 45, 445 ff., 451 f.

[2] This was followed by Eric's violent removal by poisoning, as to the lawfulness of which even the Lutheran episcopate had pronounced in the affirmative.

[3] Liturgia Svecanae Ecclesiae catholicae et orthodoxae conformis. Stockholm, 1576.

resisted these attempts at catholicising and held fast to the ecclesiastical order of 1571. The King, who was secretly converted in 1578, entered into negotiations with the Pope, through the mediation of the Jesuit **Antony Possevin**, with the object of bringing Sweden into subjection to Rome. But the Pope would not agree to what was proposed (several kinds of concessions in rites and constitution); but as John's political calculations (in Poland) failed, his zeal for this act of faith also cooled. The Jesuits were driven out, their chairs filled by Protestants. After Catherine's death, the new queen Gunnila (1585) completely did away with the influence of the Catholic party.

John held obstinately to his liturgy, but among the people this interlude had rendered the evangelical feeling consciously stronger. On his death, he was succeeded by his Catholic son Sigismund, who was at the same time King of Poland and devoted to the Jesuits. When the news reached Rome that he desired to renounce the crown of Sweden, the Pope hastened to put before his eyes the duty of restoring the Catholic religion and, by uniting the two powerful States of Poland and Sweden, of procuring *firmissimas opes ecclesiae catholicae, hostibus detrimenta inaestimabilia*.[1] But, in order to assure the Swedish throne to himself, he was obliged to promise to maintain Protestantism in Sweden, after his uncle Duke **Charles** of South Ermanland had, in the capacity of regent, convoked the **ecclesiastical assembly**[2] at **Upsala**, which abolished John's ecclesiastical institutions, adopted the CA and determined upon keeping Catholicism aloof; private persons of a different confession were only to be tolerated, as long as they kept themselves quiet. This assembly sealed the victory of the Reformation in Sweden and in its results was of the greatest importance also for the maintenance of the same in Germany.[3] Sigismund, who had immediately protested in secret against these concessions as extorted by compulsion and did not cease to favour the Catholics, was finally declared to have forfeited his authority, when he paid no attention to renewed demands, and Charles (the youngest son of Gustavus Vasa) was chosen regent and, in 1604, King, under the title of **Charles IX**. Although personally more inclined to Calvinism, in accordance with the opinion of the country, he maintained Lutheranism, and the firmly-established Lutheran church now proved itself a solid foundation of the development of the people. His son **Gustavus Adolphus** at the critical moment became the saviour of German Protestantism.

2. Poland.

Sources (continuation of p. 212). STAN. HOSII *Opp. omnia.* Colon. 1584. 2 vols. *Epist. Hosii in Acta hist. res gestas Poloniae illustr.* IV. Cracoviae, 1879; IX. 1, 1886. *Consensus in fide relig. Christ.* . . . *Sendomiriae sancitus.* Heidelb. 1605. *Acta conventus Thoruniensis.* Varsav. 1646.

---

[1] THEINER II. *Urk*, p. 83.

[2] On the character of the assembly as a "concilium," which Charles subsequently wanted to dispute in the interests of his Calvinistic leanings, cp. HILDEBRAND p. 115 ff.

[3] Hence the Swedish Church rightly celebrates the centenary of the "Uppsala möte."

Literature: F. HIPLER, Hosius in KL VI 295 ff. Biography by EICHHORN. Mainz, 1854. For Vergerio's journey to Poland in 1556/1557 see SEMHRZYCKI in Altpreuss. Monatsschr. XXVII. Sendomir: D. E. JABLONSKI, *Hist. cons. Sendom.* Berol. 1731. ERBKAM in RE XIV 128 ff. NIEMEYER, p. 553 ff. SCHAFF I 581 ff.; the Colloquy at Thorn: ERDMANN in RE XV 636 ff. O. IKIER, *Das Coll. charit. zu Thorn.* Halle, 1889. C. KRASICKI, *De societatis Jesu in Polonia primordiis.* Berlin, 1860. KLEINWÄCHTER, Gericius in ZhGes. Prov. Pos. V. 219 ff.

However favourably matters had developed themselves for the Evangelicals during the reign of **Sigismund II. Augustus**, yet here also in the meantime a saviour of the Catholic Church had arisen in the person of the Erasmian **Stanislaus Hosius** (Bishop of Culm from 1549-1551, and afterwards Bishop of Ermland), who became more and more decidedly a supporter of Catholic interests. In 1551 he had laid before the provincial synod of Petrikau a *Professio fidei catholicae*, to which all present assented by oath (afterwards worked up into the *Confessio catholica*, 1557, Works I 1 ff.); in 1555 he asked the Pope to send Jesuits into the country and to appoint a nuncio. Paul IV. did not now hesitate to instruct the King by letter as to the correctly Catholic attitude towards heretics;[1] **Aloysius Lippomani** made his appearance as nuncio, and demanded from the King the heads of eight or ten of the chief Protestants, but his conduct excited such wrath, that he soon asked to be recalled.[2] The evangelical cause suffered from the want of prominent leaders and differences of view. In addition, the evangelicals in Great and Little Poland and Lithuania gave themselves special constitutions. The Calvinists in the country certainly found an admirable champion and representative in John a Lasco (or Laski), who had been called in by them.[3]

Full of vigour and conscious of his aim, he endeavoured to procure for the reformed congregations of Little Poland greater constitutional independence in face of the Church of the Bohemian Brethren, to repel the advance of anti-Trinitarianism, while at the same time promoting a friendly understanding with both

---

[1] Raynaldi Annales ad an. 1556. Tom. XXXIII 596, 599, 601.

[2] Vergerius, Dialogi IV, fol. 82: Correspondence of Duke Christopher with Vergerio, p. 135, 138 f.

[3] John a Lasco was born in 1499, and belonged to a most distinguished Polish family. The nephew of the Archbishop of Gnesen and designed for the highest ecclesiastical dignities, he made the acquaintance (1524), during a humanistic voyage of study, of Erasmus (ZhTh 29, 608 f.), Faber Stapulensis, Farel, Oecolampadius, Zwingli and others: he left his home in 1538 just when the bishopric of Cujavia was offered him, in order to be able openly to declare his adherence to Protestantism, and, after a period of wandering, had succeeded in finding religious occupation in East Friesland (Emden) as superintendent of the Friesian Church, which he provided with regulations in the spirit of Calvin (The Emden Catechism, 1546). Driven out from there after the Interim, he had placed his services at the disposal of a fugitive congregation in England (p. 210), with which, having been expelled by Mary, he in vain sought refuge in Denmark and North Germany, until Emden again offered him refuge; but the battle-cry raised by Westphal against the Calvinist doctrine of the Eucharist, and the sharpening of differences in the matter of confessions rendered his position difficult. He returned home in 1556.

Lutherans and Bohemians and the necessary task of a Polish translation of the Bible. What caused him special distress was that the gravest charges were brought against him from Lutheran Germany (Er. Alberus,[1] Brenz), and Paul Vergerio was even sent from Wurtemberg to Poland to warn people against him (FRA II. XIX 224 ff.). When he died in 1560, he left his views as an inheritance to the Polish congregations. In 1565 the "reformed" broke away from the Unitarians at the Synod of Petrikau, and compelled them to form a church community of their own (RE XI 509). But, in 1570, Lutherans (amongst whose clergy Philippism predominated), Reformed and Bohemian Brethren, united in a **federated union** in a **Consensus at Sendomir**: the representatives agreed to a consensus as to the *praecipua capita fidei* (the Trinity, Christology, Justification, etc.), united in common recognition of the formula of the Confessio Saxonica (1551, CR 28, 415 ff.) in regard to the Eucharist, mutually protested their orthodoxy, but at the same time reserved to themselves independence of rites. On the strength of this they arranged a peaceful, brotherly juxtaposition of the three branches, who were mutually to respect their acts of ecclesiastical discipline and discipline over their clergy as well as the parochial rights: at the same time the three participating churches were to be mutually represented and their elders were to meet in conference. After the death of Sigismund Augustus, the last of the Jagellons (1572), the difficulties of the election of a King for Poland began. The general confederation now made arrangements to secure its rights in view of future elections. The diet of Warsaw (1573), at which the Catholic clergy themselves recognised the necessity of a compromise, introduced into the *pacta conventa* (to which every new King had to take an oath) the *pax dissidentium*, i.e., the isonomy of all dissenting religious parties, while, just as at the religious peace of Augsburg, the right of deciding the confession of their peasantry was reserved to the noble lords. If Protestantism had hitherto gained the upper hand, the Catholic reaction now began. Hosius (cardinal since 1561) had introduced the Jesuits (Braunsberg, 1564), whose educational institutions soon became of high importance for the Polish nobility; if the nobles were again won over to Rome, the country parishes were bound to follow. Thus the evangelicals only found protection where the the nobles steadfastly adhered to the evangelical confession. Under **Sigismund III.** (1587-1632), the pupil of the Jesuits, who during his reign settled in all the more important towns, a period of special severity set in, in which in the cities also (Cracow, Dantzig, Thorn) Protestantism was obliged to yield to force. Yet the personally tolerant **Vladislaus IV.** (1632-1648) still felt the need of introducing as far as possible a religious union or at least approximation, and, acting on the advice of **Bart. Nigrinus,** who had successively gone over from the Socinians to the Lutherans, then to the "Reformed," and now to the Catholics, arranged the "amiable" **religious discussion at Thorn,** to which the Romish-Jesuit party willingly assented, relying upon the want of union amongst the Protestants and hoping for an opportunity of propagating their doctrines; a mutual understanding according to them meant a return to the mother Church. The Elector Frederick William as Duke of Prussia and the Duke of Courland were invited to take part in it as vassals. The confessional opposition amongst the evangelicals had become more accentuated since the majority of the earlier Philippists had gone over to Calvinism and decided Lutherans (Gericius in Posen and

---

[1] Cp. SCHNORR V. CAROLSFELD, *E. Alberus*, Dresden, p. 156 ff.

others) had taken their place. In 1595, the quarrel that threatened had been with difficulty averted by the renewal of the Consensus of Sendomir at the **Synod of Thorn.** Gericius, who protested against the Consensus, was deposed and excommunicated by the Synod, defied the verdict for a short time with his congregation, but then obeyed a call to foreign parts. Abraham Calov of Danzig now frustrated the intention of summoning the peaceful Calixtus as spokesman of the Danzigers on the Lutheran side, whereupon the great Elector deputed him to attend a discussion at Königsberg; but he was completely set aside at Thorn, and the leadership bestowed upon the acute Hülsemann of Wittenberg. The Catholics were then allowed to feast their eyes on the sight of the Lutherans (who had first hindered the commencement of the discussion by petty grumbling) beginning to dispute with the Reformed their claim to be adherents of the CA. The *Colloquium caritativum* (of Thorn) became *irritativum*, from which those who took part in it finally separated with mutual irritation. Above all, peace amongst the evangelical parties was destroyed: general synods no longer took place, the Lutherans dropped off from the consensus of Sendomir.

3. Hungary and Transylvania.

Literature (see above, p. 214): Arch. f. siebenb. LKunde, NF XIX 581 ff.; for Pázmány, see F. BALOGH in RE XI 398 ff.

The attempt, made in 1561, to introduce the Jesuits into Hungary failed and in 1567 they again abandoned the forlorn hope; a similar attempt made by Sigism. Báthóry in Transylvania in 1585 ended with its failure in 1588. After 1586, they recommenced their work in Hungary with better success, so that they were soon able to venture to pass from proselytising to inciting to deeds of violence. The Emperor Rudolph's generals (Barbiano in Hungary, Basta in Transylvania which had been resigned by Báthóry to Rudolph) were inclined to exterminate Protestantism. Yet, even in 1600, a Jesuit report was able to announce: *Centuplo et amplius excedunt numero haeretici catholicos, non tamen sunt potentiores* (Arch. f. sieb. LK XIX 590). In 1604, Rudolph committed the violence of arbitrarily adding to the articles of the diet of Pressburg a twenty-second Article: that the King desires to extend the Roman Catholic religion in all his countries and confirms all enactments that had been issued since the time of Stephen the Holy for the protection of Catholicism. **The evangelical cause now combined with the defence of the violated constitution of the country:** the nobles (not only the evangelical) rose against Rudolph, made the Transylvanian prince Stephen Bocskai prince of Hungary and proclaimed complete equality of rights for those of the Catholic, Augsburg, and Helvetic confessions. At this critical moment for the house of Habsburg, Archduke Matthias, as the representative of the house, brought about the **peace of Vienna** in 1606, which removed the arbitrary additional article of 1604 and assured freedom of religious belief to the Protestants, without, however, in any way injuring the Catholic Church. When Rudolph persistently protested against this peace,[1] the diet of Pressburg in 1608 inserted it amongst the laws of the country, and the

---

[1] Paul V. warned him *ne in maximum praeiudicium religionis catholicae licentiam hanc concederet.* Archiv. XIX 604.

Hungarians rendered homage to Matthias, who compelled his brother to cede Hungary to him; on tne 19th of November he was crowned, on the basis of a capitulation, in which he promised complete religious liberty to the Protestants. A **Lutheran** synod at Sillein (Syn. Solnensis) which met in 1610 now arranged the constitution (three superintendents), the form of religious worship, and the Confession (acceptance of the Formula of Concord). A second synod (1614) completed the organisation of the Lutheran Church. Meanwhile, the Catholic cause had found an extraordinarily clever literary champion in the person of the convert, the Jesuit **Peter Pazmany** (Archbishop of Gran, died 1637),[1] whose winning personality was successful in bringing back the most distinguished noble families (such as the Esterházys) to the Catholic Church. These wealthy lords of the manor were followed by thousands of their subjects, mostly under compulsion. But even the Jesuit pupil Ferdinand II., at his election in 1618 confirmed the Peace of Vienna on oath. But when he immediately afterwards proceeded to set it aside, the Protestants again sought aid from Bethlen Gábor, who again assured equal liberty to the three Confessions. The war between him and Ferdinand was ended in 1621 by the Peace of Nikolsburg, at which he renounced the royal title, while Ferdinand was obliged to reconfirm the Peace of Vienna. During the time of peace that ensued, the Lutherans held their third synod (1622) and legally arranged the official duties of the superintendents and the functions of the ministers. But the recatholisation of the nobility made continued progress, supported by the educational institutions of the Jesuits and their University founded in 1637 at Tyrnau.[2] As early as 1634 the majority of the diet were Catholic. In 1637, Ferdinand III. again confirmed the Peace of Vienna, but it was understood to mean that it guaranteed religious liberty but no churches, and hence the building of new churches was forbidden. Transylvania was again obliged to afford protection. Prince George Rákóczy, pressing on victoriously to Pressburg, in 1645 extorted the **Peace of Linz,** which guaranteed complete religious liberty (with churches, bells and cemeteries), and, in 1647, was solemnly ratified as a law of the land to counteract the intrigues of the Jesuits (see the text in Borbis, p. 61 ff.). The reformed students, who had hitherto directed their course to Heidelberg, now turned towards Holland (Franeker) during the Thirty Years' War: there they came in contact with both Independency and Anabaptism, which occasioned violent struggles, especially in reference to severer or milder ecclesiastical discipline and the constitution of the Church at home.

---

[1] Especially in his *Wegweiser zur göttlichen Wahrheit* (Kalauz, 1613), written in Hungarian.

[2] Ephemerides Colleg. et Acad. Tyrnav von 1636-1640 in Arch. XIX 628 ff.; in which for instance we read, Jan. 31st, 1637: Duo Calvinistae studiosi fuerunt et logica exclusi, quod noluerint fieri catholici.

CHAPTER FIFTH.

The Condition of Germany after the Religious Peace of Augsburg.

Sources and *Literature:* General: FR. V. RAUMER, G. *Deutschlands I* 1558-1630 in HTb II 1 ff. J. JANSSEN, *G. d. d. Volkes*, Vols. IV-VI. M. RITTER, *Deutsche G. im ZA der Gegenref.* I. Stuttg., 1889. A. HUBER, *Gesch. Oesterreichs* IV. Gotha, 1892. A. KÖHLER, *Der Augsb. Religionsfriede und die Gegenref.* in JdTh 23, 563 ff. L. v. RANKE in HpZ I (1832) 223 ff. G. WOLF, *Zur G. d. d. Protestanten* 1555-1559. Berl., 1888. SAFTIEN, *Die Verhandll. Ferd. I. mit Pius IV. über den Laienkelch.* Gött., 1890. KNÖPFLER, *Die Kelchbewegung in Baiern.* München, 1891. SCHWARZ in JGG XIII. SICKEL in AÖG XLV. TH. WIEDEMANN, *G. d. Ref. u. Gegenref. im Lande unter d. Enns;* 5 vols. Prag., 1879-1886. A. WOLFF, *Gesch.-Bilder aus Oester. I.* Wien, 1878. TH. V. OTTO, *G. d. Ref. im Erzherz. Oester. unter Max II.* Wien, 1889. W. E. SCHWARZ, *Briefe und Acten zr. G. Max' II.;* 2 parts. Paderb., 1889, 1891. MAURENBRECHER in HZ 7, 351 ff.; 32, 263 ff. REIMANN in HZ 7, 23 ff. SCHLECHT in JGG XIV 1 ff. STIEVE, *Die Politik Baierns;* 2 vols. München, 1878, 1883. P. DREWS, *P. Canisius.* Halle, 1892. O. BRAUNSBERGER, *Entst. u. erste Entwickl. der Katechismen des sel. P. Can.* Freib., 1893. Biography of PFAUSER in STROBEL, *Beitr. z. Lit.* I 255 ff, L. KELLER, *Die Gegenref. in Westf. u. am Niederrhein;* 2 vols. Leipz., 1881, 1888; the same in HZ 63, 193 ff. C. PREGER, *Pankraz v. Freiberg.* Halle, 1893. SCHORNBAUM, *Ref.-Gesch. von Unterfranken.* Nördl., 1880. H. HEPPE, *Die Restaurat. des Katholicismus in Fulda, auf d. Eichsf. u. in Würzb.* Marb., 1850; the same, ZhTh 27, 376 ff.; the same, *Das evg. Hammelburg u. dessen Untergang.* Wiesb., 1862. For Julius Echter see LOSSEN in FdG 1883, 352 ff. VON WITZINGERODE-KNORR, *Kämpfe und Leiden d. Evangelischen auf d. Eichsf.* I and II. Halle, 1892, 1893. L. MAYR-DEISINGER, *W. D. v. Rauttenau, EB v. Salzb.* München, 1886. GINDELY, *Rudolf II.;* 2 vols. Prag., 1863, 1865. *Nuntiaturberichte,* 3 Abth. I. *Der Kampf um Köln,* edited by J. Hansen. Berl., 1892. F. W. BARTHOLD in HTb, NF I 1 ff. M. LOSSEN, *Der Köln. Krieg.* Gotha, 1882. F. v. LÖHER, *Gesch. d. Kampfes um Paderb.* Berl., 1874. A. HÜSING, *Der Kampf um die kath. Rel. im Bisthum Münster,* 1883 (K. ZELL) in HpBl 38, 953 ff. A. KLEINSCHMIDT, *Jakob III., Markgraf von Baden.* Frankf., 1875 (add STIEVE in REUSCHS ThLBl XI, Nr. 24, 25). F. v. WEECH in ZGOberrh. NF VII 656 ff. For Ferdinand's Counter-Reformation see F. M. MAYER in FdG 1880, 503 ff. SCHREIBER, *Max I., d. Kathol.* München, 1868 (from a Catholic point of view). F. STIEVE, *Max I. von Baiern.* München, 1882; the same, *Das kirchl Polizeiregiment in Baiern.* München, 1876; the same, *Der Kampf um Donauwörth.* München 1875; M. LOSSEN, *Die Reichsst. Donaun.* München 1866. M. RITTER, *Gesch. d. deutschen Union* 1598-1612, I.

Schaffh., 1867; the same, *Die Gründung der Union* 1598-1608. München, 1870; the same, *Der Jülicher Erbfolgekrieg.* München, 1877. C. A. CORNELIUS, *Zur G. der Gründung d. d. Liga.* Münchner HJb 1865, 130 ff. R. KREBS, *Die polit. Publicistik der Jesuiten u. s. w.* Halle, 1890. S. SUGENHEIM, *G. d. Jesuiten in Deutschl. I.* Frankf., 1847. V. LANG, *Gesch. d. Jesuiten in Baiern.* Nürnb., 1819. VIRCK, *Der Niedergang d. Protestantism.* in DevBl 1892, 141 ff.

On the basis of the religious peace a peaceful juxtaposition at first seemed rendered possible for both parties in the Empire; at first even the Protestant party, secretly favoured by the attitude of the Emperor, was able to show some increase. But it soon became evident that Romanism, restored in opposition to the Reformation and gathering its forces together, was again proceeding to the attack and developed a reaction, which obtained several successes. Peaceful ideas of reunion on the Catholic side were repelled, the confessional opposition became more and more accentuated, until finally the latter, promoted by confused political relations on the one hand, and by the fateful split and particularism in the Protestant camp, led in the Thirty Years' War to the self-laceration of Germany.

1. The Period of Suspense.

In Germany, little notice had been taken of the fact that Paul IV. had disapproved of the religious peace in consequence of its concessions to the heretics, and that, on the occasion of the resignation of Charles V. and the transference of the imperial crown to Ferdinand (1558), he had reasserted the medieval claims of the Popes in reference to the election of the Emperor and refused to recognise Ferdinand, as elected by the aid of heretics and *inconsulto Romano pontifice.* The Pope met with nothing but mockery or animosity; Vice-Chancellor Seld bluntly opposed the right of the Empire to the papal demands (see p. 242); he declared that the imperial dignity depended only upon regular election by the Electors; that all that was left to the Pope was the scrutiny of the election and subsequently the coronation, which however did not confer the imperial dignity and by no means bestowed new rights upon it; that only the Electors or States of the Empire collectively could instal or depose. Thus Ferdinand, being opposed to the demands of the Pope, found himself obliged to adopt a moderate attitude in regard to the Protestants. And in the territories of Catholic princes the widespread leaning towards Protestantism was able to voice itself—especially in Austria and Bavaria.

Thus, in 1556, the Lower Austrian States were able to combine willingness to help against the Turks with the condition of religious liberty and Ferdinand now at least openly conceded the administration of the cup to the laity: he applied to Pius IV. in order to obtain also for his son Maximilian permission for the *communio sub utraque* as the only means of keeping him to the Romish Church. The marriage of priests was almost universal and, with the Emperor's connivance, was also tolerated by the bishops. However, in 1562, the prelates themselves declared to the Emperor that the cup for the laity and the marriage of priests must be permitted. Albert, Duke of Bavaria, also found himself compelled (1556) to concede the cup for the laity to the States of his country, in order to obtain supplies from them. A large number of the Austrian monasteries were in a state of complete disorganisation.[1] Ferdinand's efforts at the Council of Trent to obtain radical reforms were influenced by the experiences obtained during visitations in Austria. At the end of 1563, he assembled at Vienna the representatives of the clerical Electors, Bavaria and Salzburg, and consulted with them as to the necessity of conceding the cup and the marriage of priests, sent an embassy for this purpose to Rome, and Pius IV. was actually persuaded, on the 16th of April, 1564, to concede the cup, subject to all kinds of reservations, in order to prevent the people from falling away from the Church. The judgments of contemporaries as to the success of this measure were very different; some said that those who had fallen away now returned to the Church in crowds; others, that even the Catholics became schismatic. Pius V. withdrew the concession in all haste. In the Silesian principalities and the city of Breslau—although dependent in fief upon the crown of Bohemia—the Reformation had so firmly established itself that Ferdinand gave it a free hand; in the rest of Silesia the Protestants also gained the upper hand.

In North Germany, in spite of the clerical reservation in the religious peace the preponderance of Protestantism especially asserted itself in the fact that vacant bishoprics were occupied by princes of the neighbouring princely houses in spite of their Protestant confession (in 1552, Frederick of Brandenburg at Magdeburg and Halberstadt; in 1550, Ulric of Mecklenburg at Schwerin; in 1554, Christopher of Mecklenburg at Ratzeburg).

Numerous Protestants made their way into the cathedral chapter; the Reformation continually extended itself even in ecclesiastical territories. (The only secular territory, which was still obliged to remain closed to it, Brunswick, opened its gates readily after Henry's death (1568) under Duke Julius [M. Chemnitz and J.

---

[1] In 36 monasteries there were found, together with 182 monks, 135 wives (or concubines) and 223 children.

Andreä]).¹ Thus, the bishoprics were certainly not changed into secular hereditary dominions, for there remained election by the chapter and they continued to exist as special territories, but the secularisation, which was completed by the Peace of Westphalia, was already prepared. Only a certain number of bishoprics, not subject to the imperial government, but freehold, were already secularised in the course of the 16th century. Thus, the bishoprics of the March of Brandenburg, Havelburg, and Lebus not only received Brandenburg princes as administrators, but the administration was combined in perpetuity with the authority of the ruler of the land, in Brandenburg in 1571, in the others in 1598. It was the same with the electoral episcopates, Merseburg, Naumburg and Misnia. The chapters asked for Saxon princes: in 1582 they even bound themselves to do this always. Misnia was completely amalgamated with the Saxon countries (1581), Naumburg and Merseburg secured special regulations. But even the bishoprics that were subject to the imperial government received Protestant administrators: Magdeburg was under the control of princes of electoral Brandenburg (Joachim Frederick carried out the complete reformation of the archbishopric in 1566), Halberstadt, Bremen, Verden, Osnabrück and Minden under princes belonging to different neighbouring houses, without being tied to any particular house.²

The religious peace had not yet entirely abandoned the idea of a final **religious union**; the object of the Ratisbon diet of 1556/1557 was to determine upon the ways and means for this purpose. A **religious colloquy**, from which, however, neither party expected anything, began at Worms in 1557; but the split which arose amongst the evangelical collocutors (the Ernestine theologians against Melanchthon and his party) and was cleverly made use of by the Jesuit Peter Canisius, so that the Gnesio-Lutherans left Worms under protest, afforded the Catholics the opportunity they desired, of breaking off what had scarcely begun.

Paul IV. praised God's mercy for having granted this success. When then, at the re-opening of the Council of Trent, Ferdinand seriously endeavoured to carry out reforms and also to bring the Protestants to a share in them, participation was decidedly refused

---

¹ Here an evangelical regular clergy was maintained, without confiscation of the money of the foundations. In 1576, the University of Helmstedt was founded. Cp. WAGENMANN in JbdTh 21, 224 ff.

² The attempt of the Premonstrants to win back the monastery of Ilfeld on the Harz in 1562 was unsuccessful. Z Harzver. XXVI.

on the evangelical side (at the Naumburg diet of princes). A small number of Catholic theologians in vain exerted themselves pacifically to build a bridge for the Protestants to return to a Catholicism which should deal seriously with reforms.

Amongst these, **Theobald Thamer** least of all deserves to be mentioned. He had formerly espoused Luther's doctrines with zeal and at the University of Marburg opposed Andrew Hyperius who inclined to the reformed doctrine of the Eucharist, but as early as 1548 began to entertain doubts of Luther's doctrine of justification and, in a spirit of rationalism, placed the revelation of God in Christ in the latter's example and ethics; soon afterwards he was deprived of office, and again approached the Catholic Church, to which he went over in 1557, after fruitless negotiations with the theological leaders of Protestantism (he died in 1569 professor at Freiburg). The first place is much rather due to **George Cassander**, a learned Dutch theologian, who subsequently lived at Cologne and Duisburg (died 1566). His idea was to recommend strongly an idealised Catholicism, by emphasising the common foundation in the Apostle's Creed and the consensus of the older fathers of the Church, by eliminating numerous abuses, as well as by conceding the cup for laymen and the marriage of priests to the Protestants. Almost at the end of his life, Ferdinand caused a *Consultatio de articulis inter Cath. et Prot. controversis* (1564) to be drawn up by him. The Helmstedt syncretism later recalled his memory. Together with him Ferdinand also consulted the Erasmian **George Witzel** who had formerly joined the Wittenbergers and then, finding the expected moral and social results of the Reformation unfulfilled, and having been personally badly treated, had abandoned Lutheranism greatly mortified and deeply disappointed. After that, driven from place to place, he exerted himself in favour of a reformed Catholicism as zealously as he railed against the Reformation, but now found his worst opponents amongst the Jesuits.[1] Finally, Mainz offered him a refuge; but he was unable to find a ready hearing for his reformatory ideas (he died in 1574). He sketched the programme of his middle course in his work: *Via regia*.[2] The two pacific reformatory writings did not come into Ferdinand's hands, but into those of **Maximilian**.

During the reign of this Emperor (1564-1576) the situation of the Protestants appeared to assume a more favourable aspect, as his leaning towards the Protestant confession was well known. This, however, had caused strained relations between him and his

---

[1] Witzel, in 1565, writes to Cassander that the Jesuits were worse enemies than the Lutherans, *hypocriticumne magis ambigo an malitiosum hominum genus, virulentius exosos nos infestant, quod ecclesiae faciem hanc deformem, non aliam, quam ut est hodie, defensam velint, emendationem huius omnino nolint, ne Seraphicae suae societatis daemonizomeno instituto deesse videantur.* (Illustr. et clar. vir. epp. sel. 1617 p. 280 f.)

[2] For Thamer, see SALIG, *Hist. der CA* III 199 ff. NEANDER, *Th. Th., Repräsentant und Vorgänger moderner Geistesricht.* Berl., 1842. HOCHHUTH in ZhTh 1861. CASSANDRI Opera. Paris, 1616. WITZEL's Werke. I. Cöln., 1559. RE XVII 241 ff.

father; he had kept with him an evangelical court-preacher (Pfauser), whom he had been obliged to dismiss since Ferdinand insisted upon it, and made no secret of his aversion to the Jesuits;[1] his relations to Frederick III. of the Palatinate had also brought him near to the Protestants. His position as Emperor certainly kept him back from decisive steps; he endeavoured to stand superior to parties; although aggressive behaviour was not to be feared from him, the policy of the Habsburgs made him a promoter of Catholic interests. At the diet of Augsburg (1566)[2] he wanted to discuss the religious compromise again, but on the representations of the papal legate Commendone he dropped this point, and the Electors also declared that all attempts at agreement should be abandoned for the future. Nevertheless, he endeavoured to obtain from Pius IV. for his countries, on the one hand the concession of the marriage of priests, and on the other the subjection of the Protestants to episcopal jurisdiction; but when the Pope refused and his States only demanded liberty for the CA the louder, and his plans of a religious compromise (Provost Eisengrein and Joachim Camerarius) were rejected by both parties, he finally (August 18th, 1568) promised his nobles by word of mouth, for themselves and their dominions, the free exercise of the Lutheran worship and confirmed this freedom to them in 1571 in spite of the counter-pressure, which Pius V., Philip II. and Albert of Bavaria had attempted to exercise. David Chytraeus of Rostock provided the Austrians with a ritual that exhibited many peculiarities. Archduke Charles, Maximilian's brother, against his will and under pressure of necessity, also guaranteed the same liberty in Styria (1572), Carinthia, Carniola and Görz (1578).

In many German districts semi-reforms had at least taken place; for instance, in Cleves, where, under Duke William, the old reformatory ideas of an "Erasmian" kind were firmly adhered to,[3] and in the bishoprics of Münster and Paderborn, which, although they had nominally remained Catholic, nevertheless sheltered many evangelical congregations and allowed the old order of things to be relaxed in theory and practice; Protestant usages also found admission (the cup to the laity and the marriage of priests).

---

[1] Cp. Fontes rerum Austriacarum XIX 126 ff., and also the questions laid before Melanchthon by Pfauser in 1556 by order of Maximilian.

[2] JGG X 525 ff. WIEDEMANN I 351 ff.

[3] For the state of affairs in the Church, see the account of 1562 by John Pollius in Zberg. GV IX 162 ff.

2. The Counter-Reformations.

But the forces of reaction were already in existence and equipping themselves for battle. The diet of Augsburg (1566) may be looked upon as the turning-point of the history of Catholicism in Germany, where the papal legate Commendone succeeded in uniting Bavaria, Brunswick, and the ecclesiastical princes in common action. It was evident that the Council of Trent had again given the Catholic cause a fresh foothold. In addition, Spanish policy was now active on the Lower Rhine. Under the influence of Duke Alba, Duke William of Cleves had been (since 1570) urged on to Roman Catholicism, being observed, influenced and watched from Spain. In Münster, a loyal partisan of the policy of restoration was appointed bishop (1566). The interest, which German affairs gradually awakened in the Curia, and which had increased more and more since Caraffa's time (p. 250), developed, particularly in Gregory XIII (1572-1585) into the liveliest eagerness to recover the ground lost in Germany, and an energy was now displayed from Rome, which, half a century earlier, would have stifled the Reformation in its beginnings (p. 251 f.).

The Jesuits had established a firm footing at Ingolstadt since 1549 with the assistance of William IV. of Bavaria, at Vienna since 1551 under Ferdinand, and soon also in Prague, Cologne, Treves, and Dillingen; the Collegium Germanicum at Rome (founded 1552) trained men, brought up in Jesuit principles, to reconquer their native land for the Church of Rome. The Dutchman **Peter Canisius** had already commenced his clever, energetic and well-directed activity; in the Bishop of Augsburg, Cardinal **Otto Truchsess**, he found a hierarch, who afforded him intelligent and zealous support; in Bavaria, Austria and Bohemia he created firm bases of operation for the Order and, with the aid of the companions of his Order, strove to bring back the people to Catholic discipline, putting this piety that appealed to the senses before those who had become unaccustomed to Catholic devotion and recommending it by preaching and instruction. It was also of great importance to restore the honour of Catholic learning at the Universities, and thereby to train a new generation of clergy to bring up the sons of persons of rank in obedience to the Church, to lay special stress upon the struggle against heretics as a duty imposed by the faith in the bishops' sees and the courts of princes.

In 1555, the large Catechism appeared, which had been written by Canisius at the instance of Ferdinand and published in his name. This work, called *Summa doctrinae Christianae*, at first intended for the instruction of students, was the first of a long series of catechismal works for which the Catholicism of the restoration is indebted to his clever pen. Without being directly polemical, with the assistance of numerous passages from the Bible and evidence from the fathers (especially Augustine), and clever handling of the schoolmen, this work sets forth clearly and definitely, in a mild and edifying form, the doctrine of the Catholic religion in contrast with all innovations. A "very small" (1556) and then a fuller "small" Catechism (1559, in Latin and German) provided fixed rules for the education of the Catholic youth and made Canisius the instructor of Catholic Germany.¹ In **Bavaria,** Albert V. adopted decided measures. In 1558, an examination of belief was opened at the instigation of the Jesuits and in the course of a visitation thirty-one Articles (CR IX 640 ff.) were put before all suspected clergy, as to which they were examined by the commission. (Against these Melanchthon wrote (1559) *Responsiones ad impios articulos Bavaricae inquisitionis*).² Albert then proceeded further and caused all his officials and subjects to bind themselves to the Catholic faith. In the struggle with his States that held Protestant views he had recourse more and more decidedly to the ruthless employment of measures of repression. **The territorial principle, to which the Reformation was indebted for so many victories, now began to show its double-edged nature.** Albert excluded his Protestant nobles from the States of the country, compelled his evangelical subjects to emigrate, and required from officials and University lecturers that they should take the oath to the *Professio fidei Tridentinae* (see p. 247). The ecclesiastical princes at first followed his example. Thus (1572), Balthasar von Dernbach, Abbot of **Fulda,** prince of the empire, whose territory had become practically Protestant, who had his chapter as well as his knights against him, proceeded with force and cunning, until he was compelled by them to resign (1577). After his reinstallation by the Emperor and empire (1602) he extirpated Protestantism root and branch. Already, in 1574, **Electoral Mainz,** without troubling about Ferdinand's "Declaration" of 1555 (see p. 161), had begun to reconquer **Eichsfeld,** which was for the most part evangelical, with the assistance of the Jesuits. At Maximilian's death, the Protestants were in retreat along the line; the Catholics had advanced to a position of attack. In **Austria,** the condition of the Protestants changed, when **Rudolph II.** (1576-1612), who had been brought up in strictly Catholic principles at the court of Philip II., came to the throne. Indolent and capricious, accessible to papal and Spanish influence, he at first however only proceeded against **the cities;** in 1577, he confirmed religious liberty to the nobles. The indifference, which had become almost universal in the episcopal sees, now gradually disappeared. When **Gebhard Truchsess of Waldburg,** Archbishop of Cologne, induced by his relations with the canoness Agnes von Mansfeld, whose brothers pressed for a formal marriage, went over to the Lutheran Confession and in spite of the Reservatum ecclesiasticum wished to continue in his post,³ but at the same time to proclaim "free choice of religion" to his subjects, his hazardous venture was wrecked upon the resistance, which he met with from the strengthened Catholicism.

---

¹ But the dark side of Jesuit zeal speedily showed itself: presumption and thirst for power, which desired to thrust all others aside, misuse of the confessional for inquisitorial purposes, etc. Thus, as early as 1573, the Franciscan **John Nas** reproaches them with telling the people that no one could give absolution *ad salutem, nisi esset Jesuita,* with asking the maid at confession what her mistress was doing, what sort of company her master kept, etc., of asking innocent maidens about fleshly things and the like. Cp. J. JUNG, *Zur Gesch. der Gegenreform. in Tirol.* Innsbr. 1874, p. 17 f.

² Not in CR, but in his Opera. Witeb. I. 360 ff.

³ His predecessor Salentin von Isenburg had resigned, by dispensation from the Pope, in order to marry.

Deposed and excommunicated by the Pope (to whose initiative it was due that the domestic policy of Bavaria was most closely combined with the Catholic policy of restoration, while the Emperor prudently held back), only lukewarmly supported by the Protestant princes (especially Electoral Saxony), his cause was actively taken up by the reformed (and consequently out of sympathy with the Lutheran princes) Count Palatine John Casimir alone, and he was unable to assert himself against the Bavarian Prince Ernest who had been elected by the chapter. With the aid of the latter, the complete reaction under Jesuit guidance now gained the day in Cologne; but the archbishopric became crown land for Bavarian princes. The example of a principle of **mutual toleration of Confessions of faith,** which went beyond territorialism, whereby the terrors of the Thirty Years' War might perhaps have been avoided, was thereby suppressed. **Julius Echter von Mespelbrunn** (1573-1617), bishop of **Würzburg**, had certainly entertained ideas of restoration at the commencement, but had supported the chapter and knights of Fulda against their abbot, and in the interests of the increase of his own power had taken over the administration of the foundation after his expulsion; being thereby brought into conflict with Pope and Emperor, he had been obliged to rely for support upon the Protestant nobles of the chapter and the Protestant States of the empire, and to hold back his plans of recatholisation. He had been on friendly terms with the Elector Gebhard, without however approving of his plans. But, after 1584, he thoroughly rooted out the Protestantism that still held the preponderance in the territory, only allowed a choice between the mass and emigration, and drove out 120 Lutheran preachers; and, within the space of a year, the Jesuits, who unweariyingly carried out their mission, snatched 62,000 souls from Protestantism. In a similar manner, the counter-Reformation now made a clean sweep also in other bishoprics; in Paderborn under Theodore von Fürstenberg (1585), in Münster under Ernest of Bavaria (1588), in Salzburg under Wolf Dietrich von Raittenau[1] (1588), in Bamberg (1595).

3. The Presages of the War of Religion.

Various efforts were now made to bring about the **conversion** of evangelical princes. In 1573, Canisius took counsel (but to no purpose) with the Duke of Bavaria concerning the conversion of the Elector Augustus of Saxony. In the case of **James,** Margrave of Baden-Hochberg, the efforts of the convert Pistorius (1590) were successful and made a stir[2] which was increased by the discussions (Pistorius and J. Andreä) connected with them. Only his death, that followed almost directly afterwards, prevented the extirpation of Protestantism in the country that fell to the share of his kinsmen. The Jesuit pupil, Archduke **Ferdinand** (nephew of the Emperor Maximilian II. and son of Mary of Bavaria), educated at Ingolstadt and inspired by his guardian William V. of Bavaria,[3] who

---

[1] In his case it was evident that the "restoration" Catholicism was capable of combining with a highly unspiritual mode of life.

[2] Sixtus V. celebrated this first victory over a German prince by a magnificent procession, which he accompanied barefoot. STIEVE, *Die Politik Baierns.* I. 30.

[3] During his reign it was said to be more dangerous to speak of the Jesuits' janitor than of the Duke himself. STIEVE, I 414.

was devoted to the Jesuits, with hatred of Protestantism and filled with the conviction, that the prosperity of his reign depended entirely upon his zeal for the Catholic Church, took a vow in 1598 before the altar at Loretto, to make at all costs Catholicism the dominant religion in his States. Since 1599, he had expelled all Protestants from his hereditary lands of Styria, Carinthia and Carniola. **Maximilian I.**, Duke of Bavaria, had been brought up with him in the same spirit. His father, in order to be able to devote himself better to the care of his spiritual welfare, resigned in his favour in 1595, and the son, during his long reign (1595-1651), transformed Bavaria into a model Jesuit state.¹ In order to win over Philip Louis of Neuburg, the Count Palatine—an attempt which at the time was unsuccessful—he caused **a religious discussion** to be held at **Ratisbon,** at which the Jesuits Gretzer and Tanner opposed the Lutherans J, Heilbrunner and Aeg. Hunnius of Wittenberg; the bitter feeling which was fostered, apart from that, by controversial and insulting writings of all kinds was only aggravated by it.² Political tension on both sides increased, as well as the feeling that something threatening was intended on the Catholic side. In the Lutheran imperial city of **Donauwörth,** where the toleration of the Catholic monasteries was expressly stipulated, but with the reservation that processions might only take place inside the city with banners lowered, the Abbot repeatedly protested against this traditional limitation and complained to the imperial privy council, when the magistrate (in 1605) refused to allow flying colours. When the monks, while the matter was still pending, again carried out the procession in 1606, they were insulted by the populace. The Emperor thereupon entrusted Maximilian of Bavaria with the protection of the Catholics in that place and with the execution of his mandate; he speedily made preparations and as soon as the ban was pronounced, occupied the city (1607), kept it, in spite of the protests of the Swabian party against the violation of the constitution of the empire, as security for the expenses of the campaign of execution, and, by a frivolous evasion of the religious peace step by step suppressed the exercise of the Protestant religion. The feeling of insecurity in matters of justice increased; followers of Rome even publicly disputed the equality of rights or the continuance of the Augsburg religious peace. They declared that the Pope could grant a dispensation from oaths which were injurious to Christendom.³ The Emperor Rudolph had indeed commissioned

---

¹ Secret spies to watch the officials and even more secret spies to watch the spies themselves were appointed after the model of the Jesuit system of instruction.

² The dispute turned essentially upon the rule of Christian doctrine and the judge in disputed questions of belief (The Scriptures or the Pope ?). As the Jesuits, in spite of their dialectical cleverness, were as a matter of fact driven more and more into a corner, the discussion was broken off by Maximilian under pretence that the opponents had insulted the Pope. The theme of these negotiations had the effect of promoting the sharp development of the orthodox doctrine of inspiration. Cp. TRÖLTSCH, *Vernunft und Offenbarung bei J. Ger. und Mel.* Gött. 1891, p. 28.

³ J. P. WINDECK, *Prognosticon futuri status,* Colon. 1603; in the 2nd part, *Deliberatio de haeresibus extirpandis, Aufwecker der Geistlichen,* Münster, 1603. Before this, GEORG EDER, *Das goldene Vliess.* Ingolst. 1579; the writings of the Jesuit SCHERER, ROSENBUSCH and others. In 1585, L. Osiander writes his *Warnung vor der Jesuiten blutdurstigen Anschlägen,* cp. Blätter für württ. KG 1892, 62 ff.

Archduke Ferdinand to give tranquillising assurances in regard to the religious peace at the diet of Ratisbon (1608) to the Protestants who were made uneasy by the Donauwörth affair, but he thought himself bound to obey God (*i.e.*, the Jesuits) rather than the Emperor, and suppressed these communications.

The result of this was **separate alliances**; on the 4th of May, 1608, a number of Protestant princes entered into a **union** at Ahausen, for mutual protection against further violations of the constitution of the empire. At the head of it was Frederick IV. Elector of the Palatinate; other members of the union were John Frederick Duke of Wurtemberg, the Frankish Margraves, Philip Louis, Count Palatine of Neuburg, consequently only a part of the Protestants (reformed and Lutheran); others held back, Saxony agitated against it. The union was threatened by the Catholic **League** of 1609, formed under the energetic guidance of the vigorous, shrewd, and ambitious Maximilian of Bavaria. The confusion was further increased by the dispute about the succession in Jülich-Cleves with its numerous, contradictory claims. At the Dortmund agreement (1609), John Sigismund of Brandenburg and Philip Louis of Palatine-Neuburg took possession of the inheritance, while the Emperor favoured the claims of Electoral Saxony.

Meanwhile, in the Austrian States, the incapacity of the Emperor Rudolph, his hesitation between obstinacy, passion and indolence caused the States of Austria and Hungary (while he was living in retirement at Prague) to entrust the conduct of affairs to his elder brother **Matthias,** who, in order to have a support against the enraged Emperor, made very great concessions to the Austrian Protestants, and in particular guaranteed liberty of religious worship to the burgher classes. The Bohemians now also extorted from Rudolph the Bohemian Royal Charter (1609), which has been called the most liberal religious edict issued in the 17th century.

> But a *Consilium de statu religionis in Germania* explained shortly and concisely why the *exstirpatio haereticae pestis* in Germany was now bound to be very easy: 1. Protestantism is split up into a number of factions. 2. Germany lacks a prominent Protestant ecclesiastical leader. 3. The vices, with which they had hitherto justly reproached the Romish party, have now become indigenous to them. 4. Calvinists and Lutherans are consuming one another in hatred and abuse.[1]

---

[1] Printed in STROBEL, *Beitr. z. Lit.* I 179 ff.

CHAPTER SIXTH.

The Thirty Years' War and the Peace of Westphalia.

Literature: A. GINDELY. *Gesch. des 30jähr. Krieges.* 4 vols. Prag, 1869-1880; the same, *Die Gegenreformation und der Aufstand in Oberösterr.* in SBWA 118. PESCHECK in Laus. Mag., 1840, 376 ff. TH. TUPETZ in SBWA 102, 315 ff. L. SCHWABE, *Kursächs. KPolitik 1619-1622* in NA sächs. Gesch. XI 182 ff. K. G. HELBIG, *Der Prager Friede* in HTb 3. F. 9, 573 ff. PESCHECK, *Gesch. d. Gegenreform. in Böhmen.* II. SUGENHEIM, *Gesch. d. Jesuiten in Deutschland.* I. ZIEGLER, *Die Gegenref. in Schlesien.* Halle, 1888. OPEL, *Die Wahl Leop. Wilh.s zum Bischof von Halberstadt 1628:* Halle, 1891. J. G. v. MEIERN, *Acta pacis publica der westf. Friedensverhandll.* 6 parts. Hann. Götting. 1734-1736. J. ST. PÜTTER, *Geist des westf. Friedens.* Gött. 1795. HINSCHIUS, in RE XVI 829 ff. M. KOCH, *G. d. deutschen Reichs unter Ferd. III.* II. Wien, 1866. THOLUCK, *Das kirchliche Leben des 17 Jhs.* Berl. 1861. 1862. BIEDERMANN, *Deutschl. im 18 Jh.* II 27 ff.; K. F. HANSER, *Deutschland nach dem 30jähr. Kriege.* Leipz. 1862.

The tension of the "confessional" opposition finally led to a bloody decision in the most fearful of all religious wars.[1] The Bohemian Royal Charter, together with the "Agreement" of the Catholic and Protestant States which went side by side with it and was afterwards differently interpreted by both parties: the acceptance by Bohemia of the Jesuit pupil Ferdinand II., whose conscience was in the hands of the Jesuits (p. 372): the acts of oppression, as the Protestant Bohemians considered the demolition of their recently-built church at Klostergrab and the shutting up of the one at Braunau: these and other things created the thundercloud, which burst in the deed of violence that took place on the 23rd of May, 1618, at the Castle of Prague. The **Bohemian** War, the first act of the bloody drama, with the sudden overthrow of the royal power of the youthful "Winter King" Frederick V. of the Palatinate meant the persecution, partly the annihilation of Protestantism in Bohemia, Moravia, Austria, and Silesia.

---

[1] As to the part the Jesuits took in the war by advancing large sums of money to the Catholic League cp. ABA XVI 101 f.

The short-sightedness of Electoral Saxony, which, on the advice of the chief court-chaplain Hoë von Hoënegg,[1] entered into the league with the Emperor against the hated Calvinism, was unable to save the Bohemian Lutherans from the fanaticism of the counter-Reformation. The papal nuncio Carlo Caraffa directed the deeds of violence against the conquered. The deeds of heroism performed by the Lichtenstein dragoons, the Croats and other wild warriors upon a defenceless people now drove the heretics back in crowds to the mass and confessional; their tormentors then caused it to be certified that they had returned to the Catholic religion "without force or compulsion." In the rear of the victorious armies of the Emperor and the League marched the Jesuits, one of whom was able to boast in Bohemia of having brought back more than 33,000 evangelicals to the Church. The Royal Charter was torn up; Bavaria was rewarded for its assistance with the Upper Palatinate and the dignity of an Electorate. The second act, the Lower-Saxon-Danish war, brought about the imperial **Edict of Restitution** (1629), which was not Richelieu's work, but was extorted from the hesitating Emperor at the instance of the League in spite of Wallenstein's dissuasion. It shows the Catholic interpretation of the religious peace of Augsburg. It contests—1. With the Protestants the legality of their confiscation of ecclesiastical benefices not held directly under the Crown. It declares—2. That the Protestants had maintained possession of archbishoprics and bishoprics contrary to the "ecclesiastical reservation." 3. That the declaration of Ferdinand I. (p. 161) in favour of Protestant subjects in "spiritual" States[2] is invalid. 4. That commissioners ought to be sent into the empire to restore the properties of the Church. 5. That the religious peace only concerned the Catholics and the adherents of the "unaltered" Confession of Augsburg. The edict, which deeply affected the ownership of property by the evangelical States, was as a rule successfully carried out. In many cases, however, Wurtemberg offered a successful resistance. But soon a dispute arose concerning the possession of the restored properties amongst the interested Catholic parties, the old Orders, the Emperor and the Bishops, all of whom desired the restored monasteries for themselves. The Catholic party of action desired to see most of it made over to the Jesuits to found colleges and schools. Magdeburg, Halberstadt, and also Bremen were awarded to the Emperor's son,

---

[1] Cp. BRECHER in ADB XII 541 ff.; NAsächs. G. XI 299 ff.
[2] *i.e.*, States under spiritual princes.

the Archduke Leopold William, and Lutheran prebendaries elected the Catholic prince; Bavaria and Austria contended for Verden and Minden. But this campaign of annihilation against Protestantism, which now violently opened the eyes of the Lutherans (Electoral Saxony), was checked by the bold advance of **Gustavus Adolphus** in the renewed war (the third act), in which it was now a question of the political power of the Habsburgs, and in which France, the Italian princes, and indirectly also Pope Urban VIII rendered assistance to Protestantism. In the case of Gustavus, there is as little doubt that he advanced to the attack to save the evangelical princes and peoples, carried on by belief in his mission, as that he desired the reward of his victories in lasting conquests (as fiefs) on the Baltic coast and in the possession of further German territories in pledge. After his death (Nov. 6th, 1632), Swedish military discipline, which had hitherto been carefully maintained,[1] fell to pieces; the war became generally a predatory war.

After the battle of Nördlingen, Electoral Saxony concluded (1635) the **Peace of Prague** with the Emperor. Thereby the Protestants were assured the possession of the ecclesiastical properties not held directly under the Crown which they had acquired before 1552; in the case of those not so held things were to remain in statu quo for 40 years, and then the state of things of 1627 was to be considered as the valid one. But, as many reformed princes remained excluded and Sweden continued to fight in alliance with France against Habsburg, the war was continued in a fourth act, until general exhaustion led to peace negotiations with France and the Pope at Münster, with Sweden at Osnabrück, and finally, on the 24th of October, 1648, to the **Peace of Westphalia.** A deputation from evangelical and Catholic States laid the complaints of both parties side by side (Hanser p. 96). The chief questions were: whether the *Reservatum ecclesiasticum* was binding on the Protestants and whether the right of reformation assigned to the rulers of the land in 1555 should not go beyond the limit of 1555. It was of importance to the Protestants to do away with the limitations, which had been imposed by the Edict of Restitution and the Peace of Prague, and to the Catholics to defend their ownership of the church properties held by them since the Edict of Restitution. At last, after lengthy negotiations, chiefly through the energetic and

---

[1] Cp. Gustavus Adolphus's reprimand to his officers in ZdGG I 258.

shrewd diplomacy of the imperial minister Trautmannsdorff an agreement was reached and determined upon :[1]

1. Equal rights of the religious parties, especially the Catholics and the adherents of the Confession of Augsburg in the Empire. In relation to the Empire and the Catholics, the " Reformed " were to be recognised as belonging to the latter party; consequently neither the Formula of Concord nor the Variata abolish adherence to the Confession of Augsburg. All religious matters were to be settled, not by the majority of votes of the States of the empire, but by agreement between Catholic and evangelical States. An exception was only made in favour of the existing state of possession in the case of the ecclesiastical States held directly under the Crown (prelacies [bishoprics and abbeys] and foundations). The original Catholic demand, that all ecclesiastical rights and privileges belonging to a State of the empire which had fallen into Protestant hands since the Treaty of Passau (all church properties for instance) should be restored, was the less able to be granted, since in many cases the secularisation of ecclesiastical territories was needed, in order to satisfy the indemnity claims of the different belligerent princes,[2] and besides, the Protestants had complete mastery in the North German episcopal territories that were concerned. But, in order to prevent any further handing over of ecclesiastical property held directly from the Crown into evangelical hands, occupation dating from the year 1624 (where possible, the 1st of January of that year) was fixed as the normal *terminus:* occupation during that year was to remain undisturbed: the same rule was also made in regard to the possession of other ecclesiastical properties (held indirectly under the Crown). Further

2. The secular States of the empire, by virtue of the right of supremacy, were allowed the **Right of Reformation,** by virtue of which they are justified in refusing the professors of another Confession permission to sojourn in their territories. But this was granted under definite limitations, which showed greater regard for the personal rights of the subjects. (*a*) In this case also 1624 was regarded as the normal year; the subjects of a different confession are to be allowed to exercise their form of worship according as they have adopted it on any day of this year, but (*b*) those who are unable to appeal to any such legal title, or who have only adopted a different confession from that of the ruler of the country after the conclusion of peace are, as may be thought fit, either to be **tolerated** (with liberty of domestic worship and taking part in the public services of their persuasion in the neighbourhood, the right of acquiring property, following a civil profession, and of honourable burials) or,

---

[1] See also RIEKER, *Die rechtliche Stellung d. evg. K. Deutschlands.* Leipz. 1893, p. 275 ff.

[2] Sweden received (in addition to Upper Pomerania, the island of Rügen and part of Lower Pomerania) the archbishopric of **Bremen** and the bishopric of **Verden;** Brandenburg, in addition to the rest of Lower Pomerania, the bishoprics of **Magdeburg** (in reversion, as soon as the Saxon administrator Augustus should be dead), **Halberstadt, Camin, Minden;** Mecklenburg, the bishoprics of **Schwerin** and **Ratzeburg;** Brunswick, alternate occupation of the bishopric of **Osnabrück** by an evangelical prince of the house, and, in addition, the monasteries of **Walkenried** and **Gröningen;** Hesse-Cassel, the abbey of **Hersfeld.**

if compelled to emigrate (that is to say, if they prefer it) their property is to be left untouched. The treaty contained in addition to this

3. Special regulations as to the relations of Lutherans and Reformed **to one another,** since in contrast with the Catholics they were regarded as a single party,—regulations, in which the old territorial idea was completely **broken up.** At first the state of things that existed at the time of the conclusion of the peace is to prevail. Should the ruler of the country change his confession, or if the country should fall to the lot of a prince of another confession,[1] the latter, while he is to have the right of instituting a court service of his confession for himself and of granting the exercise of their religion to any community already existing in the country and which passed over to him with it, on the other hand is to leave unmolested the public religious exercise of the confession hitherto authorised, as well as the hitherto prevailing ecclesiastical ordinances and property. In this case, the choice of their schoolmasters and clergy is expressly left to the communities.

Innocent X. protested against the peace,[2] declared it *ipso iure* invalid and null and void, since it had been concluded without the approval of the Pope, and further, expressly condemned its articles, to which he declared no one was bound, even if he had sworn to them. His protest, however, was unsuccessful, the more so as, in the preamble of the instrument of peace, it was expressly provided that no contingent protest, whether made by clergy or laymen, should have weight.

But the Emperor would not allow the extension of the peace to the Austrian hereditary lands; the existing exercise of religion was only assured to the **Silesian** mediate principalities (Brieg, Liegnitz, Münsterburg, Oels) and the city of Breslau. In addition, the Silesian and Lower Austrian nobility received a few very limited concessions. Only three evangelical churches were allowed to the immediate Silesian duchies outside the walls of Schweidnitz, Jauer, and Glogau. For the evangelicals in Hungary, see p. 362. Neither party was satisfied. Amongst the Catholics, some condemned the peace as a sacrifice of the inalienable claims of the Church. Others at any rate complained of excessive loss and were of opinion that there must have been more to be obtained. The Protestants were dissatisfied that the ecclesiastical reservation had not been abandoned and that for the moment land possessed by them must be given up.

---

[1] As in the case of Pomerania, Magdeburg, Halberstadt, and Minden in Brandenburg.

[2] In the bull *Zelo domus Dei* (Nov. 26th, 1648). BM XV 603. "This protest was no mere formality, as one is inclined to consider it, but a loophole left for the Catholics to recover the lost properties and rights of their Church." (Koch II 526).

It was only the exhaustion of Germany that secured the continuance of the peace. But Paul Gerhard sang

> Gottlob nun ist verschollen—
> Das edle Fried und Freudenwort.

This peace extorted from the Catholics by the pressure of the long war confirmed the legal relations of the two churches in the empire. Certainly, it soon became evident, how many causes of disagreement, further dispute and persecution, still remained. Above all. the life of the Church was bound to feel the fearful ravages and after-effects of the war, which no treaty could undo.

The devastating results of the protracted war interfered radically with the state of affairs in the Church. It was in great part carried on with fearful cruelty by hired soldiers, who, taking no patriotic interest in the cause which they served, led a life that varied between the severest deprivations of a miserable existence and unrestrained luxury and debauchery, and, partly from greed of gain, partly from bestial lust and savagery, frightfully maltreated all classes and families. The devastations of the war led to the most fearful lack of the barest necessaries, raging diseases aggravated the evil. Numerous villages totally disappeared, hundreds of dwelling-houses lay waste in the cities, over almost the whole of Germany. It took several generations before the inhabitants reached their previous number, and a still longer time before the towns regained their former prosperous condition. Naturally, many church and parish systems were broken up, many of the clergy fled or lost their lives; it was against them that the soldiers' mania for persecution was usually directed at first. In Wurtemberg, over a hundred church ministers perished within a few years; in the Palatinate, only thirty reformed ministers out of 350 were left after the war. Vacant posts remained unfilled for years or were administered by young and incompetent people. Many colleges and schools were closed altogether or at least for a time. At the Universities, the means and naturally also the moral condition of the students sank to a low ebb. Dullness and demoralisation overspread the land. The "Simplicissimus" of Grimmelshausen (1669)[1] throws a lurid light upon the low standard of the culture of the people, whole families of which had grown up with scarcely any regular education amidst the licentiousness of the war and military life, without any idea of a regular civilian life and an assured peaceful activity. The increased need certainly lent an air of seriousness to many minds and brought to maturity many virtues of Christian self-sacrifice and charity, but in consequence of its long continuance, produced an enervating and destructive effect upon the feelings of the community; selfishness and cowardly anxiety about a bare livelihood took possession of many, while others sank into a condition of dull vegetation or into melancholy and distress. To this must be added the lack of an elevating national consciousness in these struggles, in which the German families rent each other in pieces and at the same time became the arena of foreigners. The ideal side of the religious contest retired more and more

---

[1] Edited by A. KELLER in StlV 33 and 34.

into the background. The Peace of Westphalia sealed the alienation of entire portions of the Empire and the completion of the territorial particularism of the princes. The old supremacy of the States of the empire under the Empire changed into the modern sovereignty. The empire was divided into nearly 300 sovereign territories, from Electors downwards to petty free imperial cities and sovereign abbacies, besides the mass of almost sovereign properties belonging to the Knights of the empire. Lack of a feeling of patriotism, narrowness of intellectual vision, pedantry, and a stunted life lay heavily upon all sides on the people. Not that there was an absolute lack of important, princely personalities, who zealously bestirred themselves to heal the wounds of their countries religiously and morally, materially and intellectually. The **great Elector,** whose court and government form a wholesome contrast to those of his father, George William, who displayed his extravagance and luxury in the midst of the stress of war; the pious, simple, morally pure Duke **Ernest** of Saxe-Gotha, who devoted his care to his subjects both economically and by renewing the system of church and school and who still lives in the mouth of the people as "Bet-Ernst,"[1] and others may also here be mentioned. The numerous small courts in many cases also promoted the intellectual development of this and the following period and gave support to mental talents.[2] But, the injurious influences, the invasion of French ideas, the servile imitation of Louis XIV., and the growing demoralisation of the courts still by far preponderated. The cleavage was widened by the separation of the people from the learned, and the corruption of taste and language became complete in the secular literature of the time.

---

[1] Cp., in addition to the biographies of GELBKE (Gotha, 1810) and BECK (Weimar, 1865), KEHR, *Pädag. Reden.* Gotha, 1881, p. 102 ff. J. MÜLLER's edition of his "*Special-bericht.*" Zschopau, 1883, and O. DEVRIENT in Zthür. GVer. 1882, 1 ff.

[2] See Leibnitz's words in BIEDERMANN II 37.

SIXTH DIVISION.

The internal Condition of the Evangelical Churches.

CHAPTER FIRST.
The Constitution.

Sources and *Literature*(see pp. 74 and 181). In addition, R. SOHM, *KRecht*. I. Leipz. 1892. G. SCHLEUSSNER in ZKG VI 390 ff. K. B. HUNDESHAGEN, *Beiträge zur KVerfassungsgesch.* I. Wiesb. 1864, p. 186 ff. K. RIEKER (p. 378). H. HOCHHUTH, *G. d. hess. Diöcesansynoden 1569-1634*. Cassel, 1893.

Luther's religious idea of the Church was naturally accompanied by the contestation of the *ius divinum* of any historical church constitution. Christ alone is the Lord of his congregation, he governs it by his word,—not by the compulsion of secular law, but by the internally superior power of truth; no dogma established by man has power over the Christians' conscience. Their right is the Gospel; the only power which exercises power in the Church is the power of the Word. Only one thing is bound up in this church of Christ[1] from its foundation as a necessity of its existence; the *Ministerium verbi*, which plants and propagates the Word and the Sacrament within the congregation. Ecclesiastical government and the ministry **are identical.** Nevertheless, even Luther could not evade the task of endeavouring to find for this spiritual empire

---

[1] The establishment of the office of preacher according to Luther (EA 17, ²387) took place at the **death** of Christ; the God who has reconciled the world to him also wills that the word of reconciliation should remain continually in his community. At the same time, Luther during his lifetime held fast to the principle that the **holders** of the *Ministerium verbi* receive their office "at the command and with the assent" of the community (1544 EA ²20, II 222), as the keys are handed over by God not to a definite class, but to the community of the faithful. In the Confessions of faith the double train of Luther's ideas (divine foundation and the mandate of the community) did not attain such clear statement as in his writings; the succeeding development of the Lutheran Church then allowed the one side of its doctrine of office to become completely extinct.

of Christ forms of its earthly existence. This first came practically forward in the necessity of **calling** preachers, since the previous instruments, the bishops, had proved themselves worthless; the practical cessation of episcopal jurisdiction then again set tasks which, in rapid and continuous development, led to the interference of the rulers of the country (visitations, superintendents, consistories). Luther adopted from the Catholic canonical law the idea of the **parish**; he made no *tabula rasa*, but supported the new edifice on the existing parish divisions and churches, their endowment, their offices (ministers and chaplains [deacons]); the result of this was the preservation of the rights of patronage. The superintendents nominated by the rulers of the country supervised ministers and churches, and also at the commencement took over the control of matrimonial affairs which had hitherto been settled at episcopal officialities, until they gave occasion for the establishment of **consistories** (composed of legal and theological members[1]), after the ruler of the country had previously interfered in many ways in church affairs. The idea of the **established Church** as a central organism of superintendence asserted itself in the introduction of an ordination act (1535), as a central **Confessional Church** in the establishment of doctrinal obligations for clergy and teachers. The religious ignorance and moral barbarism, in which the Reformation had previously found the Christian people, led to these established churches being considered in the first place as **institutions for the training of the people** by discipline and instruction, and the pastors as teachers of those under age and those who needed instruction. Thereby, Church affairs received an authoritatively legal character, in which the idea of assisting the congregation itself to independence, faded away: ecclesiastical discipline frequently became ecclesiastical police. Two dangers threatened this state of things: the arbitrariness of the pastors or the interference of the secular power with the internal sphere of the Church.

The **ban** (excommunication) offered special difficulty, to which were attached civil disadvantages in accordance with traditional views, together with exclusion

---

[1] In Electoral Saxony, the institution of such a board was discussed in 1538, and its activity commenced in 1539; cp. MEJER, *Zum KRechte des Ref. jhs*, p. 1 ff. SOHM has endeavoured (I 610 ff.) to establish a difference of opinion between Luther and Melanchthon on this point: that it was Melanchthon's, not Luther's ideas that in this case obtained the lead in the Lutheran Church; but he reaches this result by regarding **Melanchthon's** *Reformatio Witeb.* (p. 151) as the expression of Luther's very own ideas.

from the Sacrament. The principle was adhered to, that in this case it was a question of an inalienable right of the Christian community, in virtue of the power of the keys, not only to exclude obstinate and notorious sinners for a time from partaking of the Sacrament, but also from the Christian community itself. But who were to be the mouthpieces of the Church in this instance? Could the individual minister pronounce it without the assent and support of the community? and what was to be done in case those concerned, the community to which he belonged, paid no heed? The Schmalkaldic Articles declared the so-called greater excommunication to be a civil punishment, which in no way concerned the ministers of the Church, but on the other hand allowed the Church the privilege of pronouncing the *excommunicatio minor* (exclusion from the Sacrament and the *communio ecclesiae* until the offender reformed). The *Tractatus de potestate papae* (p. 354, 74) indeed declared that the pronouncing of this sentence was allowed to each individual pastor (*pertinere ad omnes pastores*), in connection with which, according to the clear declarations of the Reformers, the pastors were regarded as acting, not in opposition to the community, but with the assent of the community (CR III 965 *adhibitis in hoc iudicium senioribus in qualibet ecclesia;* see further Luther's *Tischreden* [Forstem.-Binds.] II 352 f. CR IV 548). The ban, which at first had generally fallen into disuse, was to be again established in accordance with the desire of the clergy on the issue of ecclesiastical ordinances; but Nuremberg for instance (in 1533), when its church ordinance was established, had succeeded in bringing about the erasure of the article of the ban (Möller, Osiander, p. 169 ff.). On this point the city authorities in particular showed themselves very difficult to please. But, as the need grew, the consistories now appeared as the proper representation of the community,[1] in whose name they were to discharge the office of the keys; only the first *gradus admonitionis* were left to individual pastors, the *sententia excommunicationis*, on the other hand, was pronounced by the consistory, and the pastor then had only to announce it. The ban was certainly thereby withdrawn from the intolerable arbitrariness of the pastors—the Flacians especially had ruthlessly governed their community by the aid of the ban—but[2] at the same time also changed into ecclesiastical police orders; the consistory condemned as an ecclesiastical court by the side of the secular court, and, like the latter, also employed external means of punishment. The treatment of **marriage** affairs also caused the greatest difficulties: a conflict arose between the statutes of canonical law firmly adhered to by the jurists and the views of the reformers (*e.g.* in the treatment of the validity of secret betrothals and obstacles to marriage). It was not until the ecclesiastical ordinances, drawn up by theologians, but decreed by the rules of the country, made fresh positive matrimonial laws that this split between jurists and theologians disappeared. Still, in the **question of divorce**, the conflict still continued between the claim of the theologians—that the word of God alone could be valid in this case—and the force of circumstances and the need of the authorities, to ordain divorces beyond these limits. The result was a law of divorce, which gave itself out as biblical, which, by the side of the ground for divorce afforded by adultery also artificially interpreted that of *desertio malitiosa* from Corinthians I. 7, and now

---

[1] Cp. the consistorial ordinance of Jena, 1569, RICHTER, KOO II 325.

[2] *E.g.* **Hesshus** at Magdeburg; cp. HUMMEL, *Epistolarum semicent.* Halae, 1778, p. 29.

included under the head of *quasi desertio* all that appeared to render separation necessary. And yet it was impossible to prevent stricter and laxer practice continually coming into conflict in spite of formal unity in the matter of theory.

The danger to the Church, which lay in the part assumed by the authorities, had been already keenly felt by Luther: *Satan pergit esse Satan; sub Papa miscuit Ecclesiam politiae, sub nostro tempore vult miscere politiam Ecclesiae* (de Wette V 596)! Melanchthon, in his displeasure at the existing state of things, had even frequently longed for the restoration of episcopal government; even Luther, in return for a reunion with a Romish church that allowed free scope for the exercise of the Gospel, would have approved of the bishops, although only as "episcopal restraint." But the process of development necessarily pressed further upon the path that had been taken and even set aside the leanings towards episcopal constitution, which showed themselves here and there under specially favourable conditions; in Prussia, the States of the country certainly endeavoured to maintain the episcopal office against the prince; but it became extinct in 1587 at the death of John Wigand; two consistories took over the administration of the Church. In Brandenburg the episcopal office disappeared even more quickly (p. 137). The conversion of Hermann von Wied, Archbishop of Cologne, to reformatory principles might have been of the highest importance for the evangelical church constitution, but his authority collapsed in 1547 and with it this evangelical church edifice. Amsdorf's Naumburg episcopate lasted an equally short time (pp. 147 f. 153).

Elsewhere, the beginnings of a **synodal** constitution had entered into life. In **Hesse** the superintendents (with limited episcopal privileges) together with a number of chosen pastors formed the general synod as a highest court. But this latter was not summoned after 1582, and Landgrave Maurice in 1610 established the consistory at Marburg as the organ of his fairly sovereign ecclesiastical rule. Even the clergy of Pomerania for a time maintained a clerical government of the teaching class represented by yearly synods and under the guidance of the superintendents, in regard to which the prince's position was that of a secular administrator who merely executed the resolutions of the synods. But, after 1593, no other general synod was held and, soon afterwards, the personal (episcopal) rights of the (general) superintendents in this case also passed over to the consistories.

This development was furthered on the one hand by the territorialism of the rulers of the country that had been permitted by the religious peace of Augsburg, and, on the other, by the general tendency of the time to development of absolute princely power.

The course of the development of territorial church organisation was followed by the **theory** that established and justified it. Melanchthon became the first theorist of the evangelical church constitution. Under the title of *Custodia utriusque tabulae*, the right was claimed for the authorities, after personally deciding for the true doctrine, to forbid all false doctrine and false worship in the country and to punish any public appearance of these "crimes" (as blasphemy). The confession and worship of a country depend, consequently, upon the decision of the conscience of the prince[1] (*cuius regio, eius religio*)[2]; for the public peace requires that only **one** doctrine (the true) should be tolerated in the land. But, in addition, the holder of governmental authority has to be considered as *praecipuum membrum ecclesiae* and, *cessantibus episcopis*, is under an obligation *iuvare alios ut emendetur ecclesia* (CR III 244; Art. Smalc., p. 350, 54). When, then, the religious peace of 1555 suspended the episcopal jurisdiction, in regard to the evangelical territories, until further notice, the experiment suggested itself, on the evangelical side to make a **transfer** of it to the evangelical rulers of the country (*see* Richter KOO II 349); consequently, the ecclesiastical government of the ruler of the country began to be confirmed not only theologically, but also by the law of the empire, and the *ius episcopale* of the ruler of the country, which now appeared a right that had been **historically acquired**, was now spoken of. The so-called **episcopal system**, which however appears in two different forms, is the result of this new idea of regarding the ruler of the country as the assign of the Catholic bishops. The jurist **Matthias Stephani** (*Tract. de iurisdictione* 1611), renouncing Melanchthon's theological confirmation, simply taught the **devolution** of the episcopal authority to the Protestant rulers of the country by virtue of the law of the empire, so that they administer the executive powers *iure proprio*, and those of the bishops *concessione imperatoris ad interim*, both completely distinct in reality, and only accidentally combined in the same subject. On the other hand, **Reinkingk** (*Tract. de regimine seculari et ecclesiastico*, 1619) and **John Gerhard** (in the Loci theologici, *locus de magistr. polit.*) harked back to Melanchthon, in so far as they made of the devolution a **restitution**[3] of the ecclesiastical sovereignty granted to the rulers of the country, but usurped by the bishops, which consequently belongs to the princes *iure proprio*, not only by consent of the empire and as *provisorium*. In this acceptation the episcopal system was again combined in Gerhard with the *custodia utriusque tabulae*. But in both

---

[1] For this purpose he would naturally have recourse to the advice of theologians, but these need not necessarily belong to the church of his country, and, finally, everything as a matter of fact depends upon his personal decision. Even the authorities are subject to the *necessitas confessionis*.

[2] This formula occurs in Joachim **Stephani**, *Institt. iur. can.*, 1599, I 7.

[3] Sohm, *KRecht* I 663, erroneously affirms that this expression is not to be found in Gerhard; but cp. Joh. Gerh. loc. XXIV § 179.

acceptations, at the same time great stress is laid upon the fact that this ecclesiastical authority belonging to the ruler of the country is bound by the decisions of its consistory as the voice of the **teachers** (*doctores*) in Gerhard by the **doctrine of the three orders** (oeconomicus, politicus, ecclesiasticus), each of which is bound to recognise the divine right of the other, while the governing class is also bound to recognise the judgments of the teaching class (to which is exclusively granted *cognoscere doctrinam*). Consequently, the development goes on, on the one hand the declaration of the accidental, historical form of the ecclesiastical government of the prince of the country as **normal** in principle, and at the same time the sanctioning of the *dominium* of the teaching class in the consistorial constitution.[1]

A similar development of the constitution also took place in the **German reformed** territories, so far as the princes came into consideration as their protectors; in this case also ecclesiastical government by the rulers of the country predominated. Certainly, we find here the beginnings of a **presbyterial** communal arrangement, which were suggestive of the original ideas of the Reformation, but were now almost entirely driven back on Lutheran soil, and on the other hand were here brought into connection with the exercise of ecclesiastical discipline. Frederick III. of the Palatinate, by an edict of 1570, instituted ecclesiastical colleges, the duty of which was to look after the external and internal well-being of the communities and exercise ecclesiastical discipline; the pastor was here united with the " censors." But these were appointed by the ecclesiastical government of the ruler of the country, the electoral " Church Council," for life. Similar arrangements were also made in Nassau and elsewhere.[2] Only on the Lower Rhine was a presbyterial and synodal constitution (realising **Calvin's** intentions) secured, in opposition to the consistorial constitution.

Zwingli, although he theoretically bestowed the ecclesiastical authority upon the individual congregation (Kilchhöre), relying upon his favourable experience of the Council of Two Hundred at Zürich (Opp. III 1, 337), regarded the civil authorities of the republican cantons, to a certain extent the organ of the Christian people (by means of the fiction of the tacit assent of the whole), as the natural directors of church affairs and placed the government of the Church in their hands, whereby the ministers of the divine word were only

---

[1] The Wittenberg judgment of 1638 (in BÖHMER, Ius eccles. I tit. XXXI § 43) shows how the *ius episcopale* was regarded, on the theological side, as only the form, under which the **teachers** *de facto* governed the Church.

[2] Jac. Andreä also in 1554 desired the like for Wurtemberg, but hesitation on the part of Brenz rendered the attempt fruitless. HARTMANN and JÄGER, *J. Brenz* II 285 ff. HEPPE, *Die presbyt. Synodalverfassung.* ²1874, p. 39 ff.

consulted, and, in case any should act contrary to God's word, were to raise their voice. These authorities were to carry on affairs in place of the as yet immature democratic ecclesiastical community. But the people approved of the new ecclesiastical government without opposition, especially as it was carried on with cautious consideration for the locality and individuals. There now only remained to the congregation the right of objecting (such objection to be confirmed) to a minister appointed by the council. The duty of maintaining ecclesiastical discipline also, originally so intended by Zwingli that the ministers together with the congregation should excommunicate and exclude sinners, was transferred with his approval to the authorities, who were to punish vices and maintain order: the ecclesiastical jurisdiction in marriage affairs devolved upon the "court of discipline" (1525),[1] in which members of the great and small council (consequently the civil authorities) sat with two clergymen. In the country parishes the "Ehegaumer," the so-called "Kirchenstillstand,"[2] affords a kind of representation of the congregation: persons chosen to exercise supervision over sins of immorality. They have to admonish transgressors repeatedly, and, if without success, to denounce them to the authorities for punishment.

Even after Zwingli's death, no alteration was made in this respect and his regulations were passed on to the other German cantons.[3] Certainly, the time very soon came, when this state churchship, which was hailed with such joy, was felt by the truest friends of the Church as a harsh oppression.

According to **Calvin's** theory[4] (see above, p. 181 f.), Christ has prescribed a definite constitution for the Church. There must always be four offices in the Church: pastors, teachers, elders and deacons. The *doctores* busy themselves with the *interpretatio scripturae*, and

---

[1] See p. 56.

[2] So called from its members remaining together in the Church for consultation when the rest of the congregation left it after the conclusion of service. HUNDESHAGEN, *Beiträge* I 215.

[3] Cp. HUNDESHAGEN, *Die Conflicte . . . . in der bernischen Landeskirche*. Bern, 1842, p. 36 ff.

[4] *Instit. christ. rel.* (1539) VI 3 cp. Ephesians IV, 11. Apostles, Prophets and Evangelists are, according to him, the extraordinary officials of the period of the foundation of the Church. Calvin, who, from a Church point of view, had no fatherland, and who felt himself, far less keenly than Zwingli, a member of the State as a whole, was unable to share Luther's love and submissiveness to the institutions of his country: cp. HUNDESHAGEN, p. 39.

are the protectors of the pure doctrine of the Church (without pastoral functions); the relief of the poor is the duty of the deacons; the pastors serve the individual congregation with the Word and Sacrament, and, united as a synod, have to pronounce judgment in questions of doctrine; the elders (who form, in conjunction with the pastors, the consistory, are the governors of the Church (*gubernatores*) by virtue of the administration of ecclesiastical discipline, which only controls spiritual means of punishment. In reference to the State, stress is laid upon the independence of the Church; yet it is the vocation of the State to protect the Church, and the vocation of the Church to strengthen the State in its struggle against what is bad. Preachers, presbyters and deacons are chosen by the congregation under the direction of the clergy, *ne quid vel per levitatem vel per mala studia vel per tumultum a multitudine peccetur*. But this theory underwent in practice (*Ordonnances*, 1541) **considerable modifications,** while at the same time important concessions were made to the civil authorities. The clergy carried out the choice of pastors, the little council (that is, the State officials) **confirmed** it, the congregation only had to give its assent. The pastors were further to be visited by a mixed commission (clergy and members of the Council). The elders were elected in such a manner that two were taken from the small Council, four from the Sixty, and six from the Two Hundred, as to which it was assumed, that Geneva would tolerate no one as a citizen, who did not assent to the Word of God, *i.e.*, the reformed faith (a reformed national religion). The Consistory, as the organ of moral discipline, was to abstain from all encroachments upon civil jurisdiction, and on the other hand to remain untouched in its spiritual authority: but as this moral discipline did not think it possible to dispense with means of enforcing right and power of punishment, the consistory, after representations and admonitions, referred matters to the civil magistrates for punishment.

Calvin's ideas were realised in greater purity in the French congregations, since these had not to arrange at all with a Christian executive power, but the State rather assumed a hostile attitude towards them. In its origin ecclesiastically **democratic,** the constitution soon developed itself as ecclesiastically **aristocratic,** in that the right of election of the lay elders, consequently co-optation, was conceded to the *consistoire*. Above the *consistoire* was the *colloque*, above the latter the provincial synod, and above that the national synod. The provincial synod appointed the clergy; all that remained to the congregation was a right of rejection. The constitution took a similar form in Scotland and the Netherlands. Of an essentially similar character also was the congregational constitution bestowed by John a Lasco in 1550 upon the London congregation of foreigners;[1] yet the latter has a part in the election of ministers; this right is still more vigorously maintained in the ordinance bestowed upon the congregation of foreigners in Frankfort-on-the-Main in 1554 by Valerandus Polanus.[2] The reformed congregations of the **Lower Rhine,** before they joined the Netherland exiles (see p. 313), had also built themselves up upon a decidedly **presbyterial** foundation.[3] The presbyteries, the members of which go out of office every year, but are re-eligible, are chosen from a list of candidates proposed. The presbyteries unite (as a rule twice a year) in the classical synod, at which supervision is exercised over the presbyteries, ecclesiastical discipline, heresies, and matters connected with schools and the poor. Only those who have vowed to submit to the discipline of the Church are looked upon as duly authorised members of the Church. Even the clergyman is subordinate to the discipline of the presbytery. This discipline deals with idolatry, superstition, contempt of God, heresy, blasphemy, disobedience to the elders and authorities, cheating (getting into debt), robbery, habitual drunkenness, luxury and the like, especially sins against the 6th (and 7th) commandments. The last resource of church discipline is excommunication, which, according as in each case a public scandal is in question or not, is pronounced in the consistory or publicly (in certain eventualities also public penance). The congregations keep in touch with one another by means of church reports and correspondence. The political decisions of the Jülich-Cleves war of inheritance procured an essential recognition of these self-governing churches, however fearfully Wolfgang William Count Palatine (who had become a Catholic) had oppressed the evangelical congregations in the war. The favourable issue rested upon the arrangements of the parties who concluded the agreement, according to which John Sigismund and his successors held firmly to the *status quo* (consequently, also showed tolerance for the Catholics), in order not to give their opponents a pretext for the suppression of the evangelical congregations. Certainly the Brandenburg electors asserted their *ius episcopale* against this reformed free church, and conformably to it asserted not only a right of supervision, but also a certain influence in ecclesiastical matters, still however with an essential maintenance of the presbyterial-synodal constitution; but the congregations thankfully accepted the patronage and protection which the ruler of the country now offered them.

---

[1] Richter KOO II 99 ff. 101.
[2] Richter II 149 ff. 159.
[3] K. Krafft, *Die Stiftung der bergischen Prov.-Synode*, 1589. Elberfeld, 1889.

CHAPTER SECOND.

The Devotional Life.

Sources and *Literature:* (see above p. 46; 74 ff.;). KLIEFOTH, *Lit. Abhandlungen.* 8 vols. Schwerin 1854 ff. ²1868 ff. DANIEL, *Cod. lit. eccl. univ.* Vols. II and III. Lips. 1851 ff. H. JACOBY, *Liturgik der Reformatoren.* 2 vols. Gotha 1871. 1876. GOTTSCHICK, *Luthers Anschauungen vom christl. Gottesdienst.* Giessen 1887. RIETSCHEL, *Luther und die Ordination.* ²Wittb. 1889. W. CASPARI, *Die evg. Confirmation.* Erl. u. Leipz. 1890. VON SCHUBERT, *Die evg. Trauung.* Berl. 1890. G. E. STEITZ, *Privatbeichte und Privatabsolution der luth. K.* Frankf. 1854. For further authorities, see the Notes.

The preaching of the Word of God, understood in a new way closely adapted to the nature of the times, which had forced its way into the heart of public worship, was bound to bring about a reorganisation of the latter. *Diligens verbi Dei praedicatio est proprius cultus Novi Testamenti* (Luther EA opp. v. a. XIX 161). In this, all the Reformers are agreed. On the part of the Lutheran Reformation, however, in contrast to the stormy and radical innovations of Carlstadt, the traditional forms of worship (mass, vespers) were preserved and a very conservative mode of procedure adopted —at first, not out of any admiration for these traditions, but in order to protect the people from any breach of ecclesiastical usage: at first, the idea was only to remove the most offensive portions, but later, to introduce more radical alterations in the direction of simplification. The traditional liturgies were **revised** according to an essentially different view of the nature of worship.

If Luther found the meritoriousness of a man's own **action,** conformity to law and ceremonial, prevailing in the Romish form of worship, on the other hand, according to him, all divine service was bound to enter into the closest relation with **faith,** as its **confirmation** in thanks and prayer and its **advancement** by the Word and Sacrament. Abundant holding forth of the Word as much as possible in daily additional services (*Von Ordnung des Gottesdienstes in der Gemeinde*, 1523, WA XII 31 ff.), restoration of the *sacramentum* of the Lord's Supper in place of the *sacrificium* of the Romish mass (involving the striking out of the sacrificial prayers and acts of the mass—*Offertorium* and *Canon missae*), **loud** utterance of the Sacramental words, the cup for the laity, the abolition of the "abomination" of low mass, the use of German congregational hymns; in addition, the accentuation of the principle of liberty, which neither knows nor tolerates any "necessary law" in this sphere; employment of the German language as the language of public worship (*Formula missae et communionis*, 1523, WA XII 197, closely adhering to Catholic forms: *Deutsche Messe*, 1526),[1] more freely than in accordance with tradition (see p. 46 and 77). But the influence of the Catholic model is shown in the fact that, in spite of the dominant position which is given to preaching, the idea is still firmly adhered to that a complete divine service is a Communion Service and culminates in this "office." This already gave rise to inconveniences in the 16th century: for, even under Luther's eyes in Wittenberg, the larger non-communicating portion of the congregation left the Church before the Communion,[2] the culminating point became actually **a supplement** of the preaching service. At the same time, the **paedagogic** valuation of the service had a very decided effect on practice ("those who are already Christians, need no external service");[3] in place of the subject of the celebrating congregation "the young people and the mass of the poor" are considered as an object of education. This occasioned, with regard to the Latin pupils, an obstinate adherence to the use at the same time of the Latin language in liturgy and choral singing, especially in the additional services particularly intended for the scholars; hence, catechismal exercises included in the service; hence, the German hymn made its way, under the point of view *ut habeat et populus quod discat* (Apol., p. 250). In external usages (altars and candles, priestly vestments, images, organ playing) Luther, in spite of his vigorous polemic against Romish outward forms, practically acted in a conservative spirit, with due understanding of the symbolical and with love of the arts. Only all magic (consecration of bells, water, palms and the like) is energetically ejected. At Communion, he at first retains in opposition to Carlstadt the not unobjectionable **elevation**; and it is not until 1543 that it disappears in Wittenberg and is also unable to maintain itself elsewhere. But in all the principle prevails: "Such ceremonies may not be our masters, as if it were a sin to act otherwise. For we Christians desire to be and must be masters of such ceremonies, that they grow not above our head as articles of belief, but they must be subject to us and serve us, when, where, in what way, and as long as we desire." (De Wette V 541.) Clearly, from the outset there is a distinction between the far simpler, plainer, more sober type of divine service in the Lutheranism of south-west Germany and the liturgically conservative type, richer in forms, of north Germany and Franconia. In regard to **baptism**, Luther at first adhered almost without alteration to the Catholic ritual translated by him into German (*Taufbüchlein* 1523 WA XII 38 ff.)[4]; but in 1526 he cleared this Sacrament of its overgrowth of symbolical acts (the act of breathing, salt, spittle, etc.), and abbreviated the exorcisms, while others went further and did away with exorcism altogether (Hesse, Wurtemberg, the Palatinate, certain towns); some also made the attempt, to arrange the rite of baptism independently and without dependence upon the Catholic ritual.

---

[1] Cp. the annotated edition in BA VII 161 ff.
[2] *Post contionem maior pars populi abivit.* KOLDE, *Anal. Luth.* 228.
[3] Cp. BA VII 165.
[4] G. KAWERAU in ZkW X 407 ff.

But the struggles with Calvinism, which reckoned the abolition of exorcism in the forefront of its "reformatory" demands, now caused the latter to be firmly adhered to with the greatest obstinacy as a "confessional" mark of distinction; thus, in Saxony (p. 297), Thuringia, where J. Menius, in the struggle with George Merula (1551) defended[1] exorcism dogmatically as an effective instrument of the Church in Prussia, where the church ordinance of 1558 certainly abolished it, but that of 1567 restored it after many disturbances and dismissals from office.[2] As for the **festivals,** the festival of the Saints with its frequently insipid legend was bound naturally to lose its importance with the worship of the Saints; however, the days consecrated to Mary that were based upon biblical history (the Purification, Annunciation and Visitation) were preserved as festivals of Christ, together with the days of the Apostles, and in like manner those of John the Baptist, Stephen, Michael (as a festival of angels and schoolchildren), frequently also of Laurence; local saints also were not forgotten (St. Antor in Brunswick, St. Ansgar in Hamburg). Bugenhagen created a "reformatory" feast by the church ordinance of Hamburg. Stress was laid upon the **paedagogic** value of adhering to the alternation and order of church festivals, in conformity with the foundation of the Christian faith. The traditional **Pericopes,** in spite of the fact that Luther clearly recognised the deficiencies in their selection, were at first retained as a makeshift out of regard for the majority of "unlearned" pastors who were in need of a postil, then, when this practice was assailed from the Calvinistic side, defended as a valuable possession. **Sunday** was maintained as a free but indispensable church ordinance of equal devotional and social importance in opposition to any legal conception of it and against the theory of a change of the Old Testament Sabbath into Sunday. But the interest of the clergy, to have Sunday rest and divine service protected by church police, in the second half of the 16th century led to an obscuration of the Lutheran, also of the evangelical doctrine of Sunday that had passed into a confession.[3] The **ordination** of the clergy by laying on of hands had lost its sacramental character; the **call** in conformity with the ordinance creates and legitimises the holders of the office of minister. Thus, at first a rite of ordination could be entirely left out of the question; in 1525, Luther adopted a solemn introduction of the clergy into office, after 1535, also an ordination distinct from this, as *publicum testimonium vocationis*, which then at the same time received the importance of a *confirmatio* by the church hierarchy and a *commendatio ministerii*. After that time, many disputes took place as to the necessity of this rite and the importance of the laying on of hands (Nuremberg, 1543, Pomerania, 1547 ff.).

---

[1] SCHMIDT, *J. Menius* II 110 ff.

[2] Cp. F. KOLDEWEY, *Der Exorc. im Herzogthum Braunschw*. Wolfenbüttel, 1893.

[3] Cp. G. KAWERAU in GGA 1892, p. 552. Sunday marriages, in particular, which gave offence to the clergy and with their banquets were prejudicial to the afternoon service and, with their preparations, also to the morning service, were the occasion of this. Justifiable zeal against this custom at once suggested that the divine command in regard to the Sabbath should be referred directly to the Sunday festival. An instance is afforded by the Rostock controversy 1557 ff.; J. WIGGERS in Jb. d. Ver. f. Mecklb. Gesch. XIX 65 ff. In 1550, there had already been a similar dispute in Stralsund *de sanctificatione Sabbathi*. MOHNIKE, *Joh. Frederus III.* Strals., 1840, p. 6 ff.

The reception of this act of ordination took place in the case of individual Lutheran national churches at very different times—in Wurtemberg, not till 1855. John Frederick's bold idea (1537) of entrusting four commissions (Wittenberg, Tübingen, Strasburg, Magdeburg) with the examination and ordination of all the clergy, remained a mere project (ZKG XIII 512). In **private confession** pastoral comfort of the conscience was combined with the paedagogic aim of an investigation of the religious knowledge of the members of the congregation. An act of **confirmation** only made its way into a small portion of the Lutheran churches. Under Bucer's influence, it proceeded from Strasburg (1534) to Cassel (1539) and so to the whole of Hesse (1566) as a "sacramental" bestowal of the *spiritus fortitudinis* through the medium of the laying on of hands; in Brandenburg (1540) it was attempted to secure its continuance as an episcopal right, which however had to be abandoned; in Pomerania (since 1544) it can be shown to have been a solemn admission to the first reception of the Holy Communion. The majority of the Lutheran churches held with Luther that the exercise of the Catechism, that is to say, the yearly Catechism examinations of the young were the proper confirmations. Extraordinary importance was attached to the education of the youth in the Christian doctrine; numerous Catechisms appeared, amongst which the palm must undoubtedly be awarded to Luther's large and small Catechisms (1529, p. 79); Catechismal sermons, exercises and repetitions in church, at school and at home helped to characterise it.

The attempt to recatholise the Protestant form of worship by means of the **Interim** awakened, amongst the decided Lutherans, a feeling of the danger to evangelical Christianity in the maintenance of the so-called Adiaphora, and encouraged the struggle for emancipation from suspicious ceremonies that were a heritage from Catholicism; but the excitement that soon afterwards grew up against Calvinism again worked in the opposite direction.

The Lutheran service had a special source of wealth in the German evangelical **hymn**[1] which, in addition to its immediate use in public worship, became of inestimable value to the religious life of the people and domestic edification by the side of the Bible, the Catechism, and the German homily. If, in the Middle Ages, in spite of numerous German spiritual hymns, German **hymnology** had only reached scanty proportions, it remains one of Luther's chief merits that he early recognised in this matter the need and desire of the people and endeavoured to satisfy it (after 1523 the *Formula missae* WA XII 218). He himself[2] went on collecting, working, translating, composing new hymns (1524, *Etlich Christlich Lider, Lobgesang und Psalm* [the so-called *Acht-*

---

[1] PH. WACKERNAGEL, *Bibl. d. deutschen KLiedes*. Frankf. a. M. 1855; the same, *Das deutsche KLied von Luther bis Nic. Hermann*. Stuttg. 1841; the same, *Das deutsche KLied*. 5 vols. Stuttg. 1862-1875. J. MÜTZELL, *Geistl. Lieder d. evg. K. aus dem 16 Jh*. 3 vols. Berl. 1855. E. E. KOCH, *Gesch. des KLieds*. ³Vols. I-III. Stuttg. 1866 ff.

[2] PH. WACKERNAGEL, *Luthers geistl. Lieder*. Stuttg. 1848. BACHMANN in ZkW V 159 ff.

liederbuch]; the Erfurt Enchiridion (1524) with 25 German hymns, 18 by Luther; John Walther's *Chorgesangbüchlein* (1524) with 32 German hymns). Psalms, Latin hymns, medieval canticles, the Catechism, parts of the mass (Credo, Sanctus) afforded him the opportunity of more or less free work; thus, he produced the penitential hymn of evangelical Christendom *Aus tiefer Noth*, its joyful song of the glory of the Gospel *Nu freut euch liebe Christen gmein*, its hymn of offence *Ein feste Burg*, its children's Christmas hymn *Von Himmel hoch* and others.[1] Others early followed his example: **Paul Speratus** (died in 1551 evangelical bishop of Pomesania at Marienwerder), who in his *Es ist das Heil uns kommen her* created the popular poetical doctrine of belief,[2] **Nic. Hovesch** (Decius) of Stettin, who composed the German Gloria (*Allein Gott in der Höh sei Ehr*)[3] and the German Agnus (*O Lamm Gottes unschuldig*), **Laz. Spengler**, town clerk of Nuremberg (died 1534) with *Durch Adams Fall ist ganz verderbt* (cp. FC p. 574), **Graumann** (Poliander) with *Nu lob mein Seel den Herren*, the Joachimsthal Cantor **Nic. Hermann** and many others. In the Low German district also, together with translations from High German, we have many original hymns (**Nic. Boye** in Meldorf, **J. Freder** in Hamburg and Stralsund, **Andr. Knöpken** in Riga, **H. Bonnus** in Lübeck). This fountain of song was not choked up even during the sway of the vigorous controversial theology at the end of the century of the Reformation, and, in the midst of repulsive theological quarrels, the religious impulse of the Reformation frequently continues to operate with surprising earnestness and vigour. **Barth. Ringwald** (died 1598) of Neumark, **Nic. Selnecker**, and **Ludw. Hembold** (died 1598 at Mühlhausen in Thuringia) characterise this period of certainly intermittent originality but yet of considerable edifying value in setting its impress upon the period of the Reformation. The oppressions of the time taught a **Valer. Herberger** (died 1627 at Fraustadt at Poland: *Valet will ich dir geben*) and the otherwise extravagant zealot **Phil. Nicolai** (died 1608 at Hamburg: *Wachet auf, ruft uns die Stimme, Wie schön leucht't uns der Morgenstern*) their songs of hope. In the latter a new note is sounded, a sensual magnificence of colouring and sensations of individual, mystic love of Jesus, which stand out in a remarkable manner as distinct from the ecclesiastical lapidary style of the period of the Reformation and its harsh earnestness: cp. also **J. M. Meyfart** (died 1642 at Erfurt) with his hymn so full of yearning: *Jerusalem, du hochgebaute Stadt*. After **M. Opitz** wrote his treatise *Von der deutschen Poeterei*, the influence of the same soon became traceable in the form of the spiritual song-writing, while at the same time the terrors of the Thirty Years' War impelled people to an inward grasping of the consolation of faith, and hence to hymns of the Cross and consolation. The chief representative of these is **Joh. Heermann** (died 1643 at Köben);[4] *Zion klagt mit Angst und Schmerzen, O Gott, du frommer Gott, Herzliebster Jesu, was hast du verbrochen*, and many others. Also the admirable lyricist **Paul Flemming** ranks amongst the ecclesiastical hymn writers with his *In allen meinen Thaten*.

---

[1] He proved his call to be a Christian national poet in his historical national song of the first Dutch martyrs (see pp. 46 and 197): *Ein neues Lied wir heben an*.

[2] Budde in ZprTh XIV 1 ff.

[3] Bachmann in ZKW I 480 ff.

[4] P. Wackernagel, *Joh. Heerman's geistliche Lieder*. Stuttg. 1856.

By the side of ecclesiastical poetical art a *musica sacra*[1] entered into the composition of new melodies and the cultivation of figurate-music for several voices (John Walther in Torgau), the theologian Lucas Osiander in Stuttgart, Seth Calvisius in Leipzig (died 1617), **Hans Leo Hassler** of Nuremberg (died 1621), Melchior Vulpius of Weimar (died 1616), Michael Praetorius of Wolfenbüttel (died 1621), **John Eccard** of Königsberg and Berlin (died 1611). Everywhere the schools provided the church choirs, princes and towns vied with each other in beautifying the service with part song; the playing on the organ, which supported the choral singing and competed with it in artistic adornment of the service, was supplemented by instrumental music,[2] so that the services, especially those in the towns, were abundantly equipped from a musical point of view on festival days, and were almost overburdened by extensive "concertgiving." But, together with the *figuraliter* of artistic singing, the *choraliter* of the Gregorian liturgical singing was also industriously cultivated in the altar singing of the clergy, the introits, responsories, and psalm-singing of the choir-boys. The congregation sang its German hymns (mostly from memory without book) **without organ accompaniment,** under the leadership of the cantor with the boys; it was not until the end of the period that the organ gradually began to become the instrument of the singing of the congregation.[3]

In the **reformed** churches the development of public worship was different. In Zürich, a *Taufbüchlein*[4] (by Leo Jud) certainly appeared in 1523, which like the Lutheran was in the main a translation of the Catholic ritual. But here the Reformation soon adopted the tendency to a more decided abolition of Romish ceremonies, symbolism and representation. Altars and images,[5] crucifixes and lights, had been removed since 1524, a similar point of view to Carlstadt's being adopted. Not a remodelling of the service of the mass, but an abolition of the same and the substitution for it of a celebration of the Communion, new and peculiar, although using the building material of the mass, and besides to be kept only at a few fixed dates (in Zürich at Christmas, in Passion Week and at Whitsuntide) was what was aimed at. The clergy bring the bread and wine to the members of the congregation who remain seated in their places, and each then conveys it himself to his mouth. The usual Sunday service

---

[1] C. VON WINTERFELD, *D. evg. KGesang.* 3 vols. Leipz. 1843-1847. L. SCHÖBERLEIN, *Schatz des lit. Chor-u. Gem. gesanges.* 3 vols. Göttingen, 1864-1872.

[2] Especially employed by **Heinr. Schütz** of Dresden (died 1672). HEROLD, *Alt-Nürnberg in seinen Gottesdiensten.* Gütersl. 1890, and VON LILIENCRON, *Lit.-musik. G. d. evg. Gottesdienste von 1523-1700.* Schlesw. 1893. give a clear representation of the liturgical and musical development of the Lutheran services.

[3] RIETSCHEL, *Die Aufgabe der Orgel im Gottesdienste bis in das 18 Jh.* Leipz. 1892.

[4] Cp. the liturgy in NIEMEYER p. 72 ff.; further, HUNDESHAGEN, *Beiträge zur KVerfassungsgesch.* I 176 ff.

[5] In order to explain Zwingli's attitude towards the Old Testament prohibition of images, we must refer to his experiences at Einsiedeln, the place of pilgrimage. The harsh attitude also of the later generation to the question of images is clear from BULLINGER's judgment of 1570 f. in FRIEDLÄNDER, *Beiträge zur Ref.-G.* p. 226 ff., 235 ff.; *Relinquendum* [in templis] *omnino nihil, unde postea exoriatur rursus superstitio.*

is, on the other hand, essentially a preaching service (*Ordnung die Predigt anzufahen und zu enden*, Zürich 1529); intercessory prayer, Lord's Prayer, preaching (thanksgiving-prayer for the departed), confession of sin, and the vow of absolution. According to Lavater's account (*De ritibus et instit. eccl.* Tigur. 1559), it is characteristic that, before the third bell, which calls the congregation together, public sales of properties, articles lost and found are announced by some one commissioned for the purpose; married men, who have left their wives, are summoned to appear before the marriage-court; after the third bell, the authorities make known their regulations affecting the citizens (this use of the church as a place of proclamation for public purposes is also frequently found in the 17th and 18th centuries in the Lutheran Churches). Zwingli declares (*fidei ratio* 1530,) that ceremonies which do not conflict with the word of God and are free from superstition, should there really be any such, might be tolerated for a while for charity's sake, but that the object aimed at must be the abolition of all ceremonies. It appeared only natural that the Romish choral singing was dropped, and also that the organ which supplied the artificial music was obliged to give way; but even **congregational singing** was not allowed after 1527; Zwingli, although himself a poet and musician,[1] was afraid of the spiritual being blunted by the sensual; common, or in other words, alternate utterance of the prayers by a male and female chorus was introduced in its place. Zwingli's conception of Sunday was entirely free: time and place are subject to us, not we to them. Idleness is not worship of God: hence, work on Sunday after the conclusion of the service would be more agreeable to God than vicious idleness. The believer is above the Sabbath (*Schlussreden* of 1523 Art. 25 and its interpretation). Private confession and absolution are not commanded by Scripture; general public confession and public general absolution are sufficient; in addition, private advice and consolation of consciences. A spiritual preparation for the Lord's Supper and the proper equipment thereto precedes the days of celebration. Ordination is limited to the introduction of the clergy by laying on of hands. But Zwingli's purism was not imitated everywhere in German Switzerland.[2] In Bâle the organ was certainly obliged to remain silent, but Oecolampadius was decidedly in favour of **congregational singing** and in 1526 introduced the singing of German psalms. Yet, in other places, even this restriction was broken through, much was adopted from the Lutheran Church hymns and original additions made (by **Ambr. Blarer**, Zwick,[3] and others; in 1553, the St. Gall hymn-book; in 1536, the Constance hymn-book by John Zwick with 150 hymns (amongst them 67 psalms). Finally, in 1598, the Council of Zürich decided upon the introduction of congregational singing.

In **Geneva**,[4] Calvin's *Formes des prières et chants ecclésiastiques* (1542) settled the form of divine service; the preaching service offers confession of sins, psalm-singing, free prayer, preaching, intercessory prayer with the Lord's prayer, song and benediction; on Communion Sundays the confession of faith leads

---

[1] O. MYCONIUS says of him: *In musicis supra aetatem excellebat*.

[2] RIGGENBACH, *KGesang in Basel*. Basler Beiträge IX 327 ff. GÖTZINGER, *KGesang in St. Gallen* in St. Galler Lit. Beitr. II. H. WEBER, *KGesang Züricks*. 1866; the same, *Gesch. des KGes. in der deutsch-ref. Schweiz*. Zürich 1876. ODINGA, *Das deutsche KLied der Schweiz im Ref. zeitalter*. Frauenfeld 1889.

[3] See SCHELHORN, *Sammlung f. d. Gesch. I.* (Nördl. 1779), p. 41 ff.

[4] E. DOUMERGUE, *Essai sur l'histoire du culte réformé*. Paris, 1890.

from the preaching service, the sermon at which deals with the Communion, to the sacramental words, to which is added a long, doctrinary admonition. In 1538, Calvin, during his banishment in Strasburg with Farel, had worked at a collection of French psalms and had himself translated some for this purpose. **Clement Marot**,[1] valet de chambre at the Court of Francis I., hitherto an erotic poet, produced a considerable number in 1540 and 1543; after his death Beza, at Calvin's instigation, continued this work, so that the complete Psalter was enabled to appear in 1562; it was divided into twenty-five weeks and always sung through in order. **Claude Goudimel** (died 1572), Palestrina's tutor, composed for the melodies of the Psalms simple harmonies for four voices in uniform movement, and thereby rendered possible four-part singing, which however Calvin would not allow at divine service; Goudimel accordingly only recommended it "for private use at home."[2] The Lutheran **Ambrose Lobwasser**, professor of Law at Königsberg, made an unpoetical translation of the French psalter into German (Leipzig, 1573), and his version, notwithstanding that several far better collections of German psalms had already appeared, was generally adopted in the German reformed churches, thanks to the compositions of Goudimel; in German Switzerland it also drove out the more abundant 16th century treasury of hymns and thereby kept back the contributions of the Reformation to the store of German church singing for a considerable period.

In Bâle, the crypto-Lutheran antistes Simon Sulzer had endeavoured, since 1558, to introduce Lutheran usages, such as organ-playing and private confession, private baptism and the communion of the sick, but met with an energetic resistance, since "signs of the Papacy" were at once scented by the people.[3] The organ had also been destroyed in many places in the Netherlands in 1566 on the occasion of an outbreak of iconoclasm, but had been preserved in the northern states. The synod of Dort (1578) demanded its abolition, but the authorities defended it and allowed it to be played before and after divine service. After 1637 it came into use when singing was going on, and the synod of Delf (1638) now declared it to be an Adiaphoron, reviving thereby, however, a violent controversy. In the Palatinate it did not find admission again until after 1655. The reformed purism in the matter of worship found its most decided characterisation amongst the English Puritans, in opposition to the "papist" service of the English established church and in combination with the opposition of Presbyterianism to a new hierarchy (see above, p. 334). **Preaching**, which had made its way into the centre of divine service, and had attained to fresh honour, was industriously, almost superabundantly employed. The new subject matter had at first broken up the traditional scholastic form of preaching. Luther's sermons were living testimonies of the faith adopted by him from the Scriptures and found again in them throughout, popular to the point of violence, adapted to the times in their attack upon Rome and

---

[1] DOUEN, *Cl. M. et le Psautier huguenot;* 2 vols. 1878, 1879; add TH. DUFOUR in *Revue crit. d'histoire et de Litt.* 1881. C. J. RIGGENBACH in RE XII 355 ff.

[2] Musical instruments, according to Calvin, belong to the *Instruction puérile de la Loy*, in the New Testament; God desires to be honoured "d'une façon plus simple."

[3] G. LINDER, *Simon Sulzer.* Heidelb. 1890, p. 50 ff.

enthusiasts, upon the sins of high and low. His " heroic " manner of preaching, that was entirely due to his personality, was certainly little adapted for a model for the rising generation of theologians, but found, especially amongst the Gnesio-Lutherans, many an important imitator, who knew how to preach with popular vigour, impressive earnestness, and the aggressive zeal of polemical controversy. Melanchthon likewise, by instruction and his own example, had made preaching serviceable to doctrinal purposes by means of the **local method** and found many pupils. Together with the development of a new corporate scholastic theology scholastic (synthetic) methods of preaching,[1] rapidly settled, which fell back upon scholastic models, developed themselves. The sphere of sermons grew dangerously, Luther's warnings against preachers, who could not leave off soon, was forgotten; pomp and show of theological learning, the bombast of allegorically emblematic comparisons, as the preaching of the Middle Ages had matured it, above all, the "confessional" polemics of the evangelical confession and parties set against one another made their entrance and robbed preaching of its religiously edifying effectiveness. We may see how rapidly this change took place, if we compare the homely children's catechismal sermons of the Brandenburg-Nuremberg church ordinance of 1533 or the unpretentiously popular sermons of James Andreä of 1560 with the series in which Polyc. Leyser (1590) treated the whole catechism in a polemical spirit "against the Calvinists." There is no need for surprise that, in consequence of these controversial sermons, the weekday services soon lost their edifying value in regard to the people which had been expected from them, and that they gradually ceased to be attended. Yet, in later times also, there was no lack of preachers of original power. If pericope-preaching prevailed at the Sunday services of the Lutheran church, the reformed preaching of Switzerland from the outset emancipated itself from this tradition, selected by preference sermons upon the books of the Bible in order and thereby impressed more deeply upon preaching the stamp of practical interpretation of the Scriptures. In the cathedral of Münster, in place of the *Horae Canonical*, meetings of the clergy took place for edifying exegetical discourses upon the biblical books (prophecy = collegium biblicum). Calvin instituted something similar in the *Conférence*—biblical discussions held every Friday, at which those present could put questions, which were at once answered.

An important preaching theorist arose at Marburg in the person of **Andrew Hyperius**[2] (died 1564), whose merit consisted in the fact that he referred preachers to the Scriptures themselves as the true and abundant source of all *inventio;* but at the time, during the preponderance of dogmatic interests, he secured little attention; on the other hand, his reference to Timothy II, 3, 16, led people to attach a fivefold practical application to preaching, which was then exercised in many ways in true formalistic fashion.

As the evangelical churches in Germany, like those of most other countries, had entered into an abundant, frequently superabundant inheritance of ecclesiastical buildings, there was little opportunity for the development of a special **Protestant style of building.**[3] Towards the end of the Middle Ages,

---

[1] Andr. Pancratius, *Methodus concionandi.* Wittb. 1571; Schleupner, 1610; Hülsemann, 1625, and other editions.

[2] *De formandis concionibus sacris.* Marb. 1553.

[3] Cp. K. E. O. FRITSCH, *Der KBau des Protestantismus.* Berlin, 1893. C. GURLITT, *G. d. Barock-Stiles.* Stuttg., 1889.

Catholic ecclesiastical architecture, by laying out **churches with porticoes** and galleries, had provided spaces which took account of the importance of preaching and could easily have been adapted to the needs of the evangelical congregation.¹ The monastery and cathedral churches, with their arrangements for the choir, deep spaces shut off from the space allotted to the congregation, caused greater hindrances.² The fixing of the evangelical church service as an assembly of the congregation at first led to the construction of fixed seats which, in view of the traditional place of the chancel, were obliged to be arranged near one of the central pillars of the long nave, which in accordance with custom was usually adhered to, and partly of revolving seats. But the question of the place most proper for the chancel also soon led to independent attempts; the chancel was frequently pushed forward to the side of the altar, and, occasionally, both were placed in the centre of one of the long sides (the castle chapel at Stuttgart, 1553), or chancel and organ were removed behind the altar (as in the Wilhelmsburg at Schmalkalden in 1590); even the arrangement of the chancel in front of the altar space shut off by a rood-loft was attempted (Lauenburg-on-the-Elbe, 1590).³ The central building also came into use in the reformed districts (Hanau, 1622). Of the most important church buildings, to which our period can point, the Church of Christ at Tondern (1591) and the Church of Mary at Wolfenbüttel (1608) still show strongly the after-influence of the Catholic model, in the former case by a " rood-loft " shutting off of the choir from the body of the church, in the latter by the arrangement of the altar in a deep space for the choir, which, later, rendered necessary the insertion of a second altar nearer the congregation. Architecturally speaking, the constructive traditions of Gothic were combined with the forms of the late Renaissance. Free from the power of tradition, large ecclesiastical buildings, which took into account the latest requirements of divine service, arose on reformed soil. In the Netherlands, the medieval position of the chancel close to a central pillar of the long nave was preserved, but an extensive building, which transformed the Catholic " long house "⁴ into a (three-naved) " cross house " (*e.g.*, the Zuider and Wester Churches of Amsterdam, 1603 and 1620) was erected upon it. Round the chancel the elders had their seats; in front of it was the desk, from which the precentor led the singing of the Psalms. As Communion was celebrated here on covered tables, a larger part of the space allotted to the congregation was provided with movable chairs. in place of which the tables were set up on Communion days.

---

¹ Cp. C. GURLITT, *Kunst und Künstler am Vorabend der Reformation.* Halle, 1890.

² Luther says (Lauterbach's Tagebuch, p. 43) that the great five-naved churches were *inconvenientes ad praedicationem*. " Fine solid churches with low arches are the best *pro concionatoribus et pro auditoribus; non enim finalis causa est illorum templorum rugitus et boatus chorantium, sed verbum dei illiusque praedicatio.*" Churches like St. Peter's at Rome, or the cathedrals of Cologne and Ulm are *inopportuna*.

³ An attempt was certainly made, by constructing two rectangular adjacent wings, the common part of which afforded space for altar, chancel, font and organ, to make room for as many church-goers as possible and at the same time to keep the sexes strictly apart (Freudenstadt, 1601).

⁴ The " long house " and the " altar house " formed the stem, the " cross house " the arms of the cross, in Catholic churches.

CHAPTER THIRD.

The Development of the Theological Spirit from the time of the final Confessional Settlement.

1. Lutheran Scholastic Theology.

Literature: DORNER, *Gesch. d. prot. Theologie.* München, 1867. THOLUCK, *Lebenszeugen der luth. K.* Berl. 1859; the same, *Der Geist der luth. Theologen Wittenbergs.* Hamb. 1852; the same, *Das kirchl. Leben des 17. Jhs.* I. Berl. 1861. G. FRANK, *Gesch. d. prot. Theologie.* I. Leipz. 1862. HEPPE, *Dogmatik d. deutsch. Protestantismus im 16 Jh.* 3 vols. Gotha, 1857. W. GASS, *Gesch. d. prot. Dogmatik.* I. Berl. 1854. B. PÜNJER, *Gesch. d. christl. Rel.-Philosophie seit der Ref.* Vol. I. Braunschw. 1880.

The **controversial Theology**, which was devoted to the defence of the "pure doctrine," as firmly established in the confessions, against every deviation from it in its own camp and against all the theologies of other confessions, to a very considerable extent absorbed ecclesiastical sympathies. The "praeceptor Germaniae" still exercised a powerful posthumous influence in theological schooling as well as in the formation of a system, as much by his philosophical text-books as by the theological forms of expression in his *loci theologici*. The victorious Lutheranism, which had overcome Philippism and had dimmed the recollection of Melanchthon, did not suspect to how great an extent it was supported by him from a dogmatic point of view. Aristotle, the hated of Luther, begins to be highly esteemed even amongst Protestant theologians by a new Scholasticism as the teacher of a method of argument which proceeds in accordance with the strict forms of Logic and the rules of the syllogism. Not that philosophy offers dogmatics positive speculative impulses; but by its scientific character it makes it possible *tradendis legibus definitionum, divisionum, methodi et argumentationum, ut distincte et ordinate res exponere, evidentius easdem confirmare et adversarios pressius refutare theologus possit.*[1] The efforts of the Parisian philosopher **Peter Ramus** (de la Ramée), who went over

---

[1] J. GERHARD, *Methodus studii theol.* Jenae, 1620, p. 99.

to Calvinism and lost his life in the massacre of St. Bartholomew, to improve and simplify the Aristotelian Logic and facilitate the study of Logic, met with great approval in Switzerland and Germany, especially amongst the teachers of the colleges in the Rhine land and Westphalia and the French " Reformed," but the strict scholastic spirit, on the reformed (Beza) as well as on the Lutheran side, rejected him; the Leipzig philosopher John Cramer was deprived of office in 1591 for Ramism. The work of the Paduan Aristotelian Jac. Zabarella (died 1589) *De methodo* exercised a special influence upon methodology.

In **Martin Chemnitz** (died in 1586, while superintendent at Brunswick),[1] the pupil of Melanchthon, who in dogmatics had educated himself up to a decided Lutheranism, dogmatics are still free from the above thorny and formalistic spirit. **Aegidius Hunnius** (superintendent and professor at Wittenberg, died in 1603), in a series of dogmatic monographs, acutely developed the theology of the Formula of Concord. **Leonhard Hütter** (Hutterus, professor at Wittenberg, died in 1616), the champion of the Concord against the "reformed" Hospinianus (p. 289), composed by order of the Elector of Saxony a *Compendium locorum theologicorum*, which was intended to oust Melanchthon's *Loci* from the schools. The masterpiece of the "local" method adopted by Melanchthon was produced by the Jena theologian, **Joh. Gerhard** (died 1637);[2] it is equally distinguished by the abundant store of quotations relating to dogmatics taken from all periods, by completeness in the treatment of articles of doctrine, by the clearness of its developments and the moderation of its judgments, also by the continuous development which becomes noticeable in many points and, not least, by the pious sentiments and religious sympathies of the author. (Yet the same man also worked as a devotional writer with great success). Here the formalism of the school took a back place behind the earnestness of positive reflection. In consequence of the uninterrupted controversy with both Papists and "Reformed," the liking for the *argumentatio syllogistica* continually found fresh nourishment; by means of this artifice, Aeg. Hunnius, at the Ratisbon Colloquy (1601) drove the Jesuit Gretser into a corner (p. 373). But a David Chytraeus already found himself obliged to concede that the charge brought by those of other countries was not unfounded,—that the theology of the time was *mere scholastica, in qua nihil pietatis appareat*.

The recovery of the Holy Scriptures through the Reformation was welcomed: they were accepted as the *unica norma, ad quam ceu ad Lydium lapidem omnia dogmata exigenda sunt et iudicanda* (cp. the thoroughly evangelical propositions FC 570 ff., 632 ff.). Luther had freed exegesis from the triflings of the fourfold meaning of the Scriptures: *simplici, purae primariaeque verborum significationi niten-*

---

[1] Besides the *Examen Concilii Tridentini 1565-1573*, see his *Loci theologici* published by Polyc. Leyser in 1591.

[2] *Loci theologici*, 9 vols. 1610-1621; Tüb. 1762-1781; Berol. 1863 ff.

dum est—figura nihil probat (WA VIII 63)[1] and Melanchthon proclaims the rule: *Non potest Scriptura intelligi theologice, nisi ante intellecta sit grammatice* (CR XX 790). But the fresh draught of a Luther from these springs, and even the earnest and fruitful exegetical efforts of a Brenz and others were continued with little energy. Certainly, **Flacius** Illyricus, in his *Clavis scripturae sacrae* (1567) had struck into a good path in the matter of hermeneutics; but the dogmatically polemic tendency of the age prevailingly brought the Scriptures forward as a collection of *dicta probantia* for the doctrine as established in the confessions; the Symbols stand *de facto*—in spite of all statements to the contrary made on principle—as a law of interpretation **above** the Scriptures. However noteworthy the attempts made by Luther himself in the direction of maintaining differences of value within the Scriptures themselves by means of religious treatment of their centre Christ, and however clearly he recognised the human and hence earthly incomplete side of the Bible, his work would nevertheless have been impossible, had it not been able to employ the generally recognised authority of the letter of the Scriptures as that of the Word of God, both as a positive superstructure and as a weapon against every attack. It was natural that his successors in the struggle against the authorities, which Rome advanced against them, should announce that the Scriptures contained the absolute, legally doctrinal authority, and hence speedily repressed Luther's new method of treatment, but at the same time also practically subordinated the interpretation of the Scriptures to the doctrinal law of the Symbols (under the title of the *analogia fidei*).

Lucas Osiander in his *Biblia latina* indeed produced a great commentary on the whole Scriptures (1573-1586), Victor. Strigel *Hypomnemata in omnes libros Novi Testamenti*, David Chytraeus of Rostock (died 1600) a number of voluminous commentaries, and Erasmus Schmidt of Wittenberg (died 1637) distinguished himself by his Latin translation of the New Testament with notes, as by his large concordance to the New Testament, while J. Tarnor of Rostock (died 1629) equally devoted his attention to exegesis; also, the work akin to humanism on the linguistic side of interpretation was carried on by Joachim Camerarius (died 1574), Flacius and others, and found a valuable compilation in the *Philologia sacra* of Salomo Glassius (professor at Jena, then general-superintendent at Gotha (died 1656). But the organic comprehension of

---

[1] *Solo literali sensu pugnandum est, qui et unicus est per totam Scripturam. Nihil Origenes, nihil Hieronymus, nihil omnes, qui plures sensus dederunt.* 1521 EA opp. v. a. V 297. Cp. also Opp. exeg. lat. XIII 110, where Luther raises a protest in the matter of exegesis against *tota Alexandrina schola.*

biblical ideas and historical intelligence were lacking; dogmatics stifled exegesis. Even the magnificent ecclesiastical and historical undertaking of **Flacius**, in which he had the co-operation of Wigand, Judex and others, the *Magdeburger Centurien* 1559-1574 (Vol. I. p. 9) had in the main judged history in accordance with dogmatic standards; the succeeding period remained without any more important historical production. It was Calixtus who first asserted fresh historical points of view.

2. The mystical and practically-religious Current.

Sources and *Literature:* For Weigel, see L. PERTZ in ZhTh 27, 3 ff.; 29, 49 ff.; J. O. OPEL, *V. Weigel*, Leipz. 1864; H. SCHMIDT in RE XVI 677 ff.; A. ISRAEL, *V. W.s Leben und Schriften*. Zschopau 1888 (also KAWERAU in ThLZ 1888, 594 ff.). For Böhme, see his Works, Amsterdam 1682. HAMBERGER, *Die Lehre des Philosoph. J. B.* München 1844; FECHNER, *J. B.s Leben und Schriften*. Görl. 1857. HARLESS, *J. B. und die Alchymisten*. Berl. 1870; SEPP, *Geschiedkund. Nasporingen* II 137 ff. B. PÜNJER, *Gesch. der Rel.-Philos.* I 180 ff. For Rosenkreuzer and Andreä see HOCHHUTH in ZhTh 33 and 34; HOSSBACH, *J. V. Andr.* Berl. 1819. WURM, Calv 1887. For John Arndt, see WALCH, *Einleit. in d. Rel.-Streitigkeiten innerhalb d. luth. K.* III 171 ff. G. B. SCHARFF, *Suppl. hist. litisque Arndianae*. Witt. 1737. F. ARNDT, *J. Arndt*. Berl. 1838.

By the side of such representatives of corporate theology stand men, in whose works certain impulses of religiosity, which had been repressed by theological development, found, more or less secretly, satisfaction. The religious subjectivity, which had been powerfully excited in the Reformation period and which, when freed from external authorities, seeks light and satisfaction in directly turning to God and illumination through him—consequently, mystic enthusiasm—,was repressed in the "confessional" churches as fanaticism, but, at the same time, the vigorous certainty of salvation in justification by faith was threatened by the zeal for the defence of pure doctrine, and the spirit in many ways benumbed by the letter of a new scholastic theology. Accordingly, an **undercurrent**, in which the mystic impulse felt itself provoked against all fixed and objective churchdom and asserted itself with indifference against the historical portion of biblical Christianity, did not cease to exercise a reactionary influence.

The Lutheran pastor **Valentine Weigel** (died in 1588 at Zschopau in Misnia), during his lifetime certainly refrained from giving publicity to his mystical ideas of the outer and inner man, of mystic tranquillity and of the divine foundation in man (the Christ in us), which he tacked on to neo-platonic ideas and those of the natural philosophy of a Paracelsus, and which, consistently carried out, would disintegrate historical Christianity—he even went so far as to sign the Formula of Concord; but after his death his writings were circulated (by his

Cantor Weickart and others) in MS. amongst circles of similar views and were published after 1609 (at Halle and Magdeburg, *Der güldene Griff, Kirchen-oder Hauspostill* and others[1]). Much that was akin to his ideas, but also much that was foreign to them (especially of an apocalyptic nature) was now foisted upon him by others. The appearance of these writings naturally gave great offence to corporate theology; mystically fanatical ideas were since then branded with the name of Weigelianism. The mystic theosophy of the pious Görlitz shoemaker **James Böhme,** the *philosophicus teutonicus* (died 1634), (who, independent of Weigel and rich in speculative merit as well as serious efforts to keep his ideas of natural philosophy in connection with ecclesiastical Christianity, wrote, however, under the influence of the writings of Paracelsus on the one hand and of Schwenkfeld on the other), worked in a similar way; his *Aurora oder die Morgenröthe im Aufgang* was circulated in MS. after 1612 (printed 1634). He then remained silent for seven years, accused by the *Oberprediger*[2] and prohibited by the authorities from writing any more. In 1619 he resumed writing, suffered fresh attacks, but finally found absolution at Dresden and patrons amongst the nobles of Silesia. With the desire for mystic profoundness and fervour, which feels dissatisfied with the orthodox doctrinal treatment of religious questions and is repelled by the ultra-zealous feelings and often worldly behaviour of the theologians, and with confidence in the inner light is combined a bold speculation, struggling after expression, which in an agnostic spirit mixes up religious experiences with natural processes: the partiality for the secret and the marvellous with sincere piety, to the exclusion of secret forces in the philosopher's stone and alchemistic visions.

In the struggle with such a dull mystic theosophy the prevailing theology was more and more inclined to scent and resist in all deeper emotions of religious immediacy a spirit of fanaticism hostile to the church.

The *Allgemeine und Generalreformation der ganzen Welt* together with the *Fama Fraternitatis des löblichen Ordens des Rosenkreuzes* (Cassel, 1614) caused great excitement; these were followed by the *Confessio Fraternitatis RC* (1615),[3] and the *Chymische Hochzeit Christiani Rosenkreuz. Anno* 1459 (1616). A general search after the secret bond of mystico-alchemistic tendency described in these writings, and which it was pretended had existed for two hundred years, began to be carried on, in consequence of which partly fanciful, partly false combinations arose, which under this name allured or exploited the credulous. "Weigelianism" fused with fanciful "Rosicrucianism," mysticism combined

---

[1] He most effectively represents his mysticism, to which the Church is a stranger, in the *Dialogus de Christianismo*, in which the "pupil" (a Weigelian) discusses with the "preacher" (a representative of scholastic theology) the nature of Christianity, refers from the human authorities to Christ, from the Aristotelian Melanchthon to Luther's oldest writings, from the Confession of Augsburg to the Scriptures and belief, from the *Notae ecclesiae* to the inner word, finally dies without confession or Sacrament, is buried in the field, but receives divine testimony that he is in the light.

[2] [The chief ecclesiastical authority.]

[3] Both reprinted at Frankfort, 1827.

with alchemistic secret knowledge.¹ Originally, as already Herder assumed, it had been a case of nothing more than a play of fancy with a strongly satirical tendency to lash the traffic in secrets and the alchemy of the age: *ludibrium plane futile et quod inanitatem curiosorum prodat* (Autobiogr. Andreaes. p. 10). There is no doubt that **Joh. Val. Andreä**, the grandson of James Andreä, a remarkable and highly-intellectual man, who had a clear insight into the abuses of the age, and was superior to others of his time, had a great deal to do with these writings, in which he was perhaps assisted by his fellow students: for him this was the purifying completion of the writings of the period of youth.² Andreä, born in 1586, deacon at Vaihingen 1614, superintendent at Calw 1620, court-preacher and consistorial councillor at Stuttgart 1639, abbot of Bebenhausen, 1650, of Adelberg, 1654, where he died in the same year, was a singular man in many respects; he was far-seeing, a man of comprehensive and many-sided education, averse to dead formalism, in the midst of the misery of the Thirty Years' War and the brutalising influence of the time filled with the liveliest desire for religious renovation and moral discipline as the desire of the Church—the man, whom Spener would gladly have awakened from the dead, and whose importance has been recognised by Herder. In his Autobiography³ he declares that, filled by ardent love for the cause of Christianity, and yet always meeting with hindrances where he endeavoured to promote this *via plana*, he has endeavoured by a round-about way, *ea arte, ut per lusum et ingeniosa allectamenta seria agerem et Christianismi amorem propinarem*.⁴ Thus, he selects turns and phrases of varied kind, *e.g.*, in the romance of the Christian State *Reipublicae Christianopolitanae descriptio*.⁵ He is deeply penetrated with a sense of the abuses of the established churchdom under the rulers of the land (Apap, 1631, reprinted at Leipzig, 1827). He feels the need of a friendly union of truly Christian persons (*christiana societatis idea 1620*); and the closer union between such that really took place is the positive counterpart of the caricature of the Rosicrucian League. Amongst those, with whom he sought such a connection, we may mention, in addition to Joh. Gerhard and the famous schoolmaster J. Amos Comenius, **John Arndt**, the author of the *Vier Bücher vom wahren Christenthum* (1605-1609), and of the *Paradiesgärtlein*, pastor at Badeborn in Anhalt (p. 306), then at Quedlinburg, Brunswick and Eisleben, and lastly general-superintendent at Celle (died 1621). Andreä's words: " he who now seeks an upright life is reviled as an enthusiast, a Schwenkfeldian, an

---

¹ HOCHHUTH has collected the literature of the Rosicrucians in ZhTh 33, 253 ff., 34, 301 ff. For sectarians from these circles in Schleswig-Holstein cp. CARSTENS in Z. f. Schlesw.-Holst. G. XXI 375 ff.

² In his autobiographical records (p. 10) he confesses to the *Chymische Hochzeit;* but he also knows the origin of the *Fama Fraternitatis* and the *Confessio*, although he may not have been the sole author of them. The *Generalreformation* is a translation from the *Ragguagli di Parnasso* (I 77), by the satirist Boccalini, whom Andreä valued very highly. Cp. GUHRAUER, *Joach. Jungius.* Stuttg. 1850. p. 53 ff.; the same, ZhTh 22, 298 ff.

³ Published in Latin by RHEINWALD. Berol. 1849, p. 47.

⁴ Cp. Grimmelshausen's similar self-justification for his Simplicissimus StlV 65, 24 f.

⁵ Cp. also his allegorical epic poem *Die Christenburg* published by GRÜNEISEN in ZhTh Vl 231 ff.

Anabaptist," were fulfilled in the case of Arndt, who, immediately after the appearance of the first book, *Vom wahren Christenthum* (1605), was attacked by a Brunswick fellow-minister. The insistence upon personal sanctification was regarded as an obscuration of justification, the striving after Christian perfection as fanaticism, the fostering of the intercourse of the faithful with God and Christ in a manner tinged with Tauler's mysticism as a renewal of enthusiasm. In contrast to the widespread, dry and reasoned orthodoxy, which so often proved unfruitful in regard to the religiously moral life, a certain mystic absorption and pietistic narrowness was a necessary complement; the holy earnestness of practical piety, which here gave utterance to itself, was, in the demoralisation of the times, a fruitful source of godliness for thousands. Arndt was violently reproached for having adapted (Book II. cap. 34) a portion of Weigel's *Gebetbüchlein* (without knowing the author of the book, which at the time only circulated in MS. form). After his death, the disputatious Chancellor of Tübingen, Professor Luc. Osiander the younger, attacked his book as the "book of hell" (*Theologisches Bedenken* 1623);[1] these attacks continued throughout the whole of the 17th century,[2] although many, like Joh. Gerhard, took the side of the author, and as a matter of fact the work served to foster piety in thousands. Besides, there was no lack of men of unassailable orthodoxy, who saw the serious injury that was produced by the false certainty of the possession of the pure doctrine and the pure form of worship; cp. the *Oratio de novo*[3] *evangelio* by **Tarnor** ot Rostock (in J. G. Pfeifer, *Variorum theologorum miscell. theol.* Lips. 1736). Also **Joh. Matth. Meyfart's** struggle against "Pennalism"[4] in his *Christl. Erinnerung von Erbauung und Fortsetzung der Academ. Discipline* (1636) deserves special notice, in so far as it threw a lurid light upon the moral condition of the Universities and the race of theologians that was growing up and made men's consciences keener; at the instigation of Höe, Electoral Saxony caused the book to be confiscated.

3. Fresh Controversies.

Literature: For Huber, see WIGGERS in ZhTh 8, 1, 114 ff.; SCHWEIZER, *Centraldogmen* I 501 ff.; G. FRANK, I 271 ff. For the Cryptics and Kenotics, see WAGENMANN in RE VII 640 ff. THOLUCK, *Das kirchl. Leben* I 21 ff.

In spite of the limits drawn by the Formula of Concord, there was no lack of violent differences inside orthodox Lutheranism itself, in view of the tendency of this theology to regard the decisions

---

[1] Cp. F. Arndt, p. 205 ff.

[2] Cp. e.g., the Danzig controversies ZhTh 24, 43 ff.

[3] Especially confidence in church-going and the Sacrament, instead of in faith in Christ. Cp. Hans von Schweinichen's declaration: "Accordingly God has ordered: Strive first of all after the Kingdom of God . . . . as I have followed this command and zealously kept the first of January at Church." *Denkwürdigkeiten*, ed. OESTERLEY. Bresl. 1878, p. 516. G. WITZEL had already (1539) given a satirical description of the evangelical, whose motto is: "What sayest thou to me of life? We have the doctrine pure and unadulterated." (*Drey Gesprechbüchlein* Bl. B 4 b.).

[4] [A system of fagging.]

in regard to salvation and damnation as the chief points of dogmatic decisions.

The Formula of Concord had not been able to do away with the contradiction between **particular divine election** and **universal grace.** With the Reformers, it adhered to the idea that the definite number of those who become blessed is chosen by God's free grace and pre-destined to eternal life, but in like manner, in order to avoid the harshness of the Calvinistic *decretum absolutum* in reference to the rejected, also maintained the postulate, that God's grace is universal, that He has not created a portion of mankind for condemnation by Him without any regard to personal decision. This point of view was supported by Jak. Andreä against Beza at the **Mömpelgard Colloquy** (1586); in opposition to the reformed predestination dogma, people became accustomed, on the Lutheran side, to lay stress upon the universality of God's grace and the fault of those who were condemned, while at the same time, in regard to the pious, the idea was excluded that their election was in any way conditioned by their personal behaviour, and consequently in any sense merited by them. **Samuel Huber,** a minister who had been deprived of office at Berne owing to his opposition to the Calvinistic doctrine of predestination after a disputation with Beza (1588), had then become a Lutheran minister at Wurtemberg and finally found employment in Wittenberg, believed he could improve the method of instruction by teaching the universality of grace and also the **universal** divine **election** of all to salvation, the success or non-success of which was simply conditioned by the believing or impenitent and unbelieving conduct of men; certainly the presupposed idea of an actual election was thereby abandoned.[1] **Aegidius Hunnius** entered the lists against him and was impelled to place the decisive factor in election and rejection in the behaviour of the natural man (already **foreseen** by God) in opposition to the announcement of salvation. But as this behaviour, owing to the universally unavoidable resistance of man (corrupted by original sin) to divine things, cannot consist in an inward turning to belief in God, which indeed can only be an effect of divine grace, greater or less attention and readiness must be regarded as decisive, which the **unregenerate** shows to the external Word, or the greater or less proportion of **obstacles,** which are put in the way of acceptance of the Word. Huber was deprived of office in 1595 as a teacher of heterodoxy; after that time, he in vain endeavoured here and there to find recognition and a fresh sphere of activity.

The christological controversies between the theologians of Giessen and Tübingen caused greater stir. Out of the symbolical doctrine of the *communicatio idiomatum* sprung the thorny question whether Christ, in his condition of humiliation in accordance with his human nature had voluntarily **emptied himself** of certain divine qualities (*e.g.*, his world-ruling omnipotence), or whether he made use of them **secretly** : whether $\kappa \acute{\epsilon} \nu \omega \sigma \iota \varsigma$ (thus Mentzer and Feuerborn

---

[1] Bestendige Bekantnus D.S.H. Ob Gott durch seinen Sohn J. Chr. nur allein etlich wenig Menschen oder zumal alle Menschen . . . erwehlet und verordnet habe, 1595, ²1598.

of Giessen) or κρύψις (thus Hafenreffer and L. Osiander of Tübingen) is correct. The uninterrupted κτῆσις was recognised on both sides, but the former denied the continual χρῆσις. The theologians of Electoral Saxony, led by Hoë von Hoënegg, thought themselves obliged to deal the decisive blow in the heated controversy. In accordance with the resolutions of an assembly of Leipzig and Wittenberg theologians at Dresden, Hoë (or Höpfner?) composed, and the Elector John George promulgated, a *solida decisio* (Lips. 1624) which was to form the basis of instruction in Saxony. In Hesse-Darmstadt, also, this decision, which in the main decided in favour of the Giesseners, was adhered to. The necessities of the war gradually caused the opposition of the Tübingeners to die away. But opponents jeered at the "Lutheran cat-fight."

4. The Reformed Theology.

Until the end of the year, **Th. Beza** was the recognised continuer of Calvin's work in reformed districts. The interest in the exegetical study of the Scriptures, called forth by Calvin's thoughtful commentaries (to large portions of the Old Testament and all the New, with the exception of the Revelation), which thoroughly examined the text and investigated its connection, was fostered as a labour of love by Beza in his New Testament with an old and modern Latin version and exegetical remarks (1565), and by Tremellius and Francis Junius of Heidelberg in their Latin version of the Old Testament. In the learned commentaries of **Joh. Piscator** (died 1629) of Herborn, exegesis here also entered into the service of dogmatics, while **Hugo Grotius** (died 1645)—vigorously attacked from the Lutheran side and not even recognised by the "reformed" as one of their body—rendered yeoman service to the cause of historical exegesis. (Cp. the important theological productions in the circle of the Arminians). The learned men of France, the Netherlands and Switzerland devoted themselves to the study of the Old Testament and, in connection therewith, also to that of the Oriental languages (Drusius died 1616 at Francker, Louis de Dieu died 1642 at Leyden, John Buxtorf, father (died 1629) and son (died 1664) and in these undoubtedly surpassed the Lutheran theology. In like manner, in the province of Church History and ecclesiastico-historical criticism, **Rud. Hospinianus** (Wirth: died in 1626 a professor of Zürich) opposed Catholicism in investigations, in particular, of the rites and constitution of the old Church, and Lutheranism in the matter of the Eucharistic controversy.[1] In **Gerardus Joannis Vossius** (professor at Leyden, Dort and Amsterdam, died 1649) we have a polymath, who equally distinguished himself in the province of the humanities and theology, and as an historian specially took up the investigation of the history of dogmas.[2] French Calvinism was able to point to a **David Blondel** (died at Amsterdam in 1655), who gave considerable trouble to

---

[1] Opera: Genf 1681, 7 Fol.
[2] Opera 1695 ff., 6 Fol.

Romanism by proving the spuriousness of the pseudo-Isidorus, and on the other hand unmasked the fiction of Pope Joan; the Anglicans to the learned patriotic writer **James Usher**,[1] Archbishop of Armagh and Primate of Ireland (died 1656) who temperately endeavoured to defend the episcopalianism of his church against both the papal system and the Presbyterians on the basis of comprehensive historical investigations. The dogmatically "confessional" spirit was in this case especially prominent in the Netherland theology which tried conclusions with Arminianism,—most decidedly in the Pole **Joh. Maccovius** (Makowsky) of Franeker (died 1644), whose scholastically syllogistic method became the subject of serious investigations at Dort; the synod certainly supported his orthodoxy, but blamed his method as too complicated and scholastically modelled upon that of the Jesuits. Nevertheless, this method of teaching, corresponding to the character of the time, continued for a time victorious. The French dogmatist and controversialist, **Dan. Chamier** (professor at Montauban, died 1621), author of the bulky *Panstratia Catholica*,[2] may be put by the side of Makowsky and also of **Franz Gomarus** (see below).

5. Arminianism and the Synod of Dort.

Sources: EPISCOPIUS: Opera, 2 vols. Amst., 1650, 1665. UYTENBOGAERT, *De kerckelicke Historie* (up to 1619). 1646 Fol.

Literature: Coolhaes: biography by H. C. ROGGE, 2 vols. 1856. Coornhert: biography by MOORREES. Schoonhoven, 1887; C. LORENTZEN. Jena, 1886. Uytenbogaert: biography by H. C. ROGGE, 3 vols. Amst., 1874-1876. ZhTh 13, 1, 63 ff. Episcopius: PHIL. A LIMBORCH, *Hist. vitae S. Episc.* Amstelod., 1701. ZhTh 13, 1, 95 ff. The Remonstrance: BENTHEM (p. 196), p. 635 ff.; WALCH, *Rel.-Streitigkeiten ausser der luth. Kirche.* III 540 ff.; A. SCHWEIZER, *Centraldogmen*, II 66 ff.; SCHAFF, I 516 ff. Dort: *Acta Syn. Dordr.* Leyden, 1620. The Statement of Hesse: ZhTh 23, 234 ff. JOH. HALESII, *Hist. Conc. Dordrac.*; translated by Mosheim, Hamb., 1724. BENTHEM, p. 367 ff. NIEMEYER, p. 690 ff. SCHAFF III 550 ff. Grotius: Niceron, *Nachrichten* I 31 ff. JAC. REGENBOOG, *Hist. d. Remonstranten* (Dutch, 1774), German, Lemgo., 2 parts, 1781. Adr. a CATTENBURGH, *Biblioth. Scrip. Remonstrantium.* Amst., 1728. For Amyraut, cp. A. SCHWEIZER in Tüb. th. Jbb., 1852, 41 ff.; the same, in RE I 356 ff. EBRARD in Ref. KZ 1853.

In contrast with the growing spirit of strict Calvinism, a theologically milder, more liberal tendency had already shown itself at an early date amongst the laity and clergy in the Netherlands, *e.g.*, in D. V. Coornhert, a notary of Haarlem and a pious preacher of tolerance (he was especially severe against the doctrine of original sin and the defence of the burning of heretics), and in

---

[1] Cp. NICERON, *Nachrichten* I 1 ff.

[2] On the Lutheran side J. Gerhard provided a similar arsenal for the struggle with Rome, by collecting the testimony of Catholic writers to confirm the evangelical doctrines: *Confessio Catholica*. Jenae 1633-1637. 4 vols.

Caspar Coolhaes, preacher at Leyden (he opposed Calvin's doctrine of predestination; all who accept the main truths of Christianity are brothers; defended the rights of the authorities over the Church). The Amsterdam preacher, **Jac. Arminius**, from 1603 professor at Leyden, now entered into violent controversy with his colleague **Franz Gomarus** as the opponent of the Calvinistic doctrine of predestination.[1] The tendency to turn back from dogmatically fixed doctrine to the simpler biblical form of doctrine and therewith to dogmatic indefiniteness and liberalmindedness soon showed itself as a further difference; a more pacific disposition (even in regard to Rome) and, in the then condition of things, even in the interest of the latter, the accentuation of the claim of the **authorities** to the control of the Church were prominent.

After the death of Arminius (1609), **Simon Episcopius** and Beza's pupil, the highly respected preacher at the Hague, **Uytenbogaert** took over the leadership of the Arminians. On the 14th of January, 1610, they drew up the so-called **Remonstrance**, the five articles of which teach the conditionality of predestination, and describe faith as the work of grace, the effect of which, however, is not irresistible, and grace is liable to be lost. Oldenbarneveld received the document, and, after some time, presented it to the States of Holland. Uytenbogaert now also published a tractate on the rights of the authorities in ecclesiastical matters. The opponents, so it declared, desired the equalisation and collateral position of the Church in regard to the State; experience has already condemned this system; the only possible thing now remaining is the superiority of the State, which is under God but above the Church. It is the duty of the State to see to it, that the Church does not, by quarrelling and useless doctrine, deprive the people of the training for a devout life. The States afterwards forbade controversy as to the rights of the authorities, and declared that the preachers of this party should not be censured by their opponents, and that, in the question of predestination, nothing more should be asked for from candidates for the ministry than the contents of these articles. The Gomarists, however, came forward in 1611 at a conference at The Hague as vigorous **Counter-Remonstrants**, and disputed with the authorities the right of interfering in this question of doctrine. Negotiations between the parties at the request of the States (Delf, 1613) were as fruitless as a decree (Jan. 1614), which invited peace and ordered such "profound moot-points," as that of predestination, not to be brought into the pulpit. Neither party was content with this. The people, otherwise so quiet, became still more violently excited by the question in dispute. In Amsterdam and other places the result was a violent interruption of the religious services of the Remonstrants. The Calvinists pressed for a decision by means of a national synod. It was a matter of supreme importance that

---

[1] On the side of Arminius, one could appeal to the widely circulated work of the Dutch **Anastasius Veluanus**, *Der leken Wechwijser.*, Strassb., 1554, who was a decided opponent of the doctrine of predestination and in many respects also appears as his forerunner. See MOLL in Kerkhistorisch Archief I.

political factions now joined these ecclesiastical parties; the opposition of the Stadtholder, Maurice of Orange, who strove for a centralised authority at the expense of the provinces and of the aristocratic-republican party of the system of confederation (Oldenbarneveld) which laid stress upon the rights of the provinces and found its chief support in the States of Holland, by far the most powerful of the States. Maurice, although hitherto favourably disposed towards his court-preacher Uytenbogaert and who had no personal interest in the dogmatic controversy, now espoused the cause of the counter-Remonstrants and made use of their popular democratic power. They demanded a decision by means of a national synod; their power, supported by Maurice by means of political measures (the abolition of aristocratic town-magistrates and the like) obtained the majority in the States-General of 1617 (Gueldres, Zealand, Friesland, Groningen): Holland and Utrecht-Oberyssel protested emphatically that, to say nothing of the danger of deciding the dogmatic question before them by means of a synod, a victory by a majority of votes of the other States was not valid in religious matters, since, by virtue of the Union of Utrecht, the *imperium circa ecclesiastica* was clearly conceded to **individual** provinces. (Besides, the ecclesiastical controversy was limited only to these two provinces). But agitation and Maurice's policy gained over the more important towns even of these States; Holland was finally left by itself. Maurice broke the last resistance by a *coup d'état*—the imprisonment of the most important leaders of the aristocratic-republican party, Oldenbarneveld, Grand pensionary[1] of Holland, Hugo Grotius pensionary of Rotterdam, and some others, against whom a political suit was brought. Oldenbarneveld was executed in May, 1619, as he would not ask for mercy; Grotius was condemned to imprisonment for life and confiscation of his property, but was set free through his wife's cleverness.

At the **Synod of Dort,** whose decision in the matter of dogma was to be foreseen under these circumstances, the foreign members of the reformed Churches were also invited: for the most part they were represented: the English episcopal, the Scotch, delegates from Germany, the Palatinate, Hesse, Wetterau, Bremen, Emden, German Switzerland and Geneva. The French "reformed" were forbidden to take part in it "*instinctu Jesuitarum.*" The Elector of Brandenburg sent no representatives, out of regard for his Lutheran subjects; scruples also were expressed elsewhere. The Anhaltines, being regarded as Arminians, were not invited. The president was **Bogermann,** preacher of Leeuwarden, a zealous Calvinist and supporter of the punishment of heretics (translator of Beza's essay *De haereticis a civili magistratu puniendis*).[2] Sibrandus Lübbert, professor at Franeker, and Gomarus, at the time in Groningen,

---

[1] [The president of the States-General of Holland. The pensionary of a Dutch *town* was its syndic or legal adviser.]

[2] On the other hand Anastasius Veluanus had already taught: *De rechte Christenheit en vervolcht niemant:* and Uytenbogaert had already, when a student at Geneva, made no secret of his opposition to Beza in this point.

showed especial zeal. The Remonstrants, who, in accordance with a resolution of the synod, appeared on the 6th of December, 1618, were at the outset treated as accused persons, on whom the synod was to pass judgment. Simon Episcopius, supported by twelve others, undauntedly championed his cause. The Synod held 154 sittings from November 13th, 1618, to May 9th, 1619. The negotiations lasted until January 14th, 1619, with the Remonstrants, who then, as they would not consent to submit to the synod, and declared it to be in reality partisan and schismatic, were dismissed as convicted liars: "*Dimittimini, ite, ite!*" "God will judge between us and this synod" (Rogge, Uytenbogaert II 512). The synod, not without difficulty, since amongst the foreign representatives from England and Germany a large number were averse to the Calvinistic extreme, established the orthodox doctrine of particular predestination (*immutabile propositum; causa gratuitae electionis est solum dei beneplacitum; non ex praevisa fide aut aliqua bona qualitate et dispositione*), the particular value of redemption and the impossibility of grace being lost (avoiding, however, an express supralapsarian mode of teaching)[1] under five heads[2] with ninety-three canons altogether. The vote of censure upon the Arminians (in which, however, the Hessians and Anglicans did not join, as they could not permit any judgment upon persons) declared that they should be excluded from all ecclesiastical offices as disturbers of the Church. The Synod summoned the heads and demanded from them their signature to the *Acte van Stilstand* (a promise to abstain from all active interference in the affairs of the Church) and banished them, when they refused it. The provincial synods, the classes and presbyteries behaved in like manner: they laid the Articles of Dort,—eventually, the *Akte vom Stillstand*—before the Arminian members and then banished them. Only an extraordinarily small number agreed to the written promise demanded of them. The States-general expelled the refractory.

---

[1] Of the other resolutions we may note: A new translation of the Bible, in which (against Gomarus), the Apocrypha were to be preserved, but put *after* the New Testament; exclusion of the Epistle to the Laodiceans; control over home, school, and church catechisations; *in singulis pagis scholas constituendas* in the interest of the Church; teachers bound to the doctrine of the Church.

[2] 1. De divina praedestinatione; 2. de redemptione; 3. 4. de conversionis modo; 4. de perseverantia sanctorum.

In the question of the Constitution, the Synod (*i.e.*, the Dutch members) accepted in the main the collective constitution which had previously been sketched out at the Synod at the Hague (1586). This however did not receive the confirmation of the States-general. The result was now not a general, but only a provincial ecclesiastical ordinance. Besides the confession, mutual representation at the provincial synod formed a bond of unity. But still the synodal constitution prevailed; only the provincial synods, formed out of the deputies of the classes, require, in order to be held, the approval of the States-general, which send two commissioners.

The expulsion and persecution of the Arminians caused the formation of the so-called **Rhynsburgers** or **Collegiants** by the three brothers Van der Codde. The meeting of those who held the views of the Remonstrants without their banished preachers in this case led to a rejection in principle of the office of the ministry, and to the emphasising of the voice of the spirit after the manner of the Quakers and to Anabaptist ideas, even to the rejection of ecclesiastical confessions.

The banished leaders of the Arminians (Episcopius, Uytenbogaert) now found refuge in Brabant, especially in Antwerp and consequently under Spanish rule; and subsequently, some few even in France (1621), although the Calvinists there had accepted the resolutions of the Synod of Dort. Arminian colonists found a welcome with Duke Frederick III. of Holstein-Gottorp and founded Friedrichstadt. But, even in Holland, after Maurice's death (1625) the severity against them relaxed, when his brother Frederick Henry succeeded him. Their meetings were tolerated; in 1630, they were allowed to build a church in Amsterdam and in 1634 to establish a gymnasium (seminary) for the training of their religious teachers, at which a number of famous savants gave their services, at first **Episcopius** himself. He at once drew up a confession approved by the preachers of his party (*Confessio sive declaratio sententiae Pastorum, qui in foederato Belgico Remonstrantes vocantur*, Herder-Wiici, 1622; Opp. II 2, 69),[1] which however contained an express protest against being bound by symbols.[2] Together with him, Uytenbogaert exercised great influence in regard to the Church. A presbyterial synodal constitution was established: the synod held its meetings yearly at Amsterdam and Rotterdam alternately. In comparison with the small number of their community (in 1841, they had 20 churches and six chapels of ease) the number of their great theologians and

---

[1] Also in Benthem, p. 660-821.

[2] On the opposition of certain Remonstrant clergy to every symbol, see ROGGE III 38.

learned men is remarkable: Hugo Grotius, Gerhard Joh. Vossius (p. 409), Curcellaeus,[1] Limborch,[2] Clericus,[3] Wettstein.[4]

Their effect was that of a scientifically liberating leaven. Their opposition to the Calvinistic doctrine of orthodoxy and its exclusion of theological progress rested generally on a far lower estimate of the abstract fixation of the doctrine of belief and the tendency to withdraw from the speculative to the religiously practical and moral—from differences of doctrine to what was common to Christianity—certainly at the risk of a levelling moralism. The spirit of Erasmus continues working amongst them. Grotius has the merit of having liberated exegesis from the fetters of dogmatics. As they abandoned blunt Augustinianism and hence weakened the opposition to the Catholic doctrine, divergences soon became observable in the doctrine of the Trinity,[5] and although, in the 17th century, they defended themselves against the charge of Socinianism, they still entered into a more friendly relation with it, as dogmatically speculative differences lost their importance.

The Synod of Dort, which also settled the limits in regard to Lutheranism,[6] marked for the reformed churches the foundation of a **Scholasticism** that developed itself in these strict forms. A stately succession of dogmatists, Gomarus, Maresius, Maccovius, Gisb. Voetius (died 1676), developed a Calvinistic orthodoxy, which yet did not cause the absence of sound linguistic knowledge nor of the warm forces of life.

From the conflicts with Arminianism it is easy to understand that the harmless attempt of Professor **Moyse Amyraut** of Saumur (*Traité de la prédestination*, 1634)[7] aroused suspicions, especially in Holland and Switzerland, as he attempted to support the doctrine of Dort by assuming in addition a *gratia universalis hypothetica* (*sub conditione fidei*), according to which God desired the salvation of all men, if only all could believe, but in which the actual salvation of mankind remains founded simply on the real particularism of divine predestination."

---

[1] ZhTh 13, 1, 101 ff.
[2] ZhTh 13, 1, 106 ff.; RE VIII 683 ff.
[3] ZhTh 13, 1, 109 ff.
[4] ZhTh 9, 1, 73 ff.; 13, 1, 115 ff.; RE XVII 18 ff.
[5] Episcopius is already a decided "Subordinatian," but at the same time an opponent of the Socinians.
[6] Besides the Netherlands, Switzerland, the Palatinate, the French churches and the English Puritans accepted its resolutions.
[7] Also his *Doctrinae Calvini de absol. reprob. decreto defensio* (1641) and *Specimen animadversionum in exercitationes de gratia univ.* (1648).
[8] *Gratia* **obiectiva** *offert hominibus id quod est credendum;* **subiectiva** *mentem ita comparat, ut admittere atque amplecti queat id quod offertur. Illa exposita patet omnibus, haec paucis indulgetur, ex electionis proposito descendit.* In regard to

6. The Peacemakers and G. Calixtus.

Sources and *Literature*: A. DE DOMINIS, *De republ. ecclesiastica*. Lond., 1618 (written before his flight). *Causae profectionis suae*, 1616, in STRUVE, *Bibl. libr. rariorum*. I. Jenae, 1719; p. 116 ff. Against him, *Censura s. facult. theol. Parisiensis*, 1618. For his life: J. H. M. ERNESTI, *Ueber das Recht der Hierarchie auf Censur*. Leipz., 1829. REUSCH, *Der Index*. II 401 ff. F. JUNII, Opera. Gen., 1607; I 677-762. *Treuherz. Vermahn. d. Pfälz. Kirchen* in GOLDAST, *Polit. Reichshändel*. Frank., 1614; p. 894 ff. F. LÜCKE, *Ueber Alter, Verf., ursprüngl. Form . . . des Friedensspruches In necessariis*, etc. Gött., 1850; the same; StKr 1851, 905 ff. For Duraeus, see *Dict. of Nat. Biogr*. XVI 261 ff.; RE III 774 ff. E. L. TH. HENKE, *G. Cal. u. seine Zeit*; 2 vols. Halle, 1853, 1860. H. SCHMID, *Gesch. d. synkretist. Streitigk*. Erl., 1846. W. GASS, *G. Calixt und der Synkretismus*. Bresl., 1846. *Calixts Briefw.*, edited by HENKE. Halle, 1883; add two *Nachträge*, 1835 and 1840.

There was now no lack of voices, which, in view of the pressing necessity of the Protestants and the injury done to practical Christianity by controversial theology, were raised in the endeavour to restore a peaceful attitude of mind and drive back the spirit of strife. Certainly, all the pacific efforts which had been made to tone down or bridge over the opposition between Rome and the Reformation, as far as they had hitherto been possible, appeared perfectly hopeless in face of the increased tension in the relations of the opposing parties. Several religious conferences between Jesuits and Protestants only served the purpose of making converts. When the Archbishop of Spalatro, Marcus Antonius de Dominis, came forward with ideas such as Cassander (p. 358) had shortly before asserted, he at once quarrelled with the post-Tridentine, Jesuitical Catholicism that opposed all fitful efforts for peace: he fled to London, where he went over to the Anglican Church, and was enticed back to Rome by Gregory XV., where he ended his life in prison in 1624; his corpse was burnt by the hangman. If the Jesuits occasionally showed themselves friendly to the Lutherans, it was only to make use of them against the Calvinists

---

this particular election Amyraut is in complete agreement with his Calvinistic colleagues; he only deviates from them in that he affirms the universalism of the death of Christ for all, in case they believe, and in like manner God's universalist plan of salvation in sending Christ into the world; "a synthesis of simply ideal universalism to a firmly maintained real particularism." According to Ebrard's idea, Amyraut essentially taught a *reprobatio* of the godless on the ground of their petulant obstinacy that had been foreseen from eternity, whereby God's universalism suffers a restriction; but this is a misconception.

and to keep open the internal breach in' Protestantism. But, between the two evangelical parties, after the separation, neither union nor equitable recognition of a broad common basis, such as might have led to a co-operation to their common interest, was possible. The spirit prevailing in Lutheranism immediately drew monstrous, odious conclusions from the dogmatic ideas of the Calvinists, in order to throw a lurid light upon the soul-corrupting errors of the latter. On the whole, there existed on the "reformed" side more inclination and a certain political impulse to recognise brothers in the Lutherans, even if tainted with some papistical leaven and not yet sufficiently radically reformed.

On the Lutheran side, we need only mention as characteristic of the prevailing spirit (cp. p. 297, 8) Polyc. Leyser's Essay: *Ob, wie und warum man lieber mit den Papisten Gemeinschaft halten solle, denn mit den Calvinisten* [whether, why and how one should rather hold communication with the Papists than with the Calvinists] (1602, republished by Hoë in 1620 in justification of the policy of Electoral Saxony): pacific voices were not indeed wanting, but they seldom obtained a hearing. It was different on the "reformed" side. At the Mömpelgard Colloquy (1586) the Calvinists demand that, *quum in fundamentis Christianae religionis . . . . inter nos adversus Pontificios conveniret*, not only should all bitterness and invectives be abandoned, but also *ut datis citra diversarum sententiarum praeiudicium adversus communem hostem fraternitatis dextris concordiae conciliandae studeretur*—but without success.[1] Later also, the **French** Calvinists again endeavoured to meet the Lutherans—the latter were to be drawn into a union of all the reformed churches, a confession to be agreed upon, all controversy to be forbidden—at the Synod of Tonneins (1614); but the struggle on the reformed side against Arminianism and the orthodox tendency thereby promoted (Synod of Dort) were unfavourable to the continuance of such efforts. Nevertheless, the Synod of Charenton (1631) declared the Lutherans orthodox and wanted to grant them admission to Communion. Amyraut also preached energetically the possibility of an understanding with the Lutherans, who had always held the same fundamental religious opinions (RE I 359). Similar pacific tendencies showed themselves in Germany in **the Palatinate. Franc. Junius** (Du Jon of Bourges) wrote at Heidelberg (1592) an *Eirenicum de pace ecclesiae catholicae inter Christianos, quamvis diversos sententiis, religiose procuranda*. In 1606 followed the "Sincere Exhortation of the Churches of the Palatinate to all the evangelical churches in Germany: that they may yet heed the great danger, which threatens them as well as us from the Papacy, and one day, in a Christian and brotherly spirit, help us to remove or allay the internal, unnecessary dispute, which has already been sufficiently investigated." The divergences of the Lutherans were certainly declared to be "errors," but such "as could be regarded with leniency for the sake of Christian love." The efforts of **David Pareus** (professor at Heidelberg, died 1622) deserve special mention: in his *Irenicum sive de unione et synodo Evangelicorum concilianda* (1614) he recommended a *pius syncretismus* (= *conventio amicabilis*) of the Evangelicals

---

[1] FRIEDLÄNDER, *Beiträge zur Ref.-Gesch.* p. 161.

against the common enemy. Nothing was to be binding in the Church which did not necessarily follow from Holy Scripture: but in the fundamental articles the Evangelicals were at one. Hütter, N. Hunnius and others rudely rejected the proffered hand of brotherhood. **Rupertus Meldenius** wrote his *Paraenesis votiva pro pace ecclesiae ad theologos Aug. Conf.* (about 1628) at first only in view of the spirit of strife in his own camp, not with direct unionist tendencies. The name is certainly assumed: amongst others, G. Calixtus has been suggested. The author attributes the numerous losses of Protestantism sustained in the falling away of its members first and foremost to the fatal love of strife, which misled many simple souls; where is certainty to be found at all, if the *doctores* carried on an embittered strife about questions which were said to be of the greatest importance: thereby the door is opened to Antichrist. His advice is, not to imperil the practical interests of piety. Here we first (?) meet the expression: *In necessariis unitas, in non necessariis libertas, in utrisque charitas.*[1]

The attempt proved fruitless to bring about an understanding between Lutherans and "Reformed" at the **Leipzig Religious Conference** (1631, the theologians of Electoral Saxony [Hoë], of Brandenburg [Bergius] and Hesse), at which negotiations were at least carried on dispassionately and an effort was made to settle how far the different parties were agreed (Niemeyer 653 ff.). The Scotch Presbyterian **John Duraeus** (Dury) (formerly preacher to the English mercantile community at Elbing, after that in England, where his ideas met with a favourable reception amongst the Latitudinarians, then in numerous journeys and negotiations on the Continent) intervened with well-meant proposals for the promotion of the peace of the Church, which tended, not syncretistically, to the fusion of confessions, but to the bringing out and accentuation of the agreement in fundamental points and in increasing the importance of the practical aims of piety. Yet they met with distrust and opposition amongst the leaders of the Lutherans (*e.g.*, Nic. Hunnius, superintendent at Lübeck, *Ministerii Lubecensis theologica consideratio pacificatoriae transactionis a Duraeo tentatae*). Notwithstanding, he continued indefatigably his pacificatory efforts: he died at Cassel in 1680.

He had found someone to understand him at the University of **Helmstedt,** where a revision of the system drawn up by orthodox Lutheranism had been taken in hand by **George Calixtus,** a man of wide views and more liberal theological training. This caused him to break through the limits set by Lutheranism in the interest of the reunion of the separated members of the Church of Christ and to look outside for the foundations of an oecumenical Christianity. Melanchthonian traditions, personal acquaintance with prominent members of other confessions, and the influence of earnest historical studies which led him beyond the narrow bounds of the "confessional" horizon were combined in him with a pacific frame of mind, which sought a basis of agreement

---

[1] About the same time MEYFART wrote, *De concilianda pace inter ecclesias per Germaniam evangelicas.* Schleusingae, 1628.

amongst the hostile confessions, and raised him above his Lutheran contemporaries, but at the same time evoked their distrust.

> George Calixtus (Callisen), born in 1586 at the Schleswig village of Meddelbye (near Tondern), the son of a minister who had been Melanchthon's pupil, was indebted for his education to the University of Helmstedt, which, in spite of its rejection of the Formula of Concord, possessed in Dan. Hofmann a strictly Lutheran controversial theologian, but at the same time in Joh. Caselius a humanist of the old stamp with many-sided intellectual sympathies and in Corn. Martini an able Aristotelian. Attracted especially by the latter, Calixtus here received an impulse to historical enquiry, in particular the thorough study of the fathers of the Church. Scientific journeys of several years enlarged his view, brought him into closer contact with both Catholic and reformed theologians and taught him to know and appreciate impartially the theology and ecclesiastical systems of other confessions, although he always condemned the *religio pontificia vel Jesuitica* as an irreconcileable adversary. From 1614 until his death (1656) he exercised at the University of Helmstedt, as a professor of theology of increasing reputation for learning, an influence on numbers of students, who formed his school.

What distinguished him from his corporate colleagues was, in the first place, **the pacificatory disposition,** which led him to recognise and appreciate faithful, sincere Christians not only in his own confession, but also outside it. He indeed adheres to the Lutheran doctrine, with trifling Melanchthonian modifications of the orthodox dogmatism, but Catholics and "Reformed," as well as Lutherans, should know that they possess **the essential thing** in their **common substance of belief.** He desires that this common possession should be recognised as alone necessary to salvation; on the basis of this great *consensus* the mutual hatred of Christians may be stilled; it will then be the business of the theologians, to discuss the manifold *dissensus* of the confessions and where possible to bring about a compromise. He supported these ideas in the controversy with Rome, in order to deprive of their weight the Romish special doctrines that went beyond this common possession of Christians. But these ideas also have their root in the erroneous view that it was a question, between Protestantism and Catholicism, of a large concordant substructure, on which the two confessions only built other structures in different ways. Further, he championed the idea of **capability for further education** in contrast with the Lutheran theology of self-satisfaction, which thought it needed nothing more. The historical character of his studies further leads him to supplement the onesidedness and exclusiveness of the Protestant principle of the Scriptures by the tradition of the old Church and to turn the latter effectively against the Romish Church itself. The

Church as a whole has a promise that it does not err. The more it is divided, the more the boundary between truth and error is obliterated in it; hence a special authority for settling what is of fundamental importance in Christianity is to be attributed to the old undivided Church, while the credit of being a bond of union for all Christians is to be accorded to the old Church *consensus quinquesecularis*, which is represented to the laity in the Apostles' Creed. From this consensus of the old Church he combats Socinianism and, with equal energy, learning and acuteness, the Catholic defence of the Papacy.[1]

If this supplementing of the evidence of the Scriptures by the tradition of the old Church brought upon him the reproach of Crypto-Catholicism, he still less obtained indulgence for regarding the Calvinists as closely connected brothers, with whom he is at one on all fundamental points, in spite of the energy with which he champions the Lutheran special doctrine against them. At the Colloquy of Thorn (p. 362) he was obliged to submit to be rejected by heated orthodoxy as the co-religionist of Hülsemann and (in particular) of Abr. Calov and to be driven over to the side of the "reformed" as their adviser. His historical enquiries (monographs dealing with the history of dogma), his treatment of Ethics, to which he devoted a separate work, as **theologia** *moralis* (1634), as a branch of theology and not as belonging to practical philosophy, his sharp separation of what is within the ken of philosophy from what is only knowable by revelation, his dogmatically unprejudiced treatment of the Old Testament,[2] the stress laid by him upon good works as a condition of piety, lastly, his theoretically and practically altered attitude (especially towards Calvinism), make him an "innovator," who was highly honoured in his school (Conrad Hornejus, Joachim Hildebrand,[3] Ulric Frederick Calixtus. H. Conring),[4] and found others to carry on his work (but, after a short time, with failing intellectual force), who indeed introduced healthful corrections for his age, but yet did not hit the point, which reformatory importance might have given his work. He strives to reach the simple from the scientifically complicated, religious happiness from theology;[5] but still he only grasps at an older, and certainly Catholic formulation, the recognition of which would have obscured **the advantage, which the Reformation had brought.**

---

[1] His learned contestation of celibacy (*De coniugio clericorum*, Helmst. 1631) caused special excitement.

[2] A more liberal idea of the doctrine of inspiration is also observable: cp. THOLUCK, *Das kirchliche Leben*, I. 32.

[3] Niceron, *Nachrichten* XVIII 302 ff.

[4] Niceron XV 214 ff.

[5] W. GASS called it "the revolt of religious against dogmatic happiness" (*Calixt*, p. 11).

CHAPTER FOURTH.

The Influence of the Reformation upon Morality and Education.

Literature: The **charges** against it are collected in DÖLLINGER, *Die Reformation*, and J. JANSSEN, *Gesch. des deutschen Volkes.* Vols. IV and VI. KÖHLER, *Die Bestrebungen der evg. Fürsten des 16 Jhs. zur sittlichen Erneuerung des Volkslebens* in ZhTh 45, 266 ff. UHLHORN, *Christl. Liebesthätigkeit* III. W. KAWERAU, *Die Reformation und die Ehe.* Halle, 1892. SOLDAN, *Gesch. der Hexenprocesse,* ²revised by H. HEPPE; 2 vols. Stuttg., 1880. HARTFELDER, *Mel. s Aberglaube* in HTb 6, F. VIII. Count MIRBACH-HARFF in FdG 1881, 615 ff. HANSER, *Deutschland nach dem 30 jährigen Kriege.* Leipz., 1862; p. 285 ff. A. RHAMM, *Hexenglaube und Hexenprocesse, vorn. in den braunschw. Landen.* Wolfb., 1882. M. OSBORN, *Theatrum diabolorum* I. Berl., 1893. R. CALINICH, *Aus dem 16 Jh.* Hamb., 1876. H. BECK, *Die Erbauungslit. d. evg. K. Deutschlands* I. Erl., 1883. H. HOLSTEIN, *Die Ref. im Spiegelbild der dramat. Lit. des 16 Jhs.* Halle, 1886.

By parties most distinct from one another—Catholics as well as Anabaptists and Separatists—the charge has been brought against the Reformation,—that it destroyed morality and discipline, paralysed "charitable" life, and also arrested the development of science and art. Many, disappointed at the lack of good results, deserted Luther's cause and then accused the evangelical preaching of faith of being the cause of the mischief. Luther himself, towards the end of his life, frequently made increasingly bitter complaints of the evangelical people; and it is easy to obtain, from the evangelical sermon literature, a gloomy picture of brutality and demoralisation, of moral depravity and licentiousness. Certainly, profound abuses are unmistakable. Luther's preaching of faith was misinterpreted by a large number as the means of coming to a comfortable arrangement with God; when the prospect of the reward and meritoriousness of good works ceased, the impulse to procure guarantees of salvation by works dried up, and love, as the unselfish fruit of belief, in many cases disappeared. And no wonder; for new and (especially) higher moral motives do not at once come into operation in the same proportion as the old, which they have displaced. There comes a time when the old motives disappear, while the new manifest their power only in few cases. The leaven at first works gradually. Further, every ecclesiastical revolution which takes away from a people ecclesiastical custom and ecclesiastical uses exercises a disorganising effect upon the masses, as this custom had been to thousands the substitute for a conscious, religious life. Thus, in particular, the districts which during the 16th century went through manifold changes of religion here and there and by the ordinance of the ruling authorities, experienced a severe loss in ecclesiastical stability.¹ The tendency to dogmatic controversy, which the Reformation so soon adopted, absorbed much religious force, drove preaching and the instruction of youth upon unfruitful paths, and produced an orthodoxy, which was only too often a caricature of true Christianity.² At the same time, the new territorial churches were frequently obliged to content themselves with very imperfectly educated clergy; and Luther on many occasions consoled himself with the thought that defects in a man's mode of life were more tolerable than defects in "faith and doctrine" (EA 8 ²142). The country clergy, in particular, were at the outset recruited from the artisan class and for a long time there remained a body of clergy of the second class in theological training and the culture of morals.

Of the clergy, about 1750 in number, who were ordained at Wittenberg 1537-1560, the smaller half came from the University, a quarter from the schoolmaster's desk; but they also included cloth-makers, tailors, shoemakers and the like. But the number of students increased from year to year, and in 1608 Leonhard was able to repel, as a Jesuit lie, the assertion that "common and ignorant laymen," uneducated artisans were called to the office of preacher amongst them.³ The Church Ordinance (1580) of Electoral Saxony, however, complained of candidates for ordination, who allowed themselves to be "trained to a

---

¹ Cp., *e.g.*, for the Upper Palatinate, WITTMANN, *Gesch. d. Ref. in der Oberpf.*, p. 71, 101 ff. For Anhalt, see DUNCKER, *Anhalts Bekenntnissstand*, pp. 138, 165, 181, 224, and often.

² Perhaps the worst instance is afforded by the Lutheran poet and historian **Michael Lindener**, who wrote the most obscene jest books of the 16th century and also translated Savonarola's religious works, while he was himself an industrious theological and ascetic writer. He says of himself: "This same poet was pious; but when he had had a drink, he was a filthy beast." Cp. ALG VII 434 ff. The wild Margrave Albert of Culmbach also affords a psychological riddle; a first-class robber-knight and incendiary, he never mounts his horse without a pious utterance and the legend of the hymn-book even declares him to be the composer of the glorious "Was mein Gott will."

³ RIETSCHEL, *Luther und die Ordination*, p. 83 ff. FR. RUDOLPHI, *Gotha diplomatica*. Frkf. 1717. I 162. CALINICH, p. 8.

number of certain questions" (for the examination preceding ordination) by students, and also that the patrons in the country endeavoured to instal their clerks or tutors in the livings, in order that they might further be enabled to make use of them for all kinds of private services. (Richter, KOO II 430 f.)

Social and economical difficulties were caused by the marriage of the clergy; the income of their posts in many cases was insufficient, much church property was dissipated during the first years of storm and stress, many sources of income ceased of themselves, and there was little inclination in the congregations to take the needs of the case sufficiently into account. Hence arose considerable strife between pastors and congregations and complaints of the greed of the former. At the same time, especially in the Lutheran churches, the treatment of the congregations as a people in need of instruction which had to be directed by its pastor and the exaltation of the functions of the office of preacher impelled the clergy only too easily to an autocratic use or abuse of the office and to the development of an unseemly consciousness of the same.

But, notwithstanding all these abuses, we must not overlook what had actually been accomplished by preaching, catechismal instruction and the confessional, in the direction of the work of educating the people. Although rough in form and for the most part of a homely kind, an honourable class of citizens grew up as the result of this work: new ecclesiastical usages became naturalised; a people was brought up, which was well acquainted with the Word of God, in whose houses Christian usages took firm root. Communion, which, under the Pope, was required as a law of the Church once every year from every Christian at Easter, and hence with hardly any exception was not desired more frequently, —or if so, was refused by the priests (KL III 370 ff.), has now lost its compulsory force. Hence, even if there is no lack of people who now stay away for years (cp. *e.g.* EA 21, 148), on the whole an **elevated** desire for "the delightfully comforting food of poor afflicted souls" (EA $4,^2$ 495) is perceptible and a new **custom** in the matter of the Eucharist becomes naturalised, which as a rule leads to the table of the Lord four times a year. Luther's doctrine of the fulfilling of Christianity in the call has elevated the work of the citizens: nothing more was now heard of a higher Christianity of the perfect, who are separated from the "world." Married life has received its full, unassailable right and therewith a new consecration. The evangelical parsonage has taken the place of the impure celibacy of the priests as a new power of culture. The gloriousness of the "dear holy home church" and the praise of the Christian housewife are brought before the eyes of the German people in sermon, drama, and "marriage mirrors," and in spite of the "Grobianism" [coarseness] in which the popular wit of the tavern, celibatarian cynicism and the frivolous efforts of humanistic poets met together, evangelical ideals exercise an elevating moral effect upon domestic life as well as upon public decency. Public scandals of social life, such as the numerous "secret marriages" are done away with, brothels put down.[1] Professional mendicancy is combated, fresh regulations in regard to the poor are drawn up. When the administration of the Church was transferred to the authorities, it became a matter of conscience for the latter to provide for the moral and religious welfare of their subjects. The legislation of the country works as a rule very energetically in the cause of the protection of ecclesiastical life (*e.g.* regulations for Sunday) and the moral education of the people. Then, the Thirty Years' War exercised a terribly devastating effect. After the overpowerful religious movement became a source of danger to the humanistico-scientific in the first years of the Reformation, the latter itself pressed Humanism into its service as a valuable auxiliary.

The old Universities were reorganised on the Wittenberg model, and[2] new ones were added: Marburg 1527, Königsberg 1544, Jena 1548, Helmstedt 1575, Altdorf 1578, Herborn 1584, Giessen 1607, Rinteln 1619, Strasburg 1621. In 1550, Wittenberg again had about 2,000 students.

Numerous high schools arose, a new school-system began to flourish, which, under the intellectual aegis of Melanchthon, endeavoured to combine the reformatory and humanistic ideal, *pietas* and *eloquentia* (the latter considered as the grammatical certainty to be obtained from the Classics and as a knowledge of the subject, a capacity for correct judgment as well as clearness of expression). By the side of territorial churchship was developed (after 1543 in the Duchy of Saxony) a **territorial school-system** in the established and royal schools provided with secularised monastic property, for the purpose of supplying the country with capable forces in the matter of ecclesiastical and secular government. Wurtemberg arranged (1559) its country school-system on a uniform plan; here also the monasteries were changed into academies. But the German Bible, Catechism, and church hymns exercise an improving influence upon **the school training of the people**, which was at first provided for in the towns generally,

---

[1] Vergerius strikingly compares (1562) the favourable condition of affairs in Protestant Germany with the secret immorality in Rome itself that was tolerated by the Popes and taxed as a branch of industry. HUBERT, *Verg.s public. Thätigk.* p. 200. We may further bear in mind the description given by Aeneas Sylvius of the state of morals in Catholic Vienna in the 15th century (ZhTh 45, 267), in order to obtain the correct standard of comparison. M. Ambach and J. Rath (in 1543 and the following years) carried on a highly instructive controversy regarding the admissibility of dancing as an amusement: see Bl. f. württ. KG 1893, p. 43 ff.

[2] HARTFELDER, *Melanchthon als Praeceptor Germaniae.* Berl. 1889, p. 506 ff.

and more slowly in the country.[1] In the villages it was thought sufficient that the clerk should teach the Catechism and practise German singing; then reading, writing and arithmetic gradually followed. Luther had set up a goal for Christendom, which cannot be reached without a national school; but the way to this was not travelled all at once, and the time for a compulsory national school was not yet come. Wittenberg, however, vigorously takes the lead; every village is to have its "German" school; and everywhere the work is on the way. At the beginning of the 17th century the paedagogue **Ratke** (Raticius) proclaimed the principle of general school education—*Nullus puer aut puella praetereatur*, and the Weimar school ordinance of 1619 adopted it. What a glaring contrast, on the other hand, is shown by the procedure of the Jesuit authorities in Bavaria against the spread of the school system in town and country after 1578, especially their aversion to the national school in accordance with the principle of "reducing the number of schoolmasters as far as was practicable and possible."[2]

Again, although **superstition** was successfully combated in the more limited sphere of worship and the religious relation of man to God, yet it was far from being generally done away with in the life of the people. The clearly defined attitude taken up by Luther in reference to contemporary astrological superstition was not shared by Melanchthon, who rather strove to give a scientific confirmation to casting horoscopes and the like (CR XI 261 ff. and often). General respect was paid to portents and prodigies, comets and other celestial signs as indications of the destinies of men; the significance attached to dreams plays an important part in the life of a Melanchthon.[3]

The Reformation took over the most fantastic, coarsely materialistic belief in the devils and evil spirits without a break from the Middle Ages. Not only is all Luther's battle of belief in his eyes a personal struggle with the cunning and assaults of the corporeal Satan, in which the field is taken against the vices and immoralities of the age as against so many separate devils (the devils of drunkenness, cursing, marriage and the like), but the return to the Scriptures also assisted the Evangelicals to bring the demonology of the Bible into a new, forcible and close connection with the dark and uncanny popular belief in devil's leagues of witches and enchanters, in changelings, ghosts, and demoniacal influence on men and animals and the like; cp. **Jod. Hocker's** Essay, *Der*

---

[1] It is incorrect to make Luther (on the ground of EA ²17, 420) the herald of compulsory education. According to the context, he only strongly impresses upon the authorities the right and duty of keeping at school the talented sons of poor parents (in the interest of the rising generation of preachers) and of assisting them by scholarships. **Francis Lambert** of Avignon prescribes a general school for the people, at least for boys, in the *Reformatio ecclesiae Hassiae* (1526); but this ordinance was not carried out (p. 79).

[2] Cp. KLUCKHOHN in HZ 31, 343 ff.

[3] For the superstition of the courtiers of John Frederick, see NA sächs. Gesch. X 146 ff.

Teuffel selbs (Ursel, 1568), which was sent out as an introduction to the demonological compilation *Theatrum diabolorum* (Frankf. 1569). Luther, the miner's son, had not grown up for nothing under the influences of lower popular mythology. Thus, the late medieval **trials of witches** experienced a Protestant after-growth, in which a confused theological system is perniciously combined [1] with a system of justice that is led into false paths (treating it as *crimen exceptum*) by the "witches' hammer" (Malleus maleficarum),[2] continually fresh confessions extorted by torture are obliged to confirm and establish the correctness of the system followed in a horrible vicious circle, and a bulwark of misbelief is erected, in which the executioners always think they are doing God's will. The worst persecutors of the witches were the small territorial lords, the period of the most luxuriant growth of this perversion of justice that of the Thirty Years' War. In the little Catholic country of Drachenfels, 92 persons were put to death for witchcraft and sorcery out of about 800 inhabitants in about three years; in the town of Würzburg, from 1627-1629, 219 persons. Both confessions here walked in the same paths; the most convinced supporters of the criminal system pursued were to be found on the Catholic (**Jean Bodin**, 1579, the **Jesuit** Delrio 1599) as well as on the evangelical side (the "reformed" **Erastus,** 1578, the Lutheran **Bened. Carpzov,** 1635). The evangelically-minded physician at the Court of Cleves, **Joh. Weier** (Wier), 1563, in vain lifted up his voice against it (*De praestigiis daemonum*),[3] and **Ant. Praetorius** of Frankfort in 1629 boldly testified against the "unchristian, illusive and unsafe" practice of the employment of torture; Catholic writings like those of the Jesuits **Tanner** (died 1632) and **Fr. v. Spee** (*Cautio criminalis*, 1631, but only printed anonymously in Protestant Rinteln)[4] equally failed to make any impression; the protest (1592) of the enlightened Catholic priest **Corn. Loos** against the "new alchemy" of the persecution of the witches cost him incarceration and a disgraceful recantation. At the same time, these opponents for the most part avowed a belief in witches, and only contested the manner of the judicial process against them, which proceeded from the assumption that all the accused were really guilty and made even the innocent guilty by means of the rack.

A valuable means of awakening evangelical piety and morality was afforded by the almost superabundant **devotional** literature, to which, in addition to the theologians (from learned academicians like John Gerhard to simple ministers), numerous laymen of all classes (crowned heads as well as pious widows) contributed. If in these there is much that is bombastic and typologically overdone and unpalatable to modern taste, we must not forget the importance of a book of preaching, devotion and prayer for the building up of a pious national life. The new spirit of evangelical piety is also widely circulated in the dramatic literature of the time.

The **school-comedy,** which was everywhere fostered, took possession of the fresh material; above all, biblical history, which it knew how to germanise in its own manner with much *naïveté*, and at the same time drastically in

---

[1] Cp. *e.g.* the Bavarian enactment of 1611 in ZdCG II 92 ff.

[2] Cp. Vol. II. p. 545; a German extract is given by J. M. SCHWAGER, *Vers. einer Gesch. der Hexenprocesse.* I. p. 57-228. Berl. 1784.

[3] A vigorous polemic against Wier's "Defence of Sorcerers and Witches" in WIDMANN-PFITZER's *Faustbuch,* 1674, StBlV 146, 66.

[4] The German translation (Frankf. 1649) was the work of a Protestant.

all seriousness and frequently with coarse humour; further, the great events of the Reformation itself afforded profitable material, which was brought before the eyes of the people in manifold variations in praise of Luther and as a warning against the Roman Antichrist; to these must be added the most important and most suitable themes of popular life, the praise of pious marriage, the warning picture of a dissolute life and the like. Homely and far removed from higher dramatic conception, the Muse of the drama yet exercised great influence by its impressive sermons and as an instructor of the people. The popular style and radically sound, cheerful piety of a Hans Sachs has certainly never been attained by later generations; theological views were for the most part expressed with pronounced diffuseness and verbosity.

SEVENTH DIVISION.

The Smaller non-Catholic Groups.

CHAPTER FIRST.
The Waldensians.

Sources and *Literature:* CH. SCHMIDT in ZhTh 22, 250 ff. J. HERZOG, *Die röm. Waldenser.* Halle, 1853, p. 333 ff. E. ARNAUD, *Hist. des Protestants de Provence.* Paris, 1884, I 3 ff. Entirely under the influence of the Waldensian legend: PERRIN, *Hist. des Vaudois.* Genève, 1618. J. LEGER, *Gesch. d. Waldenser*, translated by VON SCHWEINITZ. Bresl., 1750. A. MONASTIER, *Hist. de l'égl. Vaudoise;* 2 vols. Genève, 1847. F. BENDER, *Gesch. d. Waldenser.* Ulm, 1850. A. MUSTON, *L'Israel des Alpes.* Paris, 1851.

The Waldensians, already strongly influenced in the second half of the 15th century by contact with the Hussites, after that time had within them as a cause of disagreement the fact that, while some of them pressed forward under Hussite influence, the other, on the contrary, upheld their medieval character as a Catholic sect, not so much separated from the Church in the matter of dogma as in point of constitution. In the first party, the German, especially the neighbouring Swiss Reformation asserted the influence of its spirit. A Piedmontese Waldensian clergyman named Martin travelled to Germany, and took home with him reformatory writings. But a decided step in advance was taken by the French Waldensians of Provence and Dauphiné. These sent (1530) George Morel and Peter Masson to Oecolampadius, who in turn sent them on to Bucer; they described the condition of their congregations and their confession of faith and asked for advice and instruction. Oecolampadius's advice was very decided; he urged them to take up a clear position, while Bucer's tendency to compromises and concessions made itself characteristically prominent. On his journey home Masson suffered martyrdom at Dijon, Morel fortunately reached home with the documents; as a decided supporter of the Reformation, he declared to the Brethren, *in quot et quantis erroribus versarentur, in quos veteres ipsorum ministri eos coniecissent*, but met with considerable opposition in his desire for reform. At the instance of the French Waldensians a six days' **Waldensian Synod** took place in September, 1532, at Chanforans in the valley of Angrogne, in which the tempestuous Farel and two other Swiss pastors took part, at which it was resolved, to abandon entirely all participation in the Catholic service; fresh provisions were made in regard to doctrine (also predestination), worship and life (against auricular confession, prohibition of marriage and the celibacy of the clergy, against private revenge; swearing by God allowed), which indicated a **complete evangelical transformation of the old Waldensianism.**

Naturally a strong opposition party was not wanting; two clergymen left the meeting with a protest, and then betook themselves as spokesmen of this party to the Bohemian Brethren, on the plea that they were commissioned to obtain their opinion as to the innovations. They also obtained a document, in which the Brethren testified their disapproval of the new resolutions. This caused a second synod to be held in August 1533 in the valley of St. Martin, which confirmed the resolutions of the previous year: the two clergymen thereupon retired into private life. Certainly, the change in accordance with the model of the Swiss Churches was only slowly carried out. It was not rapid amongst the French Waldensians of Provence, who now openly severed themselves from the Romish Church, and thereby at first experienced an increase, but now found themselves abandoned to merciless persecution. They first transmitted to Cardinal Sadolet, and then also (1543) to Francis I. confessions of faith of an essentially reformed character.[1] In 1535 persecution broke out against them in Provence: in vain (with Farel and Viret) they called upon the German Protestants to intercede with King Francis. The persecution was renewed with special cruelty in 1545, when about 4,000 of them were murdered or dragged upon board the galleys, 22 villages were reduced to ashes: the intervention of Strasburg with Francis I. was sharply rejected; it was told not to interfere with what concerned his subjects. However, about 4,000 of them managed to make their escape to the Alps, whence some of them subsequently returned home. The Reformation was carried out more slowly amongst the Waldensians of Dauphiné, who were not subjected to persecution till 1560, and amongst those of Piedmont, who first openly practised evangelical preaching after 1555, and, although at first threatened by the French government at the time were not seriously persecuted: however, when in 1559 the valleys were given back to Savoy, their time of trial arrived. They offered armed resistance and, after

---

[1] The former may be found in Latin in PANTALEON, *Martyrum hist.* Basil. 1563 p. 130 ff., the latter in ZhTh 22, 256 ff. The Eucharist is *une saincte memoire et action de graces des benefices que nous avons recue par sa mort et passion, qu'on doibt faire ensemble en foy et charité*. Bullinger (1545) gives them the character: *Illi recte sapiunt et sanctissime vivunt: nostram religionem nostraque dogmata receperunt in omnibus* (CR 40, 79).

severe losses, obtained free exercise of their religion within definite limits at the peace of Cavour. In the face of fresh oppressions, they combined in the *Union des vallées* (1571) which denotes the definitive victory of the Reformation in their body. But from that time also commences amongst them the ugly attempt to remodel their own history in a twofold direction: on the one hand, they carried back their origin to the Apostles, on the other, they smuggled their evangelical method of teaching into their medieval documents and post-dated by centuries the youthful productions of their literature, until, in our days, German investigations (Dieckhoff and Herzog) discovered these falsifications of history and then gradually, even amongst the Waldensians themselves, although not without violent reluctance on their part, discredited these legends.

The Waldensian colony amongst the Calabrians also favoured the Reformation, but was subsequently entirely annihilated by the power of Rome. When, in 1630, the plague had raged in the valleys of Piedmont, the Waldensians found themselves compelled to accept French pastors: with the alteration of the language of divine service was combined a closer adherence in worship to the model of the Church of Geneva.

CHAPTER SECOND.

Utraquists and Bohemian Brethren.

Literature: J. CAMERARIUS, *Historica narratio de fratr. orthod. ecclesiis in Bohemia,* etc. Heidelb. (1605). BOROVY, *Die Utraquisten in Böhmen* in AÖG XXXVI. PALACKY, *Gesch. v. Böhmen,* V. 2. CZERWENKA, *Gesch. d. evg. K. in Böhmen.* II. Bielef. u. Leipz. 1870. GINDELY, *Gesch. der böhmischen Brüder.* Vol. I. Prag. 1857; the same in FRA II, XIX. FRIND, *KGeschichte Böhmens.* IV. For the hymn-books of the Bohemian Brethren, see R. WOLKAN, *Das deutsche KLied der böhm. Brüder.* Prag. 1891; and the *Epistola Fratrum ad Frideric. III.* in Camerarius p. 286 ff. S. SVOBODA, *Der Prager Landtag von 1575* in ZkTh 1893, p. 193 ff. 385 ff.

Luther, in the summer of 1522, had sought to enter into connection with the Bohemian **Utraquists**, by writing to the diet assembled at Prague: he declared that he had proved in his writings their good claim in opposition to Rome: now, when the Gospel was making itself felt with fresh vehemence, it was their duty to stand firm and not to allow themselves to be deprived either of the utraquistic Communion or the blessed memory of their martyrs Huss and Jerome (de Wette II, 225 ff.; Enders III, 432). In fact, the influence of the Reformation now made itself felt here, while an evangelically-minded party arose. A member of the same, the clergyman **Gallus Cahera**, in the summer of 1523 visited Wittenberg and so gained Luther's confidence that he induced him to encourage the Utraquists, in an essay *De instituendis ministris* (end of 1523, WA XII 160 ff.), which was dedicated to the town council of Prague, to break loose from the hitherto existing dependence of their clergy upon the consecration of the priests by Catholic bishops (which, chiefly sought after in Italy, could only be obtained under an ambiguous denial of their utraquist standpoint),[1] to create for themselves an independent office by election on the part of the congregations, and, eventually, to place men like Cahera at the head of their ecclesiastical system and to cause their clergy to be ordained by such. In fact, Cahera, at the re-election to the consistory of the Utraquists, was chosen as one of the administrators, and subsequently pastor at the Teyn church at Prague; their assembly at Prague (February, 1524) passed resolutions decidedly friendly to reform. But Cahera's attempt to do away with the celibacy of the priests met with resistance, and the ambitious and sordid man[2] rapidly completed his conversion to the Catholic party and endeavoured by means of negotiations with Rome to assure his dominant position. Under his direction the

---

[1] Cp. the ridicule of these *presbyteri Italici* of the Utraquists by the Bohemian Brethren in their *Apologia verae doctrinae.* Viteb. 1538, E 2 b.

[2] He finally became a beerhouse-keeper.

evangelical party was persecuted ; the resolutions of the assembly of 1525 again rejected the reformatory influence in their doctrinal regulations. After the Utraquists had vainly negotiated with Bishop Nausea at Vienna with a view to the ordination of their clergy unfettered by limitations, they endeavoured to obtain ordination at Prague, since in 1561 the archiepiscopal see was again occupied, and, at the request of the archbishop, sacrificed the Communion of children which was still usual amongst them. But when the archbishop also required of them the right of examining the candidate for ordination and the *professio fidei Tridentinae* (p. 247), this connection was again dissolved. In ever-increasing numbers clergymen, unconsecrated or ordained by evangelical consistories appeared in their ranks, just as they were unable to offer a successful resistance to the intrusion of the marriage of the priests. The Reformation, contrary to the intention of the leading circles, made its way irresistibly into their congregations, and destroyed the untenable position of the *Compactati*, but also broke away more and more from their congregations. In 1577, only 15 Bohemian noblemen still avowed their adherence to them ; in 1589, only 7 royal towns saw their ecclesiastical officials in the Utraquist consistory. Lutheranism, on the other hand, met with a friendly reception, above all in the **German** parts of the country, in the royal towns, further, in the entire mining district, where German miners formed the chief part of the population ; in like manner, the German nobles furthered the cause of the Lutheran reformations (Count Schlick and others). Lutheranism pressed forward **exercising a German influence** and extended itself from the German frontiers, continually advancing and driving Utraquism forward in all kinds of transitions to the Lutheran Reformation. After the battle of the White Mountain the counter-Reformation abruptly put an end to Utraquism.

But also the **Moravio-Bohemian union of brethren** was affected by Luther's influence and thereby driven to fresh developments. The Brethren, who at the end of the 15th century had entered into connection with the Waldensians, had then turned their eyes full of hope towards Erasmus, to whom they had sent a deputation in 1511 and whose powerful intercession they had invoked on behalf of their persecuted congregations. He had prudently declined to intervene (Camerarius p. 125 f.). They now greeted Luther's appearance with far livelier hopes. **Luke of Prague,** who first put in order the hitherto confused dogmas of the brethren, was at their head from 1518 to 1528.

Paul Speratus, who was at that time in Iglau in Moravia, first brought the Brethren into contact with Luther (1522), by acquainting him with their doctrine of the Eucharist[1] (the spiritual presence of Christ, whose body remains in Heaven; the rejection of the adoration of the Sacrament). Luther replied and at the same time asked that their doctrine of the Eucharist might be put before him more exactly in a special treatise. He now received writings of theirs of all kinds (including their Catechism, and the Senior, Luke, sent him

---

[1] ENDERS III 363 f., 397 ff.

by the brothers **Horn** (Roh) and the hymn-writer **Mich. Weisse** a tractate *Von der siegreichen Wahrheit*. But as Luther was not completely satisfied by these, he answered them with *Vom Anbeten des Sacraments* (1523), in which he warned them against a merely symbolical conception of the Eucharist, but treated adoration itself as a subsidiary matter. At the same time he expressed himself partly approvingly, and partly in a spirit of criticism and instruction, concerning different points of their teaching and practice (against their coordination of works to faith, their adherence to the seven sacraments and the prohibition of the marriage of the clergy, their contempt for a learned education of the latter, and so forth). Luke replied (1524), strictly adhering to their peculiarities and vigorously condemning the morally offensive mode of life, which was produced in Germany by Luther's preaching of faith and liberty; the life of the Wittenberg students had given the Brethren a bad idea of the fruits of evangelical freedom. The difference between the Brethrens' seclusive view of life and that of the Reformer was here characteristically and sharply prominent. The combination of the two parties was broken off and remained in abeyance until the death of Luke in 1528, who as decidedly rejected the influence of the Zwinglian doctrine.

Luke was succeeded in the seniority by **Martin Skoda,** his co-religionist, who however lacked the power to offer an equally vigorous resistance to innovations. Young Brethren betook themselves to Wittenberg for study, where they learnt to know and appreciate Luther's doctrine and evangelical freedom; when Luther's adherent, **John Horn,** succeeded in 1532, he and **Bened. Baworinsky** entered into relations with the former. The result was at first a period of **approximation to Lutheranism.** Celibacy was abolished, although only a few made use of this liberty, the writings of Luke were disavowed by the Brethren; their *Apologia verae doctrinae*, dedicated to the Margrave George of Brandenburg, appeared at Wittenberg in 1532 with a preface by Luther. They protested against Zwingli's doctrine of the Eucharist, but did not go over completely to Luther, limiting themselves to the undecided formula of a "sacramental" presence. Their peculiar custom of repeating the ceremony of baptism in the case of the members of their community on coming of age was abandoned by them (*magnorum virorum in Ecclesia Christi sententiam secuti*) at the Synod of Jungbunzlau[1] 1534, an act of self-defence, to prevent themselves being regarded as Anabaptists; laying on of hands after previous instruction was substituted for it. The connection with Luther was vigorously supported by **John Augusta** who had great influence in the union; their confession, drawn up for King Ferdinand in 1535, in which they attempted to prove themselves co-religionists

---

[1] Cp. *Apologia verae doctrinae* 1538, Bl. B. 2.

of the adherents of the Confession of Augsburg, appeared in 1538 with Luther's preface, who, in spite of many differences in doctrine, as well as in mode of life, regarded with approval the earnest and capable people, and, in dealing with them, abandoned something of his dogmatic demands. In 1540, negotiations were also commenced in Strasburg with Bucer, whose doctrine of the Eucharist approximated nearer to theirs than Luther's; also, the simplicity and plainness of the Strasburg service pleased them. Through Bucer they made the acquaintance of Calvin. The time of Lutheranising for the Brethren ceased with Luther's death; the writings of their Luke were restored to honour, and they felt, so far as they were obliged to seek adherence to the churches of the Reformation, their closer relationship to Calvinism.

The political change brought about by the Schmalkaldic War, in which the nobles amongst the Brethren sided with the Evangelicals against Ferdinand, brought bitter persecution upon them after times of peace. On the 18th of September, 1547, Ferdinand did away with the toleration that had hitherto been shown towards the Brethren; their petitions to him and the Emperor were refused a hearing. Augusta, by fearful tortures and, subsequently, sixteen years' imprisonment, became the martyr of the Brethren. Fifteen hundred of them decided to emigrate to Poland: when they were at first refused admission here, the majority went on to Prussia, where Albert allowed them to settle in return for their renouncing some of their special customs which were regarded with suspicion by the Lutherans. In places where the Lutheran Church and ministry was in existence, they were simply to join the Lutheran congregation: where they founded new villages, their own ministers were to be confirmed for them by the Lutheran bishops. A theological examination of their preachers took place before a commission at Königsberg, which established their agreement with the Confession of Augsburg; subsequently (March 19th. 1549) an ecclesiastical law was issued for their incorporation. Bishop Speratus of Pomesania, in whose district they were settled, also showed himself their true friend. Here, they were to amalgamate with the Church of the country, but in 1574 they returned home. Those who remained behind in Bohemia conceived fresh hopes, when the evangelical tendencies of the successor to the throne, Maximilian II., became known to them. In 1555, they sent **Blahoslaw**, the priest of the Brethren, to Vienna, who conveyed their petition (especially for the release of Augusta) to Maximilian by means of his court-preacher Pfauser. Maximilian made friendly promises, but was for a time powerless. The nobles amongst the Brethren protected their co-religionists on their estates, but the political situation compelled them to amalgamate with those of Lutheran views amongst the Bohemian States and at the same time dragged the Brethren still deeper into the political current.

Still, only about a tenth of the population confessed the Catholic faith.[1] But, in 1551, Ferdinand had already sent nine young

---

[1] ZkTH 1893, 391.

Bohemians to Ignatius, the general of the Jesuits, to be educated. In 1555, **P. Canisius** reconnoitred at Prague, where a college, and soon also a Jesuit school with a theological seminary for young nobles and a *seminarium pauperum* were founded. The Jesuits gained a footing in Moravia in 1558. In view of the Catholic reaction, the Brethren united (1575) with the Lutherans in the **Confessio Bohemica,** in which the express rejection of Calvinism was omitted. (But at the same time, with the victory of Lutheranism over Melanchthonianism in Germany the connection of the Brethren with German Lutheranism was destroyed; they now still only saw in the "reformed" their nearest co-religionists).

Rudolph the Second's avowedly Jesuitical sympathies promoted the further union of the parties which communicated *sub utraque*. In 1609, the united Evangelicals again laid their confession of 1575 before the King, obtained its recognition in the **Charter of religious liberty,** and then united under a common consistory at Prague, at which the Brethren, however, secured certain privileges for themselves. The Thirty Years' War brought upon them the heaviest persecutions after the brief days of victory, in which the bishop of the Brethren had consecrated Frederick V. of the Palatinate, the "Winter King," King of Bohemia. Cruelly proscribed in Bohemia and Moravia, they resolved to emigrate. The old Moravio-Bohemian *unitas fratrum* was practically annihilated in 1627, after the Bohemian section of the evangelical national Church of Bohemia had almost become extinct in 1609. Scattered remnants of them found admittance in Great Poland, especially Lissa, under the protection of the Counts Leszinsky. Here they formed a **Moravio-Bohemian Church of exile** distinct from the **Polish Unity** (pp. 213, 361). Meanwhile, they had found a highly intellectual leader, strong in the faith, in the Moravian **Amos Comenius** (born 1592), who had completed his studies at Herborn and Heidelberg, and, driven from Fulneck to Moravia, organised a congregation and school system at Lissa. After 1632, he managed this union as senior, after 1648 also as bishop. By his educational writings (*Janua linguarum reserata; Orbis pictus; Didactica magna*, in which he worked up his contemporaries' manifold proposals of reform to the comprehensive plan of an education of the people, equally moral and religious, completely adapted to human nature and depreciating the sensual view) he gained a European reputation and rendered the highest services to Bohemian literature.

Finally (1656) driven out from Lissa with his congregation, even in foreign parts (he died at Amsterdam in 1670) he never lost an opportunity of interceding for his oppressed brethren, and at the same time firmly maintained the pacificatory idea of the *unitas fratrum* as a valuable heritage at the time of narrow-minded quarrelsomeness. From 1656 the Moravio-Bohemian Unity only existed in pitiful remnants; yet Comenius still kept a look out for an evangelical reawakening of his nation, and hence continued the episcopal consecration resting his hopes on his son-in-law **Peter Jablonski** (died in 1670, court preacher at Memel); his son, **Dan. Ernest Jablonski**, in like manner received Bohemian episcopal consecration at Lissa in 1699, and, as preacher at the Prussian Court and chosen senior, loyally interceded for the Bohemian "Diaspora."[1] This branch of the Church of the Brethren gradually died out. Yet, in Bohemia as in Moravia itself, scanty remnants of the Brethren survived, in spite of all persecutions; some of these Bohemians, under the influence of German pietism, emigrated in the 18th century, and were well received at Berlin as well as in Upper Lusatia. In 1722 members of the Moravian branch arrived at Berthelsdorf, where the "renewed unity" showed its adherence in many ways to the past.

The community, which had long possessed the Bible in the language of the people, set up an especially honourable memorial in the splendid work, the **Kraliz Bible** (1579-1593) in six volumes with notes, which, after Blahoslaw had translated the New Testament, was completed by eight learned brethren at the expense of Baron John of Zerotin; it was equally distinguished for its fidelity to the original text and its pure and popular language.

In 1501 the Bohemian Brethren had collected their Czech hymns in a hymn-book unfortunately lost. In 1531, Mich. Weisse brought out a first collection in the **German** language, partly free imitations of Latin originals, partly containing original hymns. In 1544, the hymn-book appeared revised by John Horn, who, in particular, altered the communion hymns in conformity with the approximation to Luther and added fresh ones.[2] Then, in 1561, followed the great Czech "Cancional," and (in 1566) a new German hymn-book containing 456 hymns, which, together with numerous pieces of poetry, borrowed from Swiss and Lutheran books, at the same time added many original Czech hymns to the German church hymn-book. Much of their treasury of hymns passed over into the hymn-books (especially the Low German) of the Lutheran Church.

---

[1] [Its object was the evangelisation of the State Churches of Europe.]

[2] Cp. SCHELHORN, *Samml. für die Geschichte* I (Nördlingen, 1779), p. 349 ff.

CHAPTER THIRD.

The Anabaptists.

The Baptist Congregations after 1535.

Literature (see above, p. 88): H. OTTIUS, *Annales Anabaptistici*. Basel, 1672. HOCHHUTH, *Landgr. Philipp u. die Wiedertäufer* in ZhTh 28, 538 ff.; 29, 167 ff. For Huter, see J. LOSERTH in AÖG 78, 427 ff.; the same, in Z. allg. G., 1884; the same, *Deutschböhm. Wiedertäufer* in Mitth. d. V. f. G. d. Deutschen in Böhmen, XXX 404 ff.; the same, *Der Anabaptismus in Tirol*. Wien, 1892.

Anabaptism generally was heavily weighted by the prejudice, which, since the events that had taken place at Münster, caused Catholic and evangelical circles to see in every one of its adherents a subverter dangerous to the common welfare. Certainly, here and there traces of the "libertine"-antinomian spirit showed themselves and discredited the whole body, but "the genuine Anabaptists were ashamed of the Münster fanaticism."[1] But only a few, like Philip of Hesse, discovered **distinctions** between them and recognised that by the side of those "who proceed to action and attack with the sword" stood the great multitude of "simple pious people," who could only be reproached with "error in belief."[2] The

---

[1] SEPP, *Kerkhist. Studiën*, p. 78.

[2] OTTIUS, *Annales anabapt.*, 131. Even Bucer does not advise that capital punishment, which certainly the law of God demands from all who "fall away from true religion and persuade others to do the like," should be enforced against *those* Baptists, "in whom no sedition, heinous sin or godless mind can be found, but merely a simple conviction that they hold their error to be entirely God's truth and command." An attempt should be made to instruct such persons with true earnestness; if they continue obstinate, they are neither to be driven from the country, as that would be only sending them to others, nor punished by imprisonment, as this would not improve them, but they are to be made to carry on their work in their houses or in places, **where they will be unable to mislead anyone.** It is the duty of the authorities to do their utmost to prevent the latter. ZKG VII 472 ff. (1546). Cp. the resolutions of the Oberlanders in Memmingen 1532, KEIM, *Schwäb. Ref.-G.*, p. 259. A. Blarer successfully attempted the method of instruction in Esslingen in 1532. KEIM, Reform.-Blätter d. Reichsstadt Esslingen, p. 74 f.

majority of the Baptists had indeed nothing to do with the spirit shown at Münster. Certainly, in 1536, the most diverse evangelical authorities, whom Philip consulted as to their opinion, urged him to intervene more vigorously, assuring him that he might justly proceed against them with the sword, to protect the pure doctrine; he did not, however, abandon the path of friendly instruction and the attempt to convince them by the Scriptures. Nor was he entirely unsuccessful; thus, he won over several of their leaders (Peter Tasch and others), who in their turn drew others after them. But his mode of procedure was exceptional. In 1536, three Baptists were beheaded in Jena, after Melanchthon had argued with them in vain; for "it is necessary to enforce the most rigorous penalties against the obstinate, and although some few may not be malicious folk, the pernicious sect must be suppressed" (CR III 16). Even Luther became appreciably more severe in his judgment; he declared that it was a disgraceful thing and worthy of death that they, who had received no call, should lay hands upon the office of ministers who had been duly called (de Wette VI 152, ZhTh 28, 560 ff.). Another difficulty from which Anabaptism suffered was its **want of uniform organisation.** The congregations in Moravia and the Tyrol had no connection with the Dutch and Friesians on the North Sea; to these must be added the Swiss, Palatine, and numerous petty congregations scattered here and there. Yet there was no lack of efforts to bring them in touch with one another and secure mutual support. But even the congregations in the same country suffered from **divisions,** in which, owing to the undogmatic character of their Christianity, there were fewer differences in the matter of doctrine than peculiarities in the exercise of excommunication, divorce laws, and greater or less separation from the world (in the matter of clothing and the like). In regard to dogma, the only important point is that the Moravian Anabaptism, on the irruption of anti-Trinitarian elements from Italy in 1562, **rejected** this spirit as foreign, and in the 12 Articles of the Apostolicum firmly adhered to the union with the rest of Christendom[1]; that further, the (semi-docetic) view, that the flesh of Christ did not proceed from Mary, but was engendered by the spirit of God, although widely circulated by **Menno Simonis** (p. 129), had not the effect of causing division amongst the different

---

[1] FRA 43, 646 f.

circles of the Brethren. An assembly of delegates at Strasburg in 1555 resolved upon an arrangement in accordance with the principle (*Proverbs*, XXV, 27), "Enquire not after the things, which are too hard for thee"; it was proposed simply to acknowledge Christ as the Son of God and the incarnation of the Word, but to omit all discussion of the question how Christ became man. On the other hand, considering the preponderatingly social character of their idea of Christianity, all questions of the Christian mode of life were bound to become burning ones and such as readily conduced to separation.

For instance, in regard to the question, how far excommunication is to be put in force in reference to the intrusion of new fashions in clothes, the strict "Flemings" were at variance with the more liberal "Waterlanders"; clothes without buttons, only with hooks and with pockets only on the inside (Matt. 10, 10) became in Switzerland, and later also in the Palatinate, the characteristics of distinct congregations. Subsequently, the question whether tobacco-smoking was allowed, became the subject of serious discussions. "Excessive zeal without discretion, excessive narrowness of the spiritual sphere of vision, narrowmindedness and blind adherence to principle frequently perverted the beneficial effect of moral discipline into the opposite, while too often encroaching upon the personal rights of the members of the congregation."[1]

Their history continued to be a martyrology, in many countries (*e.g.* Bavaria) without alleviation, in others with intervals of rest; only in isolated cases did they meet with an uncertain tolerance. In Protestant Holland, their readiness to come forward in time of need with large offerings of money procured them the protection of William of Orange against the zeal of the Calvinists. As in Holland and East Friesland, so also in Moravia they found for some considerable time a more or less endurable existence, while the neighbouring Bohemia, whither they had migrated in large numbers, especially since 1528, refused to tolerate them.

In Moravia, the Tyrolese **James Huter** at first came forward as their most prominent leader. When Ferdinand, in 1535, wanted to wipe them out of Moravia by force, he wrote a manly letter to the governor of the province and accused Ferdinand, "the enemy of divine truth," before God.[2] After this, he fled to the Tyrol, where he was betrayed into the hands of his enemies and was put to death with fearful tortures in 1536.[3] During the Schmalkaldic

---

[1] A. Brons, p. 178.
[2] Ottius, p. 75 ff.
[3] FRA 43, 122 ff.

War, the Brethren went through terrible times, and in the Thirty Years' War they were expelled altogether (1622).[1] In Moravia they gained the reputation of being excellent colonists, agriculturists and vintagers; poverty and mendicancy were unknown amongst them; discipline, order, loyalty and honesty procured them a good name and a respected position. The education of their children in common schoolrooms under sisters who were appointed for the purpose was peculiar to them. They now went on to Hungary and Transylvania. Reformed Switzerland treated them with continuous intolerance and endeavoured to get rid of them by fines, banishment, confiscation of their property, imprisonment, and sometimes even by punishing them with death, but was unable to overcome the movement which quietly continued to spread its influence further. As late as 1614 Zürich ordered a Baptist to be beheaded.

The signs of a gradually changed attitude towards Baptism showed itself in the various attempts during the second half of the 16th century to gain an intellectual victory over Anabaptism by means of **religious discussion**. Bucer, at the wish of the Landgrave Philip, had already engaged in a somewhat protracted theological "hearing" with the leaders of the Hessian Anabaptists in 1538 (ZhTh 28, 626 f.). In 1554, the Reformed, under the leadership of **Micronius**, held a discussion at **Norden** with **Menno Simonis** on the incarnation of Christ.[2] The (fruitless) **Emden** disputation (1578), which the Count of East Friesland had arranged, was protracted for several months.[3] In like manner, in 1598, **Acronius** disputed with the Anabaptist **Peter of Cologne** at **Leeuwarden**. These discussions were regarded as victories for Calvinism, and gave the reformed synods the opportunity of renewing their warning against the Baptists as a pernicious evil. The Palatinate also became the theatre of similar discussions. In 1557, Otto Henry arranged a disputation at **Pfeddersheim**; but the Anabaptists complained of a biassed rendering of their utterances in the protocols. Subsequently, Frederick III. invited them in 1571 to **Frankenthal**[4]

---

[1] To the number of about 70,000 according to MERIAN, *Topographia Bohemiae, Moraviae, et Silesiae*. Frankf. 1650, p. 96; GINDELY, *Gesch. des 30-jähr. Krieges*. Zweite Abtheilung. Prag. 1880, p. 565 reckons the number at only 2,000.

[2] Both sides, basing their arguments upon passages from the Bible, fought over the physiological question, whether *mulieribus natura nullum insit semen*, whether only *agrorum instar semen duntaxat excipiant, mulieribus nihil ad foetus materiam conferentibus*, or whether *mulieri aeque ac viro semen tribuitur*. Cp. CRAMER, *M. Simons*, p. 107 ff. OTTIUS, p. 123.

[3] Protocol. Dath is, alle Verhandelinge des Gesprecks tho Embden mit den Wedderdöpern, de sich Flaminge nömen. Embden, 1579.

[4] Protocol, dat is de gansche Handlinge des Gesprecks te Franckenthal, 1571 (Dutch translation of the official protocol, Heidelberg, 1571). KLUCKHOHN, *Friedrich III.*, p. 385 ff. In 1567, the Anabaptist Leonh. Dax underwent an examination at Altz, of which Cramer gives an account **at the end** in SCHELHORN'S *Samml. für die Geschichte*. I (Nördl. 1779), p. 381 ff.

to a fresh discussion which was carried on without bias, and in which **Peter Dathenus**, as a reformed theologian, argued with the layman **Diebold Winter** (who was profoundly versed in theology), **Rauf Bisch** and others; an interesting conflict between evangelical scholastic theology with its syllogistic artifices and a lay biblicism, which was frequently driven into a corner by theological artifice, but instinctively sought a far more correct position than the new scholastic theology. For instance, in the chief discussion—the importance of the Old Testament for the Christian—in which Dathenus most vigorously supported the thesis that "Abraham and the prophetic Church of the Old Testament maintained and acknowledged the very same concerning the Articles of belief (Apostolicum) as we also believe and acknowledge at the present day,"[1] whereas the other two, while fully recognising the preparatory, prophetic significance of the Old Testament, refused "to derive Christ and his justice from Moses." The repugnance of the Baptists to all dogmatic formulation that went beyond the Scriptures continually entered into conflict with the ready-made formulas of a developed scholastic doctrine and, as may easily be understood, found in the latter neither intelligence nor advances. Their simple "we do not know," given in answer to so many questions, as to which the theologian thought he knew so much, could not possibly find favour. Even the pious Elector Frederick at last came to look upon the Anabaptists as "evil rascals," whose quiet activity he could only tolerate as long as they practised their devotions at home, but forbade their preaching and baptising under threat of severe punishment. These religious discussions, however, showed the Baptists the value of a higher education for their "exhorters" and "teachers," who always held their office as an honorary one; they began to attach greater importance to education in language, and then in theology. But it was not until 1675 that, in Holland, the preachers were paid and an educational institution was founded.

In addition to the rejection of Infant Baptism and their congregational discipline shut off from the world, the attitude of the Anabaptists towards the authorities, military service and the oath is characteristic of all their circles. They recognise in the authorities a divine order of things, but one subordinate to that of Christ. "In the perfection of Christ **the ban** alone is employed to admonish and exclude him who has sinned." Consequently, he who belongs to this perfection of Christ can only follow the example of Christ, who would not judge the adulteress, nor settle an inheritance; should a brother be elected to an office of authority, he must follow Christ, who fled when men wanted to make him a King. Authority is government according to the flesh; Christians have only a government according to the Spirit.[2] Thus, while Anabaptism continued full of respect in its attitude towards the existing

---

[1] Protokoll, p. 79.

[2] See p. 89; FRA 43, 43 f.; also Zwingli, Opera III 388 ff. For Melanchthon's admirable remarks on these ideas, see CR III 24 f.

authorities and avoided all resistance to or employment of legal procedure, its followers settled their affairs amongt themselves and met the injustice which they experienced from others by simply passive endurance of it. (However, in times of persecution, the Brethren assisted many of their co-religionists to flee from prison, while more consistent Baptists declined to escape for conscience sake.) While such was the unbending attitude taken up by the community of the perfect towards the civil regulations, they yet succeeded, wherever they found the barest toleration, in attaining a position of comfort by their industry, simplicity and retiring disposition.

The Baptists also contributed a substantial addition to the religious songs of the 16th century; as is only natural, their **martyr**-songs in the nature of ballads, for which Luther's song of martyrs (p. 395) serves as a model, take first place. "The tendency of all is *moral;* the sanctification of man and its preservation in life and death are almost their only subjects." "Love is the great and inexhaustible theme of these songs; for love alone is the distinguishing mark of the children of God." A German collection of their songs appeared in 1583; one in Dutch had been already published.[1]

But, where Baptism obtained tolerance as a sect, "the original religious freshness and enthusiasm gradually grew less, a barren mechanism of holy manners confined life within narrow bounds; the congregations no longer had the strength to bring forward new forms. Thus, in the end, the strict limits, which separated the Brethren from other religious congregations and the world, no longer contained anything which would have been worth the most anxious care for its preservation."[2]

2. New Prophets.

(A) **David Joris** (see above, p. 128).

(B) **Henry Niclaes (Nicolas).**

Literature: NIPPOLD in ZhTh 32, 323 ff.; 473 ff.; the same in Gelzer's Monatsbl. XXIII 15 ff. VAN SLEE ADB 23, 573 f.

The founder of the "Family of Love," **Henry Niclaes**, affords a singular example of pantheistically antinomian mysticism. Born in 1500 or 1501 at some place unknown—according to some authorities, Münster—and brought up as a strict Catholic, the boy very soon gave evidence of his visionary tendencies. Luther's writings made no impression upon him, but his own study of the Bible led him to independent religious speculations, while outwardly he

---

[1] Cp. KOCH, *Gesch. des KLieds.* [3] II 141 ff. Much information and numerous specimens may be found in FRA 43; WACKERNAGEL, *Das deutsche KLied.* V 677 ff.; LILIENCRON in ABA XIII 1, 121 ff. p. 124.

[2] A. HEGLER, *Geist und Schrift bei S. Frank.* Freib., 1892, p. 3.

observed the forms of Catholic devotional zeal. He carried on business as a merchant and early established a household. Having been imprisoned for trading with non-Catholics but soon released, he migrated to Amsterdam (about 1528); here also he was imprisoned, but, on giving sufficient proofs of his adherence to Catholicism, was again released. In 1540, he received a call as a prophet by special revelation, being at the same time bound to commit his revelations to writing. He soon withdrew to Emden, where he carried on an extensive business until 1560, and at the same time had frequent visions (his "Journeys into the land of Pietas"). Partly through his personal influence, and partly by means of numerous writings printed abroad and privately circulated with the greatest secrecy he gathered together adherents here and there in the countries which he visited on business (especially England and Holland). Gradually he aroused the opposition of both the evangelical clergy and the anabaptist leaders. When the Council of Emden intended to imprison him, he opportunely withdrew, but sent in a defence, in which he roundly denied the authorship of his writings and all sectarian tendencies. Notwithstanding, his property was now seized, and he himself prosecuted. After a short stay in Kampen and Cologne he transferred his sphere of operation to England, where he also found the largest following. A split had already begun to show itself amongst his faithful ones, and many became doubtful of his prophethood. He died in the seventies; his sect disappeared from the Continent after 1614; in England, a defence of it appeared as late as 1649, after Elizabeth had previously, in 1580. issued a proclamation against it.

His writings,[1] partly in verse, full of arbitrarily allegorical treatment of the Scriptures, proclaim the age of **Love,** which now commenced after the age of the law and faith. He himself is the prophet of this age of perfection. He who participates in it undergoes mystic deification in complete self-sacrifice of his own will in obedience to the priests of the household of love; such a one is no longer concerned with the law, as he can no longer sin. The new community, separated from the world, is organised as a strict hierarchy; under the bishop (Niclaes) and his twenty-four elders are six classes of priests. These priests "disembarrass themselves" of secular marriage. The priesthood has no property of its own, but lives upon the tithes of the community. The latter has its own calendar; a year beginning fourteen days before Easter and comprising thirteen months of twenty-eight days each, with four great periods of festivity each lasting ten days; Saturday and Sunday are in addition the holy days of their meetings. Niclaes combines with the older anabaptist enthusiasm the central idea of the perfect Kingdom of God as a kingdom in which the spirit (not the letter) and the importance of the prophethood are the chief factors; also, according to Van Slee, the rule that the members of the House of Love should not be baptised before the age of thirty. It can no longer be demonstrated, to what extent the fall from the dizzy height of pantheistic self-deification into fleshly antinomianism ("In the heavenly Jerusalem no one will be ashamed of his nakedness") took place at the secret meetings of the House of Love; but it is very probable that the serious accusations of its opponents were not unfounded. In addition to this charge and that of self-deification, the hypocrisy with which they posed to the outside world as members of the public church societies met with especial censure.

---

[1] For a list, see ZhTh 32, 331 ff.

CHAPTER FOURTH

Anti-Trinitarians and Socinians.

1. The first Anti-Trinitarians.

Literature: CHR. SANDIUS, *Bibliotheca Anti-Trinitariorum.* Freist., 1684. STAN. LUBIENIECIUS, *Hist. Ref. Polonicae.* Freist., 1685. F. TRECHSEL, *Die protest. Antitrinitarier.* 2 vols. Heidelb. 1839. 1844. BENRATH, *Ref. in Venedig.* Halle, 1887; the same, *Ochino.* ²p. 267 ff. C. SCHMIDT, *Blandrata* in RE II 491 ff. MOSHEIM, *Anderw. Versuch einer vollst. und unpart. Ketzergesch.* Helmst., 1748; the same, *Neue Nachr. von Servet.* Helmst., 1750. HEBERLE in Tüb. ZfTh 1840. H. TOLLIN, *Das Lehrsystem M. Servets.* 3 vols. Gütersl., 1876-1878; the same, numerous writings and essays, many of which are mentioned in RE XIV 160 f.; add PÜNJER in ThLZ 1877, 199 ff. A. V. D. LINDE, *M.S.* Gron., 1891. P. SCHAFF, *Hist. of the Chr. Church* VII 681 ff. New York, 1892. F. SOCINI, *Ad amicos Epistolae.* Racov., 1618. E. LUCKFIEL, *Der Socinianism. u. s. Entwicklung in Grosspolen,* in ZhGesellsch. f. d. Prov. Posen VII 115 ff. RITSCHL, *Lehre von der Rechtfertigung* ²I 334 ff. H. SCHMIDT in RE XVI 388; HARNACK DG III 682 ff. N. FOCK, *Socinianismus.* 2 parts. Kiel, 1847; the same, in ZhTh 15, 2, 83 ff.

However comprehensively Luther had criticised the traditional doctrine of the Church, it had never occurred to him to extend his criticism to the central dogma of the Church as it had existed since the Council of Nicaea—the doctrine of the Trinity. Certainly on several occasions he had openly discussed the awkwardness of the expression "Three in One" (EA ²9, 1. 12, 408. 6, 358), and also on occasion abandoned the term ὁμοούσιος (WA VIII 117), but it was folly on the part of his Catholic opponents to denounce him as an Arian. He had indeed **found a different way** from the trinitarian speculation of the schoolmen to attain to the knowledge of God : " no one shall taste the Godhead except as it consents to be tasted—that is, it must be treated of in the **manhood** of Christ " (EA 35, 334), and it was quite in the same sense that Melanchthon at first withdrew the question of the Trinity from human speculation and designated it as simply an object of our devotion (p. 36, 7). But it was just the central position that Christ won in his eyes as the mediator of salvation, the revealer of God and the way to the Father that, for him, gave the formulas of ecclesiastical Christology and the doctrine of the Trinity new life.[1] The recognition of the

---

[1] Luther's **religious** interest in this Christology is expressed, *e.g.*, in 1544 in the proposition : *Tantae molis erat perditum hominem redimere, ut talis et tanta victima pro eo esset necessaria.* EA opp. v. a. IV 472. On the one hand, *lex, peccatum, gratia* (p. 36, 7) remain for Luther the Alpha and Omega of all theology (compare his last controversial writing [1545]. Leipz. 1893, p. 11), yet, on the other hand, the article of the Trinity is for him the highest, that *de incarnatione filii Dei summus post articulum Trinitatis* (E. A. *l. c.* 478).

fact that Greek philosophy had exercised its influence upon the doctrine of the fathers of the 3rd century (p. 39) was not applied to this article of their doctrine; rather, in Luther's opinion it was established as firmly as a rock, that this Nicaean doctrine was the pure expression of the testimony of the Scriptures.[1] And, together with the scholastic development and confirmation of his doctrine of the Eucharist (p. 85), the subtle distinctions of the doctrine of the two natures acquired for him the closest theological interest.

Nevertheless, in the intellectual revolution of the years of the Reformation the attack on the chief fortress of the Catholic dogma did not fail to be made. The most different currents met here: pantheistic mysticism, offshoots of the later medieval nominalism, moralistic and critico-humanistic enlightenment.

The CA already found itself obliged to enter a protest against *Samosatenos neotericos*. It thereby attacked a number of suspicious manifestations, which **Anabaptism** had brought into prominence. In 1525, a voice had made itself heard at Antwerp, which identified the Holy Ghost with human intelligence (de Wette II 641, III 62). In the same year some painters stood before the tribunal at Nuremberg and confessed that they "thought nothing of Christ." In 1527, Rhegius complains of the doctrine of an Anabaptist, that Christ is "only a teacher of Christian life." Amongst the so-called Nicolsburg Anabaptist Articles we find the following principles (? due to Hetzer): Christ is conceived in original sin; Mary is not the mother of God, but only the mother of Christ; Christ is not God, but only a prophet on whom the word of God is bestowed.[2] In the same year, A. Althamer testifies from Nuremberg, that he himself has heard some people who called Christ only "a prophet and a sinner." Hetzer had also composed a treatise attacking the divinity of Christ, the publication of which was only prevented by his imprisonment and Zwingli's intervention. A. Blarer threw the MS. into the fire. Osiander, exaggerating, in 1529 even treats it as a common but esoteric doctrine of the Baptists, "that they deny the article of the Trinity." The same complaint also comes from East Friesland.[3]

Further, a young master of arts, **John Campanus** of Jülich, who had lived at Wittenberg since 1528, in the spring of 1530 handed the theologians there a treatise on the Trinity, "*Contra Lutheranos et omnem post Apostolos mundum*," which, in Melanchthon's judgment, contained *misera monstra dogmatum*; it disputed the personality of the Holy Ghost and looked upon Christ (like the Arians) as

---

[1] Hence, according to him, every deviation from the doctrine of the Athanasian creed is a revolt of the human understanding against the Scriptures (EA 23, 274).

[2] Roth, *Augsb. Ref. Gesch.* p. 216. StKr 1886, 167.

[3] Cp. especially Plitt, *Einleitung in die Augustana* II 152 ff. Further, Steitz, G. *Westerburg*, p. 141; cp. also, for Strasburg, ZhTh 30, 30: for Esslingen, Keim, Ref.-Blätter, p. 74 f.

begotten by the Father *infra aeternitatem*. The Elector of Saxony caused him to be imprisoned.[1] On his return home, he published (in 1532) his immature and arrogant speculations in his treatise "Göttlicher und heiliger Schrifft Restitution."[2] But Luther frankly expressed his joy, when he heard the (false) news that Campanus had been put to death at Liege by the episcopal criminal tribunal (de Wette IV 121. CR. II 228). He died in 1574 after many years' imprisonment.

2. Michael Servetus.

Far more important and productive of results was the appearance of the Spaniard **Michael Servetus**, whose treatise **De Trinitatis erroribus** (1531) was printed at Hagenau.

As the statements, which this martyr to anti-Trinitarianism subsequently made in regard to his life, are in many cases contradictory, so hardly anything certain is known in regard to his youth,—the place of his birth (Tudela or Villanova?), the year of his birth (1509 or 1511?), the course of his education (law-student at Toulouse?).[3] It is certain that in 1530 he was present at the coronation of the Emperor at Bologna and at that time had relations with Quintana, the imperial confessor. In the autumn of 1530, he approached Oecolampadius in Bâle, who gave him a friendly reception and endeavoured (but in vain) to wean him from his anti-Trinitarian ideas. Rejected at Bâle, Servetus brought out from Strasburg, (where Capito, who always "had a special partiality for foreign visitors" admitted him into his house),[4] his audacious controversial essay *De Trinitatis erroribus* (1531) at Hagenau, to the great indignation of the Strasburgers as well as the Swiss, who hastened to refuse all association with him. Certainly, in the preface to his second work *Dialogorum de Trinitate libri II*, Servetus now endeavoured to weaken the bad impression, which had been created by the first, which latter he excused on the score of his *imperitia* and the *incuria typographi*. But as a matter of fact the

---

[1] KÖSTLIN II 330 f. and the authorities, p. 666. For his doctrine, see especially CR X 132 f.

[2] [Restoration of the divine and holy Scriptures], a summary of which is given in SCHELHORN, Amoenit. lit. XI 78 ff.

[3] What TOLLIN, in ZwTh XX and XXI, ZhTh XLV and often, claims to have discovered about Servetus's earlier life and RIGGENBACH (RE XIV 153 ff.) has appropriated in the main features, is uncertain and in part a fanciful combination.

[4] Capito was seriously suspected of approving Servetus's views; Servetus subsequently directly affirmed, *que Capito estoit d'accord avec luy*. TOLLIN (*Servet und die oberländ. Reformatoren*. Berl. I 1880) has drawn far-reaching conclusions from this, against which GERBERT (*Geschichte der Strassburger Sectenbewegung*. Strassb. 1889, p. 129 ff.) has rightly raised objections. The only correct statement in Tollin's work is that Capito shrank from all "inquisitive" questions in the matter of the Trinity.

dialogues represented the same standpoint. But, at the same time, he withdrew from Germany and at first endeavoured, by assuming another name (Mich. Villanovanus) and pursuing a different occupation, to escape the consequences of his writings which were condemned in both ecclesiastical camps as blasphemy. His writings made a special impression upon Melanchthon. The latter indeed condemned his details as *confusas imagines*, which by themselves did not mean much; but still they announced to him *quales tragoedias excitabit haec quaestio ad posteros, εἰ ἔστιν ὑπόστασις ὁ λόγος, εἰ ἔστιν ὑπόστασις τὸ πνεῦμα*. They taught him that the adversary with whom evangelical dogma must have a serious explanation was Paul of Samosata (consequently dynamistic monarchianism). The old Church had not sufficiently answered him. And, while he now took occasion from Servetus to treat henceforth in his *Loci* the doctrine of the Trinity in detail in the spirit of the old writers, he confidentially imparted to Camerarius: *Ego me refero ad illas Scripturae voces, quae iubent* **invocare** *Christum, quod est, ei honorem divinitatis tribuere, et plenum consolationis est. τὰς δὲ ἰδέας τῶν ὑποστάσεων καὶ διαφορὰς ἀκριβῶς ζητεῖν, οὐ πάνυ συμφέρει* (CR II 630, XXI 353 ff.).

As a corrector for the press at Lyons, Servetus edited a reprint of Pirkheimer's Ptolemaeus with many valuable additions of his own, then directed his literary efforts to the province of medicine, and also repaired to Paris to study the same (the University registers do not confirm his subsequent assertion that he took his doctor's degree in that faculty). The student came into collision with the faculty, since he delivered lectures upon *astrologia iudiciaria*, i.e., astrology as the science of human destinies; we here find the bold critic in the service of the grossest superstition! After practising for some time in Charlieu, he found occupation in 1540 as a physician in Vienna, at the same time editing literary works for the Lyons press (reprints with his own additions). Here he again returned to his theological studies, revised his older works with additions, and composed his life's work: **Christianismi Restitutio.** In 1545, he had entered into correspondence with Calvin in regard to this work and its ideas; the latter sent him his *Institutio*, which Servetus returned with marginal glosses, together with a portion of his own manuscript. In 1546 the correspondence ended; Calvin abruptly shook off the "arrogant" man, and declared: *Si venerit* [to Geneva] *modo valeat mea auctoritas, vivum exire nunquam patiar!* The opportunity of keeping his word was destined to come. Servetus had had his *Restitutio* secretly printed in 1553[1]; no sooner had Calvin seen the book, than (February 26th) he caused Servetus to be denounced by a third party to the Catholic inquisitor at Lyons.[2] But "Villanovanus," at his first examination, denied both the authorship and his identity with Servetus. Calvin now handed to the Inquisition Servetus's letters of 1545-1546 and a portion of his marginal glosses to the copy of the *Institutio*, which clearly proved his anabaptist views, which served as further

---

[1] The author denoted himself by the initials M.S.V.; but on p. 199 he had betrayed his name. Hence, it appears incomprehensible that Melanchthon should consider Campanus to be the author. CR VIII 175.

[2] Notwithstanding, Calvin afterwards sophistically denied the fact with the remark, whether it was credible literas inter eos ultro citroque volitare, quibus non minus est inter se dissidium quam Christo cum Belial? CR XXXVI 479.

material for accusation. After this, Servetus was imprisoned in Vienne, and at his examination was in the greatest straits, from which he endeavoured to escape by declaring that years before he had only carried on a dialectic joke with Calvin in the character of Servetus. He fortunately succeeded in escaping from prison on the 7th of April; on the 17th of June, the inquisition was executed at Vienna upon him *in effigie* and upon his writings. After vainly endeavouring to reach the Spanish frontier, on his flight to Italy he touched at Geneva on the 14th of August, where he was arrested at the instigation of Calvin, whose amanuensis came forward as his accuser (according to the *ius talionis*). After this, Calvin, with a zeal that leaves a melancholy impression, hurried on the judicial process, intensely excited when the Council hesitated about settling the matter off hand in accordance with his intentions, supported by the entreaties of his friends, that Servetus should be handed over to death. It was not until the Swiss towns of Berne, Zürich, Bâle, and Schaffhausen, before which the Council laid the documents, had given their assent by their theologians who had already been most energetically instructed by Calvin and their councillors, that he pronounced judgment on the 26th of October, to the effect that Servetus deserved *estre bruslé tout vif*[1]; the next day the punishment was carried out.

Servetus's doctrines are set forth most completely and in their most developed state in his *Restitutio*.[2] It is a mistake to regard him as a modern theologian, "a child of the 19th century" (**Tollin**), as if he were a rationalist; it is only occasionally that we find such expressions as *fides vera esse non potest sine intellectu et cognitione* (Rest. 41). In his speculations he is a pantheistic (Neo-) Platonist, who attempts to adapt the Gospel of John to his theory of ideas, and amongst the teachers of the Church, sees in Origen and Clement of Alexandria the supporters of true ecclesiastical tradition. He **raises himself above** his Trinitarian opponents by the recognition of the fact that in the New Testament the historical Jesus, but not the divine Hypostasis is the subject of all christological attributes; further, by the lively recognition of a progress of revelation from Old to New Testament, finally, by the sure knowledge that the Christology of Nicaea did not prevail from the commencement in the Church—it is a tragical fact that Calvin confounded this better knowledge by a quotation from the Pseudo-Justin *de expositione fidei*—as well as by the perception of the fact that the scholastic

---

[1] Calvin informs us: *genus mortis conati sumus mutare, sed frustra* (CR 42, 567), but the judicial documents are silent as to any proposition of the kind.

[2] In this (*de trinit. V.*) he also brings forward the theory of the lesser circulation of the blood; but the accidental character of this exposition makes it doubtful, whether he really discovered it. See the passage in question and others in Niceron, Nachr. IX 340 ff.

Christology, in spite of all dialectic efforts, does not arrive at a true human nature of Christ.[1]

Christ is to him the highest manifestation of God, the true θεοφανία; *nemo patrem videt nisi in Christo,* and "to believe" is, according to his view, to behold this manifestation of God in Christ *internis oculis.* But these assertions of his are widely different from those of the Reformers that sound similar; for they are not intended to serve the soteriological interest, but are the formulas of a pantheistic[2] speculation, for which God is the omniform essence of things that expresses itself in countless *modi,* the *Logos* the *modus par excellence,* the original *modus,* the principle of all other *modi,* the *locus idearum.* After this *Logos* has manifested itself in a number of historical phenomena, sometimes only as a voice, sometimes as a visible form, it becomes a real phenomenon, humanly corporeal. The Christology of Servetus harks back from the ecclesiastical doctrine, as he imagines, to the pure doctrine of the Scriptures, in reality to the Alexandrine *Logos*-speculation, with an alloy of Neo-Platonism and Cabalism. His soteriology exhibits individual traces of the influence of the reformatory doctrine, but characteristically diverges from it in its hostile attitude towards the *servum arbitrium,* and in its support of the meaning of salvation and the meritoriousness of works.[3] His doctrine of Baptism (certainly not to be explained from Anabaptism, but only from his biblicism) is confused: *Sequitur fidem baptismus, in quo per Spiritum S.* **vivificatur** *fides* (Rest. 448); it is only after his thirtieth year that a man is capable of receiving Sacrament. His doctrine of the Eucharist is in equal conflict with the *transsubstantiatores,* the *impanatores* (Luther) and the *tropistae* (Zwingli), but differs from Calvin's in its mystic character: the Eucharist serves for the generation of the heavenly body, *Christi corpus in nobis tunc facit incrementum.* In his keen, but also coarse polemic against the ecclesiastical doctrine of the Trinity, as he had it before him especially in Thomas Aquinas (*triceps quidam Cerberus,* Rest. 77; *pro uno Deo habetis tricipitem Cerberum* CR 36, 750), every suspicion of the religious value, which it had just received again in Luther's faith, is lacking; he sees in it only a trick of scholastic extravagance. To destroy and uproot this doctrine, therefore, is called by him a *restitutio christianismi.* His study of ecclesiastical history shows him the invasion of anti-Christianity in three forms: The doctrine of the Trinity, the Papacy, and Infant Baptism (the age of Constantine). It is from this date accordingly that he reckons the 1260 apocalyptic days (years)[4] and is consequently certain that the days of Antichrist have run their course and that the millennium of Christ is near at hand. In the consciousness that he may—that he must announce the commencement of this time as a prophet, he sends forth his work. It is his special consolation, that martyrdom in the service of Christ brings with it special places of honour in Heaven.

---

[1] Cp. TOLLIN, *Thom. v. Aquino, der Lehrer Servets* in ZwTh XXXVI.

[2] *Dii vere nos efficimur participatione deitatis Christi, facti vere participes divinae naturae. Internus noster homo est de coelo et de substantia Dei.* (Rest. 196).

[3] *Illusi sunt hodie, qui magica quadam cognitione, quam vocant fidem, se solos iustos existimant, cum tamen veram Christi fidem ignorent. Qualemcumque fidei excellentiam quis adipiscatur, ex hoc nunquam vere sequetur, quin charitatis actus et bona opera suam mercedem habeant, quoquo modo ex tali fide ea nasci ipse contendat. Omnium eximia est ac maxima charitas . . . perfectioni futuri seculi magis propinqua.* Rest. 354.

[4] Cp. Revelations, 11, 2.

If we now consider how fanatically Calvin attacks this opponent of the church doctrine of the Trinity, how he seems unable to breathe again until he is assured that the Council has pronounced and carried out the sentence of death, we are confronted by the question: What is the reason of the sinister energy exhibited in his hatred? Certainly, a personal antipathy may have unconsciously played its part against the man, who had formerly attempted so arrogantly to instruct and play the schoolmaster over him; also, the longer the trial lasted, the more it became for him a decisive **trial of strength**, whether he was still master in Geneva—he threatened to leave the city, if he did not carry the day: but still it was also for him a question of the consciousness that he had a mission to fulfil in Geneva. Bullinger writes to Calvin that "God has here afforded the opportunity *ecclesiam expurgandi a labe seu foeditate haerescos.*" "*Totus orbis videat, Genevam Christi gloriam cupere servatam*" (CR 42, 621, 604). In fact, it was a question of maintaining in its purity Romanic Calvinism, which was dangerously attacked on different sides (especially by the Italian exiles) by anti-Trinitarianism, **the entire religious possession**, which was protected by the dogma of the Trinity, being thereby endangered. However dark the shadows appear, which in this case fall upon Calvin, however repulsive to us the correspondence of the Swiss theologians in this business, it was **a question of life and death**, as far as the existence of Calvinism was concerned. The funeral pile of Servetus was the preservation of Calvin's work.

Not only did Calvin's colleagues in Geneva unanimously sign the apology for this deed (*Defensio orthod. fidei de s. Trinitate*, 1554, CR 36, 453 ff., in which is discussed the question *An christianis iudicibus haereticos punire liceat*, 461 ff.), but also the *Confessio gallica* 1559, (Schaff III, 368), and the *Confessio helvetica posterior* (1556, Schaff III 241) mention Servetus by name and thereby expel anti-Trinitarianism once for all from their churches. The humanistic, more free-thinking circles of Switzerland (especially **Castellio** in Bâle)[1] and the circles of the Italian

---

[1] Under the pseudonym of Mart. Bellius, he wrote *De haereticis an sint persequendi* (March, 1554). Calvin and Beza at once guessed the author (CR 43, 95, 97, 134). Castellio had already excited great displeasure by his preface to his Latin Bible (Feb. 1551, addressed to Edward VI.): *si quis a nobis in aliquo religionis vel puncto dissidet, eum damnamus et per omnes terrarum angulos linguae stilique iaculo petimus:* we do not indeed kill him ourselves, but hand him over to Pilate. *Et haec omnia Christi nos studio et iussu et nomine facere clamamus!* He demands; *doctrina ignorantiam pellat—non ut carnifici mandetur provincia doctoris!* This moving appeal for toleration has been translated into German in C. A. Crusius, *Gnomon.* Leipz. 1774, p. 131 ff.

exiles commenced an agitation against Calvin's act, and railed at the new Pope and the new Inquisition in Geneva, but in vain; not only did Beza cleverly and eloquently support Calvin;[1] Melanchthon also, at Calvin's earnest request, upheld him and did not fail, both in public and private, repeatedly to stigmatise Servetus as a blasphemer and to preach the right of the Christian authorities to extirpate such abominations (CR VIII 362, X 851 ff., XII 696 ff., XXIV 501).

3. The Italo-Polish Anti-Trinitarians.

Anti-Trinitarianism pressed forward irresistibly from **Italy**: on the one hand, the critical and philosophical influences of the culture of the Renaissance impelled thinkers to examine also this mystery of the Papacy,[2] partly to deny it flatly in rationalistic fashion, partly to revive the speculations of the Trinitarian controversies of the old Church; on the other hand, Anabaptism, which had been transplanted to Italian soil since about 1540, soon took an abruptly anti-Trinitarian turn. In September, 1550, an anabaptist Council attended by sixty deputies was secretly held at Venice (p. 227), which agreed to the propositions: Christ is no God but man, the offspring of Joseph and Mary, but full of divine powers. He died in order to reach God's justice, *i.e.*, the summit of his goodness and compassion and promise. They introduced amongst the Italian fugitives to Switzerland their increasingly anabaptist and anti-Trinitarian ideas and came forward with them in the form of doubts, as to which they sought instruction.

Thus, the physician **George Blandrata,** who had been physician-in-ordinary at the Court of Sigismund I. of Poland, now fleeing from Pavia before the Inquisition, repaired to Calvin, whom he pressed with his sceptical questions and objections, without allowing himself to be convinced by his instructions (CR 37, 325 ff.).[3] **Alciati, Gentile, Gribaldo** and others strengthened the anti-Trinitarian group in the Genevese Italian community, so that Calvin drew up a confession, which all the members of this community were obliged to accept on the 18th of May, 1558, and to sign with the proviso that, whoever deviated from it, should be looked upon as a perjurer (CR 37, 385 ff. 45, 168 ff. 176. 236. 256 f.). Alciati and Blandrata, who had come forward as spokesmen of the anti-Trinitarians, feeling themselves no longer safe in Geneva, tried the ground in Berne and Zürich. Not feeling safe even here, Blandrata again directed his steps towards Poland. Gentile, who had signed against his will, but then felt

---

[1] *De haereticis a civili magistratu puniendis.* August 1554.

[2] In 1545, Melanchthon mentions certain theological questions, which the Italians had put before him, as to which he complains: *Multum est* **Platonicarum** θεωρῶν *in Italica theologia.* CR V 767.

[3] The editors (37 p. xxxii) certainly deny, but without visible reason, that this work is the reply to the questions propounded in 45, 169 ff.

compelled to make his convictions known (CR 37, 389 ff.), was condemned to do ignominious penance as a perjured teacher of heterodoxy, and then arrested by the city authorities (CR 37, 415 ff.). However, he managed to escape, was imprisoned on Bernese territory, but released after a closer examination of his doctrines. He also now hastened towards Poland, but, having imprudently allowed himself to be again seen in Switzerland, was again imprisoned and, in 1566, beheaded at Berne as a perjured teacher of heterodoxy. Gribaldo saved himself by a confession of faith that satisfied his opponents in Switzerland, and died (1564), without being further molested, although looked upon with suspicion.

The lawyer **Lelio Sozzini**,[1] who in 1547 had fled to Zürich, where he lived after 1548 with Pellican, warned by the fate that had overtaken Servetus, was contented with veiling his dissent from the ecclesiastical doctrine of the Trinity and "satisfaction" in the form of cautiously doubting questions with a request for instruction. In Zürich he was regarded as "a pious and learned man;" it was not until after his death (1562) that it was discovered how decided an attitude he had already assumed. **Ochino** also, but not until he had left Switzerland, in his *Dialogi* (1563) composed in Poland, revealed the fact that the doubts of the Italian circle had at least made a strong impression upon him: although he formally **defended** the doctrine of the Church, he did so with the significant avowal that it stood as much in need of a fresh examination in the light of the Scriptures as the Catholic doctrine of the Eucharist, and proposed the question (although only *disputando*) whether this doctrine had a practically religious significance.

In Switzerland, anti-Trinitarianism had been robbed of its strength by the departure of some and the death of others. Its further development henceforth took place on the soil of **Poland** and **Transylvania.** The Polish nature, humanistically trained and emotional, now showed itself most readily accessible to this scepticism, as it had always been to Italian influences. Stancaro's controversy regarding the intercession of Christ (p. 217, CR 37, 333 ff.) helped to clear the way for criticism of the Church doctrine. The freedom of the press which prevailed there and the right of free worship at home, which had been extorted from the nobles, was very favourable to the spread of the new doctrines. The Italians at first joined the **reformed** group amongst the Poles, and soon found in **Peter Gonesius,** who had read the works of Servetus, a zealous co-religionist, who in 1558, at the Synod of Brzesc, put forward an essay against Infant Baptism and also found patrons and followers amongst the nobility. Blandrata, against whom Calvin in vain issued a warning (CR 45, 378), who had been appointed superintendent of the reformed church in Little Poland, cautiously promulgated his anti-Trinitarianism under the cloak of a biblical mode of expression; having fallen under suspicion, he again saved himself by an ambiguous confession, and then again entered the service of the Court as physician-in-ordinary. Meanwhile, anti-Trinitarianism continued its propaganda, and in 1561 extorted a synodal resolution that preachers should abstain from terminology not taken directly from the Scriptures. Anti-Trinitarianism also made its way into Lithuania, protected by the powerful Starost John Kiszka and secured a hold upon a number of reformed churches. The Cracow preacher **Gregory Pauli** now carried the opposition to the church

---

[1] [Laelius Socinus of Siena] : TRECHSEL II, 137 ff.

doctrine (which at first had an Arian tinge) further—to a denial of the pre-existence of Christ. Having been deprived of his office, he founded an independent unitarian congregation. After vain attempts to check the split in the reformed congregations, the diet of Petrikau (1565) brought about an open breach by a colloquy between Trinitarians and anti-Trinitarians.[1] The Unitarians now adopted an independent church constitution and founded synods and schools of their own.

But the new Unitarian Church was still by no means in general agreement in the attitude it assumed; its members laid stress upon the unity of God, and, in their Christology, had recourse to undefined biblical turns of speech; in the doctrine of Baptism, the rejection of Infant Baptism was to the fore, while in regard to the Eucharist, they harked back to Zwingli. In the doctrine of salvation a moralistic conception asserted itself. But, in the main question, an Arian party, which firmly maintained the pre-existence of Christ, but looked upon his relation to the Father as strictly "subordinate," now entered into a struggle with a moderate party, which dropped the pre-existence but upheld the childbirth of the Virgin and attributed divine honour to the deified man, while both attacked an opposition, which now gave up the supernatural childbirth and the adoration of Christ. The latter opinion found an energetic supporter in **Francis David** (Davidis), the superintendent of the Transylvanian Unitarians (here the separation from the "reformed" had taken place in 1568). Blandrata, who had vainly attempted to make him change his opinions, finally caused him to be imprisoned, but thereby brought about the open separation of the Unitarians into *Adorantes* and *Non-adorantes*.

While matters were in this state of confusion, **Fausto**, the nephew of Lelio Sozzini, vigorously interfered, established the distracted party on a firm structure and thus developed the clearly developed form of **Socinianism** out of the chaos of anti-Trinitarian Anabaptist tendencies.

4. Socinianism.

Fausto Sozzini,[2] born at Siena in 1539, a young lawyer, had fled from the Inquisition in 1559; the secret literary legacy of his uncle (Epist., p. 17) led him into anti-Trinitarianism,—a legacy, to the fulfilment of which he subsequently devoted all the energies

---

[1] The Romish party (Hosius) promoted the cause of the anti-Trinitarians in so far as it freely supported the view that neither the doctrine of the Trinity nor of Infant Baptism could be proved from Scripture alone.

[2] Faustus Socinus.

of his life. At first, a post at the Medicean Court kept him tied; but the theological impulse in him became so powerful, that in 1574 he joyfully sacrificed brilliant prospects, secretly left house and home, devoted four years in Bâle to further study and literary work,[1] and then obeyed Blandrata's summons (1578) to Transylvania. But the split amongst the Unitarians there and the violent proceedings against Davidis drove him (in 1579) from there to Poland (Cracow). Here he was at first obliged to fight for his admission into the Unitarian community, as he refused to accept their Anabaptism (Epist. 363 ff.). His next work had for its object **to undo the connection of Unitarianism with Anabaptism** and then to bind Unitarianism firmly together in theory and practice by overcoming both the Arian party and that of the Non-adorantes (Epist., p. 186 ff.). He drove out the Anabaptist party, in 1600 the community solemnly rejected Non-adorantism, the Arian party submitted. In 1598, the Jesuits celebrated a triumph; some Cracow students seized the sick "arch-heretic," with the intention of burning him to death, and he was only saved by the intervention of a professor. After that time he lived under the protection of a nobleman at the village of Luclawice until his death in 1604. In the year following appeared the Rakow (larger) Catechism, Confession and text book in one, begun by him and completed by Val. Schmalz; a small children's Catechism was added to it. The union of the Unitarians as "Socinians" was thereby crowned with success. A considerable number of friends and pupils continued the work in his spirit, amongst them many Germans[2] (Schmalz of Gotha, Ostorodt of Goslar, the Franconian

---

[1] A criticism of the church doctrine of "satisfaction" in his essay *De Jesu Christo servatore* (printed 1594) and a criticism of the doctrine of death as a consequence of the Fall in *De statu primi hominis*.

[2] At the University of Altdorf the physician **E. Soner** (died 1612) secretly propagated Socinianism. See further what took place at Heidelberg (p. 302). The treatise by the Silesian **Mart. Seidel** (*Origo et fundamenta relig. christ.* ZhTh 6, 192 ff.) found at Halle in 1587 went still further in rejecting all positive dogmas and attempting to prove that the Messianic prophecies indicated quite a different picture of the future from that which was "fulfilled" in Christ. The treatise *De tribus impostoribus* (printed in 1598, probably also earlier), the author of which is to be looked for neither among the Socinians, nor among the Calvinists but among the enlightened Catholics of Italy, preached scepticism towards all the foundations of religion generally. (Editions by F. W. GENTHE, Leipzig, 1833; E. WELLER, Heilbr., 1876; cp. MÖLLER in RE VI 708 ff.; TENTZEL, *Curiöse Biblioth.* 1704, p. 487 ff.)

John Crell, the noblemen von Schlichting and Baron von Wolzogen
and others). They had their most important community in Rakow
(in the Palatinate of Sendomir, founded in 1569), where an academic
college of their own provided a school and university education for
the rising generation, where most of their writings were printed,
and their general synod met every year. After the anabaptist
element had separated from it, Socinianism only exercised a power
of attraction upon the upper, humanistically educated circles.
In 1627, the Jesuits succeeded in stirring up the mob against the
Socinian church and community at Lublin; on the 1st of May,
1638, the same party, seizing upon some youthful excesses against
a crucifix as an excuse, obtained from the Senate at Warsaw,
by a violation of the course of justice, the sentence that the school
at Rakow should be demolished, the Socinians deprived of their
church, their printing works done away with, their preachers and
teachers proscribed. Certainly, on the part of the Protestants, a
protest was raised against this glaring violation of justice, although
they were by no means sorry to see the annihilation of the
Unitarians. The "Sarmatian Athens" sank into a village. The
school which was established once again in Kissielin was destroyed
in 1644. At the religious colloquy of Thorn (p. 362) the Socinians
again attempted to join in the discussion as a dissenting party that
enjoyed equal rights with the rest, but were rejected as unbidden
guests. By a resolution of the diet of 1658 they were completely
expelled from Poland as a "secta Ariana." The remnants of the
communities made their escape, partly to Transylvania, where
they subsequently survived even worse times as a church union, while a
small band reached the March and Prussia, where they were tacitly
tolerated; in the Netherlands they attached themselves partly to
the Mennonites,[1] partly to the Remonstrants, in whose ranks they
were gradually merged. From Holland Unitarianism forced its
way to England in the 17th century; although threatened in 1648
with the death penalty by a resolution of Parliament, it could not
be extirpated. At first, however, its adherents did not formally
separate from the established church.

In Socinus's mode of thought the Scotistic-Pelagian tendency of Scholasticism
is combined with humanistic criticism of the Catholic dogma; it is, as HARNACK
admirably puts it, "the destruction of Catholicism, which it was found possible

---

[1] Cp. the title of *docti Menonistae* given to the Socinians by Justus Lipsius,
RITSCHL, *Lehre von der Rechtfertigung*[2] I 323.

to effect on the basis of the result of Scholasticism and the Renaissance, without deepening and vivifying religion" (DG III 655). The credit of the Scriptures is not shaken, but the New Testament is the only standard authority in them, the credibility of which is proved on external grounds as well as in the person of the founder of the religion of the New Testament, who is justified by his miracles and resurrection. The New Testament, again, attests the trustworthiness of the Old. Thus, in this case, the Christian religion is made plausible to the human understanding as a **book-religion**. This understanding is the logical, which declares all that elevates itself dialectically to be a false conception; there is no question of asserting the facts of experience in contrast to the world of the supernatural, hence miracles and prophecies give no offence. It is thus a question of rational supernaturalism. God would have revealed himself in vain, if our intelligence could not grasp the revelation; in it certainly much is **supra** *rationem et humanum captum*, but there is nothing **contra** *rationem sensumque communem*. The faith, which the Scripture teaches, is before all faith in the existence and just recompense of God. As man, being by nature mortal, could not of himself find the way of salvation, which depends only upon the will of God, it must be pointed out to him by the Scriptures; it demands from us an acknowledgment of God and Christ, combined with a pious life. The doctrine of the Trinity is subjected to a keen criticism, in which Socinus's exegesis successfully raises itself above the dogmatically fettered exegesis of his opponents. In the matter of Christology, the idea, only hypothetically expressed by Duns Scotus, that God could also have redeemed us by a man, is seriously considered; Christ, in consequence of his wonderful conception a man of an extraordinary kind, invested with divine wisdom and power, raised from the dead and elevated to equal power with God, and hence worthy of adoration,[1] is considered essentially as a prophet; as such he has made the law of greater importance, promised us eternal life, set us the example of moral perfection and confirmed it by his death. Baptism and Communion appear as the ceremonial commandments of the New Testament, as symbols and confessions, that is to say, tokens of remembrance.[2]

However greatly Socinus's biblicism may have been mistaken in the rejection of the pre-existence of Christ and obliged to have recourse to exegetical acts of violence, to an equal extent the brilliant article of his theology, his dialectical criticism of the doctrine of satisfaction is acute and plays the part of a pioneer, in so far as it endeavoured to work out a juridically valid equivalent for the sin of mankind. His (Scotistic) idea of God rejects generally the necessity of satisfaction for God; the punishment of an innocent person is repugnant to the justice of God. It is most contradictory to combine remission of sins and satisfaction for sins, since the one excludes the other. Substitution is inconceivable in the case of personal punishment, since it would be the height of injustice to permit the former. The suffering of the innocent is never the suffering of punishment. Further, the supposed substitution in his suffering

---

[1] Epist. 272 ff. Christ now possesses *summam in angelos et in homines et in ipsos daemones potestatem*, and hence is able *aliquid efficere vel largiri* for those who call upon him. *Occasio Christi invocanda est, cum quis in aliqua* **necessitate** *est constitutus, qua divina* **ope** *indigeat*.

[2] Infant Baptism is not in accordance with biblical evidence, but may be tolerated by Christian love as *error inveteratus*, out of consideration for the weak.

our death, saves no one from this death, as experience teaches. The dragging in of the *obedientia activa* is on the one hand worthless, since Christ was bound to this for his own person, and on the other highly contradictory, since thus a double payment of the same debt is received. Since, further, the Godhead is incapable of suffering, the death of Christ regarded as an act of substitution only possessed the value of the sacrifice of a single human life, and consequently could not suffice for the whole world. But if the substitution were equivalent in itself, it would necessarily exercise its effect unconditionally, not only upon faith. This theory, besides being unreasonable and unbiblical, also has a destructive effect upon the moral energy of man. This was an attack, which was irrefutable on the basis of the attacked **juridical** conception of the satisfaction of Christ. This criticism had an immediate result upon Arminian dogmatics (Hugo Grotius), in which the equivalence of the act of Christ was abandoned. Certainly, Socinus also speaks positively of a **merit** of the death of Christ, but only in an improper sense; out of regard for the Epistle to the Hebrews, he even teaches a heavenly priesthood of Christ and an *expiatio peccatorum* taking place in Heaven, but only as a specially powerful assurance of divine forgiveness, as a merciful liberation from the punishment of sin and an indication of Christ's own life, crowned with heavenly reward, in order to stir us to follow in his footsteps. In spite of the biblical colouring of ideas, the doctrine of Socinus is **the breaking up of religion into rational knowledge of God and morality;** not one of the religious conquests of the Reformation is here made use of; it is only a critical analysis of medieval theology, in spite of the undeniable advance shown by his biblical exegesis in numerous individual cases.

CHAPTER FIFTH.

Mystic Spiritualism.

1. Sebastian Franck.

Literature: An ample review in Alemannia V 135 f. MERZ in RE IV 603 ff, C. A. HASE, *S. Franck v. Wörd.* Leipz. 1869: NIPPOLD in Jen. LZ 1876. Nr. 22; F. WEINKAUFF in Alemannia IV 24 ff., V 131 ff., VI 49 ff., VII 1 ff.; the same in ADB VII 214 ff.; F. LATENDORF, *S. F.s erste Sprichwörtersamml. von 1532.* Poesneck, 1876, p. 341 ff. A. HEGLER, *Geist und Schrift bei S.F.* Freib., 1892. CHR. SEPP, *Geschiedkund. Nasporingen.* Leiden, 1872. I 158 ff. E. TAUSCH, *S.F. und seine Lehrer.* Halle, 1893. A list of his writings in HASE, p. 295 ff.

Together with the enthusiastic opposition of Baptism, which as a searching **popular** movement opposes to the Reformation a different ideal of moral life and a different programme of the union of the congregation, and together with the theologically critical opposition of the anti-Trinitarians which originated in the circles **of the learned,** the opposition of solitary minds is aroused; these assert the principle of **religious subjectivity,** the individually personal character of religious feeling in opposition to the historically limited **Churchdom,** the **spiritual** character of Christianity in contrast with **the Scriptures.** They are **the Spiritualists** amongst the opponents of the Reformation. No one exhibits this contrast so clearly and consistently, and hence so uniquely, as **Sebastian Franck** of Donauwörth. The idea of the inwardness of religion in him breaks through every kind of churchdom, makes him an opponent of every theological system, of every form of worship and every organised community. On principle he renounces the Church of Luther like every other: "in our times three chief forms of belief have arisen, which have a large following, the Lutheran, the Zwinglian, and the Baptist; **the fourth is already on the way:** all formal preaching, ceremony, Sacrament, excommunication, and calls to the ministry will be done away with as unnecessary: simply an invisible spiritual Church, gathered together amongst all peoples in unity of the spirit and faith and governed only by the eternal visible Word of God without any external means, will be established."[1] Hence, he consistently does not attempt to found a new ecclesiastical community, and to gain followers in this sense, but limits himself as a literary man to find readers who can understand and adopt his ideas.

    Sebastian Franck, born in 1499 in the imperial city of Donauwörth, received a theological and humanistic training at the University of Ingolstadt (Alem. VII 4) and at the Dominican college of Heidelberg. After having been a Catholic priest in the episcopate of Augsburg (about 1524), he entered the service of the Lutheran Reformation as preacher at Gustenfelden in the diocese of Nuremberg. Having become friendly with the Ansbach reformer **Andr. Althamer**, he had freely revised (1528) the Diallage ($\delta\iota\alpha\lambda\lambda\alpha\gamma\dot{\eta}$, reconciliation of the disputed passages in the Scriptures) of the latter (directed against **Denk**). He fought for the right understanding and use of the Scriptures, but also for the spirit which alone can rightly interpret the Scriptures, and in his little book *Vom Laster der Trunkenheit* (Of the vice of drunkenness) had given sympathetic expression to his complaints that a genuine apostolic community, which put excommunication in force against sinners, was nowhere to be found. "If a minister of the word observes that a man is not improved by the Gospel, but only misuses it to glorify and cover the shame of the flesh, he does not remain there . . . he remains mute and is silent or hurries away" (Bl. Ca). His alarm at the absence of moral results from evangelical preaching at first causes him (like the Baptists and Schwenkfeld) to set his hopes upon the establishment of an ordinance of excommunication and discipline; but his development soon goes beyond this, for it is just the Scriptures, on which all evangelical preaching relies, that are the occasion of the fleshly abuse and worldly sentiments that prevail in the congregations. Thus, having rapidly made up his mind, he resigns his office, and at first lives a retired life at Nuremberg. His disapproval of the violent measures taken against the Baptists brings him under the suspicion of favouring Baptist principles, with which, however, he is only in agreement in his criticism of the churches of the Reformation. In 1529, he migrates to tolerant Strasburg, whence he is expelled in 1531 on account of his outspoken critical judgments upon Erasmus, Luther, the Eucharistic controversy, the persecution of heretics and the like in his *Chronica, Zeitbuch und Geschichtbibel*; for some time he supports himself in Esslingen as a soap-boiler; after 1533 he lives in Ulm, occupied with literary work; here also he is persecuted by the clergy (M. Frecht), and, at Melanchthon's instigation, by letters from the Landgrave Philip to the Council of Ulm, but manages to support himself as a printer until 1539. Being finally expelled, he turns towards Bâle, where he continues his writing and printing. In 1542 (1543) he dies here. Together with Luther, he enjoys the reputation of being the best and most popular prose writer of the Germans of his time, who knew how to make the most of history and the proverbs of the people as morally educating and religiously edifying factors (in spite of much defective criticism), a popular writer of the first rank and a patriot such as few were in his days, and who in addition took up a position outside the strife of parties like no other man of his time.

---

[1] *Chronika und Beschreibung der Türkey.* Nürnb., 1530, Bl. K. 3b.

To the **misuse of the Scriptures** is due all the corruption of religion, and it is just the Reformation that has made a paper idol of them. Everyone explains them as he pleases, everyone makes them a shameful pretext for vice. The splitting of Christendom into sects is the consequence of this misuse of the Scriptures. But, even positively, they are not adapted to be the highest authority of the Christian, for they are in the letter full of contradictions, and contain, understood literally, much that is unworthy of God : they certainly require, but do not give new life. At no time have those who are learned in the Scriptures been the best Christians. The New Testament is preaching **by word of mouth**,[1] it is spirit, but not letter. Therefore eternal happiness is not bound by the letter of the Scriptures. In the letter divine truth cannot find its full expression at all, for God cannot be confined in any creature. It depends upon the moral and religious nature of man (spirit or flesh) whether he finds God or the devil in the Word. Accordingly, he combats the papacy of the Scriptures, in order to raise objections against the external formalities of religion generally. (At the same time he firmly adheres to the inspiration of the Scriptures, but only complete possession of the spirit and personal experience make a man capable of understanding them ; only the spirit finds in the letter of the Scriptures the Word of God.)

The authority of the religious man is the **interior, spiritual Word** (= the Spirit of God), which speaks to our soul ; this is effective force and necessary for salvation. It is implanted in him together with his creation in the image of God. Not only God's law, but all the chief articles of Christian belief are given with this religious, moral disposition of man, and to all peoples without respect of persons. Certainly sin has concealed and dimmed the light of ·the soul, but not completely extinguished it ; it continues working as a "token in the mind." If man gives himself up to the creature, his ear becomes deaf to the inner word, but where tranquillity, the Sabbath of the soul, is, there the voice is heard and appropriated, the heart becomes subject to the Word by internal constraint, and that *Plerophoria* enters which is the surest thing of all that is sure ; the will of God becomes free personal conviction, the knowledge of God and self are one. At the same time, Franck attempts to arrive at an appreciation of the revelation of God in Christ. As the world no longer understood the divine, God reminded it of it, by himself becoming incarnate ; what Christ brought us, was already in us, only we were not conscious of it. "In Christ every form of God became visible and appeared," in his life and teaching he shows how God feels towards us and how we should feel towards Him ; thus, according to Augustine (*de trin*, 4, 6)[2] he is *sacramentum et exemplum* of the Christian. Owing to his generation from God and Mary Christ's flesh bears a double nature in itself: it is born of spirit and flesh ; but the spiritual flesh in it overcomes the flesh that had its origin in Mary until the flesh is completely deified in his exaltation. As the "immovable God is angry with no one," in the Passion of Christ it is a question only of the healing of our evil conscience, of the removal of our hostility to him. But all that Christ did in the flesh and became for us goes beyond itself: we must here also press forward from the flesh into the spirit, from the Christ for us to the Christ in us, from Christ

---

[1] They are Luther's ideas (WA XIII 259), of which he here shows a peculiar appreciation.

[2] Ed. Maurina, Venet. 1723 VIII 813 G.

as the Sacrament in the flesh to Christ as our example in the spirit (in his life and Passion). As he here leads us from the historical Christ to the spirit, so he leads us by the doctrine of the *Logos* to the unconscious Christianity of the world outside the Christian: the Platonists and the moral philosophers of antiquity are to him a testimony to the effects, which the Word has at all times exercised upon the hearts of men. The apostolic community does not appear to him the model which the Christian community of all succeeding time should strive to imitate, but a stage in the childhood of Christianity, which still needed external ceremonies (Sacraments) and hence through God's condescension received such a puppet-show.

Franck, whose positions are first and foremost intended to be the antithesis of Lutheran churchdom, learnt much from Luther, but he exaggerated the subjective character of the religion which Luther taught him,[1] to the depreciation of all objective factors. Hence he goes back beyond Luther to German mysticism and thence to (Neo-) Platonism, but yet in such a manner that there is always an after-echo of Lutheran influences in him. At the same time, this versatile man, open to influence from all quarters, received varied impulses from many of his contemporaries, Denk, Bünderlin (a co-religionist of Denk),[2] Schwenkfeld, Staupitz and others, but also from Erasmus, Cornelius Agrippa and others.[3] All these impulses are intermingled with a Spiritualism which grasped in an inimitable manner the personal character of all religion, the **essence** of religious **certainty,** but fails to supply an adequate answer to the question, **how** such a religion **arises**: which, more than any other, recognised and strove against the bitter abuse, to which Luther's boasting of the Word and stress upon the need of Christ for us were exposed, and championed important evangelical truths against the identification of the Word and Gospel of God with the letter of the Scriptures, but at the same time, in its dualism of Scripture and spirit came into conflict with a fundamental idea of the Reformation. Later generations have carried out his ideas further, consciously and unconsciously. In the 16th century, he found amongst evangelical citizens a considerable circle of readers, wherever discontent was felt with the papacy of the theologians.

Luther himself despised him as an "enthusiast" and "spiritualist," "whom nothing pleases but spirit, spirit, spirit, who has no regard for the Word, the Sacrament, or the ministry"; at the same time, he condemns him as a querulous

---

[1] The idea of religion itself is borrowed by him from Luther's beautiful words: *Vivendo, imo moriendo et damnando fit theologus, non intelligendo, legendo aut speculando*, WA V 163: cp. Gulden Arch. 1538 240 b.

[2] A. NICOLADONI, *Joh. Bünderlin von Linz.* Berlin, 1893.

[3] TAUSCH has collected a full list of such influences in his work.

censor without positive ideas and (unjustly) as a dishonourer of the female sex.[1] An official declaration of the Lutheran theologians was issued against him (and Schwenkfeld) in March, 1540, at Schmalkalden, in which it is justly made a matter of reproach against him that: *multa colligit ad Scripturae auctoritatem extenuandam et iubet spiritum quaeri omisso verbo;* his proposition (taken from Cicero), "there is only **one** sin," with which he referred from individual sins to the sinful tendency of the soul, is rejected by them as an unauthorised intermingling of Stoic morality: to his spiritual kingdom of Christ, which numbers members amongst "sects" of all kinds, they bluntly oppose, as the *unica Ecclesia Christi*, the church of pure doctrine and pure worship (CR III 983 ff.)

2. Caspar Schwenkfeld.

Literature: Works not completely collected in *Der 1. Theil der christlichen orthodoxischen Bücher C. Schw. s.* Frankf. 1564. Epistolary: I. *Christl. lehrh. Missiven.* II. 1. *Sendbriefe von der päpstlichen Lehre;* 2. *Sendbriefe, die er auf der Lutherischen Glauben geschrieben.* Frankf. 1566 and 1570. Fol. ERBKAM, p 357.; the same, in RE XIII 776 ff. O. KADELBACH, *Gesch. C. v. Schw. u. der Schwenkfelder.* Lauban, 1860; A. F. H. SCHNEIDER, *Ueber den gesch. Verlauf. der Ref. in Liegnitz.* Berl. 1860 (Progr.). O. HAMPE, *Zur Biogr. C. S. s* (up to 1539). Jauer 1882 (Progr.).). ERDMANN in ADB 33, 403 ff.; GERBERT, *Strassb. Sektenbewegung,* p. 132 ff. JOH. WIGAND, *De Schwenkfeldismo.* Lips. 1587. A. BAUR, *Zwinglis Theologie* II 245 ff.

Notwithstanding the many points of contact between Franck and Schwenkfeld, which has caused both as a rule to be named and judged together by their contemporaries, the difference between them is, that only the latter is **theologically** interested, endeavours to gain influence over contemporary theology, does his utmost to develop a dogmatic theory and to defend it on all sides,[2] and that Schwenkfeld only abandons the evangelical congregations from necessity, not on principle, like Franck, in order to gather round him immediately a new conventicle-community. Hence there existed and still exists at the present day a community of Schwenkfeldians, while Franck was never able to form a community.

Born in 1489[3] at Ossig in Silesia, of an old noble family now extinct, Schwenkfeld, in 1506, attended the University of Cologne and other academies; about 1510, he entered the service of the Court at Oels as equerry, then served at Brieg (1515) and soon afterwards at Liegnitz at the Court of Duke

---

[1] EA 63 384 ff. LÖSCHE, *Anal. Luth.* p. 60. As he gathered no sect round him, Luther and others thought that he exercised a waning influence. Speratus's contemptuous verdict is: "In his case it is idle chattering; he speaks just like a child." (TSCHACKERT, *P. Speratus,* p. 61.)

[2] "Schw. had met de godgeleerden van professie, Fr. mit het godsdienstige volk to doen." SEPP, *Geschiedk. Naspor,* I 161.

[3] Cp. HAMPE, p. 6.

Frederick II. In 1519, he had already been won over to the cause of the Gospel by Luther's writings and maintained intimate relations with the Silesian friends of the Reformation. Defective hearing caused him to retire into private life at Ossig (1521); his life was henceforth devoted to zealous study of the Bible and correspondence in the interests of the Reformation. In December, 1521, he rode to Wittenberg, was present during Melanchthon's negotiations with the Zwickau prophets (p. 38), and made the acquaintance of Carlstadt. Urged by Schwenkfeld, John Hess of Breslau decided openly to support the cause of Luther, and, in 1523, Duke Frederick gave a free course to the Reformation at Liegnitz. However, Schwenkfeld, when defending himself in a letter to the Bishop of Breslau (January, 1524) protested vigorously against being called a "Lutheran." Soon afterwards, his *Ermahnung des Missbrauchs etlicher furnehmster Artikel des Evangeliums* appeared, in which he already looks with suspicion upon the dangers, which the importance attached to justification by faith alone brings with it, and complains of the formal belief of men, their service in the letter without living spirit, and the want of life in the spirit. Meanwhile, he had found a vigorous supporter of his views in **Val. Krautwald**, who was in office at the cathedral at Liegnitz in 1523, and had formerly been a canon of Neiss and notary of the episcopal chancery. In the course of the year 1525, Schwenkfeld developed his peculiar doctrine of the Eucharist, which he pretends to have received by "visitation from above." Christ means: my body is this, namely, bread, spiritual food; my blood is this, namely, spiritual drink. Krautwald at first opposed this, but, on the 16th of September, allowed himself to be won over and then furnished him with the scientific confirmation of the new interpretation. Provided with his *Quaestiones contra impanationem* and a letter of Krautwald, Schwenkfeld now rode again to Wittenberg, discussed the Eucharist with Luther, Jonas and others, and desired the institution of the ban.[1] Meeting with a friendly reception, but really rejected,[2] he went on to propagate his doctrine of the Eucharist in his native place and thereby to drift farther away from the cause of Luther. His old friend Hess now turned decidedly against him; but he betook himself from Luther to Tauler and the "German theology" (Vol. II., p. 469) and now developed, with ever-increasing clearness, his view of "the inner true word of God, which is God himself and must precede the outer, figurative word." Oecolampadius, who hailed in Schwenkfeld an ally against Luther's doctrine of the Eucharist, had a work of his printed at Bâle.[3] Schwenkfeld advised his Liegnitz followers to abstain for a time from Communion altogether, until the true Christian community (Stillstand) should have established itself; soon the report spread that he also desired to do away with infant baptism. Duke Frederick, who was unsuccessful in founding a University owing to the disturbed state of things, felt anxious whether, as advised by Schwenkfeld, he was on the right path; Schwenkfeld at first calmed him; but when Ferdinand, King of Bohemia, urged on by John Faber, began to worry the Duke about him, Schwenkfeld preferred to

---

[1] Cp. besides the Epistolar II 2 nr. 1. ENDERS V 277, 294, 330. *Sunt molestissimi et garruli* was Luther's complaint against the two Silesians.

[2] On April, 1526, followed Luther's written rejection of his theories, de Wette III 123 (where it is wrongly dated).

[3] *De cursu verbi Dei, origine fidei et ratione iustificationis.* Zwingli published a second work by him soon afterwards.

leave Silesia (1529). He betook himself to his adherents in South-west Germany—to Strasburg, where first Capito, and then M. Zell, welcomed him in their own house. But Schwenkfeld's aversion to the organised Church, his ideas as to the conventicle, his contempt for all "ceremonies," even the Sacraments, brought about at the Synod of Strasburg (June, 1533, which was devoted to the unifying of the ministers and taking up a position against the sectarians) a disputation with him, which here also shook his position. He left the town voluntarily. This was the beginning of a wandering life for him (Esslingen, Augsburg, Spires, Ulm). A conference at Tübingen (1535) with Bucer, Blaurer and Frecht[1] led to an agreement, in which toleration was promised him, in return for his pledge, not to attempt to destroy the Church. But when, at the instance of Frecht, the theological meeting at Schmalkalden publicly branded him (together with S. Franck) as heterodox owing to his doctrine of the flesh of Christ,[2] his wanderer's life changed into that of a fugitive. In 1543, he in vain endeavoured to approach Luther with a view to common hostility against the Swiss, but he bitterly repulsed the "fool possessed by the devil" (de Wette, V 613).[3] Attempts at approaching other evangelical leaders also proved unsuccessful. Notwithstanding, Schwenkfeld gathered together and edified his followers by indefatigable literary activity and contended with the most opposite theologians of both the Lutheran and Catholic churches, until a gentle death led him to peace at Ulm (1561).

His doctrine is a renewal of German mysticism under the influence of the formulas of reformatory doctrine and gives especial keenness to the Christological controversy in regard to the Eucharist. The tranquillity of the soul, faith as an inner feeling and communication of the nature of God to men, justification as an internal making-just (*Gerechtmachung*); then, the theory which reminds us of M. Hofmann (p. 93), that Christ's manhood does not proceed from the "creaturely" world, but is flesh sanctified by Mary's regeneration, hence capable of deification, but which now as divine cannot enter into any connection with the earthly elements of the Eucharist, are characteristic articles of his theology.[4]

His followers in Silesia (especially amongst the peasants) gathered together after his death (after 1570) in small congregations, which grew by union with the remnant of the Anabaptists after 1589. They maintained themselves in the

---

[1] Württemb. KGesch. Calw. 1893, p. 353.

[2] Here, on the evangelical side (the Wittenberg degree-oath, 1533 [p. 108] contains this same triad) the Apostles, Nicene and Athanasian Creeds were combined as the *symbola vere tradita in verbo Dei*. CR III 985. **Alexander Alensis,** *Summa theologiae*, pars III qu. 69, 2 and 5 already teaches: *tria sunt symbola, Apostolorum, Patrum* [*Nic.*], *Athanasii*.

[3] By distorting his name into *Stenkfeld* Luther forged for the controversialists a cheap and convenient weapon against him; cp., *e.g.*, B. SCHLÜSSELBERG, *Catalogus haereticorum* pars X.

[4] Cp. also RITSCHL, *Rechtfertigung*. I,[2] p. 318 f.

neighbourhood of Goldberg, until a Jesuit mission (1720) forced the majority of them to emigrate, first to Saxony, then to Holland, England and, lastly, America (Philadelphia). The small remnants which stayed behind, were guaranteed toleration by Frederick the Great, when Silesia became Prussian, but gradually died out. In the duchy of Prussia, where he had kept up a correspondence since 1525, Schwenkfeld gained an influential supporter in **Friedr. v. Heideck**,[1] by whom **Duke Albert** was temporarily estranged from Lutheranism. A number of Masovian clergy became Schwenkfeldians: **Speratus**, as Bishop of Pomesania, caused their leader, **Peter Zenker**, to be suspended by the Synod of Rastenburg (1531). Then the duke arranged a colloquy at Rastenburg, at which Schwenkfeld's Liegnitz friend, **Fab. Eckel**, argued with Speratus and Poliander in the name of the party (December, 1531). The Schwenkfeldians claimed the victory and Albert forbade the publication of the protocols desired by Speratus. Luther, like the Zürich theologians, now endeavoured at this critical period to gain influence over the duke. After four years of uncertainty, the collapse of the Münster Baptist kingdom caused Albert definitively to withdraw his protection from Spiritualism: Lutheranism was now able to confirm its authority.[2] In Wurtemberg, Duke Christopher adopted (1554) severer measures against the Schwenkfeldians: but here, as in the Rhenish Palatinate, it was just this persecution which brought about a firmer conventicle union of his adherents, traces of whom were still to be found in the 17th century.

A number of religious hymns also owed their origin to the Schwenkfeldians, some of which found their way into evangelical collections of hymns through the Constance and Strasburg hymn-books.[3]

---

[1] Cp. Tschackert's, "*Neudruck der Christlichen Ermahnung*" Heidecks. Königsb., 1892.

[2] Cp. Tschackert, *Urkundenb.* I 184 ff.; the same, *P. Speratus.* Halle, 1891, p. 50 ff.

[3] A. F. H. Schneider, *Zur Literatur der Schw.schen Liederdichter.* Berlin, 1857. Koch, *Geschichte des KLiedes,* [3]II 151 ff.

INDEX.

Abercromby, 346.
Acronius, 440.
Acta Sanctorum, 257.
Adelmann, 27.
Adolf, Count of Mörs, 314.
Adorantes, 453.
Adrian VI., 42, 168, 222.
Aepinus, 157.
Aerschot, Duke of, 320.
Agnes of Mansfeld, 371.
Agricola, John, 78, 84, 105, 155, 158, 279.
—— Stephen, 99.
Agrippa, Cornelius, 461.
d'Ailly, Peter, 9, 25, 83.
Ainsworth, 354.
Alane (Alesius), Alexander, 143, 337.
Alba, Duke, 153, 319, 326, 354, 370.
Albert V. of Bavaria, 366, 369, 371.
—— of Brandenburg, Margrave, 153, 160, 422.
—— of Mainz, Cardinal, 11, 36, 71, 80, 134, 136, 138.
—— of Mansfeld, 46, 72.
—— of Mecklenburg, 46, 138.
—— of Prussia, 46, 72, 76, 138, 282, 434, 465.
Alberus, Erasmus, 59, 157, 361.
—— Matthew, 83.
d'Albret, Jeanne, 193, 326.
Alcantara, Petrus of, 269.
Alciati, 451.
Aleander, Jerome, 28, 33.
Alexander VI., 273, VIII, 251.
—— Alensis (schoolman), 464.
—— of Parma, 320.
Allegri, Vitt., 249.
Allen, W., 334.
Altemps, Cardinal, 241.
Althamer, A., 445, 459.
Altieri, Balthasar, 225.
Alumbrados, The, 269.
Ambach, M., 424.
Amling, Wolfgang, 306.

Amsdorf, N., 10, 35, 46, 124, 147, 157, 280, 295, 385.
Amyraldus, Moses, 415.
Anabaptists, 36, 64, 88 ff., 125 ff., 197, 206, 216, 227, 433, 437 ff. 445, 451, 454.
Andreä, James, 286, 289, 292 ff., 301, 303, 324, 367, 372, 387, 399, 406, 408.
—— Joh. Val., 406.
—— Laurent. 168.
Anjou, Duke of (Alençon), 327
Anne of Cleves, 206.
—— of Denmark, 346.
Anti-Trinitarians, 444 ff.
Antony of Bourbon (Navarre) 193.
Apologia, The, 113.
Aquaviva, 231, 264.
Aquila, Casp., 105.
Arcimboldi, 11.
Aresen, 167.
Aristotle, 10, 20, 401.
Arminianism, 322, 347, 349, 410.
Arminius, J., 411.
Arndt, J., 306, 406.
Arran, Count of (J. Hamilton) 338.
Arthur of England, 200.
Articles, the twelve, of the peasantry, 67.
Attritio, 12, 245, 259, 267.
Augustus, Elector, 148, 284, 287, 290, 297, 372.
Augusta, John, 433.
Augustine, Augustinianism, 39, 258, 370, 415.
Autos de fé, 317.

Bajus, M., 258.
Bancroft, R., 335, 348.
Ban (excommunication), 26, 130, 179, 182, 203, 302, 333, 383, 439, 459.
Barbiano, 362.
Barnabites, 229.

Barnim of Pomerania, 123.
Baron, Peter, 335.
Baronius, Caes, 257, 271.
Bartholomew, Massacre of Saint, 251, 323 ff.
Bassi, Matteo de, 229.
Basta, 362.
Bathóry, 362.
Battenburg, 128.
Baworinsky, Bened., 433.
Beaton, David, 338.
—— J., 338.
Becanus, Mart., 263.
Beier, Chancellor, 104.
Bellarmine, R., 248, 256, 259, 263, 327.
Bellay, Du, 192.
Benedetto de Mantova, 222.
Bergen, book of, 293.
Bergius, 418.
Bernard, St., 9.
Bernières, Jean de, 269.
Bertano, 244.
Berthelier, Ph., 173.
Bérulle, Cardinal, 271.
Beuckelssen, Jan (John of Leyden), 127.
Beza, Th., 175, 177, 185, 187, 193, 195, 213, 323, 398, 402, 408, 409, 412, 450.
Bible, translations of: Bohemian, 436; Croatio-Illyrian, 217; Danish, 165; Dutch,413; English, 201, 205; French, 177; German, 34, 92; Hungarian, 215; Italian, 221; Spanish, 316; Swedish, 169; Wendish, 217.
Bidembach, 292.
Biel, 9.
Billik, 152.
Bisch, Rauf, 441.
Blahoslaw, 434.
Blandrata, G., 213, 451.
Blarer (Blaurer), Ambr., 45, 82, 122, 397, 437, 445, 464.

Blarer (Blaurer), Th., 93.
Blaurock, 65, 90.
Blondel, D., 409.
Bobadilla, 230.
Bocskai, 362.
Bodin, Jean, 426.
Boehme, James, 405.
Bogermann, 412.
Boleyn, Anne, 200 ff.
Bolland, John, 257.
Bolsec, Jerome, 182, 184.
Bomelius, Henry, (Bommel), 196, 313.
Bomhover (Bomhauer), 12, 43.
Bonner, 206, 208, 210, 330.
Bonnus, Herman, 130, 395.
Book of Discipline, 341, 344.
—— of Sports, 347.
Boquin, 301 ff.
Bora, Catherine von, 69.
Borja, Francis, 232.
Borromeo, Carlo, 189, 250.
Bosio, A., 257.
Bothwell, J., 343.
Boucher, 328.
Bownd, N., 347.
Boye, Nic., 395.
Boyneburg, 205.
Brederode, 319.
Breitinger, 35.
Brenz, J., 46, 69, 75, 81, 84, 95, 99, 122, 124, 152, 158, 282, 301, 324, 333, 361, 387, 403.
Bres, Guido de, 198.
Bresnitzer, 269.
Brethren of Charity, 271.
—— Bohemian, 46, 90, 213, 431.
Breviarium Romanum, 248.
Briçonnet, 172.
Brismann, 46, 138.
Browne, G., 336.
Browne, Robert, 354.
Brownists, 354.
Brucioli, 221.
Brück, 105, 279.
—— the Younger, 288.
Brunsfels, O., 59.
Bucer, 45, 82, 85, 99, 109, 112, 116, 124, 134, 140, 144, 148, 151, 155, 172, 176, 184, 192, 209, 278, 312, 331, 394, 428, 438, 440, 464.
Buchanan, 339.
Buchholzer, 137.
Buckingham, 349.
Bünderlin, 461.
Büren, Daniel von, 287.
Bugenhagen, 35, 77, 80, 84, 93, 104, 123, 131, 133, 158, 166, 393.

Bulls: Exsurge Domine 1520, 26; Decet Romanum pontificem 1521, 29; Non opus esse credimus 1526, 70; Regimini militantis 1540, 231; Licet ab initio 1542, 223; Laetare Hierusalem 1514 150; Cum ex apostolatus officio 1559, 250; In sacrosancta and Iniunctum nobis 1564, 247; Ex omnibus afflictionibus 1567, 258; Provisionis nostrae 1579, 258; Inter gravissimas 1582, 251; In coena Domini 1627, 254; In eminenti 1642, 260; Zelo domus Dei 1648, 379.
Bullinger, 117, 171, 184, 187, 195, 209, 216, 301, 334, 339, 396, 429, 450.
Buscoducensis, Nic., 312.
Busenbaum, 265.
Buxtorf, John, 409.

Cahera, Gallus, 431.
Cajetan, 15, 71, 255.
Calendar, Revision of the, 251.
Calini, 247.
Calixtus, G., 362, 404, 416 ff.
—— U. F., 420.
Calov, Abr., 362, 420.
Calvin, John, 140, 171-187, 192 ff., 198, 209 ff., 221, 276, 281, 288, 300 ff., 324, 332, 339, 355, 356, 361, 387 ff., 398, 409, 447 ff., 450.
Calvisius, Seth., 395.
Camaldolites, 228.
Camerarius, 369, 403, 447.
Campanella, Th., 274.
Campanus, John, 445.
Campeggi, 43 ff., 106, 109 ff., 140, 201 ff., 214, 223.
Campell, Ulr., 188.
Canisius, Peter, 233, 300, 358, 367, 370, 372, 435.
Canus, Melchior, 232, 240, 256.
Capito, 46, 57, 82, 92, 109, 124, 140, 172, 446, 464.
Capuchins, 229.
Caraccioli, Galeazzo, 224.
—— nuncio, 28.
Caraffa, see Paul IV.
—— Carlo, 376.
Carlos, Don, 343.
Carlowitz, Christ. von, 155.
Carlstadt, 10, 17 ff., 27-35, 61, 84, 87, 164, 391, 396, 463.

Carnesecchi, P., 226.
Carpzov, J. B., 426.
Carranza, Barth., 317, 331.
Cartwright, Th., 335, 354.
Casale, 201.
Casas, Bart. de las, 273.
Caselius, Joh., 419.
Casimir of Brandenburg-Ansbach, 77.
Cassander, George, 358, 368, 416.
Cassiodoro de Reina, 316.
Castellio, Seb., 182, 450.
Catechismus Romanus, 247.
Catharine of Aragon, 200 ff.
—— of Medici, 192, 323, 338.
—— of Sweden, 358.
Cazalla, Augustin, 317.
Celtes, 50.
Cerri, 274.
Cervino, 238.
Chamier, Daniel, 410.
Chandieu, Ant. de, 194.
Chantal, Madame de, 269.
Charles V., 23 ff., 27, 29 ff., 38, 41 ff., 70 ff., 73, 95 ff., 103 ff., 106 ff., 115 ff., 123, 131 ff., 137, 140, 142, 146, 149, 158, 165, 169, 177, 191, 193, 196, 200, 207, 214, 221, 238 ff., 312, 316, 365.
—— of Baden, 292.
—— I. of England, 348, 357.
—— IX. of France, 323 ff.
—— of Guelders, 118, 149, 195.
—— of Savoy, 173.
—— IX. of Sweden, 358 ff.
—— Archduke, 217, 343, 369.
Chatel, 264.
Chemnitz, Mart., 281, 289, 292, 366, 402.
Chieregati, 41 ff.
Christian I. of Denmark, 164.
—— II. of Denmark, 136, 164 ff., 168.
—— III. of Denmark, 166 ff.
—— I., Elector of Saxony, 297.
—— II., Elector of Saxony, 297.
Christopher of Mecklenburg, 366.
—— of Wurtemberg, 122, 185, 226, 285, 289, 301, 324, 465.
Chrysostom, 257.
Church Constitution, 382 ff.
—— Hymns, 394, 436, 442, 465.
—— Music, 249, 496.
Chytraeus, D., 281, 285, 292, 369, 402.

INDEX

Cisnero, Garcia, 230.
Clarenbach, Ad., 121.
Clement, of Alexandria, 448.
—— VII., 43 ff., 59, 70, 97, 103 ff., 111, 115, 119, 131, 154, 168, 175, 192, 197, 201, 221, 225.
—— VIII., 233, 248, 252, 259, 328, 346.
—— XIV., 231.
Clément, Jacques, 327.
Clericus, 415.
Clichtoveus, 58.
Cochl(a)eus, Joh., 31, 33, 58, 68, 110, 114, 123, 140, 148, 152.
Codde, van der, 414.
Coelestinus, 288.
Colet, John, 200.
Coligny, Francis de, 193.
—— Gaspard de, 193, 324.
Collegiants, 414.
Collegium Germanicum, 233.
—— Romanum, 233.
Colonna, Vittoria, 225, 229.
Comander, 188.
Comenius, Amos, 406, 435.
Commendone, 241, 369.
Common Prayer book, 208.
Concord, Swabian, 292; Swabio - Saxon, 292; Wittenberg, 124, 307; Wurtemberg, 122.
Condé, Louis, 193, 324, 327.
Confession of Augsburg, 104.
—— Variata, 140, 278, 285, 301, 305, 307, 310, 378.
—— Bâle, 125.
—— Belgica, 198, 313.
—— Bohemica, 435.
—— Csengerina, 216.
—— Gallica, 194, 313.
—— Helvetica I., 125.
—— —— posterior, 187, 216.
—— Montana, 216.
—— Pentapolitana, 216.
—— Remonstrantium, 414
—— Saxonica, 158.
—— Scoticana, 341.
—— —— posterior, 344.
—— Sigismundi, 310.
—— Wesaliensis, 312.
—— Wirtembergensis, 158.
Confirmation, 394.
Confutatio, 110, 113.
Congregatio de auxiliis gratiae, 259.
Congregationalism, 354.
Conring, H., 420.
Consensus Dresdensis, 290.
—— ministerii Bremensis ecclesiae, 306.
—— pastorum Genevensis ecclesiae, 185.

Consensus of Sendomir, 361.
—— Tigurinus, 184, 281.
Consistories, 385.
Consul, Steph., 217.
Contarini, G., 140 ff., 221, 223.
Convention of Cassel, 294; Frankfort, 243; Lichtenburg, 292; Quedlinburg, 294; Schmalkalden, 293; Torgau, 292; Zerbst, 290.
Coolhaes, C., 411.
Coornhert, D. V., 410.
Cop, Nic., 175.
Copernicus, 253.
Cordatus, Conrad, 279.
Cordier, Maturin, 174.
Corpus Julium, 287, 296.
—— Misnicum seu Philippicum, 287, 311.
—— Wilhelminum, 287.
Corvinus, Ant., 138.
Cosimo II. of Florence, 226.
Cotta, Ursula, 8.
Council of Mantua, 131; Vicenza, 135; Trent, 133, 150, 158, 237 ff.; Bologna, 154, 239.
Counter-Remonstrants, 411.
Couraud, 180.
Covenant, 340, 344, 350, 352.
Coverdale, 200, 205, 209.
Cowell, 348.
Cracow, 291.
Craig, J., 343.
Cramer, John, 402.
Cranmer, Thomas, 202, 205 ff., 331, 336.
Crato von Crafftheim, 291.
Crell, John, 455.
Crescentio, Cardinal, 240.
Cromwell, Oliver, 357.
—— Thomas, 205.
Cronberg, Hartmuth von, 45.
Crotus Rubianus, 21, 61.
Cruciger, 99, 139, 155, 158, 279.
—— the younger, 291.
Crypto-Calvinism, 287, 291, 296, 307.
Curcellaeus, 415.
Cureus, John, 291.
Curio, Coelius Secundus, 225.
Custodia utriusque tabulae, 386.

Dalmatin, 217.
Darley (Darnley), 343.
Dathenus, Peter, 313, 441.
David (Davidis), Francis, 453.
Dax, Leonh., 440.
Delfino, 241.
Delrio, 92.
Denk, 35, 92, 461.
Dernbach, Balth. von, 371.
De tribus impostoribus, 454.

Dévay, Matth. Biró, 215.
Devotional literature, 426.
Diana of Poitiers, 192.
Diaz, John, 152, 316.
Diepold, 46.
Diet of Augsburg (1518), 15; (1525), 72; (1530), 102; (1547), 154; (1555), 161; (1566), 187.
—— of Copenhagen (1530), 165.
—— of Nuremberg (spring, 1522), 41; (autumn, 1522), 41; (1524), 42.
—— of Odensee (1527), 165.
—— of Petrikau (1526), 213; (1555), 213.
—— of Ratisbon (1532), 119; (1541), 140, 146; (1546), 152; (1556 - 57), 367; (1608), 373.
—— of Spires (1526), 73; (1529), 97; (1542), 146; (1544), 150.
—— of Strengness (1523), 168.
—— of Worms (1521), 29; (1545), 151.
Dietenberger, 34, 58, 255.
Dieu, Louis de, 409.
Disputation of Bâle, 57; Berne, 82; Leipzig, 17.
Divine Service, 391.
Divorce, 384.
Dominis, M. Ant. de, 416.
Dortmund, Agreement of, 374.
Drusius, 409.
Dryander, see Enzinas.
Dudley, Lord, see Leicester.
Dürer, 33.
Dungersheim, 94.
Duns Scotus, 268.
Duperron, 262.
Duplessis-Mornay, 329.
Dupuy, 262.
Duraeus (Dury), Joh., 418.
Duvergier, 260.

Eber, P., 158.
Eberlin of Günzberg, 45.
Eccard, Joh., 396.
Eccius dedolatus, 20.
Ecclesiastical architecture, 400.
Eck, Joh., 15, 17 ff., 26 ff., 58, 81, 91, 105, 110, 114, 140, 255.
—— Joh. von, 30.
Eckel, Fab., 465.
Eder, G., 373.
Edict of Nantes, 326.
—— of Nîmes, 329.
Edinburgh Agreement, 340.
Edward VI., 207 ff., 224, 330, 336, 338, 450.

Egmont, 319.
Egranus, Joh. Silv., 27.
Ehem, Chancellor, 303.
Einarsen, Gisser, 167.
Eisengrein, 369.
Eitzen, Paul von, 295.
Elevation, 392.
Eliä, Paul, 164.
Elizabeth, Queen of England, 201, 203, 207, 264, 267, 331 ff., 336, 340, 345, 346, 443.
—— Queen of Spain, 326.
—— Electress of Brandenburg, 136.
—— of Calenberg, 138.
—— of Rochlitz, 136, 144.
Emmius, Ubbo, 129.
Emser, Jerome, 19, 34, 58, 255.
Engelbrechtson, Oluf, 167.
English Nuns, 236.
Ennius, 54.
Enzinas, Franc. (Dryander), 209, 316.
Episcopalianism, 348, 383 ff.
Episcopius, Sim., 411.
Epistolae virorum obscurorum, 10, 21.
Erasmus, 10, 21, 28, 33, 51, 58, 79, 86, 91, 196, 200, 208, 255, 316, 360, 415, 432, 459, 461.
Erastianism, 322, 352.
Erastus, 302, 322, 426.
Ercole d'Este, 177, 221.
Eric XIV., 358.
—— of Brunswick, 72, 134, 136.
—— the Younger, 138, 153, 320.
Ernest of Bavaria, 372.
—— of Brandenburg, 310.
—— of Brunswick, 72, 98, 106.
—— of Gotha, 381.
—— Frederick of Baden, 307.
Erskine, Lord, 340.
Escobar, 265.
Essen, John of, 46, 197.
Esterhazy, 363.
Estius, W., 257.
Etcetera-oath, 350.
Eucharist, 62, 83, 99, 124, 172, 176, 184, 209, 245, 278, 283, 304, 333, 392, 397, 449, 463.
Exercitia spiritualia, 230, 234.
Exorcism, 297, 306, 312.

Faber (Fabri), Joh., 54, 58, 64, 68, 79, 81, 110, 114, 215, 463.
—— —— Peter, 230, 233.
—— —— Stapulensis, 172, 175, 190, 360.

Fagius, 209, 331.
Family of Love, 442.
Farel, W., 57, 82, 173, 177, 184, 191, 360, 398, 429.
Farnese, Alexander, see Paul III.
—— Paul III.'s grandson, 151.
Feldkirchen, 27.
Ferdinand the Catholic, 229, 315.
—— I., 41, 44, 67, 74, 92, 97, 99, 103, 115, 117, 134, 136, 139, 146, 150, 153, 155, 159 ff., 214, 225, 241, 247, 365, 370, 376, 433, 439, 463.
—— II., 217, 363, 372.
—— III., 363.
Festivals, 393.
Feuerborn, 408.
Filliucius, 265.
Fink, 309.
Fisher, John, 58, 85, 204.
Flacius Illyricus, 158, 257, 280, 286, 288.
Flaminio, Marcant., 222.
Flemings, 439.
Flemming, P., 395.
Fleisteden, P., 121.
Fonzio, Bart., 221.
Forge, de la, 176.
Formula of Concord, 289 ff.
Foscarari, 247.
Fox, 205.
Francis I., 23, 29, 70, 135, 146, 150, 160, 175, 177, 190, 226, 398, 429.
—— II., 193, 194, 323, 341.
—— II. of Brunswick, 72, 106.
—— II. of Waldeck, 127, 148.
Franck, Seb., 458, 464.
Frankfort, Truce of, 131.
—— Recess of, 283, 286.
Frecht, M., 156, 459, 464.
Freder, Joh., 395.
Frederick I. of Denmark, 73, 93, 165, 168.
—— II. of Denmark, 296.
—— III. of Holstein, 414.
—— II. of the Palatinate, 140, 150, 155, 285.
—— III. of the Palatinate, 187, 285, 300, 304, 313, 369, 387, 440.
—— IV. of the Palatinate, 303, 309, 374.
—— V. of the Palatinate, 510, 375, 435.
—— II. of Liegnitz, 463.
—— the Great, 465.
—— the Wise, 15, 20, 24, 26, 32, 37, 41, 46, 62, 67, 77, 164.
—— Duke of Saxony, 136, 297.

Frederick, Margrave of Brandenburg, 158.
—— Archbishop of Bremen, 306.
—— Henry of Orange, 414.
—— William, great Elector, 361, 381.
Frith, J., 200, 204.
Froment, A., 173.
Fürstenberg, Th., 372.
Fuggers, 11.
Funck, 282.
Furcíro, 247.

Gábor, Bethlen, 363.
Galileo, 253.
Galle, Peter, 169.
Gallicanism, 260 ff.
Galicius, Ph., 188.
Gallus, Nic., 146, 158.
Gardiner, 205, 210, 331.
Garnet, 346.
Gedicke, 310.
Gentile, 451.
George of Anhalt, 143, 143, 148.
—— of Brandenburg, 46, 98, 101, 106, 116, 142, 433.
—— Archbishop of Bremen, 286.
—— of Pomerania, 123.
—— of Saxony, 19, 37, 41, 68, 71, 96, 123, 134, 144.
—— Ernest of Henneberg, 292.
—— Frederick of Baden, 303.
—— William of Brandenburg, 309.
Gerbel, Nic., 99.
Gerhard, Joh., 257, 386, 402, 407, 410, 426.
—— Paul, 380.
Gericius, 362.
Gerson, 9.
Ghent, Agreement of, 320.
Ghislieri, see Pius V.
Giberti, 220.
Gil, Juan, 316.
Giustiniani, Paul, 229.
Glanaeus, Jodocus, 305.
Glapion, 30.
Glareanus, 51.
Glassius, Sal., 403.
Goltwurm, Casp., 304.
Gomarus, Fr., 410, 412, 515.
Gonesius, P., 452.
Gonzaga, Card., 241.
—— Giulia, 221.
Gorka, 213.
Gothus, Laur. P., 358.
Goudimel, Cl., 398.
Granvella, 140 ff.
—— Ant. Per., 318, 343.

INDEX 471

Graumann, see Poliander.
Gray (Grey), Jane, 330.
Grebel, Conr., 55, 64, 90.
Gregory XIII., 251, 258, 260, 317, 326, 334, 370.
— XIV., 248, 252.
— XV., 253, 274, 416.
Gretser, 373, 402.
Gribaldo, 451.
Grimani, Marino, 252.
Grimmelshausen, 380.
Grocyn, William, 200.
Gropper, John, 140, 148.
Grotius, Hugo, 409, 412, 415, 457.
Gruët, Jac., 182.
Grumbach, Argula of, 45.
— W. von, 288.
Grunthler, 225.
Grynaeus, Sim., 176, 180, 215, 303.
Güttel, 45.
Gueux, 319.
Guignard, 264.
Guise, Claude of, 193.
— Francis of, 193, 195, 324.
— Henry of, 327.
— Charles of, 193, 195, 324, 326, 327.
— Mary, 193, 338.
Gunnila, 359.
Gunpowder Plot, 264, 346.
Gustavus Adolphus, 359, 377.
— Vasa, 73, 93, 164, 168, 358.

Hafenreffer, 409.
Hales, John, 347.
Hall, Joseph, 349.
Haller, Bert., 56, 82, 186.
Hamel, 258
Hamilton, Archbishop, 338.
— P., 337.
Hans of Denmark, 164.
— von Küstrin, see John, Margrave.
Hardenberg, A. R., 186, 281, 286.
Hassler, H. L., 396.
Hausmann, Nic., 77, 123.
Hedio, 46, 57, 99.
Hedwig of Poland, 212.
Heermann, Joh., 395.
Heideck, Frederick of, 465.
Heidelberg Catechism, 301, 306, 308, 313, 314.
Heilbrunner, 373.
Heitfeld, 314.
Held, 133 ff.
Helding, Mich., 155.
Helmbold, L., 395.
Henry of Bouillon, 329.

Henry of Brunswick, 72, 134, 136, 147, 151, 366.
— VIII. of England, 58, 70, 83, 144, 199 ff., 208, 211, 330, 332, 337.
— II. of France, 158, 186, 192.
— III., 262, 264, 325.
— IV., 194, 252, 261, 264, 298, 327, 349.
— II. of Mecklenburg, 46, 72, 138.
— II. of Navarre, 191.
— of Saxony, 136, 279.
— Julius of Brunswick, 296.
Herberger, V., 395.
Herborn, general synod of, 305.
Herdessianus, Chr., 296.
Heresbach, Conrad of, 120, 148, 311.
Hermann, Nic., 395.
— Count of Mörs, 314.
— von Wied, 147, 153, 385.
Hervát, Jos., 215.
Hess, John, 84, 463.
Hesshus(en), T., 185, 285, 288, 291, 292, 296, 301, 313, 384.
Hetzer, 35, 55, 92, 100, 445.
Heusenstamm, Seb. von, 150.
Hildebrand, Joachim, 420.
Hocker, Jod., 425.
Hoë of Hoënegg, 376, 409, 417.
Hoen (Honius), C. H., 83, 197.
Höpfner, 409.
Hoffmeister, John, 152.
Hofmann, D., 419.
— M., 93, 126, 166, 169, 197, 464.
Honter, 214.
Hoogstraten, 26.
Hooker, R., 348.
Hooper, Joh., 209, 334.
Horn, Count, 319.
Horn (Roh.), Joh., 433, 436.
Hornejus, Conr., 420.
Hosius, Stan., 241, 300, 358, 453.
Hospinianus, 309, 409.
l'Hospital, 195, 324.
Hotman, Fr., 326.
Hovesch, Nic. (Decius), 395.
Howard, Cath., 206.
Huber, Sam., 408.
Hubmaier, 64, 90, 91.
Hülsemann, 362, 399, 420.
Huguenots, 193.
Hulst, Fr. von der, 197.
Hunnius, Aeg., 298, 308, 373, 402, 408.

Hunnius, Nic., 418.
Huss, 19, 31, 431.
Hussites, 91, 212.
Huter, Jac., 439.
Hutt, Hans, 93.
Hutten, Ulrich von, 22, 38, 59.
Hütter, Leon., 402, 418, 422.
Hyperius, A., 307, 368, 399.

Images, 36, 55, 63, 319, 349, 392, 396.
Independency, 354.
Index librorum prohibitorum, 247, 286, 317.
Indulgences, 11.
Innocent IX., 252.
— X., 254, 265, 379.
— XI., 274.
Inquisition, 223, 317, 319.
Interdict, 204, 252.
Interim, of Augsburg, 155.
— of Leipzig, 157, 280.
— of Ratisbon, 140.
Irenaeus, Chr., 288, 297.
Isabella of Transylvania, 215.
— of Spain, 315.
Isenburg, Salentin von, 371.
Ius episcopale, 386.

Jablonski, D. E., 436.
— Peter, 436.
Jäger, John, see Crotus Rubianus.
Jagow, Matth. von, 136.
James V., 337.
James VI. (I.), 264, 339, 343, 350, 354.
— of Baden - Hachberg, 307, 372.
Jansen, Corn., 259.
Jerome, 10, 255.
— of Prague, 431.
Jesuits, Order of, 3, 218, 232, 246, 257, 263, 274, 359, 363, 370, 375.
Jesuits, female, 236.
Joachim I., 11, 24, 32, 71, 136.
— II., 135, 140, 143, 147, 150, 158, 281.
— Ernest of Anhalt, 292, 306.
— Frederick of Brandenburg, 309, 366.
John the Steadfast, 46, 68, 72, 77, 95, 101, 104, 111, 118, 446.
— III. of Jülich - Cleve, 120, 148, 311.
— of Brandenburg (Hans von Küstrin), 137, 153, 156.
— of Anhalt, 143.

John, son of George of Saxony, 136.
—— —— of Frederick I. of Denmark, 166.
—— III. of Sweden, 358.
—— VI. of Nassau-Dillenburg, 304.
—— Casimir, 293, 297, 302, 306, 372.
—— Christian of Brieg, 311.
—— Frederick of Saxony, 77, 106, 120, 122, 132, 136, 141, 146, 150, 157, 192.
—— der Mittlere, 284, 288, 394, 425.
—— of Wurtemberg, 374.
—— George I. of Anhalt, 306.
—— —— of Brandenburg, 309.
—— George of Saxony, 409.
—— Sigismund of Brandenburg, 309, 374, 390.
—— —— of Transylvania, 215.
—— William of Saxony, 288, 291.
—— Ciudad, 271.
Johnson, Francis, 354.
Jonas, Justus, 35, 60, 99, 104, 138, 209, 463.
Joris, Joh. Dav., 128, 197, 442.
Juan de la Cruz, 269, 271.
Jud, Leo, 35, 53, 55, 396.
Julius II, 11, 201.
—— III., 158, 240.
—— of Brunswick, 289, 292, 296, 366.
Junius, Francis, 303, 319, 409, 417.

Kaiser, 82.
Käser, L., 94.
Kautz, 93.
Κένωσις, 408.
Kessler, Joh., 57.
Kettenbach, Joh., 45.
Khaireddin Barbarossa, 131.
Khlobner, 217.
Kirchner, 288, 297.
Kiszka, Joh., 453.
Klebitz, W., 285.
Knipperdolling, 127.
Knöpken, A., 46, 395.
Knothe, 212.
Knox, J., 209, 331, 339, 347.
Knudson, 164.
Körner (Cornerus), Christ., 292.
Kolb, Fr., 82.
Kraliz Bible, 436.
Krautwald, Val, 463.

Krell, Nic., 297 ff.
Κρύψις, 409.
Krzycki, 212.
Kunz, 179.

Lainez, Diego, 230, 240, 258, 324.
Lambert, Francis, of Avignon, 45, 79, 106, 337, 425.
—— preacher, 206.
Landenberg, Hugo von, 51.
Lang, John, 45.
Languet, H., 326.
Lapide, Cornelius a, 258.
Lasco, John a (de), 184, 209, 210, 213, 360, 390.
Lassus, Orl., 249.
Latimer, Bishop, 205, 208, 331.
—— Lord, 207.
Latitudinarianism, 347, 418.
Latomus, 34, 196.
Laud, W., 349 ff.
Lavater, 397.
Laymann, 265.
Lazarists, 271.
Le Gras, 272.
Leicester (Dudley), 343.
Lemoine, 267.
Leo X., 11, 14, 24, 26 ff., 29, 42, 191, 220.
Leon, Luis de, 269, 317.
Leopold, William, 377.
Less, 258, 265.
Leszinsky, Counts, 435.
Leyden, John of, see Beuckelssen.
Leyser, Polyc., 293, 297, 399, 417.
Lichtenstein, Leon. von, 88.
Liga, League, 70, 327, 374.
Lindener, Mich., 422.
Link, 36, 45.
Lip(p)omani, 240, 360.
Lobwasser, A., 398.
Loists, 197.
Loos, Corn., 426.
Lopez, Gregory, 269.
Lotzer, Seb., 67.
Louis XII. of France, 177.
—— XIII. ,, 329.
—— XIV. ,, 260, 381.
—— IV. of Hesse, 303, 308.
—— V. ,, 308.
—— V. of the Palatinate, 135.
—— VI. ,, ,, 293, 302.
—— II. of Hungary, 74, 214.
—— of Wurtemberg, 292, 303.
Loyola, Ignatius, 223, 228 ff., 253, 258.
Lübbert, 412.
Luke of Prague, 432.
Luther, Hans, 7.
—— Margaret, 7.

Luther, Martin, 1-152 passim, 164, 168, 171, 184, 190, 194, 195, 200, 202, 209, 212, 217, 220, 223, 225, 255, 276, 290, 295, 299, 303, 308, 316, 356, 359, 368, 382, 391, 399, 401 ff., 421, 431, 438, 442, 449, 459, 463.

Maccovius, 410, 415.
Magni, Joh., 168.
—— Peter, 170.
Magnus, Duke of Mecklenburg, 138.
Maidalchini, Olympia, 254.
Maistre, Le, 261.
Major, G., 152, 155, 158, 280, 295
Malaval, Fr., 269.
Maldonatus, 257.
Malebranche, 271.
Malvenda, 152, 155.
Manuel, Nic., 56.
Manz, Fel., 64, 90, 94.
Marbach, Joh., 185, 303.
Marburg Articles, 100, 105.
Maresius, 415.
Margaret of Denmark, 163.
—— of Navarre, 175, 177, 191.
—— of Parma, 318.
—— of Savoy, 197.
—— of Valois, 325.
Mariana, 233, 264.
Marini, 247.
Marnix, Phil. von, 319.
Marot, Cl., 398.
Marsilius, 1.
Martin, Waldensian, 428.
Martini, Corn., 419.
Martyr, Petr. (Pietro Martire), 185, 209, 222, 224, 281, 323.
Mary of Bavaria, 372.
—— the Catholic, of England, 185, 198, 200, 207, 210, 312, 330, 336, 339, 360.
—— of Medici, 262.
—— Stuart of Scotland, 193, 194, 332, 334, 338.
—— of Hungary, 197, 214.
Massillon, 271.
Masson, P., 428.
Mathys, Jan, 126.
Matthews (Rogers), 205.
Matthias (Emperor), 362, 374.
Maulbronn, Formula of, 292.
Maurice, Elector, 143, 147, 150, 155, 159, 240, 287.
—— Landgrave, 308, 385.
—— of Orange, 321, 412, 414.
Maximilian I., 23.
—— II., 159, 241, 243, 247, 288, 366, 368, 372, 434.

INDEX

Maximilian I., of Bavaria, 373.
Mayenne, Duke of, 326.
Mayor, John, 339.
Medina, Barth. de, 266.
Megander, 179.
Melanchthon, 20, 25, 37, 60, 69, 79, 95, 98, 104, 110, 112, 124, 133, 137, 139, 145, 148, 151, 155, 158, 171, 180, 185, 192, 202, 205, 209, 213, 216, 221, 225, 255, 264, 276 ff., 291, 295, 300, 304, 312, 316, 367, 371, 383, 399, 401, 419, 424, 438, 441, 447, 451, 459, 463.
Melander, Dion, 145.
Meldenius, R., 418.
Melville, A., 344, 347.
Mendoza, Cardinal, 315.
Mening, 305.
Menius, Just., 99, 124, 280, 393.
Mennonites, 129, 455.
Mentzer, 408.
Merula, G., 393.
Mespelbrunn, Jul. Echter von, 372.
Meyer, Joh., of Knonau, 53.
—— Mark, 130, 166.
—— Seb., 54, 56.
Meyfart, J. M., 395, 407, 418.
Michelsen, 165.
Micronius, 210, 440.
Mill, W., 340.
Miltitz, K. von, 17, 26.
Milton, 355.
Mirus, 297.
Missale, 248.
Missions, Catholic, 273.
Mörlin, Joach., 280.
—— Maxim., 304.
Molina, Louis, 259.
Monheim, Joh., 311.
Monita privata (secreta), 233.
Montague, R., 348.
Monte del, Cardinal, see Julius III.
Montmorency, 192.
Morata, Olympia, 225.
More, Thomas, 200, 202.
Morel, Fr. de, 194.
—— G., 428.
Morone, Giov. de, 221.
Mosellanus, 11.
Münzer, Th., 36, 62, 88, 93.
Muret(us), 324.
Murner, Th., 58, 81.
Murray, James Stuart, 340, 343.
Musaeus, Sim., 280.
Musculus, Andr., 280, 290, 293.
—— W., 124.

Mutianus, Conr., 8, 61.
Myconius, Fr., 45, 99, 124, 205.
—— Oswald, 51, 125, 172.
Mylius, 298.
Myritsch, Melch., 197.

Nádasdy, 215.
Nas, Joh., 371.
Naumburg Diet of princes, 241, 284, 301, 368.
Nausea, 432.
Neri, Philip, 235, 271.
Neuser, 302.
Niclaes, Henry, 442.
Nicolai, Phil, 395.
Nigrinus, Barth., 361.
Nobili, Rob., 274.
Non-adorantes, 453.
Norfolk, Duke of, 205.
Northumberland, Duke of (Warwick), 211, 330.
Noviomagus (Eob. Geldenhauer), 304.
Nuremberg, Truce of, 119.
—— "standard" books, 261.

Oath of allegiance, 264, 346.
Occam, 9, 25.
Ochino, 209, 222, 224, 452.
Oecolampadius, 27, 45, 57, 81, 83 ff., 92, 98, 117, 125, 172, 177, 278, 360, 428, 446, 463.
Oldenbarneveld, 322, 411.
Oldendorp, Joh., 130.
Olevianus, Casp., 301, 305.
Olevitanus, Rob., 175, 177.
Opitz, M., 395.
Oratorians, 271.
Oratory of Divine Love, 220.
Ordination, 383, 393.
Organ, 396.
Origen, 39, 448.
Osiander, Andr., 46, 48, 92, 95, 99, 124, 147, 205, 217, 282, 445.
—— Luke, 292, 294, 303, 373, 396, 403.
—— —— the younger, 409.
Ostorodt, 454.
Ostrorog, 213.
Osuna, Francis of, 269.
Otho, Ant., 280.
Otto Henry, 123, 147, 185, 285, 440.

Pack, Otto von, 96.
Pacta conventa, 361.
Pagi, Ant., 257.
Paleario, Aonio, 222, 225.
Palestrina, 249, 398.
Palladius, P., 167.
Pancratius, A., 399.

Pappus, Joh., 296.
Paracelsus, 405.
Paraguay, Jesuit missions in, 274.
Pareus, Dav., 303, 417.
Parker, Matthew, 201, 333.
Parliament, short, 350.
—— long, 351, 356.
Parr, Catharine, 207.
Passau, Treaty of, 160.
Paul III., 131, 135, 142, 144, 149 ff, 158, 222, 225, 230, 232, 238, 273.
—— IV. (Caraffa), 162, 193, 222, 226, 240, 249, 317, 332, 360, 365, 367, 370.
—— V., 252, 265, 346, 362.
Pauli, Greg., 452.
Paul of Samosata, 447.
Pax dissidentium, 361.
Pázmány, Peter, 363.
Peace of Amboise, 324.
—— of Barcelona, 103
—— of Boulogne, 326.
—— of Cambray, 103.
—— of Cappel, 117.
—— of Cavour, 430.
—— of Crespy, 150.
—— of St. Germain, 325.
—— of Kaaden, 122.
—— of Linz, 363.
—— of Longjumeau, 325.
—— of Madrid, 70.
—— of Montpellier, 329.
—— of Nicolsburg, 363.
—— of Prague, 377.
—— of Vienna, 362.
—— of Westphalia, 377.
Pelargus, Chr., 310.
Pellican(us), Conr., 51, 57.
Perez, Juan, 316.
Pericope, 393, 399.
Perrin, Ami, 183.
Pescara, 70.
Petavius, Dion., 257.
Peter of Cologne, 440.
Petersen, 165
Peterson, Laurence, 170, 358.
—— Olaf, 296.
Petraeus, 168.
Peucer, C., 288, 291, 306.
Pezel, 290, 304 ff.
Pfauser, 369, 434 ff.
Pfeffinger, 155, 279, 281.
Pfeiffer, H., 63, 67.
Pflug, Jul. von, 140, 147, 153.
Philip II., 106, 159, 194, 198, 241, 246, 250, 317, 323, 326, 327, 330, 343, 369, 371.
—— III., 252.
—— of Brunswick-Grubenhagen, 72.

31

Philip of Hesse, 46, 68, 72, 79, 95 ff., 106, 108, 111, 118, 122, 127, 133, 137, 139, 140, 143 ff., 146, 149, 151, 153, 157, 159, 224, 289, 304, 307, 437, 440, 459.
—— III. of Nassau-Weilburg, 304.
—— of the Palatinate, 123.
—— of Pomerania, 123.
—— Louis of Palatine-Neuburg, 374.
Philips, Ubbo, 129.
Pierius, Urb., 297.
Pierluigi, son of Paul III., 154, 239.
Pighino, 240.
Pirkheimer, 20, 27, 61, 84, 92, 447.
Piscator, 305, 409.
Pistorius, 140.
—— the son (Jesuit), 372.
Pithou, P., 262.
Pius IV., 226, 241, 247, 250, 333, 366, 369.
—— V., 226, 247, 250, 258, 260, 317, 334, 336, 339.
Planitz, 37.
Planta, 189.
Platonism, 39, 449, 451.
Plessis-Mornay, Du, 194.
Plettenberg, W. von, 138.
Poach, 280.
Poinet, 210.
Polanus, Valet., 390.
Pole, Cardinal, 211, 222, 225, 238, 331.
Polentz, George von, 76.
Poliander, 68, 395.
Pollius, Joh., 369.
Possevin(us), Ant., 359.
Praecipuum membrum, 386.
Praetorius, Abd., 280.
—— Ant., 426.
—— Mich., 396.
Preaching, 398.
Predestination, 10, 40, 60, 178, 184, 187, 295, 301, 306, 311, 335, 341, 408, 411, 415.
Presbyterianism, 334, 341, 344, 353, 357.
Prierias (di Prierio), Silv., 13, 15.
Priests of the Mission, 271.
Probabilism, 266.
Probst, Jak., 45, 197.
Professio fidei Tridentinae, 247, 432.
Proles, 8.
Propaganda, 275.
Prophecy, 342, 399.
Pruystinck, Eloy, 197.

Prym, 352.
Psalm-singing, 397.
Pucci, 51.
Puritanism, 334, 346, 357.
Puteanus, see Dupuy.

Queiss, Erh. von, 76.
Quietism, 268.
Quignon, 208.
Quintana, 446.
Quiroza, 316.

Radziwill, Prince, 213.
Raittenau, Wolf. Dietr. von, 372.
Rákóczy, George, 363.
Rakow Catechism, 454.
Ramus, P., 401.
Rangoni, 120.
Ratichius (Ratke), 425.
Ratisbon, League of, 44.
Ravaillac, 264, 329.
Raynaldus, Oder., 162, 257, 271.
Reformatio Sigismundi, 66.
Reinhard, Anna, 53.
—— Mart., 164.
Reinkingk, 386.
Religious Colloquy (see also Disputation).
Religious Colloquy, Altenburg, 288.
—— —— Baden, 81.
—— —— Hagenau-Worms, 139.
—— —— Heidelberg (1584), 303.
—— —— Leipzig (1631), 418.
—— —— Maulbronn, 290, 301.
—— —— Mömpelgard, 408, 417.
—— —— Poissy, 323.
—— —— Ratisbon (1541), 140; (1601), 373.
—— —— Thorn, 362, 420, 455.
—— —— Worms (1540), 129; (1557), 283, 367.
—— —— Zürich (1), 53; (2), 55, 64; (3 and 4), 65.
—— Peace of Augsburg, 161.
Remonstrance, 411.
Remonstrants, 411, 455.
Renata (Renée) of Ferrara, 177, 221, 225.
Reservatum ecclesiasticum, 161, 371, 376.
Restitution, Edict of, 376.
Reuchlin, 8, 10, 20.
Rhegius, Urb., 45, 84, 123, 445.
Rhenanus, B., 51.
Rhynsburgers, 414.
Ricci, Matt., 274.

Richard Simmern, Count Palatine, 303.
Richelieu, 262, 329, 376.
Richer, E., 262.
Ridley, 208, 210, 331.
Ringwald, B., 395.
Rink, Melch., 88.
Rites, Chinese, 274.
—— Malabar, 274.
Rizzio, Dav., 343.
Robinson, John, 354.
Rode, H., 83, 87, 197.
Rodriguez, 230.
Rogers, J., 205, 209.
Rohan, Duc de, 189.
Rollius, Nic., 313.
Rosenbusch, 373.
Rosicrucians, 405.
Rossaeus, 328.
Rothmann, B., 126.
Roussel, G., 175, 190.
Royal Charter (Majestätsbrief), 374, 435.
Rudolph II., 252, 362, 371, 374.

Sa, Eman., 265.
Sabbath, 347, 353, 393.
Sachs, H., 45, 427.
Sadolet(i), Ja., 181, 220, 223, 429.
Sala, Margaret von der, 144.
Sales, De, 189.
—— Francis de, 269.
Salesian Women, 269.
Saliger, Joh., 281.
Salmeron, Al., 230, 233, 240.
Salmuth, 297.
Sam, Conr., 46.
Samson, Bern., 51.
Sanchez, Th., 265.
Sarcerius, Er., 281, 304.
Sarpi, P., 252, 262.
Savonarola, 422.
Schall, J. A., 274.
Schappeler, Chr., 67.
Schatzger, 58.
Schenk, Ja., 279.
Scherer (Jesuit), 373.
Schlichting, Von, 455.
Schlick, Counts, 432.
Schlüsselberg, 288.
Schmalkaldic Articles, 132.
—— League, 115.
Schmidt, Er., 403.
—— Conr., 55.
Schmaltz, Val., 454.
Schnepf, Erh., 122, 152, 304.
School Comedy, 426.
—— Institutions, Evangelical, 424.
—— Jesuit, 235, 425.
Schütz, H., 396.
—— Court-preacher, 291.
Schwabach Articles, 100, 104.

INDEX

Schwarzenberg, John of, 213.
Schweinichen, Von, 407.
Schweiss, Al., 111.
Schwenkfeld, 94, 405, 462.
Scultetus, Alr., 310.
—— Jerome, 13.
Seidel, M., 454.
Seld, 242, 365.
Selden, J., 352.
Selnecker, 134, 278, 286, 289, 293, 298, 395.
Sendomir, Consensus of, 361.
Sepulveda, 273.
Serafino, Fra, 221.
Seripando, 241.
Servetus, M., 182, 225, 446.
Seymour, Jane, 205, 206.
Siber, H., 185.
Sickingen, 22, 30, 38.
Sigismund I. of Poland, 72, 137, 212, 451.
—— II. Augustus, 213, 360.
—— III., 361.
Silvanus, 302.
Simon VI. of Lippe, 309.
—— VII., 309.
Simonetta, 241.
Simonis, Mennon, 129, 198, 438, 440.
Sisters of Charity, 272.
Sixtus V., 248, 252, 263, 327, 372.
Skoda, Mart., 433.
Socinians, 415, 453 ff.
Somerset, Duke of, 207, 211, 338.
Soner, E., 454.
Sophia, Electress, 297.
Sorores angelicae, 229.
Soto, 155, 331.
Sozzini (Socinus), Fausto, 453.
—— —— Lelio, 452.
Spalatin, G., 29, 77, 105.
Spangenberg, Cyr., 288.
Spee, Fr. von, 426.
Spengler, Laz., 27, 45, 395.
Speratus, P., 46, 76, 395, 434, 462, 465.
Spiera, Franc., 226.
Staffort Book, 307.
Stancaro, 217, 452.
Staupitz, 8, 16, 461.
Sten Sture, 164, 168.
Stephani, Joach., 386.
—— Matth., 386.
Stiefel, 45.
Stör, 57.
Stössel, 286, 291.
Storch, Nic., 37.
Strafford (Wentworth), 351.
Stratner, 137.
Strauss, Ja., 62, 77.
Strigel, 284, 286, 403.

Stübner, Marc., 37.
Stumpf, Sim., 55, 64.
Sturm, Ja., 99, 116.
—— Joh., 296.
Suarez, Fr., 265.
Sully, 329.
Sulzer, Sim., 398.
Sunday Festivals, 342, 347, 393, 397.
Superattendents, Superintendents, 79, 341, 383.
Superstition, 425.
Supremacy, Act of, 203.
—— Oath of, 333, 336.
Surrey, Earl of, 207.
Sylvester, Joh., 215.
Sylvius, Aen., 424.
Symbols, three oecumenical, 464.
Symbolum Apostolicum, 420, 438.
Syngramma Suevicum, 84.
Synod of Antwerp (1566), 313.
—— of Brzesc, 452.
—— of Chanforans, 429.
—— of Charenton (1631), 417.
—— of Delf, 398.
—— of Dillenburg (1578), 305.
—— of Dort (1578), 314, 322, 398; (1618-19), 307, 310, 322, 412, 417.
—— of Emden, 313.
—— of the Hague, 414.
—— of St. Martin, 429.
—— of Middleburg, 305, 314.
—— of Petrikau, 361.
—— of Sillein, 363.
—— of Strasburg, 464.
—— of Thorn, 361.
—— of Tonneins, 417.
Synods, evangelical, 305, 385.

Tamburini, 265.
Tanner, 373, 426.
Tarnov, J., 403, 407.
Tasch, P., 438.
Tast, Herm., 166.
Tauler, 9, 407, 463.
Tausen, Hans, 165.
Teresa de Jesus, 269.
Terillus, 265.
Tersteegen, 270.
Teschenmacher, 313.
Tetrapolitana, 109.
Tetzel, 11 ff.
Thamer, Theob., 368.
Theatins, 222, 229.
Theology, German, 9, 463.
Thomas, Thomism, 142, 222, 244, 247, 258, 449.
Thomassin, 271.
Three Orders, Doctrine of the, 387.

Tiene, Gaetano von, 222.
Tillet, Du, 175.
Timann, Joh., 186, 281, 286.
Toletus, 265.
Torgau Articles, 105.
—— Book of, 292.
Trautmannsdorff, 378.
Tremellius, 209, 303, 409.
Treves, Elector of (Greiffenklau), 31, 38.
Tripmaker, 126, 197.
Trolle, 164, 168.
Truber, Primus, 217.
Truchsess, Gebhard, Archbp., 371.
—— Otto, Card., 370.
Tübingen Book, 292.
Tyndale, W., 200, 205, 337, 354.
Tyrants, Murder of, 264, 346.

Ulric of Mecklenburg, 285, 366.
—— of Wurtemberg, 67, 97, 121.
Ungnad, Hans, 217.
Uniformity, Act of, 332.
Union, of 1609, 374.
—— Church, 310, 417 ff.
—— des vallées, 430.
Upsala möte, 359.
Urban VIII., 236, 253, 260, 262, 265, 275, 377.
Ursinus, Zach., 301, 305.
Usher, 352, 353, 410.
Utraquists, 19, 46, 431.
Utenhove, 210.
Utrecht, Union of, 320.
Uytenbogaert, 411, 414.

Vadian(us), Joach., 51, 54, 57.
Valdés, Alf. de, 71, 106, 221, 316.
—— Juan, 221, 224.
Valer, Rodr., de, 316.
Valla, Laurent., 22.
Vehus, 31.
Veltwyck, Gerh., 140.
Veluanus, A., 411, 412.
Vergerio, P. P., 131, 189, 217, 225, 324, 361, 424.
Vermigli, see Peter Martyr.
Vincent, Women of St., 272.
St. Vincent de Paul, 271.
Viret, Pet., 173, 178, 184, 185, 429.
Voes, H., 46, 197.
Volprecht, 48.
Vorst, Van der, 133.
Vossius, G., 409, 415.
Vulgate, The, 244, 248, 256.
Vulpius, Melch., 396.

Waldensians, 90, 177, 185, 428 ff.
Wallenstein, 376.
Walther, Joh., 395.
Ward, Mary, 236.
Warham, Archbp., 201.
Warwick, see Northumberland.
Waterlanders, 439.
Weickart, 405.
Weier (Wier), 426.
Weigel, Val., 404.
Weimar Confutation, 284.
Weisse, Mich., 433, 436.
Wentworth, see Strafford.
Wesel, National Meeting at, 313.
Wesenbeck, 286.
Westminster Assembly, 352 ff.
—— Catechism, 353.
—— Confession, 353.
Westphal, Joach., 185, 281, 360.
Wettstein, 415.
Whitaker, 335.
Whitgift, 335.
Wiclif, 1, 31, 60, 199.
Widebram, 291, 305.
Wiener, Paul, 217.

Wigand, 280, 286, 288, 291, 292, 385, 404.
William III. of Bavaria, 94, 370.
—— IV., 233.
—— V., 372.
—— IV. of Cleve, 149, 311, 369.
—— IV. of Hesse, 289, 296, 308.
—— (the Rich) of Nassau, 304.
—— of Orange, 304, 319, 439.
—— Archbp. of Riga, 138.
Williams, Roger, 356.
Wimpina, 14.
Windeck, J. P., 373.
Winter, Diebold, 441.
Wishart, G., 338.
Witches' Hammer, 426.
Wittgenstein, Count, 305.
Witzel, G., 136, 255, 368, 407.
Wolff, Ambr., see Chr. Herdessianus.
Wolfgang of Anhalt, 72, 98, 106, 116, 123.
—— of Zweibrücken (Bipont) 156, 301.
—— William, Count Palatine, 390.

Wolmar, Melch., 175.
Wolsey, 201, 204.
Wolzogen, Freiherr von, 455.
Worms, Edict of, 32, 41.
Wullenwever, Jürg., 130, 166.
Wyttenbach, Thom., 51, 57.

Xavier, Francis, 230, 232, 253, 274.
Ximenes, Franc., 315.

Zabarella, Ja., 402.
Zanchius, 302.
Zaorowski, Jerome, 233.
Zápolya, 97, 118, 215.
Zasiius, 61.
Zell, Matth., 46, 464.
Zenker, Peter, 465.
Zerotin, Joh., 436.
Zingg, Fr., 54.
Zütphen, H. von, 45, 197.
Zwick, Joh., 397.
Zwilling, Gabr., 36.
Zwingli, 49, 57 ff., 81 ff., 92, 94, 99, 109, 117, 125, 150, 171, 176, 184, 188, 197, 206, 209, 276, 288, 360, 387, 396, 433, 445, 449, 453.

www.ingramcontent.com/pod-product-compliance
Lightning Source LLC
Chambersburg PA
CBHW021427300426
44114CB00010B/689